Using dBASE® 5 for Windows™, Special Edition

Diane Tinney

Paul McFedries

Gordon Padwick

Ed Jones

Gerry Litton

Sherry L. Matsen

Yvonne Johnson

Chris and Betty Bolté

Using dBASE 5 for Windows, Special Edition

Library of Congress Catalog No.: 94-68084

ISBN: 1-56529-630-3

97 96 95 94 4 3 2 1

Interpretation of the printing code: the rightmost double-digit number is the year of the book's printing; the rightmost single-digit number, the number of the book's printing. For example, a printing code of 94-1 shows that the first printing of the book occurred in 1994.

Publisher: David P. Ewing

Associate Publisher: Don Roche, Jr.

Managing Editor: Michael Cunningham

Product Marketing Manager: Greg Wiegand

Associate Product Marketing Manager: Stacy Collins

Credits

Publishing Manager
Nancy Stevenson

Acquisitions Editors
Thomas F. Godfrey III
Jenny L. Watson

Product Director
Kathie-Jo Arnoff

Production Editors
Judy Brunetti
Virginia Noble

Copy Editors
Jill D. Bond
Jodi Jensen
Andy Saff
Susan Christophersen
Kellie Currie
Christine Prakel
Rebecca Whitney
Lisa Gebken

Technical Editors
Charles Miedzinski
Michael Watson
Warren Estep

Acquisitions Coordinators
Deborah Abshier
Patricia J. Brooks

Book Designer
Amy Peppler-Adams

Cover Designer
Jay Corpus

Technical Specialist
Cari Ohm

Graphic Image Specialists
Teresa Forrester
Dennis Sheehan
Clint Lahnen
Jason Hand

Imprint Manager
Kelli Widdifield

Production Team
Angela Bannan
Claudia Bell
Kim Cofer
Juli Cook
Karen Dodson
Chad Dressler
Terri Edwards
DiMonique Ford
Aren Howell
Bob LaRoche
Beth Lewis
Wendy Ott
Maxine Dillingham
Nancy Sears Perry
Kris Simmons
Michael Thomas
Tina Trettin
Karen Walsh

Indexer
Charlotte Clapp

Editorial Assistants
Jill L. Stanley
Michelle Williams

Composed in *Stone Serif* and *MCPdigital* by Que Corporation

About the Authors

Diane Tinney is proprietor of The Software Professional, a business that provides education, development support, and consulting on a variety of Windows and DOS applications. Diane specializes in the integration of Windows products, and specifically, database implementation and integration. Most recently, Diane authored Que's *Paradox for Windows Programming By Example,* and contributed to *Using Paradox 4.5 for DOS,* Special Edition and *Using Microsoft Office,* Special Edition.

Paul McFedries has been a computer programmer for over 20 years and, as a principal in Lone Wolf Software, specializes in database applications. He has a degree in mathematics, but has been able to live a normal life anyway. McFedries has written or coauthored over 15 books on topics such as dBASE, FoxPro, Access, and Windows. He lives in Toronto, where he indulges his hobbies of desktop video production, 3-D animation, and relaxing at the beach.

Gordon Padwick is a consultant who specializes in Windows applications. He is the author of many books and magazine articles about word processing, spreadsheets, graphics, desktop publishing, and presentation software, and about industrial computer applications. In addition, he presents computer training courses, provides computer applications support, and does custom programming. Gordon is a graduate of London University and has completed postgraduate studies in computer science and communications. He is a Senior Member of the Institute of Electrical and Electronics Engineers.

Ed Jones is the author of over 30 database, spreadsheet, word processing, and technical books. He has also published articles in *Databased Advisor, DBMS,* and *Lotus* magazines. Jones provides consulting, planning, software development, and training for federal government agencies, law firms, and other corporate environments in the greater Washington, D.C., area. He has designed and provided personnel management software to an installed base of approximately 100 companies nationwide.

Gerry Litton is the author of numerous books on microcomputer software. With more than 30 years in the computer industry to his credit, he now works as a professional consultant. A former professor of computer science at the University of San Francisco, Litton resides in Oakland, California.

Sherry L. Matsen is involved in computer and software setups, and customized software design on an ongoing basis with clients. Among the packages she has worked with are Quattro, Excel, Word, Ventura, and PowerPoint. Her strongest and most utilized skill is in dBASE IV where she has written custom applications for gold assay labs, car dealerships, marinas, motels, and others.

Yvonne Johnson has been involved in teaching and writing about PCs since they first came into use. For 12 years she owned and operated a successful computer training school. During that time she authored all the training material for the school and wrote several books published by Que and other publishers. After selling the school, she now devotes more of her time to writing, consulting, and programming. Her training and writing background has made her exceptionally well-versed in database, word processing, graphic, spreadsheet, presentation, integrated, and publishing software.

Betty Bolté has been an editorial and software training consultant for several years, operating in the central Indiana area. She writes her own computer training materials, and enjoys writing articles and editing other writers' work.

Chris Bolté has been working with personal and mini-computers for over 15 years. He has written several database applications in network environments, and has experience in dBASE, SQL, ORACLE, and other popular programming languages. He has performed training for software packages designed for various customers, and has written design, maintenance, and user manuals for many different applications.

Trademark Acknowledgments

We'd Like To Hear From You!

As part of our continuing effort to produce books of the highest possible quality, Que would like to hear your comments. To stay competitive, we *really* want you, as a computer book reader and user, to let us know what you like or dislike most about this book or other Que products.

You can mail comments, ideas, or suggestions for improving future editions to the address below, or send us a fax at (317) 581-4663. For the on-line inclined, Macmillan Computer Publishing now has a forum on CompuServe (type **GO QUEBOOKS** at any prompt) through which our staff and authors are available for questions and comments. In addition to exploring our forum, please feel free to contact me personally on CompuServe at 76507,2715 to discuss your opinions of this book.

Thanks in advance—your comments will help us to continue publishing the best books available on computer topics in today's market.

Kathie-Jo Arnoff
Senior Product Development Specialist
Que Corporation
201 W. 103rd Street
Indianapolis, IN 46290

Contents at a Glance

Contents

8 Entering, Editing, and Viewing Data 145

9 Creating Basic Queries 167

Introduction

Today, information is money. Those who have information and can extract the right information quickly when it is needed far excel those who can't find the information. It's no surprise then, that the computer has been enlisted to help manage data inputs and outputs. Database software has traveled from the mainframe to the mini and down to the micro computer. dBASE was one of the first database applications designed for the micro computer. World-wide, more people use dBASE to manage their data on micro computers than any other single database.

dBASE for Windows is a powerful database management application that mere mortals can use. Unlike many software applications that ignore the installed user base, dBASE for Windows is mostly compatible with earlier DOS versions of dBASE. Even the dBASE for Windows programming language is downwardly compatible (except for a few DOS-oriented commands that are no longer needed in the Windows environment).

dBASE for Windows helps you manage your informational needs in a graphical Windows environment. You can store, edit, and extract information when you need it and in the form that you need it. You can create forms and reports that look just like the forms and reports that you use in your current business. And, if you'd like to, you can create turn-key database applications complete with custom menus, dialog boxes, and buttons. You can even link your dBASE application to other applications via DDE, OLE, and SQL extensions.

Using dBASE 5 for Windows, Special Edition, helps you exploit the features of dBASE for Windows and practically apply them to your environment.

Who Should Use This Book?

Using dBASE 5 for Windows, Special Edition, is geared toward PC users who need a tutorial reference to dBASE for Windows. The authors of this book recognize that your learning time is limited. The focus is on getting you up to speed quickly so that you can be productive immediately. Then, as you have time, you can build on your practical experiences and fine-tune your skills by moving on to intermediate and advanced concepts.

This book assumes you are familiar with Microsoft Windows but not necessarily familiar with dBASE. If you are new to database concepts and dBASE, this book is ideal for you. If you are upgrading to dBASE for Windows from a DOS version, you will find this book puts you on the fast track for taking advantage of the new features.

How This Book Is Organized

Using dBASE 5 for Windows, Special Edition, is designed to complement the documentation that comes with dBASE for Windows. Beginners will find the step-by-step information in this book helpful. Experienced users will appreciate the comprehensive coverage and expert advice. After you become proficient with dBASE for Windows, you can use this book as a desktop reference.

Using dBASE 5 for Windows, Special Edition, is divided into four parts:

Part I: Learning dBASE for Windows Fundamentals

Part II: Power Skills in dBASE for Windows

Part III: Integrating dBASE for Windows with Other Applications

Part IV: Building dBASE Applications

Part I introduces you to dBASE and describes the fundamental concepts. Chapter 1 introduces the key features in dBASE for Windows. If you are a user of a DOS dBASE product, you should read Chapter 2, which provides you with important information on moving from dBASE for DOS to dBASE for Windows. The remaining chapters in Part I provide you with a solid foundation in database concepts, creating databases, queries, forms, and reports.

Part II builds on your foundation skills and takes you to the next level of expertise. Chapter 12 introduces you to relational database concepts. Chapter 13 shows you how to use the Expression Builder. Chapters 14–17 teach you how to manipulate data and cover advanced skills in creating forms, reports, and queries. The last chapter discusses multiuser (networking) issues.

Part III explores the dBASE integration features. Chapter 20 shows you how to import and export data. Chapter 21 explains how to use OLE and DDE with dBASE. Chapter 22 provides information on using dBASE in a client/server environment. The last chapter presents a "real-world" scenario that illustrates how to put the dBASE integration features to work for you.

Part IV adds the power of dBASE programming to your interactive dBASE skills. dBASE for Windows incorporates object-oriented, event-driven programming extensions into the existing dBASE language. Chapter 23 reviews the key components of the dBASE programming language. Chapter 24 explains the new approach to designing a dBASE for Windows application. Chapter 25 shows you how to use the Command window. Chapters 26 and 27 cover the Program Editor and the Debugger. Chapter 28 explains how to write program modules. Then the remaining chapters show how to work with data, tables, forms, and other objects to automate database tasks.

This book also includes three appendixes of useful reference material. In Appendix A, you will find information about using your old dBASE III and dBASE IV applications in dBASE for Windows. Appendix B gives you tables of handy shortcut keys. And Appendix C is a handy reference to the more than 170 properties in dBASE for Windows.

Conventions Used in This Book

dBASE for Windows enables you to use both the keyboard and the mouse to select menu and dialog box items: you can press a letter or you can select an item by clicking it with the mouse. Letters you press to activate menus, choose commands in menu, and select options in dialog boxes are printed in boldface type, as in the following example: "open the **F**ile menu and choose **O**pen."

Names of dialog boxes and dialog box options are written with initial capital letters. Messages that appear on-screen are printed in a special font, as in the following example: `Variable undefined`. New terms are introduced in *italic* type. Text that you are to type appears in **boldface**.

Some lines of code are too long to fit within some of the margins in this book. A special line-wrap icon (➥) is used to indicate when two or more lines of code are typed as one line.

Uppercase letters are used to distinguish file and directory names.

Tip
This paragraph format suggests easier or alternative methods of executing a procedure.

dBASE for Windows includes SpeedBars for your convenience. By clicking a button on a SpeedBar, you can execute a command or access a dialog box. The button icons in the margins indicate which button you can click to perform a task.

Note

This paragraph format indicates additional information that may help you avoid problems or that should be considered in using the described features.

Caution

This paragraph format warns the reader of hazardous procedures (for example, activities that delete files).

Troubleshooting

This paragraph format provides guidance on how to find solutions to common problems.

◀ "Section title," p. xxx

▶ "Section title," p. xxx

Using dBASE 5 for Windows, Special Edition, uses margin cross-references to help you access related information in other parts of the book. Right-facing triangles point you to related information in later chapters. Left-facing triangles point you to related information in previous chapters.

Part I

Learning dBASE for Windows Fundamentals

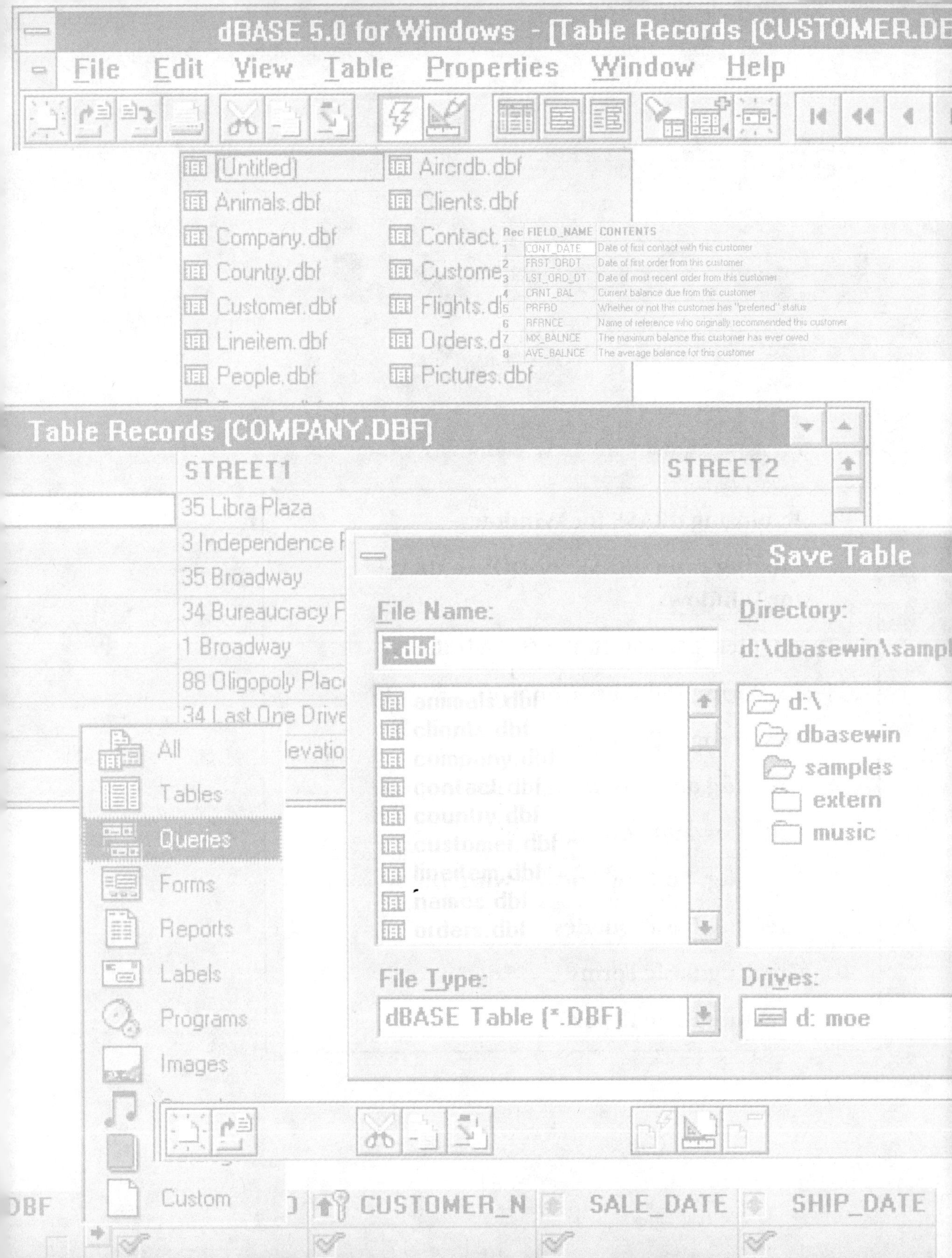

dBASE 5.0 for Windows - [Table Records (CUSTOMER.DE
File Edit View Table Properties Window Help
(Untitled)
Aircrdb.dbf
Animals.dbf
Clients.dbf
Company.dbf
Contact.
Country.dbf
Custome
Customer.dbf
Flights.d
Lineitem.dbf
Orders.d
People.dbf
Pictures.dbf
Rec FIELD_NAME CONTENTS
1 CONT_DATE Date of first contact with this customer
2 FRST_ORDT Date of first order from this customer
3 LST_ORD_DT Date of most recent order from this customer
4 CRNT_BAL Current balance due from this customer
5 PRFRD Whether or not this customer has "preferred" status
6 RFRNCE Name of reference who originally recommended this customer
7 MX_BALNCE The maximum balance this customer has ever owed
8 AVE_BALNCE The average balance for this customer
Table Records (COMPANY.DBF)
STREET1
STREET2
35 Libra Plaza
3 Independence P
35 Broadway
34 Bureaucracy P
1 Broadway
88 Oligopoly Plac
34 Last One Drive
levatio
Save Table
File Name:
*.dbf
Directory:
d:\dbasewin\sampl
d:\
dbasewin
samples
extern
music
File Type:
dBASE Table (*.DBF)
Drives:
d: moe
All
Tables
Queries
Forms
Reports
Labels
Programs
Images
Custom
CUSTOMER_N
SALE_DATE
SHIP_DATE

Chapter 1

Exploring dBASE for Windows

dBASE for Windows is Borland International's most recent implementation of dBASE. It not only offers a wealth of improvements over its DOS-based predecessors, but it also maintains full compatibility with existing dBASE for DOS applications. New users can get up to speed quickly, creating the tables, forms, queries, and reports necessary to manage information and obtain the answers to their database questions. Experienced dBASE developers will find the familiar dBASE language is still available to them, along with a host of extensions to that language that take full advantage of the event-driven Windows environment.

In this chapter, you learn about the following:

- General features of dBASE for Windows
- dBASE for Windows Interface
- dBASE for Windows Navigator
- Tables, queries, forms, reports, and programs
- System requirements

Looking at the Features of dBASE for Windows

dBASE for Windows is more than simply a DOS version of dBASE transported to the Windows environment. The features provided by dBASE for Windows appeal to a wide range of skill levels, so you should be able to become comfortable with the product quickly, whether you are a novice or an experienced developer. The following sections introduce the major enhancements and features provided by dBASE for Windows. Figure 1.1 shows dBASE for Windows at work. In this figure, two tables containing data are visible simultaneously, and the Navigator—a dBASE for Windows feature that helps you manage your data in a visual way—is partially visible.

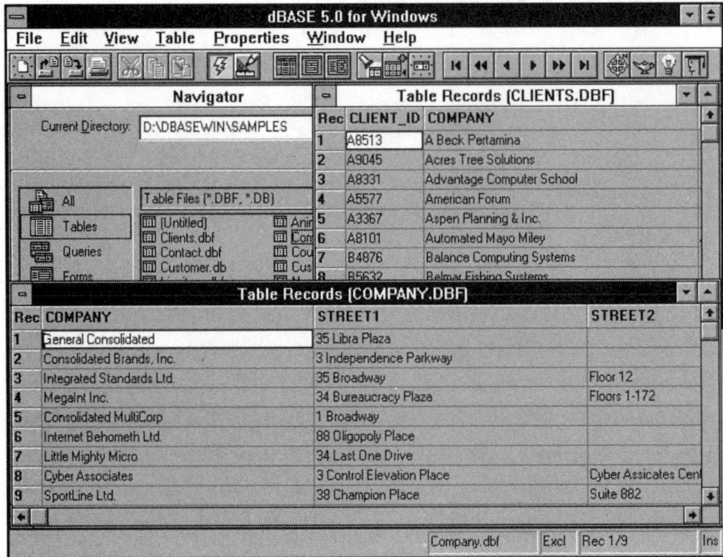

Fig. 1.1 An example of dBASE for Windows at work.

Compatibility with dBASE for DOS

A high degree of compatibility with existing dBASE III PLUS and dBASE IV applications is a major strength of dBASE for Windows. The compatibility claimed by many "dBASE-compatible" products varies significantly from the level of compatibility offered by dBASE for Windows.

Applications claiming to be dBASE-compatible routinely require you to make changes to many lines of program code before these applications can run a program originally written in dBASE III PLUS or dBASE IV. dBASE for Windows, on the other hand, is designed to run most of your existing programs while requiring only minimal changes to the existing program code. You can quickly convert existing dBASE applications to run under the Windows environment; later, as time permits, you can enhance those applications to utilize the bells and whistles inherent to Windows.

True compatibility with earlier dBASE versions is an important factor when you consider the thousands of custom applications written with the older DOS versions of dBASE. Often, these applications were written by individuals who have long since left the job, but the faithful application is still in use. With dBASE for Windows, you don't have to rewrite most program code to run a dBASE III, dBASE III PLUS, or dBASE IV program. You can become comfortable with dBASE for Windows before you begin the task of changing the code behind your programs to take full advantage of the Windows environment.

Relational Query-by-Example

dBASE for Windows has a relational query-by-example feature that is provided as an integral part of the program. This feature enables you to interactively create and implement complex *queries,* which are search questions that you pose to your database in order to retrieve specific data. These queries can use single tables, or they can be fully relational and use multiple tables. You can even save queries for future use, so that later you can ask the same types of questions about your data and retrieve answers based on the latest available data.

dBASE for Windows queries are interpreted by dBASE into familiar dBASE commands. You therefore have the option of using the query-by-example facility to ask specific questions about your data or using dBASE commands to compose your queries. dBASE for Windows can use queries stored in its own format or stored in the query formats of dBASE IV and dBASE III PLUS.

Language Enhancements

On the programming side, dBASE for Windows is a superset of dBASE IV, with a number of commands added specifically to take advantage of the Windows environment. A new DEFINE command has dozens of available clauses that enable you to control the appearance or behavior of a Windows object, such as list and option boxes, Browse windows, and form backgrounds.

Mouse Support

The capability to use the mouse adds another level of ease to older dBASE programs. Unlike some other dBASE-compatible packages, dBASE for Windows lets you offer a mouse-controlled interface that your dBASE for DOS applications can take advantage of without you having to rewrite the programs.

About the dBASE for Windows Interface

When you first start dBASE for Windows, you see the two windows shown in figure 1.2: the Command window and the Navigator. (If either of these windows was closed by the last person using dBASE for Windows, they may not be visible when you start the program. You can bring either window into view by opening the **W**indow menu and choosing either Navigator or Command. These two windows, along with the menus, are your way of communicating with dBASE for Windows.

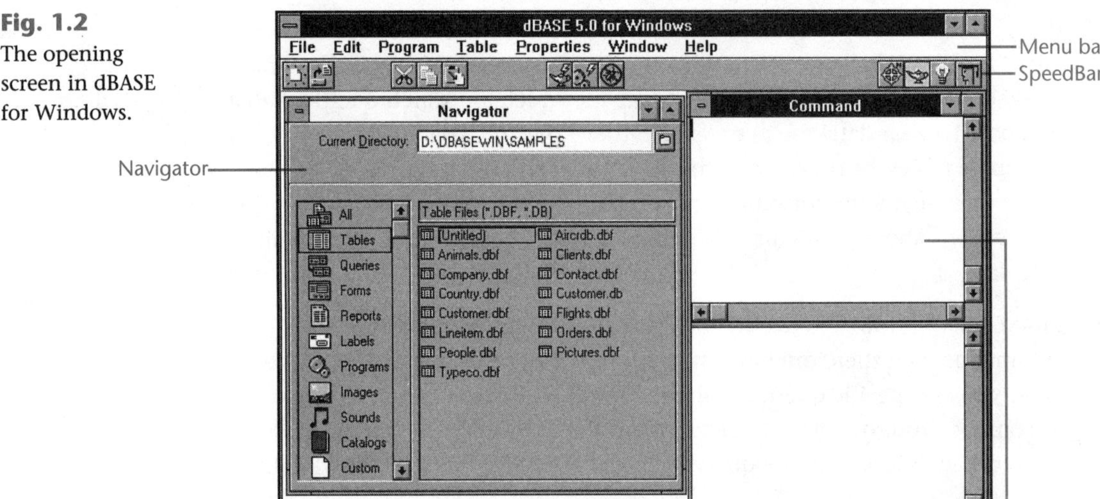

Fig. 1.2
The opening screen in dBASE for Windows.

The Navigator and the Command window work with the menu bar and the SpeedBar to give you access to the power of dBASE for Windows and to tell you what is going on within the program.

The Command Window

If you worked with earlier versions of dBASE, you can type the commands you are familiar with in the Command window. As you enter commands, the results of those commands appear in the lower portion of the Command window. If you have used earlier versions of dBASE for DOS, you use the Command window in the same way you used the dot prompt. You also can run existing dBASE programs by typing the familiar DO command in the Command window, followed by the name of the program. The program then runs in the lower half of the window. You can think of the Command window as a tool for those who want to work with dBASE the "old-fashioned" way—using interactive dBASE commands and running dBASE for DOS program files.

The Menu Bar

The menu bar provides pull-down menu commands for common tasks, such as saving changes to the objects with which you work or printing reports. These menus vary at times, depending on what type of object you are working with, but the following menus are always visible:

- **F**ile. You use the options shown on this menu to create, open, close, save, and print various types of files, including tables, forms, and reports.

- **E**dit. You use the options on this menu to make changes to data. The **E**dit menu includes the Undo and Redo commands to undo the last operations you performed; the Cut, Copy, and Paste commands to perform Windows cut-and-paste operations; and, in most cases, a Select All command that you can use to select items with which you are working. The **E**dit menu also may contain additional commands, which vary depending on where you are in the program.

- **P**roperties. You use the options on this menu to modify the various properties, or default behaviors, of different objects. You can now use the **P**roperties menu to modify many of the environmental settings that you changed using the SET commands in earlier versions of dBASE.

- **W**indow. You use this menu to arrange the various windows that appear on the desktop when you are working in dBASE.

- **H**elp. You use this menu to obtain help on using the various features of dBASE for Windows.

The SpeedBar

Many of the frequently used menu commands can be initiated in either of two ways: by choosing the command from the pull-down menu or by clicking the equivalent button on the SpeedBar. Like the menus, the SpeedBar changes depending on the area of dBASE for Windows in which you are working. When you start dBASE for Windows, you see the SpeedBar shown in figure 1.3. The buttons contained on this SpeedBar are identified in table 1.1.

Fig. 1.3
The initial SpeedBar buttons.

Table 1.1 Buttons on the Initial SpeedBar

Button	Button Name	Purpose
	New Document	Opens a pop-up menu from which you can choose a new object to create (table, query, index tag, form, report, label, program, or catalog)
	Open File	Displays the Open File dialog box, which you can use to open various types of files
	Cut	Cuts selected data and moves it to the Windows Clipboard
	Copy	Copies selected data to the Windows Clipboard
	Paste	Pastes the contents of the Windows Clipboard at the insertion pointer location
	Execute	Executes the command line entered in the Command window
	Do	Executes a program file
	Debug	Compiles a program file and loads it into the debugger
	Navigator	Moves the focus to the Navigator window
	Command	Moves the focus to the Command window
	Expert	Uses an Expert to create a form
	Tutor	Runs an interactive tutorial

The SpeedMenus

dBASE for Windows also makes use of SpeedMenus, which are various pop-up menus that appear when you right-click particular objects through-out the program. You can use these menus to quickly perform different operations on the object in question. For example, if you right-click a table, a pop-up menu appears with choices for adding, deleting, finding, and replacing records within that table.

The Navigator

You might want to think of the Navigator as the tool of choice for those who prefer to work in the "new Windows way." The Navigator provides a familiar Windows interface to the objects you work with in dBASE: the tables, queries, forms, reports, and so on. You can design objects or use them from the Navigator—you can open tables and forms, execute queries, print reports, and run dBASE programs. You can work with your files directly from the Navigator, or you can organize your files by dragging and dropping them into open dBASE catalogs. You can also run files by dragging them from the Navigator into the Command window.

The upper portion of the Navigator contains a text box with the name of the current directory and a Folder button that, when you click it, displays a Choose Directory dialog box. You can use this dialog box to choose the current directory. This feature is equivalent to using the SET DIRECTORY TO command in the dBASE language.

Tip
To open the Navigator if it is not visible, pull down the **W**indow menu and choose Navigator.

The lower portion of the Navigator has two halves: a Categories list on the left, which provides a filter to determine what types of files are visible, and a Files list on the right, which contains a list box showing graphic representations of all the files in the selected category. As you click to select any of the file types in the left half, the corresponding files of that type appear on the right. If you click the Queries icon in the Categories list, for example, all queries in the current directory are then visible in the Files list, as shown in figure 1.4. (In this example, the Navigator window has been maximized to occupy the entire main window.)

After you select the object type you want to work with from the Navigator's Categories list, you can use the mouse to perform a number of operations on a specific object from the Files list. If you right-click any object in the list, a SpeedMenu opens for that object, and you can then choose an action from the choices in the SpeedMenu.

Each file shown in the Files list has a default run mode and a default design mode. You can switch directly to these modes by double-clicking an object (to enter the run mode), or by double-right-clicking the object (to enter the design mode). If you double-click a table, for example, the table opens in a Browse window; you can then add to or edit the data in the table. If you double-right-click the same table, a Table Structure window opens in which you can change the design of the table. Double-click a form, and the form opens containing a record. Double-right-click the form, and a design window opens in which you can modify the form's design. Double-click a program, and the program runs in the Command window. Double-right-click the program, and it opens in an editor window where you can make changes to the program. The item called Untitled—which appears under each category in the Navigator window—provides a way for you to create new items in that category. You can click the Tables icon in the Categories list, for example, to display all tables; then you can double-click the Untitled item to open a new table for design.

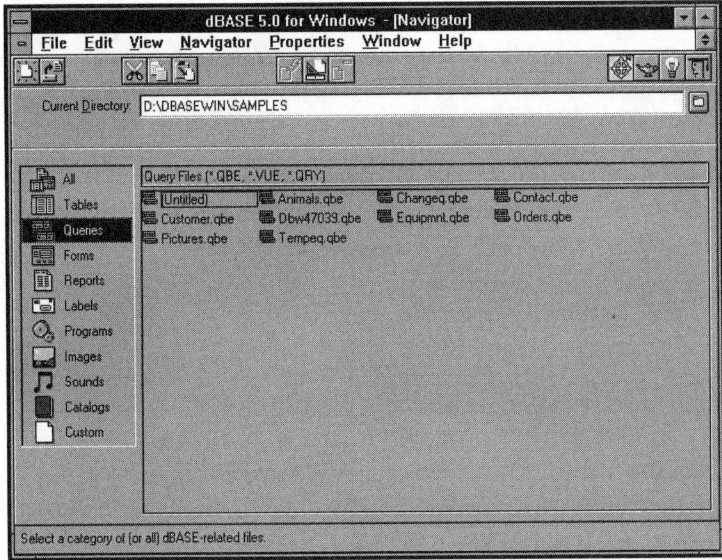

Fig. 1.4
The Navigator, showing all queries in the specified directory.

Note

Keep in mind that you double-click an object when it is the size of an icon (*iconized*), not when the file is open. You do not double-click an object that is already open.

You can also create *catalogs* from the Navigator, which provide you with a way to organize the various files you use as you work with a particular database task. In a way, catalogs can be thought of as "storage containers" or "filing folders" that help you organize all the files you commonly use for specific jobs. dBASE for Windows catalogs are fully compatible with dBASE IV catalogs and are much improved over the awkward feel they had in earlier versions of dBASE for DOS. When you create a new catalog, its window is identical to the Navigator window, but it displays only the items that have been placed in that catalog. Consequently, after you become comfortable using the Navigator, you will find it easy to work with catalogs.

About the Navigator Categories

Each category in the Navigator uses a different icon to identify the files in that category. These icons can be thought of as the objects you work with in dBASE for Windows. The following sections explain the Navigator categories in greater detail.

Tables

The Tables category displays all dBASE (*.DBF) and Paradox (*.DB) files. From the Navigator, right-click any table to open the SpeedMenu, which has the following options:

> *Table **P**roperties* displays a dialog box that contains various properties for the table (such as its size in bytes, and the last date any edits were made to the table's data).
>
> ***D**elete* removes the selected table and any associated tables from the disk. dBASE asks for confirmation before doing so.
>
> ***E**dit Records* opens the table in an Edit window so that you can view the data one record at a time. Choosing **E**dit Records is equivalent to entering EDIT in the Command window.
>
> ***A**dd Records* opens the table in an Edit window with a new blank record so that you can begin adding data. Choosing **A**dd Records is equivalent to entering APPEND in the Command window.
>
> *Design **T**able Structure* opens the Table Structure window with an existing table in the window. You can then make the desired changes to the table's structure. Choosing Design **T**able Structure is equivalent to entering MODIFY STRUCTURE in the Command window.

Queries

The Queries category displays all query files. In dBASE for Windows, query files include dBASE for Windows .QBE files, dBASE IV .QBE and .VUE files, and dBASE III PLUS .QRY files. In dBASE for Windows, you use query files to provide selected subsets of data in response to questions that you ask about your data. With a national mailing list stored in a table of names and addresses, for example, you may want to see all records from a particular state, and you may want only certain fields (such as just the name, city, state, and phone numbers) from the table. A query can provide these kinds of results, such as all names and phone numbers for all residents of Idaho.

If you double-click the Untitled item while the queries are displayed in the Navigator, a new query opens, and you can design the query to obtain the data you need. If you double-click an existing query in the Navigator, the query runs, and the selected records and fields are made available to the dBASE environment. If you right-click any query, you open a SpeedMenu with the following options:

*Query **P**roperties* displays a dialog box that contains various properties for the query (such as its size in bytes, and the last date any edits were made to the query).

***D**elete* removes the query from the disk (dBASE asks you for confirmation before doing so).

***R**un Query* runs the query.

*Design **Q**uery* opens the Query Designer with the existing query so that you can make necessary changes to the query's design.

***E**dit as Program* opens the query in the form of a dBASE program, which you can then edit as necessary.

Forms

The Forms category displays all screen form files. (In earlier versions of dBASE for DOS, these screen form files were known as *format files*.) When you select this category from the Categories list, the Files list displays all dBASE for Windows form files (.WFM) and all dBASE for DOS format files (.FMT). In earlier versions of dBASE, forms were commonly used to view and edit data. You can use forms for these purposes in dBASE for Windows, but you can also use forms in dBASE for Windows for other tasks, such as creating switchboards with command buttons that users can click to carry out specific tasks.

If you double-click the Untitled item while the forms are displayed in the Navigator, the Form Designer opens with a new form, and you can design the form to view the desired data. If you double-click an existing form in the Navigator, the form opens. If you right-click any form, you open a SpeedMenu that has the following options:

*Form **P**roperties* displays a dialog box that contains various properties for the form (such as its size in bytes, and the last date any edits were made to the form).

Delete deletes the form from the disk (dBASE asks you for confirmation before doing so).

Run Form runs the form.

Design Form opens the form designer with the existing form, and you can make necessary changes to the form's design. Choosing Design Form is equivalent to using the MODIFY SCREEN command in earlier versions of dBASE.

Edit as Program opens the form as a dBASE program, which you can then edit as necessary.

Reports

The Reports category displays all report files. When you select this category from the Categories list, the Files list shows all dBASE for Windows report files (.RPT and .FRG) and all dBASE for DOS report files (.FRM and .FRG). If you double-click the Untitled item while the reports are displayed in the Navigator, the Report Designer opens with a new report, and you can design the report to obtain the data you need. If you double-click an existing report in the Navigator, the report opens in Print Preview mode, and you can print the report. If you right-click any report, you open a SpeedMenu that has the following options:

Report Properties displays a dialog box that contains various properties for the report (such as its size in bytes, and the last date any edits were made to the report).

Delete removes the report from the disk (dBASE asks you for confirmation before doing so).

Run Report runs the report. Choosing **R**un Report is equivalent to using the REPORT FORM command in earlier versions of dBASE.

Design Report opens the Report Designer with the existing report, and you can make necessary changes to the report's design. Choosing De**s**ign Report is equivalent to using the MODIFY REPORT command in earlier versions of dBASE.

Labels

The Labels category displays all label files. When you select this category from the Categories list, the Files list shows all dBASE for Windows label files (.RPL and .LBG) and all dBASE for DOS label files (.LBL and .LBG). If you double-click the Untitled item while the labels are displayed in the Navigator, Crystal Reports opens with a new label. You can design the label to produce the size or style of mailing label you want. If you double-click an existing label in the Navigator, the label opens in Print Preview mode, and you can print the labels. If you right-click any label, you open a SpeedMenu with the following options:

*Label **P**roperties* displays a dialog box that contains various properties for the label (such as its size in bytes, and the last date any edits were made to the label).

***D**elete* removes the label from the disk (dBASE asks you for confirmation before doing so).

***R**un Labels* actually runs the label. Choosing **R**un Labels is equivalent to using the LABEL FORM command in earlier versions of dBASE.

Design Labels opens Crystal Reports with the existing label, and you can make desired changes to the label's design. Choosing Design Labels is equivalent to using the MODIFY LABEL command in earlier versions of dBASE.

Programs

The Programs category displays all dBASE for Windows, dBASE IV, and dBASE III program (*.PRG) files. You can execute programs using the equivalent of the dBASE DO command, or you can compile programs for later use. You can also create new programs or change existing ones. If you double-click the Untitled item while programs are displayed in the Navigator, a Program Editor window opens, and you can create a new program. Double-click an existing program, and the program runs. If you right-click any program, you open a SpeedMenu that has the following options:

*Program **P**roperties* displays a dialog box that contains various properties for the program (such as its size in bytes, and the last date any edits were made to the program).

***D**elete* removes the selected program from the disk. dBASE asks for confirmation before doing so.

*D**o*** runs the program. Choosing D**o** is equivalent to using the DO command in the dBASE language.

*De**b**ug* loads the program into the dBASE for Windows debugger so that you can track how the program runs.

Design Program opens the Text Editor window so that you can make changes to an existing dBASE program. Choosing Design Program is equivalent to using MODIFY COMMAND in earlier versions of dBASE.

Images

The Images category displays all graphic image files with .PCX and Windows bitmapped (*.BMP) file extensions. In dBASE for Windows, you can store images in OLE fields, or you can place them in forms or reports as design elements. If you double-click the Untitled item while images are displayed in the Navigator, Windows Paintbrush opens, and you can create a new graphic using the appropriate Windows Paintbrush techniques (see your Windows documentation for details). If you double-click a named image file, the Image window opens with the image displayed. If you right-click any image, you open a SpeedMenu that has the following options:

Image Properties displays a dialog box that contains various properties for the image (such as its size in bytes, and the last date any edits were made to the image file).

Delete removes the image file from the disk (dBASE asks you for confirmation before doing so).

Display Image opens the image in a view-only window.

Design Image opens the image in Windows Paintbrush, where you can make modifications to it.

Sounds

The Sounds category displays all sound files with Windows Wave (*.WAV) file extensions. In dBASE for Windows, you can store sounds in OLE fields, or you can place them in forms or reports as OLE objects that you can click to play the sounds. If you double-click the Untitled item while sounds are displayed in the Navigator, the Windows Sound Recorder opens, and you can record sounds using the appropriate Windows Sound Recorder techniques (see your Windows documentation for details). If you double-click a named sound file, the Windows Sound Recorder opens with the file loaded for editing or playback. If you right-click any sound, you open a SpeedMenu that has the following options:

Sound Properties displays a dialog box that contains various properties for the sound file (such as its size in bytes, and the last date any edits were made to the sound file).

Delete removes the sound file from the disk (dBASE asks you for confirmation before doing so).

Play Sound uses the PLAY SOUND command (a part of the dBASE language under dBASE for Windows) to play the sound, using whatever sound driver was installed during your Windows setup.

Design Sound opens the Windows Sound Recorder with the selected sound file loaded for editing.

Catalogs

The Catalog category displays all dBASE for Windows and dBASE IV catalog (*.CAT) files. In dBASE for Windows (as in dBASE IV), you use catalogs to group files together that are associated with a given database task. Some competing database managers use projects or folders to accomplish the same purpose.

Suppose that in dBASE you have a mailing list application. As part of that application, you have a table of data containing names and addresses, a form used to edit the data, a report used to print a listing of all the names, and a label used to print mailing labels. You also have two different queries so that you can retrieve users by a particular state and by a particular ZIP code. Each of these objects is stored in a separate file. You could place all these objects in a single catalog. Then, when you open that particular catalog, you see only those objects created for the mailing list, and not the objects created for other database tasks.

If you double-click the Untitled item while the catalogs are displayed in the Navigator, a Create Catalog dialog box appears. You can then use the options in the dialog box to create a new catalog file. If you double-click an existing catalog in the Navigator, that catalog is placed into use, and you see only the files stored in that catalog. If you right-click any catalog, you open a SpeedMenu that has the following options:

Catalog Properties displays a dialog box that contains various properties for the catalog file (such as its size in bytes, and the last date any edits were made to the catalog file).

Delete removes the catalog file from the disk (dBASE asks you for confirmation before doing so).

Open Catalog opens an existing catalog and causes files created from that point on to be added to that catalog.

An Overview of the Common Objects

Although you work with a number of items, or objects, in dBASE for Windows, you are likely to work with these five types more than any others: tables, queries, forms, reports, and programs.

Tables

dBASE for Windows uses the common relational database model in which data is stored in a series of tables. In each table, rows contain the individual records and columns contain the individual fields. In figure 1.5, the Name, Street, City, State/Prov, and ZIP/Postal code data contained in the fifth row of the table make up a *record*. The categories NAME, STREET, CITY, STATE_PROV, ZIP_POSTAL, and COUNTRY are all *fields*.

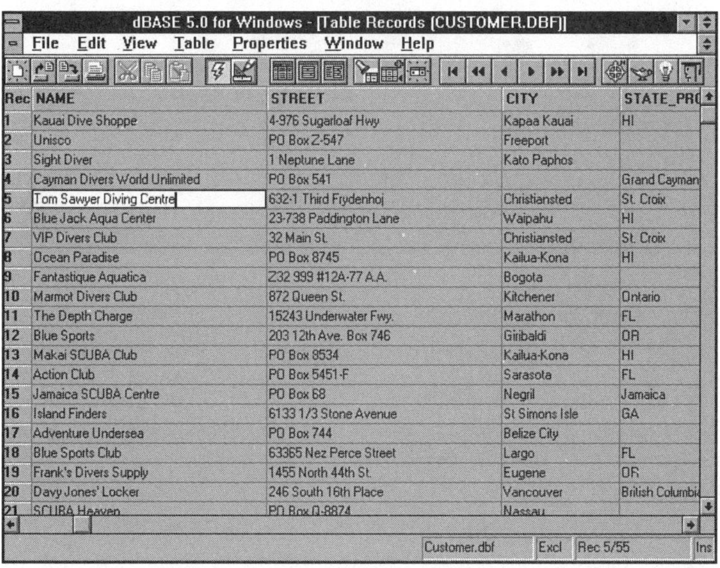

Rec	NAME	STREET	CITY	STATE_PR(
1	Kauai Dive Shoppe	4-976 Sugarloaf Hwy	Kapaa Kauai	HI
2	Unisco	PO Box Z-547	Freeport	
3	Sight Diver	1 Neptune Lane	Kato Paphos	
4	Cayman Divers World Unlimited	PO Box 541		Grand Cayman
5	Tom Sawyer Diving Centre	632-1 Third Frydenhoj	Christiansted	St. Croix
6	Blue Jack Aqua Center	23-738 Paddington Lane	Waipahu	HI
7	VIP Divers Club	32 Main St.	Christiansted	St. Croix
8	Ocean Paradise	PO Box 8745	Kailua-Kona	HI
9	Fantastique Aquatica	Z32 999 #12A-77 A.A.	Bogota	
10	Marmot Divers Club	872 Queen St.	Kitchener	Ontario
11	The Depth Charge	15243 Underwater Fwy.	Marathon	FL
12	Blue Sports	203 12th Ave. Box 746	Giribaldi	OR
13	Makai SCUBA Club	PO Box 8534	Kailua-Kona	HI
14	Action Club	PO Box 5451-F	Sarasota	FL
15	Jamaica SCUBA Centre	PO Box 68	Negril	Jamaica
16	Island Finders	6133 1/3 Stone Avenue	St Simons Isle	GA
17	Adventure Undersea	PO Box 744	Belize City	
18	Blue Sports Club	63365 Nez Perce Street	Largo	FL
19	Frank's Divers Supply	1455 North 44th St.	Eugene	OR
20	Davy Jones' Locker	246 South 16th Place	Vancouver	British Columbi
21	SCUBA Heaven	PO Box Q-8874	Nassau	

Fig. 1.5
The records and fields of a table.

dBASE for Windows permits a number of different data types for your fields. You can have alphanumeric fields (used to store any combination of characters, including numbers), numeric fields (used to store data that is calculated), floating number fields, date fields, logical fields (used to store yes or no values), and memo fields (used to store large amounts of text).

Creating a table in dBASE for Windows is a simple task. You can enter the CREATE command in the Command window, or you can double-click the Untitled option in the Navigator when Tables are displayed. With either method, you see a Table Structure window (see fig. 1.6) in which you can specify the names of the fields and the field types to be contained in your table. After you have designed the necessary tables, you can use the various icons of the Navigator and the various SpeedBar buttons to open the tables—and to open the forms that enable you to easily work with the data in those tables.

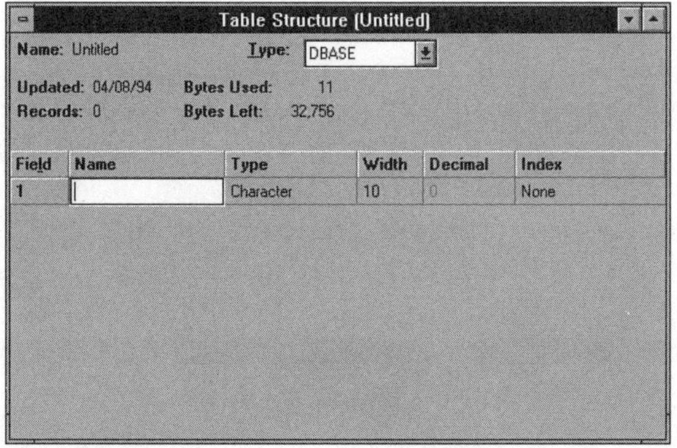

Fig. 1.6 Example of the Table Structure window.

dBASE for Windows is a *relational database*. A relational database lets you have more than one table open at a time, and the tables can be linked by means of a common field. Suppose you have a customer orders database that has one table containing customer names and addresses and another table containing orders for various customers, and both of these tables contain a Customer ID field. In dBASE, you can establish a link between the two tables so that every time you view a record with a particular customer's name and shipping address, you can also see all the orders for that customer.

Queries

► "Designing a Database," p. 79

Retrieving the data you require to perform a specific task—such as all orders for a specific customer, all sales during the month of June, or all employees reporting to a particular manager—is most easily accomplished through queries. The word *query* literally means *to ask*, and in dBASE for Windows, you use relational query-by-example (or QBE) to ask questions of the tables in your databases. Figure 1.7 shows an example of a query in dBASE for Windows. If you are familiar with the query-by-example used in Borland's Paradox, you can see that dBASE for Windows' query-by-example is similar. And if you are familiar with the use of the SET FILTER TO, SET RELATION TO, and INDEX ON...FOR commands in the dBASE language, you can think of relational QBE as a graphical implementation of the features of all three of those commands. Queries enable you to combine data from related tables and then filter the data so that you obtain the specific information you need.

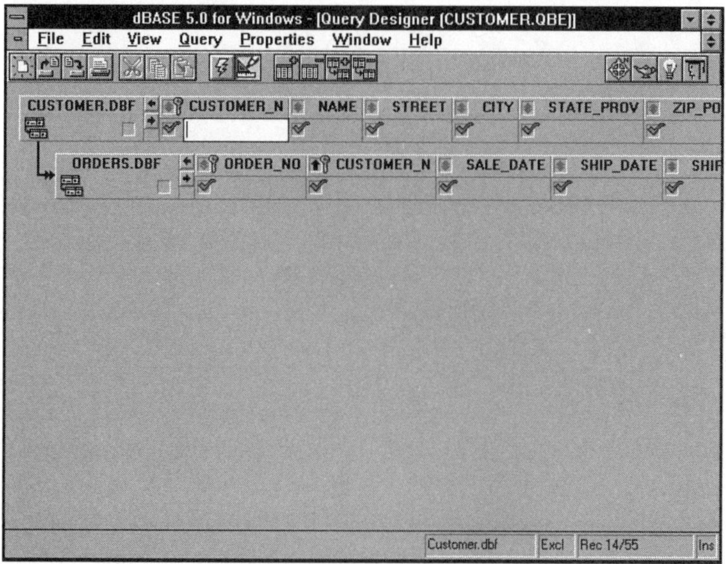

Fig. 1.7
Example of a query in dBASE for Windows.

Forms

You can use dBASE for Windows' Form Designer to build custom forms, including forms that resemble the paper-based ones commonly used in your office. You can use these forms to simplify data entry and editing. You can control data entry by omitting unnecessary fields and only including ones that are appropriate for the particular situation. You can also add *calculated fields*, which are fields that show a calculation based on the contents of another field. In addition, you can enhance the appearance of forms by adding lines, rectangles, or pictures as graphic elements. Forms can also show simultaneously data from multiple tables in a database.

Forms are part of developing applications in dBASE for Windows. You can add command buttons to a form, and these buttons can be used to execute commands written in the dBASE language. You can also change the *properties* (characteristics), of the various objects you place on a form in order to control the behavior of the form. Figure 1.8 shows an example of a form in dBASE for Windows.

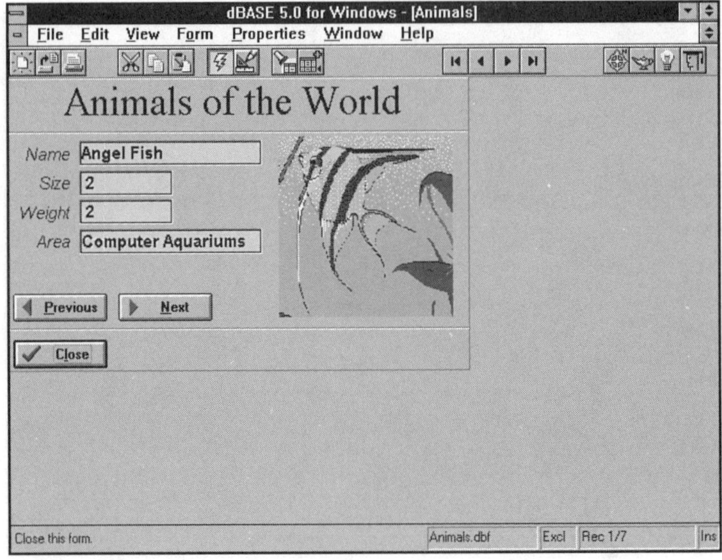

Fig. 1.8
An example of a dBASE for Windows form.

Reports

Reports are the end result of most databases, whether those reports consist of a single record presented on-screen or hundreds of pages of printed data. As with forms, you can design reports in dBASE to show data from a single table or from multiple related tables. Your reports can provide detailed subsets of data, or they can provide overall summaries. And you can use the Report Designer window to quickly create a report that meets your specific requirements. Figure 1.9 shows an example of a report in dBASE for Windows.

Programs

Programming in dBASE for Windows consists of creating and running programs, which are simply files containing dBASE commands. (Programs are also known as *command files*.) Any computer program is a series of instructions written to tell the computer how to perform a specific task. In dBASE, these commands are written to a disk file that is retrieved and run when you want to run the program. Each time you run the program, dBASE executes the list of commands in sequential order, unless the program specifies otherwise.

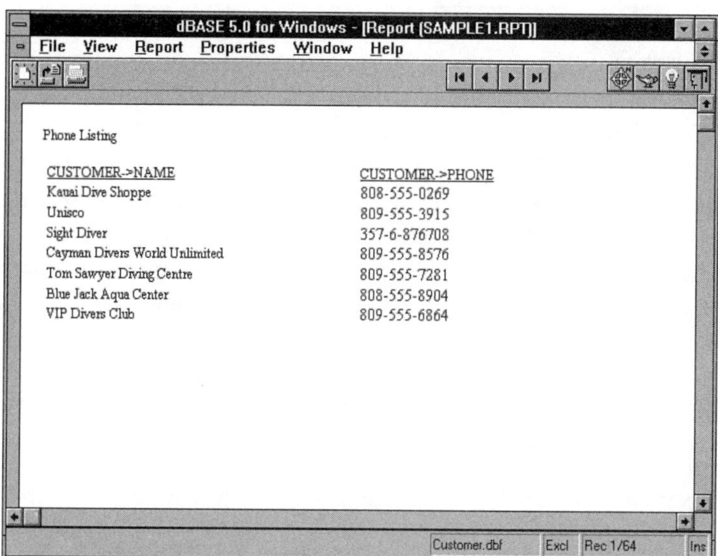

Fig. 1.9
An example of a report in dBASE for Windows.

How dBASE for Windows Compares to the Competition

dBASE for Windows is just one of a number of relational database managers on the market, but its heritage makes it a unique product with a very specific slant. In creating dBASE for Windows, Borland's goal was to provide a way to bring dBASE applications into the Windows environment, thereby offering all the advantages of Windows to newly developed applications. At the same time, Borland wanted to maintain full compatibility with older dBASE for DOS applications.

A number of excellent database products are currently on the market, including Borland's own Paradox for Windows and dBASE IV, along with others, such as Microsoft's FoxPro and Access. Each of these products provides full relational database management, programming languages for application development, and other high-end features. The strength of dBASE for Windows is its compatibility with the dBASE language you may have used over the years, as well as its compatibility with the thousands of dBASE programs and applications already on the market.

An important difference between dBASE for Windows and the various versions of dBASE for DOS that came before it is the added visual nature of the program. With all earlier versions of dBASE, you commonly used dBASE commands to perform the desired operations. Menu systems, first introduced with dBASE III, offered more options in dBASE III PLUS and in dBASE IV, but many users continued to do most of their work using the famed dBASE *dot prompt.* Although dBASE for Windows doesn't force you to give up those commands if you know them, you can easily perform much of your work by manipulating objects through the Navigator and with the SpeedBar buttons.

System Requirements

To use dBASE for Windows, you need an IBM-compatible computer running Windows version 3.0 or higher. Although you can run Windows with as little as 2M of RAM, dBASE for Windows requires at least 6M of RAM, but 8M is recommended. A mouse is also required for some operations. If you are using dBASE for Windows on a local area network, refer to the appropriate network documentation (packaged with your dBASE documentation) for more information about using the program on a network.

Specifications

Specifications for dBASE for Windows include the following (these are theoretical maximums; practical maximums may be less depending on the memory installed in your PC):

Maximum size of table: 2 billion bytes

Maximum fields per table: 1,024

Maximum size of a character field: 254 bytes

Maximum size of a record: 32,767 (including the _DBASELOCK field)

Maximum number of tables that can be placed in a query or report: 225

From Here...

You may want to refer to the following chapters for additional information about the concepts discussed in this chapter:

- Chapter 9, "Creating Basic Queries." Many reports are based on query data, so knowing how to create queries is essential. This chapter tells you everything you need to know to get started.
- Chapter 11, "Creating Basic Reports." This chapter gets you started on reports by covering topics such as starting Crystal Reports and navigating the Report Designer, using the Personal Trainer, and designing and printing a basic report.
- Chapter 12, "Working with Related Tables." If you plan to create multiple-table reports, read this chapter to learn about relating and linking tables.

Chapter 2

Moving from dBASE for DOS to dBASE for Windows

If you have been a user of dBASE for DOS, you may be wondering what all is involved with the switch to dBASE for Windows. It's likely that you have a number of existing tables (called *databases* in the dBASE lingo of old), along with forms, reports, labels, and possibly some programs for managing specific tasks. You may have some concerns about making the switch. You, or others in your organization, have most likely invested a great deal of time and effort into dBASE for DOS. Naturally, you want the move to dBASE for Windows to cause as little upheaval as possible, and you want to be able to take advantage of dBASE for Windows' increased functionality gradually—as time permits.

The good news is that you can take most of your work from dBASE III, dBASE III PLUS, or dBASE IV directly into dBASE for Windows—with no changes. (And rest assured that the bad news is minimal.) You can open and edit your tables, use your screens, print your reports and labels, and even run your dBASE programs—with minimal changes, if any. dBASE for Windows offers considerably more functionality than any previous version of dBASE. But you can ease your way into this functionality, using the more advanced features of dBASE for Windows as you have the time and the inclination to explore them. If you have been using the dBASE dot prompt for all your work, you can continue using the same commands—with no change—in the Command Window of dBASE for Windows.

A minor disadvantage comes into play only if you are accustomed to doing things with the menus of either dBASE III PLUS or dBASE IV. If that situation applies to you, you have to learn to use a new interface, with its own set of menus for different tasks. Because you are working with dBASE and all of its associated parts, however, you will find that many aspects of your work are familiar. Although you will still put tables to use, edit and browse among your records, and run reports and labels, you will will find that the menu options you use to perform these tasks have changed.

In this chapter, you learn how dBASE III PLUS and dBASE IV differ from dBASE for Windows in the following areas:

- Starting dBASE
- Creating tables
- Adding records
- Using forms
- Creating and using queries
- Generating reports
- Programming

Introducing the User Interface of dBASE for Windows

Assuming that you have worked with dBASE before (after all, that is what this chapter is about and you *are* reading it), you have seen one of two possible interfaces (*interface* is a fancy term for the conventions and procedures that determine how you communicate with a program). If you worked with the old workhorse, dBASE III PLUS, you probably stuck with the famed dot prompt—dBASE's way of issuing commands for everything you did. You also may have used the Assistant, a system of menus that enabled you to perform many common database tasks (see fig. 2.1).

The Assistant moved dBASE in the right direction by making dBASE easier to use (something early versions of dBASE were not known for). Many users, however, found it both awkward and limiting. You could do most common tasks through the Assistant menus, but those tasks that you could not do were often also quite necessary. Consequently, most dBASE users found themselves still resorting to the dot prompt. And although dBASE III PLUS provided a catalog feature, its use was not intuitively apparent, so users stayed away from it in droves.

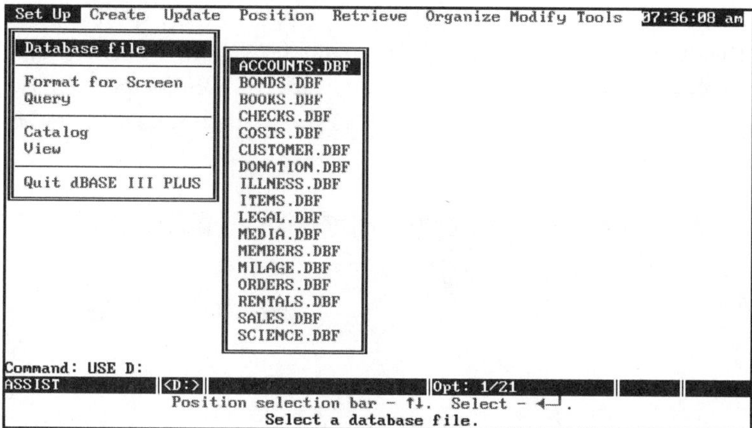

Fig. 2.1
The dBASE Assistant provided menus for most tasks in dBASE III PLUS.

Ashton-Tate, the company manufacturing dBASE at the time, heard the complaints about the limitations of the Assistant and replaced it with the Control Center in dBASE IV (see fig. 2.2). The Control Center added to the Assistant's functionality and also made catalogs more manageable. With the introduction of the Control Center, dBASE IV integrated the catalog concept into the program's menu structure, which made the overall user interface less awkward to deal with.

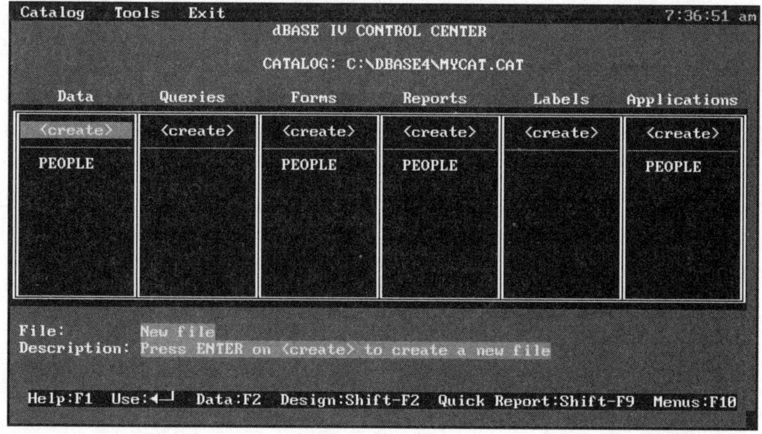

Fig. 2.2
dBASE IV's Control Center replaced the dBASE III PLUS Assistant.

dBASE for Windows offers its own user interface, which, thanks to the event-driven design of Windows, provides access to more database management power. At the same time, the dBASE for Windows user interface offers seasoned dBASE pros a familiar way to accomplish tasks. As with all Windows applications, dBASE for Windows offers pull-down menus for common tasks such as opening files, finding and editing records, creating and using forms, or printing reports. The menus enable you to do essentially what you did with the dBASE III PLUS Assistant and the dBASE IV Control Center. dBASE for Windows, however, also offers the Navigator, the Command Window, and the buttons of the SpeedBar. Figure 2.3 shows the interface offered by dBASE for Windows.

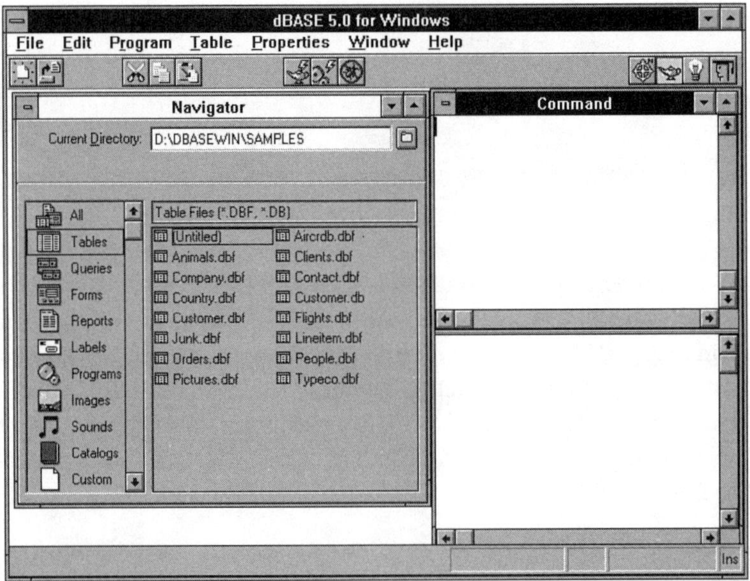

Fig. 2.3
The dBASE for Windows interface with the Navigator and Command window displayed.

In many respects, the Navigator replaces both the Control Center in dBASE IV and the catalog feature in dBASE III PLUS. Rather than being task-oriented, however, the Navigator is oriented in terms of the different types of files used by dBASE for Windows. If you click the Tables icon in the left column of the Navigator, for example, a list of tables is displayed in the right column; if you click the Reports icon, a list of available reports is displayed.

Starting dBASE for Windows versus dBASE for DOS

Starting dBASE for Windows is likely to be the area that seems the most different when you make the switch from dBASE for DOS. The Windows interface makes starting the program a little simpler. To start dBASE III PLUS or dBASE IV, you probably used an assortment of DOS commands (or possibly a batch file) to establish a DOS path, switch to the dBASE directory, and load the program. You don't have to establish a path when you use Windows because Windows' file management system performs the necessary tasks in the background. With Windows, you only have to double-click the dBASE for Windows program icon in the dBASE for Windows program group. The major difference is in the appearance of the program's interface, as described earlier and shown in figure 2.3.

Creating a Table

To create a table in dBASE III PLUS, you open the **C**reate menu and choose **D**atabase File from the menus; then dBASE asks you for a drive identifier (so that it knows where to store the file) and a name for the file. After you enter this information, you are taken to a design screen so that you can enter the specifications for the new table.

To create a table in dBASE IV, you place the cursor on the <create> entry under the Data panel in the Control Center and press Enter. A design screen similar to the one in dBASE III PLUS appears. Working across column by column, you enter the name of the field, its type, its width, and the number of decimal places. You enter these specifications for each field, and then you place the cursor on any blank field and press Enter or Ctrl+End to indicate that you are finished with the process. In the case of dBASE IV, the design screen also contains an index column that you can use to specify whether an index should be added to the field to keep the data in order. Figure 2.4 shows dBASE IV's design screen. The design screen used by dBASE III PLUS and dBASE III was virtually identical, except for the absence of the Index column.

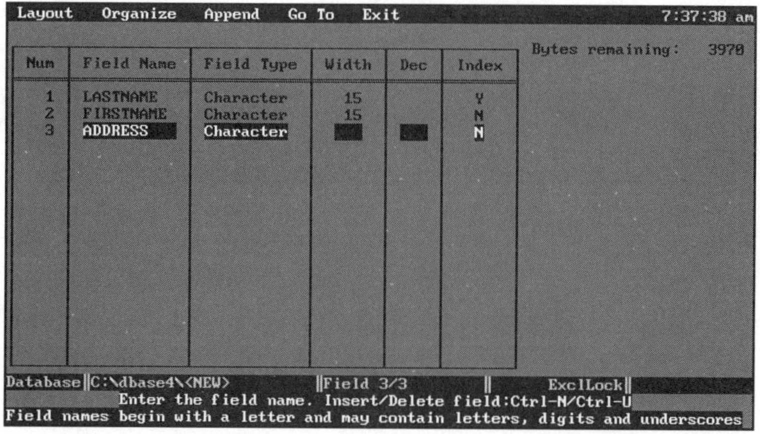

Fig. 2.4
The table design screen used in dBASE IV.

To create a new table in dBASE for Windows, you open the **F**ile menu and choose **N**ew, and then you choose **T**able from the submenu. The Table Structure dialog box appears, which is similar in overall design to the one used by versions of dBASE for DOS. Figure 2.5 shows the Table Structure dialog box. One clearly visible difference is the addition of the **T**ype drop-down list box at the top of the dialog box. You can click the arrow to open the list box and reveal its two choices: dBASE and Paradox. You use this list box to indicate the type of table you want to create: a dBASE table or a Paradox table (dBASE for Windows lets you create either type). If you are upgrading from dBASE III or dBASE III PLUS, the Index column is also new to you, but dBASE IV users are familiar with this column. The Index column lets you specify an *index*, which enables you to view or print records in a particular order based on a certain field.

▶ "Indexing and Sorting Data," p. 119

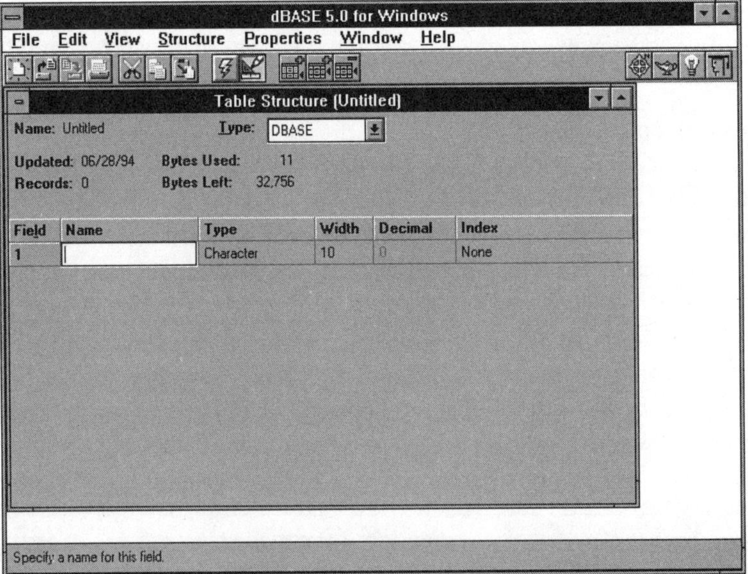

Fig. 2.5
Use the Table Structure dialog box to define the fields in a table.

Note

In all versions of dBASE for DOS, after you define the table, you can move to an empty field and press Enter to complete the process. In dBASE for Windows, if you move to an empty field during the table definition process and press Enter, dBASE displays an error message informing you that empty fields are not allowed. To complete the definition process, open the **F**ile menu and choose **S**ave.

Adding Records

To add records in dBASE III PLUS, you open the **U**pdate menu and choose **A**ppend. In dBASE IV, you highlight the name of the table in the Data Panel, press F2, choose **R**ecords, and finally, choose **A**dd New Records. With either of these methods, dBASE displays a simple on-screen form that you can use to add records to the table.

In dBASE for Windows, you can add new records by opening the **T**able menu and choosing **A**dd Records. dBASE displays a blank record from the table in a simple form, as shown in figure 2.6. You can use the mouse to add the record, or you can press Tab to move to each successive field.

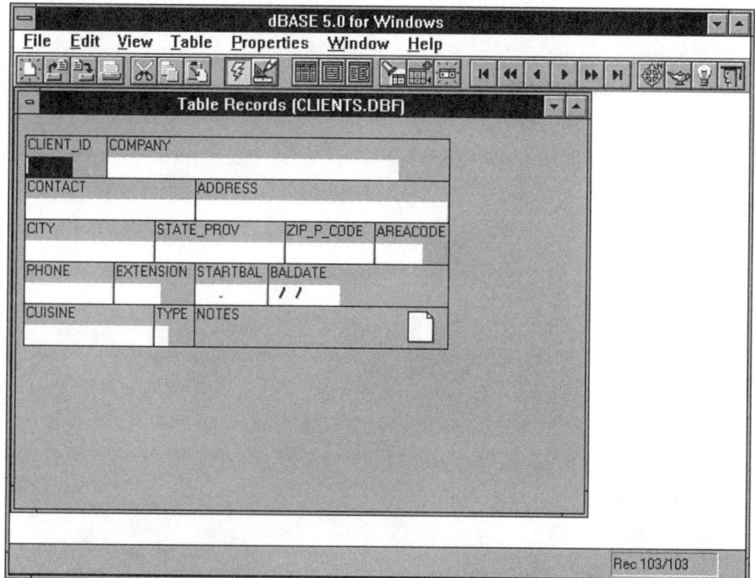

Fig. 2.6
The simple form you use to add records to a dBASE for Windows table.

One difference worth noting: In all versions of dBASE for DOS, you can press Ctrl+End at any time to indicate that you are finished adding records and ready to close the on-screen editing form. (You can also press Ctrl+W, a key combination that is a holdover from the early days of dBASE.) In dBASE for Windows, pressing Ctrl+End has no effect. Interestingly, however, the old Ctrl+W key combination still works. To close the window in which you add new records, click the window's Close box (or press Ctrl+F4—the standard Microsoft Windows key combination for closing windows) or use Ctrl+W.

In dBASE for DOS, when you want to enter or edit data in memo fields, you move the cursor to the memo field and press Ctrl+Home. You make any necessary revisions, and then you press Ctrl+End. In dBASE for Windows, however, you can simply double-click the appropriate memo field, and a window in the memo field opens. You then make the necessary additions or revisions to the field. When you are finished, you close the window in the memo field using the window's Close box (or Ctrl+F4), or you can press Ctrl+W.

Designing Forms

The way in which forms work is the first area in which dBASE for Windows differs significantly from versions of dBASE for DOS. In dBASE for DOS, you use forms to customize the way data is entered into a table. Typically, you use custom entry forms to make data entry and editing easier and more accurate. Forms can contain some fields of a table while omitting others, calculated fields can be included in forms, and forms can be placed in various locations. In any version of dBASE for DOS, you use a screen designer to create custom forms. In dBASE III PLUS, you start the process by opening the **C**reate menu and choosing **F**ormat. In dBASE IV, you highlight <create> in the Forms panel of the Control Center and then press Enter. With either version of dBASE, a form design screen appears next (see fig. 2.7).

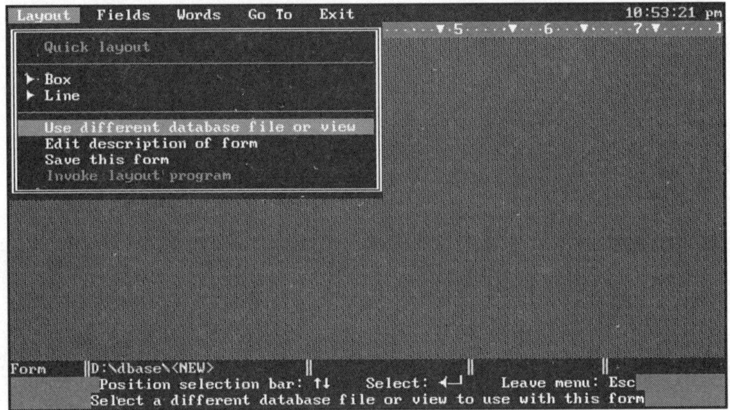

Fig. 2.7
The screen designer you use in dBASE for DOS to create custom forms.

In the screen designer, you place fields and type text (to serve as labels) in the appropriate locations, and then you use the various menu options to draw any necessary lines or rectangles. When you have finished designing the form, you save it as an .FMT file. Later, you can use that saved form to view and edit data in a table. When you save a form, dBASE (behind the scenes) creates a file that contains a series of @...SAY and @...GET program statements. When the form is put into use, the language interpreter that is part of dBASE uses these statements to control the appearance of the screen.

This form design method works well enough for simple data-entry screens. Its limitations become obvious, however, as you begin to do more complex database work. One significant disadvantage to this form design method is that there is no easy way to create *relational forms*—forms you can use to examine data stored in more than one table simultaneously. For example, perhaps you want to show more than one record from a "master" table (such as a table of customers), along with all associated records from a related table (such as all orders placed by that customer). The screen painters in dBASE for DOS were not designed to let you do this sort of thing. Of course, you can always write a program to display this type of screen, but the original intent of the screen designer was to eliminate the need for you to write programs simply to display a data-entry screen.

Another limitation of the screen designer in dBASE for DOS is that you can only create forms that are useful for data entry and editing. You cannot create menus, dialog boxes, or any of the other parts of a user interface that are common to complete applications.

To provide compatibility with your existing dBASE for DOS forms, dBASE for Windows can run your existing forms unchanged. Just like the forms you create in dBASE for DOS, the forms you create in dBASE for Windows can provide data entry and editing capabilities. dBASE for Windows forms, however, can offer a great deal more. Besides handling data-management tasks, you can use forms to provide custom windows, dialog boxes, and even complete interfaces for an application. Forms in dBASE for Windows can also contain graphic elements as part of the form design, or they can display graphic images that are stored in the fields of a table.

As an example of the flexibility possible with forms, consider the next three forms shown here. Figure 2.8 shows a form designed for a common data-entry task. Notice, however, that the form includes a graphic image of a tropical fish specimen (in this form, the image is stored in the field of a table). Also notice that the form includes its own navigation and control buttons. In this case, a portion of an application's user interface is an integral part of the form.

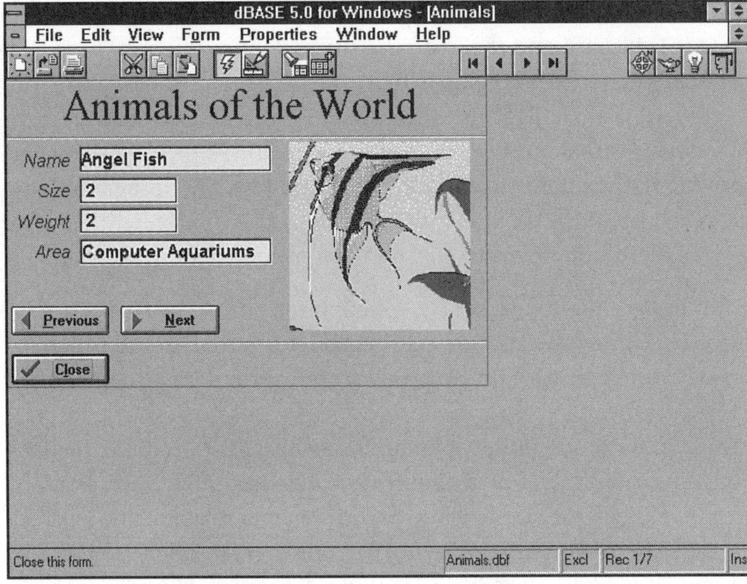

Fig. 2.8
A custom data-entry form containing a visual element and control buttons.

In figure 2.9, the form includes list boxes that can be used to look up related data contained in other tables.

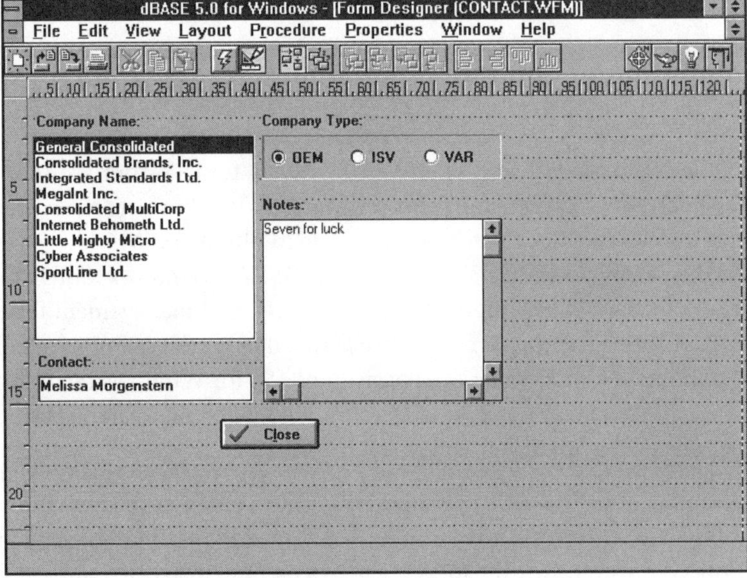

Fig. 2.9
A form design that includes scrollable list boxes that reference data in associated tables.

Finally, figure 2.10 shows a form that makes no use whatsoever of any data from dBASE tables. The form's only purpose is to serve as a programmable calculator.

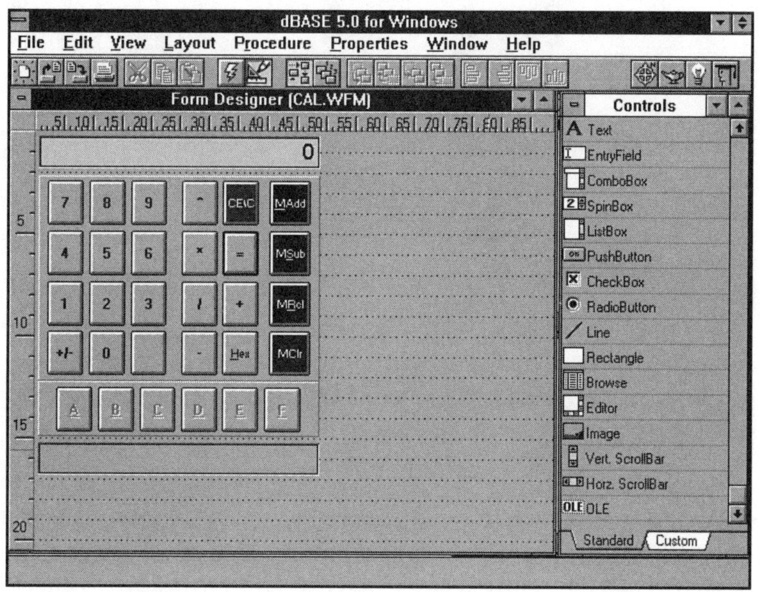

Fig. 2.10
A form design that provides a programmable calculator.

To begin designing a form in dBASE for Windows, you open the **F**ile menu and choose **N**ew, and then you choose **F**orm from the submenu. A blank window in the Form Designer appears, accompanied by the Controls window, as shown in figure 2.11.

▶ "Designing Advanced Forms," p. 335

You use the tools in the Controls Window to add various controls to the form. As you continue designing the form, you can easily check its progress by switching between the form's design and run modes. After you save the form, you can run it by double-clicking its name in the Navigator. And while you are in the design mode for any form, you can run the form by opening the **V**iew menu and choosing **R**un, or by clicking the Run icon in the SpeedBar.

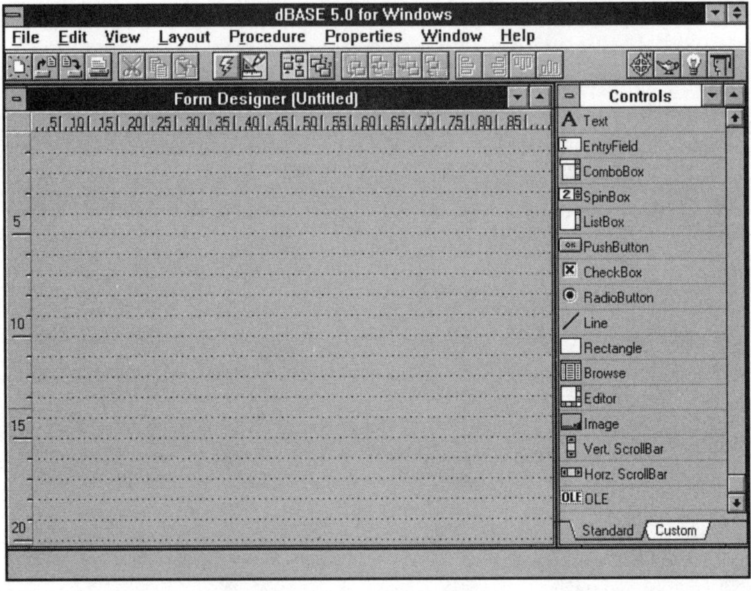

Fig. 2.11
Use the Form Designer to create new forms in dBASE for Windows.

If you want to quickly design a form that can be used primarily for data entry and editing, you can use the Form Expert (described in more detail in Chapter 10, "Creating Basic Forms"). When you first begin to design a form, you are asked whether you want to design the form manually or use the Form Expert. If you choose to use the Form Expert, you are asked a series of questions about the form and then the Form Expert produces a form based on your answers. Figure 2.12 shows a dialog box produced by the Form Expert.

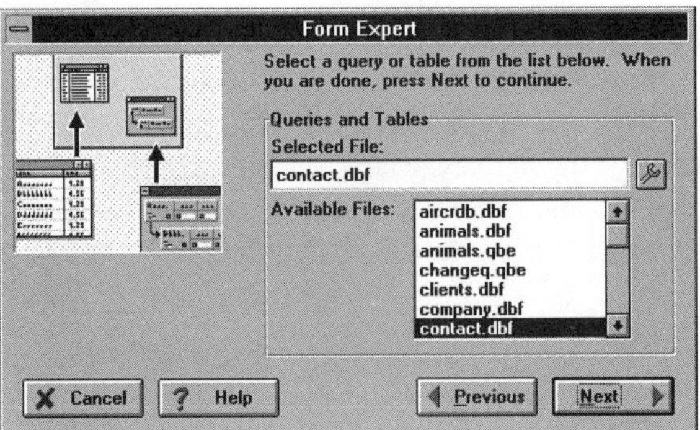

Fig. 2.12
This dialog box produced by Form Expert permits the user to select specific fields to include in a form.

If you are familiar with the Quick Form options provided in the dBASE for DOS Screen Painters, you will be pleased to know that the Form Expert provides considerably more screen design flexibility than those older facilities in dBASE for DOS. The old screen painters limited you to a single style of layout, with all fields of a table appearing by default in a form. The Form Expert, by comparison, enables you to include all fields of a table or to selectively choose fields for inclusion in the form. The Form Expert also gives you a choice of layouts and styles for the form. You can choose between columnar or row-oriented layouts, and you can select among various "looks" for the form. Figure 2.13 shows an example of a completed form created with the aid of the Form Expert.

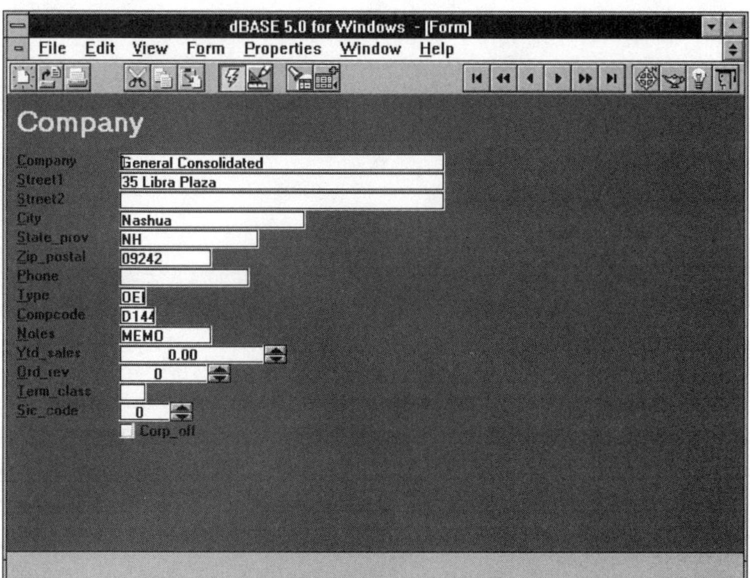

Fig. 2.13
A form created when the user answered a few simple questions in the Form Expert dialog boxes.

Creating Queries

Both dBASE III PLUS and dBASE IV provide ways for you to perform queries, which (as you learned in Chapter 1) are questions you can ask to retrieve specific sets of your data. Only dBASE IV, however, provides query-by-example—a standardized way to retrieve specific data that is now used by many database managers. dBASE for Windows also provides query-by-example, so you can define conditions and retrieve data that conforms to those specific conditions. Figure 2.14 illustrates the process of defining a query in dBASE for Windows.

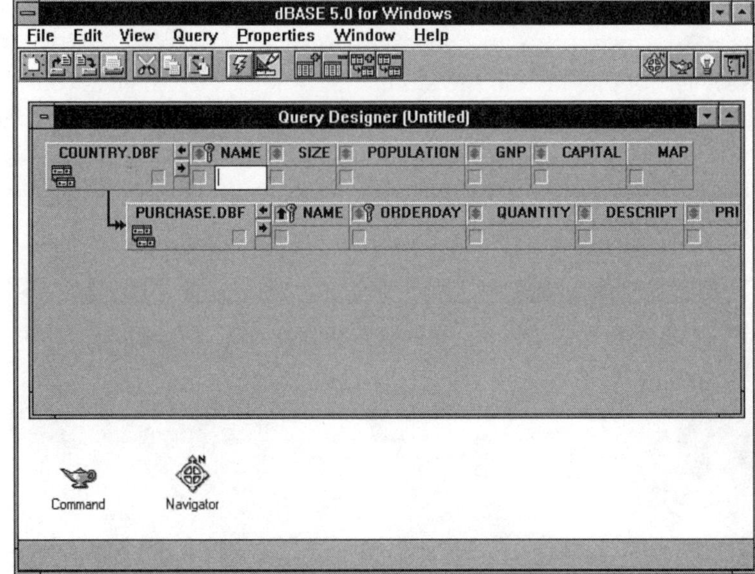

Fig. 2.14
The dBASE for Windows query definition process enables you to present only those records that meet the specific conditions you define.

To take full advantage of the Windows environment, the Query Designer in dBASE for Windows uses a visual approach to the definition of your queries. You can use the mouse to click in particular fields of the query, thereby entering the conditions that limit the records made available to the query. After you specify the conditions, you can run the query; dBASE makes available only those records that match the specified conditions. In dBASE for Windows, you can use the output from queries as a basis for forms or reports, and you can also view that output in a Browse window.

Generating Reports

The reports feature is one area that has changed significantly between dBASE for DOS and dBASE for Windows. You have to learn a new way of doing things, but you gain a great deal of flexibility and power in return for your efforts.

If you have used dBASE III PLUS, you know that its report writer provides, at best, simple columnar reports. In fact, the report writer provided with dBASE III PLUS is so limited that an entire legion of third-party products grew out of the need to circumvent its limitations. The report writer in dBASE IV is a great improvement. It provides a banded style of report designer that you can use to create many common types of reports. Nevertheless, even the version in dBASE IV has limitations. In particular, creating relational reports is a challenge in either version of dBASE for DOS. dBASE for Windows, on the other hand, includes a professional report designer, Crystal Reports, that you use to create your reports. Figure 2.15 shows a report being designed using Crystal Reports.

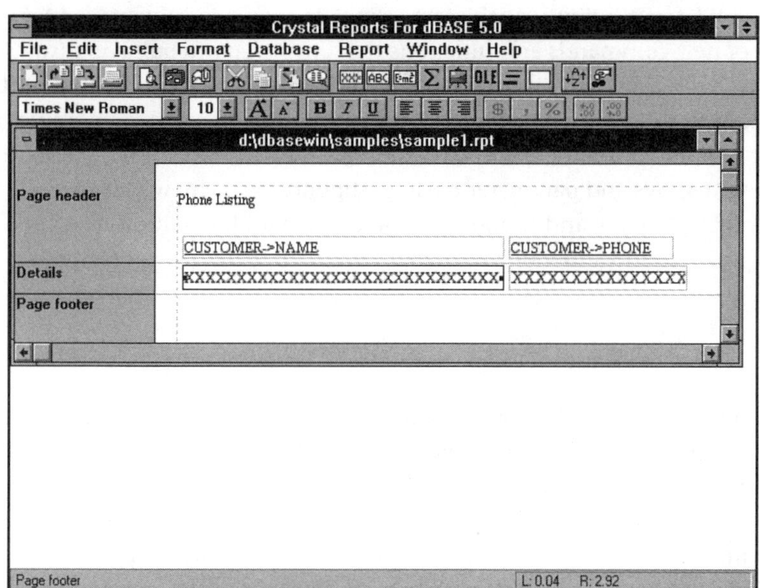

Fig. 2.15
A report in the Crystal Reports window during the design phase.

The major difference between designing reports using Crystal Reports and designing reports using dBASE for DOS is that Crystal Reports provides a design surface that matches the Windows design concepts. You don't lay out a report by inserting fields and text, as you did in dBASE for DOS, so much as you "paint" the report. In Crystal Reports, report design is much more of a free-form process than was possible in any DOS version of dBASE. Reports are based on query views, which are created using the Query Designer. Your reports can contain fields or text labels, as well as graphic design elements. With Crystal Reports, you can also create crosstab reports that summarize numeric data, something that was not possible (outside of writing program code) with earlier versions of dBASE. Although Crystal Reports is its own program, you can still run the reports that you design and save from within dBASE for Windows.

Programming in dBASE for Windows

Programming in dBASE for Windows can be as familiar as you want, as different as you want, or anywhere in between. If you have been programming in any DOS version of dBASE, you can take your programming skills directly into dBASE for Windows. At the same time, you can take advantage of an array of new commands and functions that enable you to build applications that go far beyond what was possible with dBASE for DOS. Besides supporting all dBASE for DOS program code, dBASE for Windows provides a number of advanced programming features, including a C-style preprocessor, support for enhanced arrays and parameter passing, support for the new field types (binary and OLE data), and support for Paradox tables. In addition, you can incorporate sound and video into your dBASE for Windows programs.

From Here...

Veterans of dBASE III PLUS and dBASE IV will find much in dBASE for Windows that is familiar. Granted, some features do not work the same, but neither are they terribly difficult to learn. An important point to keep in mind is that dBASE for Windows was designed to be compatible with your existing work in dBASE for DOS. The techniques you have used in the past to design and implement your databases can now, for the most part, be carried over to dBASE for Windows. You can use your past experience with dBASE for DOS as a solid foundation on which to build your new skills with dBASE for Windows.

You may want to refer to the following chapters for additional information about the concepts discussed in this chapter:

- Chapter 9, "Creating Basic Queries." Many reports are based on query data, so knowing how to create queries is essential. This chapter tells you everything you need to know to get started.

- Chapter 11, "Creating Basic Reports." This chapter gets you started on reports by covering topics such as starting Crystal Reports and navigating the Report Designer, using the Personal Trainer, and designing and printing a basic report.

- Chapter 12, "Working with Related Tables." If you plan to create multiple-table reports, read this chapter to get the lowdown on relating and linking tables.

Chapter 3

A Quick Tour of dBASE for Windows

This chapter is designed to help you get to work quickly with dBASE and your data, by showing you how to open tables, add and edit data, print very simple reports, and obtain selected responses to the questions you have about your data. To prevent you from having to enter tedious amounts of sample data, this chapter uses the sample data provided in the CLIENTS.DBF table supplied with your installation of dBASE for Windows. If you installed dBASE for Windows in the usual manner, the CLIENTS.DBF table is in the DBASEWIN\SAMPLES directory of your hard drive.

This chapter shows you how to perform the following specific tasks:

- Start dBASE for Windows
- Work with windows, menus, and dialog boxes
- Open a table in the Table Records window
- Navigate in a table
- Add records
- Edit records
- Use Form view
- Find data
- Delete records
- Create a query

- Print your data
- Use dBASE commands in the Command window

Starting the Program

To start dBASE for Windows, double-click the dBASE for Windows icon in the dBASE for Windows program group.

When the program starts, you see the windows shown in figure 3.1: the Command window and the Navigator.

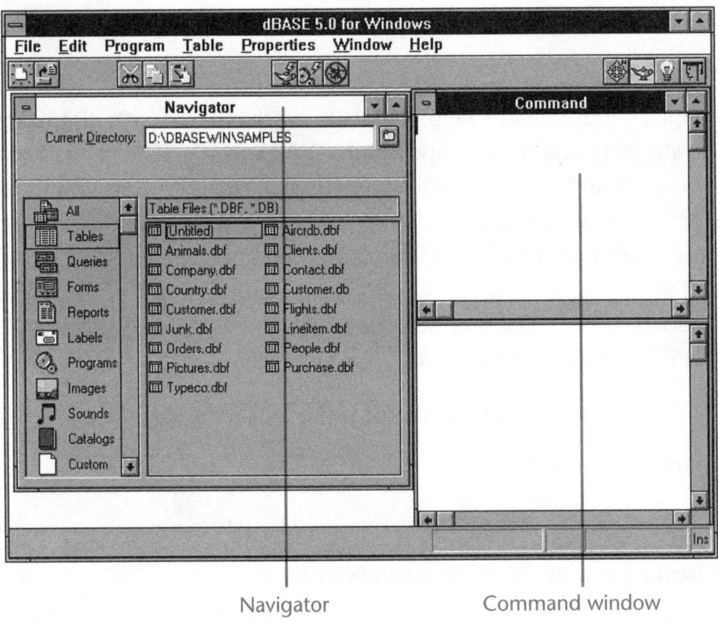

Fig. 3.1 The opening screen in dBASE for Windows.

In this chapter, you use the Navigator and the various menu options for much of your work. Toward the end of the chapter, you also work with the Command window.

About Windows, Menus, and Dialog Boxes

As with any Windows application, dBASE for Windows uses the standard Microsoft Windows items, including windows, menus, and dialog boxes.

Figure 3.2 identifies some of these items, which, when combined, compose the *user interface* that you use to communicate with dBASE for Windows.

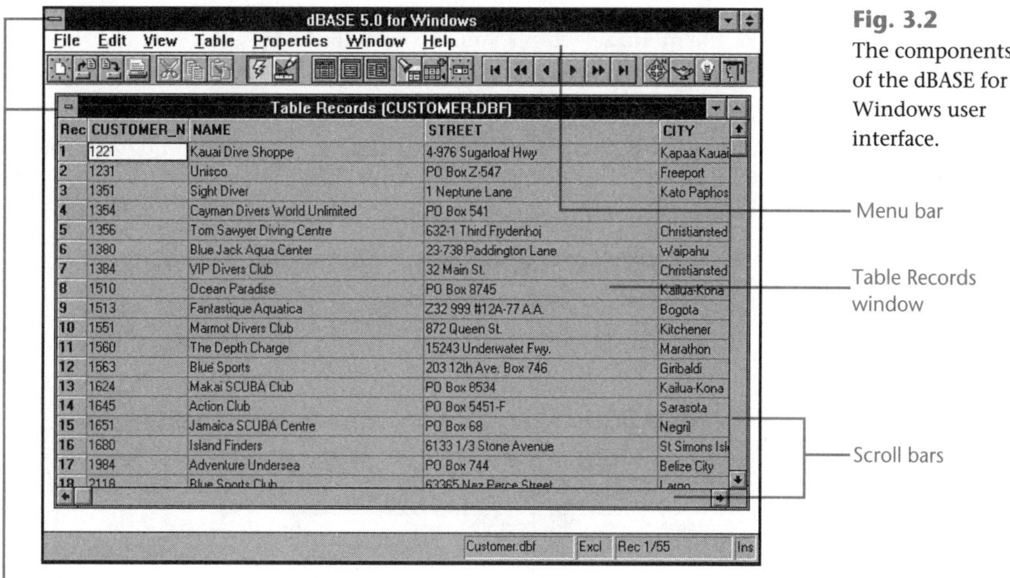

Fig. 3.2
The components of the dBASE for Windows user interface.

Figure 3.2 shows two windows: the dBASE for Windows window (which is *maximized*, or expanded to its full size), and a Table Records window containing the records of a table. As you can see in the figure, each window has a Control menu, but only the Table Records window has scroll bars. At the top of the main window is the menu bar. The menu bar offers pull-down menus with which you can access the various program options.

Note

This book assumes that you are familiar with the basics of moving and sizing windows in Microsoft Windows. If you need help with these tasks, refer to your Windows documentation.

You can use either the mouse or the keyboard to open menus and to choose menu commands. Using the mouse, click the menu's name in the menu bar, and the menu drops down. Then click the appropriate command in the menu to choose it. To open a menu using the keyboard, hold down the Alt key while you press the underlined letter of that menu in the menu bar. Then to choose an option from that menu, hold down the Alt key while you press the underlined letter for that command. For example, pressing Alt+F opens the **F**ile menu; pressing S chooses the **S**ave command.

Many of the menu selections you make in dBASE for Windows result in the appearance of a dialog box. A *dialog box* is an on-screen message box that either provides you with additional information about the task you are trying to perform or requests information from you so that the program can continue the task. Figure 3.3 shows an example of a dialog box.

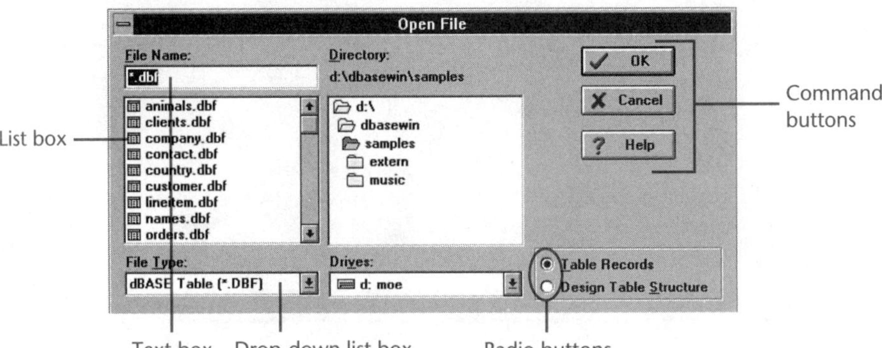

Fig. 3.3
This dialog box appears when you choose the **O**pen command from the **F**ile menu in dBASE for Windows.

Many dialog boxes have text boxes in which you can type text, such as the name of a file. Some dialog boxes also have list boxes (with which you can select one option from a number of possible options), check boxes, or radio buttons. You can click the boxes or buttons to turn on or off the indicated choices. Some dialog boxes have drop-down list boxes; in these, you click the arrow at the right edge of the box, and an expanded list of options drops down. You can then select the option you want by clicking it. In addition, most dialog boxes have command buttons, including an OK button, a Cancel button, and a Help button. You can click OK to accept the chosen options in the dialog box when you are finished selecting them, and you can click Cancel to cancel any changes you have made to settings in the dialog box. Clicking Help displays a help screen relating to the dialog box options.

The most commonly used menu commands are duplicated on the SpeedBar. The SpeedBar buttons are equivalent to choosing a particular command from a menu. Clicking the Print button in the SpeedBar, for example, is equivalent to opening the **F**ile menu and choosing **P**rint. The SpeedBar buttons change depending on the point you are at in dBASE for Windows. Figure 3.4 shows the SpeedBar that is visible when a table is open in a Table Records window.

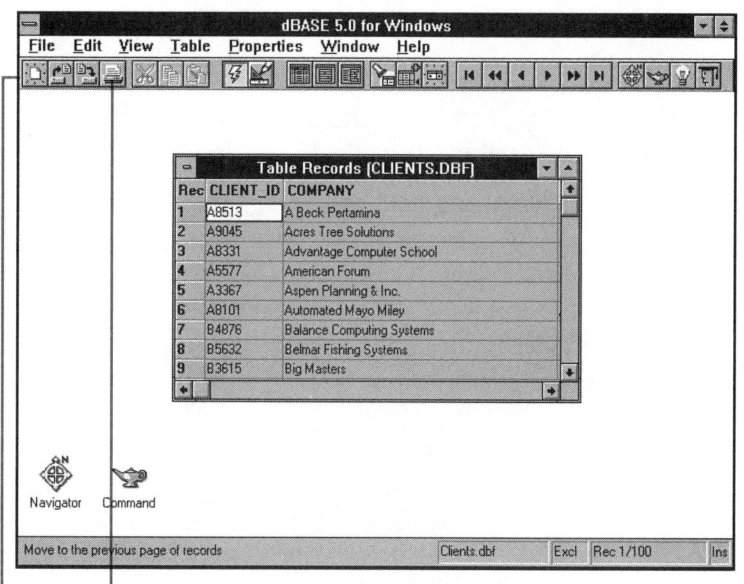

Fig. 3.4
The SpeedBar that is visible when a Table Records window is active.

Some of the buttons that appear on most SpeedBars include Cut, Copy, and Paste (the equivalents of **E**dit, Cu**t**; **E**dit, **C**opy; and **E**dit, **P**aste), the Print button (the equivalent of **F**ile, **P**rint), and the Design and Run buttons (the equivalent of pressing Shift+F2 for Design, or F2 for Run).

Tip
dBASE for Windows displays the purpose of each SpeedBar button at the bottom of the screen as you move the mouse pointer over the button.

The SpeedMenus

dBASE for Windows also makes use of SpeedMenus, which are various pop-up menus that appear when you right-click particular objects throughout the program. You can use these menus to quickly perform different operations on the object in question. As an example, if you right-click a table, a pop-up menu appears with choices for adding, deleting, finding, and replacing records within that table.

Opening a Table

Before you can work with data in a dBASE table, you have to open the table. In dBASE for Windows, you can open tables with the Navigator or by entering the USE command in the Command window. If you use the Navigator, you must first click the Tables icon in the Navigator so that all tables are visible. You then can double-click the name of the table you want to open.

Tip
Another easy way to open a table is to click it in the Navigator and then press F2.

To open the Clients table provided with dBASE for Windows, perform the following steps:

1. If the Tables category isn't already highlighted in the Navigator, click it to select it (or choose **T**ables from the **V**iew menu).

2. When the list of available tables appears in the right column of the Navigator, double-click Clients. The table opens in a Table Records window, as shown in figure 3.5.

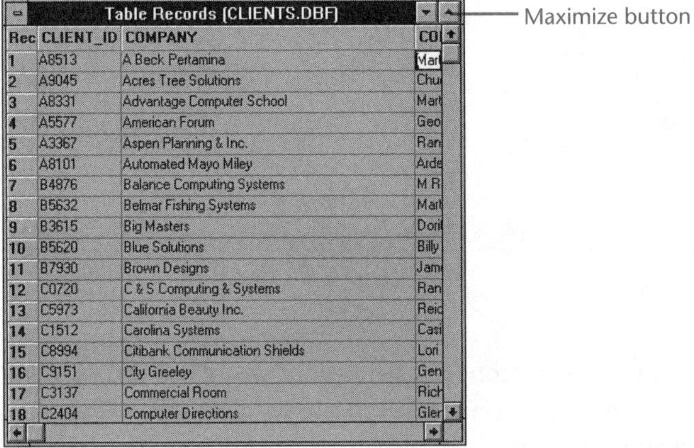

Rec	CLIENT_ID	COMPANY	CO
1	A8513	A Beck Pertamina	Mar
2	A9045	Acres Tree Solutions	Chu
3	A8331	Advantage Computer School	Mart
4	A5577	American Forum	Geo
5	A3367	Aspen Planning & Inc.	Ran
6	A8101	Automated Mayo Miley	Arde
7	B4876	Balance Computing Systems	M R
8	B5632	Belmar Fishing Systems	Mart
9	B3615	Big Masters	Dori
10	B5620	Blue Solutions	Billy
11	B7930	Brown Designs	Jam
12	C0720	C & S Computing & Systems	Ran
13	C5973	California Beauty Inc.	Reic
14	C1512	Carolina Systems	Casi
15	C8994	Citibank Communication Shields	Lori
16	C9151	City Greeley	Gen
17	C3137	Commercial Room	Rich
18	C2404	Computer Directions	Gler

Fig. 3.5
An example of a table open in a Table Records window.

3. To see more of the data in the Table Records window, maximize the window by clicking the Maximize button in the upper-right corner of the window.

When a table is viewed through a Table Records window, you see the data in the familiar row-and-column format common to database managers. Each row of the table contains a record, which is one complete set of data, such as a customer's name and address. Each column of the table contains an individual field (category of information), such as the street address or name of a city.

Navigating a Table

You can navigate a table using a number of different methods. Perhaps the most obvious is the visual method of navigation-by-mouse. You use the horizontal and vertical scroll bars and the mouse to get where you want to go.

When a table has more records than can fit in a single window, a vertical scroll bar appears at the right edge of the window. Click the scroll bar's up arrow to scroll up through the contents of the window; click the down arrow to scroll down through the contents of the window. You can also move through the data by dragging the *scroll box*, the small rectangle visible within the scroll bar. Dragging the scroll box causes movement of the cursor by an amount relative to the distance you drag the box. For example, if you click and drag the scroll box down roughly one-fourth of the length of the vertical scroll bar, the cursor moves down through approximately one-fourth of the records in the table.

If the table is too wide to fit in a window, a horizontal scroll bar appears at the bottom of the table. You can use the horizontal scroll bar in a manner similar to the vertical scroll bar. Click the left arrow to scroll to the left in the window; click the right arrow to scroll to the right. Dragging the scroll box to the left or right moves you horizontally by a relative amount, causing the columns to scroll to the left or to the right within the window.

You can also use various keys and key combinations to move around in a table. Pressing Tab moves the cursor one field to the right, except for the last field, when pressing Tab causes the cursor to move to the first field of the next record. In a similar fashion, pressing Shift+Tab moves the cursor one field to the left, except for the first field, when pressing Shift+Tab moves the cursor to the last field of the preceding record. You can use the up-arrow and down-arrow keys to move among the records of the table.

Navigating with the Table Menu Commands

You can use various commands from the **T**able menu to move around in a table. If you open the **T**able menu, you see the choices shown in figure 3.6.

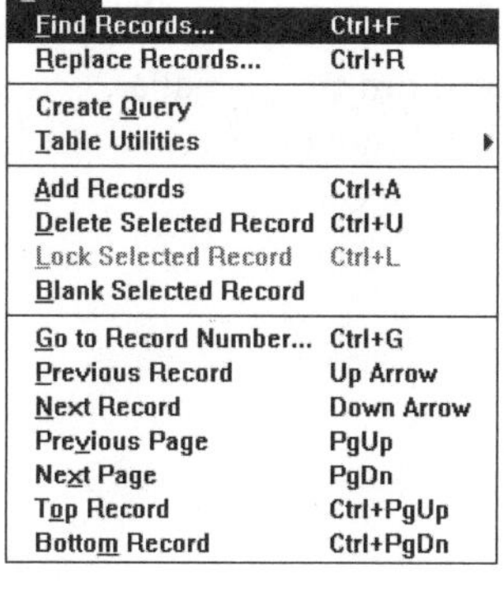

Table	
Find Records...	Ctrl+F
Replace Records...	Ctrl+R
Create Query	
Table Utilities	▸
Add Records	Ctrl+A
Delete Selected Record	Ctrl+U
Lock Selected Record	Ctrl+L
Blank Selected Record	
Go to Record Number...	Ctrl+G
Previous Record	Up Arrow
Next Record	Down Arrow
Previous Page	PgUp
Next Page	PgDn
Top Record	Ctrl+PgUp
Bottom Record	Ctrl+PgDn

Fig. 3.6
The Table menu.

Choose **P**revious Record to move the cursor to the previous record (equivalent to pressing the up-arrow key), or choose **N**ext Record to move the cursor to the next record (equivalent to pressing the down-arrow key). The Pre**v**ious Page command on the menu moves the cursor backward one full window, whereas the Ne**x**t Page menu command moves the cursor forward one full window. Finally, the T**o**p Record and Botto**m** Record menu commands can be used to move to the first or last records in the table.

Navigating with the SpeedBar Buttons

You can also move through the records in your table by using the SpeedBar navigation buttons. These buttons are identified in figure 3.7.

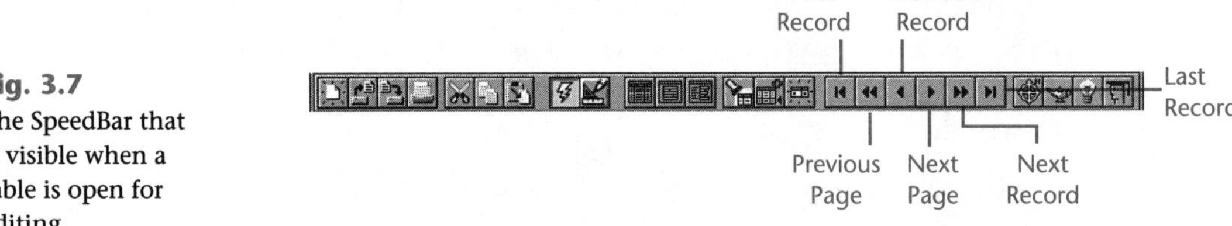

Fig. 3.7 The SpeedBar that is visible when a table is open for editing.

You can use the SpeedBar navigation buttons to perform the same tasks you perform using commands in the **T**able menu. The Previous Record and Next Record buttons, the two buttons in the center of the set of buttons, move the cursor to the previous record or the next record, respectively. The Previous Page and Next Page buttons move the cursor to the previous window and the next window, and the First Record and Last Record buttons move the cursor to the first and last records in the table.

Adding Records

To add records to a table, open the **T**able menu and choose **A**dd Records or click the Add Records button in the SpeedBar. Choose **A**dd Records from the **T**able menu now. The cursor moves to a new blank record at the end of the table, as shown in figure 3.8.

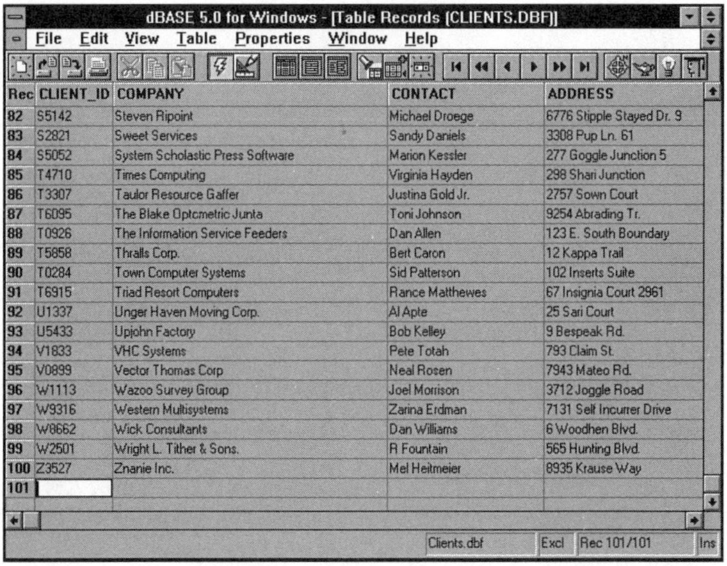

dBASE 5.0 for Windows - [Table Records (CLIENTS.DBF)]

File Edit View Table Properties Window Help

Rec	CLIENT_ID	COMPANY	CONTACT	ADDRESS
82	S5142	Steven Ripoint	Michael Droege	6776 Stipple Stayed Dr. 9
83	S2821	Sweet Services	Sandy Daniels	3308 Pup Ln. 61
84	S5052	System Scholastic Press Software	Marion Kessler	277 Goggle Junction 5
85	T4710	Times Computing	Virginia Hayden	298 Shari Junction
86	T3307	Taulor Resource Gaffer	Justina Gold Jr.	2757 Sown Court
87	T6095	The Blake Optometric Junta	Toni Johnson	9254 Abrading Tr.
88	T0926	The Information Service Feeders	Dan Allen	123 E. South Boundary
89	T5858	Thralls Corp.	Bert Caron	12 Kappa Trail
90	T0284	Town Computer Systems	Sid Patterson	102 Inserts Suite
91	T6915	Triad Resort Computers	Rance Matthewes	67 Insignia Court 2961
92	U1337	Unger Haven Moving Corp.	Al Apte	25 Sari Court
93	U5433	Upjohn Factory	Bob Kelley	9 Bespeak Rd.
94	V1833	VHC Systems	Pete Totah	793 Claim St.
95	V0899	Vector Thomas Corp	Neal Rosen	7943 Mateo Rd.
96	W1113	Wazoo Survey Group	Joel Morrison	3712 Joggle Road
97	W9316	Western Multisystems	Zarina Erdman	7131 Self Incurrer Drive
98	W8662	Wick Consultants	Dan Williams	6 Woodhen Blvd.
99	W2501	Wright L. Tither & Sons.	R Fountain	565 Hunting Blvd.
100	Z3527	Znanie Inc.	Mel Heitmeier	8935 Krause Way
101				

Clients.dbf | Excl | Rec 101/101 | Ins

Fig. 3.8
A new, blank record appears at end of the table when you choose **A**dd Records from the **T**able menu.

You can add information to the table by typing the appropriate data into each field and then pressing Tab when you have finished typing. Add the following data to the table; press Tab after each entry so that the cursor moves to the next field.

CLIENT_ID: **P4252**
COMPANY: **Pioneer Systems**
CONTACT: **Maria Ferguson**
ADDRESS: **4212 Wyldewood Way**
CITY: **Durham**
STATE_PROV: **NC**
ZIP_P_CODE: **27709**
AREACODE: **919**
PHONE: **555-2380**
EXTENSION: **252**
STARTBAL: **500.00**
BALDATE: **4/12/94**
CUISINE: **Chinese**
TYPE: **1**

After you enter the data into these fields, the cursor is located in the Notes field, which is a memo type field. If you try to type information directly into this field, dBASE beeps and does not accept the data. Data entry into memo fields requires a different technique.

When the cursor is in a memo field (as it is at this point in our current example), you are at the entry point for a *memo window,* which can hold up to 64,000 bytes of data for a single record. You can get into the memo window using either of these two techniques:

- Double-click in the memo field.
- Open the **V**iew menu and choose Fie**l**d Contents. (Note that you can also press F9.)

Use either of these techniques to open the memo window now. A window opens that has the title CLIENTS->NOTES, as shown in figure 3.9.

Fig. 3.9
An open memo field.

Tip
Users familiar with the older DOS versions of dBASE can still use the Ctrl+W key combination to exit a memo window. When you are in a memo window, pressing Ctrl+W is the same as choosing **S**ave and Close from the **F**ile menu.

In the window, you type the text of your memo field entry just as you would type text using any word processing software. Now type the following text into the memo window for the new record you just added:

This company plans to order a significant amount in the first quarter to meet a government procurement.

When you have finished typing, you can store your changes and return to viewing the table by opening the **F**ile menu and choosing **S**ave and Close.

Working in Table Layout versus Form Layout

Entering data in a table using a table layout accomplishes the task of data entry, but usually it is not the most convenient way to add data. Keeping track of all the information associated with a single record is often difficult when you are looking at a table, because as you continue to enter data and press the Tab key, parts of the data for that same record scroll off the left side of the screen. dBASE displays information in the row-and-column format of a table because the concept of a database is easier for most users to grasp when the data is viewed in this manner. The row-and-column format also makes it easier to view large amounts of information at one time. But when you are concerned with only one record (which is the case when you are adding data), you usually don't care about the other data in the table. You probably prefer to see as many fields as can fit on the screen at once.

dBASE for Windows provides flexibility by offering you a choice of two approaches to data entry. You can use the tabular approach, which you just used to add a new record, or you can use an on-screen form, which shows just one record at a time. To toggle layouts, you can either press F2, or you can open the **V**iew menu and choose **F**orm Layout. Press F2 now to switch to a form layout. The record you just added is displayed in an on-screen form (see fig. 3.10).

You use different techniques to move through records when they are displayed in form layout. Try pressing the PgUp key repeatedly; then try pressing the PgDn key a number of times. Next, repeatedly press the up-arrow and down-arrow keys. You can see that PgUp and PgDn, which in table view moved you up or down a full window of records, now move you forward or backward one record at a time. The up-arrow and down-arrow keys, which in table view moved you up or down one record at a time, now move you forward or backward one field at a time.

Fig. 3.10
The record you added displayed in a form layout.

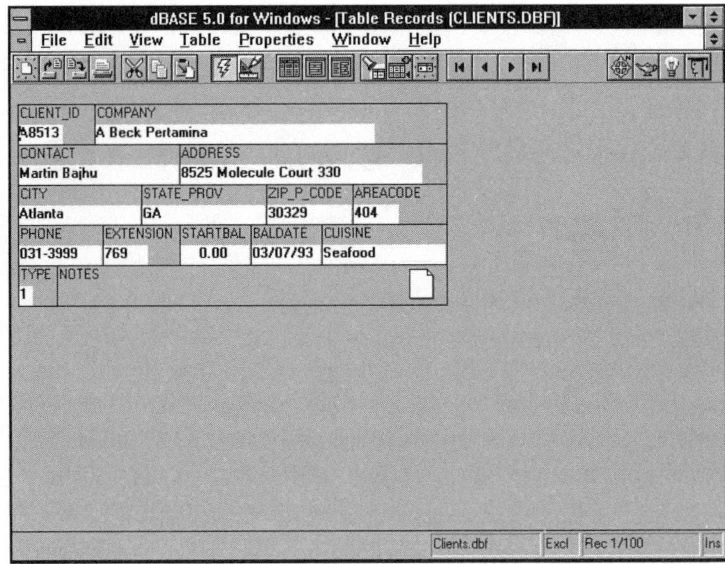

Try adding one record while you have the table displayed in the form layout. Open the **T**able menu and choose **A**dd Records (or click the Add Records button in the SpeedBar), and a blank record appears at the end of the table. Click in the CLIENT_ID field if the cursor is not already there; then add the following record, pressing the Tab key after each entry:

Tip
You can also use the Ctrl+A key combination for adding a new record.

CLIENT_ID: **W1312**
COMPANY: **Wilson Demographics**
CONTACT: **Thomas Wilson**
ADDRESS: **2300 Arlington Blvd.**
CITY: **Arlington**
STATE_PROV: **VA**
ZIP_P_CODE: **22029**
AREACODE: **703**
PHONE: **555-6370**
EXTENSION: **100**
STARTBAL: **500.00**
BALDATE: **5/15/94**
CUISINE: **Mexican**
TYPE: **1**

In this example, you can leave the memo field blank. After you have inserted the entry in the Type field, press F2 twice to switch back to table layout. Then press Home to quickly move the cursor back to the first field in the table. The two new records you added are displayed at the bottom of the table, as shown in figure 3.11.

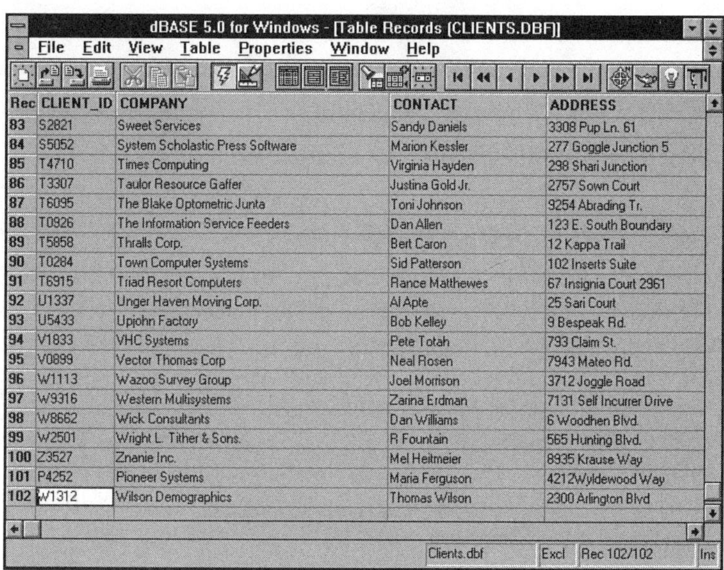

Rec	CLIENT_ID	COMPANY	CONTACT	ADDRESS
83	S2821	Sweet Services	Sandy Daniels	3308 Pup Ln. 61
84	S5052	System Scholastic Press Software	Marion Kessler	277 Goggle Junction 5
85	T4710	Times Computing	Virginia Hayden	298 Shari Junction
86	T3307	Taulor Resource Gaffer	Justina Gold Jr.	2757 Sown Court
87	T6095	The Blake Optometric Junta	Toni Johnson	9254 Abrading Tr.
88	T0926	The Information Service Feeders	Dan Allen	123 E. South Boundary
89	T5858	Thralls Corp.	Bert Caron	12 Kappa Trail
90	T0284	Town Computer Systems	Sid Patterson	102 Inserts Suite
91	T6915	Triad Resort Computers	Rance Matthewes	67 Insignia Court 2961
92	U1337	Unger Haven Moving Corp.	Al Apte	25 Sari Court
93	U5433	Upjohn Factory	Bob Kelley	9 Bespeak Rd.
94	V1833	VHC Systems	Pete Totah	793 Claim St.
95	V0899	Vector Thomas Corp	Neal Rosen	7943 Mateo Rd.
96	W1113	Wazoo Survey Group	Joel Morrison	3712 Joggle Road
97	W9316	Western Multisystems	Zarina Erdman	7131 Self Incurrer Drive
98	W8662	Wick Consultants	Dan Williams	6 Woodhen Blvd.
99	W2501	Wright L. Tither & Sons.	R Fountain	565 Hunting Blvd.
100	Z3527	Znanie Inc.	Mel Heitmeier	8935 Krause Way
101	P4252	Pioneer Systems	Maria Ferguson	4212Wyldewood Way
102	W1312	Wilson Demographics	Thomas Wilson	2300 Arlington Blvd

Fig. 3.11
The two new records added to the bottom of the table.

Editing Data in a Table

After you enter your data into a table, making changes to it is mostly a matter of finding the record you want to change, moving the cursor to the desired fields, and making the necessary changes. You can go to an existing record by opening the **T**able menu and choosing either the **G**o To Record Number or the **F**ind Record command. **G**o To Record Number assumes that you know the record number of the record you are seeking; **F**ind Record lets you search a given field for specific data.

Using the Go To Record Number Command

If you know the record number for the record you want to edit, follow these steps:

1. Open the **T**able menu and choose **G**o To Record Number. The Go to Record dialog box appears, as shown in figure 3.12.

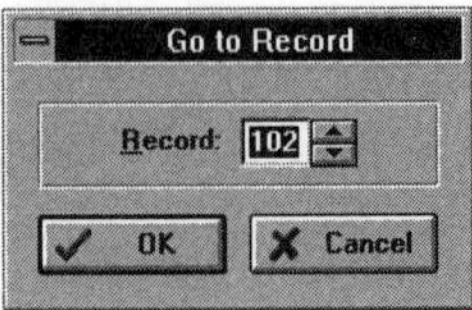

Fig. 3.12
The Go to Record dialog box.

2. In the dialog box, type the number of the record you want to go to. Alternatively, you can click the spinner arrows to increase or decrease the value in the box.

3. Click OK, and dBASE moves to the record you indicated.

Using the Find Record Command

If you don't know a record's number, but you know a specific bit of data that you can search for in a field (such as a client's contact name), follow these steps to find the record you want to edit:

1. Open the **T**able menu and choose **F**ind Record. The Find Records dialog box appears, as shown in figure 3.13.

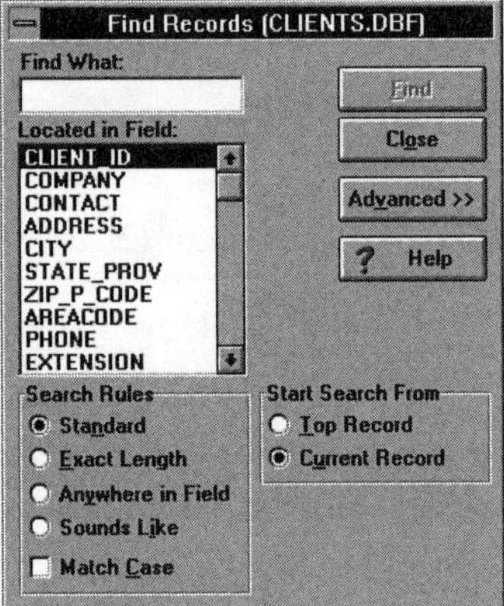

Fig. 3.13
The Find Records dialog box.

2. In the Located In Field drop-down list, highlight the field you want to search by clicking the field's name.

3. Type the value you want to find in the Find What text box.

4. Click OK, and dBASE locates the next record containing the value you specified.

After you reach the appropriate record, you can use the Tab and Shift+Tab keys to move to the appropriate field. Then use the Backspace or Del key to remove unwanted characters and make the necessary corrections.

To insert new characters between existing ones, press the Ins key to toggle it until you are in Insert mode (the letters `Ins` appear in the Status bar at the bottom of the window). Then type the characters you want to insert. Existing characters are pushed to the right to make room for the new ones. To turn off Insert mode, press the Ins key again. When you are not in Insert mode, any characters you type while you are editing a record will overwrite existing characters.

Saving Changes

During a work session with dBASE, much of the data you add and edit is stored in memory. This data is written to disk only when dBASE needs to do so, or when you close a table. When you make a change to a record, the change is not considered permanent (even in memory) until you move the cursor off that record or close the table. When you move the cursor off a record you just edited, the changes to that record are stored in memory, and you can't undo them. When dBASE needs to free some memory space, or when you close the table or exit from dBASE, the changes are written permanently to disk.

You can, at any time, force dBASE to save changes to the current record by opening the **F**ile menu and choosing either **S**ave Record or Sa**v**e Record and Close. **S**ave Record saves the changes and leaves the table open for further use; Sa**v**e Record and Close saves the changes and also closes the table. Conversely, as long as you have not moved the cursor off a record, you can discard any changes you have made to that record. To discard the changes, open the **F**ile menu and choose either Aban**d**on Record or A**b**andon Record and Close.

Tip
You can use the Ctrl+S key combination to save a record, Ctrl+W to save and close a record, and Ctrl+Q to abandon a record and close.

Deleting Records

In dBASE, you use a two-step method to delete unwanted records. First, you mark unwanted records for deletion, and then you delete the marked records with an operation known as a *pack*. Users of earlier DOS-based versions of dBASE will find this to be a familiar process. The techniques have not changed, but dBASE for Windows does provide menu options and mouse shortcuts to help you perform these tasks.

To mark a record for deletion, click the record to select it, open the **T**able menu, and then choose **D**elete Selected Record.

Tip
You can also mark records for deletion by placing the cursor anywhere in the record and pressing Ctrl+U.

Repeat this marking process for every record you want to delete. The deletions are not permanent until you perform the second part of the process—packing the table. When you pack a table, all records marked for deletion are removed, and the remaining records are renumbered accordingly.

To pack a table, open the **T**able menu and choose **T**able Utilities. From the next menu that appears, choose **P**ack Records, and a confirmation dialog box appears. Click **Y**es in the dialog box, and the pack operation proceeds.

Although this two-step method for deleting records may seem awkward to those who have not worked with earlier versions of dBASE, it has its advantages. The fact that the deletions are not permanent until you perform the pack makes it possible for you to change your mind about a deletion. Deleted records can be recalled (or, in effect, *unmarked*) as long as you have not yet performed the pack.

To recall a record marked for deletion, move the cursor to any deleted field in the record and press Ctrl+U to toggle the deleted status. The Recall Current Record command appears in the menu only when the cursor is located at a record that has been marked for deletion.

Introducing Queries

▶ "Creating Basic Queries," p. 167

▶ "Working with Related Tables," p. 261

▶ "Creating Advanced Queries," p. 425

After you store data in a dBASE table, you must have a way to regularly retrieve selected subsets of that data. Simple searches are fine when you want to find a single record and make changes to that record, but sometimes you want to formulate more complex questions relating to your data. You may want to see a listing of all clients who live in California, all sales reps who have exceeded a certain goal for the last three months, or all customers who have exceeded their credit limits. These kinds of database questions can be answered using queries. You learn more about queries in later chapters, but the following exercise gives you an idea of how you can use dBASE for Windows queries to find specific data easily.

To create a query that retrieves all the client names, contact names, and phone numbers for clients based in California, perform the following steps:

1. Open the **F**ile menu, choose **N**ew, and then choose **Q**uery.
2. An Open Table dialog box now appears. Click CLIENTS.DBF and then click OK. A new Query window appears, as shown in figure 3.14.

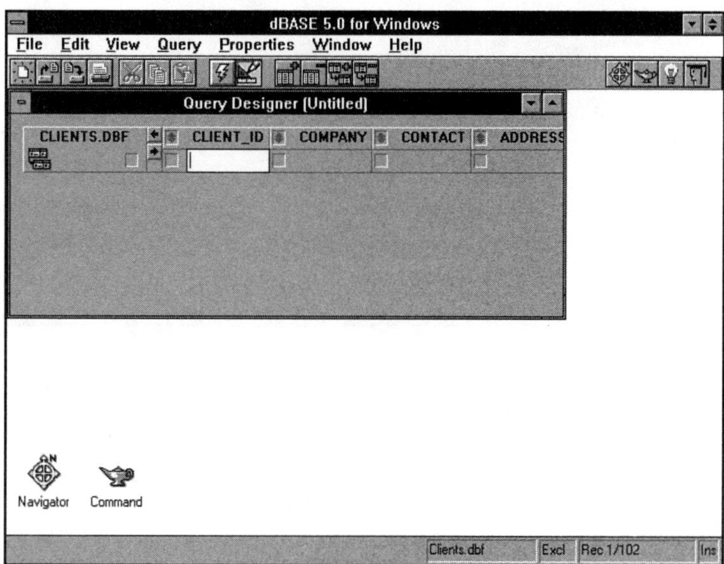

Fig. 3.14
An example of a new Query window.

3. Click the box beside the COMPANY field, and a check appears in the box.
4. Click the box beside the CONTACT field to add a check to that box, and then repeat this step for the CITY field.
5. Click the box beside the STATE_PROV field. While the insertion pointer is still flashing next to the STATE_PROV box, type the following (including the quotation marks):

   "CA"

6. Click the box under the AREACODE and PHONE fields to add check boxes to those fields. At this point, your query should resemble the example shown in figure 3.15.

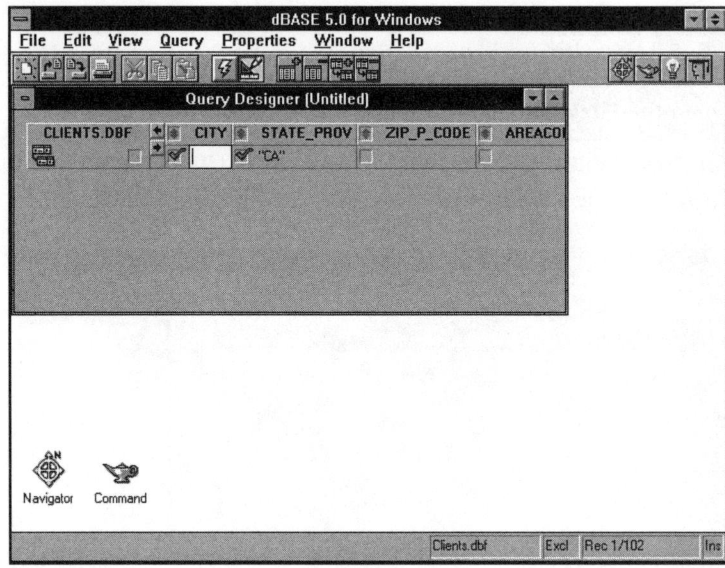

Fig. 3.15
An example of a filled-in Query Results window.

The fields you selected tell dBASE that you want to see the COMPANY, CONTACT, CITY, STATE_PROV, AREACODE, and PHONE fields from the Clients table, and you want to see only those records in which CA appears as an entry in the STATE_PROV field.

7. Open the **V**iew menu and choose Query Results. Alternatively, you can press F2, or you can click the Run button in the SpeedBar (the button containing the lightning bolt). A view of the table appears showing only the fields you selected in the query, and showing only those records in which CA appears in the STATE_PROV field (see fig. 3.16).

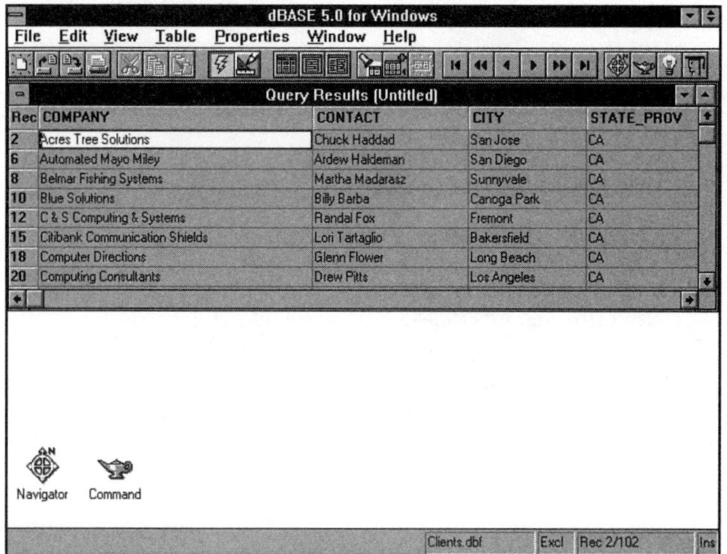

Fig. 3.16
The results of your first query.

Getting a Printout Quickly

You can quickly generate a printout of the data in the table by opening the **F**ile menu and choosing **P**rint. Turn on your printer now and try this. The Print Records dialog box appears, as shown in figure 3.17.

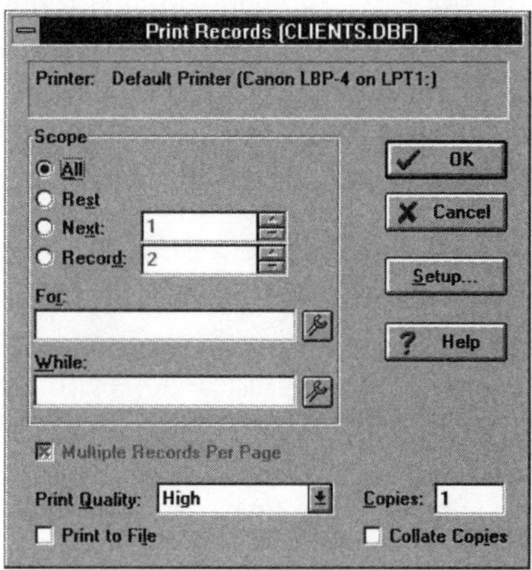

Fig. 3.17
The Print Records dialog box.

▶ "Printing a Report," p. 255

You learn more about the Print Records dialog box in a later chapter; for now, notice that the default settings cause all records shown in the current table window to be printed. Because the currently displayed table is based on a query that selected certain fields and certain records, only this selected data appears on your printout. Click OK in the dialog box to begin printing. Your printed report should show the data that is visible in the table window.

▶ "Designing Basic Reports," p.229

▶ "Creating Advanced Reports," p.385

You can utilize similar techniques to quickly generate a printout of the data in any table. After you open a table, open the **F**ile menu and choose **P**rint, click OK in the Print Records dialog box, and you get a printout containing the data in that particular table. Of course, you can create far more complex reports in dBASE using more complicated methods. Later chapters dealing with reports discuss how you can design reports containing headers and footers, customize the placement of fields, add graphic images, and incorporate other specialized techniques.

Introducing the Command Window

Up to this point, you have been performing all your work through the Navigator. A significant advantage of dBASE for Windows, however, is that it lets you use menu actions and mouse clicks (which are part of the Windows environment) along with typed commands (which are common to earlier versions of dBASE). Even if you are not familiar with earlier versions of dBASE, you may find after working with commands that you prefer to use them for much of your dBASE work. For many operations, typing a command is faster than choosing the corresponding menu option. To bring the Command window to the foreground, double-click the Close box in the Navigator; then open the **W**indow menu and choose **C**ommand (see fig. 3.18).

If you have been following along and performing the exercises in this chapter, you can see that some commands (that you did not type) already appear in the Command window. These commands were entered automatically by dBASE in response to some of your mouse actions and menu choices. For example, the SET FILTER and SET FIELDS commands were entered in response to the query you designed earlier to select certain records and fields from the table.

If you plan to enter commands directly in the Command window, you probably want to see the results of those commands as you enter them. You can see the results of dBASE commands in the lower half of the Command window.

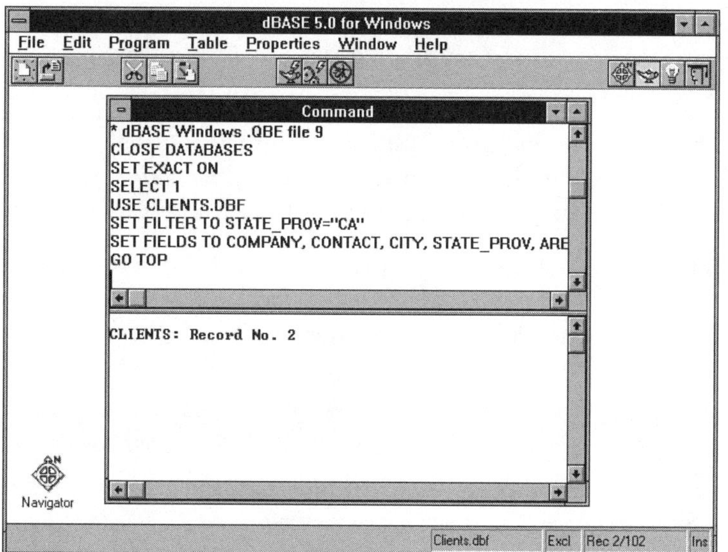

Fig. 3.18
The Command window.

Opening a Table

From the command level, you must initiate the USE command when you want to open a table and use it. Earlier, you closed the Clients table, so use the USE command now to reopen it. In the Command window, enter the following:

USE CLIENTS

You will not see any visible action, but the table is now open for you to use. To be sure that you have opened a table, you can use the LIST command to display a listing of the data contained in the table. Entering the LIST command alone causes the contents of the entire table to appear in the Command Results window. You can be selective about what you display, however, by including specified field names after the LIST command. If you add more than one field name, be sure to separate the field names with commas. To see how the LIST command works, enter the following command in the Command window:

LIST COMPANY, CITY, STATE_PROV, PHONE

dBASE responds by displaying in the Command window data from only those fields you named. If you had entered LIST without any field names, data from all the fields in the table would have been displayed. (With large tables, it can take quite a bit of time for a large amount of data to be displayed in the window. You can stop the display of data at any time by pressing the Esc key.)

You can route the output from a list command to your default Windows printer by adding a TO PRINT clause to the end of the LIST command. To try this technique, enter the following command in the Command window:

LIST COMPANY, CITY, STATE_PROV, PHONE TO PRINT

This command causes the listing you saw earlier in the Command Results window to be routed to the printer rather than to the window.

Note

If you are using a laser printer, you may have to enter an EJECT command after the LIST command in order for the printer to process the print request completely.

dBASE also lets you add FOR clauses to many commands. A FOR clause enables you to select specific data in much the same way you did earlier when you designed the query to obtain specific records. As an example, try entering the following command in the Command window:

LIST COMPANY, CITY, STATE_PROV, PHONE FOR STATE = "NY"

The Query Results window appears, as shown in figure 3.19.

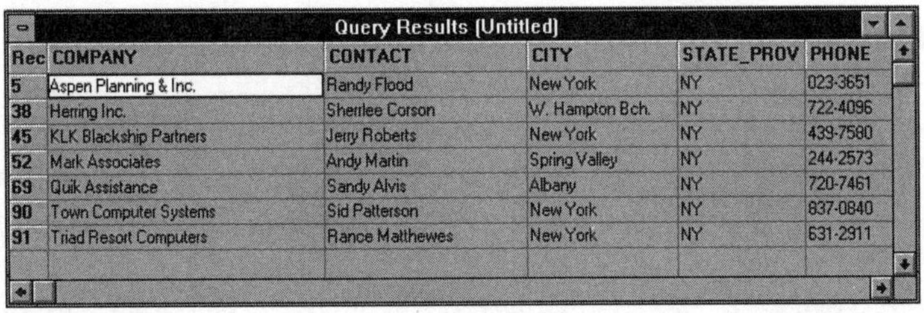

Query Results (Untitled)

Rec	COMPANY	CONTACT	CITY	STATE_PROV	PHONE
5	Aspen Planning & Inc.	Randy Flood	New York	NY	023-3651
38	Herring Inc.	Sherrlee Corson	W. Hampton Bch.	NY	722-4096
45	KLK Blackship Partners	Jerry Roberts	New York	NY	439-7580
52	Mark Associates	Andy Martin	Spring Valley	NY	244-2573
69	Quik Assistance	Sandy Alvis	Albany	NY	720-7461
90	Town Computer Systems	Sid Patterson	New York	NY	837-0840
91	Triad Resort Computers	Rance Matthewes	New York	NY	631-2911

Fig. 3.19
The results of a query entered in the Command window.

These results show how you can pair the FOR clause with the LIST command to obtain just the data you may be seeking.

Later chapters discuss other dBASE commands you can type in the Command window, along with ways you can use the Navigator and the menu commands in place of those commands. You can even exit dBASE either by typing a command in the Command window or by choosing a command from a menu. In the Command window, you can enter **QUIT** to close all open files and completely leave dBASE. If you would rather use the menus, you can open the **F**ile menu and choose E**x**it.

From Here...

Refer to the following chapters for more helpful topics regarding working with tables and your basic data in dBASE for Windows:

- Chapter 9, "Creating Basic Queries." This chapter tells you what you need to know to start creating basic queries.
- Chapter 11, "Creating Basic Reports." This chapter tells you what you need to know to start creating basic reports.
- Chapter 12, "Working with Related Tables." This chapter tells you how to relate and link tables.

Chapter 4

Exploring Database Concepts

In many ways, a database is like an expert consultant. A database stores a wealth of information about a particular topic, classifies and organizes data, updates this knowledge as new facts and figures are presented, and reports answers to questions that you ask.

With all these points of similarity, however, one major difference exists between the database and a consultant: the database has no built-in intelligence. The range of functions the database can perform is determined by the database management system that created and set the database in motion. Furthermore, every operation a database performs must be directed by someone who understands how the database management system works and, equally important, the reasons why the database was originally set up. This chapter will examine the database concepts with which you must be familiar to design and implement effective databases.

In this chapter, you learn the following:

- What a database is
- What database management is
- What a relational database is
- Basic database management concepts
- dBASE for Windows terminology

What Is a Database?

The term *database management* makes many a computer user's eyes glaze over. The concept of database management can bring to mind teams of individuals in white lab coats, slaving over giant mainframe computers containing billions of records. But this sort of analogy can be unnecessarily complex, because *database management* is nothing more than the storing of information in an organized fashion.

Every database is originally designed to solve some sort of problem. The problem may be complex or simple, or it may be a problem that regularly occurs, or one that needs a one-time solution. In any case, resolving the problem requires collecting a body of knowledge, or pertinent facts, into an organized unit. A *database* provides a way to organize facts so that they become a resource that can be used to solve a business problem. If you give some thought to common, everyday activities, you will likely discover that a database underlies these activities. Databases come into play with many common business problems, such as getting out the payroll, keeping track of expenses and revenues, sending statements to customers, ordering supplies and managing inventory, paying taxes, and so on. Success (or the lack of it) in handling these kinds of business challenges depends to a large degree on the planning that goes into organizing the information demanded by each problem.

As an example, just consider for a moment what it takes to pay the salary for the employees of an organization. If you work for an organization with more than a few employees, the accountant who writes your check probably relies on a database, and that database contains details on who you and the other employees of the company are. For you to get paid with any accuracy, the accountant has to know your name, social security number, wage rate, and the number of hours worked during each pay period. All this enables the accountant to deduce your gross rate of pay; but, assuming that the firm withholds taxes from your check, the accountant also has to know your tax rate and how many deductions you are claiming on your W-4 form.

Typically, the kind of data gathering described here is just the start of the task. If solving the payroll problem also includes deducting for contributions in a pension program, accounting for overtime pay at a different pay rate, accommodating sick leave or vacation time, or even the cost of mailing the checks to you, additional items of data about you and the other employees must be recorded.

Databases can handle more than business problems. Databases also can help you send out party invitations, balance a checkbook, organize a music collection, or plan a garden. At the technical end of the spectrum, you also find databases involved in launching satellites, curing diseases, forecasting weather, and balancing national budgets.

As you can see, a database is a collection of objects, people, events, transactions, locations, and so on. A database differs from other kinds of descriptions in that the contents are organized into specific categories. These categories are chosen specifically to address the problems that the database is designed to solve, which may limit what the database can do. In database usage, informational categories are referred to as *fields*.

Because database descriptions can range anywhere from the simple to the complex, and also because the purposes for a database can range from one to many, also understand that a database management system needs the flexibility to handle many different situations. In dBASE for Windows, you have a program that can handle complex database management tasks, but can also manage even the smallest everyday problem.

What Is Database Management?

Of course, database management involves more than simply designing a series of tables and then storing the data in those tables. The entire reason for the existence of a database is to retrieve information that answers a specific business question. And database management involves everything that is necessary to accomplish that task. After the creation of the tables, when you add new data to those tables, you are managing the database. If you later go back and search for a specific record, then edit that record, you are managing the database. When you rearrange how the information is organized, you are managing the database. And when you retrieve information meeting certain conditions (by means of a query or with a selective report), you are managing the database. dBASE for Windows provides a number of different ways in which you can perform database management. You can use the query-by-example (QBE) facility to show you all the records meeting a certain criteria, such as all addresses in a mailing list located in a specific ZIP code. You can also use QBE to retrieve data from more than one table at a time, based on a relationship between the tables. You can browse through a table one record at a time, or you can search a table for a specific value. You can generate reports that contain listings of your data in whatever format you want, and those reports can include calculations that are based on the fields of one or more tables.

In summary, the following common tasks are involved in database management:

- Adding information to the tables of the database
- Editing data in the database
- Deleting records from the tables of the database
- Arranging (by means of sorting or indexing) the records, so that the information is available in a desired order
- Searching the database for a specific record
- Querying the database to obtain an answer to a specific question about the data in the database
- Reporting on the data in the database

What Is a Relational Database?

► "Entering, Editing, and Viewing Data," p. 145

► "Creating Basic Queries," p. 167

► "Creating Basic Reports," p. 229

The area that still gives many people difficulty is in going from a simple database that utilizes a single table to a *relational database*. Simply put, a relational database is a collection of multiple tables, which allows data retrieval based on links (or relationships) among fields of these tables. The next chapter, "Designing a Database," will detail the planning that goes into relational databases, but a brief example here will serve to illustrate the point. Take the everyday business problem of managing customers and their orders for a given set of products. Any marketing organization of any size will have numerous customers. And, it is hoped, each customer will place more than one order with the organization. For each customer, therefore, the organization is faced with maintaining a record of all the orders placed by that particular customer. In this case, these two tables are classic examples of what is known as a *one-to-many* relationship. That is, for each record in one table (the one containing the customers), there are many records in the related table (the one containing the orders), as illustrated in figure 4.1.

As a relational database manager, dBASE for Windows lets you store data about the same items in several tables, and link these tables together in a way that makes sense. Also, using the QBE facility built into the program, dBASE lets you design and implement relational queries, which are used to ask questions about the data in several tables at once. It also lets you establish and manage relationships among your tables.

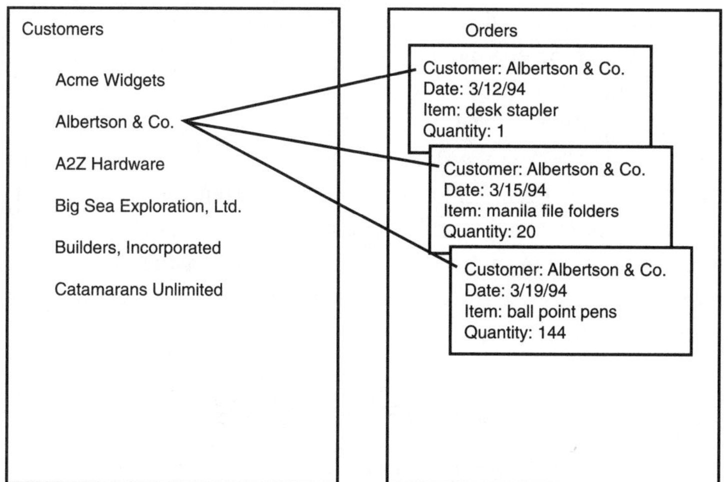

Fig. 4.1
In a one-to-many relationship, each record in one table (often referred to as the parent table) can have many related records in another table (often referred to as the child table).

Reviewing Basic Data Management Concepts

Although an organized collection of information technically defines a database, it's probably a little obvious that you'll need more than that to go on when you sit down and begin working with dBASE for Windows. With data that's stored in computer databases, the data has to be broken down into units that someone (in this case, you) must strictly define. Breaking the data into units is a necessity, because the computer has no way of knowing what's significant about the information that you are storing. When it comes to databases stored using personal computers, most programs (dBASE for Windows included) follow the general theories of relational database design, which say that your data is stored in one or more tables (along with other associated objects such as forms and reports) that make up the database.
By far the most important aspect of database design lies with the design of tables, and as the user of dBASE for Windows, how you design the tables is entirely up to you. The data in each of the tables is stored in *records* (also known as *rows* in some data management terminology), and each record is divided into individual *fields* (also known as *categories*, or *columns*). Each of the items in a specific record have something in common, and each item from a specific field has something in common. Each field, in fact, represents a specific category of data.

As an example, take the everyday example of storing your Rolodex in database form (fig. 4.2). If you were to store the contents of your Rolodex in a dBASE table, having all the data in a single field would be an unworkable solution; reports would be difficult to format, and it would be difficult to impossible to search on the basis of specific data (such as the city in which a person lives). You would probably want to use separate fields for names, addresses (including the city, state, and ZIP code), and phone numbers. As shown in the figure, each record of the table would represent a different card within your Rolodex. Each field of the table would represent a different category (such as City or State) on all of the Rolodex cards. Some examples of common fields that your tables may contain include Lastname, Firstname, Customer ID, Vendor ID, Part Number, Quantity, Date Sold, Date Ordered, Phone, Location, Description, Photo, and so on.

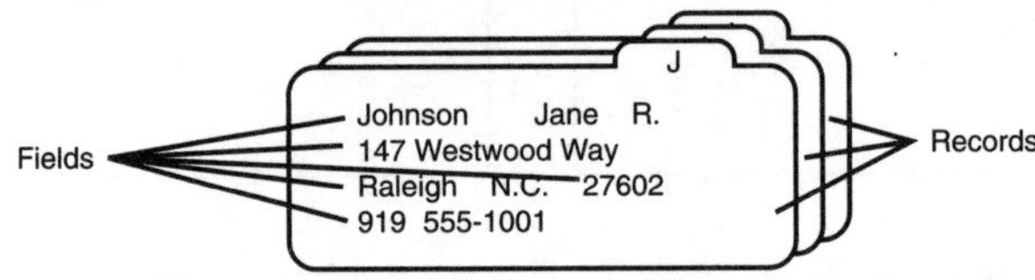

Fig. 4.2
Everyday use of a Rolodex to store names, addresses, and phone numbers demonstrates how identical data can be stored in the table of a relational database.

In addition to considering what fields are appropriate for your tables, you'll also need to identify the types of data to be stored in the fields. dBASE for Windows lets you designate fields as one of a number of possible types. These include character, numeric, floating, logical, memo, date, OLE, and binary. Later chapters will detail how you define the different field types as you design a new table. But as far as the basics of database management are concerned, it's important to be aware of the fact that you will need to identify what kinds of data you are working with, as well as what fields you will need.

Thinking of a Database Solution

A database is set up in response to a problem. In and of itself, a database doesn't solve the problem but instead provides the means to find a solution. The problem embodies the purpose behind setting up the database. The database developer has to constantly keep this purpose in mind when setting up the system.

Recognizing the problem is an important step in determining how to proceed. Choosing a database management system, setting up the informational categories that make up the database, and formulating the questions that a database answers are all important considerations. Stating the problem and outlining the requirements needed to resolve the problem are vital steps in ensuring that the resulting database system can answer the questions and perform the tasks needed to solve the problem.

In database lingo, the term *application* refers to the problem, the database set up to solve the problem, and even the solution itself. As an example, a customer database set up to handle the problem of billing customers for orders shipped can be called an *order entry application.*

Tip
Databases solve problems. The more effort you put into understanding a problem, the more useful the database becomes.

Although a typical database is set up to address a particular problem, you aren't restricted to solving only this problem. Informational categories in the database often can serve other purposes. As an example, assuming that the customer database contains the contact names and addresses of each customer, this database can also serve as the basis for other applications that require customer names and addresses, such as advertising flyers or the mailing of a products catalog. The financial information compiled by tracking the customer orders can be used to predict the coming year's profits. In this case, the same application serves as an order entry system and a mailing list management system.

By now, you probably begin to realize that some applications need more data than can be stored easily or effectively in a single table. An accounting application, for example, needs to record all the expenses and revenues for an organization during a specific time period.

The order entry database can serve as an important component of an accounting application because one category of income can be recorded, based on sales to the customers. The order entry database, however, doesn't record other income, such as dividends or interest, and doesn't account for expenses, such as utilities or rent. Recording all these items is necessary to fulfill the main purpose of an accounting application: to generate a balance sheet and income statement for the needed time period.

In theory, you could design a single, massive table to address every detail of the accounting application. In most database management systems, however, setting up a number of different databases that the full application uses to pull together the needed information may be a better method. This kind of multi-database application requires a *relational database manager*. The term *relational* refers to the fact that the component tables are logically related to one another.

Understanding dBASE for Windows Terminology

The chapter that follows will provide additional suggestions along the lines of how you should design your database. Before proceeding into the area of database design, however, you should be familiar with the terminology used by dBASE for Windows.

Database terminology is by no means standardized, and dBASE is just overcoming some interesting quirks in this regard due to its heritage. As mentioned earlier, the basic unit of data in a database is the record, which is made up of one or more fields; and, a number of records are stored in a single table. dBASE terminology uses the term *records* to describe the basic units (rows) of data stored in the table, and it uses the term *fields* to identify the individual categories of a record. So far, so good: this matches accepted database terminology fairly well.

The terminology problem comes up when you define *tables* and *databases*, particularly to veteran users of dBASE. Although standard relational database theory uses the analogy of multiple tables comprising a database, this was not always the case with dBASE. Many years ago, the original designer of dBASE for DOS (known in its first implementation as dBASE II) designed the program with the idea of tables left out of the picture entirely. What were, in effect, tables of data were instead referred to as database files, or databases. (When you opened a database for use in dBASE, therefore, you were in effect opening a table.)

To make matters worse, early versions of dBASE had no way to organize multiple database files into any kind of cohesive unit; it was up to the user of dBASE to keep track of which database files were needed for a particular application. (Later versions of dBASE, including dBASE for Windows, added a type of "catalog" feature that helped keep related files in one area, where they were easier to work with.) Recognizing that the concept of tables as parts of databases fits more neatly into the accepted realms of database management, Borland is moving dBASE terminology towards the accepted concepts of multiple tables. Throughout this book, *tables* will refer to the individual collections of the records, and *database* will refer to a collection of one or more tables.

From Here...

In this chapter, you explored the concepts involved in database management and how these concepts are important to the solution of business problems. The job of analyzing application requirements can be simple or complex, depending on the type and number of results you want the database management system to yield. The more complex the problem, the more effort you should put into carefully designing the application. To learn more about designing database applications, refer to the following chapters:

- Chapter 5, "Designing a Database." This chapter shows you how to design databases, tables, forms, and reports. It also addresses networking and multiuser concerns.
- Chapter 6, "Creating and Modifying a Table." This chapter shows you how to create a dBASE table and a Paradox table. It also shows you how to modify the structure of a dBASE table.

Chapter 5

Designing a Database

This chapter explains the underlying concepts of database design. Proper planning must be an integral part of the design and implementation of all the objects—the tables, queries, forms, reports, and programs—that make up a database.

In this chapter, you learn how to do the following:

- Plan a database
- Plan the tables
- Plan the relationships
- Plan the forms and reports
- Automate the database
- Manage the database
- Consider network and multiuser issues

Planning a Database

Too often, in the rush to meet a perceived need, proper database planning gets pushed to the bottom of the priorities list. Many database professionals tend to underestimate the importance of this crucial task, doubtlessly because it fails to generate much excitement; most find that the process of writing code, or designing objects such as the forms and reports, is far more interesting than planning databases. To rush through or entirely side-step the database planning process is a serious mistake, however, because the underlying tables that result from the planning process are the heart of any database application.

The first step in designing any successful database is to complete a thorough "needs" analysis. The only effective way to conduct this analysis is to talk to the end users—the people who will regularly use the database to accomplish a given task. Successfully automating a process is impossible unless you are familiar with that process, and talking to the users provides that familiarity.

In the world of business and government exists a class of computer professionals known as *systems analysts*. The systems analyst is a problem-solver who understands the needs of the organization and commands a set of problem-solving tools, particularly database management systems. Systems analysts take on individual problems that can be solved with a computer, choosing appropriate software tools and developing applications that are structured around those tools.

When building applications, you can use the same reasoning process as a professional systems analyst. This process entails the following steps:

1. Assemble indicators of the problem that the database is to solve.

2. Examine and analyze the issues underlying the problem.

3. Use your analysis of the indicators to formulate the problem precisely.

4. Determine the solution to the problem.

Consider as a real-world example of this reasoning process the task of planning a database system that is to track documents related to an important case at a major law firm. The scenario might unfold as described in the following sections.

Step 1: Identifying the Signs of the Problem

The first step is to identify the signs of the problem to be solved. You identify these signs by gathering information from the client (or the group of users who will work with the system regularly, as well as the management for that group). In this scenario, the signs of the problem are evident in studying the current process, a combination of manually filed documents originally written with a word processor, and some documents stored using a simple flat-file manager. Documents from both sources are haphazardly stored in manual filing systems as a resource for the case. The client expects the analyst to look at the existing systems, and design and implement a replacement.

In this example, the law firm's paralegals will make the system work, but the managing attorneys will have the final word on what you do. This step may sound like a lot of conceptual work—focus group meetings, interviews, and examinations of existing processes—because that is exactly what it requires. When you're trying to determine the basic causes of the problem that you are solving, there is no substitute for talking with the users and management.

As a designer, you must often reconcile what the users want with what management wants. In the the law firm example, the paralegals probably will want a system that has the least number of fields necessary to do the job, but the attorneys probably will want everything but the kitchen sink designed into the database. Part of your job as systems analyst is to strike a balance between these conflicting objectives.

Step 2: Examining and Analyzing the Issues

The next step is to examine and analyze the issues underlying the problem. After attending all the focus group meetings that you have planned as part of the first step, perhaps you have a series of notes describing incoming documents that are processed as part of the ongoing task. You also have comments from users regarding what they like and don't like about the existing system. You can use such notes when completing the next step.

Step 3: Formulating the Problem

In step 3, you use your analysis of the indicators to formulate the problem precisely. In this example, your analysis tells you that each series of documents has specific entities in common that you can use to establish the required tables. Your analysis also indicates that your major needs are to search for needed, relevant documents based on textual comments and to generate detailed reports of the results of the searches.

Step 4: Determining the Solution

Your understanding of the work flow at this point helps you to define specific entities for the proposed system: document numbers, dates associated with the documents, the names of persons involved with each document, and the textual comments that make up most of the documents. You have also determined that the system that you will develop must replace the current manual system, providing access to all the existing data. At the same time, the new system must provide detailed reports that show all documents based on search terms found within the textual comments or within the fields that name the persons involved. Based on this information, you can proceed to document your proposed database system, and use that documentation in its design.

Putting the Application Together

After you plan the solution, how do you put the application together? You let

Tip
To plan a database effectively, you may want to plan backward. Determine the results that you want and how you want to assemble and arrange these results. Lay out the reports that you want the database to create and use the information requirements of the reports as the basis for deciding which building blocks to include in the database.

the details of the problem determine the data requirements for both the database and the information output. Above all, you want to make sure that the "building blocks" of the database are sufficient to produce all the needed information. In the case of the law firm, you might now take the time to determine whether you will have all the data inputs necessary to obtain the required output. After you fully understand the requirements, you can proceed to the following steps, to plan the individual components of the database.

Planning the Tables

After you complete the system analysis process to define the overall problem that your organization faces (and how to address the problem so that you achieve the overall goals for the database), you're ready to break down the task into specifics. You begin by planning and implementing the tables that will store your data. Using the facts that you gathered from your needs analysis, you can organize your specifications into tables and begin to plan the relationships between the tables.

Before you begin to create the actual tables in dBASE for Windows, you should work through, on paper, the preliminary drafts of your table designs. During the first draft stage, your goal is to identify all the possible entities (or fields) that you will need for storing the distinct data that will become a part of the database.

▶ "Designing a dBASE Application," p. 537

As an example, consider the task of tracking orders as performed by an order-entry system that you must design using dBASE for Windows. At this initial stage, you examine existing forms and work with the system currently being used to handle the data. The different entities that the system must use should quickly become obvious. For example, the order-entry system may contain entities such as order ID, customer name and address, order data, shipping name and address, product name, price, and quantity sold. Each of these entities (if you determine that each is truly necessary to the overall process) will become a field within a table of your database.

At this early stage of the planning process, you need not determine whether all the entities belong in a single table or precisely how many tables you need. Instead, you need only make sure that your proposed list of the entities (fields) contains each one that your database will need.

Planning the Relationships

After you determine the needed entities, you begin to define the relationships that will exist between them. (This process also helps you divide the entities into the separate tables necessary for the overall task.) As an example, consider again the order-entry system. Your initial pass at creating a list of fields might resemble the following:

Order ID code

Customer name

Customer address

Order date

Ship date

Product ID code

Product name

Unit price

Quantity

Description

You will quickly discover (either by examining existing systems or by working with a system set up around a table that uses just these fields) that a single-table system is terribly inefficient for an order-entry system. Such a system results in unnecessary duplication of data. For example, you would have to enter the customer name and address for each order, even when the same customer orders multiple items, as figure 5.1 illustrates. In an order-entry system of any magnitude, you will find that each customer may make several orders (a one-to-many relationship) and that each order may include several items (another one-to-many relationship).

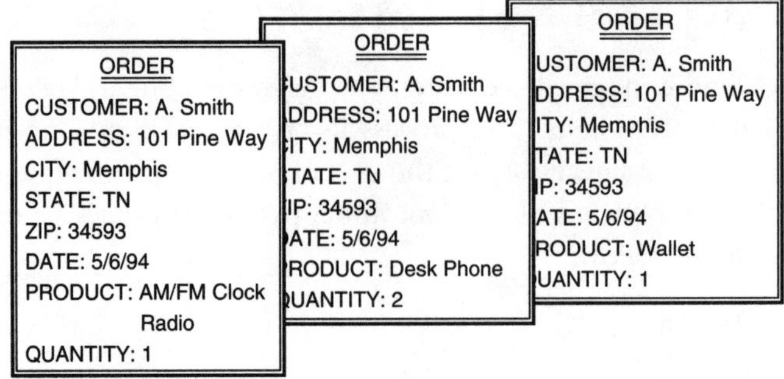

Fig. 5.1
A database in its unnormalized form (as explained shortly) results in the unnecessary duplication of data.

By carefully examining your data, you can identify all the relationships that exist between your entities, as well as the kind of relationships (one-to-one, one-to-many, or many-to-many) that exist in each case. After you consider the relationships, the proposed tables might begin to resemble the following:

Customers	**Orders**	**Order Details**	**Inventory**
Customer ID code	Order ID code	Order ID code	Product ID code
Customer name	Order date	Product ID code	Product name
Customer address	Customer ID code	Quantity	Unit price
Customer city	Product ID code	Description	
Customer state	Ship date		
Customer ZIP			
Customer phone			

In this case, by examining the data, you can easily see that relationships between multiple tables are necessary. For example, you can easily see that this order-entry system must deal with separate entities of customers and orders, and each customer has one or more orders. Figure 5.2 illustrates an example of this relationship.

As you continue examining the data, you notice that unnecessary duplication still exists. Because a single order from a customer might contain a request for more than one item, having only the two categories, as illustrated in figure 5.2, results in the repeated entry of multiple orders that have the same customer name (or number) and the same order date. To avoid this duplication, you must split the data for the orders further, into orders and order details, with each group of records under order details corresponding to a single record under orders, as illustrated in figure 5.3.

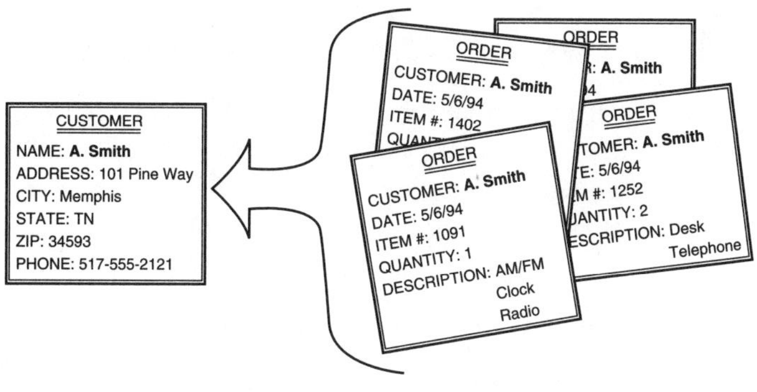

Fig. 5.2
An example of the relationship between customers and the orders placed by those customers.

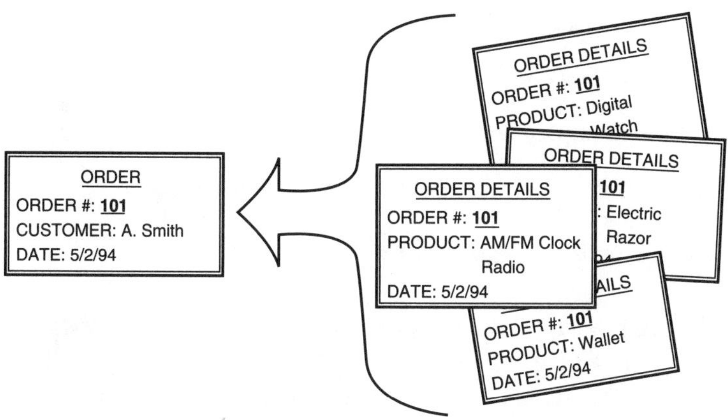

Fig. 5.3
An example of the relationship between a specific order and the details of that order.

As you continue the planning process, you also note that for each order the user must enter a description of the item. If different customers repeatedly order the same item, the user must repeatedly enter that item's description. You can eliminate this duplication by using an ID code to refer to the product and adding a separate inventory category to store the ID codes and descriptions of the inventory items.

► "Working with Related Tables," p. 261

This process of establishing relationships and eliminating redundancies by using multiple tables is called *normalization*. For more information on the subject of normalization and proper database design, you might check out some of the many texts that address the subjects, such as Jim Townsend's *Introduction to Databases* (Que) and Roger Jennings' *Database Developer's Guide with Visual Basic 3.0* (Sams).

Planning the Forms and Reports

Now that you have designed your tables, you can turn your attention to the forms and reports that the database will need. As with tables, you must plan properly when designing forms and reports; otherwise, you might create forms or reports that fail to provide your users with the information that they need.

When designing forms and reports, your basic task is to present to the user, in a clear and understandable way, the raw data in your tables. To achieve the best presentation, use either a custom form (if you want to enable the user to enter and edit data) or a report (if you want to provide a summary of data). In either case, the steps involved might resemble the following:

1. Define, on paper, the layout of the form or report.

2. Design and implement the necessary queries.

3. Using dBASE for Windows, design the form or report.

The following subsections describe these three general steps.

Step 1: Defining the Layout of the Form or Report

Before you begin laying out a form in the dBASE form designer, or before you launch Crystal Reports to design a report, you should have a specific idea of the form or report that you want. One of the best ways to clarify this idea is to outline on paper the design of the form or report. Make sure to get feedback from the users while you are still sketching the design on paper.

For example, in the order-entry system, you might need a report that prints a group of all orders processed in a given day. A preliminary design, sketched on paper, might resemble the one shown in figure 5.4.

Distribute copies of the proposed report and solicit from the potential users comments on its design, such as those shown in figure 5.4. By obtaining this early feedback, you can produce reports that you will not have to rework significantly to achieve your objectives.

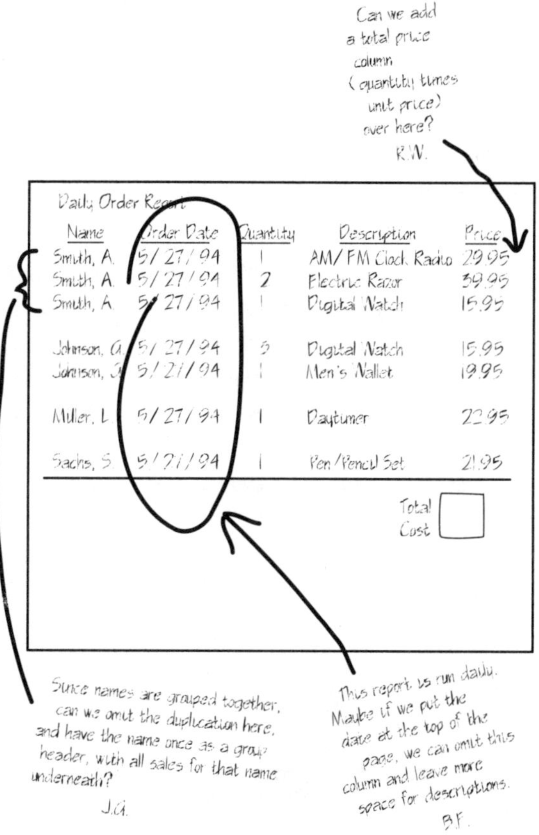

Fig. 5.4
A report's proposed design, sketched on paper, can help expose deficiencies and thus improve the design.

As a basis for designing reports, you can often use the printed output of existing computer-based or manual systems. Be aware, however, that you may not want to duplicate an existing system's forms or reports under a new system. If such a form or report has shortcomings, don't accept them as part of the new design; instead, address them as part of the redesign.

Tip
Creating a very small sample of the proposed data and building prototype forms and reports based on that data can often help highlight possible design deficiencies.

Step 2: Designing and Implementing the Needed Queries

Because dBASE now provides query-by-example (QBE) capabilities, your reports have another potential source of data besides tables. You must decide whether tables or queries should serve as the data sources for your forms and reports, and design and implement any needed queries accordingly.

For reports, you probably will want to use queries, because you rarely want a report that contains every scrap of data in a table. If your reports are of a relational nature (meaning they draw data from more than one table), basing the reports on relational queries simplifies the design process; you won't have to use any complex dBASE commands to establish the relationships, because they are established automatically when the query is executed as the report runs.

▶ "Entering, Editing, and Viewing Data," p. 145

Consider once again the example of the order-entry system. One common data-retrieval need is for a single order based on the order number, another is to examine all orders that were entered on a specific day, and a third is to examine all orders within a given range of dates. With dBASE for Windows, you can create three different queries that meet each of these needs.

Step 3: Designing the Form or Report

▶ "Using the Form Expert to Create a Blank Form," p. 203

After drafting a design on paper and creating any needed queries, you can design the form or report by using the Form Designer window (for forms) or Crystal Reports (for reports).

Figure 5.5 shows a prototype design of the report drawn in figure 5.4. This prototype was drawn with Crystal Reports, the report designer provided with dBASE for Windows.

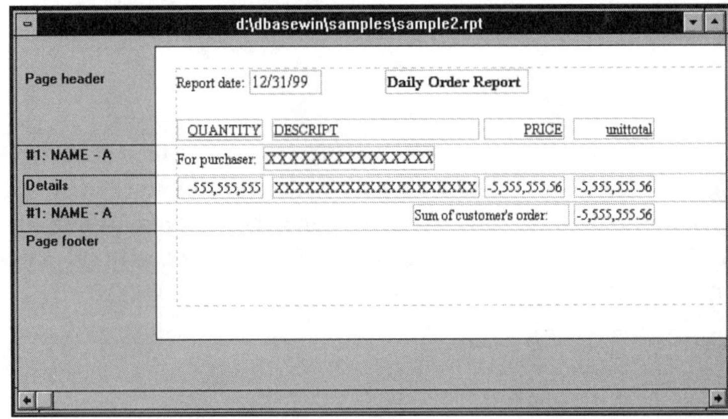

Fig. 5.5 The prototype report sketched in figure 5.4 as designed in Crystal Reports for use within dBase for Windows.

To lay out forms or reports, you use Windows-oriented drag-and-drop techniques. By using the preview options built into dBASE for Windows, you can check how the form or report appears with actual data as you continue the design process.

► "Introducing Crystal Reports for dBASE," p. 229

Automating the Database

After you design and implement the needed database objects—the tables, queries, forms, and reports—you face the most challenging task of all. You now proceed to automate the database, by designing and implementing a custom user interface that handles the database tasks that users need to perform.

You can't expect employees who have no experience with dBASE for Windows to be able to use your order-entry system to add or edit data, open the needed order forms, or print the necessary sales reports, unless each of those employees undergoes considerable dBASE training. The way around this problem is to write a dBASE program that displays a series of custom menus and dialog boxes that make it easy for users to perform the common tasks necessary to use the order-entry system. You should include menu choices and dialog boxes that add and edit customers, orders, and inventory, and that print all the reports the system provides. You must also include code that deals with the inevitable mistakes made by users.

To create such a program in the dBASE environment, you must write code. You might write such code entirely on your own, or you can use a CASE (computer-aided software engineering) based tool that helps write dBASE applications.

Tip

If you plan to develop many dBASE applications, you should investigate the various third-party CASE tools. Many of these tools make it easier to develop dBASE applications.

Again, proper planning is critical to the success of a custom application. Before you begin writing code, you must have a concrete idea of the actual needs of the application's users. The consulting world is littered with the remains of systems written by programmers who thought they knew what their clients really wanted. With proper planning, you can prevent your application from joining the ranks of such ill-conceived systems.

Managing the Database

When considering design issues, you must also keep in mind the task of managing the database. Too often, the database design and implementation process stops when the program developers deliver a working application to the client. While the program developers usually move on to other projects, the client is left handling the day-to-day task of managing the database. As part of the database planning process, you must include tools and techniques to cover the day-to-day management of the database.

Common real-world examples of these kinds of tools and techniques include the following processes:

- Index maintenance that is done on a regular basis to maximize performance during searches and reports
- Export procedures for copying selected portions of the data to other file formats and to floppy disks for use with other software
- End-of-year postings, which keep the database purged of outdated data
- Procedures for reclaiming disk space (the dBASE Pack operation) and for backing up the database

Everyday management of the database requires these kinds of common processes, and ways to handle such tasks must be an integral part of the database design.

Considering Network and Multiuser Issues

▶ "Locking Files and Records," p. 447

Because dBASE for Windows is a multiuser product, it provides tools and techniques for use on a local-area network (LAN). Like other xBASE-compatible languages, dBASE for Windows uses *record locking* and *file locking* to enable multiple users to use data safely and concurrently on a LAN. Although dBASE for Windows incorporates automatic locking, an application developer can choose to implement more restrictive forms of locking. Chapter 18 provides specifics regarding how you can control locking within a dBASE application. Be aware that your application may require such locking controls and plan accordingly, determining the levels at which you need to establish these controls.

When designing a database application that is to be used on a network, you need to utilize these locking features effectively. Probably the most common problem that you may face is *multiuser contention*—that is, what to do when multiple users try to perform the same nonsharable operation at the same time. The way that dBASE for Windows handles this problem by default may not be the most elegant (or efficient) possible way for your particular application; you need to analyze your application's needs to determine whether to utilize an alternative method.

You must also plan to handle mass updates to the database. You might choose to enable users to make such updates as needed, or you might build in some batch processes that the application will execute at certain (nonpeak) times. When making this choice, you must consider such factors as database size and disk space availability. Multiserver networks often move both users and applications from server to server at various times, so you also may have to take this into account when designing your application.

Finally, performance is always a major constraint on an application's operation on a network. What kinds of fine-tuning can you perform on your application's code to make the application run faster? Should you store a copy of the application and run it from the server (and thus decrease performance) or from the individual workstations (and thus increase performance, but also make updating the application a potential nightmare)? You need to consider each of these issues when moving your database and its application to a multiuser environment.

From Here...

As you develop your applications, remember that applications can be relatively simple—you can solve a single problem with a single database. An application can also present numerous problems that you can address with one or more databases. The job of a database management system such as dBASE for Windows is to maneuver through one or all of an application's tables to process information needs. Analyzing application requirements can be simple or complex, depending on the type and the number of results that you want the database management system to yield.

For more information about designing databases, see the following chapters:

- Chapter 6, "Creating and Modifying a Table." This chapter provides useful information about designing tables.
- Chapter 9, "Creating Basic Queries." This chapter describes how to build queries that you can use to drive your reports.
- Chapter 10, "Creating Basic Forms." This chapter details design-related information.

- Chapter 11, "Creating Basic Reports." This chapter will help you design your reports.
- Chapter 18, "Using dBASE in a Multiuser Environment." This chapter will help you design applications for use on local area networks.
- Chapter 24, "Designing a dBASE Application." This chapter explains how to design a dBASE for Windows application.

Chapter 6

Creating and Modifying a Table

Tables are a vital element of all databases. You can use dBASE for Windows to create tables in either of two formats: dBASE or Paradox. dBASE for Windows is designed so that you can treat both types of tables virtually the same—even though there are many differences between the two types.

This chapter describes the following:

- Each of the dBASE field types
- Creating a dBASE table
- Modifying the structure of a dBASE table
- Creating a Paradox table

Defining a Table's Structure

Each dBASE table—whether in dBASE or Paradox format—consists of a group of related records. Each record consists of a group of field values. When you create a new table, you define its *structure*; that is, you specify all the fields that the table is to contain. For each field, you assign a name (such as LAST for LastName) and a type (such as C, N, or L). You also assign a length to some fields; dBASE automatically assigns default lengths to the others.

◄ "Designing a Database," p. 79

As an example, here's the design of a simple table that contains name and address information:

Data Item	Field Name	Type	Length
First name	First	Character	15
Last name	Last	Character	25
Street	Street	Character	25
City	City	Character	25
State	State	Character	2
Zip	Zip	Character	10
Telephone	Phone	Character	13
Annual salary	Salary	Numeric	9,2

This design has several noteworthy features:

- As much as possible, each field name is chosen to indicate something about the information to be stored there. However, as we'll see later, the length of a field name is restricted to only a few characters, so be a little clever when choosing these names.
- Most fields require only a single number to describe their length. However, numeric fields require two values for lengths: the total length and the number of decimal digits.
- The type that you assign to each field specifies the kind of data values that you plan to store in the field. The length that you assign to a field should be long enough to accommodate the maximum size value that you ever expect to store in the field.

The values you select when first creating a new table are not etched in stone. If, while working with a table, you discover that some of your original design parameters—field name, type, or length—are inadequate, you can change them. For example, if you find that the length you chose for a FirstName field is inadequate, you can easily increase it. Decreasing the size of the field can result in a loss of data.

Before you learn how to create tables, you need to understand the various types of fields you can use in these tables. The following section describes these fields. Then, the next section will show the details about creating and using tables.

Note

Most of the remainder of this chapter focuses on tables in dBASE format. Near the end of the chapter, the differences between dBASE and Paradox tables are discussed.

Exploring the Field Types

Fields are the backbone of database information. Using dBASE tables, you can store many different types of information, including text strings (such as names and addresses), numbers, pictures, sounds, or even Object Linking and Embedding (OLE) objects from other Windows applications.

To get the most out of working with databases, you must be familiar with the capabilities and limitations of the various types of fields. This section gives you that information.

Table 6.1 lists the eight different field types available with dBASE. Notice that dBASE automatically sets the size of most field types. However, for character, numeric, and float fields, you supply the maximum length when you define the field. Usually, you select a size that is large enough to accommodate the largest value you expect to enter for that field.

Table 6.1 The dBASE Field Types

Field Type	Maximum Size	Type of Data
Character	254	Letters, digits, and other keyboard characters
Memo	Nearly unlimited*	Letters, digits, and other keyboard characters
Numeric	20 characters**	Numbers only
Float	20 characters**	Numbers only, in exponential format
Date	Fixed at 8	Dates
Logical	Fixed at 1	True/False
Binary	Fixed at 10	Binary files, such as .WAV, .PCX, and .BMP
General OLE	Fixed at 10	OLE objects supplied by other applications

**Maximum size is determined by system limitations.*

***Including sign and decimal point.*

Assigning Field Names

Tip
Be creative when assigning field names. FIRSTNAME is much more descriptive than FIELD5.

As you define each field for a new table, you must assign it a name. Each name within a table must be unique—no two fields can have the same name. Moreover, capitalization of field names is ignored, and dBASE converts field names to all uppercase letters.

A field name can be from 1 to 10 characters long. Names can include letters, digits, and the underscore character (_). A field name cannot include spaces or any other special characters, such as ?, *, and so on.

When creating a table that includes many fields, you may have some difficulty finding enough unique and meaningful field names. If you have this problem, you can create a special glossary, which is simply a list of fields and their contents. In fact, you can use a simple two-field dBASE table to store the contents of this glossary, as shown in figure 6.1.

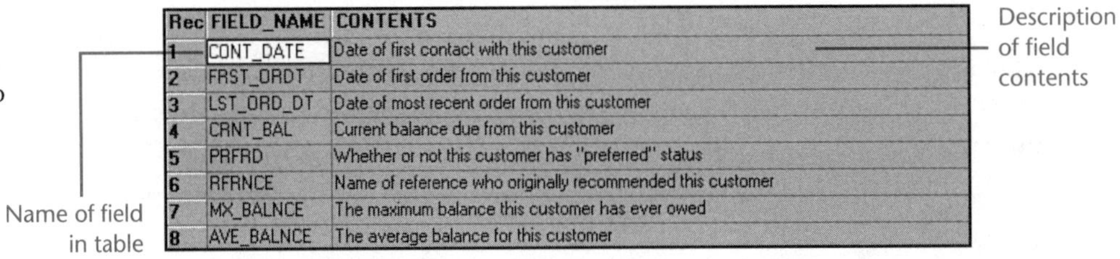

Fig. 6.1
You can use a dBASE table to store field definitions.

Rec	FIELD_NAME	CONTENTS
1	CONT_DATE	Date of first contact with this customer
2	FRST_ORDT	Date of first order from this customer
3	LST_ORD_DT	Date of most recent order from this customer
4	CRNT_BAL	Current balance due from this customer
5	PRFRD	Whether or not this customer has "preferred" status
6	RFRNCE	Name of reference who originally recommended this customer
7	MX_BALNCE	The maximum balance this customer has ever owed
8	AVE_BALNCE	The average balance for this customer

Description of field contents

Name of field in table

Character Fields

A character field can contain letters, digits, and just about any special characters that are on the keyboard, except for special control keys such as Enter, Backspace, Esc, and Tab. Because most database information consists of character strings, tables usually have more character fields than any other type of field.

You can store numbers, as well as other values, in a character field—if you don't plan to perform arithmetic on them. Examples of such numbers include ZIP codes and phone numbers. If you plan to perform arithmetic on a group of numbers, you must store the numbers in a numeric or float field.

The maximum length of a value in a character field is 254 characters. For longer values, you must use a memo field.

You can use the values in a character field as the basis of sorting the records in a table. dBASE can sort records either in ascending or descending order.

Memo Fields

Memo fields serve an important purpose in dBASE tables, because all fields except memo types are of a fixed length. For example, the longest string that you can store in a character field is 254 characters. In contrast, the length of a memo field is variable, so you can use a memo field to store extremely long text strings. For example, you can use a memo field to store a free-form history of your interaction with each of your clients.

► "Using the Text Editor," p. 220

A side benefit of memo fields is that each field value consumes only as much disk space as its length requires. For example, in a memo field, the string `Cinderella` occupies approximately 10 bytes of disk space, and the string `Now is the time for all good men to go home` occupies approximately 43 bytes of space. If the length of a character field is set to 200, however, every value stored in that field occupies 200 bytes of disk space—regardless of the actual length of the data.

You can define several memo fields for a table and store each of these fields in a single, separate memo file. This file has the same name as the original table, except that it has the .DBT extension. For example, the memo file for a CLIENTS.DBF file would be named CLIENTS.DBT.

dBASE sets the length of each memo field to 10 characters. Each 10-character value contains a pointer to the corresponding value of the memo field in the memo file.

dBASE imposes a few restrictions on the use of memo fields. First, you cannot run a dBASE query on values in a memo field. For example, you cannot ask dBASE to find all the records that contain the name *Jon Smith* in a Customer memo field. Similarly, you cannot sort a table of records according to the values in a memo field.

Tip

If you don't expect to perform arithmetic or to do numeric sorting on a group of numbers, you can define a character field for storing them.

You can usually work around these restrictions. For example, if you plan to perform queries based on various key values, you can establish one or more additional fields in which you can store the values. You can then perform the queries on the fields. The same is true for sorting. If you expect to sort a table based on a particular group of values, create a field for the values. You can then sort the records in the table based on this field.

Numeric Fields

You use numeric fields for storing groups of numbers—particularly numbers on which you plan to perform either numeric calculations or numeric sorting. dBASE can format the output from numeric fields in many different ways so that you can tailor your output to suit the requirements of specific reports.

The valid characters that you can use to enter a numeric value include the digits 0 through 9, the decimal point, and the minus sign. The maximum length that you can assign to a numeric field is 20 characters, including a sign and decimal point. When defining a numeric field, you must also specify the total number of digits to include with each number—although this number can be 0.

You can sort the records in a table according to the values in a numeric field, either in ascending or descending order.

Float Fields

A float field is similar to a numeric field in that both contain numeric values. The two types differ, however, in that a float field can store very small and very large numbers. dBASE outputs values from a float field in exponential notation. For example, the numbers 5.0×10^{15} and 5.0×10^{-15} are output as 5.0E15 and 5.0E–15.

When you define a float field, you must specify its length—up to a maximum of 20 characters—and you must also specify the number of places to the right of the decimal point.

You can sort the records in a table according to the values in a float field, either in ascending or descending order.

Date Fields

A date field provides a convenient way to store date values. As you enter dates into a table, dBASE automatically supplies the *mm/dd/yy* structure for you. dBASE also checks your input, letting you know when you enter an illegal date (such as 02/29/95).

You can sort the records in a table according to the values in a float field, either in ascending or descending order.

Logical Fields

A logical field contains yes/no, or true/false, information. You usually use a logical field to indicate the true or false status of something. Each field value is stored as either T or F, although you can enter any of the following values:

For a true value: T, t, Y, or y

For a false value: F, f, N, or n

The following are a few examples of logical fields:

Field Name	Contents
BAL_DUE	Whether a balance exists for the current customer
ADULT	Whether the record is for a child or an adult
PREFERRED	Whether the current customer has preferred status
OVERDUE	Whether a book is overdue

Binary Fields

Binary fields are one of the most innovative additions to dBASE for Windows. You can use these fields to store images and sounds. When you add a new value in a binary field, you actually store the name of the file that contains an image or sound. This file name's extension can be .PCX, .BMP, .GIF, .TIF, .WAV, or that of any standard image or sound file.

When you display a record that contains image or sound information, you can view the image or play back the sound file by double-clicking the binary field name.

► "Using DDE and OLE with dBASE," p. 487

General (OLE) Fields

You can use a general (OLE) field to store objects from other Windows applications that support Object Linking and Embedding (OLE). When you create a new record in a table that contains a general field, you either link an OLE object (from another application) to that field or embed an OLE object as part of the table record.

When you display a record that contains a general field, you can view the OLE object by double-clicking the field. Windows then launches the parent application, which in turn loads and displays the OLE object.

For example, suppose you insert a 1-2-3 spreadsheet as an OLE object in a general field. Later, when you double-click on that field, Windows will launch 1-2-3 and open that spreadsheet, which will then appear as part of the dBASE record.

Choosing the Right Field Types

When you create a new table, you must select a type for each of its fields. While doing so, you must consider the kind of data values that each field is to store. Here are a few tips to help you choose the correct field types:

- If a group of values consists of alphanumeric strings, use a character field for them if possible. If some values are longer than 254 characters, however, you must use a memo field.
- If you want to sort records based on a group of alphanumeric values, you must store the values in a character field. Consequently, each of these values must be no longer than 254 characters.
- If any of a group of numbers is too large to be written within the 20-digit limit for numeric fields, you must store the numbers in a float field.
- If you want dBASE to retain the exact values for a group of numbers, store the values in a numeric field.
- If you expect to use dBASE to perform either numeric calculations or numeric sorting on a group of numbers, store the numbers in either a numeric or float field.
- If you want dBASE to retain leading zeros for a group of numbers, such as a set of zip codes, store the numbers in a character field. dBASE removes leading zeros from numbers in numeric and float fields.

Table 6.2 summarizes the preceding information.

Table 6.2 Selecting Field Types

Type of Information	Characteristics of Data Values	Field Type
Alphanumeric	To be sorted by dBASE	Character
Alphanumeric	Less than 254 characters	Character
Alphanumeric	Longer than 254 characters	Memo
Numeric	Values within the range 0-1020	Numeric
Numeric	Values outside the range 0-1020	Float
Numeric	Exact values must be retained within dBASE	Numeric
Numeric	Values not to be used for either sorting or numeric operations	Character

Troubleshooting

When entering a value for the number of decimal places in a numeric field, I sometimes get an `Invalid decimal value...` *error message. What does it mean?*

The value you enter in the Width column for a numeric field is the total number of spaces allocated for each field value—including one place for the decimal point and one for the sign. As a result, the maximum value you can enter for the number of decimal places is 2 less than the total field width.

Tip

Use a pencil, a piece of paper, and your brain to work out the complete design for a new table before turning on your computer. You'll save a lot of time in the long run.

Creating a dBASE Table

After you have worked out on paper the design that you want for a new table, you can then implement this design by creating the actual table structure in dBASE. To accomplish this, you specify the name and type for each field—as well as the length of some fields.

Before you create the new table structure, review your design to make sure that it conforms to the following limit: The maximum length of a dBASE record is approximately 32,700 characters, except for memo fields, which can be extremely large. In other words, the sum of the lengths of all the fields that you create—except for memo fields—cannot be more than 32,700 characters.

Tip

If your table design exceeds the 32,700 character limit, you must redesign the table, possibly by breaking it into two or more smaller ones.

Defining the Table Fields

To define a new dBASE table, follow these steps:

1. If you have been working with another table, such as one of the samples that come with the dBASE software, close it now by opening the **F**ile menu and choosing **C**lose. This simplifies your work by eliminating any possible confusion from having two tables open at the same time.

2. If the Navigator is not currently displayed on your screen, as shown in figure 6.2, display it now either by opening the **W**indow menu and choosing **F**ile Viewer, or by clicking the SpeedBar's Open File View button.

3. To make life a little easier, maximize the Navigator window by clicking the button in its upper-right corner.

4. To begin creating a table, you can either click the Tables icon and then click the [Untitled] file icon, or open the **F**ile menu and choose **N**ew Table. The Table Structure window then appears, as shown in figure 6.3.

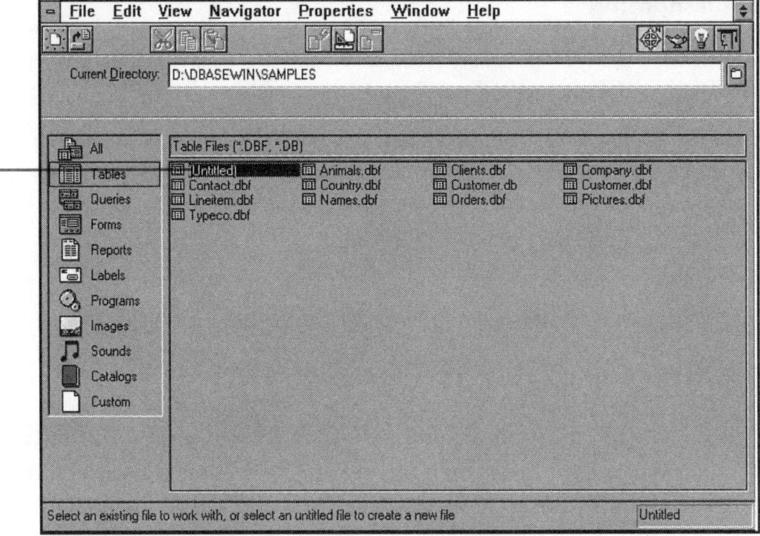

Fig. 6.2
You can begin creating a new table from the Navigator window.

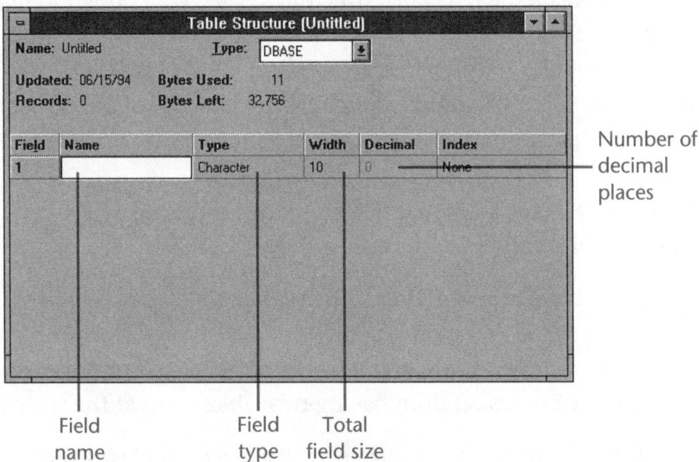

Fig. 6.3
Use the Table Structure window to specify the fields for the new table.

5. In the **T**ype drop-down list box at the top of the window, choose DBASE for the table type. You can now enter specifications for the first field.

6. Click the text box in the Name column and in row 1. Then enter the name for the first field. Remember that a name must start with a letter, must be no longer than 10 characters, and can contain only letters, numbers, and underscores.

> **Note**
>
> If you make a typing mistake, you can use the standard keys for moving the text cursor and deleting characters. You can also reposition the text cursor by clicking the mouse.

7. When you finish entering the field name, move the text cursor to the next box to the right, in the Type column. Pull down the list box, which displays the various types of available fields. Then select the one that you want to assign to this field.

8. If you chose either a character, numeric, or float field type, move to the next box, in the Width column; then enter the size (that is, the total number of characters) for this field. Note that this number must include space for a decimal point, as well as the digits to the right of the point.

9. If the field type that you selected is either numeric or float, move to the box in the Decimal column and then enter the total number of decimal places to be displayed for every number stored in this field.

10. To define another field, do any of the following:

    Using the mouse, click anywhere in the blank space below the current field list.

    Click the the SpeedBar's Add a New Field button.

    Press Tab or Enter until the new blank field appears at the bottom of the current field list.

Using steps 6 through 10, you can add to the new table as many fields as you want. As you add fields, the window should resemble the one shown in figure 6.4.

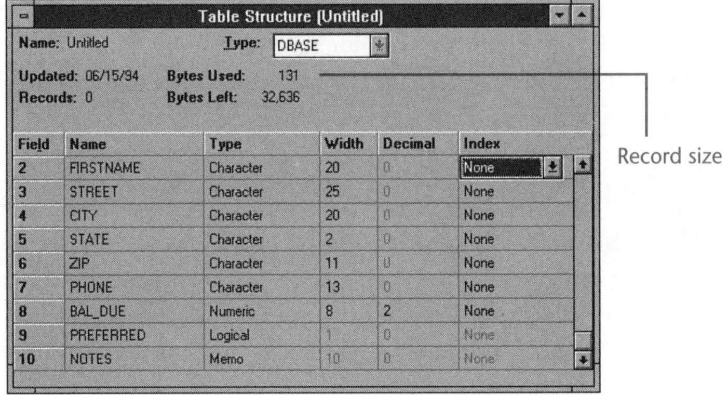

Fig. 6.4
You can define many fields for a new table.

Understanding the Table Structure Window

The Table Structure window has several noteworthy features. The Bytes Left number refers to the total amount of space, in field widths, that remains available for defining fields. When you first open this window for a new file, approximately 32,756 bytes are available. In other words, the sum of all the field widths for the table must be no greater than 32,756 bytes. Note that this same number is also the maximum size available for a single table record.

▶ "Indexing and Sorting Data," p. 119

As you define the table, the Bytes Used number shows the sum of the widths for the fields that you have defined so far. When you begin a new table, this number is 11 bytes, which is the system overhead needed for each table.

The window's Index column specifies indexes.

Navigating within a Table Definition

As you work with a field definition, you can return to previous fields to check or modify your work. If the field you want to modify is visible on-screen, you can simply click on it and then make your changes. If the field is not visible, however, you can use the keyboard operations shown in table 6.3 for navigating within a table definition.

Table 6.3 Operations for Navigating within a Table Definition

To Move to	Operation
The next entry in current field	Tab or Enter
The previous entry in current field	Shift+Tab

To Move to	Operation
The next field	Down Arrow
The previous field	Up Arrow

In addition to performing the operations listed in table 6.3, you can jump directly to a field as follows:

1. Open the **S**tructure menu and choose Go To Field Number, or press the hot key Ctrl+G. The Go to Field dialog box shown in figure 6.5 then appears.

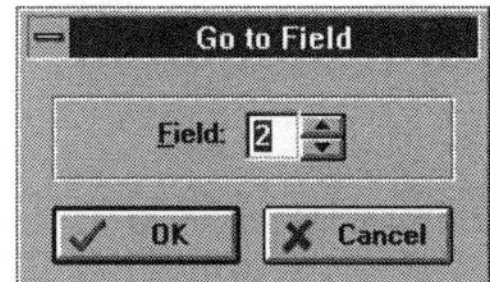

Fig. 6.5
Use the Go to Field dialog box to jump to a field.

2. Enter in the **F**ield box the number of the field.

3. Choose OK or press Enter.

Saving the Table

As you create a new table structure, it is stored temporarily in your computer's RAM memory. To preserve your work, however, you must save this structure to a new file on your hard disk.

Tip
Save your work every few minutes while you're creating a new table. That way, you won't lose too much work in the event of a computer crash or other horrible occurrence.

To save the new table to a disk file, follow these steps:

1. Click the SpeedBar's Save the Current File button, or open the **F**ile menu and choose **S**ave. The Save Table dialog box shown in figure 6.6 then appears.

2. In the File **T**ype drop-down list box, select `dBASE Table (*.DBF)`.

3. Select the disk drive, directory, and file name for the new table.

After you save the new table, dBASE returns to the Table Structure window and displays the new file name at the top of the window.

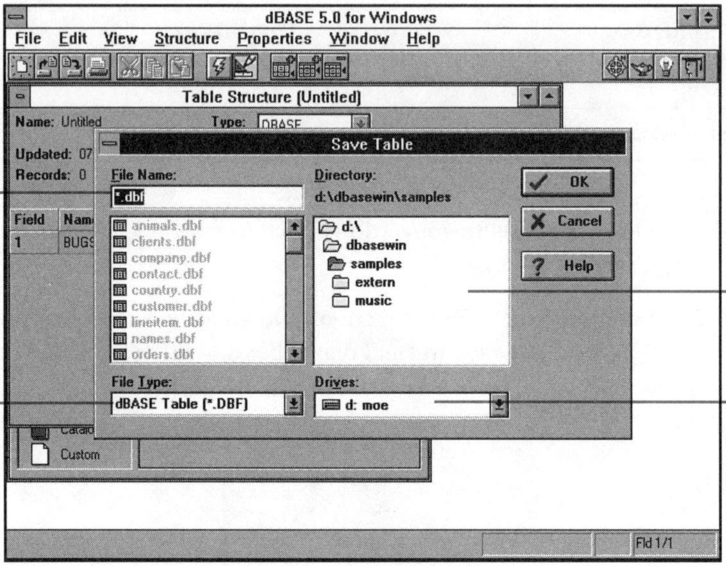

Fig. 6.6
In the Save Table dialog box, you select a file name for saving the new table.

Working with the Table Structure Window

You can alter the appearance of the Table Structure window in a couple of ways: by hiding the vertical and horizontal grid lines, and by rearranging the order of the displayed columns. These changes remain in effect only as long as the Table Structure window is currently displayed. That is, when you exit from the window and later return to it, dBASE restores both the original grid lines and column order.

Hiding the Grid Lines

If you prefer not to see either the horizontal or vertical grid lines, you can temporarily hide them by using the following steps:

1. While in the Table Designer, open the **P**roperties menu and choose **T**able Structure Window. The Table Structure Properties Inspector dialog box then appears, as shown in figure 6.7.

2. Choose whether you want horizontal or vertical lines—or both—to remain visible.

3. Choose OK.

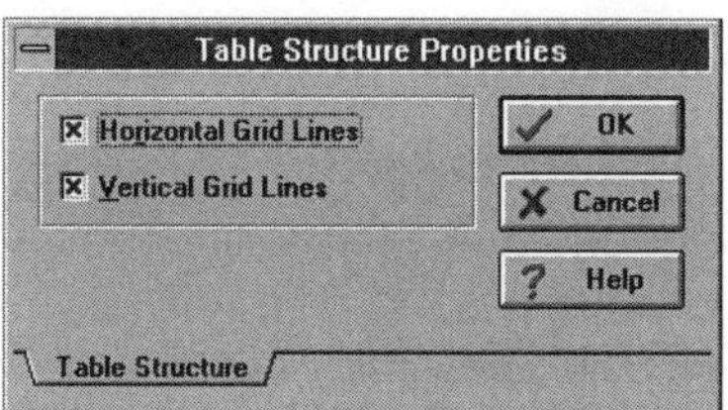

Fig. 6.7
The Table Structure Properties dialog box enables you to select the grid lines that you want to display.

Rearranging the Columns

You can temporarily rearrange the columns in the Table Structure Window. These changes remain in effect only until you exit from the window.

Tip
A check mark next to an option indicates that the lines will be visible.

To rearrange the columns, follow these steps:

1. Move the mouse cursor to the top of the column that you want to move. The shape of the cursor automatically changes to a small hand, as shown in figure 6.8.

2. To reposition the column, drag the cursor left or right. As you do, notice how the columns are rearranged.

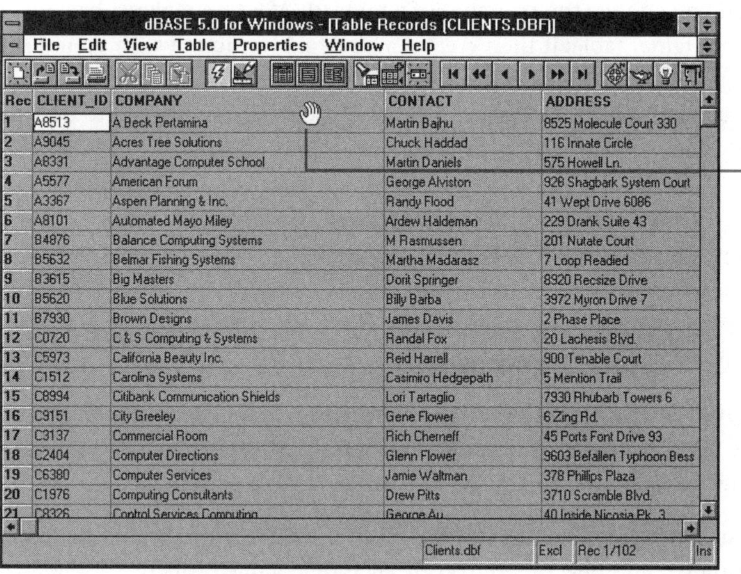

Fig. 6.8
Use the mouse to rearrange the column order.

Modifying a Table Structure

You can modify the structure of a table at any time. For example, you may want to review your definition immediately after you save the new table to a disk file, and possibly make changes to your original work.

Alternatively, you may prefer to begin adding records to the table so that you can get a preliminary feel for the table design. Later, you may decide to revise some aspects of the table structure. For example, you may realize that one field is too short, or that you should add another field to the table.

You can modify the structure of a table in any of the following ways:

- Add a new field
- Delete an existing field
- Modify the name, type, or length of an existing field
- Change the field order (that is, the order in which the fields appear in the various dBASE windows)

When you change the structure of a table, dBASE first makes a backup copy of the original table; it then creates a new table structure with your design changes. Finally, dBASE copies the data from the original table to the new one, using the field names and field order to determine where to insert each field value.

Changing Names, Field Order, and Widths

If a table is new (that is, if it does not contain any data), you can make any combination of changes to its field names, order, and widths—all at the same time. For example, you could rename one field, delete another one, and completely change the order of the fields.

If, however, you want to modify the structure of a table that contains one or more records, you must observe certain restrictions in the way you make changes. Otherwise, you could lose some or all of your data.

If you change the field order, dBASE can use the corresponding field names of the original and new tables to copy each field value properly. If you change the name of one or more fields, however, dBASE must depend on the field order in the old and new tables to determine where to copy each field value.

Therefore, if you want to make structural changes to a table that contains data, you must observe the following restrictions to guarantee that no data loss occurs:

- If you change the field order, do not change any field names.
- If you change any field names, do not change the field order, and do not add any new fields to the table. Also, do not change the widths of any of the altered fields.
- If you add any new fields to the table, do not change the width or name of any fields in the table.
- If you change the width of any fields, do not change their names and do not add any new fields.

Suppose that you want to rename the field First to FirstName, and you also want to reverse the order of the City and State fields. To apply the preceding rules while accomplishing these objectives, you would follow these steps:

1. Change the field name from First to Firstname, then save your changes to the disk file.
2. Reverse the order of the two fields, then again save your changes.

When modifying a table structure, remember that if you shorten the width of a character, numeric, or float field, the values in that field are truncated as necessary to fit into the new, shorter field. For example, suppose that you store the value ABCDEFG in a character field whose width is 7. If you change the width to 5, the original value is truncated to ABCDE.

Changing the Type of a Field

If you change the type of a field, dBASE tries to modify the contents of that field to conform to the new type. For example, suppose that you have entered the value 123 in a field. If you change the field's type from character to numeric, dBASE converts the value 123 to the number 123.00.

If dBASE cannot convert data to conform to the new type, dBASE deletes the data. For example, because dBASE cannot convert the string `xyz123abc` to a numeric format, the string is deleted from the table.

Tip
Before making any structural changes to a table, you should make a backup copy of it. Then, if you unintentionally make a mess of the table, you can recover the original copy from the backup file.

Making Changes to the Table Structure

To make any changes to a table's structure, you must display the Table Structure window on your screen as shown in figure 6.4. To display this window, either click the SpeedBar's Modify Table Structure button or open the **V**iew menu and choose **T**able Structure.

You can make a backup copy of a table in several ways. For example, you can exit temporarily to Windows (that is, without closing the dBASE window), use the Windows File Manager to make the copy, and then return to dBASE. Alternatively, you can make a copy from within dBASE itself, by following these steps:

1. Display the Table Structure window.

2. Either click the SpeedBar's Save the Current File button or open the **F**ile menu and choose **S**ave As. dBASE then displays the Save As dialog box.

3. Select a new name (and directory, if you want) for the backup file. Use a file name that you can remember—perhaps a variation on the original one.

4. Click OK or press Enter. dBASE then returns to the Table Structure window.

5. Open the **F**ile menu and choose **C**lose to close the current table (the backup table that you just created).

6. Open the **F**ile menu and choose **O**pen to reopen the original table.

To make any type of structural change to a table, you use the Table Structure window. If this window isn't visible, display it by clicking the SpeedBar's Modify Table Structure button.

When you make changes to a table structure, dBASE stores them temporarily in the computer's RAM memory. To store these changes on the hard disk, however, you must remember to finish by saving the changes to the file that contains the table; otherwise you lose your work when you exit dBASE. To save the changes, either click the SpeedBar's Save Current File button or open the **F**ile menu and choose **S**ave.

Adding New Fields

You can insert a new field anywhere you want in a table. For example, you can add the field after the last one, or you can insert it between two existing fields.

To insert a new field after the last one in a table, follow these steps:

1. Click anywhere on the blank space below the field list, click the SpeedBar's Add a New Field button, open the **S**tructure menu and choose **A**dd Field, or press Ctrl+A.

2. Press Tab or Enter repeatedly until the cursor moves to the bottom of the field list.

3. When the new, blank field appears, as shown in figure 6.9, fill in your choices for the new field.

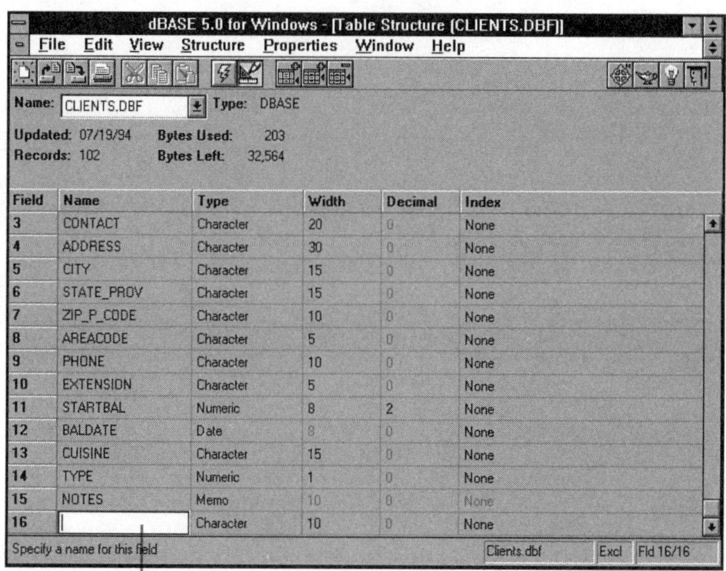

Fig. 6.9
You can insert a new field below the last one.

To insert a new field between any two fields, follow these steps:

1. Click anywhere on the field before which you want to insert the new field.

2. Click the SpeedBar's Insert New Field button, open the **S**tructure menu and choose **I**nsert Field, or press Ctrl+N.

3. After dBASE inserts a line for the new field (see fig. 6.10), you can then fill in the name, type, and width for the new field.

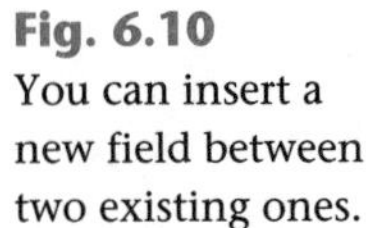

Fig. 6.10
You can insert a new field between two existing ones.

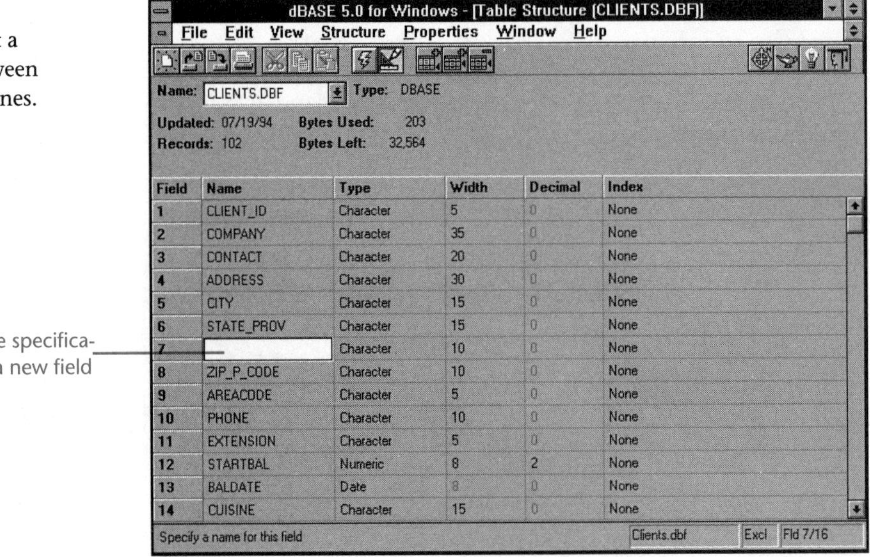

Deleting Fields

> **Caution**
>
> Remember that when you delete a field, you lose all the information stored in that field. Because deleting fields is an irrevocable step, be sure to make a backup copy of your table before continuing.

At any time during the life of a table, you can delete fields that are no longer needed. When you delete a field, dBASE discards the data for that field and then rebuilds the entire table.

To delete a field, follow these steps:

1. Click anywhere on the field that you want to delete.

2. Click the SpeedBar's Delete Selected Field button, open the **S**tructure menu and choose **D**elete Selected Field, or press Ctrl+D.

Rearranging the Fields

The order in which you originally define the fields of a table is the order in which the fields appear on many of the dBASE windows. As you work with a table, you may find that the original field order presents various inconveniences. For example, as you browse through a table, you may prefer to have certain fields grouped together.

To rearrange the field order, follow these steps:

1. Position the mouse cursor directly over the number of the field that you want to move. As you do, the shape of the cursor changes to a small hand, as shown in figure 6.8.

2. Drag the cursor up or down to reposition the field.

3. Repeat steps 1 and 2 as necessary to rearrange as many fields as you want.

4. To save your changes, either click the SpeedBar's Save Current File button or open the **F**ile menu and choose **S**ave.

When you save the changes, you permanently establish the new field order as part of the table.

Editing Existing Fields

> **Caution**
>
> Be sure to make a backup copy of the table before making any of these types of changes.

You can change the name and type of any field. You also can change the length of character, numeric, and float fields. When you make any of these changes, be sure to observe the restrictions discussed in the earlier section, "Making Changes to the Table Structure."

To modify the characteristics of a field, just click the part of the field that you want to modify and then make your changes. If you cannot see the field on your screen, you can scroll up or down until the field is visible.

> **Troubleshooting**
>
> *If I am entering records into a dBASE table, how can I switch to the mode where I can modify the table structure?*
>
> You can easily switch to the Table Structure window. Just pull down the **V**iew menu and choose the Table **S**tructure option. Then, when dBASE queries you, choose the option **O**pen Exclusive. The Table Structure window will appear, and you can make whatever changes you want. Remember, however, that your structural changes can result in loss of some of the data you've just entered—as well as any other data in the table.

Creating a Paradox Table

You can use dBASE to create a table with Paradox format. The technique is basically the same as that for creating a table in dBASE format, with the following exceptions:

- When defining the table, you choose the Paradox table type.
- The field types that you can use are different.
- The restrictions on field names and lengths are also different.

Several differences between Paradox and dBASE tables become important as you work with them:

- The rules for defining and using indexes are different.
- The maximum length for a Paradox record is 32,000 bytes, which is slightly less than the limit for dBASE tables.
- Paradox tables do not use record numbers. Instead, bookmarks are used for record identification.
- When you delete a Paradox record, you lose it immediately and permanently.

Assigning Field Names

The rules for assigning names to Paradox fields are considerably more flexible than those for dBASE fields. The maximum length for a Paradox field name is 25 characters (compared to 10 for dBASE tables). A name can contain letters, digits, spaces, and any of the special characters except for curly braces ({}), square brackets ([]), parentheses (( )). Also, you cannot use the character # by itself or the character combination ->.

Alpha Fields

The Paradox alpha field type is equivalent to the dBASE character field. The width of the Paradox alpha field can contain up to 255 characters (instead of the 254-character limit of dBASE character fields). The Paradox alpha field can contain any printable ASCII character.

Number

The Paradox number field contains number data from -10^{307} to 10^{308} with 15 significant digits and contains a sign indicating a positive or negative value. This field type is used for extremely precise calculation and should be used whenever calculations will be performed on the data. For discrete whole numbers (such as quantities), use either the long or short field type.

Money

The money field type is reserved for handling currency data. Paradox always uses six decimal places when performing calculations on currency field data and always displays the currency data with a decimal point (two decimal digits) and a currency symbol. There is no equivalent field in the dBASE field types.

Date

Dates may include any valid date (including BC dates) to December 31, 9999, and are stored in a format specified in the date tab of the IDAPI Configuration Utility. The IDAPI Configuration Utility sets many of the environmental parameters used by both dBASE for Windows and Paradox 5.0 for Windows. The Paradox date field type is equivalent to the date field type in dBASE.

Short

The short number field contains a 2-byte (16-bit) signed integer value within the range of –32767 to 32768. The data in a short field cannot contain a decimal point.

Long

The long field is a 4-byte (32-bit) signed integer. Only whole numbers are permissible (no decimal points). The range of 32-bit signed integers is from –2147483647 to 2147483647. The long field type is new to Paradox 5.0.

BCD

The numeric data in this field is stored in BCD (binary coded decimal) format. BCD numbers are used for extremely precise calculations. The BCD format guarantees that the data is stored with the maximum precision possible on the computer's hardware. As a result, calculations with BCD numbers are generally slower than with other numeric data types. The BCD field type is new to Paradox 5.0.

Logical

The Paradox logical field type is equivalent to the dBASE logical field except that values are stored as T and F instead of .T. and .F.

Memo

The Paradox memo field is equivalent to the dBASE memo field. The memo data is stored in a separate .MB table instead of the primary .DB file. The major difference between the Paradox memo field type and the dBASE memo field is that as many as 240 characters of the Paradox memo field will be stored in the primary .DB table. The exact value is determined by the Paradox table structure and is specified by the developer as the table is built.

Fmtmemo

Data in the fmtmemo type of field is stored with formatting (such as font attributes like bold, underline, and italic, as well as font size) information intact. The fmtmemo field even retains carriage returns, blank spaces, and other formatting information.

Binary

The Paradox binary field type is similar to the dBASE binary field type. The data in the binary field is not interpreted or automatically processed by Paradox or dBASE and often consists of unstructured data such as sound or video data. You use a separate graphic type for graphics (video).

Bytes

Byte fields contain raw byte data such as bar code or magnetic strip data. Unlike the memo field type, byte data is stored directly in the Paradox file for fast access. (Memo data is stored in the external Paradox .MB file.) The byte field type is new to Paradox 5.0.

OLE

The Paradox OLE field is equivalent to the dBASE OLE field type. The OLE field contains data in the OLE 2.0 object format. The OLE object is easily loaded into its parent application (called the *OLE server*) for editing.

Graphic

The Paradox graphic field type is specialized for accepting graphic data in .BMP, .PCX, .TIF, .GIF, and .EPS formats. Generally speaking, data in .BMP format is accessed faster by Windows applications than other graphics formats.

Time

A time field stores the time of the day with millisecond accuracy. The value is the number of milliseconds since midnight and is limited to 24 hours.

Timestamp

The timestamp field is similar to the time field except that it contains the date as well as the number of milliseconds since midnight. The timestamp field is useful for precision time determinations.

Autoincrement

An autoincrement field begins with 1 in the first record and automatically adds 1 for each succeeding record. The value of an autoincrementing field cannot be changed or edited. If a record is deleted, the values of the other autoincrementing fields are not changed.

The autoincrement field type is often used as the primary key for Paradox 5 tables. Because the value cannot be edited, you are guaranteed that each record contains a unique value in the autoincrementing field. The autoincrement field type is new to Paradox 5.0.

From Here...

This chapter has described in detail the process of creating a new table. After you have created a new table of your own, you can begin using it. You'll find more information about using tables in the following chapters:

- Chapter 7, "Indexing and Sorting Data." This chapter describes how you can streamline a table by adding indexing and sorting capabilities.

- Chapter 8, "Entering, Editing, and Viewing Data." This chapter describes how to add, view, and manipulate records in the table.

Chapter 7

Indexing and Sorting Data

One of the main reasons for using dBASE for Windows is to be able to manage your information conveniently. Often, this involves displaying and rearranging data in a particular order.

There are many circumstances in which you may want to view a group of records in a particular order. For example, you may want to view a group of client records ordered by client last names. Or you may want to see a client list sorted by the amount owed to you by each client.

Invariably, the order in which you want to view or process a table of records is not the *natural order*, that is, the order in which you originally added the records to the table. In fact, this natural sequence is rarely of any great interest. Instead, you are usually concerned with other record sequences.

dBASE for Windows has two mechanisms for presenting records in a particular order: *sorting* and *indexing*. These mechanisms are quite different from each other, but they do have one common feature: they can both be used to generate lists of records ordered by one or more fields. For most applications, you will probably find indexing to be your preferred tool, although sorting can also be an extremely powerful tool.

In this chapter, you learn how to do the following tasks:

- Create an index for a table
- Create a sorted table
- Decide whether to use an index or a sorted table
- Arrange records sequentially

Understanding Indexes

An index for a table is a separate object that you create with dBASE for Windows. As you work with dBASE tables, you'll find many situations in which you can use indexes to great advantage.

Here are some reasons why you might choose to create an index:

- An index allows dBASE for Windows to rapidly locate and display records. This is particularly important with very large tables.
- Indexes allow you to view and print groups of records in just about any order you want. For example, you may want to create a report in which record information is displayed in order by customer last name. Or, you may need to display a group of records in order according to particular combinations of field values.
- An index can limit your view of a table to a particular subset of records.
- If you want to establish a relationship between two tables, you must use indexes.

To understand how an index works, suppose that you have created the Clients table shown in figure 7.1. In this table, each record contains information about one of your clients.

Fig. 7.1
A sample dBASE table.

LASTNAME	FIRST	STREET	CITY	STATE	BAL_DUE	LSTPMNTDAT	PREFERRE
Parker	Peter	123 Fifth Ave.	Oakland	CA	555.00	01/01/92	.F.
Smithy	Alice	14 Harrison Ave.	Berkeley	CA	0.00	08/01/94	.T.
Johnson	Noreen	31260 Gateway Blvd.	Eugene	OR	752.00	05/15/94	.T.
Stuart	Alice	888 Moraga Way	Orinda	CA	425.00	03/01/94	.F.
Ramsey	Donald	3259 Allston Way	Berkeley	CA	0.00	03/25/94	.T.
Poirot	Herman	95 Washington St.	Oakland	CA	255.00	03/25/94	.T.
Marple	Maureen	853 Patterson Way	Portland	OR	753.00	11/15/93	.T.
Henderson	Mary	1327 Mylvia St.	Berkeley	CA	0.00	06/01/94	.F.
Kent	Cleon	1 Broadway	San Franci	CA	2525.00	04/08/94	.T.
Lane	Louis	13 Kent Avenue	Eugene	OR	0.00	02/10/94	.T.
Pastina	Paul	81 Pharm Place	Orinda	CA	850.00	05/01/94	.F.
Kimmel	Ellen	21 Nance Road	Orinda	CA	255.00	03/14/94	.T.
Vance	Philo	13 Nancy St.	Portland	OR	0.00	05/05/94	.F.

Suppose that you ask dBASE to locate a particular record in this table. The problem is that the records are not lumped together in one convenient place on your hard disk; instead, they are randomly scattered at different disk addresses. For this reason, dBASE may have to thrash around the hard disk a while to find the record that you want.

The solution to this problem is to create an index, which helps dBASE to find any record almost instantaneously.

Looking for database records on a hard disk is similar to finding a book in a library. Each book in the library is analogous to a single record in a table. You could wander around the library from shelf to shelf, and perhaps you would eventually find the book that you want.

However, a much better solution is available: you can use the library's card index. Because the index cards are arranged alphabetically by author name, you can easily find your book's index card, which then points you directly to the book's location in the library. The library card index is analogous to a dBASE index for a table.

Tip
In actual practice, you never have to worry about the details of an index's structure, because dBASE for Windows handles them automatically.

To illustrate this analogy, figure 7.2 shows the structure of an index on the LastName field for the Clients table shown in figure 7.1. This index contains a set of entries, one for each record in the table. The first column for each entry contains the value of the LastName field for a record. The second column contains a pointer to that record, which contains the address of that record on the disk.

There are two interesting features about this index. First, notice that the entries are arranged in sequence by value—just as the cards in a library index are sequentially arranged. This ordering is a fundamental characteristic of all indexes, and it's a crucial one because it allows dBASE to display values from a group of records sequentially according to the values stored in the index. For example, dBASE could use the index in figure 7.2 to display the records in order according to last name values.

Index Entry	Disk Address
Armitage	AAB142
Blackowitz	CDF336
Henderson	BAC159
Johnson	GEA948
Kent	CAF921
Kimmel	BBB093
Lane	CBB329
Marple	ACC152
Pastina	BBC129
Poirot	ABA829
Ramsay	CAC324
Smithy	CAD824
Stuart	DDD924

Fig. 7.2
An index contains one entry for each record.

The second interesting feature about indexes is how they offer a quick route to finding records. Just as you can quickly locate the card for any particular book in a library index, dBASE can easily locate the entry for any particular record in an index and then read that record from the disk—again because the index entries are arranged in order. The result is that when you want to view the contents of a record, dBASE can display it in milliseconds rather than minutes.

You may wonder why dBASE needs to bother with indexes at all. After all, computers are very fast, and it shouldn't take any noticeable time to locate a particular record in a table. This is true, provided that there are only a few dozen or hundred records in a table. If you're maintaining a table containing thousands—or even tens of thousands—of records, however, even a very fast computer will seem to crawl as it searches through each record looking for the particular one you want.

dBASE indexes are even more cleverly designed than library card indexes, so that the software can locate any index entry in virtually no time at all. dBASE then uses the pointer in that entry to jump directly to the record in the table, no matter how large the table.

Looking at the Index Types

dBASE for Windows supports two basic types of indexes: those stored in production index files (.MDX), and those in individual index files (.NDX). Both of these index types help to locate records quickly, as previously described. The .NDX type, a holdover from earlier dBASE days, is still supported for compatibility with older dBASE applications.

Production Indexes

The standard index used with most tables is called a *production index*. The first time that you create an index for a table, dBASE for Windows creates a corresponding index file for the table, giving it the same file name as the table, but with the .MDX file name extension. This index file is called the *production index* for the table. For example, the name of the production index file for the table CLIENTS.DBF would be CLIENTS.MDX.

If you create more than one index for a table, they are all stored in the production index file for that table. You can create up to 47 indexes in an .MDX file.

Individual Index Files

Older versions of dBASE use a more primitive type of index, called *individual indexes*, that you must manually create, open, and close as needed. You can assign any name you want to these files, but they all have the file name extension .NDX.

To be compatible with these older software versions, dBASE for Windows can maintain this type of index file. If you use individual indexes, however, you must still create, open, and close them manually, using the Command window.

Tip
If you are creating new tables with dBASE for Windows, you will probably never need to be concerned about .NDX index files.

Note

For the remainder of this chapter, the term *index* refers to only those stored in .MDX files, unless .NDX indexes are specified.

Looking at the Main Features of an Index

The table in figure 7.2 illustrates the basic construction of an index for a table. Each entry, which corresponds to a different table record, consists of two parts—a value and a pointer. You don't need to worry about the details of how an index is constructed or works. To be able to use indexes effectively, however, you need to understand how dBASE maintains indexes.

Tip
If you are converting an older dBASE application to dBASE for Windows, you should recode the application so that it uses production indexes rather than the older .NDX type.

Automatic Index Loading and Maintenance

If you have worked with some earlier versions of dBASE, you'll appreciate how well indexes for the Windows version have been automated. Each time you open a table, dBASE for Windows automatically opens the .MDX file for the table—if it exists. Similarly, the file is automatically closed.

dBASE for Windows automatically maintains the entries in an index in order. That is, when you add a new record to a table having an index, dBASE for Windows automatically adds a corresponding entry to the index—and in the correct position within the index. Similarly, when you delete a record from a table, the corresponding index entry is automatically deleted.

Tip
An .MDX file for a table exists only if there's at least one index defined for the table.

If you change the value of a field on which an index is based, dBASE for Windows automatically changes index entries as needed. For example, suppose that your Clients file has an index based on the LastName field, and suppose that you discover that the field value for a particular record was incorrectly entered as *Style* instead of *Pyle*. When you edit this value to its correct spelling, *Pyle*, the original index entry for this record—*Style*—will be deleted, and a new one for *Pyle* will be inserted in the proper location in the index.

Note

The automatic index maintenance supplied by dBASE for Windows is an important feature. After you establish an index for a table, you can forget about the details of the index's structure, because dBASE for Windows automatically handles them for you.

The Master Index

You can create up to 47 different indexes for a table, and they are all automatically maintained whenever you add, delete, or modify records. You must, however, select which of the indexes is the current master index, which is the one that determines the order in which dBASE for Windows processes and displays records.

You can assign any existing index to be the master index, and you can switch from one to another whenever you want. For example, suppose that you have two indexes attached to the Clients file, one based on the City field and the other on the LastName field. To view the records in order by the client last names, you would make the LastName index the master index. Then, to view the records ordered by city, you would switch to the City index.

Each time you open a table, by default no index is selected as master. That is, dBASE for Windows uses the natural order of the table records.

Index Keys

As dBASE for Windows builds a new index for a table, it creates a separate entry for each record, with the entries arranged in sequential order according to their values. For example, in figure 7.2, the values shown in the first column are from the LastName field in the Clients table; consequently, the index entries are arranged by values of the LastName field.

The index values are always based on the *key* for that index. For example, the key for the index shown in figure 7.2 is the LastName field in the Clients table. In fact, a single field is the simplest type of key for which you can create an index.

You can create an index whose keys can be from any single field in a table: City, State, Bal_Due, and so on. For example, if you want to view a group of records in order by state, then you would create an index whose key is the State field.

You can also create more complex indexes, based on two or more fields, or based on a calculation involving one or more fields. In fact, you can specify highly complex keys that allow you to view your data in many different ways.

As an example of using a complex key, suppose that you want to view a group of Clients records in order by state and also by city within each state, as shown in figure 7.3. To accomplish this, you could create an index whose key is the combination of the State and City fields.

LASTNAME	FIRST	STREET	CITY	STATE	BAL_DUE	LSTPMNTDAT	PREFERRE
Smithy	Alice	14 Harrison Ave.	Berkeley	CA	0.00	08/01/94	.T.
Ramsey	Donald	3259 Allston Way	Berkeley	CA	0.00	03/25/94	.T.
Henderson	Mary	1327 Mylvia St.	Berkeley	CA	0.00	06/01/94	.F.
Parker	Peter	123 Fifth Ave.	Oakland	CA	555.00	01/01/92	.F.
Poirot	Herman	95 Washington St.	Oakland	CA	255.00	03/25/94	.T.
Stuart	Alice	888 Moraga Way	Orinda	CA	425.00	03/01/94	.F.
Pastina	Paul	81 Pharm Place	Orinda	CA	850.00	05/01/94	.F.
Kimmel	Ellen	21 Nance Road	Orinda	CA	255.00	03/14/94	.T.
Kent	Cleon	1 Broadway	San Franci	CA	2525.00	04/08/94	.T.
Johnson	Noreen	31260 Gateway Blvd.	Eugene	OR	752.00	05/15/94	.T.
Lane	Louis	13 Kent Avenue	Eugene	OR	0.00	02/10/94	.T.
Marple	Maureen	853 Patterson Way	Portland	OR	753.00	11/15/93	.T.
Vance	Philo	13 Nancy St.	Portland	OR	0.00	05/05/94	.F.

Fig. 7.3
A table displayed in order by state and city.

Knowing the Advantages of Using Indexes

Indexes are one of the cornerstones of database management, and there are many situations in which you could hardly do without them.

Displaying Records in Order

One of the most important reasons for using indexes is that they provide a means for viewing a group of records ordered in different ways. Here's why: When you assign an index for a table to be master, the index then dictates the order in which dBASE visits and processes the records in the table.

As an example, suppose that you want to display the records shown in figure 7.1, but ordered according to client last names, as shown in figure 7.4. To accomplish this, you would create an index on the LastName field, whose structure would be similar to the one shown in figure 7.2. Then, when you open both the table and the index, dBASE will use that index when working with the table, and the records will always appear in order according to last name.

Fig. 7.4
The Clients records ordered according to the LastName field.

LASTNAME	FIRST	STREET	CITY	STATE	BAL_DUE	LSTPMNTDAT	PREFERRE
Henderson	Mary	1327 Mylvia St.	Berkeley	CA	0.00	06/01/94	.F.
Johnson	Noreen	31260 Gateway Blvd.	Eugene	OR	752.00	05/15/94	.T.
Kent	Cleon	1 Broadway	San Franci	CA	2525.00	04/08/94	.T.
Kimmel	Ellen	21 Nance Road	Orinda	CA	255.00	03/14/94	.T.
Lane	Louis	13 Kent Avenue	Eugene	OR	0.00	02/10/94	.T.
Marple	Maureen	853 Patterson Way	Portland	OR	753.00	11/15/93	.T.
Parker	Peter	123 Fifth Ave.	Oakland	CA	555.00	01/01/92	.F.
Pastina	Paul	81 Pharm Place	Orinda	CA	850.00	05/01/94	.F.
Poirot	Herman	95 Washington St.	Oakland	CA	255.00	03/25/94	.T.
Ramsey	Donald	3259 Allston Way	Berkeley	CA	0.00	03/25/94	.T.
Smithy	Alice	14 Harrison Ave.	Berkeley	CA	0.00	08/01/94	.T.
Stuart	Alice	888 Moraga Way	Orinda	CA	425.00	03/01/94	.F.
Vance	Philo	13 Nancy St.	Portland	OR	0.00	05/05/94	.F.

If you want to view the same table in different ways, each with a different record ordering, you can create one index for each particular ordering. For example, suppose that sometimes you want to view the Clients table ordered according to client last name, and other times ordered according to where the clients do business. You could create two indexes—one based on the LastName field and the other on the City field. Then, to view the records either one way or the other, assign the corresponding index to be master.

Help in Finding Records

Suppose that you want to locate the record for John Zebravitch in a 50,000-record table. To accomplish this, you supply the value *Zebravitch* for the LastName field, and dBASE then searches the records until it finds the correct one.

Without the aid of an index, the search must progress linearly; that is, from one record to the next in the table. If there are 50,000 records, the search will involve reading anywhere from 1 to 50,000 of them, depending on where Mr. Zebravitch's record happens to be. Fast computers notwithstanding, this could take a significant amount of time.

If you have defined an index for the LastName field, however, dBASE can use it to locate the record in an instant or two, regardless of its physical position in the table. Here's how: Instead of searching the table itself, dBASE searches the index for the value you specify; because the index is built, the search takes a fraction of a second, regardless of the table size. When dBASE has found the entry for Mr. Zebravitch in the index, it can then jump directly to the corresponding record in the table.

Displaying Subsets of Records

In unusual circumstances, you may want to view only a subset of records in a table, perhaps in some particular order. To accomplish both objectives, you can define an index that selects just the subset you want. For example, you could create an index to display records in order according to the LastName field values, but only for those records whose Bal_Due field value is greater than $500.

You can also create an index that displays only a single record for each value of a particular field. This is sometimes called a *unique index*.

Learning How dBASE Arranges Index Entries

As dBASE builds and maintains an index, it arranges the entries in order, either numerically, alphanumerically, or by date, depending on the type of values represented by the index key. For example, if you create an index based on the field Bal_Due, which contains numeric values, the index orders records numerically. On the other hand, an index based on the LastName field is ordered alphanumerically.

When performing an alphanumeric ordering , dBASE works on a character-by-character basis, from left to right with each value, and using the following order:

- Blank space character
- Special characters (~, /, and other keyboard characters)
- Digits 0–9
- Uppercase letters A–Z
- Lowercase letters a–z

When the special characters are ordered, they conform to a pecking order called the *ASCII order*.

As an example of how this ordering works, the following list shows several values as they would appear after being ordered alphanumerically.

```
  Alpha
@1John
@2John
@John
1
```

```
15
2
25
3
350
Alpha
Beta
Gamma
abcdeeeee
abcdz
b
baaaaaa
bz
```

If parts of this list surprise you, remember that the entries are ordered character by character. In other words, first the entries are ordered on the basis of just their first characters, then their second characters, and so on. Bearing this in mind, here are a few interesting points that the list demonstrates:

- Strings consisting of digits only are nevertheless ordered alphanumerically. Because 1 comes before 2, therefore, the entry 15 comes before 2.
- The value `baaaaaa` comes before `bz`, because *a* comes before *z*.
- Strings beginning with special characters come before other strings, because special characters take precedence over both digits and letters.
- Strings beginning with a space come before those that do not.

Creating a Simple Index

The simplest type of index you can create is one whose values are based on a single field. In fact, this type of index is often referred to as a *simple index*. Any other type of index is referred to simply as a complex index, which can involve expressions referring to one or more fields.

To create an index and then assign it to be the master index is a two-step process. First, you create the index by choosing its key. Then, in a separate step, you select it as the master index.

To create an index whose key is a single field, follow these steps:

1. Display the Table Structure window, shown in figure 7.5: either click the Display Table Structure button on the SpeedBar, or open the **V**iew menu and choose Table **S**tructure.

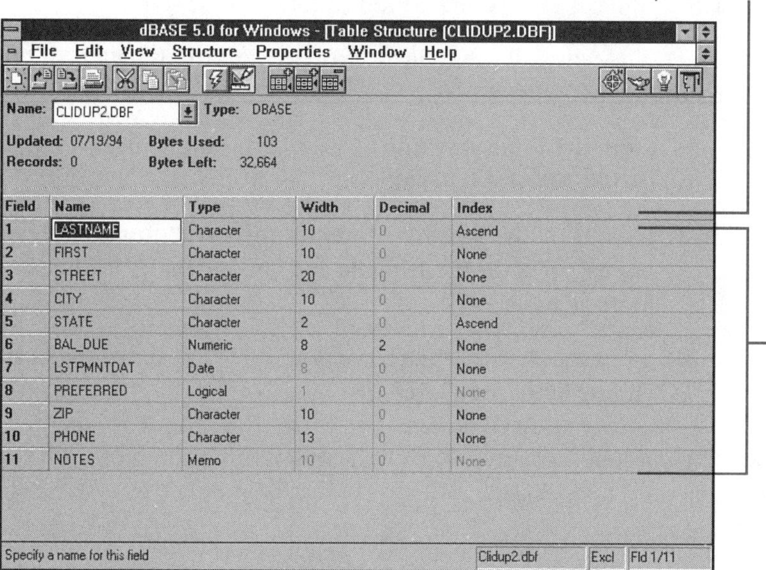

Fig. 7.5
You can use this window to create a simple index.

2. In the Index column, click the field whose values you want to use in the new index.

3. Click the arrow that appears there to pull down the Index Type list box (see fig. 7.5). Then choose whether you want the index to be ascending or descending.

4. To establish the new index, open the **F**ile menu and choose **S**ave. At this point, dBASE creates the index and stores it in the production index file (if the production index file doesn't yet exist, dBASE creates it).

Note

Avoid using very long fields as keys, especially for large tables, because the number of characters determines the required disk space for the index. If long fields are unavoidable, however, use the dBASE function LEFT( ) to select just part of the field to be the key.

Tip
To check which index is currently the master, open the Manage Indexes dialog box. The name of the master index will be highlighted.

Assigning the Master Index

After you have created an index, you can assign it to be the master index. You can do this immediately after you create it, or at any later time.

To assign an index to be the master index, follow these steps:

1. Open the Manage Indexes dialog box (see fig. 7.6) using any of the following methods:

   - From the Table Structure window, open the **S**tructure menu and choose **M**anage Indexes.

   - From the Table Records window, or when a form is displayed on-screen, open the **T**able menu and choose **T**able Utilities and then **M**anage Indexes.

   - From the Query Designer window, open the **Q**uery menu and choose **M**anage Indexes.

2. Either double-click the name of the index you want to use, or click it once and then click OK.

Fig. 7.6
Use this dialog box to select the master index.

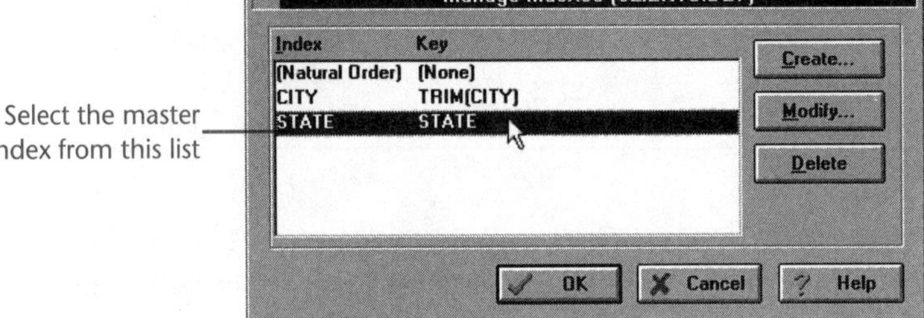

Changing the Index Name

Tip
An index name can be as long as 10 characters and can consist of any combination of letters and the underscore (_).

Each index you create must be assigned a short name. When you create a simple index, as in the previous exercise, dBASE automatically assigns the name to be that of the field on which the index is based. For example, if you create a simple index based on the LastName field, dBASE assigns it the name LastName. The name for each index appears in the Manage Indexes dialog box, shown in figure 7.6.

If you want, you can modify the name that dBASE assigns to an index, as follows:

1. Display the Manage Indexes dialog box, as described in the previous steps.

2. Click the index whose name you want to change.

3. Click the **M**odify button, and the dialog box shown in figure 7.7 will appear.

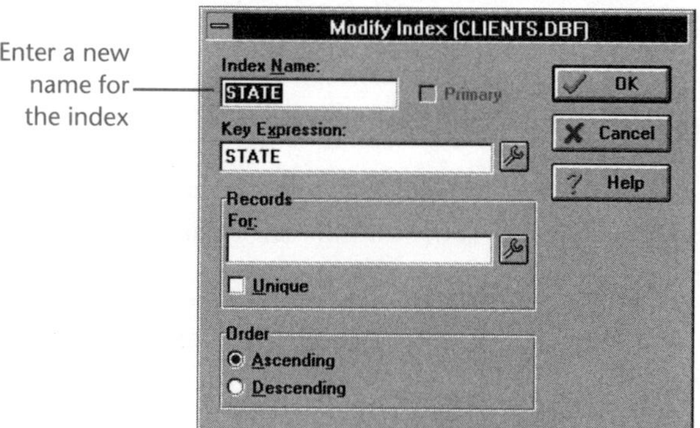

Fig. 7.7
You can modify the name of an index.

4. In the Index **N**ame text box, change the index name. You can include letters and the underscore (_) as part of a name, which can have a maximum length of 10 characters.

5. Click OK twice to have your change take effect.

Using the Index for Managing Records

After you have created an index and assigned it to be the master, it dictates the order in which dBASE processes and displays records.

To see how the new index you have created works, switch to the Table Records view: either click the View Table Data button on the SpeedBar, or open the **V**iew menu and choose Table **R**ecords. The records should now appear in order according to the values of the field on which the new index is based.

Tip
Because you'll probably be using indexes frequently, use index names that you can easily recognize. For instance, the name Lastindx might be a convenient name for an index based on a LastName field.

Note

In the Table Records view, the record number for each record is displayed in the first column. These numbers reflect the natural order of the records in the table, and they remain unchanged when the records are displayed in another order.

Creating a Complex Index

An index that's based on something more complicated than a single field is referred to as a *complex index*. To create one, you define its *key expression*, which specifies how dBASE calculates the index entry for each record.

Rules for Creating Key Expressions

A key expression can be any of the following:

- A single field name.
- A *concatenation*, or combination, of two or more field names, such as LastName+FirstName. Here, + is the dBASE concatenation operator, which combines two strings into a single one.
- An expression involving one or more fields. For example, the expression Upper(LastName) generates all uppercase entries in an index. Upper is a built-in dBASE function that converts a string to all uppercase.

You can create extremely complicated key expressions involving many field names, as well as dBASE functions and operators. When creating a key expression, however, you must be careful to conform to a few general rules:

- The maximum length of an expression is 220 characters.
- The maximum length of keys is 100 characters. For example, consider the key expression LEFT(LastName,150). The length of this expression is only 22 characters, so it satisfies the previous rule that a key expression can't be larger than 220 characters. Nevertheless, the expression is invalid because it generates keys 150 characters long, violating the 100-character maximum.

Tip
The built-in function LEFT(*field*,*N*) returns the first *N* characters of field.

- An expression usually contains at least one field name, although this is not an absolute requirement. (It's hard to imagine many keys that don't involve fields.)
- Every expression must be a valid dBASE expression.
- An expression must generate a result whose format is either numeric, alphanumeric, or date.

► "Using the Expression Builder," p. 283

Creating the Index

To create a complex index, follow these steps:

1. Display the Manage Indexes dialog box, using the steps described earlier.
2. Click the **C**reate button, and the dialog box shown in figure 7.8 will appear.

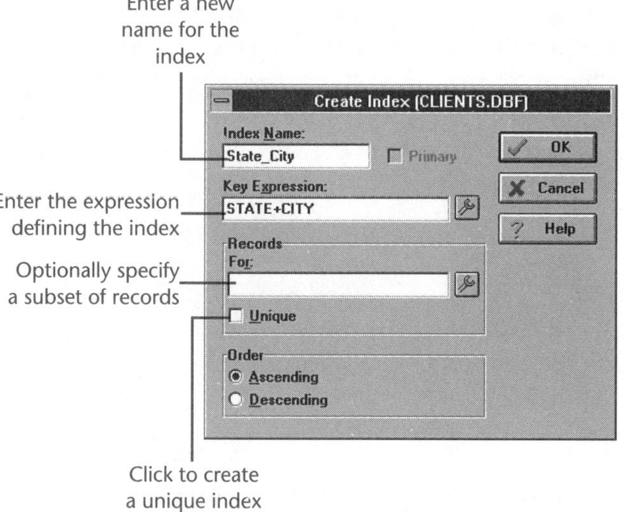

Fig. 7.8
Use this dialog box to create a complex index.

3. Enter a name for the new index in the Index **N**ame text box. You can use letters, digits, and the underscore (_) character, up to a maximum of 10 characters.

▶ "Using the Expression Builder," p. 283

4. Choose whether you want the index to be ascending or descending.

5. You can enter an expression directly in the Key E**x**pression text box. Or you can click the Tool button next to the text box to display the Build Expression dialog box shown in figure 7.9. Then build the expression you want. An expression can include field names, and dBASE operators and functions. When you're done using the Expression Builder, exit by clicking the OK button.

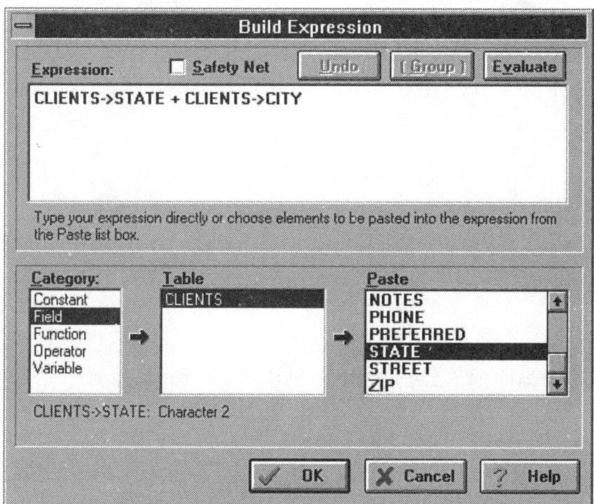

Fig. 7.9
You can use the Expression Builder to help create an expression for an index.

▶ "Creating Basic Queries," p. 167

6. If you want to limit the scope of the index to a particular subset of records, include a limiting expression in the For text box. You can enter the expression directly, or you can use the Expression Builder by clicking the button next to the For text box. For example, to limit the scope to those records for which the value of the State field is CA, you would enter the following expression:

```
State="CA"
```

> **Caution**
>
> Use the **U**nique option with care. Otherwise, you may miss records you expect to see.

7. To force the index to display only the first of a group of records having the same key value, click the **U**nique option.

> **Note**
>
> If a key involves a good deal of calculation, index creation could take quite a bit of time, particularly for large tables.

8. When you are finished defining the index, click the OK button. dBASE will build the index and then add it to the production index file for the table.

Managing an Index

Occasionally, you may need to modify or delete an index that you have created. These operations are quite straightforward, usually requiring a few keystrokes.

Modifying an Index

After using an index for a while, you may decide to modify part of its definition. You can change its name, key expression, or any other part of its definition.

To modify the definition of an index, follow these steps:

1. Display the Manage Indexes dialog box.

2. Click the name of the index you want to modify.

3. Click the **M**odify button, and you'll see the dialog box shown in figure 7.10. Notice that this box shows the current options assigned to the index.

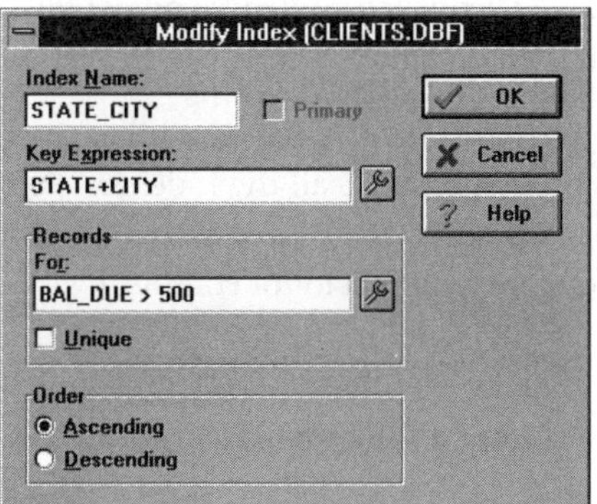

Fig. 7.10
Use this dialog box to modify the definition of an index.

4. Make whatever changes you want to the index definition.

5. Click OK twice. dBASE will update the index definition and rebuild the index as needed.

Deleting an Index

If you no longer need a particular index, you can delete it. When dBASE removes an index from a production index, there is no effect either on any of the records in the table or on any of the remaining indexes.

Deleting an index is not as dangerous an operation as deleting records, because when you delete an index the original data is not affected. Furthermore, if you later decide that you really didn't want to delete the index, you can easily recreate it, using the steps described earlier in this chapter.

To delete an index, follow these steps:

1. Display the Manage Indexes dialog box.

2. Click the name of the index you want to delete.

3. Click the **D**elete button, then click OK.

Rebuilding an Index

You may occasionally notice that when you open an index for a table the records are not displayed according to the key expression of the current master index. This type of problem usually occurs with .NDX indexes, for the following reason. If you fail to open an .NDX index for a table while you add or delete (or in some cases modify) records, your changes won't be reflected in the index, which will no longer be useful.

The production index, which is automatically maintained by dBASE for Windows, may occasionally become corrupted by power failures, hardware problems, or perhaps even cosmic rays.

Tip
Whenever you even suspect that an index isn't working properly, rebuild it.

dBASE contains a built-in mechanism for rebuilding the indexes in a production index file. This process rebuilds all the indexes—possibly a lengthy operation if either the table is very large or one or more of the key expressions are complex and therefore require a lot of computing.

To rebuild a production index, follow these steps,

1. Open the table having troublesome symptoms.
2. Switch to a view displaying data.
3. Open the **T**able menu and choose **T**able Utilities and then Reinde**x**.

dBASE will delete the current indexes.

Rebuilding an .NDX index requires a different procedure, as follows:

1. Open the table.
2. Open the Command window.
3. Open the .NDX index by typing the command **Set Index To *indexname***.
4. To rebuild the index, type the command **Reindex**.
5. Exit from the Command window.

▶ "Working with the Command Window," p. 545

Troubleshooting

One of the indexes doesn't work, even after it's been reindexed.

On rare occasions, an index becomes so corrupted that reindexing won't work. If this happens to an index stored in a production index file, you'll need to delete the .MDX file—usually from the Windows File Manager. Then, you'll need to redefine every index. If this happens to an .NDX file, delete the file, then redefine it.

As I continue to work with a table, my computer seems to take longer and longer to process the records.

The more indexes you create for a table, the longer it takes dBASE to perform various tasks, such as adding, deleting, and updating records, because each index has to be maintained in sync with the table. Deleting unnecessary indexes may improve performance.

Looking at Index Examples

This section shows various examples of creating indexes. Most of these examples use the table shown earlier in figure 7.1, in which each record contains information about a single client.

Displaying Records by Values of Balance Due

Because the Bal_Due field contains the necessary information, you simply need to create an index on this field. The key expression would simply be the field name, Bal_Due. Note that dBASE recognizes that the key expression generates numeric values, and it therefore arranges them in numeric order.

Displaying Records in Order by State and City

This example illustrates how to create a key expression based on two fields, State and City. To display records in order, first according to state and then within each state according to city, you use the following key expression:

```
State+City
```

Here, the plus sign (+) is a dBASE *concatenation operator*, which combines two strings into a single one.

The problem with this key is the following: If capitalization isn't used consistently for all values in the State and City fields, the displayed order may not be correct. Here's why: when dBASE orders a group of values, it distinguishes between uppercase and lowercase. For example, the two values *San Francisco* and *SAN Francisco* would be treated quite differently during the ordering process.

You can eliminate this potential problem by using all uppercase letters for every value that goes into the index. To accomplish this, use the following key expression instead of the one shown earlier:

```
Upper(State+City)
```

Here, the built-in function Upper forces every value in the index to be all uppercase. Notice that the original values in the table are not changed; only the values created and stored in the index are converted.

Ordering by City and Date

Suppose that you want to order a group of records first by city, and then within each city by date of last payment. To accomplish this, you must combine both the fields City and LstPmnDat into a single key expression. There's a slight problem, however: every value within an expression must be the same type, and the City and LstPmnDat fields contain different types of values.

To solve this dilemma, you must use the dBASE function DTOS, which converts date values into their character string equivalents. Here are the key expressions to use:

```
City + DTOS(LstPmntDat)
```

When the DTOS function converts a date value, the result is in the format YYYYMMDD. These values can then be ordered meaningfully by ascending or descending order.

Indexing Long Values

Tip
Use the LEFT() function anytime you want to conserve disk space, provided that the shortened key values are adequate to properly order the records.

Suppose that, to accommodate a few clients with extremely long names, you set the size of the LastName field size to 50 characters. You can create an index on this field, using the key expression LastName. Because of how dBASE sets up its indexes, however, each key value will occupy approximately 50 bytes of storage space on the hard disk. If your table has thousands of records, this could represent an enormous amount of wasted disk space—all to accommodate a few very long names.

You can eliminate most of this waste by using the dBASE function LEFT( ) to select just the first few characters in each name for the index entries. The resultant key expression is the following:

```
LEFT(LastName,10)
```

Each key expression will use only the first 10 characters of each LastName value, so each index entry will occupy only 10 bytes of hard disk space, rather than 50.

In the Clients table shown in figure 7.1, the Preferred field, defined as Logical type, is used to distinguish between ordinary clients and those who have a particularly good reputation for reliability and trustworthiness. Suppose that you want to list all the Clients records so that all the preferred customers are grouped together. As usual, you can accomplish this by creating an index on the Preferred field. You must perform a little groundwork, however, because key expressions cannot contain logical values.

The trick is to use the dBASE function IIF( ) in the key expression, as follows:

```
IIF(Preferred, "T", "F")
```

The IIF function works as follows: If a value in the Preferred field is .T. (logical *true*), then the IIF function generates the character value T. Otherwise, it generates the character value F. These two values, T and F, are the ones stored in the index, so when the index is made master, the Clients records are separated into two groups.

Sorting Tables

In some situations, you may want to create a copy of a particular table, but with the records physically rearranged in a particular way. You can accomplish this by using dBASE's *sorting* feature, which allows you to copy records from one table—the source—to another table—the target.

When you create a new table with a dBASE sort, it contains all the fields from the original table. You can choose which fields are to be used for sorting the records, however, and you can also select which subset of records are to be copied.

Sorting and indexing have one thing in common: both processes offer a mechanism for viewing records in a particular order. The circumstances in which you should use indexes and sorting are very different, however. In some cases, you should definitely use indexes, whereas in others you'll need to use sorted tables.

When to Use a Sorted Table

Because there are certain similarities between creating a sorted table and creating an index, you should have a clear picture of when a sorted table is the correct tool to use. Here are the most common situations:

- *Rearranging a table*—If you need to rearrange the physical order of information in a table (that is, the natural order), then you would run a dBASE sort operation to generate a new table in the required order.

- *Using a temporary table*—In some circumstances you may need to create a duplicate of part or all of a table, so that you can then massage the duplicate information without disturbing the original. One way to accomplish this is to use the sort feature to create the duplicate table, copying only those records with which you want to work.

- *Exporting data*—If you want to export part or all of a table to another application, you can use the sort feature to select the data from the original table and copy it to a new one for export.

When Not to Use a Sorted Table

In day-to-day operations with a table, when you want to view and work with a group of records in different sort orders, you should almost always use indexes. The following are the reasons why you normally don't create sorted tables for these purposes.

- *Hard disk space requirements*—When you sort a table of records, the end result is a new table that contains copies of the original records, but in a different order. This new table will occupy almost exactly the same amount of disk space as the original table. On the other hand, when you create an index for the table, it usually requires much less disk space than the original table.

- *Searching operations*—Because of how dBASE operates, many of its searching operations can be significantly speeded up when used in conjunction with an index.

- *Table updating*—When you add, edit, or delete records in a table, dBASE automatically updates the indexes for the table (except .NDX index files). By contrast, when you add or delete records in a sorted table, dBASE does not automatically maintain the table in sorted order.

Creating a Sorted Table

To sort a table, follow these steps:

1. To begin, open the original table and switch to a view that displays records.

2. Open the **T**able menu, choose **T**able Utilities, and then choose **S**ort Records. You'll then see the Sort Records dialog box shown in figure 7.11.

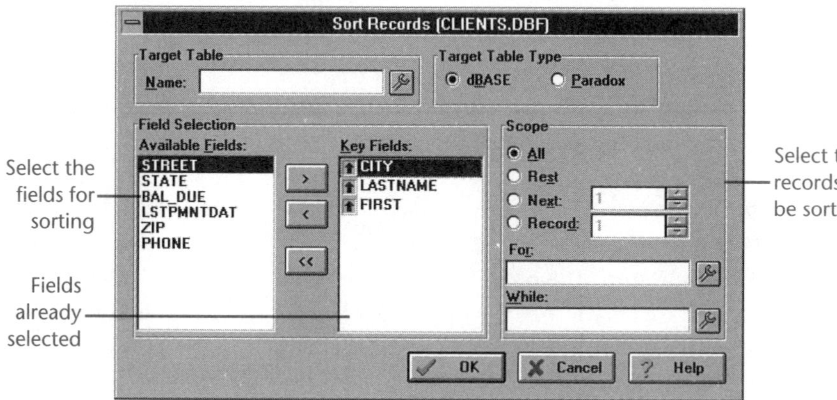

Fig. 7.11
Select the options for creating a sorted table.

3. In the **N**ame text box, enter the full name and path of the file for the new table. Alternatively, you can click the Tool button next to this text box, then use the Save File dialog box shown in figure 7.12 to select the disk drive, directory, and new file name.

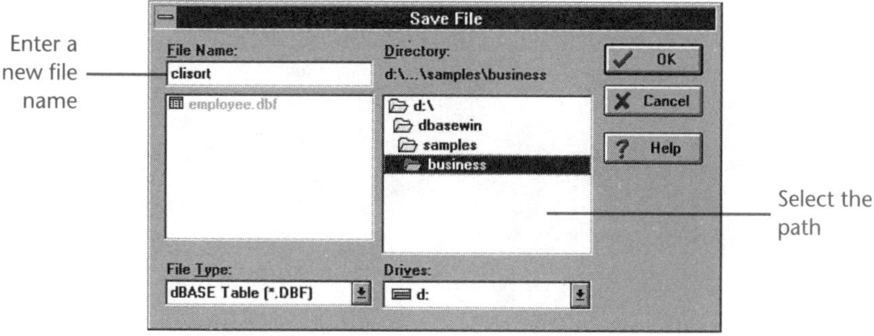

Fig. 7.12
Use the Save File dialog box to select a name and path for the new table.

4. Using the options in the Scope box, select the records you want to be copied, as follows:

   All copies all records in the table.

   Rest copies the remaining records, starting with the current position of the cursor on the View Records window.

Next copies the next n records, where n is the number that you select in the text box to the right of this option.

Recor**d** skips the first *n* records, where *n* is the number that you select in the text box to the right of this option.

5. From the Available **F**ields list box, select the fields you want to be used for sorting. To select a field, either double-click it or click once and then click the > button. The order in which the fields appear in the **K**ey Fields list box determines the field order for sorting. To insert a field between two fields in the **K**ey Fields box, click the field you want to insert; click the field before which you want the new field to be inserted; and then click the > button. To delete a field from the **K**ey Fields box, click it and then click the < button.

6. Select the sort order for the new table. For each field, click its corresponding arrow to pull down the list of choices, as shown in figure 7.13. Then select the type of sorting that you want. Note that you can choose either case-sensitive or case-insensitive sorting for alphanumeric fields.

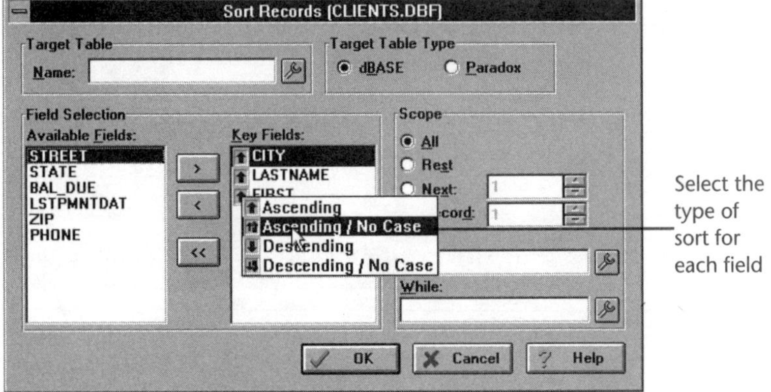

Fig. 7.13
Select the sort order for each field.

► "Using the Expression Builder,"p.283

7. To select a subset of records from the original table, enter an expression in either one or both of the Fo**r** and **W**hile text boxes. To use the Expression Builder to help create the expression, click the Tool button next to each box. If you don't fill in either box, all records in the original table will be copied.

8. When you're done selecting options, click OK to have dBASE create the new table.

From Here...

Table indexes are powerful tools and they can help you in many different ways as you use dBASE for Windows. To find out more about areas in which indexes can be helpful, you may want to read the following chapters:

- Chapter 9, "Creating Basic Queries," and Chapter 17, "Creating Advanced Queries." Both chapters describe how to find subsets of records within a table.

- Chapter 11, "Creating Basic Reports," and Chapter 16, "Designing Advanced Reports." These chapters deal with creating reports for outputting database information.

- Chapter 12, "Working with Related Tables." This chapter shows how to use multiple-table databases, where indexes play an essential role.

Chapter 8

Entering, Editing, and Viewing Data

In this chapter, you learn how to enter data in your table, edit that data, and then view the data. You learn how to use the Browse Layout, Form Layout, and Column Layout, how to set criteria for viewing your data, and how to save or abandon the changes you make.

Specifically, you learn how to perform the following tasks:

- Open and close tables
- View data in Browse Layout, Form Layout, and Column Layout
- Use the Table Records Properties
- Add, edit, and delete records
- Print tables
- Save and abandon edits
- Work in a multiuser environment
- Work with catalogs

Opening and Closing Tables

In order to add, view, or edit records in a table, you first must open the table. When you open a table, all associated files—.MDX (index files) and .DBT (memo files), for example—open automatically.

To open a table from the Navigator, follow these steps:

1. Click the Tables entry in the first column of the Navigator. This column displays the various areas you may want to access, such as Tables, Queries, Forms, and so on.

2. Double-click the name of the table you want to open in the second column of the Navigator (see fig. 8.1).

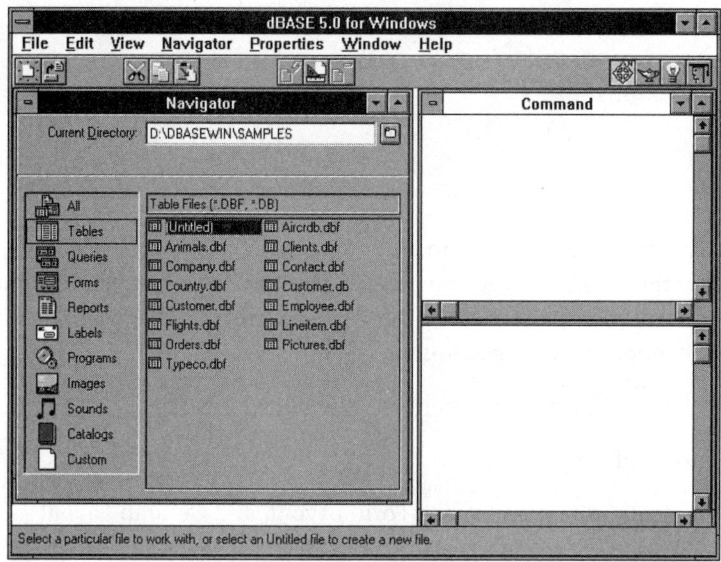

Fig. 8.1
Choosing a table from the Navigator.

To open a table file using the menus, open the **F**ile menu and choose **O**pen. The Open File dialog box appears, as shown in figure 8.2. You can either type the name of the table you want to open in the **F**ile Name text box and press Enter, or you can double-click the table's file name in the **F**ile Name list box.

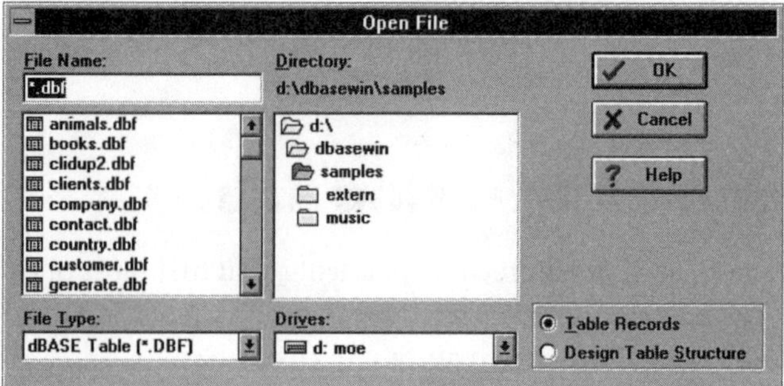

Fig. 8.2
Choosing the name of a table from the Open File dialog box.

To open a table called COMPANY.DBF stored in the DBASEWIN\SAMPLES directory, for example, follow these steps:

1. Open the **F**ile menu and choose **O**pen.
2. Specify the correct drive and directory, in this case D:\DBASEWIN\SAMPLES.
3. To select the COMPANY.DBF table, double-click the file name or type the name in the **F**ile Name text box and then choose OK.

When you close the table, your changes are saved automatically. You can use either of the following methods to close the table in which you are working:

- To close a single table, double-click the Control box of the table's window. Alternatively, you can open the **F**ile menu and choose **C**lose. The window closes and your changes are saved automatically.
- To close a table and exit dBASE for Windows, open the **F**ile menu and choose E**x**it. All the changes to your table are saved automatically.

Caution

Make sure you want the changes since dBASE doesn't prompt you to save changes.

Troubleshooting

When I try to open a table in dBASE for Windows, a message appears that says `Table in use`. *What is the problem?*

This message appears when the table is already in use. You can't see it because it's behind the Navigator. If you minimize the Navigator, you can see that the table is already open. Enter **Close All** in the Command window to close all open databases.

Viewing Data

Whenever you want to modify the data in your table by adding, editing, or deleting, you first must open the table you want to work with. You can view your records in three formats: Browse Layout, Form Layout, and Columnar Layout.

The Browse Layout view shows as many records as can fit in the window, and these records are displayed in rows and columns. The Form Layout view shows you one record at a time on-screen in a boxed format. The Columnar Layout view shows you one record at a time displayed vertically on-screen.

To select a view, open the **V**iew menu and choose the view you want. Alternatively, you can press F2 to toggle among the three views.

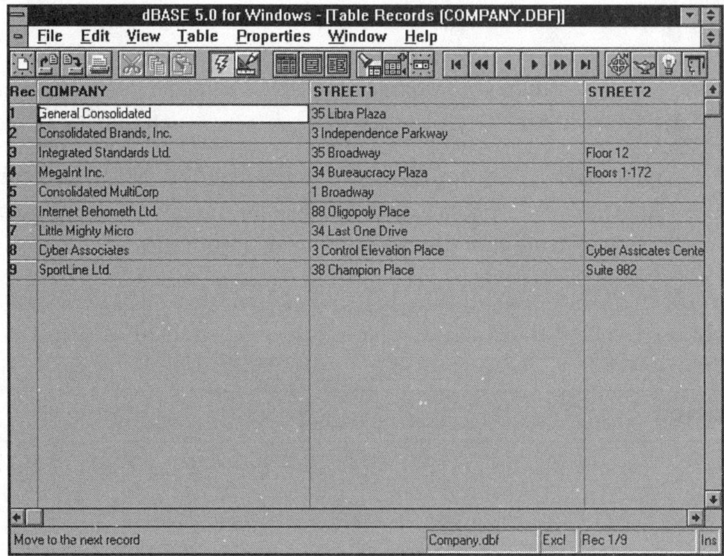

Fig. 8.3
In Browse Layout view, records appear in rows, and fields appear in columns.

Tip
When you are in Browse Layout view, several records are shown on-screen at one time. Fields appear horizontally on the screen in columns. The first column displayed is the record number and is generated by the software, so you cannot edit it.

When you select Form Layout view, only one record is displayed at a time and the fields appear in a boxed format, as shown in figure 8.4.

When you select Columnar Layout view, just as in Form Layout view, only one record is displayed at a time. The boxed fields, however, are displayed vertically on the screen, as shown in figure 8.5.

Which view you choose to work in depends on what you are doing and what your personal preferences are.

When you are looking for a specific record, Browse Layout view offers a quick way to scroll through your records. Suppose that you want to find SportLine Ltd. in the Company table. You can scroll through until you find the record. When you locate it, you can either work on it in Browse Layout view, or you can press F2 to toggle to Form Layout or Columnar Layout. When you are editing a record, especially if the table contains many fields, it is often easier to do the editing in Form Layout or Columnar Layout view.

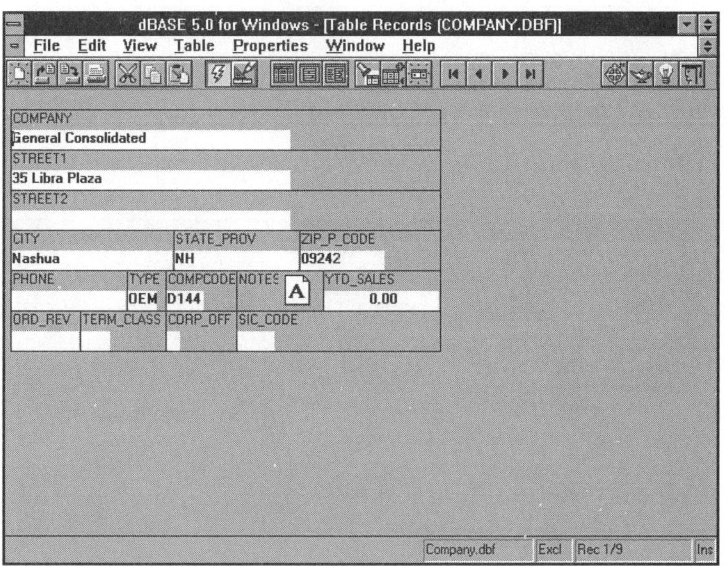

Fig. 8.4
Records are displayed one at a time in Form Layout view.

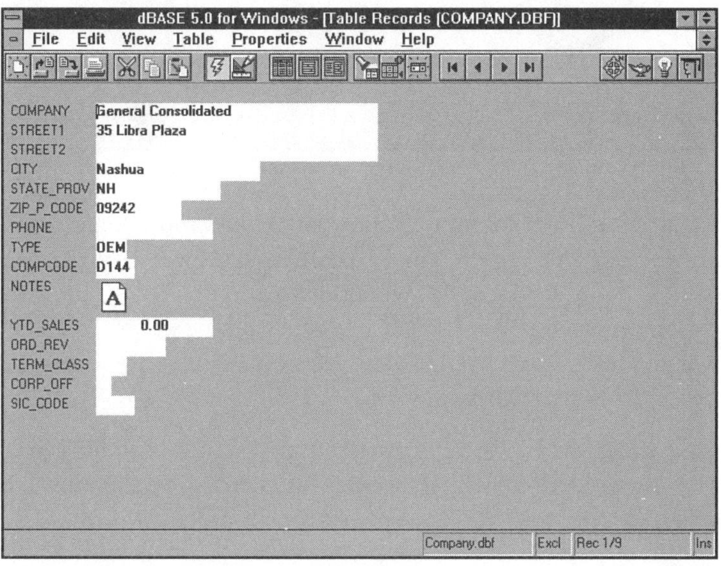

Fig. 8.5
Records are displayed one at a time in Columnar Layout view.

Tip
Remember that F2 works as a toggle among the three layouts. This gives you the benefit of the best features from all views without having to close your work.

Using the Browse Layout View

As mentioned earlier, Browse Layout view is the default view and displays records in rows and fields in columns. This view gives you a quick way to scroll through your records.

When you are working in Browse Layout view, you can make the columns wider or narrower. To change the width of columns, follow these steps:

1. Point to the column border; the arrow changes to a double-headed arrow, as shown in figure 8.6.
2. Click and drag the border to the width you want.
3. Release the mouse button when you reach the desired width.

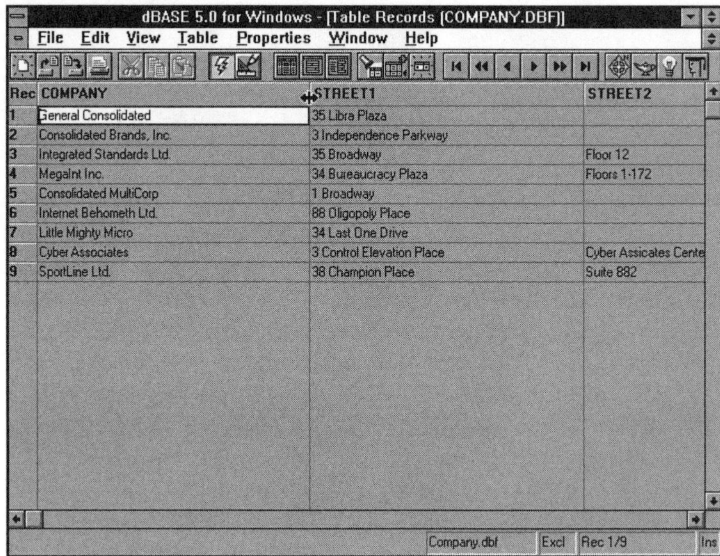

Fig. 8.6
Changing the width of a column using the mouse.

Narrowing the width of columns enables you to view more columns on-screen. If you like, you can even make a column narrower than the data in that column. In fact, you can hide columns you don't need by narrowing them down to nothing. For example, if you're working in the Company table, but you really don't need to view year-to-date sales, you can narrow that column to eliminate it from view.

When you are in Browse Layout view, you can also move columns around to make viewing easier or to make data entry faster. To move columns, follow these steps:

1. Place the cursor over the column you want to move.
2. Click the left mouse button; the pointer changes to a hand.
3. Drag the hand to the position you want to move the column to and release the mouse button. The column then appears in its new position.

If you know the record number you want to work with, you can click the Find a Specified Record button on the SpeedBar, enter the record number, and you will be taken automatically to that record. This feature is very handy when you are working in a large table. Alternatively, you can go to a specific record by clicking the right button mouse to make the SpeedMenu appear. Then click the **F**ind Records option and the Find Records dialog box appears. Enter your criteria for finding the record, and you will be taken to that record.

Tip
In View mode (but not in Design mode), you have the option of using SpeedMenu commands by clicking the right mouse button to display the SpeedMenu. You can use these commands in all three layout views.

Using Form Layout

When you use Form Layout view, a single record is shown and the fields are displayed in a boxed format from left to right. If you are editing a record, Form Layout is sometimes easier and quicker to use than Browse Layout, especially if you are working in a table that has many fields.

If you want to use Form Layout, open the **V**iew menu and choose **F**orm Layout. If you are in the Browse Layout or Columnar Layout view, press F2 to switch to Form Layout (remember F2 toggles among the layouts).

To move through the data in Form Layout view, use the Tab key (Shift+Tab to move backwards). Alternatively, you can use your mouse and click the field you want to work in.

You can move to certain other records by using these buttons on the SpeedBar:

Move to the first record

Move to the previous page

Move to the previous record

Move to the next record

Move to the next page

Move to the last record

You also can move to the next record by tabbing past the last field in the current record, or you can use the PgDn key. You can move back to the previous record by pressing Shift+Tab from the first field in the current record, or you can use the PgUp key.

Using the Table Records Properties

When you display a table, all fields and records that can fit in the window are automatically displayed. However, you may not need to view all this information at one time, so you can use the Table Records Properties to control what information you do view. The Table Records Properties lets you hide fields or omit data you don't want to view.

To use the Table Records Properties while you are in the table, open the **P**roperties menu and choose **T**able Records Window. The Table Records Properties dialog box is displayed, as shown in figure 8.7.

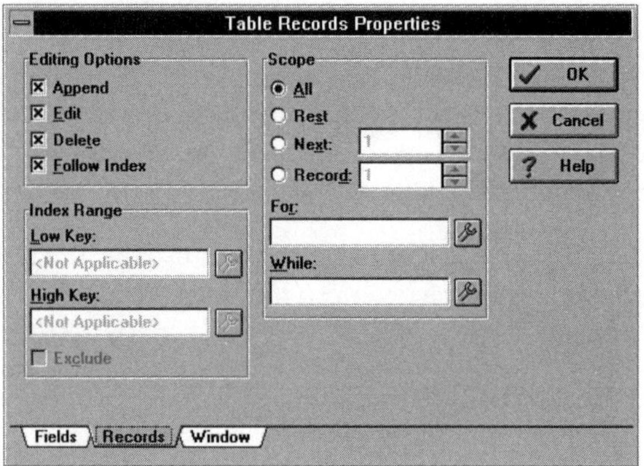

Fig. 8.7
The Table Records Properties dialog box lets you specify what information you want to view.

At the bottom of the Table Records Properties box, you can see three pages: Fields, Records, and Window.

In the Fields page of the Table Records Properties dialog box, table fields are displayed on the left in the **A**vailable Fields list box. The fields that have been selected are displayed on the right in the **S**elected Fields list box. When you first open the Table Records Properties dialog box, the program selects all the fields and displays them in the **S**elected Fields box.

Tip
If you have removed a field from the **S**elected Fields box, it appears in the **A**vailable Fields box. If you then decide you want to keep the field you removed, highlight the field and click the right-arrow button (>); the field appears back in the **S**elected Fields box.

To deselect a field, highlight the field and then click the left-arrow button (<).

You can also add calculated fields to the Table Editor. In an employee table, for example, you may have the birth dates of all employees, but you want to display their ages. To perform the calculation that enables you to display the ages, follow these steps:

1. Open the table.
2. Click the right mouse button.

3. A pull-down menu appears. From the SpeedMenu click Table Records **W**indow Properties.

► "Creating a Calculated Field," p. 425

4. The Records Properties dialog box appears.

5. Choose the Fields page.

6. Highlight the field to which you want to add the calculated information and then click Add **C**alculated Field.

7. The Calculated Field dialog box appears, as shown in figure 8.8.

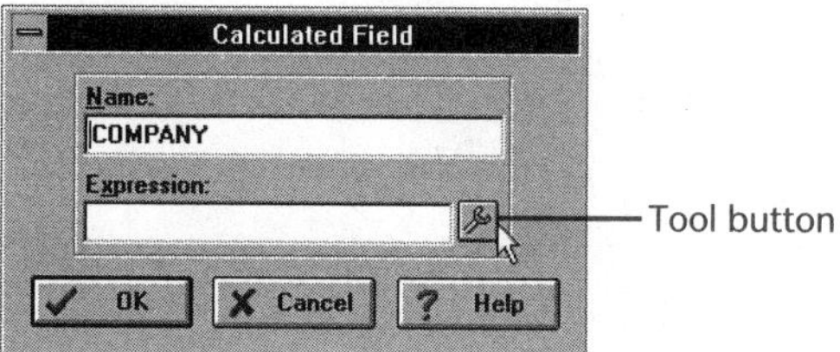

Fig. 8.8
The Calculated Field dialog box.

8. Enter a field name in the **N**ame text box (for example, you could enter Age).

9. Next, enter the expression in the E**x**pression text box or click the Tool button (see fig. 8.8) to display the Build Expression dialog box. An expression is a dBASE element that evaluates a single value. You can use field names, constants, functions, operators, memory variables, and array elements in an expression. Unless you use data conversion functions, an expression has to evaluate a single type of data (character, logical, numeric, or date). For example, if you wanted all data from January 1, 1994, you would enter the expression **MDY {01/01/94}**. If you wanted a character field called LName to appear in all caps, you would enter the expression **UPPER(LName)**.

10. After you have made your choices, click OK.

11. You are returned to the Table Records Properties dialog box, where the calculated field is shown in the **S**elected Fields list box.

12. Close the Table Records Properties dialog box by clicking OK. Your table is displayed showing the calculated field you have choosen; for example, the last name displayed in all capital letters.

◄ "Working with Objects on a Form," p. 203

You can also assign properties to fields using the Field Properties dialog box shown in figure 8.9. Assigning properties to a field enables you to set criteria and limits relating to what is acceptable to that field. For example, if you do not want to allow editing to the COMPANY field, you can assign the No Edit property to this field. To access the Field Properties dialog box, follow these steps:

1. In the Table Records Properties dialog box, highlight the field you want to assign property values to from the fields listed in the **S**elected Fields list box.

2. Click the P**r**operties button. The Field Properties dialog box appears, as shown in figure 8.9.

Fig. 8.9
The Field Properties dialog box.

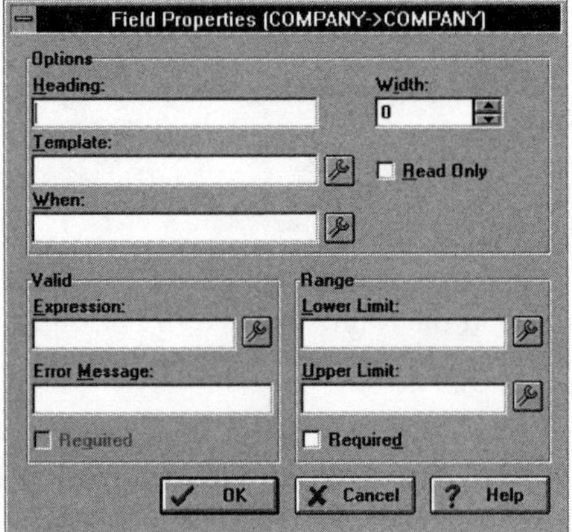

The following list explains the various options that you can modify in the Field Properties dialog box:

Tip
When you are working with expressions, and you want to ensure that your expression is correct, click the Safety Net button which is found in the Expression Builder dialog box. When this button is on, dBASE will not accept an invalid expression.

- ***Heading***—Enables you to enter a name to be displayed in the table other than the actual field name. This feature permits you to use a more detailed heading and is especially useful if the field names are abbreviated or vague. For example, the table uses the field name LN for *last name*. This abbreviation probably wouldn't mean much to anyone except the person who created the field name. To change this to display a more informative field name heading, you could type **Last Name** in the **H**eading text box. Now when the table is viewed, the heading for the LN field would be displayed as Last Name.

- *W**i**dth*—Enables you to change the width of the field so that it is displayed at a different width than when the table was designed originally. This feature can be very useful when you have to display as many fields as possible in the table view. You can narrow the width of the field (or fields) to get the most from the available space. You can change the width either by using the spinner buttons to the right of the text box to scroll to the desired width or by typing the width in the **W**idth text box.

- *Template*—Enables you to assign a template to the data in the field you choose. You can assign template specifications either by typing them directly in the **T**emplate text box or by clicking the Tool button. When you click the Tool button, the Choose Template dialog box appears (see fig. 8.10), which contains the Template Symbols and Format Functions drop-down list. Scroll through the available choices and then double-click to make your choice. If you are unsure of what a template, symbol, or format function does, highlight it in the list and a description appears in the Description box just above the Template Symbols and Format Functions box. An example of assigning a template could be to trim all trailing blanks or to convert all text to uppercase letters.

  Three pages are displayed at the bottom of the Choose Template dialog box: Character, Numeric, and Date. Each of these pages has a set of templates assigned to it. To use the assigned set of templates, click the appropriate page, and the assigned set of templates appears in the Template Symbols and Format Functions box. When you are done in the page you are working with, click OK and you are returned to the default Field Properties dialog box.

Tip
It is difficult to memorize all the templates, symbols, and format functions because there are so many of them. It is easier just to highlight a particular symbol or function in the drop-down list and read its description in the Description box (see fig 8.10).

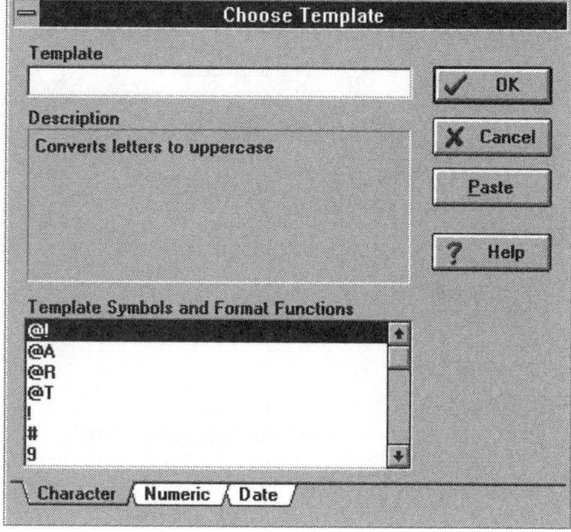

Fig. 8.10
The Choose Template dialog box with the Template Symbols and Format Functions drop-down list.

- *Valid section*—Enables you to set validating conditions that determine whether the entry in the field is valid. To set a validating condition, enter a dBASE expression in the **E**xpression text box or click the Tool button. When you click the Tool button, the Build Expression dialog box appears, which was discussed earlier in the chapter. Build your expression and then click OK. You are returned to the Field Properties dialog box.

▶ "Using the Expression Builder," p. 287

Beneath the **E**xpression box is the Error **M**essage box. Type the message in this text box that you want to be displayed if the validation conditions are not met.

Tip
An expression can evaluate only one data type. If you are using more than one data type, you must convert all the fields to a single data type.

If you click Re**q**uired, only valid values are accepted. If a range of values is acceptable, use the two text boxes in the Range section: **L**ower Limit and **U**pper Limit. To set a date range, for example, you can set the **L**ower Limit to 01/01/90 and the **U**pper Limit to 01/01/94. After you have set the range, be sure to click Re**q**uired. With the Re**q**uired box checked, a value is not accepted unless it meets the criteria you set.

When you have set all the needed criteria in the Field Properties dialog box, click OK; the Table Record Properties dialog box reappears.

Now click the Records page located at the bottom of the Table Records Properties dialog box, as shown in figure 8.11.

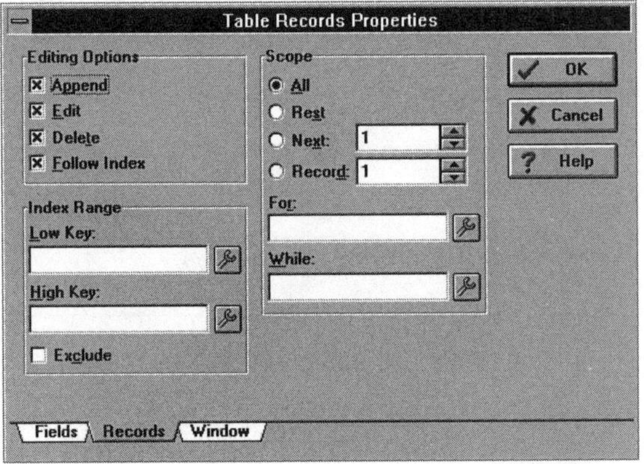

Fig. 8.11
In the Records page, you can set criteria for adding, editing, and deleting records.

In the top-left corner of the window, four Editing Options check boxes appear. The following list describes these four options:

*A**p**pend*—When this box is checked, you can add records in the table. If the box is unchecked, no new records can be added to the table.

***E**dit*—When this box is checked, you can edit existing records. If this box is unchecked, existing records cannot be changed.

Delete—When this box is checked, you can delete records in the table. If you do not want to allow deletion of records, make sure this box is unchecked.

Follow Index—When this box is checked, the cursor remains at the current position and does not follow a record to its new position. If you change the name *Zeta* to *Beta,* for example, and you sort alphabetically, the cursor does not follow the record *Beta* to its new location closer to the top of the list; instead, the cursor stays at the current position previously occupied by *Zeta.*

Beneath the Editing Options check boxes is an Index Range section that enables you to define a **L**ow Key value and a **H**igh Key value. These values can be typed in the text boxes, or you can use the Tool buttons to take you to the Build Expression dialog box. Low key values and high key values can be used to set criteria for the data. Only data that falls within that range is displayed. For example, if you want to display the records of employees hired before January 1991 but not later than January 1992, you would set the **L**ow Key value to 01/01/91 and the **H**igh Key value to 01/01/92. Only records that fall within that range would be displayed.

In the middle of the dialog box, you can see the Scope box. You use the Scope box to specify whether the options you choose are applied to **A**ll records, to the Re**s**t (of the records from this point on), to the Ne**x**t *x* records (where *x* is the number of records you designate in the text box), or to a specific Recor**d** number (which you designate in the text box). You can also set Fo**r** and **W**hile criteria. An example of setting Fo**r** criteria would be to have only the records for 01/10/94 displayed. If you click the Tool button, the Expression Builder opens, and you can build an expression.

When you have set all your criteria, click the OK button. If you want to abandon your choices, click Cancel.

Next, click the Window page located at the bottom of the Table Records Properties dialog box, as shown in figure 8.12.

In the Display section in the upper-left corner of the dialog box, you can type a title in the **T**itle text box that will be displayed in the table window. The text you type replaces the default text in the title bar. For example, you could change the default text by typing *ABC Company* in the text box.

Under the **T**itle text box are three check boxes. The following list describes these three Display options:

Toggle Layout—When this box is checked, you can switch among Browse Layout, Form Layout, and Columnar Layout.

Horizontal Grid—When this box is checked, the grid lines are visible between the columns in Browse Layout.

Vertical Grid—When this box is checked, the grid lines are visible between the rows in Browse Layout.

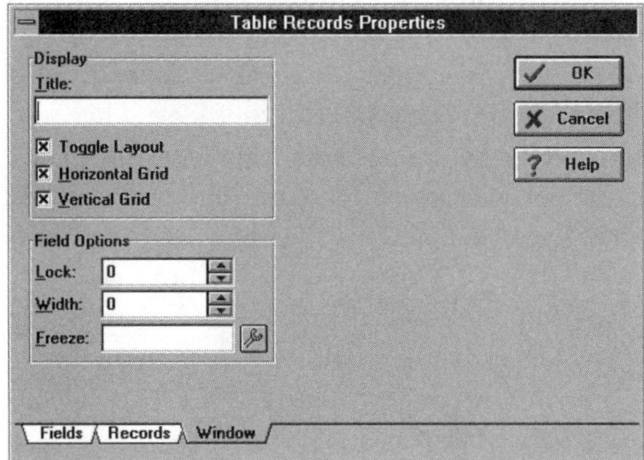

Fig. 8.12
The Window folder of the Table Records Properties dialog box.

Following the Display check boxes is the Field Options section. The following list describes these three options:

Lock—In this text box, you can designate the number of fields (from the left) that will remain stationary as you scroll through other fields in Browse Layout. For example, your table has the following fields: COMPANY, STREET1, STREET2, CITY, STATE_PROV, ZIP_POSTAL, and PHONE. If you set the lock to **1**, the COMPANY field remains in view even when you scroll through other fields. The Lock feature can be very useful, especially if you are working in Browse Layout and your table has many fields. By locking fields, you always know what record you are working on.

Width—In this text box, you can designate a global width for all columns either by typing a value in the text box or by using the spinner arrows.

Freeze—In this text box, you can designate a field that you want to freeze. When a field is frozen, you cannot edit that field. If you freeze the COMPANY field, for example, you can no longer edit that field. To freeze a field, click on the down arrow next to the Freeze text box to display a list of available fields. Highlight the field you want to freeze. The field you have selected appears in the Freeze text box.

After you have set all your criteria, click the OK button. If you want to abandon your choices, click Cancel.

Adding Records

You can add records to a table by appending a record. Appending adds the new record to the end of the table. You can do this using any one of the following methods:

- Open the **T**able menu and choose **A**dd Records.
- Press Ctrl+A.
- In Browse Layout view, go to the last record and press the down-arrow key.
- In Form or Columnar Layout view, press the PgDn key.
- Click the right mouse button to access the SpeedMenu and then choose **A**dd Records.

Using any one of these methods opens the first blank record. Type your data in the first field and use Tab to move to the next field. Again, type your data and use Tab to move on. When you tab past the last field of the record, a new empty record appears and you can repeat the procedure to add additional data.

When you enter data in a character field, any combination of letters, numbers, and punctuation is accepted.

When you enter data in a numeric field, only numbers, commas, and the minus sign are accepted.

When you enter data in a date field, you only have to type the numbers. The slash or hyphen marks which separate the month, day, and year are entered automatically.

When you enter data in a logic field, only Y, y, (Yes) N, n, (No), T, t, (True), F, f, (False) are accepted. No other entry is allowed.

When you enter data in a memo field, all letters, numbers, and punctuation are accepted.

Tip

Remember, if you have established data validation rules, the new data will be verified before it is accepted. When you establish your validation rules, make sure that they truly meet your needs.

Troubleshooting

When I try to enter data in a field, dBASE for Windows displays an error message saying that my data entry is not valid. What could be the problem?

The most likely culprit is that you have established validation rules and your data does not meet the validation rules criteria. Go to Table Properties and check your validation rules. You can then either change the rules or enter data that meets the validation rules criteria.

Editing Records

You can edit data in any of the three views: Browse Layout, Form Layout, or Columnar Layout. You can edit any record as long as the table is not designated read-only (which means that the table was set up so that it could not be edited). You also cannot edit any fields that have been frozen, and if validation criteria has been set, your edit is accepted only if it meets the criteria.

To edit a record, highlight the field you want to edit (use your mouse or the Tab key to get there). You replace all the data in the field. You can insert missing data by placing the cursor in the field and then entering characters.

To replace all or part of the data in the field, you can highlight the data and delete it. Alternatively, if you are not in Insert mode (the `Ins` message does not appear in the status bar), you can simply type over the existing data.

Deleting Records

If you want to delete records, you first must mark the records you want to delete. To mark a selected record, open the **T**able menu and choose **D**elete Selected Record. (Alternatively, you can press Ctrl+U.) This process does not delete any records; it simply designates which ones you are going to delete.

To actually delete the records from the file on disk, you must first pack them.

Caution

After you issue the PACK command, the records are physically deleted from the disk and are gone forever. You cannot retrieve them. Be very certain that you want to delete the records before you pack them.

To pack the records, use either of the following two methods:

- Open the **T**able menu and choose **T**able Utilities; then choose **P**ack Records.
- In the Command Window, type the following:

  CLOSE ALL

  SET EXCLUSIVE ON

  USE *name*.dbf *(insert the actual name of the table you are using)*

  PACK

If you change your mind about a particular record before you run the PACK command, you can unmark it. After you run the PACK command, however, the marked records are gone forever.

You can use the ZAP command to delete all the records in a table at one time. To delete all records, follow these steps:

1. Open the **T**able menu and choose **T**able Utilities; then choose **Z**ap Records.
2. When you see the message `Remove all Records?`, answer **Y**es, and the records will be deleted.

> **Caution**
>
> Be very careful when you use the ZAP or PACK command. These commands delete the data from your disk and you cannot recover it.

Printing Tables

If you want to print your table from any of the views, open the **F**ile menu and choose **P**rint. Alternatively, you can click the Printer icon. With either method, the Print Records dialog box appears, as shown in figure 8.13.

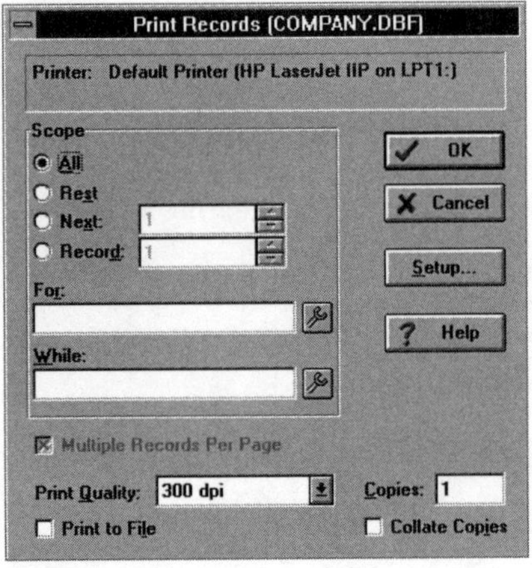

Fig. 8.13
The Print Records dialog box.

Tip
Click the **S**etup button to adjust your page orientation. Make sure that your page orientation is set the way you want it: Po**r**trait or **L**andscape. If you have several fields in your table, the information may print on more than one page.

In the Print Records Dialog Box, you can select which records you want to print. You have the following choices:

***A**ll*—Prints all records

*Re**s**t*—Prints the records from the current record on

*Ne**x**t*—Prints the next *x* number of records you choose (for example, the next four records)

*Recor**d***—Prints the record whose record number you specify

If you want to make changes to your printer setup, such as changing from portrait to landscaping printing, you can click the **S**etup button, and the Printer Setup dialog box appears. Make the changes, click OK, and you are returned to the Print Record dialog box.

When you are in Browse Layout, your records print in the table form you see on-screen. When you are in Form Layout, your records print in the single record form you see on-screen.

Saving or Abandoning Changes

dBASE for Windows automatically saves your changes when you move to a different record or when you switch between the Browse and Form layouts.

To save your changes and stay in the table, you can open the **F**ile menu and choose **S**ave Record. To save your changes and leave the table, just close the table. Your changes are automatically saved.

To abandon a change you have made, open the **F**ile menu and choose Aban**d**on Record. You must do this before you leave the record. To leave the table and abandon changes, open the **F**ile menu and choose A**b**andon Record and Close (or press Ctrl+Q).

Tip

dBASE for Windows saves your changes to memory and then saves them to disk in a group. If you want your changes saved to disk immediately as you make them, make sure that the Autosave feature is activated. To access the Autosave feature, first open **P**roperties from the menu bar, then double-click on **D**esktop. When the Desktop Properties dialog box appears, click the Table page. When the Table page is open, click **A**utosave. To exit, click OK.

Working in a Multiuser Environment

When dBASE for Windows is set up on a network, the program can handle more than one user at a time. All users are assigned access levels, and your access level determines the tasks you are permitted to perform in dBASE for Windows.

When data is being shared, one person may be updating a record while another person is using the record. To ensure that the data in the table is updated regularly, the screen is refreshed periodically. How often the screen is refreshed depends on how the refresh rate has been set in the Desktop Properties dialog box. To access the Refresh feature, first open Properties from the menu bar, then double-click on Desktop. When the Desktop Properties dialog box appears, click the Table page. When the Table page is open, enter a value in the Refresh text box. To exit, click OK.

If you are working in a multiuser environment, you must have exclusive use of the table in order to delete records. Before you can either edit or delete a record, the record must be locked. You can set dBASE for Windows to lock records automatically, by selecting **L**ock in the Table page of the Desktop properties.

▶ "Using dBASE in a Multiuser Environment," p. 443

To open **P**roperties from the main menu, click **D**esktop Properties. When the Desktop Properties dialog box appears, click the **T**able page, click the **L**ock check box, and then click OK.

If you don't have dBASE for Windows set to lock automatically, you must manually lock the record before you can edit or delete it. To manually lock a record, open the **T**able menu and choose **L**ock Selected Record (or press Ctrl+L).

If another user has already locked the record, you are asked whether you want to cancel or retry your lock.

Note

You do not have to lock a record to add records.

Working with Catalogs

You can assign tables, reports, and queries to a group called a catalog. Suppose that you want to keep all records related to teachers in one area and all records related to students in another area. You can set up a catalog called Teachers to which you assign all tables, reports, and queries related to this topic. You can do the same thing for students.

A catalog might be compared to a company in which each department has its own filing cabinet and stores its own records. Catalogs provide a great way for you to keep things organized and systematic—especially if you are working with many different tables, reports, and queries.

To set up a catalog using the Navigator, follow these steps:

1. Click Catalogs.

2. Double-click Untitled to set up a new catalog.

3. In the Create Catalog dialog box (shown in figure 8.14), enter a name for the catalog in the **F**ile Name text box.

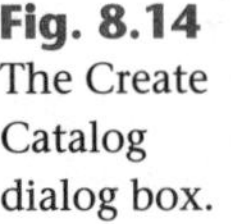

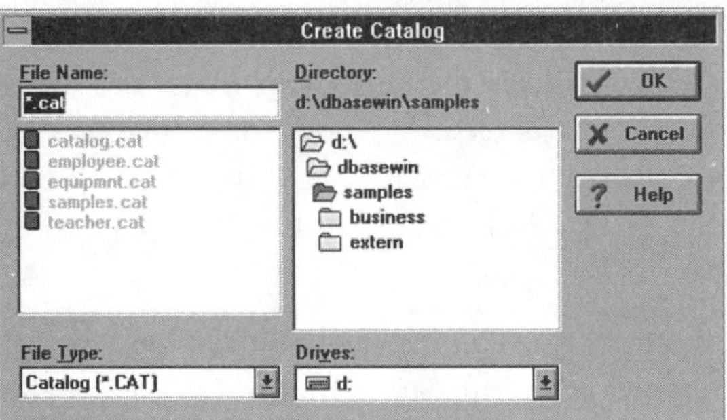

Fig. 8.14 The Create Catalog dialog box.

4. Click OK.

5. The Catalog Item Description dialog box appears and displays the Catalog Name, the Catalog Item Name, and the Catalog Description text box. In the Catalog Description text box, enter a description about the catalog you have just created. Suppose that you have just created a Teacher catalog, and it is to be used to attach all tables, queries, reports, and forms related to teachers. You might enter the following description in the Catalog Description text box: **Catalog for tracking Teacher information**.

You can create new tables, reports, or queries from within the catalog, or you can assign existing files to the catalog. To assign existing files to a catalog, follow these steps:

1. From the Navigator, click Catalog.
2. Open the Catalog you want to work with by double-clicking it.
3. From the menu bar, choose **C**atalog and then click **A**dd Item. The Add Catalog Item dialog box appears, as shown in figure 8.15.

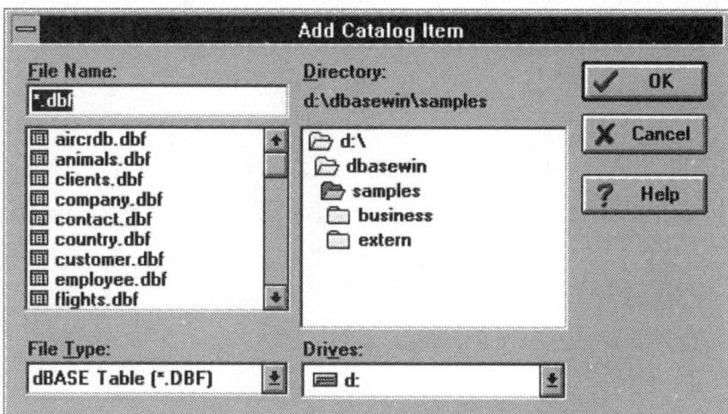

Fig. 8.15
Adding tables to a catalog.

4. Double-click a file in the **F**ile Name list box or highlight the file and click OK.
5. The Catalog Item Description dialog box appears, as shown in figure 8.16. In the Description text box, type a description of the file you have just added. Click OK.

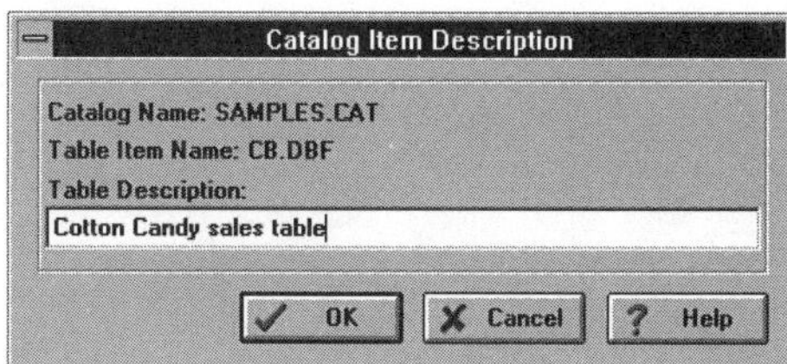

Fig. 8.16
The Catalog Item Description dialog box.

6. The file you added is now displayed in the right column in the Catalog window. When you are finished adding to the catalog, close the Catalog window.
7. To close the Catalog window, double-click the Control menu box, or press Ctrl+F4.

From Here...

You may want to refer to the following chapters for more information about the concepts discussed in this chapter:

- Chapter 13, "Using the Expression Builder." This chapter explains what an expression is, how to build an expression, and how to write and edit expressions.
- Chapter 14, "Manipulating Data." This chapter gets you started working with data subsets, generating new records, counting records, replacing data, and learning how to create field calculations.
- Chapter 18, "Using dBASE in a Multiuser Environment." If you plan to use dBASE For Windows in a network environment, read this chapter to get a better understanding of how dBASE works on a network.

Chapter 9

Creating Basic Queries

The purpose of a database is to provide information. One type of information you often need is a report, such as a weekly report of sales or inventory status. Another type of information is an answer to a specific question, such as "Which sales representatives have exceeded their quotas?" or "How many reams of copier paper do we have in stock?"

A *report* is information you require in a similar format on a regular basis, whereas a specific question, known as a *query* in database terminology, is a request for certain information. This chapter covers queries, dealing with basic queries based on a single table.

▶ "Creating Basic Reports," p. 229

▶ "Creating Advanced Queries," p. 425

In this chapter, you learn how to do the following:

- Create a query based on a single table
- Run a query to display a view
- Save and reuse a query
- Change the order of fields and records in a view
- Use conditions to include specific records in a view

What Is a Query?

A *query* is a question you ask your database. With a database that contains a table of information about books in your office or home library, for example, you can ask such questions as

- What books do I have that are written by a specific author?
- Which books cost more than $50?

- How many books did I buy last year?
- Do I have any books about databases?

You can use a query to ask for information based on any of the fields in your tables. When you use a query in this way, dBASE displays what looks like a table on your screen. The information you see is not a table, however; it is a *view* of the data in the table or tables on which your query is based. If you want, you can save the view as a table for subsequent use.

You can ask queries in two ways: you can create a query at the time you want information, or you can run a query you have previously created. In either case, dBASE creates a view containing the information you requested.

In addition to getting answers to questions, you can use queries as the basis for forms and reports, as you will discover in the next two chapters. Yet another use for queries is to edit data in tables, as explained later in this chapter.

Creating a Table to Use with Queries

Any query gets information from one or more tables. Before you start to work with queries, then, you need a table. All the examples in this and the next two chapters are based on a table that contains information about books in a library, the structure of which is shown in figure 9.1. But you can use a dBASE table you already have to experiment with queries.

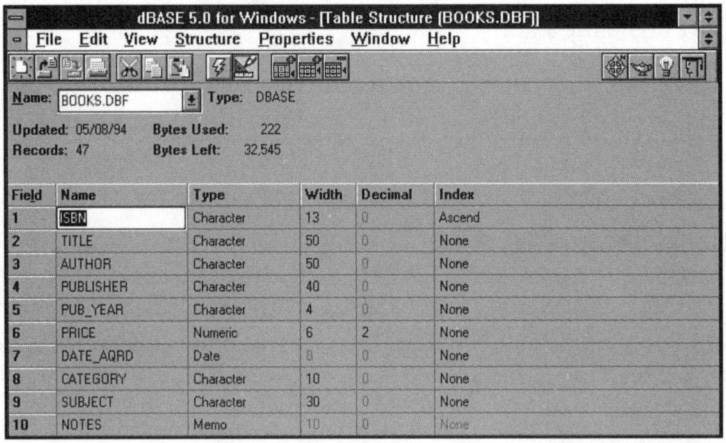

dBASE 5.0 for Windows - [Table Structure (BOOKS.DBF)]

File Edit View Structure Properties Window Help

Name: BOOKS.DBF Type: DBASE

Updated: 05/08/94 Bytes Used: 222

Records: 47 Bytes Left: 32,545

Field	Name	Type	Width	Decimal	Index
1	ISBN	Character	13	0	Ascend
2	TITLE	Character	50	0	None
3	AUTHOR	Character	50	0	None
4	PUBLISHER	Character	40	0	None
5	PUB_YEAR	Character	4	0	None
6	PRICE	Numeric	6	2	None
7	DATE_AQRD	Date	8	0	None
8	CATEGORY	Character	10	0	None
9	SUBJECT	Character	30	0	None
10	NOTES	Memo	10	0	None

Fig. 9.1
This screen shows the structure of the table used in the examples described in this chapter.

Note

ISBN, the name of one of the fields in the table, is an abbreviation for International Standard Book Number. Because every published book has a unique ISBN number, this number is ideal for indexing the table.

Opening the Query Designer Window

As in most dBASE tasks, you open the Query Designer window from the Navigator window. Do the following to open the Query Designer window in which you specify queries:

Tip
With (Untitled) selected, you can press F2 to display the Open Table Required dialog box.

1. With dBASE running, open the Navigator window, and go to the directory that contains the table on which you want to base your query.

2. Select Queries in the list of objects at the left side of the window. The window contains the Untitled query as well as the names of all existing query files.

3. Double-click (Untitled) to display the Open Table Required dialog box that lists the tables in the selected directory.

Note

An alternative to steps 2 and 3 is to open the File menu, choose New, and then in the submenu choose Query.

4. Select the table on which you want to base your query.

5. Choose OK to open the Query Designer window shown in figure 9.2.

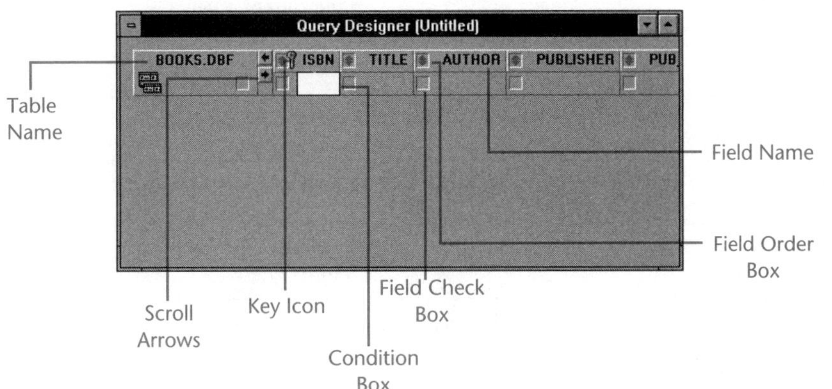

Fig. 9.2
The Query Designer window is where you design a query.

Note

An alternative way to display the Query Designer window is to start with an open table, and then click the Create New File button in the SpeedBar. Select **Q**uery from the submenu. When you use this approach, the query is automatically based on the open table.

The Query Designer window denotes key fields with a small key icon, as you can see in figure 9.2.

Note also that the Query Designer window contains a skeleton of the table on which you are basing the query. The skeleton shows the name of the table on which the query is based at the left. The remainder of the skeleton consists of short columns, one for each field in the table.

Using the Query Designer SpeedBar Buttons

Notice that the SpeedBar changes as soon as you open a Query Designer window. The seven leftmost buttons remain unchanged, but additional buttons become available. Table 9.1 lists the buttons in the Query Designer SpeedBar.

Table 9.1 Query Designer SpeedBar Buttons

Icon	Name	Purpose
	New	Create a new table, query, form, report, and so on.
	Open	Open an existing table, query, form, report, and so on.
	Save	Save the current query.
	Print	Print the code corresponding to the current query.
	Cut	Cut to the Clipboard.
	Copy	Copy to the Clipboard.
	Paste	Paste from the Clipboard.
	Run Query	Display the view resulting from the query.
	Design Query	Display the Query Designer window.

Icon	Name	Purpose
	Add Table	Add a table to the query.
	Remove Table	Remove a table from the query.
	Link Tables	Link tables in the query.
	Remove Link	Remove a table link in the query.
	Navigator Window	Activate the Navigator window.
	Command Window	Activate the Command window.
	Expert	Open an Expert.
	Tutorial	Run a Tutorial.

The actions of the New, Open, and Save buttons are similar to those in most Windows applications.

▶ "Working with the Command Window," p. 549

When you click the Print button, you get a printed copy of the dBASE commands that are executed when you run a query to display a view.

The Cut, Copy, and Paste buttons work as they do in other Windows applications. You can use these buttons to copy or move data from other windows to the Query Designer window, or from the Query Designer window to other windows. Some examples of this are mentioned later in this chapter.

The Run Query button runs the query to display a view of data in a table, as explained in more detail later in this chapter. When a view is displayed, you can click the Design Query button to return to the Query Designer window.

▶ "Creating Advanced Queries," p. 425

You use the Add Table, Remove Table, Link Tables, and Remove Link buttons with queries based on two or more tables.

You click the Navigator button to display the Navigator window.

▶ "Working with the Command Window," p. 549

The Command window button activates the Command window that displays the dBASE commands that are executed when you click buttons, choose from menus, and perform other interactive actions.

When you need help while working in the Query Designer window, you can click the Expert button to open an expert that walks you through the current task, or you can click the Tutorial button to open a relevant tutorial.

Viewing Additional Fields

Unless the table on which you are basing your query contains only a very few fields, you cannot see all the fields when the Query Designer window first appears. The window initially shows only the first few fields in the table on which the query is based. You can click the Query Designer window's Maximize button so that it fills the screen, but in most cases you still cannot see all the fields.

You have two ways to see additional fields:

- Press Tab to see additional fields to the right, or press Shift+Tab to see additional fields to the left.
- Click the scroll arrows in the skeleton to scroll the displayed part of the skeleton to the left or to the right. The scroll arrows, which are marked in figure 9.2, are between the table name and the first field name in the skeleton.

When you use either method to see additional fields, the table name at the left end of the skeleton remains in place.

Defining and Using a Basic Query

A query defines the information you want to find in your data. As you have already seen, a Query Designer window shows you the fields in the table on which the query is based. You can select which of these fields you want to see in the view of records that is displayed when you run the query. You can also specify conditions that must be satisfied in order for records to appear in the view.

Tip
Select only those fields you really need so that you can easily find the data you want in a view.

After you have defined a query in the Query Designer window, you can run that query to display a view of your data, and you can also save the query for later use.

Selecting Fields to View

To create a view consisting of only certain fields in a table, click the check boxes under the required field names in the Query Designer window, as shown in figure 9.3.

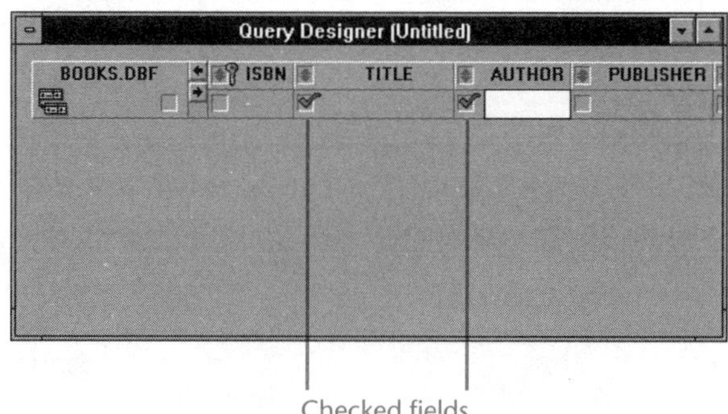

Fig. 9.3 The Query Designer window looks like this when the TITLE and AUTHOR fields have been checked for inclusion in the view.

You can, of course, choose any number of fields to view by checking those fields in the Query Designer window. Instead of checking individual check boxes, you can click the check box under the table name at the left end of the skeleton to check all fields. To remove the check marks from all fields, click this box again.

Tip
To remove a check mark from a check box, click the box again.

Running the Query

To display a view of the data, click the Run Query button in the SpeedBar. dBASE then displays a Query Results window such as the one shown in figure 9.4.

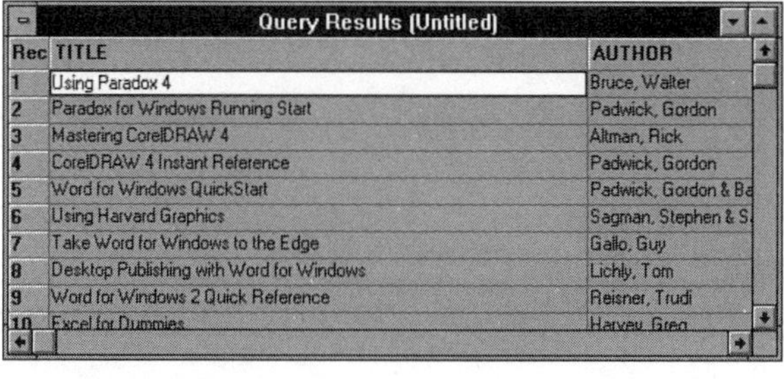

Fig. 9.4 The Query Results window shows part of the view of your data produced when you run a query.

To see a more complete view of your data, maximize the Query Results window, and drag the column boundaries between the columns to reduce the column widths, just as you can with a table. If the view consists of only a few fields, as in figure 9.5, you probably can see all the fields at once. Otherwise, you can use the horizontal scroll bar or press Tab to move from field to field.

◄ "Entering, Editing, and Viewing Data," p. 145

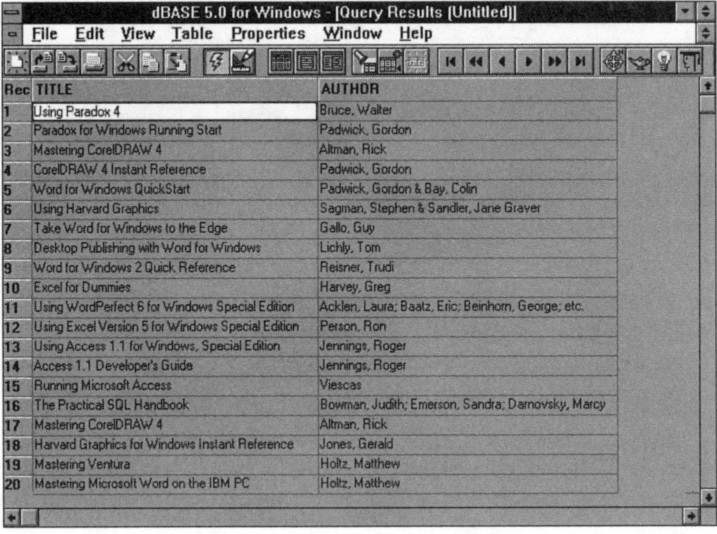

Rec	TITLE	AUTHOR
1	Using Paradox 4	Bruce, Walter
2	Paradox for Windows Running Start	Padwick, Gordon
3	Mastering CorelDRAW 4	Altman, Rick
4	CorelDRAW 4 Instant Reference	Padwick, Gordon
5	Word for Windows QuickStart	Padwick, Gordon & Bay, Colin
6	Using Harvard Graphics	Sagman, Stephen & Sandler, Jane Graver
7	Take Word for Windows to the Edge	Gallo, Guy
8	Desktop Publishing with Word for Windows	Lichty, Tom
9	Word for Windows 2 Quick Reference	Reisner, Trudi
10	Excel for Dummies	Harvey, Greg
11	Using WordPerfect 6 for Windows Special Edition	Acklen, Laura; Baatz, Eric; Beinhorn, George; etc.
12	Using Excel Version 5 for Windows Special Edition	Person, Ron
13	Using Access 1.1 for Windows, Special Edition	Jennings, Roger
14	Access 1.1 Developer's Guide	Jennings, Roger
15	Running Microsoft Access	Viescas
16	The Practical SQL Handbook	Bowman, Judith; Emerson, Sandra; Darnovsky, Marcy
17	Mastering CorelDRAW 4	Altman, Rick
18	Harvard Graphics for Windows Instant Reference	Jones, Gerald
19	Mastering Ventura	Holtz, Matthew
20	Mastering Microsoft Word on the IBM PC	Holtz, Matthew

Fig. 9.5
After maximizing the Query Results window and dragging the column boundaries, you can see more of the view.

◀ "Designing a Database," p. 79

Notice that fields in the view are in the same order as those in the original table, and also that the records in the view are in the same order as those in the original table.

Note

When a view is displayed, the SpeedBar contains the buttons available whenever a table is displayed in Browse Layout view.

Tip
Alternatively, click the Save button in the SpeedBar.

Saving Your Query

To save your query so that you can reuse it:

1. Click the Design Query button in the SpeedBar to redisplay the query in the Query Designer window.

2. Open the **F**ile menu and choose **S**ave to display the Save File dialog box.

3. Type a name for the query, and then choose OK. dBASE saves the query as a file with .QBE as the file name extension.

Tip
Because dBASE saves queries as DOS files, you are limited to eight characters in a query name.

To close the Query Designer window and return to the Navigator window:

1. Open the **F**ile menu and choose **C**lose to close the query and return to the table on which the query was based.

2. Open the **F**ile menu and choose **C**lose to close the table and return to the Navigator window.

> **Note**
>
> QBE files contain the instructions dBASE uses to display a view of information in one or more tables. These files do not contain the data displayed in views.

Running a Saved Query

After you have saved a query, you can run it from the Navigator window. Follow these steps:

1. With the Navigator window displayed, choose Queries in the list of objects on the left to see the names of existing queries, as shown in figure 9.6.

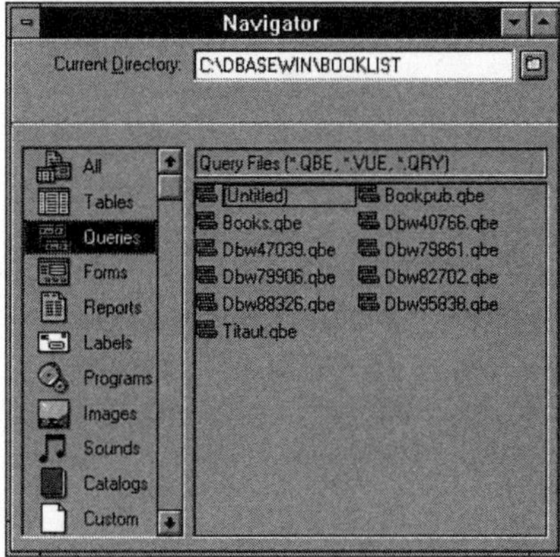

Fig. 9.6 The Navigator window contains the names of queries previously saved.

> **Note**
>
> Queries with names in the format DBW#####.QBE are those saved automatically by dBASE every time you run a query.

2. Double-click the name of the query you want to run to display a view of your data.

Tip You can right-click a query name and choose **R**un Query in the SpeedMenu to run a query.

Each time you run an existing query, the view is based on the current data in the table. If you modify the data in the table and then run the query again, the view shows the modified data.

Printing and Saving a View

◄ "Printing Tables," p. 161

After you have used a query to display a view of your data, you can print the view, and you can also save it as a separate table.

Printing a View

Tip
Alternatively, click the Print button in the SpeedBar.

You can print a view in the same way you print a table. Follow these steps:

1. With a view displayed, open the **F**ile menu and choose **P**rint to display the Print dialog box.
2. Select the records you want to print.
3. Choose OK to start printing.

Saving a View as a Table

As previously explained, a view is based on the current data in a table. At times you may want to keep a view so that you can use it as it is, even if the data in the underlying table changes. If you have a table that contains sensitive information, you may want to use a query to extract nonsensitive information from it and distribute that data in the form of a table to other people.

Follow these steps to create a table from a view:

1. With a view displayed, click the Query Design button in the SpeedBar to display the Query Designer window.
2. Open the **Q**uery menu and choose Copy Results to New **T**able to display the Save Table dialog box.
3. Enter a name for the table, and choose OK to run the query, display the view as a table, and save the table. dBASE gives the table the name you entered, using .DBF as the file name extension.
4. Open the **F**ile menu and choose **C**lose to close the table.

Note

A table created this way has the same format as any other dBASE table. When you subsequently open the Navigator window, you see this table in the list of tables.

When you save a view as a table, that table is not updated with any changes you subsequently make to the table on which the view was based.

Changing the Order of Fields and Records

The view you create, by using the method described previously, contains fields and records in the same order as those in the table on which the query was based. You can easily change the order of fields in the view, and you can arrange records in ascending or descending alphabetical or numerical order based on the contents of any field.

Changing Field Order

You change the order of fields in the view by changing the field order in the skeleton as it appears in the Query Designer window. To illustrate this, suppose you want to reverse the order of two fields. With the Query Designer window displaying a skeleton of your table, follow these steps:

1. Move the mouse pointer onto a field name. The pointer is in the correct position when it changes to the shape of a hand, as in figure 9.7.

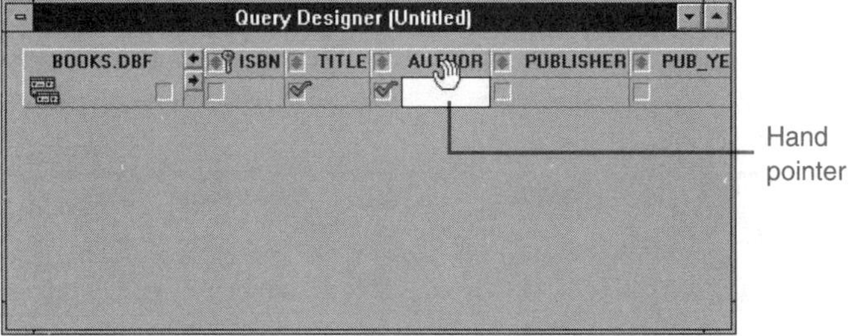

Fig. 9.7 When the pointer is on a field name, the pointer changes to the shape of a hand.

2. Press the mouse button, and drag to another field. As soon as you drag over another field name, the two field names change position (see fig. 9.8).

Fig. 9.8 After you drag one field name over another field name, the two field names change positions in the skeleton.

Now you can run the query again to see another view, this time with the two fields in the new order.

By dragging fields in the Query Designer window, you can arrange the fields in the skeleton in any order you prefer. The process of changing the order of records in the skeleton is known as *modifying the view*.

Sorting Records According to Values in One Field

Tip
The fields used for sorting do not necessarily have to be checked for inclusion in the view.

By default, records in a view are in natural order; that is, the same order as records in the underlying table. You can, however, create a view with records sorted in ascending or descending order of values in one or more fields. The order of fields can be case-sensitive or case-insensitive. dBASE can sort views based on the contents of all types of fields except Memo, OLE, and Binary.

Note

If you choose a case-insensitive sort order, records in the view are arranged in order without regard for alphabetic characters being uppercase or lowercase. If you choose a case-sensitive sort order, records are sorted with all uppercase characters having a lower value than all lowercase characters (following the order of ASCII values).

With the Query Designer window displayed, do the following to create a view with records in alphabetical order of values in a character field:

1. Point to the Field Order box immediately to the left of the name of a character or number field, and press the mouse button to display the five sort icons shown in figure 9.9. The five sort options are listed in table 9.2.

Fig. 9.9
You can choose among five sort options for each field.

Table 9.2 Sort Options

Icon	Sort Option
	Ascending sort (case-sensitive)
	Descending sort (case-sensitive)
	Ascending sort (case-insensitive)
	Descending sort (case-insensitive)
	Unsorted (natural order)

2. Drag down to highlight one of the sort icons. When you release the mouse button, the sort icon you selected appears at the left of the field name.

3. Click the Run Query button in the SpeedBar.

Sorting Records According to Values in Two or More Fields

You are not limited to sorting on only one field. When you use two or more fields, however, you have to decide the sorting priority. In a telephone directory, for example, entries are listed by people's last names. Where two or more people have the same last name, those people are listed in first-name order. Last names have the first (primary) priority, and first names have the second (secondary) priority.

When you designate more than one field to be used for sorting, the fields in the query skeleton must be in order from left to right of the sort priorities. The primary sort field must be to the left of the secondary sort field, the secondary sort field to the left of the tertiary sort field, and so on.

The table used for the illustrations in this chapter includes TITLE and PUBLISHER fields. To create a view in which records are sorted by publisher (the primary sort) and, for each publisher, by title (the secondary sort), you must first arrange the fields in the query skeleton so that PUBLISHER is to the left of TITLE. Follow these steps to sort the fields by publisher and then by title:

1. In the Query Designer window, drag the field names so that they are in priority order with the primary sort field to the left of the secondary sort field.

2. Click the check boxes of those fields you want to include in the view.

3. Select the sort order for the primary and secondary sort fields as shown in figure 9.10.

Tip
The primary and secondary sort fields do not necessarily have to be adjacent in the skeleton.

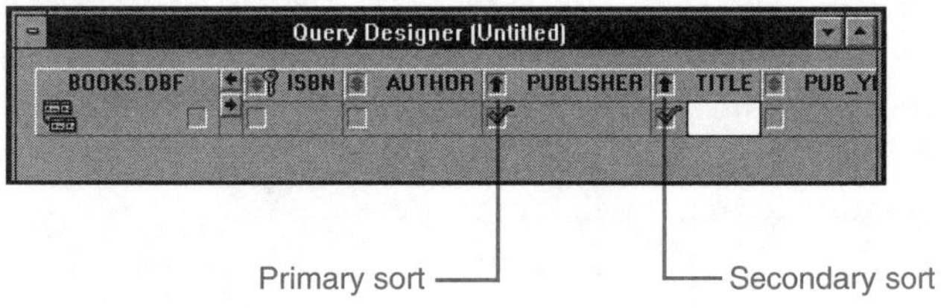

Fig. 9.10
At this stage, the skeleton has the primary and secondary sort fields in the correct order, and a sort order is selected for each of them.

4. Click the Run button in the SpeedBar to run the query.

5. Adjust the width of the Query Results window and the width of the columns so that you can see as many fields as possible (see fig. 9.11). You can also maximize the Query Results windows if necessary.

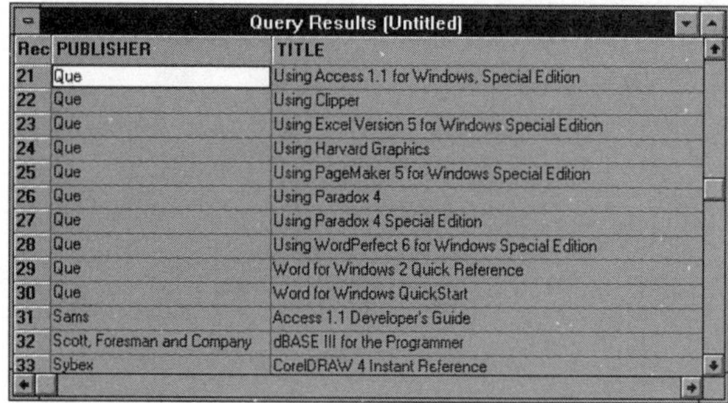

Rec	PUBLISHER	TITLE
21	Que	Using Access 1.1 for Windows, Special Edition
22	Que	Using Clipper
23	Que	Using Excel Version 5 for Windows Special Edition
24	Que	Using Harvard Graphics
25	Que	Using PageMaker 5 for Windows Special Edition
26	Que	Using Paradox 4
27	Que	Using Paradox 4 Special Edition
28	Que	Using WordPerfect 6 for Windows Special Edition
29	Que	Word for Windows 2 Quick Reference
30	Que	Word for Windows QuickStart
31	Sams	Access 1.1 Developer's Guide
32	Scott, Foresman and Company	dBASE III for the Programmer
33	Sybex	CorelDRAW 4 Instant Reference

Fig. 9.11
This view contains two fields with PUBLISHER as the primary sort field and TITLE as the secondary sort field.

You can select as many fields as you like for more levels of sorting.

Rearranging Fields in a View

Because you have to arrange the position of fields in the skeleton according to the sort priority, the field order in the view produced by the query may not be what you want. You can easily solve this problem.

After dBASE has created a view, you can change the field order on your screen, and also the order in which fields are printed. Do this in the same way you changed field order in the skeleton. Point to a field name in the view so that the pointer changes to the shape of a hand. Press the mouse button, and drag the field name to a new position. The field names, together with the data listed below them, change position on your screen. If you print the view, the fields are printed in the same order as they are displayed on your screen.

▶ "Understanding the Difference between Indexing and Sorting," p. 434

Sorting on Fields That Are Not Included in the View

Selecting which fields are to be listed in the view and marking fields to be used for sorting are independent of each other. A view does not necessarily have to include the fields on which data is sorted, and a view can include fields in addition to those used for sorting.

Using a Query to Select Records

So far, you have learned how to display views that include all records in the table on which the query is based, but not all fields in those records. dBASE also lets you choose which records to include in the view, a process known as *filtering* a table. You have several ways to create filters based on one or more fields.

Selecting Records with Specific Text in a Field

Suppose you want to create a view that contains only those records in which a field consists of specific text. In the case of a table that lists books, for example, you may want to create a view that contains books from one publisher or written by a certain author. The common data in the records you want to see is known as a *condition*. To create a view containing only those records that satisfy a certain condition:

Tip
If you don't get the records you expect in the view, check that the spelling and capitalization of the condition correspond to those in the table.

1. Display a query skeleton in the Query Designer window.
2. In the skeleton, click the name of the field for which you want to specify a condition, or click the region just under the name, to open a white Condition box for that field. Notice the flashing insertion point at the left end of the Condition box.
3. Type the condition text enclosed in double quotation marks. If you want to list books published by Que, for example, type "**Que**" in the Condition box for the PUBLISHER field.

Tip
You must enclose text within double or single quotation marks, or within brackets.

> **Note**
>
> Conditions are case-sensitive. The uppercase and lowercase letters in the Condition box must match the characters in the records you want in the view.

4. Click the check boxes of any other fields you want to include in the view, as shown in figure 9.12.

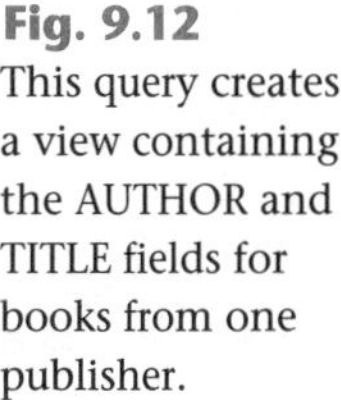

Fig. 9.12
This query creates a view containing the AUTHOR and TITLE fields for books from one publisher.

5. Run the query to display the view (see fig. 9.13).

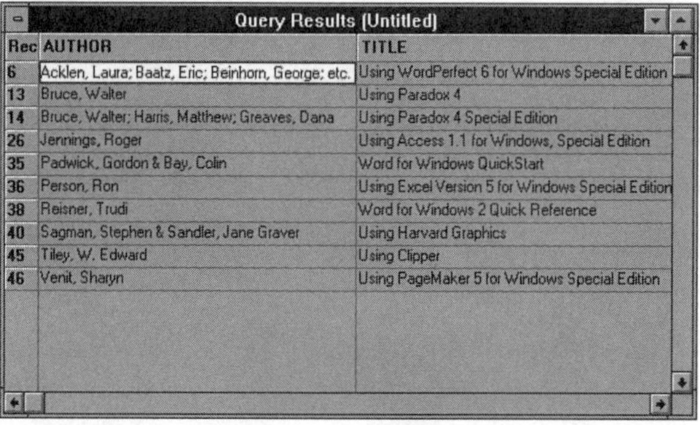
Query Results (Untitled)

Rec	AUTHOR	TITLE
6	Acklen, Laura; Baatz, Eric; Beinhorn, George; etc.	Using WordPerfect 6 for Windows Special Edition
13	Bruce, Walter	Using Paradox 4
14	Bruce, Walter; Harris, Matthew; Greaves, Dana	Using Paradox 4 Special Edition
26	Jennings, Roger	Using Access 1.1 for Windows, Special Edition
35	Padwick, Gordon & Bay, Colin	Word for Windows QuickStart
36	Person, Ron	Using Excel Version 5 for Windows Special Edition
38	Reisner, Trudi	Word for Windows 2 Quick Reference
40	Sagman, Stephen & Sandler, Jane Graver	Using Harvard Graphics
45	Tiley, W. Edward	Using Clipper
46	Venit, Sharyn	Using PageMaker 5 for Windows Special Edition

Fig. 9.13
The view shows books from only one publisher.

Tip
Include the condition field in the view initially as a testing tool; then change the query so that the condition field is no longer included in the view.

In the previous example, the view does not include the field that contains the condition. You may want to include the condition field initially so that you can confirm your query is working as you intended. After that, though, you have no reason to include the field containing the condition, because a record appears in the view only if the condition is satisfied.

This example combines record selection with sorting. In the query skeleton, the AUTHOR and TITLE fields are both set to ascending order. Because the AUTHOR field is to the left of the TITLE field, the view shows authors in alphabetical order. If the table contained more than one book for an author, those books would be shown in alphabetical order also.

Using Condition Operators to Select Records

In the preceding description of selecting records to be included in a view, you learned how to use text as a condition. A record is included on the condition that the text in a field exactly matches the text specified for that field in the query skeleton.

By using *condition operators*, you can have much greater control over which records appear in a view. Condition operators let you specify records that contain exactly a specific value, but also records in which field values are less than or more than a specific value, or records in which field values are within a certain range.

A condition operator is a character, symbol, or word that you type at the left of a condition in a Condition box. For example, if you enter "**Que**" in the PUBLISHER field of the query skeleton, the resulting view contains only those records in which the value in the PUBLISHER field is *Que*. If you enter **>"Que"** the PUBLISHER field of the query skeleton, the resulting view contains only those records in which the value in the PUBLISHER field is greater than *Que*.

Note

When evaluating Character fields, dBASE uses the ASCII values of characters. Therefore, >"Que" means text that comes after *Que* in alphabetical order.

The condition operators you can use in query skeletons are listed in table 9.3.

Table 9.3 Condition Operators

Operator	Description
>	Greater than
<	Less than
=	Equal to
<> or *	Not equal to
>=	Greater than or equal to
<=	Less than or equal to
$	Contains
Like	Pattern match

Note

When you omit a condition operator, as you did in the text example in the preceding section, dBASE assumes the presence of =. Thus the condition "Que" is equivalent to ="Que".

You can use condition operators with all types of fields except Memo, OLE, and Binary. The format in which you must use the operators differs somewhat for certain field types, as defined in table 9.4.

Table 9.4 Condition Formats

Field Type	Condition Format
Text	Enclose text within double quotation marks, single quotation marks, or brackets, as in "Que", 'Que', or [Que].

(continues)

Table 9.4 Continued

Field Type	Condition Format
Date	Enclose a date within braces, as in {5/12/94}.
Logical	Use .t., .T., .y., or .Y. for logical true. Use .f., .F., .n., or .N. for logical false.

Using Numerical Values as Conditions

You can use any of the first six operators listed in table 9.3 to create conditions that select records according to numerical values in specific fields. When the value is a number, do not enclose it in quotation marks. Figure 9.14 shows `>=20` used as the condition that the value in a field must be greater than or equal to 20.

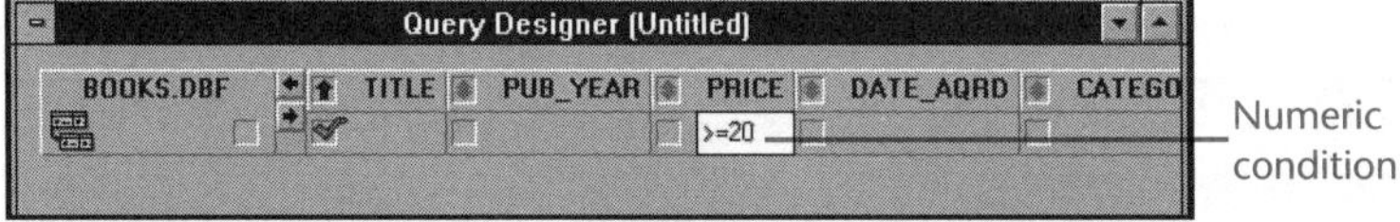

Fig. 9.14 The query specifies the condition that the price is greater than or equal to 20.

Note

If, instead of stating the condition as >=20, you typed >**20**, the view would not include records in which the value is exactly 20.

Selecting Records That Contain Certain Text

Tip You can use the $ operator to search for text in a memo field

Instead of using a condition that states the *entire* contents of Character fields, you can have a condition that selects records in which a specific field *contains* a certain string of characters. You may, for example, want to create a view containing records for all books for which the titles contain the word *Windows*. Figure 9.15 shows the condition `$"Windows"` used for this purpose.

Fig. 9.15 The condition here is that the TITLE field contains the word Windows.

Using Alphabetical Order as a Query Condition

You can define a condition so that a view contains records in which certain fields contain strings within an alphabetical range. Figure 9.16, for example, shows `>="M"` used as a condition to create a view containing those records in which the contents of the TITLE field start with *M* or any subsequent letters in the alphabet.

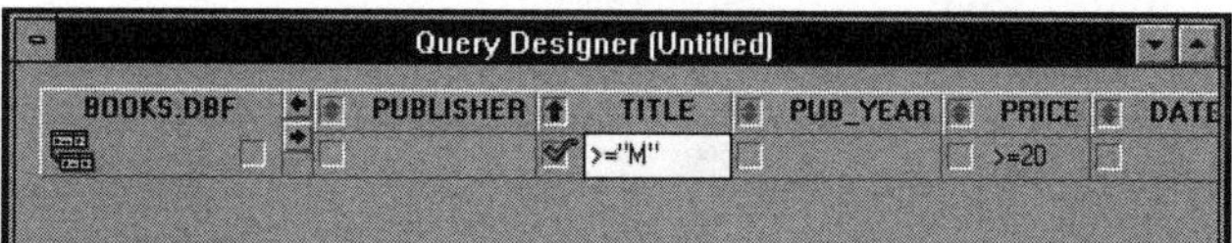

Fig. 9.16
The TITLE condition specifies records starting with M or later in the alphabet.

Note

You can enter as many characters as you need in a condition of this type—the query compares all the characters. If you enter the condition **>=Mat**, for example, the view does not contain a title starting with *Mas* but does contain titles starting with *Mat*, *Mau*, *Mav*, and so on.

Using Dates as a Query Condition

When you enter a condition in a date field, the date must be enclosed within braces. Figure 9.17, for example, shows `<={06/01/93}` used as a condition to find records in which the date field contains June 1, 1993, or earlier.

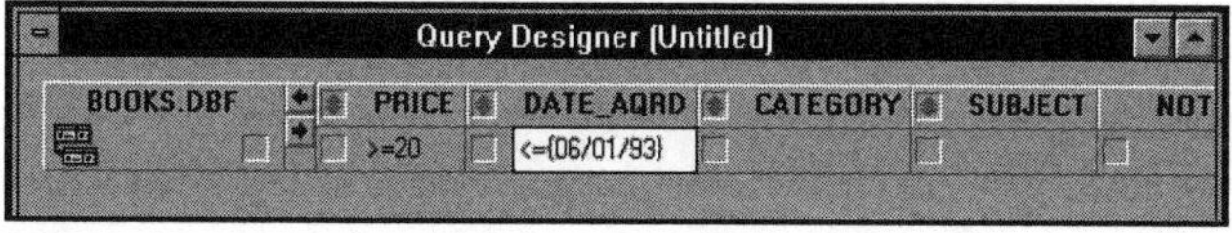

Fig. 9.17
The condition in the DATE_AQRD field specifies records containing June 1, 1993, or earlier.

Note

You can express the date in the condition as {06/01/93} or as {6/1/93}. The leading zeroes are optional.

Using Wild Card Characters in a Condition

You may need to look for records that contain a word you don't know how to spell, that may be incorrectly spelled in a table, or that may be capitalized in different ways. You can conduct such a search by using the Like operator with wild card characters.

For example, you may have a table in which a character field contains people's last names. Suppose you want to find the record for a person named

Smith. But is the person's name spelled *Smith, Smyth,* or perhaps *Smythe*? You can enter the condition **Like"Sm?th*"** to find the person's record with any of these spellings. This condition would also find names such as *Smithson.*

Table 9.5 defines the wild card characters.

Table 9.5 Wild Card Characters

Character	Represents
?	Any one character
*	Any number of characters, or no characters

The following examples illustrate some of the ways in which you can use wild card characters:

- `Like"J??n"` represents such strings as Jean, John, and Joan, but not Jan, Jon, or Jn. The reason is that each ? represents one, and only one, character.
- `Like"J*n"` represents such strings as Jean, John, Joan, Jan, Jon, Japan, or even Jn, but not Jay, Jazz, or Jane. The reason is that the * can represent any number of characters, including none. Also, any character after the * must be present in the field in the record.

Note

The ? wild card acts the same way it does in DOS. The * wild card behaves a little differently. In DOS, all characters after * are ignored, which is not the case in dBASE.

Figure 9.18 shows the Like condition operator and the * wild card used to look for records of books about CorelDRAW. The condition finds records in which the last four characters of the name are capitalized or not and any characters appear before the word.

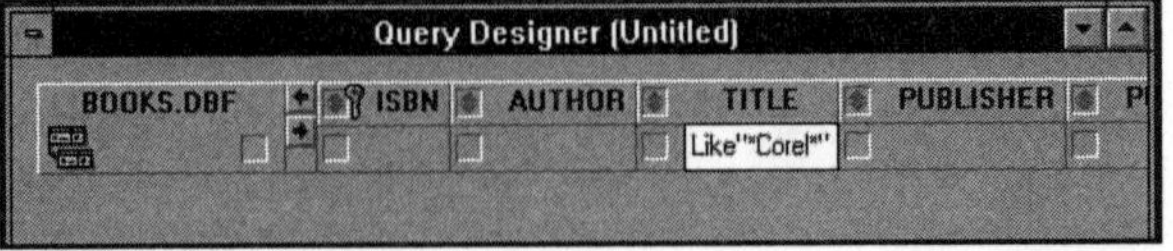

Fig 9.18 This condition specifies titles in which Corel is preceded by and followed by any characters.

Selecting Records Based on Two Conditions

You are not limited to using only one condition to select records in a view. When you use two or more conditions, you can do so in two ways:

- *AND conditions.* A record is displayed in the view only if all conditions are satisfied.
- *OR conditions.* A record is displayed in the view if one or more conditions are satisfied.

The following examples show how you can use two conditions, but you can use the same technique to combine more than two conditions.

As an example of an AND condition, you may want to see the books you purchased since the beginning of 1993 that cost more than $20. To create a query for this purpose:

1. Open the Query Designer window.
2. Enter a date condition in a date field in the skeleton, remembering to enclose the date within braces.
3. Enter a numeric condition within a numeric field. Figure 9.19 shows an example of these two conditions.

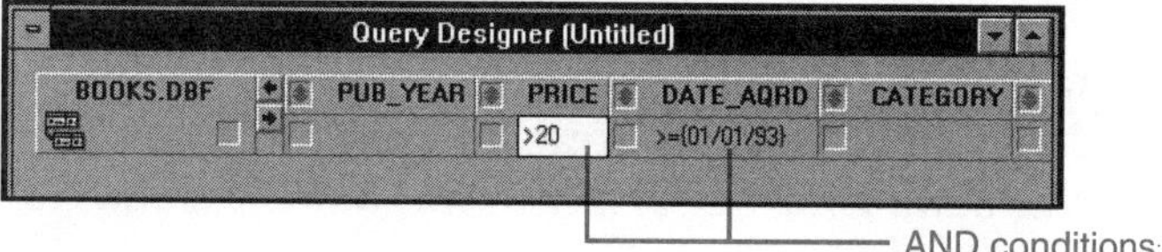

Fig. 9.19 These conditions select books purchased on or after January 1, 1993, and that cost more than $20.

When you define conditions in this way, every condition must be satisfied in order for a record to be included in the view. In the preceding example, the condition that a book cost more than $20 *and* the condition that it was purchased since 1/1/93 must be satisfied.

As an example of an OR condition, you could create a view containing records of books purchased after the beginning of 1993 or (as well as) books costing $20 or more.

To specify an OR condition, the query skeleton has to have two or more rows of conditions. You add a row to the skeleton by pressing the down-arrow key on your keyboard. You can add as many rows as you need. To delete a condition row, delete all conditions in the row and press the up-arrow key.

To define an OR condition:

1. Open a Query Designer window.
2. Press the down-arrow key to create a second row of conditions, as shown in figure 9.20.

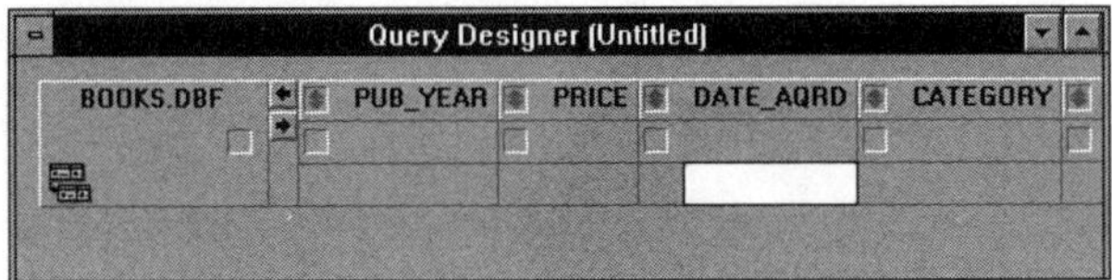

Fig. 9.20
This query skeleton contains two rows of conditions.

3. Enter a condition for one of the fields in the first row.
4. Enter another condition in one of the fields in the second row. Figure 9.21 shows conditions in two rows.

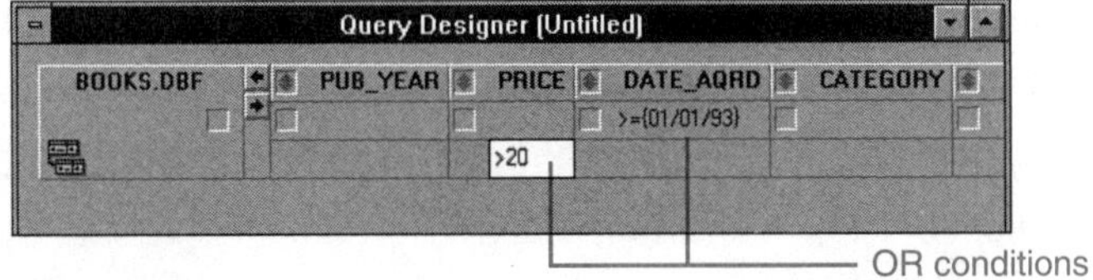

Fig. 9.21
These conditions specify books purchased on or after January 1, 1993, or those books costing $20 or more.

You can combine OR and AND conditions by defining conditions for more than one field in each row. You also can have more than two OR conditions by pressing the down-arrow key to increase the number of rows of conditions.

► "Working with the Condition Box," p. 438

You can set more complex conditions by opening the **Q**uery menu and choosing Add **C**onditions.

Checking Query Conditions for Errors

dBASE monitors the query conditions you type and alerts you if errors exist. To see this monitoring as it happens, close the current query by opening the **F**ile menu and choosing **C**lose. With Queries selected in the Navigator window, open a new Query Designer window, and then follow these steps:

1. Type **XYZ** (without enclosing quotation marks) as the condition for a character field. dBASE appears to accept what you type even though it is meaningless. (If you wanted XYZ to be recognized as text, you should have enclosed it in double quotation marks.)

2. Click another field as if you were going to define a condition for it. As soon as you click, the condition you typed in the character field becomes red to indicate an error. Also, a message in the status bar says `Variable undefined XYZ.`

dBASE has to wait until you do something to indicate that you have finished defining a condition before the program can check the condition's validity. In this case, your action of selecting another field indicated that you had finished defining the condition for the first field.

After dBASE indicates an error, you can use normal editing techniques to correct that error.

Note

After you have defined the last condition in a skeleton, always select another field even if you don't intend to define a condition for that field. In this way, dBASE checks the validity of the last condition you typed and alerts you if an error exists. If you define a condition and then immediately run the query, dBASE creates a view but ignores the invalid condition.

Using Cut-and-Paste with Conditions

As you have already seen, the SpeedBar in the Query Designer window contains the standard Cut, Copy, and Paste button that you can use to transfer data to and from the Clipboard. You can use these commands to copy conditions between different queries and also to copy data from tables to use as conditions.

Tip
You can also open the **E**dit menu and choose the Cu**t**, **C**opy, and **P**aste commands.

For example, if you have a fairly complex condition in one query and you want to use the same condition in another query, open the first query, select the condition, and copy it to the Clipboard. Then open the new query, select the Condition box into which you want to copy the condition, and paste from the Clipboard.

In a similar manner, you can copy data from a field in a table to the Clipboard, and then paste that data into a Condition box in a query skeleton.

This is probably a technique you won't use very often, but when you need to copy lengthy data, it can save you time and reduce the chance of errors.

Troubleshooting

When I run a query, the view is empty.

dBASE always finds records according to the conditions you specify, providing those conditions are valid. You may have made an error in typing the condition, or the table may not contain any records that satisfy the condition. Another possibility is that your condition may not be valid. To check for validity, return to the Query Designer window where any invalid conditions are highlighted in red.

When I run a query, the view does not contain the records I expect.

You probably have an error in your conditions. Return to the Query Designer window, and correct the conditions.

When I run a query in which I have set a date condition, the view displays more dates than it should.

You must enclose a date within braces. Return to the Query Designer window, and correct any error in the way you entered the date condition.

Editing an Existing Query

Tip
You can right-click a query name and choose Design **Q**uery in the SpeedMenu to run a query.

You can edit an existing query to create a new one. First display the query icons in the Navigator or Catalog window, and then right-double-click the icon representing the query you want to edit. dBASE displays a Query Designer window containing the query you selected. Now you can edit that query, using the methods described earlier in this chapter.

If you are working with simple queries, it's usually just as easy to create a new query as it is to modify an existing one. If, however, you have a query that contains conditions in several fields and, perhaps, has several rows of conditions, editing an existing query may be much easier than creating a new one from the beginning.

As an example of editing a query, you may want to change the one shown in figure 9.21 to give a view containing books that cost less than (instead of more than) $20. To do this, use standard editing methods to replace the greater-than symbol that precedes 20 in the second row of conditions with a less-than symbol.

After you have edited the query, you can save it as a new query so that you don't change the already existing one.

Using a Query to Edit Data in a Table

As explained earlier in this chapter, the data that a query displays in a view is, in fact, the data in one or more tables displayed in a manner dictated by the query. You need to understand that a view always contains the data that exists in tables at the time the query runs.

If your query is based on a single table and does not sort records, you can edit data in a view to change data in the table. The same is true in most cases for queries based on two or more related tables. The ability to edit data in a view in which data is sorted depends on how tables are indexed.

To see how you can edit data in a view to change data in a table, follow these steps:

1. Close any existing Query Designer windows, and return to the Navigator window.

2. Display the list of queries.

3. Double-click the name of a query that is based on a single table and does not sort records. dBASE runs that query.

4. Use normal editing techniques to make a change to a record displayed in the view.

5. Click any other record in the view. This step is necessary for dBASE to accept your edit.

6. Open the **W**indow menu and choose **1** Navigator to display the Navigator window. Alternatively, open the Catalog window.

7. Display the list of tables.

8. Double-click the name of the table on which the query you selected in step 3 was based to display that table in a Table Browse window. You can see that the change you made in the view has occurred in the table.

▶ "Working with Related Tables," p. 261

▶ "Creating Advanced Queries," p. 425

Note

If you edit data in the table and then redisplay the existing view, you do not see the change in the table reflected in the view. The reason is that a view contains the data in the table at the time the view was created by running a query. To create a view containing the changed data in the table, run the query again.

From Here...

In this chapter, you learned the basics of working with queries. You can find more information about queries in the following chapters:

- Chapter 10, "Creating Basic Forms." This chapter describes how you can create a form from a view.
- Chapter 11, "Creating Basic Reports." This chapter explains how you can create a report based on a query.
- Chapter 12, "Working with Related Tables." This chapter introduces working with two or more related tables.
- Chapter 17, "Creating Advanced Queries." This chapter discusses queries based on two or more tables and gives you more information about defining conditions in queries.

Chapter 10

Creating Basic Forms

If you are new to object-based databases, forget what you previously understood about the word *form*. In the context of dBASE for Windows, *form* has a different meaning than it has in ordinary conversation. In dBASE, a form is the principal means by which the application communicates with users.

You can use forms

- To display data that exists in tables
- To enter data into database tables (this use corresponds to the more traditional meaning attributed to the term *form*)
- As dialog boxes
- To display messages to users
- As a means of displaying other forms
- For purposes completely unrelated to databases

This chapter focuses on the first two uses of forms: displaying data in tables and providing a means to enter data into tables.

In this chapter, you learn how to do the following:

- Use the Form Expert to create a form
- Change the size and shape of a form
- Move and align objects on a form
- Change the size of objects on a form
- Use a form to display, edit, and add data to a table
- Save and print a form

Using Forms

▶ "Creating Basic Reports," p. 230

Forms are designed to be displayed on your screen. Although it is possible to print forms, you normally should use reports to display printed information from your database.

Forms consist of objects arranged in a window. For now, you need not learn the technical definition of the word *object*; instead, simply think of the word's ordinary English meaning: a synonym for *entity*. Although forms can contain many other classes of objects, the objects that this chapter emphasizes are mainly Text fields and EntryField fields.

Note

Visual Basic and other object-based environments often refer to objects as *controls*. The dBASE screens and printed reference materials use both words.

You can display forms in two modes: the *design* mode and the *running* mode. The design mode is where you place and arrange objects on a form. The running mode is where you use a form to display data from your database, edit data, and enter new data. The first part of this chapter explains how to design forms and introduces you to the design mode. The second part of the chapter tells you how to use forms and focuses on the running mode.

Figure 10.1 shows a typical dBASE window that contains a form in the design mode. This form, which is based on one that the Form Expert automatically generates from a table, contains several Text and EntryField fields, and also two SpinBox fields. The EntryField fields contain the fields' data (entries) in one record of a table; the Text fields provide titles for the form and for the individual EntryField fields. The two SpinBox fields display data from Numeric and Date fields, and also provide a convenient way to change that data.

Figure 10.2 shows the same form in running mode.

You display a form in design view when you want to add or delete fields, move them, or change their size. In design view, you can also select fonts, font sizes, and font styles, and you change the background color, field colors, and text colors. You display a form in running view when you want to work with data in the table on which the form is based. You can display data in table records, change data in records, delete records, and add new records.

This chapter covers forms that are based on a single table. To learn about forms that are based on multiple tables, see Chapter 15, "Designing Advanced Forms."

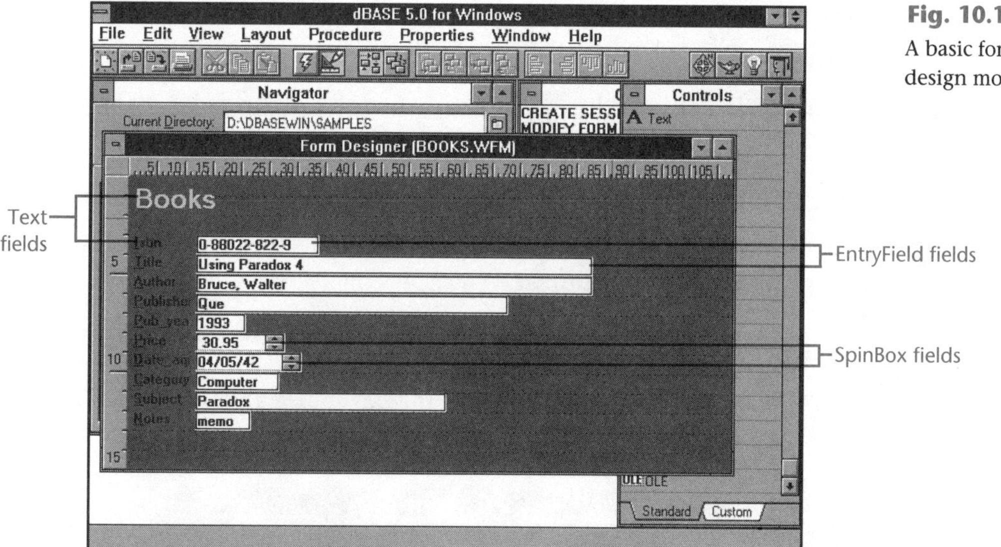

Fig. 10.1
A basic form in design mode.

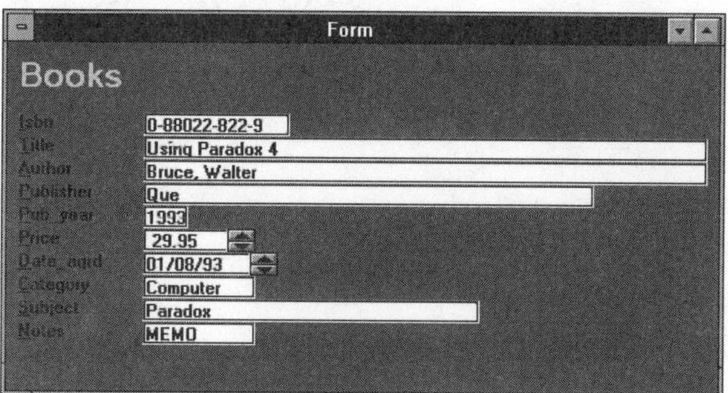

Fig. 10.2
The same basic form running with data displayed from one record of the table on which it is based.

Creating a New Form

To create a form, you place and arrange objects in a window. The principal objects on a form usually are boxes that contain data from tables, and labels for those boxes. As you will see later in this chapter, however, forms can contain many other types of objects.

The simplest way to create a form is to use the Form Expert, which offers you a series of choices.

Using the Form Expert

To begin creating a new form, do one of the following:

- Click the the SpeedBar's Form Expert button, and then click **F**orm Expert.
- Open the **F**ile menu, choose **N**ew, and then **F**orm.
- Open the Navigator window, click the Forms icon to display the names of existing forms, and then double-click the (Untitled) icon.
- In the Command window, type **Create Form Expert** and press Enter.

In each case, dBASE then displays the Form Expert dialog box shown in figure 10.3.

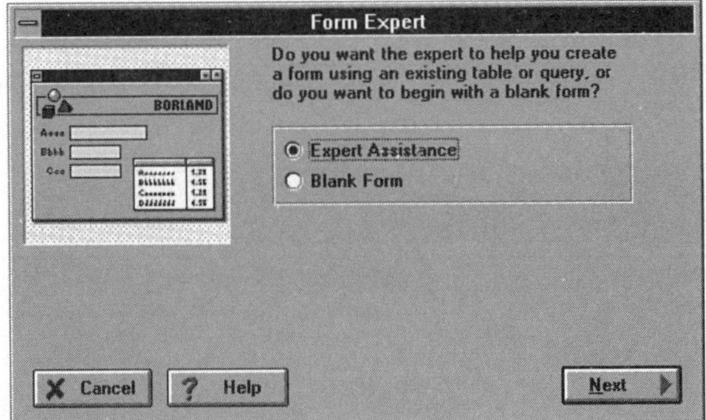

Fig. 10.3
The Form Expert dialog box is where you start to create a form.

This dialog box offers you the choice of using **E**xpert Assistance, which lets you create a form based on an existing table or query, or just starting from a **B**lank **F**orm. This chapter shows you how to base a form on a table or query.

To proceed, click the **N**ext button at the bottom of the dialog box. dBASE then displays a list of the tables and forms in the current directory, such as that shown in figure 10.4.

Select the name of the table that contains the fields that you want to include in your form, or select a query that produces a view that contains those fields. If you want to base the new form on a table or query in a different directory, click the Tool button at the right end of the Selected File text box to display the Choose View dialog box. You can use this dialog box to select a table or query from a different disk drive and directory. Click OK to return to the Form Expert. In the Form Expert, click the **N**ext button to display a dialog box that contains a list of fields such as that shown in figure 10.5.

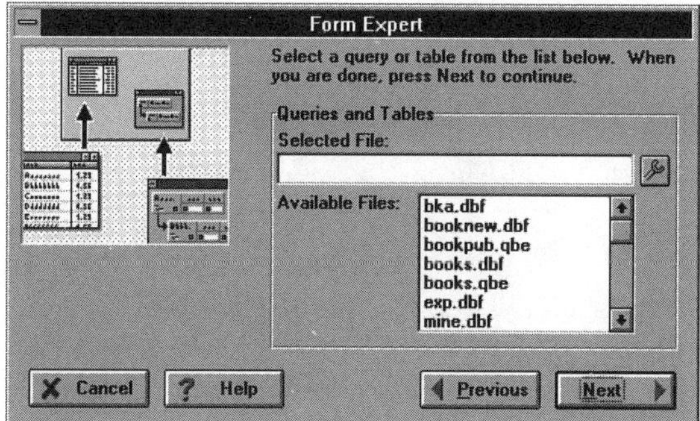

Fig. 10.4
The Form Expert offers you a choice of existing tables and queries.

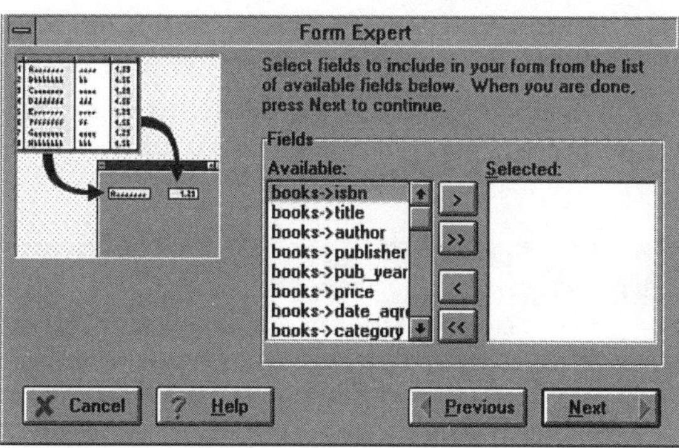

Fig. 10.5
After you choose a table or query, the Form Expert displays a list of available fields.

The Available list box of the dialog box's Fields section lists the names of the fields in the table or query that you have chosen. You can now select which of these fields you want to include in your form.

Tip
To go back to a previous section of the Form Expert, click the **P**revious button.

To select fields one at a time, click a field name in the Available list, and then click the > button between the Available and **S**elected lists to move the field into the **S**elected list. To select all fields in the Available list, click the >> button. You can move individual fields out of the **S**elected list by selecting the field name and clicking the < button. You can move all fields out of the list by clicking the << button.

Tip
Select individual fields in the order that you want them to appear in the form.

You cannot directly change the order of fields in the **S**elected list. However, you can remove a field from the list by selecting it and then clicking the < button. You can insert a field into the list by selecting in the **S**elected list the field that precedes the place where you want to insert a field, selecting the field to be inserted in the Available list, and clicking the > button.

After you have assembled in the **S**elected list the names of the fields that you want in your form, click the **N**ext button. dBASE then offers a choice of form layout schemes as shown in figure 10.6.

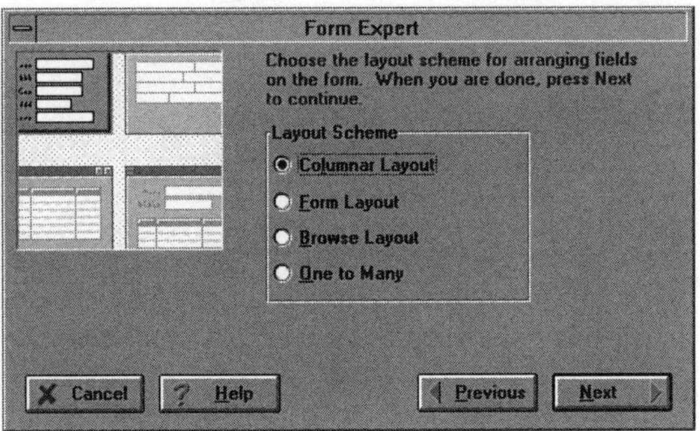

Fig. 10.6
You can use this screen to choose one of four basic form layout schemes.

The four basic layouts are shown in the top-left corner of the dialog box. When you click a form layout scheme in the center of the dialog box, the layout that you chose is highlighted in the top-left corner. Table 10.1 summarizes the layout schemes.

Table 10.1 Form Layouts

Scheme	Description
Columnar Layout	Arranges fields in a single vertical column with field names at the left.
Form Layout	Arranges fields side by side with field names above each field.
Browse Layout	Displays fields in columns with field names at the top of each column.
One to Many	Used for forms based on one-to-many linked tables. Fields from the "one" table are shown in columnar layout; fields from the "many" table are shown in browse layout.

Select the layout that most closely corresponds to the one that you want. You can easily modify the initial layout later.

After you have chosen a layout, click the **N**ext button to proceed to the dialog box shown in figure 10.7. This dialog box presents a choice of fonts, colors, and borders.

Tip
Select fonts and colors in this dialog box rather than later when you are working with the form in design view.

To change the font used in Title, Text, or Entry parts of the form, click the Tool button at the right of the corresponding line in the **F**onts section of the dialog box to display the Font dialog box shown in figure 10.8. This dialog box lists the fonts available on your computer.

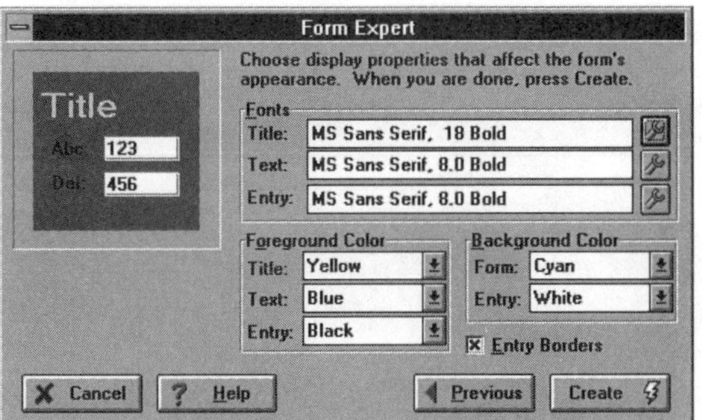

Fig. 10.7
You can use this dialog box to choose the fonts and colors for various parts of your form.

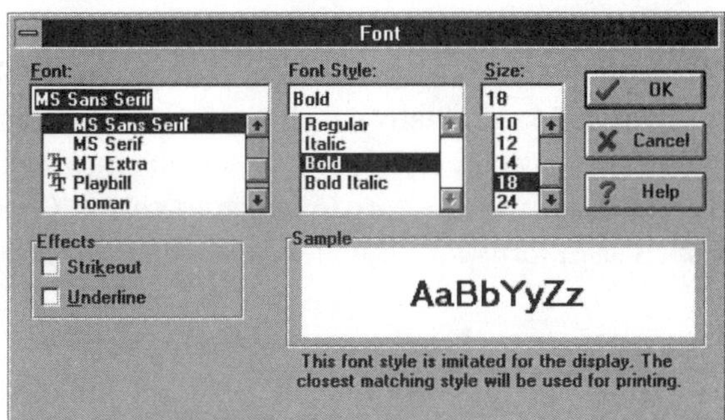

Fig. 10.8
You can use the Font dialog box to select the font, font style, font size, and font effects that you want to use in the Title, Text, and Entry parts of your form.

The Title part of the form is the name of the form that the Form Expert copies from the name of the table or query on which the form is based. The Text parts of the form are the field names that the Form Expert copies from the underlying table or query. The Entry parts of the form are the EntryFields that display data from the table or query.

To change the color of the Title, Text, and Entry parts of the form, you can open the drop-down list boxes in the F**o**reground Color section of the dialog box. In the **B**ackground Color section, you can open the drop-down list boxes to change the background color for the form and for the EntryField fields in the form.

The **E**ntry Borders check box, which is selected by default, places a rectangle around EntryField fields. If you don't want to display such rectangles, you can remove them by clicking this box and thus removing the check mark.

When you have completed making your font and color choices, click the Create button to create the preliminary version of your form, which is then displayed in the Form Designer window as shown in figure 10.9.

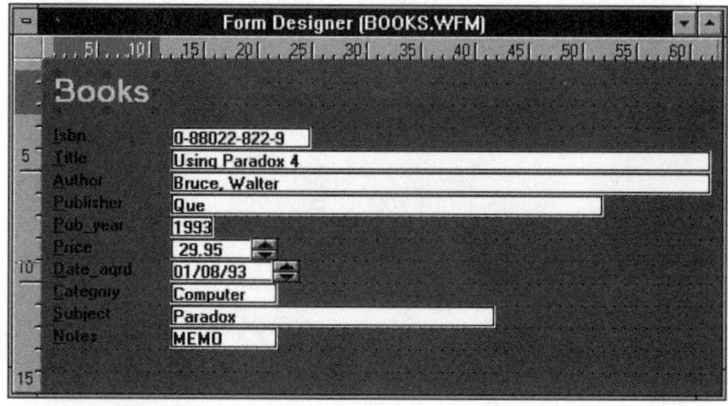

Fig. 10.9
A preliminary form design created automatically by the Form Expert.

Saving Your Form Design

At this stage, you should save your form design. To do so, open the **F**ile menu and choose **S**ave or Save **A**s. Alternatively, click the SpeedBar's Save button. In either case, dBASE displays the Create File dialog box in which you can name the form and choose the directory in which to save it. Click OK to save the file. dBASE saves each form with the file name extension .WFM.

Tip
To save a form design, you must display the form in the Form Designer window.

Working in the Form Designer Window

The Form Expert creates a preliminary design for a form and displays it on your screen as shown in figure 10.9. This preliminary design contains the following:

- A title in the top-left corner. This title is the name of the table or query on which you chose to base the form.
- The fields that you chose to include in the form, arranged in the layout that you chose, and in the order that you selected them in the Form Expert. The name of each field is the name of that field in the underlying table. The content of each field is the content of the first record in the table (in indexed order) or the first record in the view created by the query. The size of each box that contains field contents in the form depends on the field size specified in the underlying form.

Note

The title of the form and the names of fields are Text objects. The boxes that contain data from table fields are EntryField objects. The boxes that have arrows at the right are SpinBox objects.

You can change the layout of the form, and what it contains, in many ways.

Table 10.2 lists the SpeedBar buttons available when a Form Designer window is active. You use many of these buttons as you work through this chapter, and you will use others in Chapter 15, "Designing Advanced Forms."

Table 10.2 The Form Designer SpeedBar Buttons

Button	Purpose
	Create a new form or other dBASE-related file
	Open an existing form or other dBASE-related file
	Save the current form design
	Print the current form design
	Cut the selected object and save it in the Clipboard
	Copy the selected object into the Clipboard
	Insert the contents of the Clipboard at the cursor position
	Run the form
	Design the form
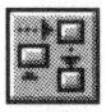	Lay out controls on the form
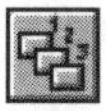	Arrange the order of controls on the form
	Place the selected control at the end of the tabbing order
	Place the selected control at the beginning of the tabbing order

(continues)

Table 10.2 Continued

Button	Purpose
	Place the selected control before the previous one in the tabbing order
	Place the selected control after the next one in the tabbing order
	Align the left sides of selected controls with the leftmost control
	Align the right sides of selected controls with the rightmost selected control
	Align the top sides of selected controls with the topmost control
	Align the bottom sides of selected controls with the bottommost control
	Open the Navigator window
	Open the Command window
	Access an Expert
	Access a tutorial

When moving existing objects or placing new objects on a form, you can use the horizontal and vertical rulers as a guide.

The array of dots in the working area of the form is an alignment grid that you can use to place objects in exact positions on the form. As you will see later, you can activate Snap To **G**rid, which automatically snaps objects to the closest grid position. You can also change the spacing of grid points, and choose whether to display the grid in the Form Designer window. When you run a form, the grid points are not visible.

Using the Form Expert to Create a Blank Form

An alternative approach to creating a form is to create a blank form and then add the objects that you want. To use this approach, you start, as before, by opening the Form Expert. Then choose the **B**lank Form option and click the Create button to create the blank form shown in figure 10.10.

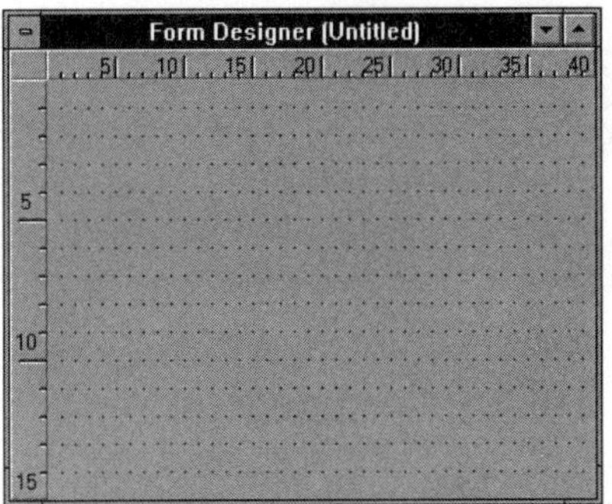

Fig. 10.10
A blank form created by the Form Expert.

If you decide to start with a blank form, you can place objects individually on that form. This chapter, though, focuses on working with a form that contains objects that the Form Expert has already placed.

▶ "Adding Objects to a Form," p. 351

Working with Objects on a Form

Tip
For forms that you intend to display or change data in tables, it is usually easier to modify forms created by the Form Expert than to create forms from scratch.

After you create a form that contains objects, you can do any of the following:

- Change the size and shape of the form
- Change the form background
- Change the grid
- Move objects
- Change the size of objects
- Add objects to the form
- Remove objects from the form
- Change the properties of objects

This chapter covers those changes that you can make by working interactively with a form. You can exercise more extensive control over a form by setting or changing properties as described in Chapter 15, "Designing Advanced Forms."

Changing a Form's Size and Shape

To change the size and shape of the form, use standard Windows methods such as dragging the borders or clicking the Maximize button. As you will see in Chapter 15, you can precisely set the size and position of the form and of objects on the form by working with its properties.

Changing a Form's Background

A form's background consists of a color and a grid, both of which you can modify to suit your preferences and needs. To change the background color, you must change the form's properties as described in Chapter 15.

To change the grid, open the **P**roperties menu and choose **F**orm Designer. This command displays the Form Designer Properties dialog box shown in figure 10.11.

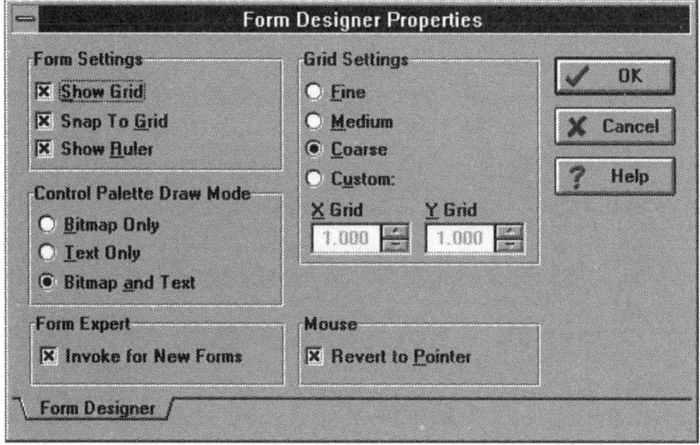

Fig. 10.11
You can use the Form Designer Properties dialog box to change the grid.

> **Note**
>
> You can also open the Form Designer Properties dialog box by pointing to a blank area within the Form Designer window and clicking the right mouse button to display the form's SpeedMenu, shown in figure 10.12. In this menu, choose the **F**orm Designer Properties option to display the Form Designer Properties dialog box.

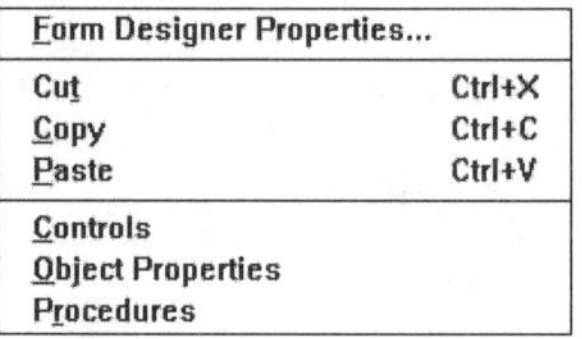

Fig. 10.12
The Form Designer SpeedMenu.

In the central section of Form Designer Properties dialog box, you can choose among three preset grid settings: **F**ine, **M**edium, and **C**oarse. Alternatively, you can choose C**u**stom to select separately the **X** grid (horizontal) spacing and **Y** grid (vertical) spacing. Grid-spacing values shown in the rulers are in increments of one tenth of an inch.

The three check boxes in the Form Settings section at the top-left of this dialog box are all checked by default. You can remove the check marks from these boxes to make the grid invisible, to turn off Snap To **G**rid, or to make the rulers invisible. When Snap To **G**rid is active, the top-left corner of objects in the form snap to the nearest grid point whenever you move them.

After making choices in this dialog box, click OK to apply the settings to the Form Designer window.

Tip
Snap To **G**rid can be active even if the grid is invisible.

Moving One Object on a Form

You can move individual objects or groups of objects. To move an individual object, such as the title of a form, follow these steps:

1. Point at the object that you want to move.
2. Click and hold down the mouse button. Handles (small black squares) appear around the object to indicate that you have selected it.
3. Move the mouse slightly so that the mouse pointer changes to the shape of a hand as shown in figure 10.13.

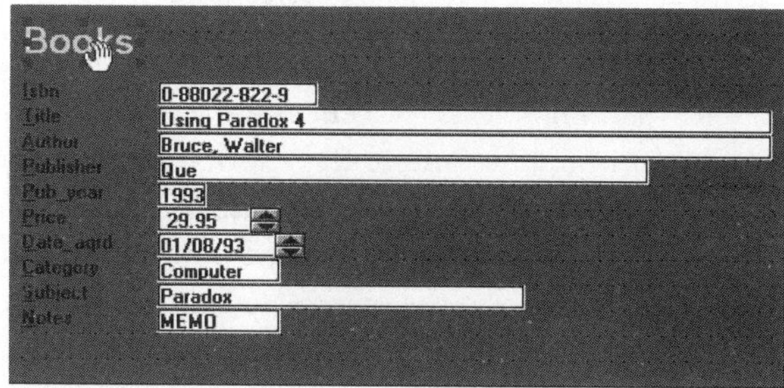

Fig. 10.13
The mouse pointer changes to a hand graphic when you select an object and it is ready to be moved.

4. Drag the object to its new position, then release the mouse button. If Snap To **G**rid is active, the object jumps from grid point to grid point as you drag; if the feature is not active, the object moves smoothly.
5. Click an unoccupied part of the window to deselect the object.

If you want to move multiple objects the same distance, you must first select each of those objects as described in the text that follows.

Selecting Objects

To move an object or work with it in other ways, you must first select it. Likewise, to work with several objects simultaneously, you must first select each of those objects.

To select a single object, point at that object and click the mouse button. When you select an object, four handles appear in each of the four corners of the selected object, and four other handles are centered the top, bottom, left, and right sides of the object. If you select only one object, that object's name appears in the Status bar at the bottom of the screen. Shaded areas in the rulers indicate the position and size of the selected object.

When you select an object by clicking it, you automatically deselect all previously selected objects on the form. As you discover in Chapter 15, "Designing Advanced Forms," the form itself, rather than objects on the form, becomes selected.

With an object selected, you can select the next object, in tabbing order, by pressing Tab, or the preceding object in tabbing order by pressing Shift+Tab. Initially, tabbing order is the order in which objects are placed on the form. As you will see later in this chapter, you can easily change the tabbing order.

Tip
With no object selected, you can select the first object in the tabbing order by pressing Tab.

To select several objects, click the first object and then hold down Shift or Ctrl while you click additional objects. To deselect one of several selected objects, hold down the Shift or Ctrl keys while you click that object.

Another way to select several objects is to enclose them within a *selection border*. To do this, point just above and to the left of the top-left object in the group that you want to select, press the mouse button, and drag until you reach a position just below and to the right of the bottom-right object. As you drag, a colored border encloses the objects. Release the mouse button to select all the objects that are completely enclosed within the selection border. If you want to deselect an object within the group, hold down the Shift or Ctrl keys while you click that object.

Note

Only objects that are *completely* enclosed within the colored selection border are selected.

To select all the objects on a form, open the **E**dit menu and choose Se**l**ect All.

Moving Several Objects on a Form

To move several objects the same distance and direction on a form, follow these steps:

1. Select the objects to be moved, using one of the methods described in the preceding section.
2. Point at any one of the selected objects, and then click the mouse button and hold it down.
3. Drag to the new position, and then release the mouse button. All the selected objects move by the same amount.
4. Click an unoccupied position on the form to deselect the objects.

Aligning Objects

When Snap To **G**rid is active, you can easily align objects horizontally or vertically on the screen. Sometimes, though, you want to position objects at other locations than grid points. To do so, turn off Snap To **G**rid before you place or move objects. When you turn off that feature, however, you may not align objects as accurately as you want.

You can align objects horizontally or vertically by using the four alignment buttons that the SpeedBar offers. For example, to align the left edges of objects vertically, you select the objects and then click the left-alignment button. This button aligns the left edges of all the selected objects vertically with the left edge of the leftmost of the selected objects.

You can use this button to align the right sides of selected objects with the right side of the object furthest to the right.

You can use this button to align the top of selected objects with the top of the topmost object.

You can use this button to align the bottom of selected objects with the bottom of the bottommost object.

Changing the Size of Objects

You can easily change the size of an object. Simply select the object, point at a handle, and drag. As you drag, the size of the object changes. If Snap To **G**rid is active, the handles snap to grid points as you drag. Although this process changes the size of the object, it doesn't change the size of text that the object contains. For information about changing text size, see Chapter 15, "Designing Advanced Forms."

Optimizing the Form Layout

You also can easily modify the initial layout of a form, as created by the Form Expert, to produce a pleasing layout for your form. Figure 10.14 shows an example of a modified form layout.

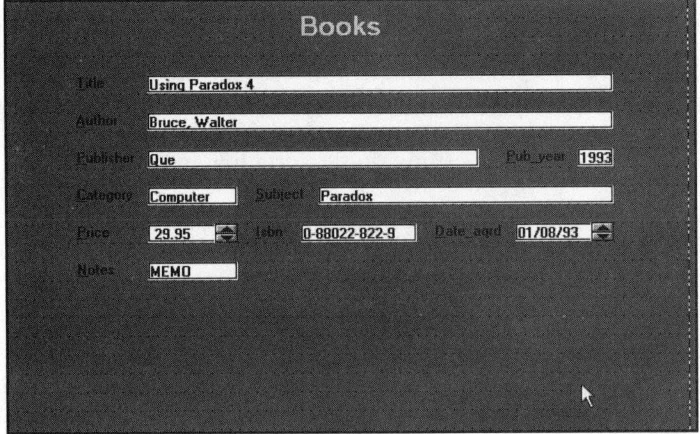

Fig. 10.14
An example of a modified form layout.

As you will see in Chapter 15, you can do much more to enhance the form. These enhancements, however, require that you work with form properties, a subject that is beyond the scope of this chapter.

Undoing an Operation

When you perform an operation in the Form Designer window, you usually can undo that action. Simply open the **E**dit menu and choose **U**ndo. You must issue this command immediately after completing the operation that you want to undo.

After you undo an operation, the **R**edo command appears in the **E**dit menu. You can choose **R**edo to return to the condition that existed before you chose **U**ndo.

Cutting, Copying, and Pasting Objects

You can use standard Windows methods to cut and copy one or more objects in the Form Designer window to the Clipboard and to paste objects from the Clipboard into a form. Such methods provide a convenient way to copy objects from one form to another and also to place into a form any graphics and other objects that you have created outside dBASE.

To implement these methods, you can use these three SpeedBar buttons or you can open the **E**dit menu and choose the Cu**t**, **C**opy, and **P**aste commands. You can also use Ctrl+X to cut, Ctrl+C to copy, and Ctrl+V to paste.

Troubleshooting

The Form Expert will not display in the Available Files list the table that I want to use.

The file that you want to use is probably in a directory other than your current one. Cancel the Form Expert and display the Navigator window. Open the Current Directory list and choose the directory that contains the table that you want to use. Then restart the Form Expert.

The alignment feature isn't working properly; when I try to right-align text fields, the right ends of the lines of text do not line up straight.

Probably the text in some text fields is not right-aligned. When you use the right-alignment SpeedBar button, you align the right edges of fields. If you want to right-align the text within those text fields, you must set each text fields Alignment property to align the text at the right end of each field. Chapter 15, "Designing Advanced Forms," explains how to right-align text within fields.

When I try to create a new form, I get a blank form rather than the Form Expert.

By default, dBASE opens the Form Expert when you start to create a new form. You may have turned off this default choice, however. From the blank form, open the **P**roperties menu and choose **F**orm Designer. Click the Invoke for New Forms check box at the bottom-left of the dialog box, and then click OK. Subsequently, when you start a new form, you will see the Form Expert.

Running a Form

So far in this chapter, you have designed a form and displayed it in the Form Designer window. To use the form, you *run* it.

To run a form, you must first display it in the Form Designer window. Then you perform one of the following actions:

- Click the SpeedBar's Run button
- Open the **V**iew menu and choose **F**orm
- Press F2

In each case, dBASE replaces the Form Designer window with the form running in a window, as shown in figure 10.15. Initially, the form shows data in the first record of the underlying table or view. Because this is the running view of the form, however, you can access data in any of the table's records. You cannot, of course, use this view to change the form's design.

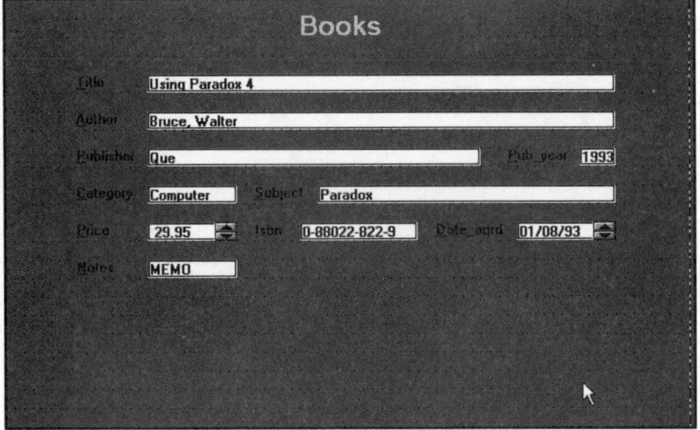

Fig. 10.15
A running form, shown maximized.

You can also run a form from the Catalog window or from the Forms section of the Navigator window by performing one of the following actions:

- Double-clicking the form's icon in the Catalog or Navigator window
- Right-clicking the form's icon in the Catalog or Navigator window to display a SpeedMenu and then choosing **R**un Form
- Selecting the form's icon in the Catalog or Navigator window and pressing F2

Another way to run a form is to type **DO** followed by the form's name (including its extension) in the Command window. For example, to run a form named Books, type **DO BOOKS.WFM.**

When you run a form, the menu bar contains only those menu items that are relevant to running a form, and the commands in certain menus differ from those available while you are designing a form. Also, some of the buttons in the SpeedBar while you are running a form differ from those displayed while you are designing a form. Table 10.3 lists the SpeedBar buttons that are available while you run a form.

Table 10.3 Form Run SpeedBar Buttons

Button	Purpose
	Create any of the primary dBASE files
	Open any of the primary dBASE-related files
	Print information in the active window
	Cut the selected object and save it in the Clipboard
	Copy the selected object to the Clipboard
	Paste the contents of the Clipboard at the current cursor position
	Run the form
	Display the form in the Form Designer window
	Search for a record
	Add a record to the form
	Go to the first record

(continues)

Table 10.3 Continued

Button	Purpose
	Go to the previous record
	Go to the next record
	Go to the last record
	Open the Navigator window
	Open the Command window
	Access an Expert
	Access a tutorial

The right end of the Status bar at the bottom of the window shows the name of the table to which the form is linked, the number of the record currently displayed, and the total number of records in the table. The left end of the Status bar provides information about the SpeedBar button to which you are pointing or about the selected menu command.

Displaying Records

When you first run a form, it displays the first record in the table (in index order) or the query on which the form is based.

To select other records, you can click the buttons near the right end of the SpeedBar, or you can open the F**o**rm menu and choose the commands in the bottom part of the menu that correspond to those SpeedBar buttons, as shown in figure 10.16.

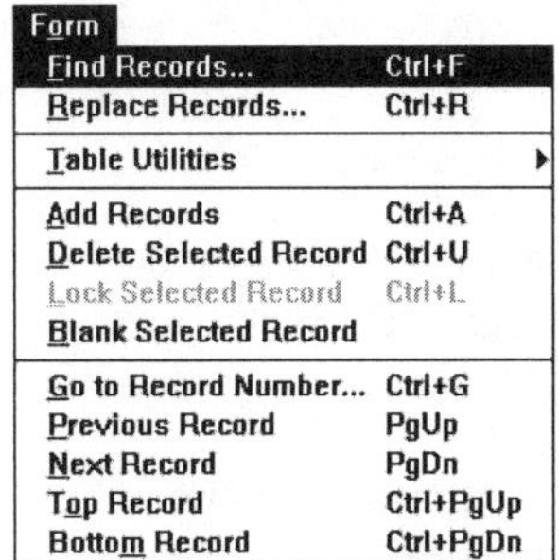

Fig. 10.16
The Form menu commands that you can use to select records.

Finding a Record

To locate a record that contains specific data, follow these steps:

1. Click the SpeedBar's Search button, or open the F**o**rm menu and choose **F**ind Records, to display the Find Records dialog box shown in figure 10.17.

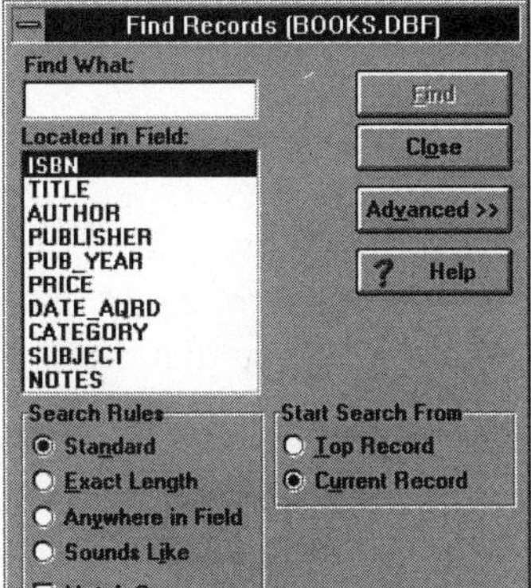

Fig. 10.17
The Find Records dialog box.

Tip
As figure 10.16 shows, you can also use shortcut keys to move from one record to another.

2. Enter into the Find What text box some or all of the data in one field of the record that you want to find.

3. In the Located in Field list box, select the field that contains the data that you entered into the Find What text box.

4. Click one of the four option buttons in the Search Rules section of the dialog box:

   - Select Sta**n**dard to search for a record in which the contents of the selected field start with the data in the Find What text box.

- Select **E**xact Length to search for a record in which the contents of the selected field exactly match (in content and length) the data in the Find What text box.

- Select An**y**where in Field to search for a record in which the contents of the selected field include the data in the Find What text box.

- Select Sounds L**i**ke to search for a record in which the contents of the selected field sound like the data in the Find What text box when you speak the words.

5. Click the Match **C**ase check box if you want to find records in which the case of the contents (uppercase or lowercase) exactly match the case of data in the Find What text box.

6. In the Start Search From section of the dialog box, choose either the **T**op Record or C**u**rrent Record option to specify where to begin the search. By default, the dialog box is displayed with the most recently used option selected.

7. Click the **F**ind button to start the search.

Tip
To view the record, you may have to drag the dialog box out of the way.

dBASE finds the record if it exists and displays its contents in the form, leaving the Find Records dialog box displayed. If dBASE cannot find a matching record, it displays an Alert box to tell you that the value was not found.

After dBASE finds the first matching record, you can display additional matching records by clicking the **F**ind button repeatedly. When you finish finding records, click the Cl**o**se button to hide the dialog box.

You can extend the scope of your search by clicking the Ad**v**anced button in the Find Records dialog box. After you do so, the dialog box expands to offer the additional choices shown in figure 10.18.

You can find information about using these facilities in Chapter 15, "Designing Advanced Forms."

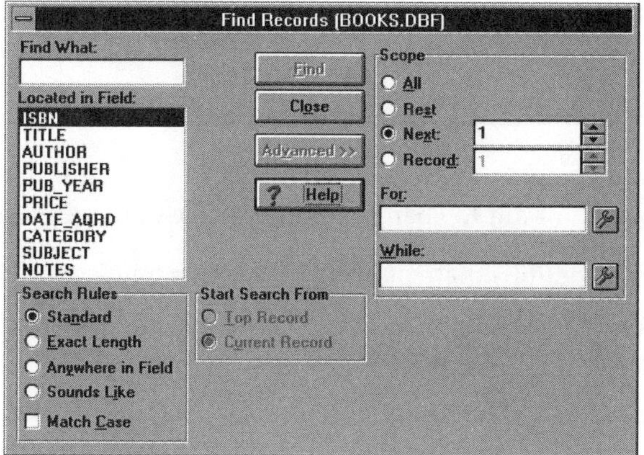

Fig. 10.18
The expanded Find Records dialog box.

Replacing Data in Records

You can use a form to locate in a table every record in which a field contains a specific value and then replace that value with a different one. You might want to perform this search and replace action, for example, when the table with which you are working contains company names and the name of one company changes.

To replace data in records, follow these steps:

1. Open the F**o**rm menu and choose **R**eplace Records to display the Replace Records dialog box shown in figure 10.19.

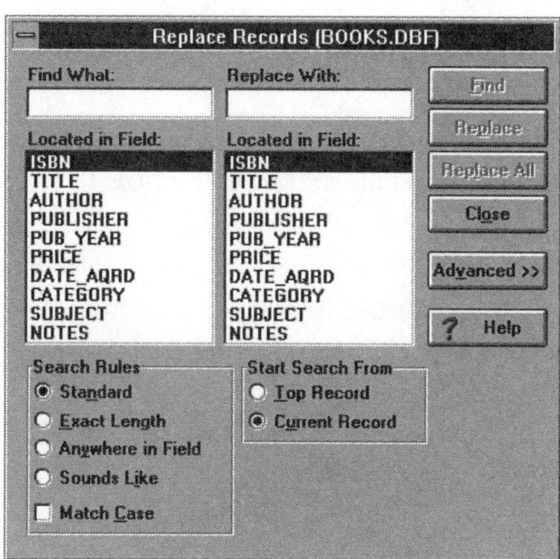

Fig. 10.19
The Replace Records dialog box.

2. In the Find What text box, type the text (or partial text) that you want to find.

3. In the Replace With text box, type the replacement text.

4. Click field names in the two Located in Field list boxes to identify the fields that you want to change and the source of the replacement data.

5. Choose the options that you need in the Search Rules and Start Search From sections of the dialog box, as you did in the Find Records dialog box.

6. Click the **F**ind button to search the records and display the first record encountered that contains the text that you entered in the Find What text, leaving the Find Records dialog box open.

7. If you want to make the replacement in that record, click the **R**eplace button. dBASE then replaces the current record and searches for the next matching record. If you do not want to replace the current record, click the **F**ind button to proceed to the next matching record. Alternatively, click the Rep**l**ace All button to replace all matching records.

> **Caution**
>
> Before you use Rep**l**ace All, be sure that you really want the specified replacement to occur in all records.

8. Repeat step 7 as many times as necessary to find, and possibly make replacements in, other records.

9. Click the Cl**o**se button to close the dialog box.

Like the Find Records dialog box, the Replace Records dialog box includes an Ad**v**anced button that you can use to access advanced methods of finding records that contain data to be replaced. See Chapter 15 for information about these methods.

Editing Records

As you have seen, you can use a form to display data in a table or to display data in a view produced by a query. This chapter has described how to use a form to display data in a single table. As you will learn in later chapters, you can also use a form to display data obtained from two or more linked tables or from a view that a query produces from linked tables.

Note

Data in tables can be displayed in a form unless the Visible property of a field is set to False, or unless a field is protected. See Chapter 15, "Designing Advanced Forms," for information about field properties, and Chapter 18, "Using dBASE in a Multiuser Environment," for information about protecting fields.

In this section, you learn how to use a form to add data to tables and to change data that already exists in tables.

If a form is based on a single table, you can easily use the form to add or change information in existing records, and to add records to the table. If a form is based on linked tables, however, you cannot perform the same actions unless you make special provisions.

▶ "Working with Related Tables," p. 259

When you run a form, you see the data in the first record of the underlying table or view. To display the record that you want to edit, you can use the methods previously described to move from one record to another. As each record is displayed, a flashing insertion point appears at the beginning of one field—the first field in the tabbing order.

Editing Character Fields

When the Form Expert creates a form, it creates EntryField objects. These objects display, in Character fields, the data of the underlying table or view, as shown in figure 10.20.

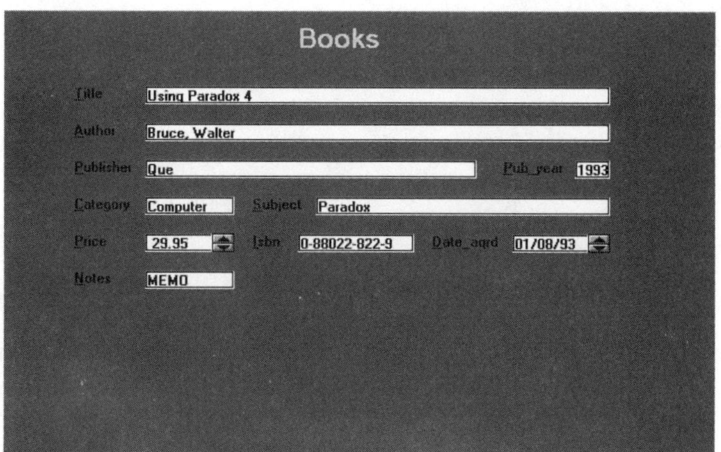

Fig. 10.20
A typical form.

To change the data displayed in an EntryField field, point exactly at the place where you want to make a change and click the mouse button to place the insertion point at that location. You then can make whatever changes are necessary by using ordinary editing techniques such as the following:

- Press the Backspace key to delete the character to the left of the insertion point.
- Press the Del key to delete the character at the right of the insertion point.
- Type characters to insert those characters at the insertion point.

As soon as you close the form or move to another field or record, dBASE saves any changes that you made.

Editing Numeric Fields

When you use the Form Expert to create a form, Numeric fields in the underlying table or view appear in the form as SpinBox objects. These objects are like EntryField objects except that they include a double-headed arrow.

You can change the data in a SpinBox object in exactly the same way that you change data in an EntryField object. You can also click the upward-pointing arrow to increase the value in the field to the next highest whole number, or click the downward-pointing arrow to decrease the value in the field to the preceding whole number.

Editing Date Fields

You can use the Form Expert to edit a table's Date fields the same way that you edit Numeric fields. You can edit a date as it appears in the form by using conventional edit techniques, or you can click the upward-pointing arrow or downward-pointing arrow to move the date forward or backward one day at a time.

Editing Memo Fields

Forms do not show the text in Memo fields. Instead, the form displays `memo` when a memo field is empty or `MEMO` if the field contains text. To display the contents of a Memo field, place an insertion point there by clicking anywhere in the field, and then press F9 to display the Text Editor window as shown in figure 10.21.

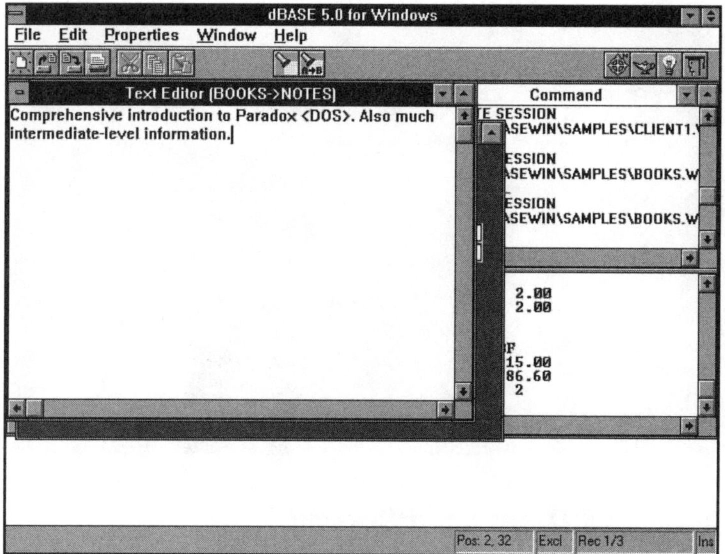

Fig. 10.21
The Text Editor window displaying the contents of a Memo field.

You can use the usual editing techniques to change the contents of the Memo field. Press F9 again to return to the form.

See the section "Using the Text Editor" later in this chapter for more information.

Adding Records

You can use a form to add new records to a table. To do so, start by adding an empty record to the table, using one of the following methods:

- Click the SpeedBar's Add a Record button.

- Open the F**o**rm menu and choose **A**dd Records.
- Press Ctrl+A.

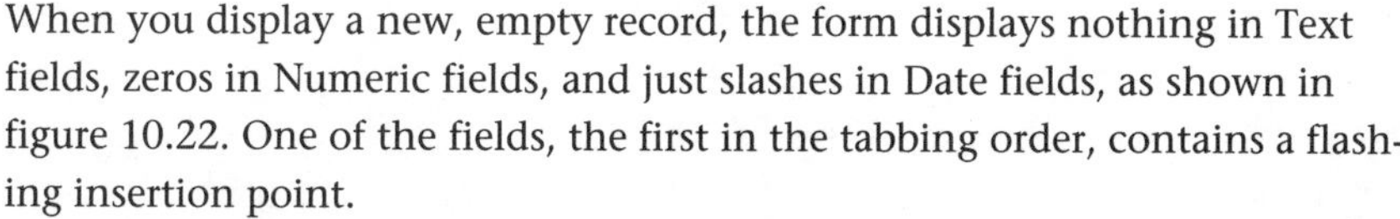

When you display a new, empty record, the form displays nothing in Text fields, zeros in Numeric fields, and just slashes in Date fields, as shown in figure 10.22. One of the fields, the first in the tabbing order, contains a flashing insertion point.

Tip
If you don't see an empty record, click the Go to First Record or Go to Last Record SpeedBar button.

To enter data into the record, start with the field that contains the insertion point and type the characters for that field. If you make a mistake, you can correct it by using the usual editing techniques. When the contents of the field are correct, press the Tab key to move the insertion point to another field. Continue until you have added all your data. Finally, commit the data to the table by moving to another record.

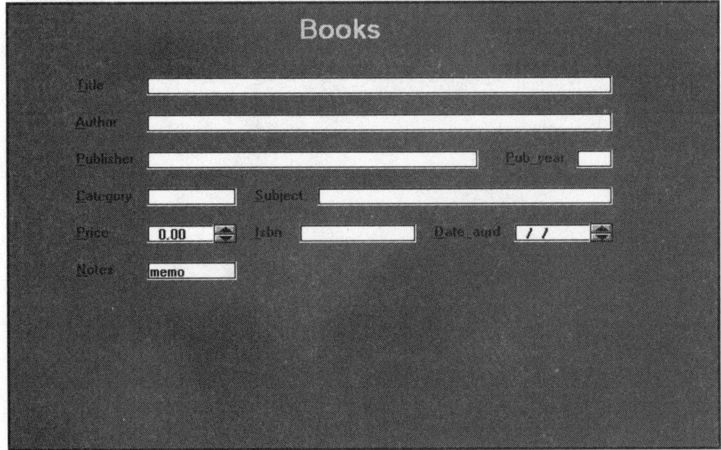

Fig. 10.22
A new, empty record in a form.

Blanking and Deleting a Record

To delete a record's data, leaving all the record's fields blank, display the record in the form, open the F**o**rm menu, and choose **B**lank Selected Record. To delete a record completely, open the F**o**rm menu and choose **D**elete Selected Record. When you *blank* a record, it stays in place but all its fields are empty. When you *delete* a record, the record and its fields are all deleted.

Using the Text Editor

dBASE for Windows provides a built-in Text Editor that you can use to edit memo fields or create and edit text files. In fact, the Text Editor is used as the basis of the Program Editor, which is used to edit program (.PRG) and form program (.WFM) files. The Text Editor provides many basic text-editing tools that you might need when editing a text file.

In addition, you can specify a different text editor to use as your default memo editor. For example, you could specify that dBASE should open Notepad whenever you edit a memo field.

Opening the Text Editor Window

When you click on a memo field, dBASE for Windows automatically opens the Text Editor window displaying any existing memo field data (see fig. 10.23). The Text Editor window enables you to minimize, maximize, resize, and move the data. To close the Text Editor window, open the **F**ile menu and choose **C**lose, or double-click the windows control box. The text entered for a memo field is saved with the table, when you save the table data.

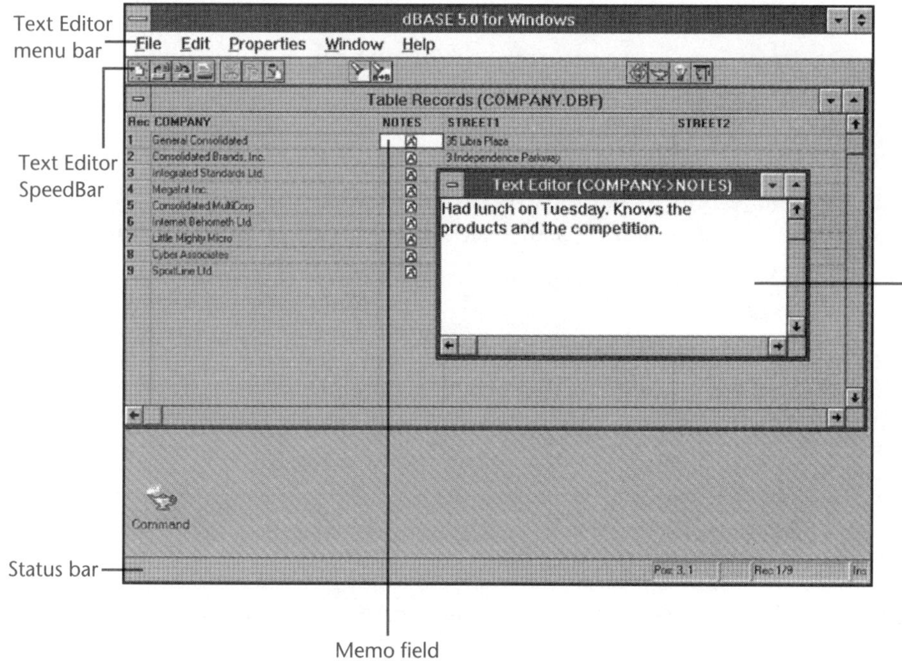

Text Editor window

Fig. 10.23
The components of the Text Editor window include a menu bar, the SpeedBar, and a Text Editor window.

To open a Text Editor window for an existing text file, follow these steps:

1. Open the **F**ile menu and choose **O**pen.
2. In the File Name text box, type or select *.TXT and press Enter.
3. Select the file from the file list box and click OK.

To open a Text Editor window for a new text file, follow these steps:

1. Open the **F**ile menu, select **N**ew, and choose **P**rogram. This opens the Program Editor, an advanced form of the Text Editor.
2. Enter the text.
3. From the **F**ile menu, choose Save **A**s.
4. Save the file with a .TXT file extension. dBASE will save it as a plain text file, and the next time you open it, the Text Editor window will appear.

◄ "A Quick Tour of dBASE 5 for Windows," p. 45

◄ "Navigating the Program Editor," p. 563

As figure 10.23 shows, the Text Editor window contains the following components:

- *Text Editor menu bar*. Contains various commands to help you work in the Text Editor window.
- *Text Editor SpeedBar*. Contains various tools to help you work in the Text Editor window.
- *Text Editor window*. Displays the text.
- *Status bar*. Displays data about your current session, such as the file name, any record locking active, record numbers, and Insert key status (insert or overwrite).

Working with the Menu Bar

dBASE changes the menu bar to provide menu options that assist you in your text-editing work. Table 10.4 describes each menu.

Table 10.4 Text Editor Window Menu Commands

Menu	Description
File	Enables you to create or open any of the primary dBASE files, close the Text Editor window, save text files, print, or exit dBASE 5 for Windows (with or without saving changes).
Edit	Contains commands for undoing, cutting, copying, pasting, and deleting text. The menu enables you to insert text from a file or copy text to a file. You can search and replace text, convert case, and join text lines.
Properties	Enables you to set Desktop and Text Editor properties.
Window	Rearranges or activates open windows.
Help	Displays help information or runs an interactive tutorial.

Note

To see two views of the same text file, open two Text Editor windows. dBASE automatically updates one window with changes made in the other. Displaying multiple views is handy when you work with large text files.

Working with the SpeedBar

When you work in the Text Editor window, the SpeedBar changes to provide options that assist you in your dBASE text-editing work. Table 10.5 describes what each button does.

Table 10.5 Text Editor SpeedBar Buttons

Button	Button Name	Action
	New	Creates any of the primary dBASE files
	Open	Opens any of the primary dBASE file types
	Save	Saves the current file
	Print	Prints the current file
	Cut	Moves the selected text or control to the Clipboard
	Copy	Copies the selected text or control to the Clipboard
	Paste	Copies the Clipboard's contents to cursor position
	Find text	Finds the specified text and moves the cursor to the first occurrence
	Replace text	Searches and replaces the specified text
	Navigator	Opens or switches to the Navigator window
	Command Window	Opens or switches to the Command window
	Forms Expert	Opens the Forms Expert
	Interactive Tutors	Opens the Interactive Tutors

Tip
You can convert text quickly to uppercase, lowercase, or initial capital letters by selecting the text, opening the **E**dit menu, choosing Con**v**ert Case, and then selecting the case you want.

Using the SpeedMenu

The Text Editor window provides a SpeedMenu feature. To access the SpeedMenu, click the right mouse button while in the Text Editor window. The SpeedMenu conveniently provides a list of the most useful commands. Table 10.6 describes the choices that the SpeedMenu offers while you are using the Text Editor window.

Table 10.6 Text Editor SpeedMenu Commands

Menu	Description
Text Editor Properties	Enables you to set Text Editor properties
Cu**t**	Moves selected text to the Clipboard
Copy	Copies selected text to the Clipboard
Paste	Copies the Clipboard's contents to the current cursor position
Find Text	Searches for the specified text
Find **N**ext Text	Searches for the next occurrence of the specified text
Replace Text	Searches for and replaces the specified text

Tip
When searching for text, press Ctrl+F to display the Search dialog box and press Ctrl+L to find the next occurrence.

Setting Text Editor Properties

Just as you can set properties for the dBASE Desktop and Command window, you can set properties for the Text Editor and change its characteristics. Open the **P**roperties menu and choose **T**ext Editor to display the Text Editor Properties inspector dialog box (see fig. 10.24). The property settings that you select are stored in the DBASEWIN.INI file.

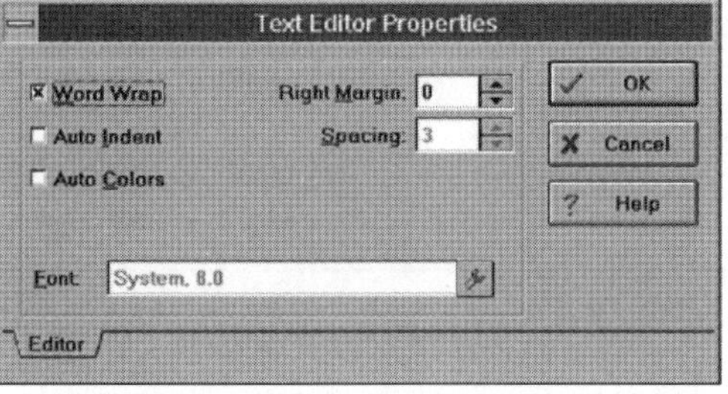

Fig. 10.24
Use the Text Editor Properties inspector dialog box to set defaults for word wrap, text indentation, colors, spacing, and fonts.

Here is a summary of the properties that you can set in the Text Editor Properties inspector dialog box:

- *Word Wrap* controls the insertion of soft carriage returns when the number of characters on a line exceeds the specified right margin. By default, **W**ord Wrap is off (unchecked).
- *Right Margin* enables you to change the right margin when **W**ord Wrap is on (checked). By default, Right **M**argin is set to 65 characters.
- *Auto Indent* controls whether new lines are automatically indented as far as the previous line. Using indentation to show the flow of logic can make your programs easier to read. The default is on (checked).
- *Spacing* controls the number of spaces to insert when the Auto **I**ndent feature is on (checked). The default spacing is four characters.
- *Auto Colors* enables you to display programming comments and literal values in different colors. By default, Auto **C**olors is on (checked). Literal values (such as text in quotation marks, braced dates, numbers, and logicals surrounded by periods) appear in blue. Syntax errors appear in red, and comments appear in grey.
- *Font* controls the font used in the Text Editor window. The default font is a monospaced font, such as Terminal or Courier. To change the font, click the Tool button and then choose the font, size, style, and effects you want.

Specifying the Default Memo Editor

By default, dBASE displays the built-in dBASE Text Editor for creating and editing memo fields. However, you can use any ASCII Text Editor, such as the Windows Notepad, to edit memo fields by changing the default Memo Editor.

To change the default Memo Editor, follow these steps:

1. Open the **P**roperties menu and choose **D**esktop.
2. Select the Files tab.
3. In the Editors section of the Desktop Properties dialog box, click the Tool button next to the **M**emo Editor text box (see fig. 10.25). The Memo Editor file-selection dialog box appears.

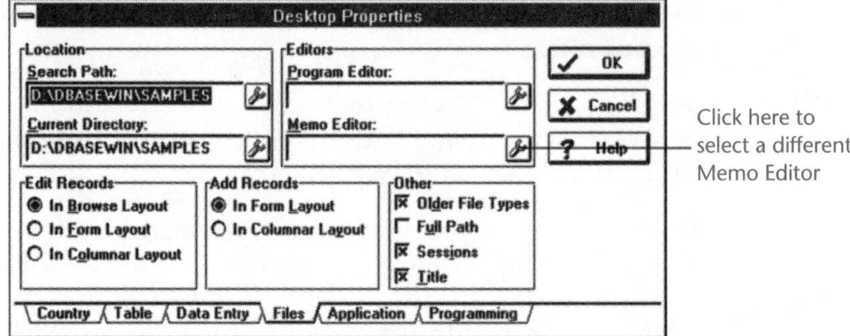

Fig. 10.25
You can use an external text editor instead of the built-in dBASE Text Editor.

4. Specify the **F**ile name, **D**irectory, and Dri**v**e of the external Text Editor you want to use. This setting is stored in the DBASEWIN.INI file.

5. Choose OK to close the Memo Editor file-selection dialog box.

6. Choose OK again to close the Desktop Properties dialog box.

Changing the Tabbing Order in a Form

You may have noticed the term *tabbing order* several times in this chapter. The tabbing order is the order in which fields are selected in a running form when you press the Tab key.

When you use the Form Expert to create a form based on a table or query, the fields appear in the order that you move them from the Available list to the Selected list. The tabbing order corresponds to this layout order.

After you move fields around on the form, the fields retain their initial tabbing order, even though they appear in a different order on the screen. As a result, when you press Tab to move from field to field while you edit a record or create a new record, fields may not be selected in a logical order.

Note

Each field has a TabStop property that, by default, is set to True. If this property is set to False, you cannot access that field by pressing the Tab key. See Chapter 15, "Designing Advanced Forms," for information about this property.

You can use four SpeedBar buttons in the Form Designer window to change the tabbing order. To do so, select a field and then choose one of the following buttons:

 Makes the selected field the last one in the tabbing order

 Makes the selected field the first one in the tabbing order

 Moves the selected field one position forward in the tabbing order

 Moves the selected field one position backward in the tabbing order

Troubleshooting

*The Save commands aren't listed in the **F**ile menu.*

When you save a form, you save its design. For this reason, you must use the Form Designer window. Switch to that window and open the **F**ile menu to access the Save commands.

While working with a running form, I can't access some fields by pressing the Tab key.

You can never access a Text field by pressing Tab, because those fields do not contain data that you can edit. The fields that you can edit, such as EntryField fields, have a TabStop property. By default, this property is set to True, which lets you select fields by pressing the Tab key. The property may have been set to False, however.

I cannot view the contents of memo fields.

To see a memo field's contents, select the field and then press F9. To return to viewing the form, press F9 again.

From Here...

In this chapter, you learned the basics of working with forms that are based on a single table. You can find more information about forms in the following chapters:

- Chapter 12, "Working with Related Tables." This chapter explains how to work with two or more related tables.

- Chapter 15, "Designing Advanced Forms." This chapter describes how to place various classes of objects on forms and how to work with properties.
- Chapter 18, "Using dBASE in a Multiuser Environment." This chapter shows you how to share forms with other users.

Chapter 11

Creating Basic Reports

As stated earlier in this book, the principal purpose of a database is to provide information. dBASE for Windows, like many other database applications, provides two ways for you to obtain information from a database: queries and reports. Queries are often informal questions you ask for which dBASE provides on-screen answers. Reports are more formal printed analyses of data.

In this chapter, you'll learn how to do the following:

- Use the Personal Trainer
- Work in the Report Designer window
- Insert database fields into a report
- Create and format a report
- Add headers and footers to report pages

Introducing Crystal Reports for dBASE

dBASE comes with a report writer provided by Crystal Computer Services, a company with many years of experience in creating specialized applications that create reports from databases. If you previously worked with a DOS version of dBASE, you probably used a separate report writer from a company such as Crystal to enhance what dBASE had to offer.

dBASE for Windows saves you the money and time involved in finding, buying, and learning how to use a specialized report writing program by including Crystal Reports in the package. Not only is Crystal Reports included, it is integrated into the dBASE for Windows environment. You'll find that the

Crystal report writer provides most, if not all, the report writing capabilities you need.

What Is a Report?

A *report* is a formatted statement of data extracted from one or more tables. As you will learn later in this book, you can create reports based on table data in various formats. This chapter, though, focuses on reports based on just one table in dBASE format.

You can use reports and forms to provide information from a table. One important difference between forms and reports is that a form is intended to be used to display information on your monitor's screen, whereas a report is intended to be printed. Another difference is that you can use a form as a means of putting information into tables, whereas you can use a report only to see what information exists in tables.

In its simplest form, a report is a little more than a printed response to a query. As you will see in this chapter, however, a report provides more extensive data formatting than a query.

Creating a Report

You can base a report on a table, a query, or even on another report. This chapter first covers basing a report on a single table. After you read Chapters 16 ("Designing Advanced Reports") and 18 ("Using dBASE in a Multiuser Environment"), you'll know how to create a report based on linked tables and on shared tables.

Before you start to create a report you should think about its purpose and answer such questions as the following:

- Who is going to read the report?
- What will those people be looking for?

After you answer these questions, you are ready to design a report that will be easy for readers to use and satisfy their needs.

The first step is to open the Report Designer window and understand what it contains.

Opening the Report Designer Window

The first step in preparing to create a report is to identify the table or query on which the report will be based. You do this by opening that table or query. You can do this from the Navigator window by selecting Tables or Queries, and then double-clicking the table or query you want to use. After that, use one of the following methods to open the Report Designer window:

- Open the **F**ile menu, select **N**ew to display a submenu, and then choose **R**eport from the submenu.
- Open the Navigator window, click the Report icon to display the names of existing reports, and then double-click the Untitled icon.

- In the Command window, type the command **CREATE REPORT** and press Enter.

Whichever method you use, after a significant delay, dBASE displays an empty Crystal Reports for dBASE Designer window with the Insert Database Field dialog box superimposed, as shown in figure 11.1. The Insert Database Field dialog box shows the fields in the most recently opened table. If you haven't opened a table, the Open Table Required dialog box appears and you can use it to select the table on which you want to base your report.

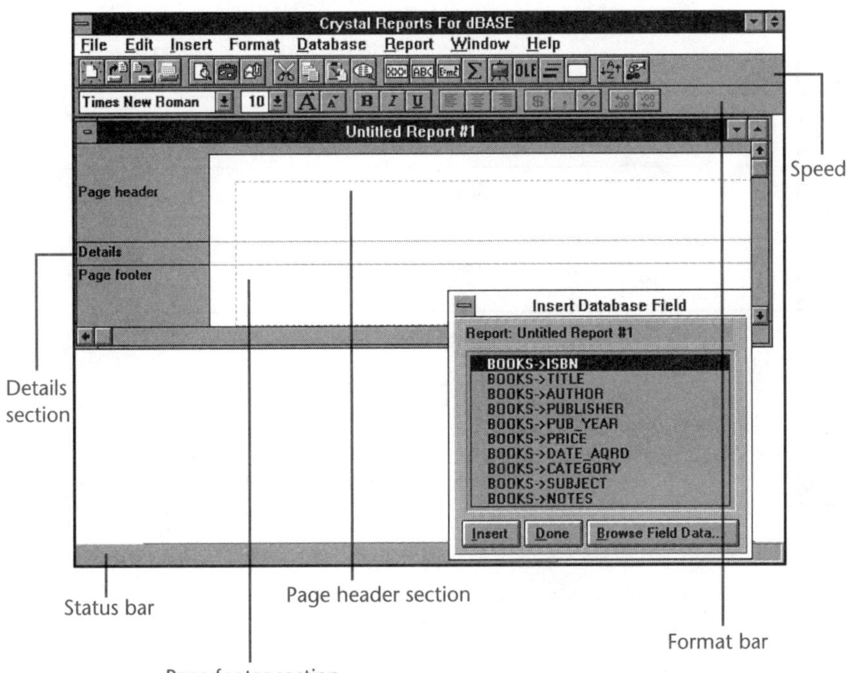

Fig. 11.1
You create reports in the Crystal Reports for dBASE Designer window shown here.

The purposes of the buttons in the SpeedBar are summarized in table 11.1.

Table 11.1 SpeedBar Buttons

Button	Purpose
	Create a new report
	Open an existing report
	Save the current report
	Print the current report
	Preview the current report
	Export the current report to a file or mail
	Mail a report
	Cut the selected text to the Clipboard
	Copy the selected text to the Clipboard
	Paste text from the Clipboard
	Select fields
 XXX	Insert a database field
 ABC	Insert a text field
 E=mc²	Insert a formula field
 Σ	Insert a summary calculation
	Insert a graphic file
 OLE	Insert an OLE object

Button	Purpose
	Draw a line
	Draw a rectangle
	Set the record sort order
	Set record selection criteria

You can use the two drop-down lists at the left end of the Format Bar to select the font and font size for selected text in a report. The purpose of the remaining buttons in the Format Bar are listed in table 11.2.

Table 11.2 Format Bar Buttons

Button	Purpose
	Increase the size of selected text by one point
	Decrease the size of selected text by one point
	Change selected text to or from boldface
	Change selected text to or from italic
	Change selected text from not underlined to underlined, or from underlined to not underlined
	Left-align selected text
	Center selected text
	Right-align selected text
	Display the currency symbol in selected number fields
	Display a thousands separator in selected number fields

Button	Purpose
%	Display a percentage symbol in selected number fields
+.0 .00	Add a decimal place to selected number fields
.00 +.0	Remove a decimal place from selected number fields

Note

You can set the currency symbol and thousands separator used with number fields in the International section of the Windows Control Panel.

The large white rectangle is the area in the Report Designer window where you create a prototype of a report. As you can see, there are three sections:

- *Page header* is where you place text and graphics fields that will appear at the top of every page of the report.
- *Details* is where you arrange the database fields that contain the details of the report.
- *Page footer* is where you place text and graphics fields that will appear at the bottom of every page of the report.

The dashed inner rectangle represents the area within the margins of printed pages.

You can, of course, change the size of the three sections and the positions of the margins. You can also choose not to display any of the sections.

When you open the Report Designer window to create a new report based on a table, dBASE displays the Insert Database Field dialog box in which all the fields in that table are listed. You select from this list those fields that you want to have in the report.

You can close the Insert Database Field dialog box by clicking the **D**one button at the bottom of the box. You can reopen the box at any time by clicking the Insert a Database Field button in the SpeedBar, or by opening the **I**nsert menu and choosing **D**atabase Field.

Choosing Optional Settings

dBASE offers many optional settings that you can select to suit your preferences while you work in the Report Designer window. You can access these options by opening the **F**ile menu and choosing Op**t**ions. This chapter assumes the settings you have are the defaults that are in place after you install dBASE.

▶ "Customizing Crystal Reports," p. 417

Giving the Report a Title

A dBASE report has two titles that you assign. One of these titles appears in the Report Designer title bar, and the other one appears on the printed pages of the report.

By default dBASE places the title "Untitled Report#1" in the title bar when you open the Report Designer window for the first time. Each time you subsequently open the window, it gives a new number to the title. These titles, however, are only temporary. Most likely, you will want to have a more meaningful title. To assign the title that appears in the title bar, follow these steps:

1. Open the Forma**t** menu and choose Report **T**itle to display the Edit Report Title dialog box shown in figure 11.2.

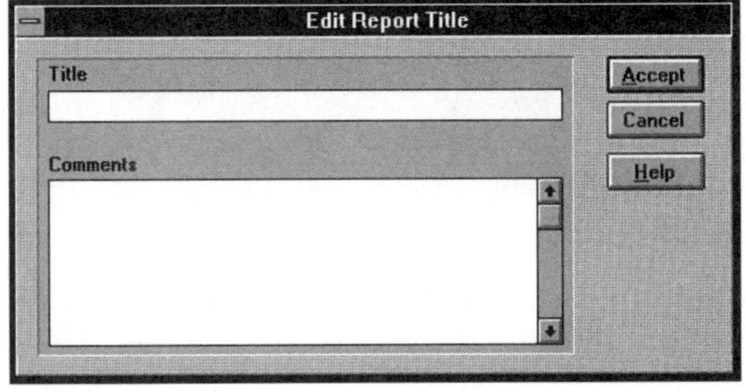

Fig. 11.2
Use the Edit Report Title dialog box to enter the title that will appear in the Report Designer window title bar.

2. Type the title you want to appear in the Report Designer window title bar.

3. Type any comments or information in the Comments box.

4. Click **A**ccept to close the dialog box and display the title in the Report Designer window title bar. The same title appears in the top line of the Insert Database Field dialog box.

Note

Whatever you type in the Comments box can be seen only when the Edit Report Title dialog box is displayed.

Refer to the section "Inserting a Text Field into the Page Header" later in this chapter for information about creating a title that is printed on every page of the report.

Selecting Which Sections to Display

By default, dBASE displays the Page header, Details, and Page footer sections in the Report Designer window. To select which sections are displayed, open the **E**dit menu and choose Sho**w**/Hide Sections to display the Show/Hide Sections dialog box, as shown in figure 11.3.

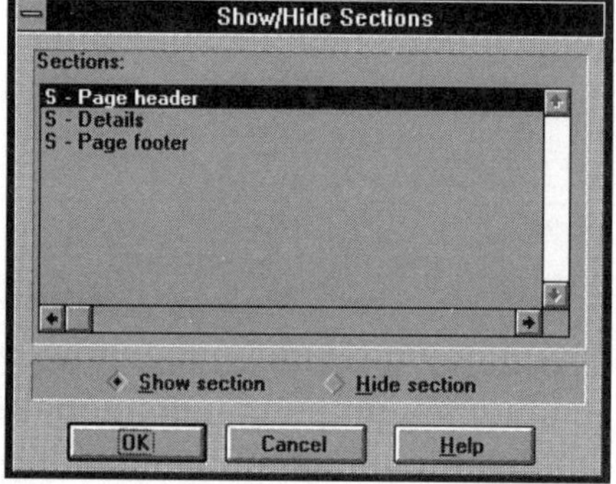

Fig. 11.3
Use the Show/Hide Sections dialog box to choose which sections of a report to display in the Report Designer window.

The Show/Hide Sections dialog box lists the three sections with *S* at the left of each to indicate that the sections are shown. To hide a section, select that section name and then click the **H**ide section option button. When you do this, an *H* appears at the left of the selected section name. If a section is already marked as hidden, click the **S**how section option button to show it.

Click OK in the dialog box to close it and return to the Report Designer window.

Inserting a Single Database Field into a Report

When dBASE first displays the Details section, there is space for only one line of fields. If you want space for two or more lines, point into the Details section and click the mouse button to place an insertion marker, then press Enter one or more times to create space for additional lines. To remove lines, press the Backspace key.

You can insert an individual database field into the Details section of a report by dragging it from the Insert Database Field dialog box. When you point to a field in the dialog box, press the mouse button, and move the mouse slightly. The pointer changes to a small white rectangle as you see in figure 11.4.

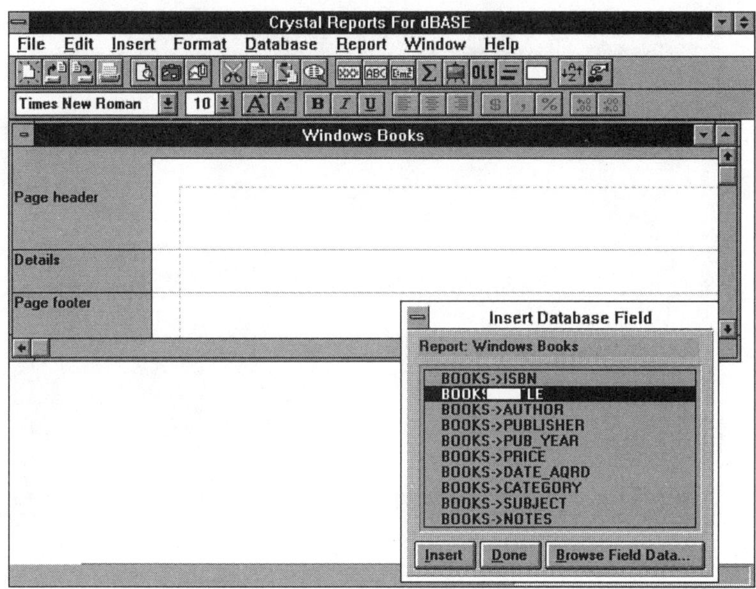

Fig. 11.4
A small white rectangle represents the field you are inserting.

Drag the white rectangular pointer out of the dialog box. As soon as it crosses the border of the dialog box, the pointer changes to an arrow and a black rectangular outline appears. This outline indicates the size of the field as defined by the table design. Drag this outline to the position where you want it to be in the Details section of the report (inside the area enclosed by the dashed margin outline), and release the mouse button.

Alternatively, you can select a field in the Insert Database Field dialog box, click the **I**nsert button to display a rectangle that represents the selected field, and drag the rectangle into the Details section.

Tip
The Report Generator does not let you insert a database field in the margin.

As soon as you release the mouse button, the field appears as a sequence of characters. The characters displayed depend on the type of field you dragged:

`xxx...`	for character fields
`555...`	for numeric fields
`12/31/99`	for date fields

When you drag a database field into the Details section, the field name appears at the bottom of the Page header section of the report, as shown in figure 11.5.

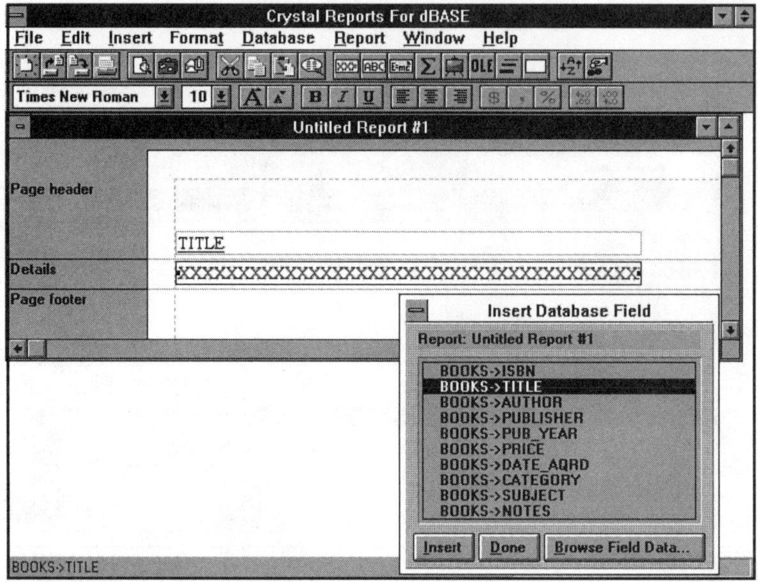

Fig. 11.5
A single database field after it has been inserted in the Details section of a report.

By using this method, you can insert as many separate database fields as you want into the Details section of a report.

Tip
Because the Report Designer does not have Undo, you must be sure to select the correct field before deleting.

Sometimes, after you insert a field into a report, you may want to remove it. If you look closely at the field in the Details section of the report, you will see small dark squares (handles) at each end. The presence of these handles indicates that the field is selected. When a field is selected, you can remove it from the report by pressing the Delete or Backspace key or by opening the **E**dit menu and choosing C**l**ear.

To select any object in the Report Designer window, such as the field name in the Page header section, point to that object and click the mouse button so that handles appear. You can then move, format, or delete that object, as explained later in this chapter.

Placing Several Database Fields into a Report

Instead of placing database fields one at a time into a report, you can insert two or more fields simultaneously. To do this, follow these steps:

1. Click one field name in the Insert Database Field dialog box to select it.

2. Hold down the Ctrl key while you click another field name to select it.

3. Repeat step 2 to select additional fields.

4. Point to any one of the selected fields, press the mouse button, and drag the multipage pointer into the Details section of the report. When you release the mouse button, the selected fields are inserted side by side in a single line of the report, as shown in figure 11.6, with the field names above them in the Page header section.

Tip
Press Esc to cancel the multipage pointer without inserting fields.

Note

Another way to select several fields is to click the first field, and then hold down the Shift key while you click another field. In this case, the two fields together with all fields between them are selected.

You can also select one field, and then hold down the Shift key while you press the down-arrow key to select consecutive fields.

Another way to insert fields into the report is to select those fields in the Insert Database Field dialog box, click Insert, and then drag the multipage pointer into the Details section.

You can repeat these steps to insert additional fields in the Details section of the report. When you finish placing fields, click the **D**one button at the bottom of the Insert Database Field dialog box to remove the dialog box from your screen.

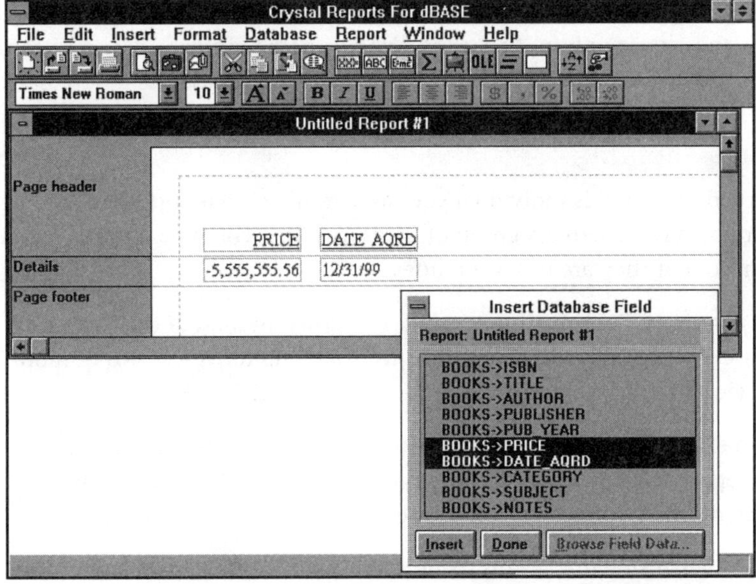

Fig. 11.6
When you insert two or more database fields, they appear in one line of the report.

Selecting and Deselecting Fields in a Report

Immediately after you simultaneously insert several fields into a report, all those fields (but not the field names) are selected, as indicated by the handles at the ends of the fields. Consequently, if you press Delete, all the fields you have just inserted are removed. In order to remove a specific field, you must select just that one field. When you remove a field, however, the field name remains. To remove a field name, you must click the name to select it and then press Delete.

There are many other operations you may want to perform on individual fields or on groups of fields. In each case, you must first select those fields.

dBASE provides several methods to select and deselect individual fields and groups of fields, as well as other objects, such as field names, in a report:

- To deselect all objects, click anywhere outside an object on the report.
- To deselect an individual object when several objects are selected, hold down the Shift key while you click that object.
- To select an object in addition to already selected objects, hold down the Shift key while you click that object.
- To select an object and, at the same time, deselect all currently selected objects, click that object.

- To select a rectangular array of objects, click the Select Fields button in the SpeedBar or open the **E**dit menu and choose Se**l**ect Fields to change the mouse pointer to a cross. Use the cross pointer to drag a rectangle around the objects you want to select, then release the mouse button.

Moving Fields

You can move fields individually, or as a group, on a report. For example, after you have inserted a group of fields in a line, you may want to rearrange them so that they are in several lines.

You can move fields by the standard Windows method of dragging with the mouse. If only one field is selected, just that field moves. If two or more fields are selected, however, all the selected fields move.

As an example, suppose you have inserted three fields in the Details section of a report and you want to rearrange them so that the three fields are in different lines. To do this, follow these steps:

1. Click inside the Details section, but not on a field, to place an insertion point just inside the left margin.

2. Press Enter twice to create two additional lines in the report, as shown in figure 11.7.

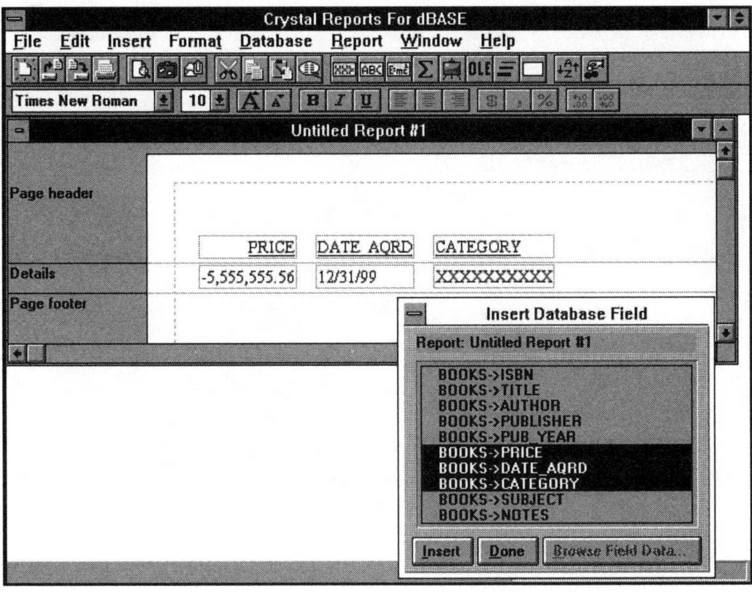

Fig. 11.7
The Details section with space for three lines of fields.

3. Point to the field you want to move to the second line and then press the mouse button to select that field.

4. Drag the field to its new position in the second line.

5. Point to the field you want to move to the third line and drag it to its new position. Now the fields are in the positions shown in figure 11.8.

Note

When you drag fields in this way, field names in the Page header section do not move.

Inserting Fields in Separate Lines

Instead of inserting fields in one row and then dragging them to separate rows, it is often faster to insert the fields directly into separate rows. If you are starting with an empty Details section, follow these steps:

1. Click in the Details section to place an insertion marker there.

2. Press Enter several times to create additional empty lines in the Details section.

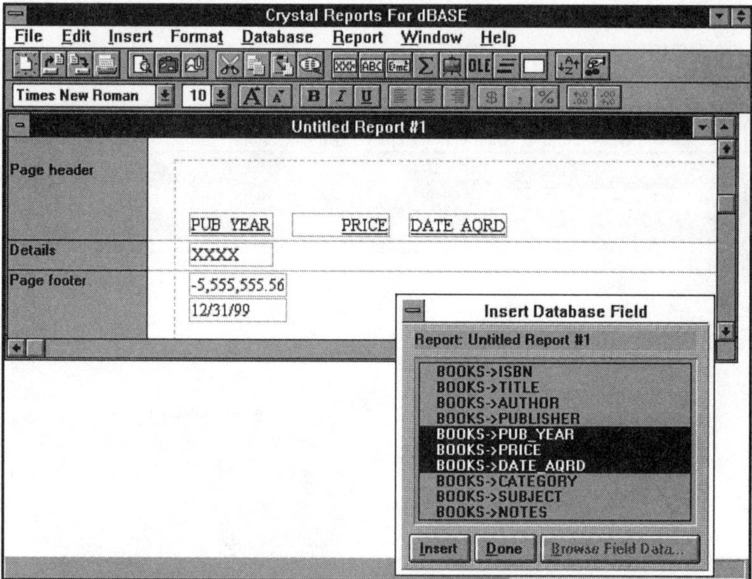

Fig. 11.8
The fields moved into separate lines.

3. If necessary, open the **I**nsert menu and choose **D**atabase Field to display the Insert Database Field dialog box.

4. Select one field in the dialog box and drag it into the Details section.

5. Select another field in the dialog box and drag it to a different line in the Details section.

6. Repeat step 5 as often as necessary.

> **Note**
>
> When you drag database fields into the Details section in this way, the field names are superimposed in the Page header section. You can delete or move field names in the same way that you delete or move fields in the Details section.

Previewing a Report

Sometimes, while you are designing a report, it's useful to see what the report will look like when it is printed. Click the Preview a Report in a Window button, located in the SpeedBar; or open the **F**ile menu, select **P**rint, and then choose **W**indow in the submenu. In either case, the Preview window appears (see fig. 11.9).

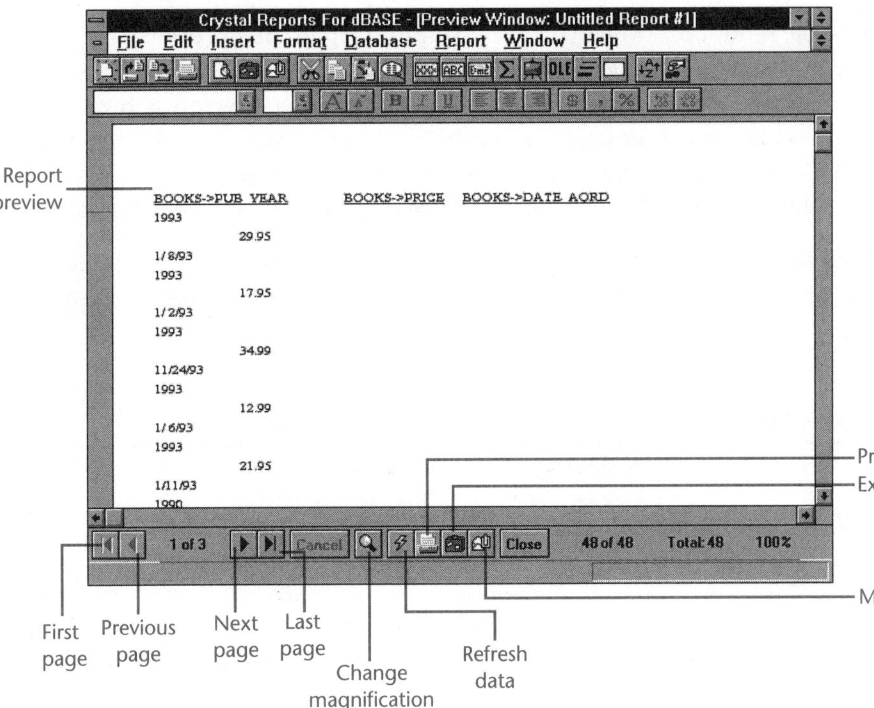

Fig. 11.9
The Preview window shows the beginning of your report as it will appear on paper.

The preview initially shows the top part of the first page of the report. You can use the vertical scroll bar to see the remaining parts of this page, and you can click the four buttons at the left end of the row of buttons at the bottom of the windows to move to other pages. To see the preview in more detail, click the Change Magnification button to switch between three levels of magnification.

If you are working in a networked configuration in which other people have access to the database and may be changing the data, you can click the Refresh Data button to show the latest version of data in the underlying table. You also can click the Print button to print the report, the Export button to export the report to a file, and the Mail button to send the report by E-mail.

After you finish examining the report on-screen, click the Close button to return to the Report Designer window.

Creating a New Report without First Opening a Table

As previously stated, a report is always based on a query. If you create a new report when a table is open, dBASE automatically creates a query based on that table and then opens the Report Designer window with the fields from that table available for inserting in the report.

If a table is not open when you start to create a report, dBASE displays an Open Query Form dialog box that lists all queries in the current directory. In this dialog box you can, if necessary, change to another directory and you can select the query containing the fields you want in your report. When you click OK in this dialog box, dBASE opens the Report Designer window with the fields in the selected directory available for you to insert into the report.

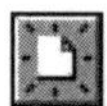

To begin creating a new report, click the Create a New Report button in the SpeedBar and then choose **R**eport, or use one of the methods in the "Creating a Report" section of this chapter.

Troubleshooting

When I try to open the Report Designer window, nothing seems to happen. Why is this?

Be patient, it takes several seconds for the Report Designer to open. If you think nothing is happening, look at the hard disk indicator on the front of your computer and you'll see it flashing, indicating that the Report module is being read from the disk.

Why don't I see all three of the Page header, Details, and Page footer sections when I open the Report Designer window?

By default, dBASE shows all three sections. If you open the **E**dit menu and choose Sho**w**/Hide sections, however, you can select which sections are shown. You, or someone else, may have done this during a previous dBASE session.

Why does my Report Designer window look different from the one shown in this chapter?

This chapter assumes default settings of many options. You can change these options by opening the **F**ile menu and choosing Op**t**ions, as described in Chapter 16, "Designing Advanced Reports."

Improving a Report

After you insert the required fields into a report, and look at a preview of it, you will probably have many ideas about how you can improve its appearance. Some of the improvements you can make are the following:

- Providing space between records
- Moving fields horizontally in a line
- Moving fields from one line to another
- Changing the alignment of data within fields

- Changing the format of numerical data
- Changing the margins
- Changing the font, font size, and font style
- Changing the color of text, text background, and text borders

These improvements are described in the text that follows.

Opening a Report

You must open a report before you can work on it. To do so, follow these steps:

1. From anywhere within dBASE, click the Open button in the SpeedBar; or open the **F**ile menu and choose **O**pen to display the File Open dialog box.

2. Open the List Files of **T**ype list at the bottom-left of the dialog box and choose Reports so that the File **N**ame list shows the names of existing reports, as shown in figure 11.10.

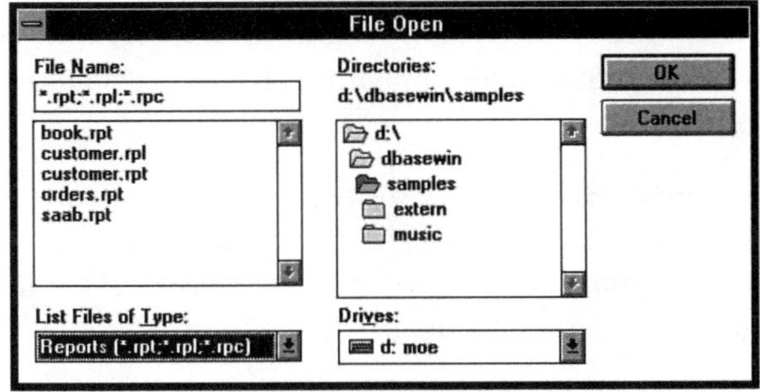

Fig. 11.10
Choose the report in the File Open dialog box.

3. If necessary, select the **d**irectory that contains the report you want.
4. Click the name of the report, and then click OK.

Providing Space between Records

The fields shown earlier in figure 11.8 completely fill the vertical space in the Details section of the report. For this reason, the report will have no space between records. To improve this situation, simply insert a blank line after the bottom line of records. To do this, follow these steps:

1. Point to the Details section, to the left of the bottom record, and click to insert an insertion point just inside the left margin.
2. Press Enter to insert a blank line after the last one.

Tip
You can increase the depth of the Details section by dragging the line that separates it from the Page footer section.

If you look at the Preview window, you will see that there is now a blank line between each record.

> **Note**
>
> You have already seen how you can select one or more fields and drag them to new positions, either within a line or between lines. Refer to the earlier section "Moving Fields" in this chapter.

Changing the Alignment of Data within Fields

When you insert a database field into a report, dBASE allocates enough space for the number of characters specified for that field in the Table Designer window. In most cases, fields contain fewer characters than the maximum allowed and those characters are usually aligned to the left end of the field. An exception to this is Numeric fields in which the data is aligned to the right. You can change this default alignment and you also can center data within fields.

You can change data alignment either in the Report Designer window or in the Preview window. In the Report Designer window, select the field you want to align and click the appropriate alignment button in the Format Bar. When you do this, the characters representing the field data move to the new alignment position.

In the Preview window, select the field you want to align in any record. When you do this, the corresponding fields in all records become selected. Then click the appropriate alignment button in the Format Bar to move the data in all records to the new alignment.

Changing the Format of Numeric Data

You can change the format of data in Numeric fields by adding a currency symbol, inserting thousands separators, adding a percent symbol, or changing the position of the decimal point. As in the case of changing alignment, you can do this either in the Report Designer window or in the Preview window.

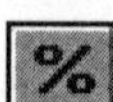

In either case, select a Numeric field and then click the appropriate button in the Format Bar. If you click the Display the Currency Symbol button, dBASE inserts a dollar sign (or other currency symbol) ahead of the numerical value. If you click the Display a Thousands Separator button, dBASE inserts a comma (or other separator) between groups of three digits to the left of the decimal point. If you click the Display a Percentage Symbol button, dBASE appends a percentage symbol to the numerical value.

> **Note**
>
> The currency and thousands separator symbols depend on the settings in the International section of the Windows Control Panel. If you have chosen English (American) as the language and have retained the default settings for that language, the dollar symbol is used for currency and a comma is used as the thousands separator.
>
> When dBASE appends the percentage symbol to a value, it does *not* change the position of the decimal point as happens in some spreadsheet applications.

If, after selecting a Numeric field, you click the Remove a Decimal Place button in the Format Bar, dBASE hides the least significant decimal digit in the data shown in the report. For example, if the value in the table from which the report derives is 12.95, after you click this button the value shown in the report is 12.9. If you click this button a second time, the value shown in the report is 12.

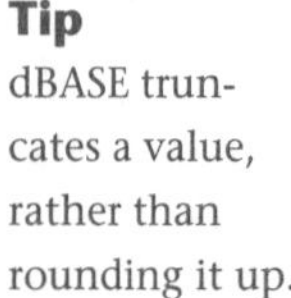

Tip
dBASE truncates a value, rather than rounding it up.

If you have clicked the Remove a Decimal Place button, and then click the Add a Decimal Place button, dBASE restores the digit that was previously in the field. For example, if a value was originally 12.95 and you click the Remove button to display it as 12.9, after you click the Add button, it will again be displayed as 12.95. If you have not previously removed decimal places, dBASE adds a zero as the least significant digit. For example, if the original value is 12.95, it becomes 12.950 after you click the Add button.

Changing the Margins

When you create a new report, dBASE uses default values for the top, bottom, left, and right margins. These margins are shown as a dashed outline in the Report Designer window.

To specify the printer on which the report will be printed and, if necessary, change the printer settings, follow these steps:

1. Open the **F**ile menu and choose Printer Setup to display the Print Setup dialog box.
2. If necessary, choose the printer on which the report will be printed.
3. Select Po**r**trait or **L**andscape orientation according to your needs.
4. Select the Si**z**e of paper on which the report will be printed and, if necessary, the **S**ource of that paper.
5. Click the **O**ptions button to display the printer options dialog box, select whatever options are appropriate for your printer, and click OK to return to the Print Setup dialog box.

6. Click OK to accept the printer.

7. Open the **F**ile menu and choose Page **M**argins to display the Printer Margins dialog box shown in figure 11.11.

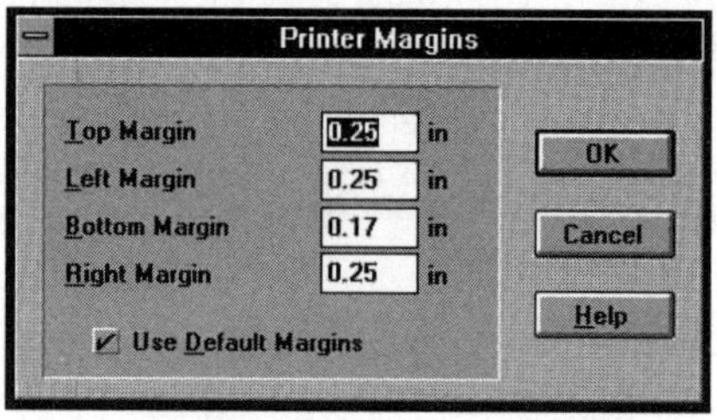

Fig. 11.11
Use the Printer Margins dialog box to set the margins.

8. Change the margin values shown in the four text boxes to suit your needs.

9. Click OK to accept the new margin values and close the dialog box.

After you have changed the margin values, you can restore the original values by displaying the Printer Margins dialog box and clicking the Use **D**efault Margins check box.

Changing the Font, Font Size, and Font Style

By default, dBASE displays and prints all the text in a report using the TrueType Times New Roman font at a size of 10 points and in Roman (normal) style. You can change the font, font size, and font style of the characters in any field either in the Report Designer window or in the Preview window. You can make these changes either by clicking buttons in the Format Bar or by opening the Font dialog box. You also can use the Font dialog box to change the color of characters.

Note

You can change the default font, font size, font style, and font color by opening the File menu and choosing Options.

Tip
You can right-click in the Report Designer window to open a SpeedMenu, and then choose Change Font.

To make any of these changes to characters in fields, first select one or more fields. Then, do one or more of the following to make changes by using the Format Bar:

- Open the font list box and select a font name.
- Open the font size list box and select a font size.

- Click the Increase Size button to increase the size of the font by one point.
- Click the Decrease Size button to decrease the size of the font by one point.
- Click the Bold button to make the selected fields bold or, if they are already bold, to unbold them.
- Click the Italic button to italicize the selected fields or, if they are already italicized, to unitalicize them.
- Click the Underline button to underline the selected fields or, if they are already underlined, to remove the underlining.

Alternatively, after selecting fields to be formatted, you can open the Format menu and choose Font to open the Font dialog box shown in figure 11.12. Use this dialog box to select character formats, as explained in Chapter 8, "Entering, Editing, and Viewing Data."

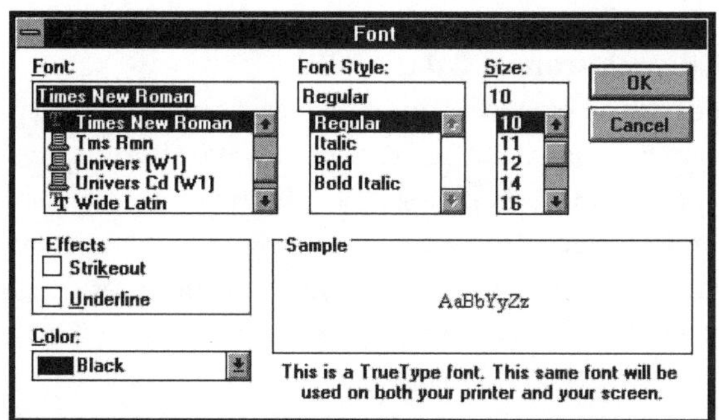

Fig. 11.12
Use the Font dialog box to format text in selected fields.

Note

When you change the font size, dBASE automatically changes the line height to suit the largest font size in that line.

◄ "Printing Tables," p. 161

Changing Field Color, Background, and Borders

By default, fields are printed in black text with no background and no borders. You can use the Format Border and Colors dialog box to change these defaults in either the Report Designer window or the Preview window.

Tip
You also can change the color of text in the Font dialog box.

To change the defaults, first select one or more fields, then open the Format menu and choose Border and Colors to display the Format Border and Colors dialog box as shown in figure 11.13.

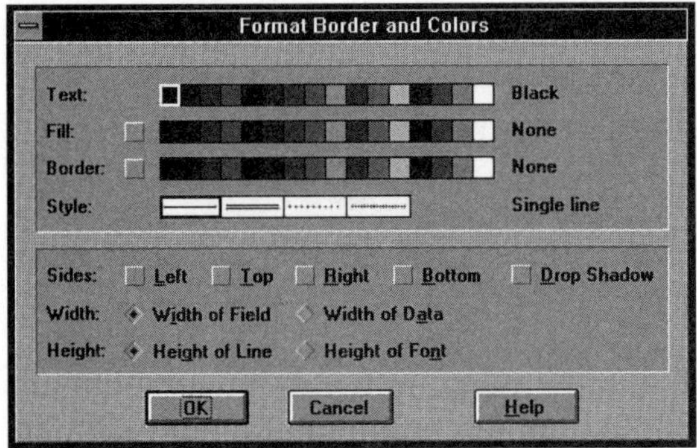

Fig. 11.13 Use the Format Border and Colors dialog box to format selected fields.

Changing Field Foreground Color

To select a color for text in selected fields, click the appropriate color button in the Text row at the top of the dialog box. When you select a color, a square appears around that color and the name of the color appears at the right. Click the OK button to close the dialog box and see the color applied to the text in the selected fields.

Changing Field Background Color

By default, fields are displayed without any background. To display a field with a background color, click the appropriate color button in the Fill row in the Format Border and Colors dialog box. When you select a color, a check mark appears in the check box at the left of the row of colors, a square appears around the selected color, and the name of the color appears at the right. Click the OK button to close the dialog box and see the background color applied to the selected fields.

By default, the background color fills the entire width of the field. If you prefer, you can apply the fill color only to the space occupied by characters in the field. To do this, click the Width of D**a**ta option button in the bottom section of the dialog box. To return to filling the entire width of the field, click the W**i**dth of Field option button.

Also by default, the background color fills the entire height of the line that contains each field. If you have two or more fields in a line and want the background fill for each field to match the font size in the individual fields, click the Height of Fo**n**t option button in the bottom section of the dialog box. To return to having the same fill height for entire lines, click the Hei**g**ht of Line option button.

To remove the background from selected fields, open the Format Border and Colors dialog box again and click the check box at the left of the row of Fill colors to remove the check mark, and then click OK to close the dialog box.

Changing Field Borders

By default, fields in a report have no borders. You can use the Format Border and Colors dialog box to add borders around selected fields. You can choose a complete rectangular border in one of 16 colors, or you can independently select any combination of the left, top, right, and bottom border edges. In addition, you can choose among four line styles and you can choose to have a drop shadow. Figure 11.14 shows some fields in the Preview window with various types of borders.

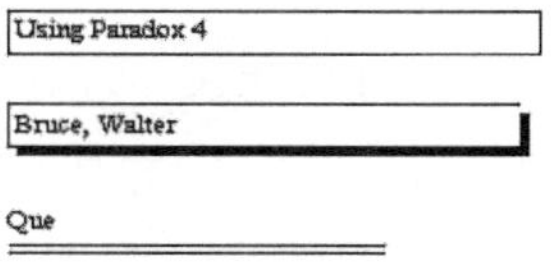

Using Paradox 4

Bruce, Walter

Que

Fig. 11.14
These are some examples of fields with borders.

To apply rectangular borders to selected fields, click one of the 16 colors in the Border row. When you do, check marks appear in the Border check box and also in the **L**eft, **T**op, **R**ight, and **B**ottom check boxes. A square marks the selected color and the name of that color appears at the right of the row of colors.

If you want only a partial border, a line under the field for example, click the appropriate check boxes in the Sides row to remove check marks in the boxes that correspond to the sides you do not want.

The line style dBASE chooses by default is single line. You can choose double line, dashed line, or dotted line by clicking the appropriate line style button. You can choose a drop shadow by clicking the **D**rop Shadow button. You must have a border on at least one side of a field in order to have a drop shadow.

As in the case of background fill colors, you can choose W**i**dth of Field or Width of D**a**ta, and you can choose Hei**g**ht of Line or Height of Fo**n**t to control the width and height of field borders.

After you specify the borders you want, click the OK button to close the dialog box and apply those borders to the selected fields.

Creating a Header and Footer

The Page header and Page footer sections of the Report Designer window are where you insert text and graphics that will appear as a header at the top of every page of a printed report and as a footer at the bottom of every page.

When you begin to create a new report, dBASE displays blank Page header and Page footer sections each with space for three lines. As you insert fields into the Details section, dBASE automatically inserts field names in the Page header section.

Working with Field Names

You can move field names and format them in the same way that you work with fields in the Details section of a report. In many cases, you will not want field names to appear in the Page header. To delete them, follow these steps:

1. Select all the field names in the Page header.
2. Press Delete, or open the **E**dit menu and choose C**l**ear.

Note

If you have inserted two or more lines of fields in the Details section, the Page header section will contain superimposed field names. You can easily select superimposed field names by clicking the Select Fields button in the SpeedBar or opening the **E**dit menu and choosing Select Fields, and then using the cross pointer to draw a rectangle around the superimposed field names.

Inserting a Text Field into the Page Header

You can insert text other than that obtained from database fields in a report. For example, most reports have a title that appears at the top of every page. This type of text is known as a *text field*. If you insert a text field in the Page header or Page footer sections of the Report Designer window, the text appears on every page. If you insert a text field in the Details section, the text appears with every record.

Note

You can insert text fields using either the Report Designer window or the Preview window, though it is usually more convenient to use the Report Designer window.

To insert a title in the Page header section, follow these steps:

1. Open the Report Designer window.

2. Click the Insert a Text Field button in the SpeedBar or open the **I**nsert menu and choose Te**x**t Field to display the Edit Text Field dialog box, shown in figure 11.15.

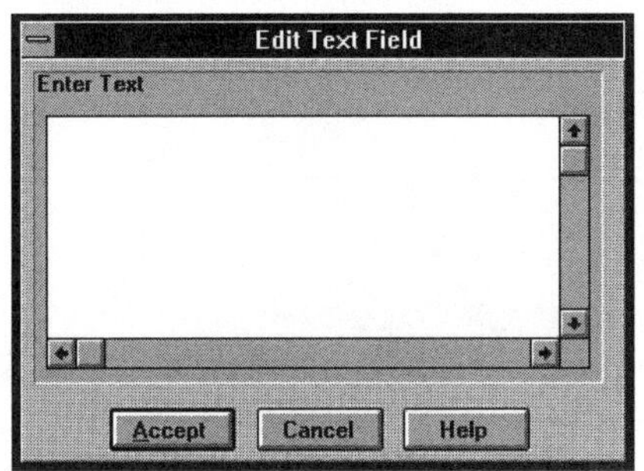

Fig. 11.15
Use the Edit Text Field dialog box to type text in a field.

3. Type the text you want to use as the title.

4. Click **A**ccept to accept the title and close the dialog box. A rectangle representing the text appears.

5. Drag the rectangle to the position where you want the title to be in the Page header section, and then click the mouse button to make the text appear inside the box.

You can select and drag the title to other positions and you can format the text either by using the Format Bar or by opening the Forma**t** menu and choosing **F**ont to display the Font dialog box.

If you click the Preview Report button in the SpeedBar, you will see the title as it will be printed. As you move from page to page in the preview, you see the title at the top of every page.

Inserting a Text Field into the Details Section

Any text field inserted into the Details section in the Report Designer window becomes part of every record. If you prepare mailing labels, for example, you normally want the same return address on every label. To do this, insert the return address as one or more text fields inserted in the Details section, as shown in figure 11.16.

Inserting Special Fields

By inserting special fields, you can easily create a report in which every page is numbered and contains the date on which the report is printed.

To print the page number and current date at the bottom of every page, follow these steps:

1. Open the Report Designer window.

2. Open the **I**nsert menu and choose Special Field to display a submenu that lists **D**ate, **P**age Number, **R**ecord Number, and **G**roup Number.

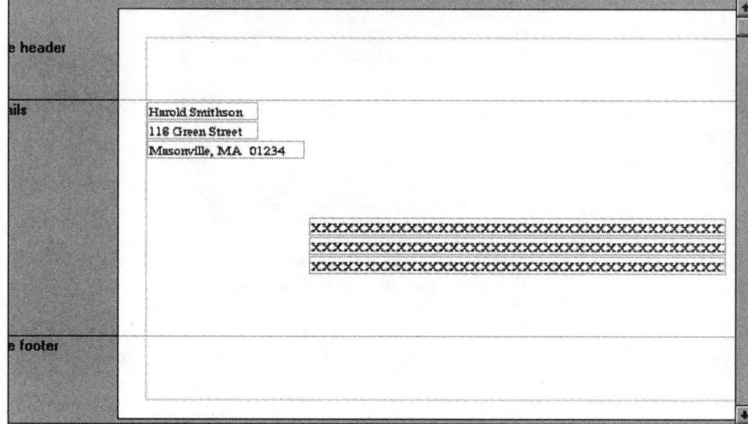

Fig. 11.16
This is an example of a Report Designer window used for printing mailing labels.

3. Click **D**ate. The submenu disappears and a rectangle appears to represent the date field.
4. Drag the rectangle to the position in the Page footer section where you want the date to appear, and then click the mouse button.
5. Repeat steps 2 and 3.
6. Click **P**age Number in the submenu.
7. Drag the rectangle that represents the page number to the position where you want it in the Page footer section, and then click the mouse button.

If you look at the preview, you will see the current date and the page number at the bottom of each page of your report.

Troubleshooting

Why are the first two or three characters missing from every line of the reports I print?

Most office printers cannot print to the extreme edges of a sheet of paper. You have probably set the margins too close to the edges of the paper for your printer. Open the **F**ile menu and choose Page Margins to change your margin settings.

Why does nothing seem to happen when I change the alignment of a field by clicking a SpeedBar button?

This is because you are working in the Report Designer window. You can see the effect of alignment only in the Report Preview window.

Why are the right five buttons in the Format Bar dimmed?

These buttons are active only when you select a Numeric field. If you select a Character field, even if the field contains only numbers, you cannot use these buttons.

Saving a Report

To save a report, click the Save the Report button in the SpeedBar or open the **F**ile menu and choose **S**ave or Save **A**s in the same way that you save other dBASE files. Report file names have .RPT as the file name extension.

Printing

You can print a report and you can also print a report definition that identifies a report's components and provides information about those components.

Printing a Report

As always, printing involves making sure the correct printer is specified and choosing appropriate setup options. After that, you can open the Print dialog box and specify which pages you want to print.

Note

If you haven't already done so, look carefully at the Preview window to verify that the report is formatted as you want it before you start printing. This is particularly important if the report contains many pages.

To print a report, follow these steps:

1. Open the **F**ile menu and choose Prin**t**er Setup to display the Print Setup dialog box.
2. If necessary, select the name of the printer you are using and choose Po**r**trait or **L**andscape orientation as appropriate.
3. Choose OK to accept the printer.
4. Open the **F**ile menu and select **P**rint to display a submenu that lists **P**rinter, **W**indow, **F**ile, and Report **D**efinitions, as shown in figure 11.17.

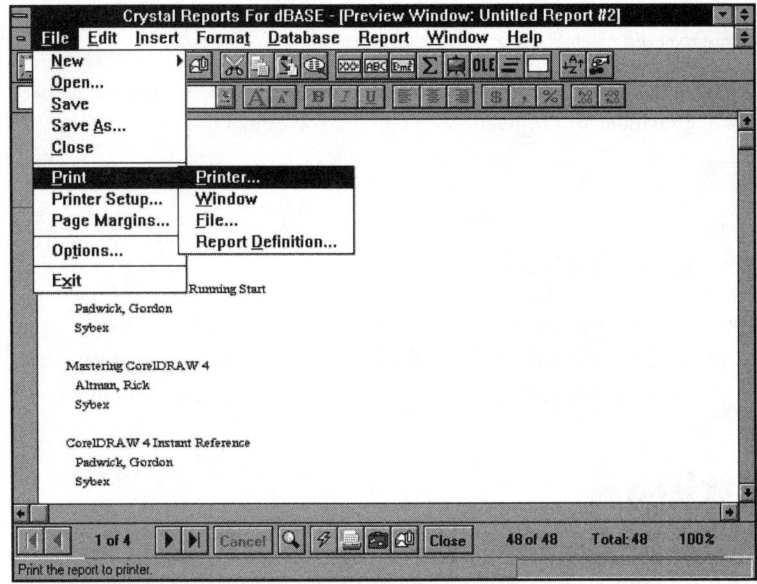

Fig. 11.17
The Print submenu.

5. Choose **P**rinter to display the Print dialog box, as shown in figure 11.18.

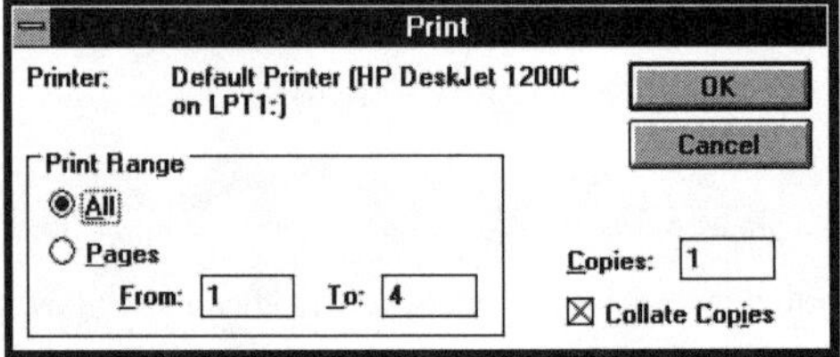

Fig. 11.18
The Print dialog box.

Note

As an alternative to steps 1 through 5, you can click the Print Report to a Printer button in the SpeedBar.

6. Choose the range of pages and the number of copies you want to print, and then click OK to begin printing.

Printing a Report Definition

A report definition, (a report about a report) identifies a report's components and provides information about those components. This definition includes informtion about the file, fields, formulas, and sections.

▶ "Customizing Crystal Reports," p. 417

To print a report definition, follow these steps:

1. Open the **F**ile menu and choose **P**rint to display the submenu.

2. In the submenu, choose Report **D**efinition to print the report definition.

From Here...

In this chapter, you learned the basics of creating reports. You'll find more information about reports in the following chapters:

- Chapter 16, "Designing Advanced Reports," for information about basing reports on linked tables, calculating values in reports, and grouping and summarizing values.

- Chapter 18, "Using dBASE in a Multiuser Environment," for information about basing reports on data shared between several users.

- Chapter 21, "Using OLE and DDE with dBASE," for information about using linked and embedded data in reports.

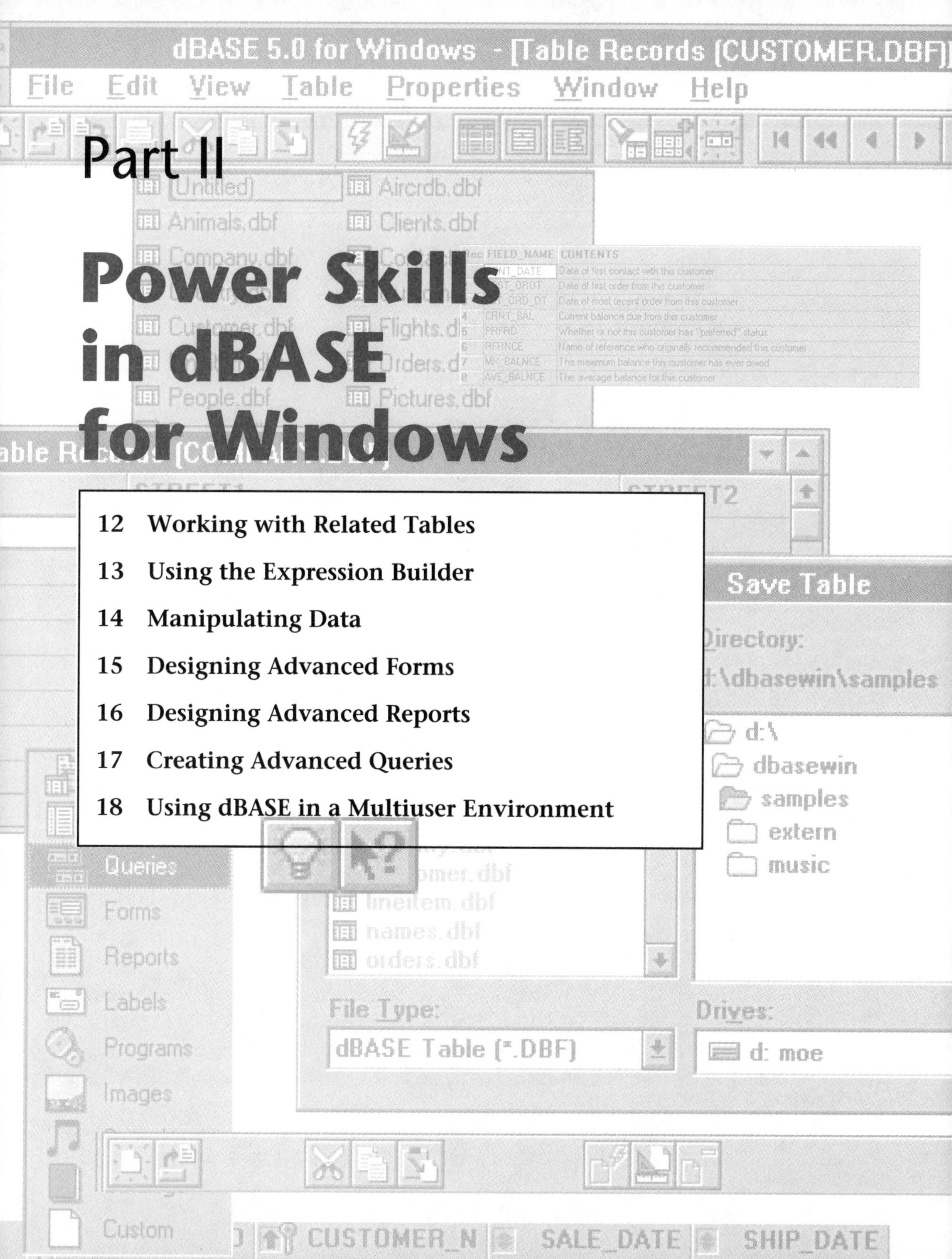

Part II

Power Skills in dBASE for Windows

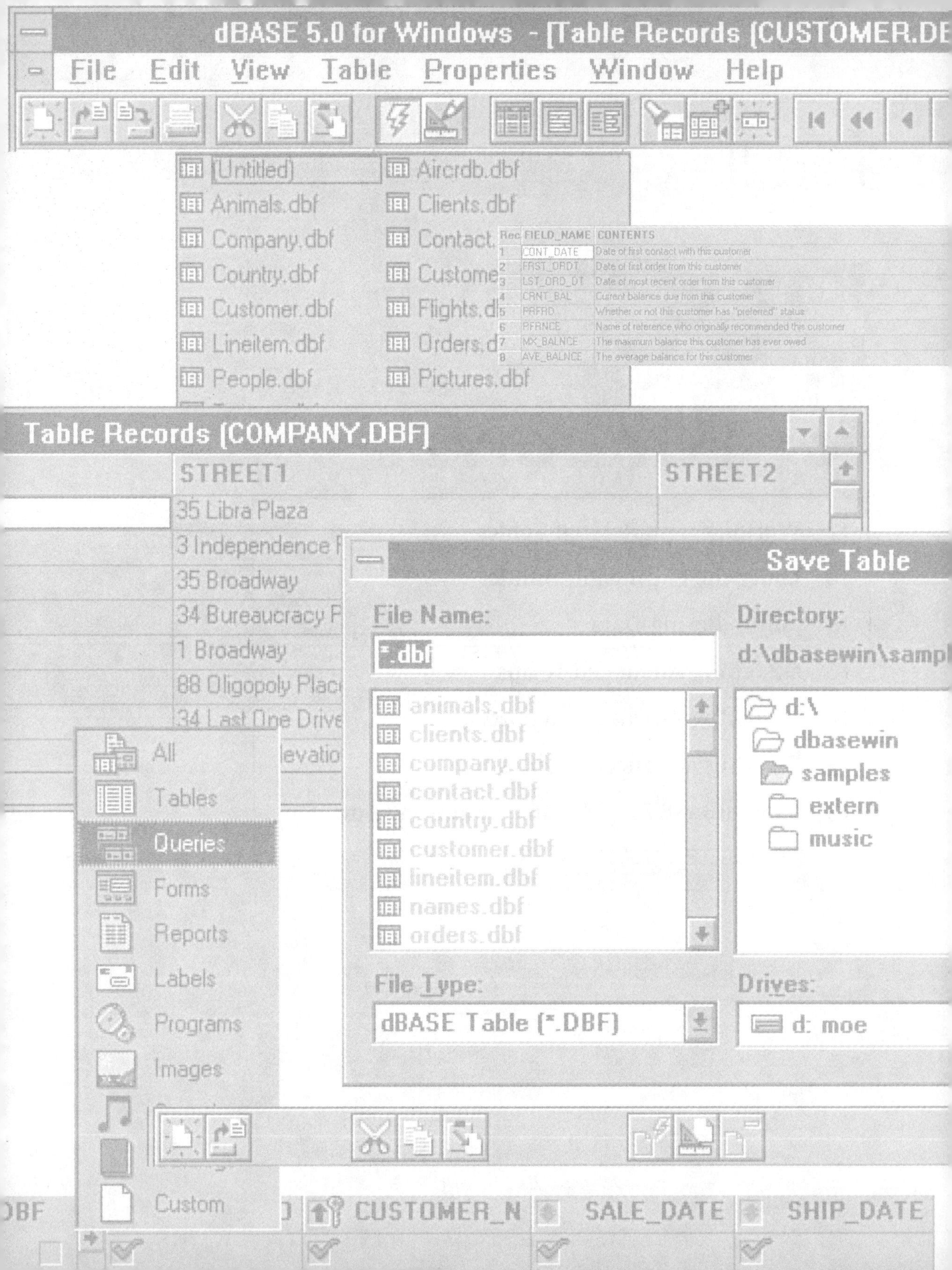

dBASE 5.0 for Windows - [Table Records (CUSTOMER.DE
File Edit View Table Properties Window Help
(Untitled)
Aircrdb.dbf
Animals.dbf
Clients.dbf
Company.dbf
Contact.
Country.dbf
Custome
Customer.dbf
Flights.d
Lineitem.dbf
Orders.d
People.dbf
Pictures.dbf
Rec FIELD_NAME CONTENTS
1 CONT_DATE Date of first contact with this customer
2 FRST_ORDT Date of first order from this customer
3 LST_ORD_DT Date of most recent order from this customer
4 CRNT_BAL Current balance due from this customer
5 PRFRD Whether or not this customer has "preferred" status
6 RFRNCE Name of reference who originally recommended this customer
7 MX_BALNCE The maximum balance this customer has ever owed
8 AVE_BALNCE The average balance for this customer
Table Records (COMPANY.DBF)
STREET1
STREET2
35 Libra Plaza
3 Independence
35 Broadway
34 Bureaucracy
1 Broadway
88 Oligopoly Plac
34 Last One Drive
Save Table
File Name:
*.dbf
Directory:
d:\dbasewin\sampl
animals.dbf
clients.dbf
company.dbf
contact.dbf
country.dbf
customer.dbf
lineitem.dbf
names.dbf
orders.dbf
d:\
dbasewin
samples
extern
music
File Type:
dBASE Table (*.DBF)
Drives:
d: moe
All
Tables
Queries
Forms
Reports
Labels
Programs
Images
Custom
CUSTOMER_N
SALE_DATE
SHIP_DATE

Chapter 12

Working with Related Tables

Most database applications (and, as you soon learn, *all well-designed* database applications) store their information in multiple tables. And although most of these tables have nothing to do with each other (such as tables of customer information and employee payroll data), at least some of the tables are likely to contain related information (such as tables of customer information and customer orders).

Working with multiple, related tables presents you with two challenges: you need to design your tables so that the related data is stored efficiently, and you need to set up links between the tables so that you can retrieve and work with the related information quickly and easily. This chapter tackles both challenges and shows you how to exploit the full relational powers of dBASE for Windows.

In this chapter, you learn to do the following:

- Understand fundamental concepts of relational databases
- Design tables for a relational database
- Link related tables
- Work with the Query Designer's link options
- Make changes to table relationships
- Remove a relation you no longer need
- Enforce referential integrity

Understanding the Pitfalls of a Nonrelational Design

Why do you need to worry about relations between tables, anyway? Isn't working with one large table easier than using two or three medium-sized ones? To answer these questions and demonstrate the problems that arise when you ignore relational database models, this chapter begins by giving you a simple example: a table of sales leads.

Table 12.1 outlines a structure for a simple table (LEADS.DBF) to store the sales leads information.

Table 12.1 The Table Structure for LEADS.DBF

Name	Type	Width	Index	Description
LEAD_ID	Character	5	Ascend	The primary key
FIRST_NAME	Character	15	None	The contact's first name
LAST_NAME	Character	15	Ascend	The contact's last name
COMPANY	Character	25	None	The company for which the contact works
ADDRESS	Character	30	None	The company's address
CITY	Character	25	None	The company's city
STATE	Character	2	None	The company's state
ZIP	Character	10	None	The company's ZIP code
PHONE	Character	13	None	The contact's phone number
FAX	Character	13	None	The contact's fax number
SOURCE	Character	10	None	Where the lead originated
NOTES	Memo	10	None	Notes or comments related to the sales lead

This structure works fine until you need to add two or more leads from the same company (a common occurrence). As you can see in figure 12.1, leads from the same company have repeating information in the COMPANY, ADDRESS, CITY, and STATE fields. (The ZIP field also repeats, as do in some cases the PHONE, FAX, and SOURCE fields.)

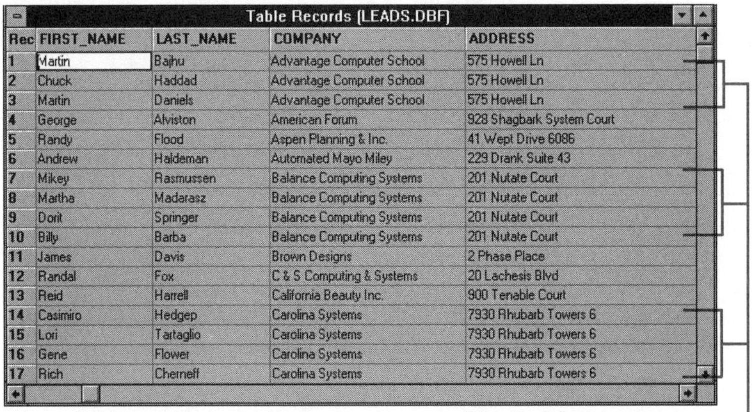

Table Records (LEADS.DBF)

Rec	FIRST_NAME	LAST_NAME	COMPANY	ADDRESS
1	Martin	Bajhu	Advantage Computer School	575 Howell Ln
2	Chuck	Haddad	Advantage Computer School	575 Howell Ln
3	Martin	Daniels	Advantage Computer School	575 Howell Ln
4	George	Alviston	American Forum	928 Shagbark System Court
5	Randy	Flood	Aspen Planning & Inc.	41 Wept Drive 6086
6	Andrew	Haldeman	Automated Mayo Miley	229 Drank Suite 43
7	Mikey	Rasmussen	Balance Computing Systems	201 Nutate Court
8	Martha	Madarasz	Balance Computing Systems	201 Nutate Court
9	Dorit	Springer	Balance Computing Systems	201 Nutate Court
10	Billy	Barba	Balance Computing Systems	201 Nutate Court
11	James	Davis	Brown Designs	2 Phase Place
12	Randal	Fox	C & S Computing & Systems	20 Lachesis Blvd
13	Reid	Harrell	California Beauty Inc.	900 Tenable Court
14	Casimiro	Hedgep	Carolina Systems	7930 Rhubarb Towers 6
15	Lori	Tartaglio	Carolina Systems	7930 Rhubarb Towers 6
16	Gene	Flower	Carolina Systems	7930 Rhubarb Towers 6
17	Rich	Cherneff	Carolina Systems	7930 Rhubarb Towers 6

Repeated data

Fig. 12.1
Sales leads from the same company have repeating information.

All this repetition makes the table unnecessarily large, which is bad enough, but it also creates two major problems:

- The data-entry clerk must enter the repeated information for each lead from the same company.

- If any of the repeated information changes (such as the company's name or address), each corresponding record must be changed.

One way to eliminate the repetition and solve the data-entry and maintenance inefficiencies is to change the focus of the table. As it stands, each record in the table identifies a specific contact in a company. But because the company information is what repeats, allowing only one record per company makes some sense. You then could include separate fields for each sales lead within the company. The new structure might look something like the one shown in table 12.2.

Table 12.2 A Revised, Company-Centered Structure for LEADS.DBF

Name	Type	Width	Index	Description
LEAD_ID	Character	5	Ascend	The primary key
COMPANY	Character	25	Ascend	The company name

(continues)

Table 12.2 Continued

Name	Type	Width	Index	Description
ADDRESS	Character	30	None	The company's address
CITY	Character	25	None	The company's city
STATE	Character	2	None	The company's state
ZIP	Character	10	None	The company's ZIP code
PHONE	Character	13	None	The company's phone number
FAX	Character	13	None	The company's fax number
FIRST_1	Character	15	None	The first name of contact #1
LAST_1	Character	15	None	The last name of contact #1
SOURCE_1	Character	10	None	Where the lead for contact #1 originated
NOTES_1	Memo	10	None	Notes or comments related to contact #1
FIRST_2	Character	15	None	The first name of contact #2
LAST_2	Character	15	None	The last name of contact #2
SOURCE_2	Character	10	None	Where the lead for contact #2 originated
NOTES_2	Memo	10	None	Notes or comments related to contact #2
FIRST_3	Character	15	None	The first name of contact #3
LAST_3	Character	15	None	The last name of contact #3

Name	Type	Width	Index	Description
SOURCE_3	Character	10	None	Where the lead for contact #3 originated
NOTES_3	Memo	10	None	Notes or comments related to contact #3

In this setup, the company information appears only once, and the contact-specific data (assuming that this information involves only the first name, last name, source, and notes) appears in separate field groups (FIRST_1, LAST_1, SOURCE_1, and NOTES_1). This structure solves the earlier problems, but at the cost of a new dilemma: the structure as it stands holds only three sales leads per company. A large firm conceivably might have more than three contacts and perhaps even dozens. This situation raises two unpleasant difficulties:

- If you run out of the repeating groups of contact fields, new ones must be added. Although adding fields might not be a problem for the database designer, most data-entry clerks don't have access to the table design screen (nor should they).
- In dBASE files, empty fields take up as much disk real estate as full ones. Making room for a dozen contacts from one company therefore means that all the records with only one or two contacts have huge amounts of wasted space.

Learning How a Relational Design Can Help

To solve the twin problems of repetition between records and repeated field groups within records, you need to turn to the relational database model. This model was developed by Dr. Edgar Codd of IBM in the early 1970s. Because it was based on a complex relational algebra theory, the pure form of the rules and requirements for a true relational database setup is quite complicated and decidedly impractical for real-world applications. The next few sections look at a simplified version of the model.

Step 1: Separating the Data

After you know which fields you need to include in your database application, the first step in setting up a relational database is to make sure each table is composed only of entities (records) from a single *entity class*. This means you must divide these fields into separate tables where the "theme" of each table is unique.

Tip
For easier table management, good database practice requires that you include a primary key field in each of your tables, whether or not you plan to use them in relations.

The table of sales leads you saw earlier, for example, dealt with data that had two entity classes: the contacts and the companies for which they worked. Every one of the problems encountered with that table (repetition between records and repeated field groups within records) can be traced to the fact that two entity classes were being combined into a single table. The first step towards a relational solution is thus to create separate tables for each class of data.

Table 12.3 shows the table structure for the contact data (CONTACTS.DBF), and table 12.4 shows the structure for the company information (COMPANY.DBF). Note, in particular, that both tables include a primary key field.

Table 12.3 The Table Structure for CONTACTS.DBF

Name	Type	Width	Index	Description
CONTACT_ID	Character	5	Ascend	The primary key
FIRST_NAME	Character	15	None	The contact's first name
LAST_NAME	Character	15	Ascend	The contact's last name
PHONE	Character	13	None	The contact's phone number
FAX	Character	13	None	The contact's fax number
SOURCE	Character	10	None	Where the lead originated
NOTES	Memo	10	None	Notes or comments related to the sales lead

Table 12.4 The Table Structure for COMPANY.DBF

Name	Type	Width	Index	Description
COMPANY_ID	Character	5	Ascend	The primary key

Name	Type	Width	Index	Description
COMP_NAME	Character	25	Ascend	The company's name
ADDRESS	Character	30	None	The company's address
CITY	Character	25	None	The company's city
STATE	Character	2	None	The company's state
ZIP	Character	10	None	The company's ZIP code
PHONE	Character	13	None	The company's phone number (main switchboard)

Step 2: Adding Foreign Keys to the Tables

At first glance, separating the tables seems self-defeating because, if you've done the job properly, the two tables have nothing in common. But the second step in the relational design is to define the commonality between the tables in a way that dBASE for Windows can understand.

In the sales leads example, what is the common ground between the CONTACTS and COMPANY tables? It's that every one of the leads in the CONTACTS table works for a specific firm in the COMPANY table. What you need, then, is some way of relating the appropriate information in COMPANY to each record in CONTACTS (without, of course, the inefficiency of simply cramming all the data into a single table).

The way you relate the tables in dBASE for Windows is to establish a field that is common to both tables. dBASE for Windows then can use this common field to set up a link between the two tables. The field you use must satisfy three conditions:

- It must not have the same name as an existing field in the other table.
- It must uniquely identify each record in the other table; that is, it must contain data that points to one, and only one, record in the other table.
- To save space and reduce data-entry errors, it should be the smallest field that satisfies the preceding two conditions.

In the sales leads example, you need to add a field to the CONTACTS table that establishes a link to the appropriate record in the COMPANY table. The COMP_NAME field uniquely identifies each firm, but it's too large to be of use. The PHONE field is also a unique identifier and is smaller, but the CONTACTS table already has a PHONE field. The best solution is to use COMPANY_ID, the COMPANY table's primary key field. Table 12.5 shows the revised structure for the CONTACTS table that includes the COMPANY_ID field. (Notice that the new field is indexed, which is a requirement to establish the link between the two tables later.)

Table 12.5 The Final Structure for CONTACTS.DBF

Name	Type	Width	Index	Description
CONTACT_ID	Character	5	Ascend	The primary key
COMPANY_ID	Character	5	Ascend	The COMPANY table foreign key
FIRST_NAME	Character	15	None	The contact's first name
LAST_NAME	Character	15	Ascend	The contact's last name
PHONE	Character	13	None	The contact's phone number
FAX	Character	13	None	The contact's fax number
SOURCE	Character	10	None	Where the lead originated
NOTES	Memo	10	None	Notes or comments related to the sales lead

When a table includes a primary key field from a related database, the field is called a *foreign key*. Foreign keys are the secret to successful relational database design. As previously mentioned, you can still link tables based on fields other than a foreign key, but foreign keys are almost always the most efficient method. The rest of this chapter assumes you'll be using a foreign key field to link your related tables.

Step 3: Establishing a Link between Related Tables

After you have inserted your foreign keys into your tables, the final step in designing your relational model is to tell dBASE for Windows to establish a link between the two tables. This step is covered in detail later in this chapter, in the section entitled "Establishing a Link between Related Tables." But first you need to understand what types of relational models exist.

Looking at the Types of Relational Models

Depending on the data you're working with, you can set up one of several different relational database models. In each of these models, however, you need to differentiate between a *child* table (also called a *dependent* table or a *controlled* table) and a *parent* table (also called a *primary* table or a *controlling* table). The child table is the one that is dependent on the parent table to fill in the definition of its records. The CONTACTS table, for example, is a child table because it depends on the COMPANY table for the company information associated with each person.

Using the One-to-Many Model

The most common relational model is one in which a single record in the parent table relates to multiple records in the child table. This model is called a *one-to-many* relationship. The sales leads example is a one-to-many relation because one record in the COMPANY table can relate to many records in the CONTACTS table (that is, you can have multiple sales contacts from the same firm). In these models, the "many" table is the one to which you add the foreign key.

Another example of a one-to-many relationship would be an application that tracks accounts receivable invoices. You would need one table for the invoice data (INVOICES.DBF) and another for the customer data (CUSTOMER.DBF). In this case, one customer can place many orders, so CUSTOMER is the parent table, INVOICES is the child table, and the common field would be the CUSTOMER table's primary key.

Using the One-to-One Model

If your data requires that one record in the parent table be related to only one record in the child table, you have a *one-to-one* model. The most common use for one-to-one relations is to create separate entity classes to enhance security. In a hospital, for example, each patient's data is a single entity class, but it makes sense to create separate tables for the patient's basic information (such as the name, address, and so on) and the patient's medical history. This design enables you to add extra levels of security to the confidential medical data. The two tables could then be related based on a common "patient ID" key field.

Another example of a one-to-one model would be employee data. You would separate the less-sensitive information such as job title and start-up date into one table, and restricted information such as salary and commissions into a second table (with the appropriate security measures in place). If each employee has a unique identification number, you would use that number to set up a relationship between the two tables.

Note that in a one-to-one model the concepts of *child* and *parent* tables are interchangeable. Each table relies on the other to form the complete picture of each patient or employee.

Using the Many-to-Many Model

In some cases, many records in one table might relate to many records in another table. This situation is called a *many-to-many* relationship. In this case, you have no direct way to establish a common field between the two tables. To see why, return to the accounts receivable application.

Table 12.6 shows a simplified structure for the table of invoice data (INVOICES.DBF). It includes a primary key—INVOICE_ID—as well as a foreign key—CUST_ID—from a separate table of customer information (which you can ignore in this example).

Table 12.6 The Table Structure for INVOICES.DBF

Name	Type	Width	Index	Description
INVOICE_ID	Numeric	5	Ascend	The primary key
CUST_ID	Numeric	5	Ascend	The foreign key from the table of customer data

Table 12.7 shows a stripped-down structure for a table of product information. It includes a primary key field—PRODUCT_ID—and a description field—PRODUCT.

Table 12.7 The Table Structure for PRODUCTS.DBF

Name	Type	Width	Index	Description
PRODUCT_ID	Character	5	Ascend	The primary key
PRODUCT	Character	5	None	The product description

The idea here is that a given product can appear in many invoices, and any given invoice might contain many products. This relationship is a many-to-many relation, and it implies that *both* tables are parents (or to put it another way, neither table is directly dependent on the other). But relational theory says that a child table is needed to establish a common field. In this case, the solution is to set up a third table—called a *relation table*—that is the child of both the original tables. In the invoice example, the relation table would contain the detail data for each invoice. Table 12.8 shows the structure for such a table. As you can see, the table includes foreign keys from both INVOICES (INVOICE_ID) and PRODUCTS (PRODUCT_ID), as well as a QUANTITY field. Figure 12.2 shows some sample data for these three tables as well as the relationships among them.

Table 12.8 The Table Structure for DETAILS.DBF

Name	Type	Width	Index	Description
INVOICE_ID	Numeric	5	Ascend	The foreign key from the INVOICES table
PRODUCT_ID	Character	5	Ascend	The foreign key from the PRODUCTS table
QUANTITY	Numeric	5	None	The quantity ordered

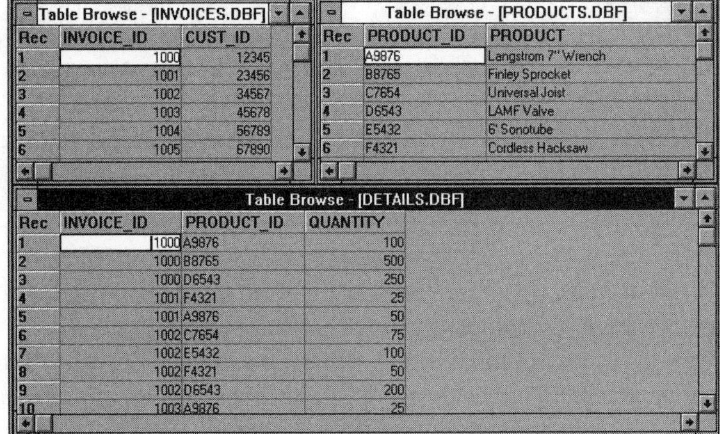
Table Browse - [INVOICES.DBF]

Rec	INVOICE_ID	CUST_ID
1	1000	12345
2	1001	23456
3	1002	34567
4	1003	45678
5	1004	56789
6	1005	67890

Table Browse - [PRODUCTS.DBF]

Rec	PRODUCT_ID	PRODUCT
1	A9876	Langstrom 7" Wrench
2	B8765	Finley Sprocket
3	C7654	Universal Joist
4	D6543	LAMF Valve
5	E5432	6' Sonotube
6	F4321	Cordless Hacksaw

Table Browse - [DETAILS.DBF]

Rec	INVOICE_ID	PRODUCT_ID	QUANTITY
1	1000	A9876	100
2	1000	B8765	500
3	1000	D6543	250
4	1001	F4321	25
5	1001	A9876	50
6	1002	C7654	75
7	1002	E5432	100
8	1002	F4321	50
9	1002	D6543	200
10	1003	A9876	25

Fig. 12.2
These three tables are connected in a many-to-many relation.

Establishing a Link Between Related Tables

Okay, you've carefully separated your data into multiple tables, established each table's parent and child roles, and added foreign keys to the appropriate file structures. Is that it? Are you relational yet? Well, close, but no cigar. dBASE for Windows doesn't assume a relationship between two files just because they have a common field. You have to combine the tables in a query and then establish a *link* between the tables.

Creating a Multiple-Table Query

◄ "Defining and Using a Basic Query," p. 172

The first thing you need to do is start a new query and load the tables you need. Follow these steps:

1. Start a new query by selecting Queries in the Navigator and then double-clicking the Untitled icon.

2. In the Open Table Required dialog box that appears, select the relation's parent table, and then choose OK.

3. Open the **Q**uery menu, and choose the **A**dd Table command; or click the Add Table button in the SpeedBar.

4. In the Open Table Required dialog box, select the relation's child table, and choose OK. dBASE for Windows displays both file skeletons in the Query Design window, as shown in figure 12.3.

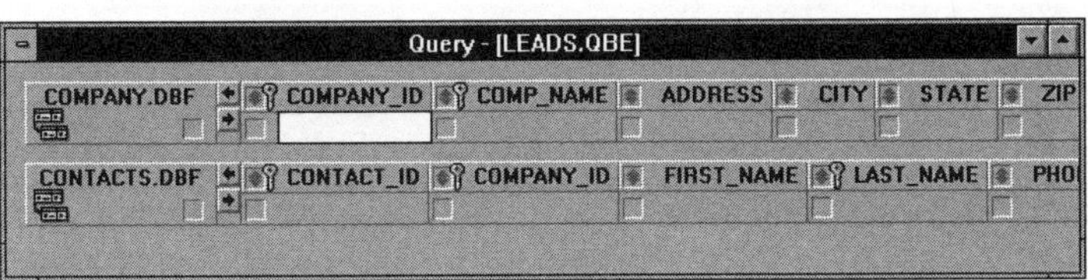

Fig. 12.3
The Query Design window shows two file skeletons.

5. Repeat steps 3 and 4 to add more tables to the query if necessary.

Linking the Tables

With your parent and child tables in the query, you now establish the link between the tables by identifying the common field used in your relation. dBASE for Windows gives you three methods from which to choose:

- Move the mouse pointer over the parent table's icon, and drag it to the icon for the child table. As you drag, the mouse pointer changes to the Create Link pointer shown in figure 12.4. You also see a line connecting the two icons.

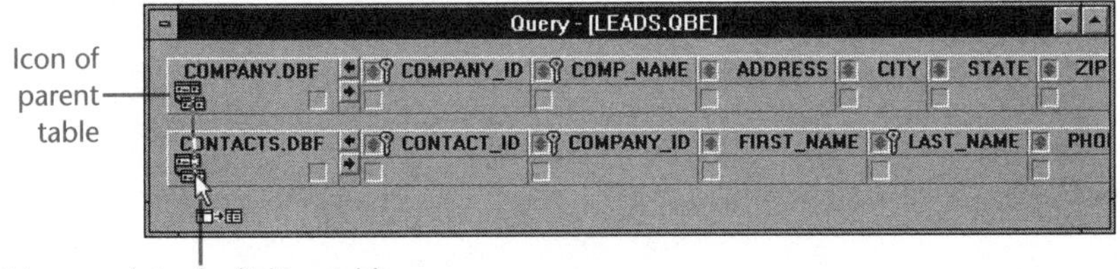

Fig. 12.4
As you drag the mouse, the pointer changes to the Create Link pointer seen in this screen.

- Activate any field in the parent table, open the **Q**uery menu, and choose **S**et Relation.

- Activate any field in the parent table, and click the Set Relation button in the SpeedBar.

Whichever method you use, you then see the Define Relation dialog box shown in figure 12.5.

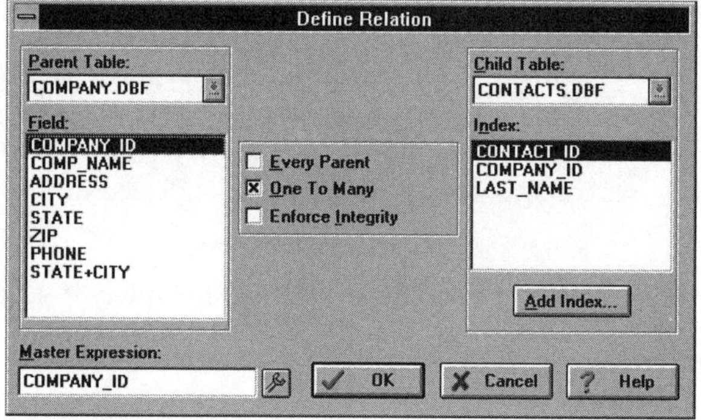

Fig. 12.5
Use the Define Relation dialog box to specify the fields to use in the link and the type of link.

Use the following steps to complete this dialog box:

1. Use the **P**arent Table drop-down list to select the parent table, if necessary.
2. In the **F**ield list, select the parent table field to use for the link. The field name appears in the **M**aster Expression text box.
3. If necessary, use the **C**hild Table drop-down list to select the child table.
4. In the I**n**dex list, select the corresponding linking field from the child table.
5. Choose OK to establish the link.

When you return to the Query Designer window, you see an arrow pointing from the parent table to the child table, as shown in figure 12.6. This arrow tells you that the two tables are linked on the common field.

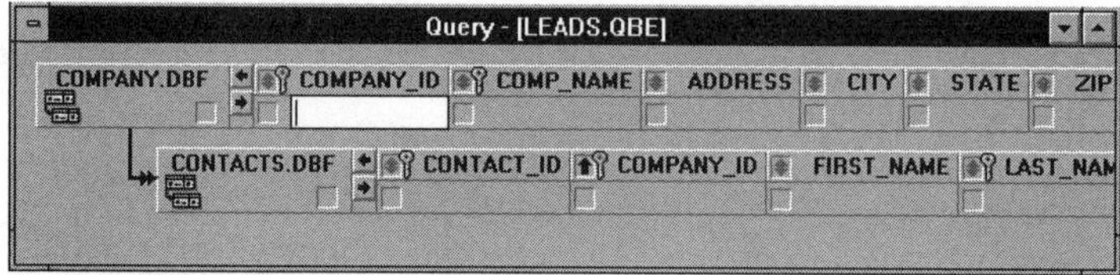

Fig. 12.6
dBASE for Windows identifies linked tables with an arrow joining the parent and child.

You also can relate tables from the Command window by using the SET RELATION TO command. First open both tables as follows:

- Open the parent table in the current work area (or open the parent table in a different work area, and then SELECT that work area).
- Open the child table in a different work area, and set its index tag to the tag used for the relation.

Now run the SET RELATION TO command, using the following syntax:

```
SET RELATION TO [<mast exp> INTO <alias 1> [ADDITIVE]]
```

Here, <mast exp> is the name of the field that is common to the parent and child tables. <alias> specifies the child table, using its alias name or its work area number. The ADDITIVE clause adds the new relation to any existing ones for the current table. If you don't use ADDITIVE, SET RELATION TO clears any existing relations before establishing the new relation.

The following commands, for example, open and link the COMPANY and CONTACTS tables:

▶ "Entering and Executing dBASE Commands," p. 568

```
CLOSE DATABASES
SELECT 1
USE COMPANY
USE CONTACTS IN 2 ORDER COMPANY_ID
SET RELATION TO COMPANY_ID INTO CONTACTS
```

To clear all relations for the current table, run SET RELATION TO without any arguments.

Linking More Than Two Tables

Linking three or more tables is, for the most part, a simple extension of two-table linking: you just add the other tables you need to the query and then drag the icons to create the links. Depending on the parent/child relationships between the tables, you could end up with one of the following three link types:

One of the tables is both a parent and a child. In this case, you use this table's parent to establish the first link, and then you link this table with its child. Figure 12.7, for example, shows a query in which the INVOICES table is both a child (to the CUSTOMER table, linked on the CUST_ID field) and a parent (to the DETAILS table, linked on the INVOICE_ID field).

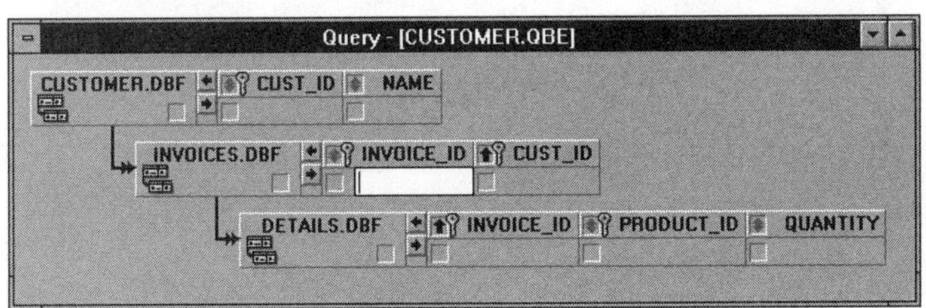

Fig. 12.7
In this query, one of the tables (INVOICES.DBF) is both a parent and a child.

One table is the parent of the other tables. In this case, you use the parent table as your basis for all the links. The query ends up looking something like the one shown in figure 12.8, where CUSTOMER is a parent to both INVOICES and SALESREP (both are linked on the CUST_ID field).

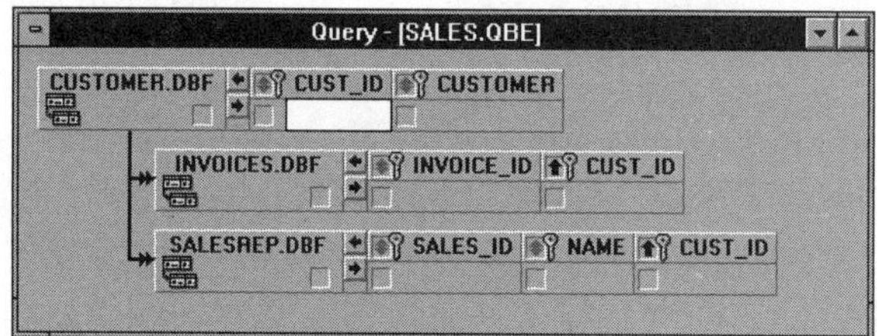

Fig. 12.8
In this query, one table (CUSTOMER.DBF) is a parent to the other tables.

One of the tables is a relation table. Many-to-many relationships are a little trickier only because dBASE for Windows handles them somewhat inconsistently. To see why, return to the previous example in which the INVOICES and PRODUCTS tables were related via the DETAILS relation table. Because INVOICES is a parent to DETAILS, you would begin by linking them on the INVOICE_ID field. PRODUCTS is also a parent to DETAILS, so you would think that you would be able to establish a link from PRODUCTS to INVOICES based on the PRODUCT_ID field. The problem is that dBASE for Windows doesn't enable a single table to be a child for two parents. Instead, you have to work backwards and use DETAILS as the parent to establish the link. Figure 12.9 shows the result. It works, but it's a little unintuitive.

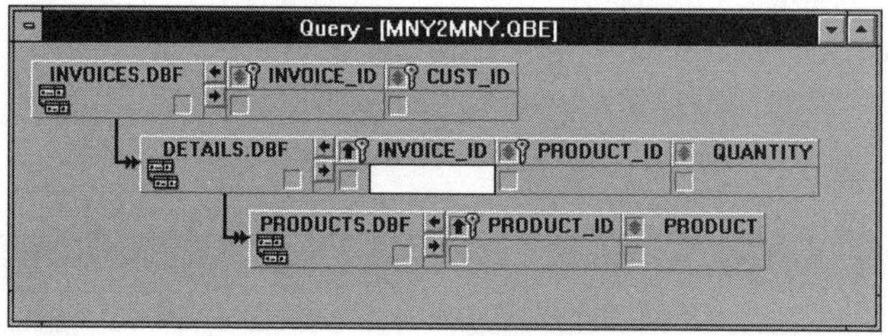

Fig. 12.9
In this query, which shows a many-to-many relation, the parent table PRODUCTS.DBF has to be used as a child to get the link to work.

◀ "Creating a Simple Index," p. 128

Troubleshooting

*The child table field I need for my link doesn't appear in the **In**dex list.*

If the correct linking field doesn't appear in the **In**dex list, you didn't index the field when you created the table. In this case, you can create the index from within the Define Link dialog box by choosing **A**dd Index. In the Create Index dialog box that appears, enter the appropriate index information, and then choose OK.

I have two tables that share a common field, but the field name in one table is different from the field name in the other table. Can I establish a link between these tables without renaming one of the fields?

Actually, dBASE for Windows doesn't require that the linking fields have the same name. As long as the fields use the same data type, you can link them without a problem.

I have a parent table that includes date information in character format and a child table that uses the normal date data type. Do I have to convert the character dates to link these fields?

Happily, no. The different data types means that you can't link these fields directly, but you *can* link them based on an expression. In this case, assuming that the parent table's date information is stored in a field named DATE, you would link the tables with the expression CTOD(DATE). (CTOD( ) is the dBASE for Windows function that converts a character value to a date value.) See "Using a Master Expression to Define a Relation" later in this chapter.

When I try to create a relation, dBASE for Windows displays an error message telling me that it can't define a "cyclic relation." What am I doing wrong?

A cyclic relation is a relation from a child table back into its parent table—a dBASE for Windows no-no.

Working with a Multiple-Table Query

◀ "Changing the Order of Fields and Records," p.177

◀ "Using a Query to Select Records," p. 181

After you have established your link, you can treat the linked tables as though they were one large table. You can add any field from the parent or child table to the view (although, typically, you won't add redundant linked fields to the view); you can index the query; you can create field expressions; you can copy the view to a new table; and so on. In fact, anything you can do in a regular, single-table query, you also can do in a multiple-table query.

When you're ready to view the combined data from the related tables, open the **V**iew menu, and choose Query **R**esults. Alternatively, you can click the Run Query button in the Query Design SpeedBar. Figure 12.10 shows a view that combines the FIRST_NAME and LAST_NAME fields from the CONTACTS table with the COMP_NAME and ADDRESS fields from the COMPANY table.

Fig. 12.10
This view combines fields from both the CONTACTS and COMPANY tables.

Query Results Browse - [LEADS.QBE]

Rec	FIRST_NAME	LAST_NAME	COMP_NAME	ADDRESS
3	Martin	Bajhu	Advantage Computer School	575 Howell Ln.
3	Chuck	Haddad		
3	Martin	Daniels		
4	George	Alviston	American Forum	928 Shagbark System Court
5	Randy	Flood	Aspen Planning & Inc.	41 Wept Drive 6086
6	Ardew	Haldeman	Automated Mayo Miley	229 Drank Suite 43
7	Mikey	Rasmussen	Balance Computing Systems	201 Nutate Court
7	Martha	Madarasz		
7	Dorit	Springer		
7	Billy	Barba		
11	James	Davis	Brown Designs	2 Phase Place
12	Randal	Fox	C & S Computing & Systems	20 Lachesis Blvd.
13	Reid	Harrell	California Beauty Inc.	900 Tenable Court
14	Casimiro	Hedgep	Carolina Systems	5 Mention Trail
14	Lori	Tartaglio		
14	Gene	Flower		
14	Rich	Chemeff		

Controlling the Records That Appear in the View

By default, dBASE for Windows assumes that you want to see every record in the child table that has a corresponding match (based on the common field) in the parent table, and vice versa. This assumption, however, might not produce the results you want. Suppose, for example, that you've linked a customer table (the parent) and an orders table (the child). Instead of seeing just those customers who have placed orders, you might want to see *every* customer.

You can control the records that appear in the view by using the following two options in the Define Relation dialog box:

Every Parent. If you activate this check box, dBASE for Windows includes every record from the parent table in the view. If you deactivate this check box (the default), only parent records that are linked to the child table appear.

One To Many. When this option is checked (the default), dBASE for Windows includes in the view every child record that is linked to a record in the parent table. If you uncheck this option, only the first child record for each matching parent record is shown in the view.

Using a Master Expression to Define a Relation

All relations are defined by a *master expression*. In most cases, this expression is simply the name of the common field. This expression is what appears in the **M**aster Expression text box in the Define Link dialog box after you select a parent table field. Often, however, just the field name is not enough to define the relation properly. The most common example is when the linking fields in the parent and child use a different data type. You may want to link on an account number field, for instance, but the parent table's ACCT_NUM field is stored in numeric format, and the child's CUST_NUM field is stored as characters. In this case, you would enter the following expression in the **M**aster Expression text box to define the relation:

```
STR(ACCT_NUM)
```

▶ "Using the Expression Builder," p. 283

This expression converts the parent's ACCT_NUM field to a string.

Another situation where the master expression comes in handy is when the data in the parent and child tables uses a different structure. For example, suppose you have a parent EMPLOYEE table with an EMP_ID field. This field contains each employee's identification number, which consists of a four-digit number followed by a division code (for example, 1234SALES). Suppose further that each division keeps a table of its own employees, and that in these tables the EMP_ID field uses only the four-digit number for each employee. In this case, you would use the following master expression to relate these tables:

```
LEFT(EMPLOYEE->EMP_ID,4)
```

For this to work properly, the EMP_ID field in the division tables must be four characters wide.

Making Changes to a Relation

After you've set up a link, you're free to make changes to the relation at any time. You might, for example, want to change the type of link or the master expression. To make changes to a relation, follow these steps:

1. Select a field in the child table's skeleton.
2. Open the **Q**uery menu, and choose **M**odify Relation.
3. In the Define Relation dialog box that appears, make your changes to the link.
4. Choose OK to return to the Query Designer window.

Removing a Relation

If you no longer need to work with the parent and child link, you can remove the relation from the query. Follow these steps:

1. Select a field in the child table's skeleton.

2. Open the **Q**uery menu, and choose R**e**move Relation, or click the Remove Relation button in the SpeedBar. dBASE for Windows removes the relation.

Note

You can, if you prefer, remove an entire table instead of just the relation from the query. To do so, select any field within the table, open the **Q**uery menu, and choose **R**emove Selected Table. You also can click the Remove Selected Table button in the SpeedBar.

Enforcing Referential Integrity

Database applications that work with multiple, related tables need to worry about enforcing *referential integrity rules*. These rules ensure that related tables remain in a consistent state relative to each other. In the sales leads application, for example, suppose that the COMPANY table includes an entry for "ACME Coyote Supplies" and that the CONTACTS table contains three leads who work for ACME. What would happen if you deleted the ACME Coyote Supplies record from the COMPANY table? Well, the three records in the CONTACTS table would no longer be related to any record in the COMPANY table. Child table records without corresponding records in the parent table are called, appropriately enough, *orphans*. This situation leaves your tables in an inconsistent state that could have unpredictable consequences.

Preventing orphaned records is what is meant by enforcing referential integrity. You need to watch out for two situations:

- Deleting a parent table record that has related records in a child table
- Adding a child table record that isn't related to a record in the parent table (either because the common field contains no value or it contains a value that doesn't correspond to any record in the parent table)

The good news is that dBASE for Windows can enforce referential integrity automatically. All you have to do is activate the Enforce **I**ntegrity check box in the Define Relation dialog box. dBASE for Windows will then warn you if you attempt an operation that will violate the integrity of the relation. For example, if you try to delete a parent record that has corresponding child records, you'll see the Alert box shown in Figure 12.11. In this case, select Yes to also delete the corresponding child records (this is called a *cascade delete*).

Fig. 12.11 dBASE for Windows displays an Alert box when you try to delete a parent record that has corresponding child records.

From Here...

If you want more information on database design, queries, expressions, or working with multiple tables, read the following chapters:

- Chapter 5, "Designing a Database," gives you the nitty-gritty on planning, designing, and building databases and tables.
- Chapter 9, "Creating Basic Queries," gives you a refresher course on query basics. You learn the layout of the Query Designer land, how to create single-table queries, how to select fields, how to add conditions, and more.
- Chapter 13, "Using the Expression Builder," helps you learn all about dBASE for Windows expressions and how to use the Expression Builder to create expressions effortlessly.
- Chapter 15, "Designing Advanced Forms," shows you how to incorporate multiple tables into a single form. This approach is a perfect way to view one-to-many relationships because the "one" side can be shown as the form fields, and the "many" side can be shown as a Browse object.
- Chapter 16, "Designing Advanced Reports," shows you how to generate relation reports based on multiple tables.

Chapter 13

Using the Expression Builder

Expressions crop up all the time in dBASE for Windows. The following list describes just a few of the areas where expressions make themselves useful:

- In the Query Designer, you can use expressions to add criteria, calculated fields, and conditions to the query.
- Indexes are defined by a tag expression.
- When you create forms and reports, you can use expressions to add calculated fields.
- Table relations are defined by a master expression.
- In Find and Replace operations, you can add an expression to narrow the focus of your search.
- You can use expressions to define subsets of records when you're sorting, deleting, recalling, or counting records, or when you're performing field calculations.
- When you're importing or exporting records, you can use an expression to define which records you want to handle.

As you can see, expressions are at the heart of dBASE for Windows; an understanding of expressions can, at the very least, make your dBASE life easier and more productive. This chapter takes you through the fundamentals of expressions, beginning with a basic tour: the definition of an expression, the elements in an expression, the different expression types, and so on. Then the chapter explains how to use what may be the handiest feature in dBASE for

Windows: the Expression Builder. This tool enables you to construct expressions piece-by-piece, test them to see whether they work properly, and then paste them into dBASE for Windows.

In this chapter, you learn about the following topics:

- Understanding expressions and what you can do with them
- Starting the Expression Builder
- Understanding the Expression Builder layout
- Creating and editing expressions
- Working with the Safety Net

What Is an Expression?

An *expression*, in simplest terms, is any combination of dBASE for Windows elements (such as field names, mathematical operators, and functions) that evaluates to a single value. An expression, in other words, is the database equivalent of a spreadsheet formula.

Like formulas, you can divide the components of an expression into two categories: operands and operators. An *operand* is the data the expression manipulates. An operand can be a field name, a constant, a function, a memory variable, or even another expression. An *operator* is the element that combines the operands mathematically or logically. If an expression is like a manufacturing process, then the operands are the raw materials that go into the process, and the operator is the method used to work with these materials to produce the final result.

This result can be a character, numeric, logical, or date value; keep in mind that you must remember the data type of the result when constructing your expressions. For example, if you will use your expression to index a character field, the expression must evaluate to a character data type. Note that only the data type of the *result* is important; you're free to mix and match data types within the expression to get the result you want.

The next few sections take a closer look at operands and operators in dBASE for Windows.

Field Names

Field names (along with constants) are perhaps the most common operands in dBASE for Windows expressions. The simplest expressions consist of a single field name. For example, when you index a field, the tag expression is just the field name itself. Similarly, when you relate two tables, the relation's master expression is the name of the field the two tables have in common.

More complex examples include adding two fields together (for example, PRICE + TAX), multiplying a field by a constant (for example, PRICE * 0.07), and using a field as a function argument (for example, STR(TOTAL)).

◀ "Creating a Simple Index," p. 128

◀ "Using a Master Expression to Define a Relation ," p. 279

Constants

A *constant* is a value that doesn't change from one iteration of the formula to the next. For example, consider the following expression that calculates the tax of an item based on the value in a PRICE field:

```
PRICE * 0.07
```

Here, the value of PRICE varies depending on the current record, but the multiplier—0.07—remains the same, making it a constant. (Constants also are called *literals* because they don't represent something else, the way a field name or variable does; with a constant, what you see really is what you get.)

Constants come in four types: *character, numeric, date,* and *logical.*

Character Constants

Character constants (or *strings*) consist of a series of zero or more characters surrounded by *delimiters* that define the beginning and ending of the constant. dBASE for Windows supports three types of delimiters: single quotation mark ('), double quotation mark ("), and square brackets ([and]). The following lines show some sample character constants using each type of delimiter:

```
'Poobah'
"Error occurred!"
[Smith]
```

Tip

A character constant with zero characters is called a *null string,* which often is used to clear fields or memory variables.

Caution

To avoid errors, don't mix delimiters in the same string. If you begin a string with, for example, a single quotation mark, you must also close the string with a single quotation mark.

Single quotation marks are used most often perhaps only because they boast the convenience of a single keystroke (double quotation marks need the assistance of the Shift key, and the square brackets are spread over two keys).

The CHR( ) function in dBASE for Windows enables you to use characters other than those you see on your keyboard. Specifically, you use CHR(<expN>) to display symbols from the ASCII character set where <expN> is a number between 0 and 255. The values 33 through 126 represent the usual keyboard characters, and the remaining values give you symbols of varying usefulness. Table 13.1 lists a few symbols you may need on occasion.

Table 13.1 Some Symbols from the ASCII Character Set

Value	Symbol
CHR(155)	¢
CHR(156)	£
CHR(157)	¥
CHR(171)	Ω
CHR(172)	º
CHR(246)	_

Tip

You can also enter ANSI characters in an expression by holding down Alt and entering the ANSI code using the numeric keypad. For example, Alt+155 gives you the ¢ symbol.

You also can use CHR(7) to beep your computer's speaker.

Numeric Constants

Numeric constants are, as you may expect, just numbers (integers and floating point values); you have no delimiters to worry about, but you must remember a few simple rules when using numeric constants:

- Don't use extra symbols such as a dollar sign ($) or a percent sign (%). Also, don't use a comma as a thousands separator (for example, enter **1234** and not **1,234**).
- You can use scientific notation for large numbers. For example, you can enter the number 3,456,000,000 as **3.456E+09**.
- Use a minus sign (–) to represent negative numbers (for example, –57).

Date Constants

Date constants are similar to character constants in that you must surround them with delimiters. In this case, you use braces ({ and }) to delimit a date constant:

```
DUE_DATE = {7/8/94}
```

The tricky part is how dBASE for Windows interprets the numbers and separators inside the braces. Most Americans read 7/8/94 as July 8, 1994. Many Canadians and Europeans, however, read the date as August 7, 1994. A Japanese may read this as the absurd date August 94th in the year 7! How does dBASE for Windows read this date? The answer depends, first of all, on the date format specified in the International settings of the Windows Control Panel (see fig. 13.1). This setting is the default used by dBASE for Windows.

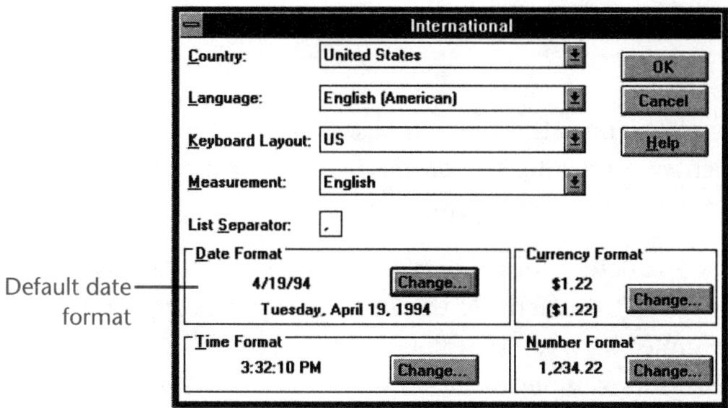

Fig. 13.1
The format selected in Control Panel's International settings determines the default date format in dBASE for Windows.

You can override the default format by making a change to the Desktop Properties dialog box. Open the **P**roperties menu, choose **D**esktop, and then select the Country tab in the Desktop Properties dialog box (see fig. 13.2).

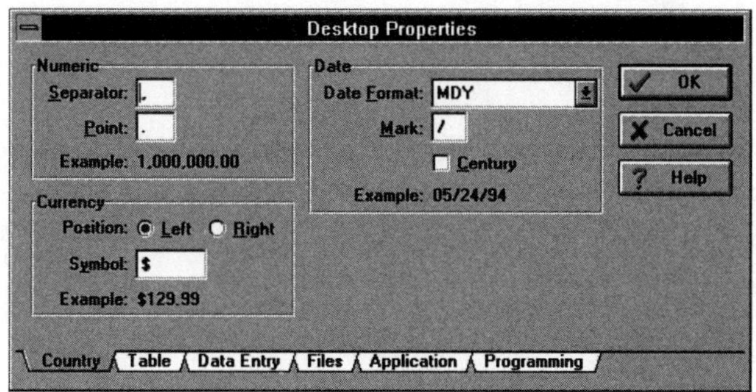

Fig. 13.2
Use the Country tab in the Desktop Properties dialog box to override the default date format in dBASE for Windows.

The Date **F**ormat drop-down list contains the six date formats recognized by dBASE for Windows. Table 13.2 summarizes each of the available formats.

Table 13.2 dBASE for Windows Date Formats

Name	Format
GERMAN	DD.MM.YY
JAPAN	YY/MM/DD
USA	MM-DD-YY
YMD	YY/MM/DD
MDY	MM/DD/YY
DMY	DD/MM/YY

The **M**ark text box determines the character used to separate the day, month, and year components in the date. The dashes (—) are the default, but periods (.) and forward slashes (/) also are common.

The **C**entury check box determines how dBASE for Windows displays the year component of the date. If you activate this check box, dates appear with four-digit years (for example, 8/23/1994); if you deactivate the box, dates appear with two-digit years (for example, 8/23/94).

Note

dBASE for Windows assumes that any date entered with a two-digit year is a date in the 20th century. If you enter **{8/23/01}**, dBASE for Windows stores the constant as August 23, 1901. If you really mean August 23, 2001, enter the date as **{8/23/2001}**.

Logical Constants

Logical values are the simplest of the literals because they have no delimiters and only four possible values exist: .T. and .Y. (or .t. and .y.) represent true; .F. and .N. (or .f. and .n.) represent false.

Troubleshooting

When I use character constants, dBASE for Windows sometimes reports a `Variable undefined` *or* `Unallowed phrase/keyword` *error. What's the problem?*

One possible cause for these errors is that you accidentally included one of the string delimiters in your constant. For example, consider the following string:

```
'What's the proper noun for a collection of crows?'
```

When dBASE for Windows evaluates a string, it begins with the first delimiter and then reads all the characters until the next instance of the same delimiter. In the preceding example, dBASE for Windows extracts only `What` as the string, and the rest of the line generates an error message. You can avoid this error by delimiting the constant with a different character than the one you need to embed in the string. The preceding example would work properly if you entered it using the double quotation mark delimiters, as this string shows:

```
"What's the proper noun for a collection of crows?"
```

You can use this same idea to embed other delimiters in a character constant:

```
'A "murder" is a collection of crows.'
[What's the word for rhinos? Why, a "crash," of course.]
```

I'm using the MDY date format and I accidentally entered a date as {1/32/94}. Why didn't dBASE for Windows produce an error?

The reason is that dBASE for Windows coerces erroneous dates into legitimate ones. In your case, dBASE converted 1/32/94 to 2/1/94, because February 1 is the "32nd" day of January. This feature can be annoying because you often miss the improper entry.

Functions

Like an expression, a *function* also takes input values (called *arguments*) and returns a result (which can be of character, numeric, date, or logical type). You can think of a function as a kind of "black-box" expression where you toss in one or more values and it spits out a particular answer. dBASE for Windows has hundreds of predefined functions that cover everything from data conversion to string manipulation.

The Structure of a Function

Every dBASE for Windows function has the same basic form:

```
FUNCTION(<argument1>, <argument2>, ...)
```

The function begins with the function name (for example, STR, DBF), followed by a list of *arguments* enclosed in parentheses. As mentioned earlier, the arguments are the function's inputs—the data it uses to perform its calculations.

For example, the SUBSTR( ) function extracts characters from a string based on three arguments:

```
SUBSTR(<expC>,<expN1>[,<expN2>])
```

The first argument—<expC>—represents the string from which the function extracts the characters (this argument may be a character field, a memo field, or a string variable). <expN1> is a number that specifies the starting point of the extraction. <expN2> is a number that specifies the number of characters to extract.

Note

To make command and function syntax easier to read, dBASE for Windows employs a modified version of the Backus/Naur Format (BNF). This format uses the following notation:

- Command and function elements (such as arguments and parameters) are usually enclosed in angle brackets: <argument>. (Although, as you see later in this chapter, dBASE for Windows leaves out the angle brackets in the Expression Builder.)
- If an element can be any expression, the abbreviation <exp> is normally used. If the element requires an expression to be a particular data type, dBASE for Windows uses the following codes: <expC> for a character expression; <expN> for a numeric expression; <expD> for a date expression; <expL> for a logical expression.
- Elements surrounded by square brackets ([and]) are optional.
- The vertical bar (|) denotes the word *or*. For example, <expC>|<memo field> means you can use a character expression *or* a memo field for this element.

For example, suppose that a table contains a PART_CODE field that consists of a three-digit number followed by a three-letter code. If you're interested in extracting the three-letter code to use in an expression, the following SUBSTR( ) function would do the job:

```
SUBSTR(PART_CODE,4,3)
```

If the current record contains *123ABC* in the PART_CODE field, the preceding function extracts *ABC*.

Rules for Entering Functions

You enter functions as you do any other data; however, you need to follow these rules:

- Type function names entirely in uppercase—this method is standard practice.
- Always enclose the function arguments in parentheses.
- Always separate multiple arguments with commas.

If you use the Expression Builder (as described later in this chapter), these conventions are handled automatically.

dBASE for Windows Function Categories

dBASE for Windows has 24 function categories. Space limitations prevent detailed explanations, but table 13.3 summarizes each category so you have some idea of what to expect.

Table 13.3 The dBASE for Windows Function Categories

Category	Purpose of Functions
Colors and fonts	Work with the dBASE for Windows colors and fonts. For example, the ISCOLOR( ) function returns .T. if the current monitor is color, and .F. if it is monochrome.
Data type conversion	Convert data from one type to another. For example, STR(<expN>) converts <expN> to a string. Similarly, VAL(<expC>) converts <expC> to a number.
Date and time data	Return, set, and work with dates and times. For example, the DATE( ) function returns the current date.
dBASE IV menus	Work with dBASE IV-style menus. PROMPT( ), for example, returns the prompt of the most recently selected dBASE IV menu item.
dBASE IV windows	Work with dBASE IV-style windows. The WINDOW( ) function, for example, returns the name of the active dBASE IV window.
Disk and file utilities	Manipulate files, directories, and disks. For example, DISKSPACE(<expN>) returns the number of bytes available on the drive specified by <expN> (where drive A is 1, drive B is 2, drive C is 3, and so on).
Environment	Monitor the dBASE for Windows environment. The MEMORY( ) function, for example, returns the number of bytes of free memory on your system.

(continues)

Table 13.3 Continued

Category	Purpose of Functions
Error handling	Trap and handle dBASE for Windows programming errors. For example, the ERROR( ) function returns the number of the most recent error.
Expressions	Work with dBASE for Windows expressions. For example, MAX(<exp1>,<exp2>) returns the greater of the two values <exp1> and <exp2>.
Fields and records	Work with and return information about the fields and records in a table. For example, ISBLANK(<exp>) returns .T. if <exp> is blank, and .F. otherwise.
Forms	Work with dBASE for Windows forms. The NEXTOBJ( ) function, for example, returns the name of the object that follows the current object in a form's tabbing order.
Input and output	Set up and manipulate input/output statements such as @...SAY and @...GET. For example, VARREAD( ) tells you the name of the input variable in the active @...GET.
Keyboard and mouse	Get mouse and keyboard information and read keystrokes. The ISMOUSE( ) function, for example, returns .T. if a mouse driver is present, and .F. otherwise.
Low-level access	Open, close, read from, and write to files directly from disk (files are not read into memory). For example, FOPEN(<expC1>,<expC2>) opens a low-level channel to the file name given by <expC1> with the file access given by <expC2> (such as *RW* for read-write access).
Memory variables	Declare and manipulate arrays and memory variables. The AFIELDS(<array name>) function, for example, stores the current table's structure data in the array given by <array name> and returns the number of fields stored.
Numeric data	Perform mathematical and financial calculations. For example, MOD(<expN1>,<expN2>) calculates the remainder (the *modulus*) when you divide <expN1> by <expN2>. For instance, MOD(YEAR(DATE( )),4)) returns 0 if the current year is a leap year.
Objects	Work with and return information about objects. LISTCOUNT(<form name>,<list name>), for example, returns the number of items in the list given by <list name>.
Printing	Return printing information. For example, PRINTSTATUS([<expC>]) returns .T. if a printer port has been set with the SET PRINTER TO command.
Programs	Work with dBASE for Windows programming constructs. The IIF(<expL>,<exp1>,<exp2>) function returns either <exp1> or <exp2> depending on the result of the logical expression <expL>. If <expL> is .T., <exp1> is returned; if <expL> is .F., <exp2> is returned.

Category	Purpose of Functions
Shared data	Work with tables in a network environment. For example, NETWORK( ) returns .T. if dBASE for Windows is running on a network, and .F. otherwise.
String data	Manipulate string data. For example, the STR(<expN>) function discussed earlier converts <expN> to a 10-character string padded on the left with blanks (if necessary). To remove these blanks, use the LTRIM(<expC>|<memo field>) string function.
Table basics	Return information about dBASE for Windows tables. The DBF([<alias>]) function returns the name of the table in the current work area (or in the work area specified by <alias>).
Table organization	Work with table indexes, sorting, and queries. For example, SEEK(<expC>|<expN>,[<alias>]) searches for <expC> or <expN> in the index order of the current table (or the table in the work area specified by <alias>).
Windows programming	Include advanced Windows programming techniques in your dBASE for Windows programs. For example, BITAND(<expN1>,<expN2>) performs a bitwise AND operation on <expN1> and <expN2>.

Variables

A *variable* is a named area of memory you can use to store and retrieve values. When dBASE for Windows encounters a variable in an expression, it uses the variable's current value when calculating the expression result. Variables are used almost exclusively in programming, so this chapter does not discuss them in any detail. This section does explain, however, that the Expression Builder recognizes two kinds of variables: System and User.

System variables are declared by dBASE for Windows, and they control certain internal aspects of the program. For example, the variable _DBWINHOME holds the drive and directory where the dBASE for Windows system files are stored (C:\DBASEWIN\, by default). Similarly, CUROBJ holds the number of the form object that currently has the focus.

▶ "Creating Memory Variables," p. 618

User variables are ones you set up yourself. You normally set up these variables in the context of a dBASE for Windows program, but you also can assign values to variables in the Command window. For example, the following statement assigns today's date—as given by the DATE( ) function—to the variable CurrDate:

```
CurrDate = DATE( )
```

Operators

As mentioned earlier, operators specify the actions to be performed on the expression's operands. dBASE for Windows groups operators into four categories: *numeric, relational, logical,* and *character.*

Numeric Operators

The *numeric operators* are, for the most part, the familiar arithmetic symbols used in mathematics. Table 13.4 lists the dBASE for Windows numeric operators, some example statements you can enter into the Command window, and the results that appear in the Results window.

Table 13.4 The Numeric Operators

Operator	Name	Command Example	Result
+	Addition	? 10+5	15
–	Subtraction	? 10–5	5
–	Negation	? –10	–10
*	Multiplication	? 10*5	50
/	Division	? 10/5	2
^ or **	Exponentiation	? 10^5	100,000

Note

You can use the addition (+) and subtraction (–) operators on date values. For example, the expression DATE( )+30 returns a date 30 days from now. Similarly, {8/23/94}–{4/20/94} returns the number of days between April 20, 1994 and August 23, 1994.

Tip

If you need to control the order of your operators, you can use parentheses: (). See the "Operator Precedence" section, later in this chapter, for details.

Relational Operators

You use *relational operators* to build expressions that compare two or more numbers, text strings, fields, or function values. The result of the expression will be .T. (true) or .F. (false). Table 13.5 summarizes the dBASE for Windows relational operators.

Table 13.5 The Relational Operators

Operator	Name	Command Example	Result
=	Equal to	? 10=5	.F.
==	Exactly equal to	? "Smythe"=="Smyth"	.F.
>	Greater than	? 10>5	.T.
<	Less than	? 10<5	.F.
>=	Greater than or equal to	? "a">="b"	.F.
<=	Less than or equal to	? "a"<="b"	.T.
<> or #	Not equal to	? "a"<>"b"	.T.
$	Is contained in	? "tab" $ "database"	.T.

Note

Remember the following points when you use the relational operators to compare strings:

- String comparisons are case-sensitive. In particular, dBASE for Windows considers uppercase letters to be *less than* lowercase. The expression "A" < "a" produces a .T. result.

- The equal to operator (=) compares strings character-by-character from the left. The comparison returns .T. if no different characters are found *or* if the string on the right runs out of characters before a different character is found. For example, the expression "Smythe"="Smyth" returns a .T. result. On the other hand, the exactly equal to operator (==) pads the shorter string with blanks so both strings are of equal length and then compares them. Therefore, the expression "Smythe"=="Smyth" is equivalent to "Smythe"="Smyth " and produces an .F. result.

- The behavior of the equal to operator (=) is determined by the value of the SET EXACT setting. Open the Properties menu, choose Desktop, and then select the Table tab in the Desktop Properties dialog box. If you activate the Exact check box, the equal to operator will behave just like the exactly equal to operator. (You also can toggle this setting by entering **SET EXACT ON** or **SET EXACT OFF** in the Command window.)

Logical Operators

The *logical operators* are similar to the relational operators in that expressions are compared and a logical value (.T. or .F.) is returned. In this case, though, the expressions being compared are themselves logical expressions. Table 13.6 lists the three logical operators.

Table 13.6 The Logical Operators

Operator	Name	Example	Description
.AND.	Logical AND	<expL1> .AND. <expL2>	Returns .T. if both <expL1> and <expL2> are .T.; returns .F. otherwise.
.OR.	Logical OR	<expL1> .OR. <expL2>	Returns .T. if one or both of <expL1> and <expL2> are .T.; returns .F. if both are .F.
.NOT.	Logical NOT	.NOT. <expL>	Returns .T. if <expL> is .F.; returns .F. if <expL> is .T.

String Operators

The *string operators* are used to concatenate (combine) two character strings. Table 13.7 gives you the details.

Table 13.7 The String Operators

Operator	Name	Command Example	Result
+	Concatenate	? "Les "+"Nessman "	"Les Nessman "
–	Concatenate with trim	? "Les "–"Nessman "	"LesNessman "

The concatenate operator (+) simply joins the two strings and leaves any trailing spaces in either string intact. The concatenate with trim operator (–) removes the trailing spaces on both strings and tacks them on to the end of the second string.

Operator Precedence

Many expressions consist of just one or two operands and a single operator. However, you often may put together longer expressions that combine many operators and operands. In these more complex examples, the order in which the calculations are performed becomes crucial. For example, consider the expression *4+3^2*. If you calculate from left to right, the answer you get is 49 (4+3 equals 7 and 7^2 equals 49). However, if you perform the exponentiation first and then the addition, the result is 13 (3^2 equals 9 and 4+9 equals 13). Even a relatively simple expression such as this can produce multiple answers depending on the order in which you perform the calculations.

To avoid this multiple-answer problem, dBASE for Windows evaluates a formula according to a predefined *order of precedence*. This order of precedence enables dBASE for Windows to calculate a formula unambiguously by determining which part of the formula it calculates first, which part is second, and so on.

Reviewing the Order of Precedence

The order of precedence that dBASE for Windows uses is determined by the various formula operators examined earlier. Table 13.8 summarizes the order of precedence that dBASE for Windows uses.

Table 13.8 The dBASE for Windows Order of Precedence

Operator	Operation	Order of Precedence
–	Negation	1st
^ or **	Exponentiation	2nd
* and /	Multiplication and division	3rd
+ and –	Addition and subtraction	4th
+ and –	Concatenation	5th
= < > <= >= <> $	Relational	6th
.AND. .OR. .NOT.	Logical	7th

From this table, you can see that dBASE for Windows performs exponentiation before addition. Therefore, the correct answer for the expression *4+3^2* is 13. Notice, as well, that some operators in table 13.8 have the same order of precedence (for example, multiplication and division); the order in which these operators are evaluated doesn't matter.

Controlling the Order of Precedence

Sometimes you may need to override the order of precedence. For example, suppose that you want to create an expression that calculates the pretax cost of an item. Consider an item you bought for $10.65, including 7% sales tax. To get the cost of the item less the tax, you use the expression *10.65/1.07*, which gives you the correct answer of $9.95. In general, the formula is as follows:

$$\text{Pretax Cost} = \frac{\text{Total Cost}}{1 + \text{Tax Rate}}$$

Suppose that you have the total cost in a field named TOTAL_COST and the tax rate in a field named TAX_RATE. Given these fields, your first instinct may be to use the following expression to calculate the pretax cost:

```
TOTAL_COST/1 + TAX_RATE
```

This expression, however, produces an incorrect result. Why? According to the rules of precedence, dBASE for Windows performs division before addition, so the value in TOTAL_COST is first divided by 1 and then added to the value in TAX_RATE. To get the correct answer, you need to override the order of precedence so the addition 1 + TAX_RATE is performed first. Surround that part of the formula with parentheses, as shown here:

```
TOTAL_COST/(1 + TAX_RATE)
```

In general, you can use parentheses to group terms together and control the order that dBASE for Windows uses to calculate expressions. Terms inside the parentheses are always calculated first, followed by terms outside the parentheses.

Caution

One of the most common mistakes when using parentheses in expressions is forgetting to close a parenthetic term with a right parenthesis. If you omit a parenthesis, dBASE for Windows generates an `Unbalanced parentheses` error. To make sure you have closed each parenthetic term, count all your left and right parentheses. If these totals don't match, you know you have left out a parenthesis.

Starting the Expression Builder

dBASE for Windows has so many operand possibilities (especially all those functions!) and so many operators that constructing even simple expressions can slow you down if you're not sure about the appropriate syntax or arguments to use.

To make everyone's life easier, dBASE for Windows includes a handy new tool: the *Expression Builder*. This feature enables you to construct expressions from scratch by picking out the operands and operators you need from lists. They're all broken down by category and type so you easily can find what you need. You can even evaluate your expression to make sure it returns the result you want.

Note

If you want to edit an existing expression, highlight the expression before starting the Expression Builder. But don't bother with this step if you're starting Expression Builder from a text box that already contains an expression. dBASE for Windows loads the expression for you automatically.

To give the Expression Builder a whirl, start it by using one of the following methods:

- In a dialog box, click the Tool button beside any text box that accepts an expression (see fig. 13.3).

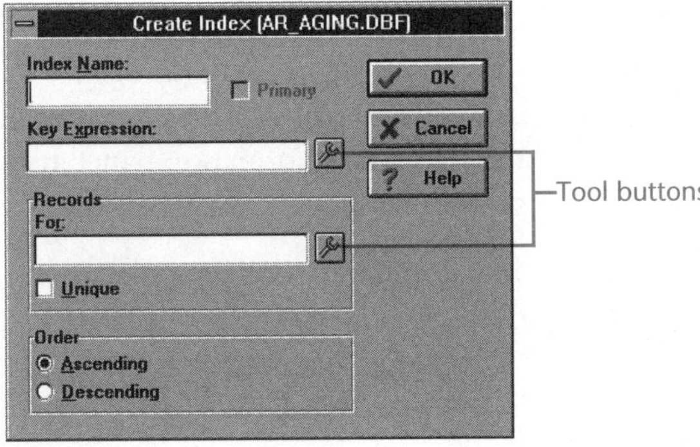

Fig. 13.3
In dialogs with text boxes that accept an expression, click the Tool button to display the Expression Builder.

- From the Command window or Text Editor, open the **E**dit menu and choose **B**uild Expression.

- Click the Expression Builder button in the Command window or Text Editor SpeedBar.

Whichever method you use, dBASE for Windows displays the Expression Builder dialog box, as shown in figure 13.4. (Depending on where you started from, the dialog box may be titled Create an Expression or Edit an Expression.)

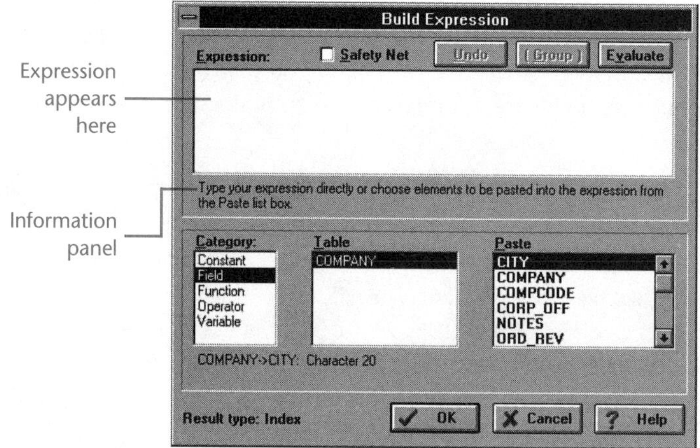

Fig. 13.4
Use the Expression Builder dialog box to create and edit dBASE for Windows expressions.

Reviewing the Expression Builder Dialog Box

Tip
You also can start the Expression Builder from the Command window or Text Editor by pressing Ctrl+E.

The Expression Builder is divided into the following four areas:

Expression This box is where you put together your expression. You can add and edit your own text or paste text from the **P**aste list. An information panel just below the **E**xpression box displays prompts and expression results.

Category This list contains the five kinds of elements you can include in an expression: Constant, Field, Function, Operator, and Variable. When you select a category, the values in the **T**ype and **P**aste lists change accordingly.

Type This box contains a list of subcategories for the item highlighted in the **C**ategory list. (If the selected category is Field, the name of this list box changes to **T**able.) For example, the Constant category has five subcategories: All, Character, Date, Logical, and Numeric. When you select a subcategory, the items in the **P**aste box change.

Paste — This box contains a list of the expression elements associated with the selected item in the **T**ype (or **T**able list). When you highlight an item in this list, dBASE for Windows displays, in most cases, a description of the item (and, if applicable, its syntax) in the information panel below the list boxes.

Note

If you select the Function category, notice that the **P**aste list seems to repeat some function names. For example, the list appears to contain two RECCOUNT( ) functions:

```
RECCOUNT
RECCOUNT.
```

The dot at the end of the second RECCOUNT tells you that this item uses a slightly different syntax. The first RECCOUNT represents the RECCOUNT( ) function that operates on the current table; the second represents the RECCOUNT(<alias>) function that operates on the table specified by the <alias> argument.

Some functions have more than two syntaxes. In these cases, the third syntax is represented by two dots, the fourth by three dots, and so on.

Building an Expression

Building an expression in the Expression Builder involves selecting elements from the list boxes and moving them into the **E**xpression area. You construct the expression one term at a time and then fill in the missing pieces (such as any constants you want to use).

Using the Basic Steps

Follow these steps to build a skeleton for your expression:

1. If you already have elements in the **E**xpression box, move the insertion point to where you want the next element to appear.

2. Use the **C**ategory list to select an element category.

3. Use the **T**ype list to select the type of element you need. If you chose the Field category in step 2, use the **T**able list to select the table with which you want to work. (The **T**able list only shows tables that were opened before you started the Expression Builder.)

Tip
You also can move an item into the **E**xpression box by double-clicking the item or by highlighting it and pressing the space bar.

4. In the **P**aste list, find the item you want to add to the expression and then drag it into the **E**xpression box.

5. Repeat steps 1–4 until you have all the elements you need for your expression.

Filling In the Expression Placeholders

After you have your expression skeleton in the **E**xpression box, you need to flesh it out by replacing any *placeholders* with actual data. These placeholders generally take one of two forms:

Tip
If you need to edit the expression, highlight the text and use the following shortcut keys: Ctrl+X to cut, Ctrl+C to copy, Ctrl+V to paste, and Ctrl+Z to undo.

- If you added a constant from the **P**aste list, dBASE for Windows inserts into the expression either the appropriate delimiters (for example, " " for character constants) or a sample value (for example, 0 for numeric constants). If delimiters were pasted, position the insertion point between the delimiters and type your constant; if a sample value was pasted, replace the value with the actual constant you want to use.

- If you added a function from the **P**aste list, dBASE for Windows inserts the function name followed by the argument syntax in parentheses. In this case, you need to replace the generic arguments with the actual data you want to use. Highlight the entire argument and then type the correct data or use the list boxes to select another expression element.

For example, figure 13.5 shows an expression where the first placeholder in the LEFT function (`expC ¦ memo field`) is about to be replaced by a field. Figure 13.6 shows the expression with all the placeholders replaced with actual data.

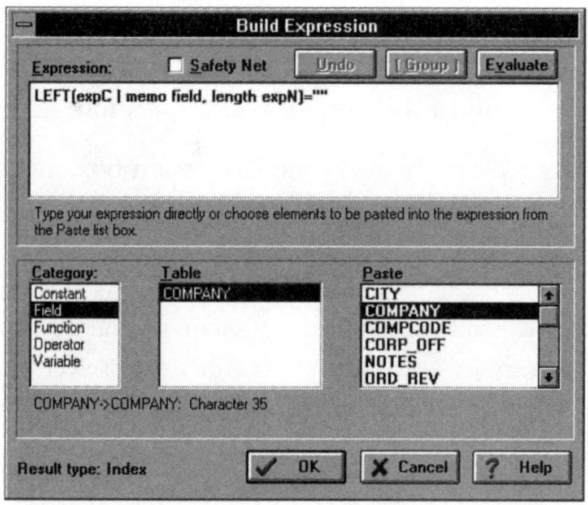

Fig. 13.5
An expression where a placeholder is about to be replaced by a field.

Caution

Make sure you replace each placeholder with a value that has the same data type as indicated by the placeholder. For example, an *expC* placeholder must be replaced by a character value.

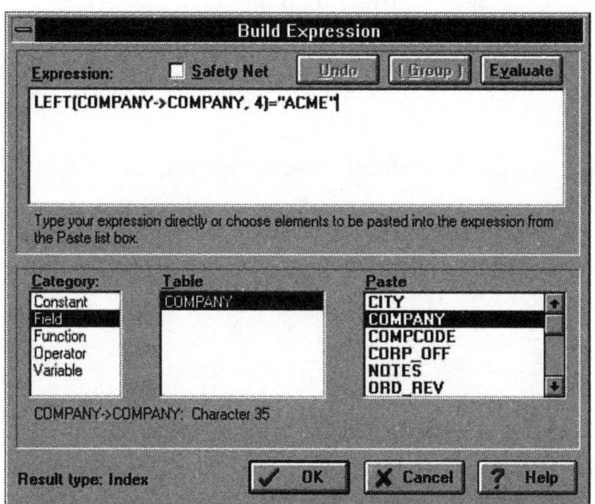

Fig. 13.6
The expression with all the placeholders replaced.

Working with a Net: Using the Safety Net

If you're unfamiliar with dBASE for Windows expressions and syntax, the Expression Builder can quickly become confusing as you try to get the expression elements in the right place and convert the placeholders to actual data. To help out, the Expression Builder offers a *Safety Net* feature that enables you to construct error-free expressions more easily. The following list describes some of the advantages you get with the Safety Net:

- The **E**xpression box insertion point moves only between elements rather than between individual characters, helping you to position the insertion point correctly.

- You can't type directly in the **E**xpression box. Instead, you can insert elements using only the **P**aste list, and you can add constants using only a separate text box. In either case, dBASE for Windows monitors what you add and checks the expression to make sure you maintain the correct syntax.

- When you add elements, dBASE for Windows uses color codes to signify the placeholders. In particular, operand placeholders (such as function arguments and constant values) appear in yellow text. If you happen to forget an operator, dBASE for Windows inserts an *Op* code in white text. Figure 13.7 shows an example.
- The information panel below the **E**xpression box tells you how many placeholders you have left to replace.
- dBASE for Windows will not let you choose the OK button until the expression is valid.
- You can use the **U**ndo button to reverse your most recent action.
- You can use the (**G**roup) button to add parentheses around selected elements to establish precedence.

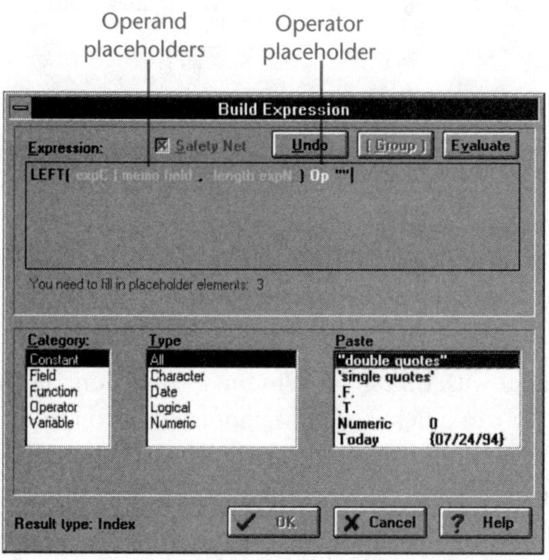

Fig. 13.7
With the Safety Net on, dBASE for Windows displays placeholders in yellow or white text.

Activating the Safety Net

To turn on the Safety Net, simply activate the **S**afety Net check box. The **E**xpression box background turns gray and the **U**ndo button becomes active (if, that is, the expression has anything to undo). If the **E**xpression box contains an invalid expression, the OK button dims.

> **Note**
>
> You can activate the Safety Net only if the **E**xpression box is empty or if it contains a valid expression.

Replacing Placeholders with the Safety Net Active

Filling in placeholders with the Safety Net uses slightly different techniques than the ones explained earlier.

If you're replacing a function argument, first click the argument. Depending on where you clicked, the insertion point moves to the left or right of the argument text (which side doesn't matter). Then select an expression element from the **P**aste list. dBASE for Windows replaces the argument with your selection.

Tip
The insertion point can be hard to see with the Safety Net on, so you also can select an argument by double-clicking it.

If you're filling in a constant, click the placeholder and start typing or just right-click the placeholder. In either case, dBASE for Windows displays a text box in which you type the constant you want to use (see fig. 13.8). Then press Enter.

To replace an operator placeholder, click `Op`, select Operator in the **C**ategory list, select a type from the **T**ype list, and then select an operator from the **P**aste list.

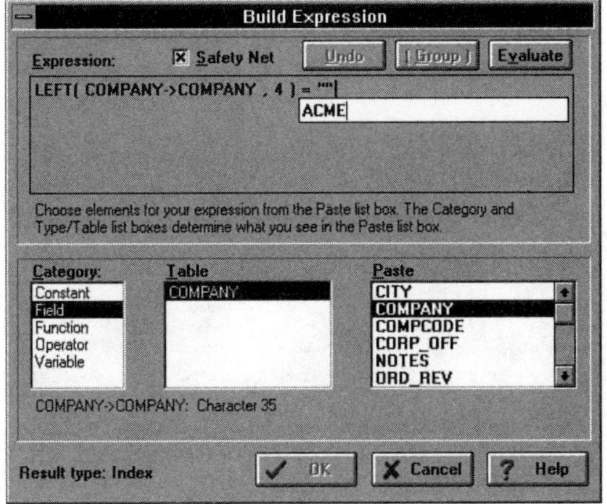

Fig. 13.8
dBASE for Windows displays a text box so you can type the value you want to use to fill in a constant placeholder.

II

Power Skills

Tip
As you replace the placeholders, keep an eye on the information panel below the **E**xpression box. The message updates with each replacement to let you know how many placeholders are left to fill in.

Grouping Elements to Establish Precedence

If the Safety Net is inactive, you establish precedence by surrounding the appropriate operands and operators with parentheses, as discussed earlier in this chapter. If the Safety Net is active, you can use the (**G**roup) button to establish precedence for part of the expression (that is, surround one or more elements with parentheses).

Begin by highlighting the elements you want to group together. Then choose the (**G**roup) button. dBASE for Windows surrounds the highlighted terms with parentheses.

Evaluating an Expression

To check your progress, you can ask dBASE for Windows to evaluate your expression. This review lets you know if the expression is calculating correctly and if the result is the correct type. To try this step, just choose the E**v**aluate button. dBASE for Windows displays the result in the information panel below the **E**xpression box. If the expression is valid, you see the value of the expression; otherwise, dBASE for Windows displays an error message (see fig. 13.9).

> **Note**
>
> If your expression includes a field, dBASE for Windows evaluates the expression based on the value of the field in the current record.

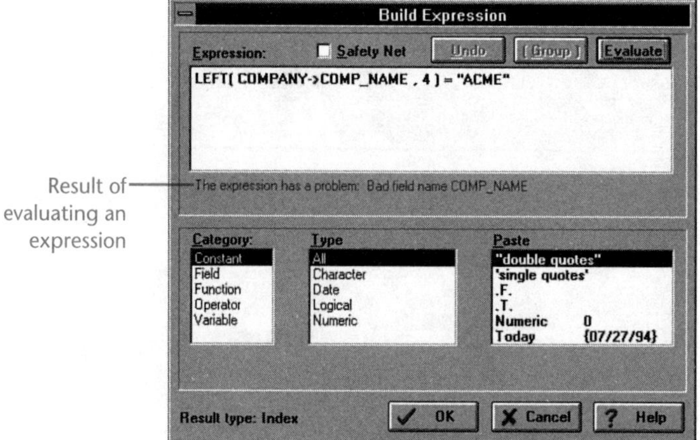

Fig. 13.9
When you choose the E**v**aluate button, dBASE for Windows displays the result or error message in the information panel below the Expression box.

Pasting the Expression into dBASE for Windows

After you finish working with the Expression Builder, choose the OK button to insert your newly constructed expression into the window or dialog box where you started Expression Builder.

> **Note**
>
> You probably should evaluate your expression before inserting it back into dBASE for Windows. Then Expression Builder has the chance to give the expression a once-over and alert you to possible problems.

From Here...

The following chapters discuss topics that use expressions in one form or another:

- Chapter 7, "Indexing and Sorting Data." This chapter covers indexes—which are defined by an expression called a *tag expression*—and sorting, where you can use expressions to restrict the sorted records.
- Chapter 9, "Creating Basic Queries." This chapter tackles query basics, including expression-based operations such as filtering records.
- Chapter 12, "Working with Related Tables." This chapter discusses table relations and shows you how to use a *master expression* to define the link between tables.
- Chapter 14, "Manipulating Data." This chapter shows you how to work with subsets of table data. In particular, you learn how to set up For and While conditions that are defined by expressions. You then put this knowledge to work in finding and replacing data, counting and deleting records, and performing field calculations.
- Chapter 15, "Designing Advanced Forms" and Chapter 16, "Designing Advanced Reports." Both chapters show you how to utilize expressions to create calculated fields. Chapter 15 also discusses using expressions to validate data entry.
- Chapter 17, "Creating Advanced Queries." This chapter takes queries to a higher level and, in particular, extends the idea of using expressions to filter the data and add conditions.
- Chapter 20, "Importing and Exporting Data." This chapter shows you how to import data from other database management systems and how to export dBASE for Windows data. You can use expressions to define the records you want imported or exported.
- Part IV, "Building dBASE Applications." Expressions are a fundamental part of dBASE programming, so they show up in most of the chapters in Part IV.

Chapter 14

Manipulating Data

Conventional wisdom claims that, in the 90s, "information is power." This may not be entirely true, however. Certainly dBASE for Windows offers no shortage of information. Whether you create the tables and enter the data yourselves, query other tables, or import files from an external database system, you have information up to your eyeballs. So where's the power?

The secret is that power resides not in the information itself, but in the ability to *manage* that information. Staring up at a mountain of data can be both intimidating and frustrating. You *know* what you need is in there somewhere, but you need to mount a veritable Everest expedition to get at it. You can regain the upper hand, however, if you know how to knock that mountain down to a molehill.

This chapter shows you how to do just that. Not only will you learn basic data manipulation chores such as counting records, performing field calculations, and finding and replacing data, but you'll see how to restrict these operations to subsets of your data.

In this chapter, you learn to do the following:

- Generate new records automatically
- Work with subsets of your data
- Count the records in a table or query
- Perform calculations on your data
- Find and replace data
- Delete records from a table or query

Generating New Records

Before we look at how you can decrease your information overload, let's check out a handy command that serves the opposite function: it actually *creates* new data for you automatically. Why would you want to do such a thing? Well, the most common reason would be to put a database system through its paces to try to shake out the flaws.

For example, suppose that you've created a query and it works fine in your test table that contains a few dozen records. If you then want to test the query performance on a 10,000-record table, presumably you have better things to do with your life than enter 10,000 records. dBASE for Windows, however, *doesn't* have anything better to do, and its **G**enerate Records command will happily perform this chore for you.

Tip
You can generate up to 1 billion records and up to 2 gigabytes of data.

To try this out, open the table for which you want to generate the new records. Then open the **T**able menu, choose **T**able Utilities, and then choose **G**enerate Records. You'll see the Generate Records dialog box, as shown in figure 14.1. Use the **R**ecords spin box to enter the number of new records you want to create. When you choose OK, dBASE for Windows appends the number of records you specified to the table. Each field is filled with random data of the appropriate data type (see fig. 14.2). (Memo fields are also created, if necessary, but they're not filled with data.)

Note

To generate records from the command line, use the GENERATE <expN> command, where <expN> is the number of new records you want to add. (<expN> must be an integer between 1 and 1 billion.) If you leave out <expN>, dBASE for Windows displays the Generate Records dialog box.

Fig. 14.1
Use the Generate Records dialog box to enter the number of new records you want to add to the table.

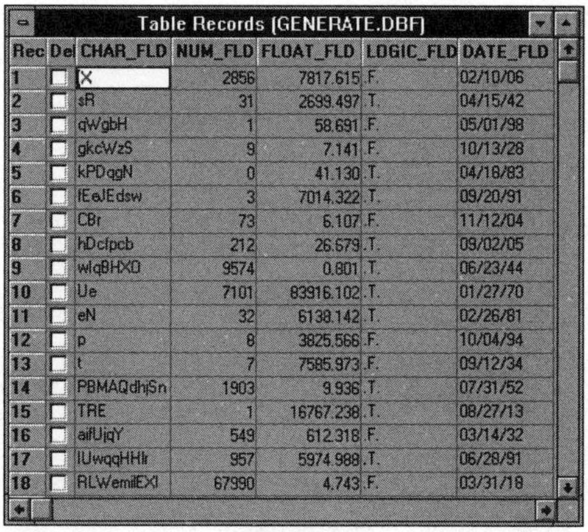

Table Records (GENERATE.DBF)

Rec	Del	CHAR_FLD	NUM_FLD	FLOAT_FLD	LOGIC_FLD	DATE_FLD
1	☐	X	2856	7817.615	.F.	02/10/06
2	☐	sR	31	2699.497	.T.	04/15/42
3	☐	qWgbH	1	58.691	.F.	05/01/98
4	☐	gkcWzS	9	7.141	.F.	10/13/28
5	☐	kPDqgN	0	41.130	.T.	04/18/83
6	☐	lEeJEdsw	3	7014.322	.T.	09/20/91
7	☐	CBr	73	6.107	.F.	11/12/04
8	☐	hDcfpcb	212	26.579	.T.	09/02/05
9	☐	wlqBHXD	9574	0.801	.T.	06/23/44
10	☐	Ue	7101	83916.102	.T.	01/27/70
11	☐	eN	32	6138.142	.T.	02/26/81
12	☐	p	8	3825.566	.F.	10/04/94
13	☐	t	7	7585.973	.F.	09/12/34
14	☐	PBMAQdhjSn	1903	9.936	.T.	07/31/52
15	☐	TRE	1	16767.238	.T.	08/27/13
16	☐	aifUjqY	549	612.318	.F.	03/14/32
17	☐	lUwqqHHlr	957	5974.988	.T.	06/28/91
18	☐	RLWemilEXl	67990	4.743	.F.	03/31/18

Fig. 14.2
The **G**enerate Records command fills each field with random data of the appropriate data type.

II

Power Skills

Working with a Subset of Records

Most database tasks are relatively straightforward when you're working with a small table or query, but they grow increasingly complex and time-consuming as the number of records you're dealing with increases. To help out, dBASE for Windows lets you work with subsets of table or query records. For example, in an indexed table, you may want to delete every record from the current record to the end of the table. Or you may want to sum the invoice amounts for a particular customer. dBASE for Windows gives you three methods for defining table or query subsets:

Scope—Selects a range of records to work with. This could be only the current record, every record in the table, only the next 10 records, and so on.

For condition—Selects all records in the table or query that meet the criteria you specify.

While condition—Selects all records that meet the criteria you specify, starting with the current record and ending with the first record that doesn't match the criteria.

Tip
In most cases, you can combine these methods. For example, you could define a range of records with which to work, and then use a For condition to manipulate only specific records within the scope.

Commands That Work with Subsets

In dBASE for Windows, you define your data subsets in the context of specific commands. In all cases, you'll follow these generic steps to work with a subset of data:

1. Open the table or query that contains the data and either Browse the table or display the query results.

2. Select the data manipulation command that you want to run. (See the list in table 14.1 for commands that let you define subsets.)

3. Use the command's dialog box to define the subset of data with which you want to work.

4. Run the command.

Table 14.1 lists the dBASE for Windows commands that work with subsets of data.

◄ "Managing an Index," p. 134

◄ "Sorting Tables," p. 139

► "Exporting Data," p. 471

► "Importing Data into a Table," p. 479

Table 14.1 dBASE for Windows Commands that Work with Subsets of Data

Command	Description
Properties, Table Records Window	Sets properties for the Table Records window, including displaying the subset only
Table, Find Records	Finds a record within the subset
Table, Replace Records	Finds and replaces data within the subset
Table, Table Utilities, Manage Indexes	Indexes data using a For condition
Table, Table Utilities, Delete Records	Marks for deletion records defined by the subset
Table, Table Utilities, Recall Records	Recalls deleted records defined by the subset
Table, Table Utilities, Append Records From File	Imports records from another file based on a For condition
Table, Table Utilities, Export Records	Exports to another file records defined by the subset
Table, Table Utilities, Sort Records	Sorts records defined by the subset
Table, Table Utilities, Count Records	Counts records defined by the subset
Table, Table Utilities, Calculate Records	Performs field calculations on records defined by the subset

For example, figure 14.3 shows the Records tab of the Table Records Properties dialog box that appears when you open the **P**roperties menu and choose **T**able Records Window. The Scope group contains the controls you use to define your subset. The next few sections look at each of these controls in detail, using the Table Records Properties dialog box as an example.

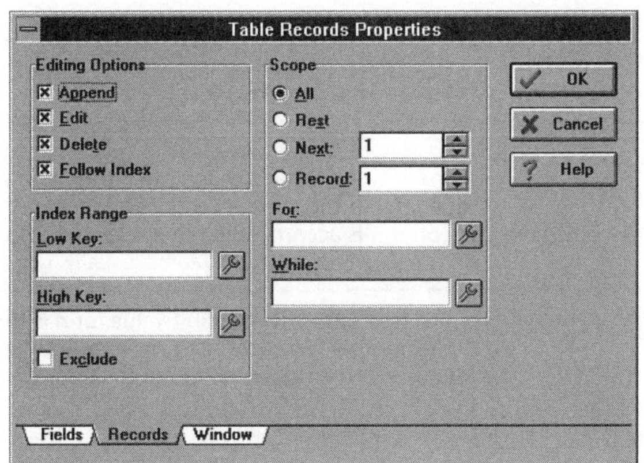

Fig. 14.3
You use the controls in the Scope group to define the subset of data with which you want to work.

Understanding Scope

In dBASE for Windows, *defining the scope* for a command selects the range of records on which you want the command to operate. This range can be as large as the entire table, as small as a single record, or anything in between. It's important to remember that a command's scope is based on the *position* of the records within a table or query and has nothing to do with the actual data contained in the records (as happens with the For and While conditions). The position of each record, of course, depends on whether the table is in natural or indexed order. Therefore, if you define your scope to be, say, the next ten records in a table, the range of records will be defined as follows:

- If the table is in natural order, the subset will include the current record and the next nine record numbers.
- If the table is in indexed order, the subset will include the current record and the next nine records in the index order.

dBASE for Windows gives you the four scope options outlined in table 14.2.

Table 14.2 dBASE for Windows' Scope Options

Option	Defines the Scope to Be
All	All the records in the table or query. In this case, dBASE for Windows always executes the command starting from the first record, regardless of the current position of the record pointer. This is the default scope in the Table Records Properties dialog box.
Rest	From the current record to the last record in the table or query.

(continues)

Table 14.2 Continued

Option	Defines the Scope to Be
Ne**x**t *n*	The *n* consecutive records starting with the current record. If there are less than *n* records remaining, the scope is from the current record to the end of the file. This option is accompanied by a spin box you can use to select a value for *n* (the default is usually 1).
Recor**d** *n*	Record number *n*. The default value for *n* is the current record number. To avoid an error message, make sure that *n* is less than or equal to the total number of records in the table or query.

Note

When you're working in the Command window, many functions and commands accept the keywords ALL, REST, NEXT <expN>, and RECORD <expN> (where <expN> is a number or numeric expression) to define the scope. For example, the following command marks the next 10 records in the active table for deletion:

```
DELETE NEXT 10
```

Working with For Conditions

Instead of selecting records based on their position in a table or query, you'll often need to select them based on their content. For example, you may want an average of the invoices where the ACCT_NUM field is "12-3456", or you may want to Browse only those records with a DATE field that contains values prior to January 1st, 1990.

To set up a For condition, dBASE for Windows provides a text box in which you can enter any valid expression. The current command will then operate on only those records that meet the expression criteria. (Remember that you can combine scope and For clauses; therefore, technically, the For expression selects those records that satisfy the condition *and* fall within the current scope.)

◄ "Using the Expression Builder," p. 283

For example, suppose that you want to Browse only those records where the ACCT_NUM field equals "12-3456". In the Table Records Properties dialog box, you'd enter the following expression in the Fo**r** text box:

```
acct_num="12-3456"
```

Here's an English-language equivalent of such a For condition:

```
Browse those records for which ACCT_NUM is equal to "12-3456"
```

When you run the command, dBASE for Windows moves to the first record in the current order (or the first record in the scope) and then moves sequentially through each record. Along the way, it tests each record to see whether it meets the For condition. If the record does not satisfy the criteria, it is ignored; if it does meet the condition, the command is executed on the record.

Note

To define a For condition when working in the Command window, many dBASE for Windows functions and commands accept the parameter FOR <*condition*>, where *condition* is any legitimate expression. For example, the following command counts the number of records that contain "ACME" in the CUST_NAME field, and stores the result in the AcmeTotal variable:

```
COUNT FOR "ACME" $ cust_name TO AcmeTotal
```

Working with While Conditions

Selecting records based on a While condition is similar to using a For condition. In both cases, the selection is based on the content of the records, and you enter an expression that defines which records you want the command to operate on. The differences lie in how the two conditions dictate where a command begins and ends:

- In a For condition, the command begins at the first record in the current table sequence (or the first record in the scope) and ends at the last record in the sequence.
- In a While condition, the command begins at the current record and ends when the command encounters a record that does not satisfy the While expression.

You'll normally use While conditions in conjunction with an index, as follows:

1. Index the table or query using a key whose fields match those you'll be using in the While condition's expression. This ensures that the records you want to process appear consecutively.
2. Find the first record that matches the expression.
3. Choose the command and enter the expression in the While text box. When you execute the command, dBASE for Windows will process the consecutive records that match the expression and stop at the first record that doesn't match.

Tip
STR( ) converts a number to a 10-character string padded on the left with blanks. Therefore, you should always use LTRIM( ) (or the TRIM( ) function) to remove these excess blanks.

For example, suppose that you want to Browse all the invoices where the customer name (CUST_NAME) is "ACME" and the invoice amount (AMOUNT) is less than $100. You first index the table using the following key expression:

```
cust_name + LTRIM(STR(amount))
```

This expression will order the invoices by customer name and then by amount. After finding the first "ACME" record with an invoice amount less than $100, you display the Table Records Properties dialog box and enter the following expression in the **W**hile text box:

```
cust_name = "ACME" .AND. amount < 100
```

Here's the English-language equivalent for this condition:

```
Browse records while CUST_NAME equals "ACME" and AMOUNT is less
than 100
```

Note

It's sometimes not obvious whether you should use a For condition or a While condition with your commands. Although it's tough to come up with hard-and-fast rules for this kind of thing, there are a few guidelines you can use:

- If your table is ordered in such a way that the records you want to process appear consecutively, use While.
- If your table is small- to medium-sized, For is faster because you don't need to order the records or find the first record to be processed.
- If you're dealing with very large tables (for example, a few thousand records and up), For can bog down under the weight; therefore, While is usually the better choice.

Note

Many Command window functions and commands accept the parameter WHILE *<condition>* to define a While condition. As usual, *condition* is any legitimate dBASE for Windows expression.

Counting Selected Records

Perhaps the most basic data you can extract from your table is the number of records it contains. The simplest case is the total number of records in the table (which is most easily had from the Status bar's `Rec <current>/<total>` display).

More usefully, you may want to know how many records in the table meet a certain criteria. For example, in a table of accounts receivable aging, you may want to know how many invoices are more than 90 days past due. Or you may want to know how many clients you have with the last name *Smith*. You could create queries for these questions and then see how many records appear in the query results, but dBASE for Windows gives you an easier method: the Count Records command.

To check this out, open the table you want to use, pull down the **T**able menu, choose **T**able Utilities, and then choose Cou**n**t Records. dBASE for Windows displays the Count Records dialog box, as shown in figure 14.4. Use the controls in the Scope group to select a scope or to enter Fo**r** or **W**hile expressions. When you're done, choose OK. dBASE for Windows calculates the total and displays the results in a dialog box (see fig. 14.5) and in the Status bar. Choose OK to remove the dialog box and return to the table.

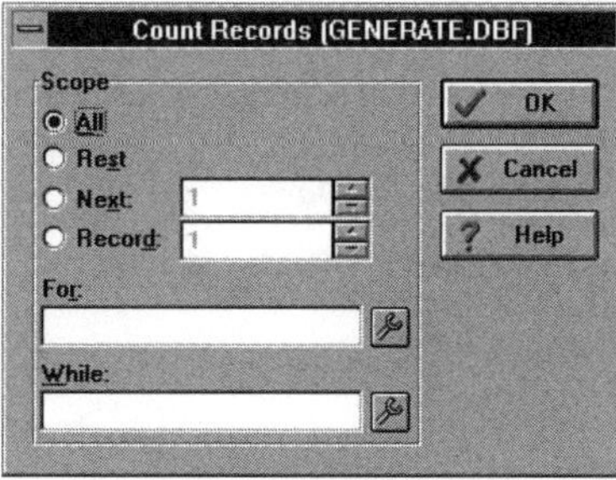

Fig. 14.4
Use the Count Records dialog box to enter the scope and conditions for the records you want to count.

Fig. 14.5
dBASE for Windows displays a dialog box showing you the count of the selected records.

Note

The Command window lets you use the COUNT command to get a quick count of table records. Here's the syntax for this command:

```
COUNT [<scope>] [FOR <condition 1>] [WHILE <condition 2>] [TO<memvar>]
```

You use the <scope> and the FOR and WHILE conditions as described earlier in this chapter. Use TO <memvar> to store the count in a memory variable. For example, the following command counts the number of records where the DATE_DUE field is greater than 90 and stores the result in a variable named DeadBeats:

```
COUNT FOR date_due > 90 TO DeadBeats
```

▶ "Entering and Executing dBASE Commands," p. 556

Troubleshooting

When I choose OK in the Count Records dialog box, the count doesn't appear in the Status bar.

dBASE for Windows' SET TALK property is probably set to OFF. This property needs to be ON to see the counts in the Status bar. You can use either of the following methods to adjust this property:

- Open the **P**roperties menu and choose **D**esktop. In the Desktop Properties dialog box, select the Programming tab, activate the **T**alk check box, and then choose OK.
- Enter **SET TALK ON** in the Command window.

Tip

You can also use the RECCOUNT([<alias>]) function to return the total number of records in the table given by <alias>.

Instead of getting a simple count, I'd like to know how much disk space a subset of records takes up. Is there any way to calculate this?

Sure. You just multiply the record count by the RECSIZE( ) function, which tells you the size of each record in the table. For example, the following commands count the number of records where the LAST_NAME field contains "Smith", store the result in a variable named SmithCount, and then multiply SmithCount by RECSIZE( ). The result, in bytes, appears in the Results window:

```
COUNT FOR last_name = "Smith" TO SmithCount
? SmithCount * RECSIZE( )
```

Performing Field Calculations

If you have tables that contain numeric or float fields, dBASE for Windows lets you perform calculations on these fields. For example, suppose you have an accounts receivable aging table that stores the amounts for invoices that are between 1 and 30 days past due in a float field named *DUE_1TO30*. You may want to know, for instance, the maximum invoice amount in this field, the average amount, or the sum of the invoices.

Using Calculate Records

You could create a report that would perform these calculations for you, but dBASE for Windows' Calculate Records command can do it faster. To see how it works, follow these steps:

1. Open the table with which you want to work.
2. Pull down the **T**able menu, choose **T**able Utilities, and then choose Ca**l**culate Records. You'll see the Calculate Records dialog box appear, as shown in figure 14.6.

Caution

Make sure that the current table has at least one numeric or float field before running the Calculate Records command. Otherwise, dBASE for Windows displays an error message.

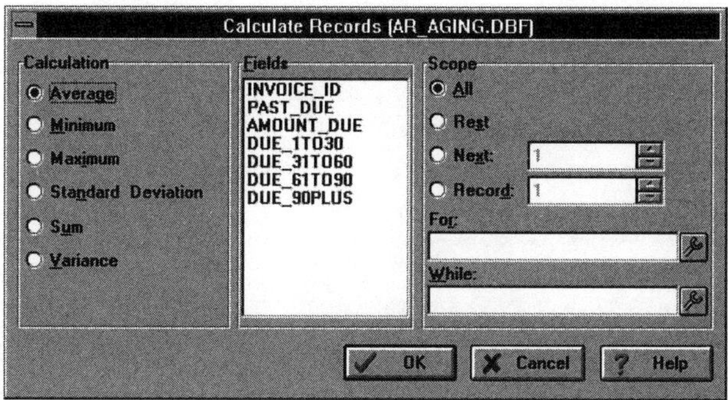

Fig. 14.6 Use the Calculate Records dialog box to select the calculation to use and the fields and records with which to work.

3. Select the type of calculation to perform. The Calculation group holds the six operations described in table 14.3.

Table 14.3 The Calculation Types Available in the Calculate Records Dialog Box

Radio Button	Calculates
Avera**g**e	The average value in the chosen fields over the selected records. A float value is returned.
Minimum	The smallest value in the chosen fields over the selected records. The returned value uses the same data type as the field.
Max**i**mum	The largest value in the chosen fields over the selected records. The returned value uses the same data type as the field.
Sta**n**dard Deviation	The standard deviation of the values in the chosen fields over the selected records. A float value is returned.
S**u**m	The total of the values in the chosen fields over the selected records. A float value is returned.
Variance	The variance of the values in the chosen fields over the selected records. A float value is returned.

4. Use the **F**ields list to highlight the numeric and float fields that you want to include in the calculation.

5. If you want to work with a subset of the table data, use the Scope controls to select the scope and the Fo**r** and **W**hile conditions.

6. Choose OK. dBASE for Windows performs the calculations and then does two things:

   - It displays the calculation results in a dialog box (see fig. 14.7).
   - It displays the number of records involved in the calculation in the Status bar.

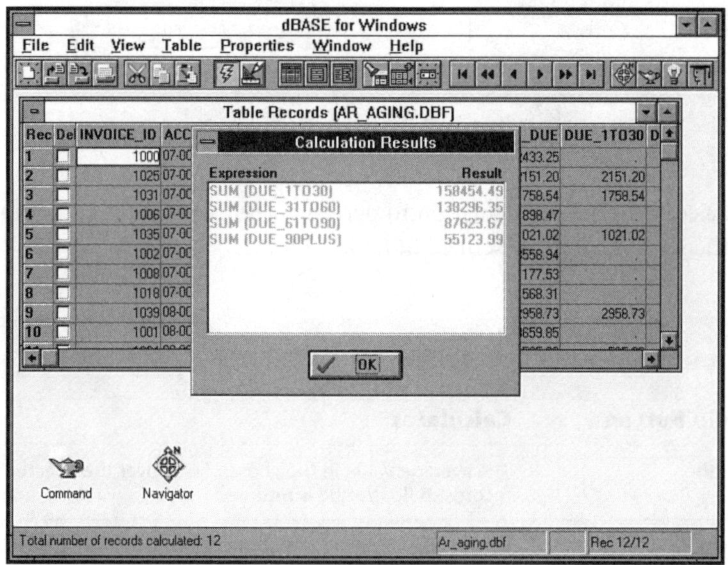

Fig. 14.7
dBASE for Windows displays the calculation results in a separate dialog box.

Using Functions

dBASE for Windows offers several functions that enable you to perform calculations for the Command window. For example, the CALCULATE function most closely emulates the Calculate Records command:

```
CALCULATE <function> [<scope>] [FOR <condition 1>] [WHILE
➥<condition 2>] [TO <memvar> ¦ ARRAY <array>]
```

For <function>, you can use any of the following functions (search for CALCULATE in the dBASE for Windows online Help system to see the full syntax of each of these functions):

AVG( )	Calculates the average of a specified numeric or float field
CNT( )	Counts the number of records of the current table
MAX( )	Calculates the maximum value of a specified field
MIN( )	Calculates the minimum value of a specified field
NPV( )	Calculates the net present value
STD( )	Calculates the standard deviation of a specified field
SUM( )	Calculates the sum of a specified field
VAR( )	Calculates the variance of a specified field

dBASE for Windows also includes four other functions that perform calculations by themselves (that is, without using the CALCULATE function): SUM( ), AVERAGE( ), MAX( ), and MIN( ).

Troubleshooting

I'm trying to use the Average calculation, but it keeps reporting inaccurate results.

You probably have blank entries in the field you're using for the calculation. dBASE for Windows treats blanks as zeros, and these zeros can throw off an average. To tell dBASE for Windows not to include blanks in the calculation, add the following to the For condition text box:

.NOT. ISBLANK(<field>)

Here, <field> is the name of the field you're using in the calculation.

Finding a Record

If you need to find some data in a table that has only a relatively small number of records, it's usually easiest just to scroll through the table using your mouse or keyboard. But if you're dealing with a few hundred or even a few thousand records, don't waste your time rummaging through the whole file. dBASE for Windows has a Find Records feature that lets you search for a key word or phrase in any field to find what you need.

For example, suppose that you have a table of products and you need to find the item with the serial number 1234567. No problem. You simply tell dBASE for Windows to look in the SERIAL_NUM field (or whatever it's called) and find the value *1234567*. Similarly, if you want to find a customer named "Fly By Night Travel," you search in the CUST_NAME field for, say, *fly by* or *night travel* (if you want, you can tell dBASE for Windows to match only part of the name and to ignore uppercase and lowercase).

Cranking Up the Find Record Command

Tip
The keyboard shortcut for the Find Records command is Ctrl+F.

From the Table Editor, open the **T**able menu and choose the **F**ind Records command. In the Find Records dialog box that appears (see fig. 14.8), use the Find What text box to enter the text string you want to find. You can also make use of the following controls in the Find Records dialog box:

Located in Field	This box contains a list of all the fields in the table and the currently selected field will be highlighted. If this isn't the field you want to search in, use this list to highlight the correct field.
Sta**n**dard	Activate this button to find records where the selected field begins with the search text. This is the default.
Exact Length	Activate this button to find records where the selected field matches and is the same length as the search text.
An**y**where in Field	Activate this button to find records where the search text matches any part of the selected field.
Sounds L**i**ke	Activate this button when you're not sure about the spelling of the search text. See "Understanding Sounds Like Searches" later in this chapter for the full scoop on the Sounds Like option.
Match **C**ase	Activate this check box to find records that exactly match the case of the search text. For example, if you check this option and enter "**ACME**" as your search string, dBASE for Windows will ignore records that contain the strings "Acme" or "acme".

Tip
You can save yourself a step by moving into the field you want to use for searching *before* running the Find Records command. This ensures that the field will be highlighted automatically whenever you begin your searches.

Top Record — Activate this button to begin the search from the first record in the table.

C**u**rrent Record — Activate this button to begin the search from the current record.

Ad**v**anced >> — Choose this button to expand the Find Records dialog box to the one shown in figure 14.9. The new options let you define the scope for the search and set up For and While conditions (as explained earlier in this chapter). You can use these options to speed up the search by restricting dBASE for Windows to a subset of the table records.

Tip
As a general rule, make your search text only long enough to uniquely identify the particular field value you want to find.

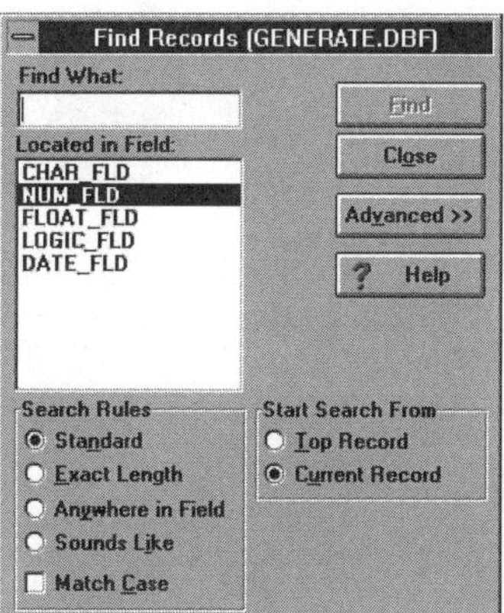

Fig. 14.8
Use the Find Records dialog box to search your table for a particular text string.

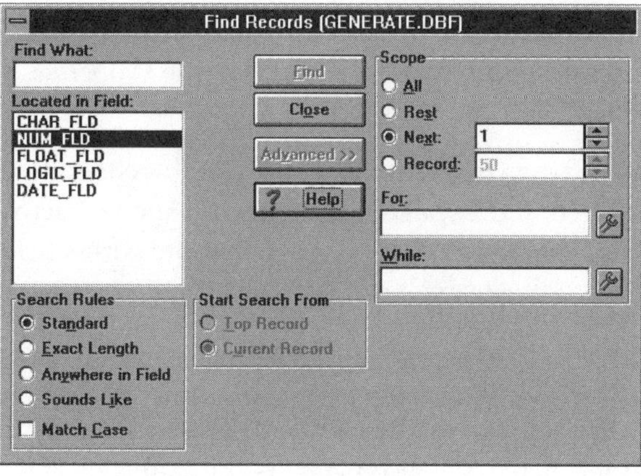

Fig. 14.9
The expanded version of the Find Records dialog box includes the controls for defining the scope and setting For and While conditions.

When you've entered your search options, choose the **F**ind button. dBASE for Windows moves to the top of the table and begins searching from there (unless you selected the C**u**rrent Record button, restricted the scope of the search, or entered a While condition; in these cases, dBASE for Windows begins searching from the current record).

If it finds a match, dBASE for Windows highlights the record (you may need to move the Find Records dialog box to see this). If this is the record you want, choose Cl**o**se to return to the table. If you're looking for a different record, you can continue searching by repeatedly choosing the **F**ind button until you get to the record you want.

Note

After dBASE for Windows finds the first match, subsequent searches for the same text extend only from the current record to the end of the table. This means that, after the last match, dBASE for Windows does *not* wrap around to the top of the table and start over. Instead, it displays an alert message telling you the search value was not found.

If dBASE for Windows can't find the search text, it displays an alert box to let you know (see fig. 14.10). Choose OK to return to the Find Records dialog box.

Fig. 14.10
If dBASE for Windows can't find your search text, it displays an Alert box to let you know the bad news.

Setting Search Options

The Desktop Properties dialog box gives you two options that affect how dBASE for Windows performs its searches. Open the **P**roperties menu, choose **D**esktop, and then select the Table tab.

The **N**ear check box governs what dBASE for Windows does when a search doesn't find a match. If the search field is indexed and you activate the **N**ear option, dBASE for Windows moves to the first record with a field value that most nearly matches the search text.

The **E**xact check box controls how dBASE for Windows compares two strings. In a search, the normal comparison process begins with dBASE for Windows comparing the first letter of the current field value with the first letter of the search text. If they match, the second letters are compared, and so on. The comparison can proceed in one of three ways:

- If different letters are found, the comparison is unsuccessful.
- If the letters in the search text exactly match those in the field value, the comparison is successful.
- If the letters in the search text match the *beginning* of the field value, the result of the comparison depends on the state of the **E**xact check box: if **E**xact is unchecked, the comparison is successful; if it's checked, the comparison is unsuccessful.

  For example, if **E**xact is unchecked, a search text of "Smith" will match a field value of "Smithers" (because "Smith" matches the first five letters of "Smithers"). If **E**xact is checked, the two strings don't match.

Note that both **N**ear and **E**xact also control the behavior of search functions such as SEEK and LOCATE.

Tip
For Command window searches, use LOCATE to find a value in a nonindexed table and either SEEK or SEEK( ) to find a value in an indexed table.

Searching with Wild Cards

For more flexible searches, you can use the dBASE for Windows *wild-card characters*. The question mark (?) substitutes for a single character in a word. For example, consider the search text *Re?d*. This tells dBASE for Windows that you want to find values that begin with *Re*, end with *d*, and can have any letter or symbol as the third letter. For example, this string would find any of the following: *Reid*, *Read*, and *Reed*. As another example, the search string *A????* would find only five-letter words that begin with *A*.

The other wild-card character is the asterisk (*), which substitutes for a group of characters. For example, searching for **carolina* will find *North Carolina* and *South Carolina*.

Understanding Sounds Like Searches

If you're having trouble finding a record that you know is in a table, it may be that you're simply misspelling the word (or, quite possibly, the word may be misspelled in the table). For example, suppose that you're looking in a LAST_NAME field for *Macmillan*. dBASE for Windows won't find what you want if the record was entered as, for example, **McMillan, McMillen,** or **MacMillin.** Wild cards won't help much and it's time-consuming to try all the possible combinations. The solution is to use the Sounds Like feature to look for a *phonetic* or *sounds like* match.

dBASE for Windows' Sounds Like search is based on the Russell Soundex algorithm. This algorithm converts a text string into a four-character code that gives you, approximately, the phonetic representation of the word.

In theory, similar-sounding words such as *Macmillan* and *McMillen* will have the same phonetic code; therefore, a Sounds Like search will find these values and anything that sounds like them.

The Soundex algorithm works by ignoring the "unreliable" components of a word (that is, those parts that play a lesser role in determining the overall sound of the word) and concentrating on the "hard" sounds that distinguish one word from another. Here's how it works:

1. Use the first letter of the word as the first letter of the Soundex code (this is called the *prefix character*).
2. Examine the word's remaining letters individually from left to right to determine the other three digits in the Soundex code. These digits range from 0 to 6 and they're coded as follows:
   - Leading spaces are ignored.
   - The vowels and the letters H, W, and Y are ignored unless they're the first letter of the word or they separate repeating consonant sounds.
   - The remaining consonants are assigned a code from 1 to 6 as follows:

Code	Letters
1	B, F, P, V
2	C, G, J, K, Q, S, X, Z
3	D, T
4	L
5	M, N
6	R

   - If the word contains consecutive consonants that produce the same code, only the first consonant is coded; the rest are ignored. The exception to this occurs when the consonants are separated by a vowel or the letters H, W, or Y. In this case, both consonants are coded. For example, SS would be assigned the value 2, but SOS would be coded as 22.

3. Stop the process when any of the following occur:

   - The Soundex code is four characters long (including the prefix).
   - There are no more characters in the word to process. If the Soundex code contains fewer than four characters, the rest of the code is filled with zeros.
   - When the first nonalphabetic character is reached.

Note

Because of the extra processing required, Sounds Like searches can be painfully slow on large tables. If you plan to use the Sounds Like feature frequently, you should create a Soundex index for the table. For example, if you'll be searching in a field named CUST_NAME, create an index with the following tag expression:

```
SOUNDEX(CUST_NAME)
```

SOUNDEX(<expC>) is the dBASE for Windows function that converts the string <expC> into a Soundex code.

◄ "Creating a Simple Index," p. 128

II

Power Skills

Troubleshooting

I'm using a large table and my searches are lightning quick on some fields and slow as molasses on others.

The speed of a search varies greatly depending on whether or not the field you're using is indexed. Indexed field searches are super-fast because Find can take advantage of the inherent efficiency and speed in the index itself. In a nonindexed field, dBASE for Windows has to trudge through each record to look for the search string. If you're going to use an indexed field for the search, be sure to set it as the master tag before running the Find Records command.

Tip
Use the SOUNDEX() function to perform Soundex searches from the command window. For example, SEEK (SOUNDEX ("macmillan")) runs a Soundex search for "macmillan".

Finding and Replacing Data

One of the dBASE for Windows commands you'll probably come to rely on the most is Replace Records. This command tells dBASE for Windows to seek out a particular bit of data and then replace it with something else. This may not seem like a big deal for a record or two, but if you need to change a couple of dozen instances of *St.* to *Street*, it can be a real time-saver.

Tip
The keyboard shortcut for the **R**eplace Records command is Ctrl+R.

The good news is that replacing data is very similar to finding it. You begin by opening the **T**able menu and choosing **R**eplace Records. You'll see the Replace Records dialog box, as shown in figure 14.11. As before, you enter the data for which you want to search in the Find What text box. Use the Replace With text box to enter the replacement text. The other options are similar to those in the Find Records dialog box—including the scope options you get when you select the Ad**v**anced button. (In fact, the Search Rules controls you selected in the Find Records dialog box are carried over to the Replace Records dialog box.) When you're ready to go, select one of the following buttons:

> **Caution**
>
> If the table is indexed, be sure to close any active index before replacing data. Replacing data in an indexed field can have unpredictable (and often disastrous) consequences.

Tip
Before choosing Rep**l**ace All, rearrange your windows so that you can see the field you're using for the replacement. This lets you eyeball the new field values to make sure that things still look reasonable before you commit to the changes.

Find	Choose this button to find the next matching record without performing the replacement.
Re**p**lace	Choose this button to replace the currently highlighted data and then move on to the next match.
Rep**l**ace All	Choose this button to replace every instance of the search text with the replacement value. If you choose this button, dBASE for Windows will display a dialog box that shows you the number of records that will be affected and asks whether you're sure that you want to commit your changes (see fig. 14.12). If you're sure, choose **Y**es.

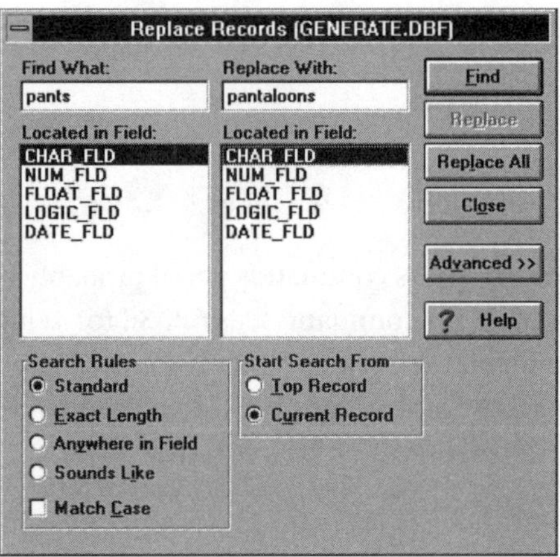

Fig. 14.11
Use the Replace Records dialog box to search for and replace data in a table.

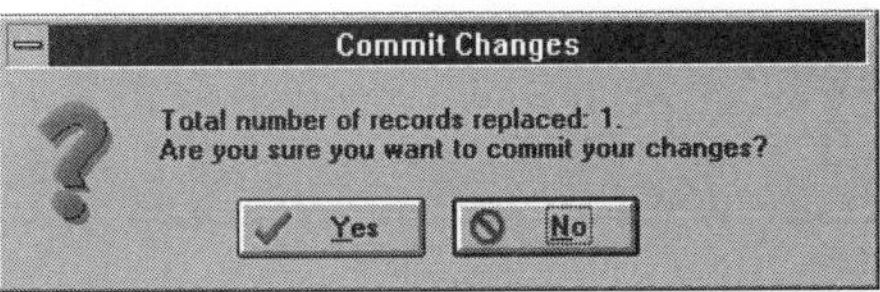

Fig. 14.12
When you select the Replace All button, dBASE for Windows displays this dialog box to tell you how many records will be affected and to ask whether you want to continue.

Note

If you need to perform global replacements in one or more fields, using the REPLACE command from the Command window is probably the fastest way to go. Here's a simplified version of the REPLACE syntax:

```
REPLACE <field> WITH <exp> [<scope>] [FOR <condition 1>] [WHILE
<condition 2>] [REINDEX]
```

This command replaces values in the field given by <field> with the value given by the expression <exp> (you can enter multiple fields and expressions). Use <scope>, FOR, and WHILE to restrict the replacement to a subset of records. If you include the REINDEX parameter, dBASE for Windows reindexes the table after the replacement is complete.

For example, the following command replaces each instance of "Smyth" in the LAST_NAME field with "Smith":

```
REPLACE last_name WITH "Smith" FOR last_name = "Smyth" REINDEX
```

Deleting Multiple Records

If you have a table that contains records you no longer need, you should delete them to save disk space and make the table easier to work with. dBASE for Windows has four commands that relate to record deletion (open the **T**able menu and choose **T**able Utilities to see these commands):

Delete Records	Marks records for deletion
Recall Records	Unmarks records previously marked for deletion
Pack Records	Permanently removes the marked records
Zap Records	Deletes all records from a table

The next few sections look at each command in detail.

Marking Records for Deletion

The first step in deleting records in dBASE for Windows is to *mark* the records for deletion. This step doesn't actually remove the records from the table. Instead, it merely points out which records are deletion candidates. This gives you a chance to look at the marked records and see if any records you need have been marked by accident. If so, you can easily recover them (as you'll see in the next section).

◀ "Deleting Records," p. 160

This precautionary step isn't usually necessary when you're deleting one record at a time (as you learned how to do in Chapter 8, "Entering, Editing, and Viewing Data"). But the **D**elete Records command lets you mark for deletion multiple records in one fell swoop based on a defined scope or on For and While conditions. A slight mistake in defining your subset could have disastrous consequences; therefore, the ability to recall marked records is a big-time blessing.

To delete multiple records from the current table, open the **T**able menu, choose **T**able Utilities, and then choose **D**elete Records. dBASE for Windows displays the Delete Records dialog box, as shown in figure 14.13. Use the usual options in the Scope group to specify a scope or to set up Fo**r** and **W**hile conditions. When you're finished, choose OK. dBASE for Windows marks the selected records for deletion and displays the marks in the Del column of the browse layout (see fig. 14.14).

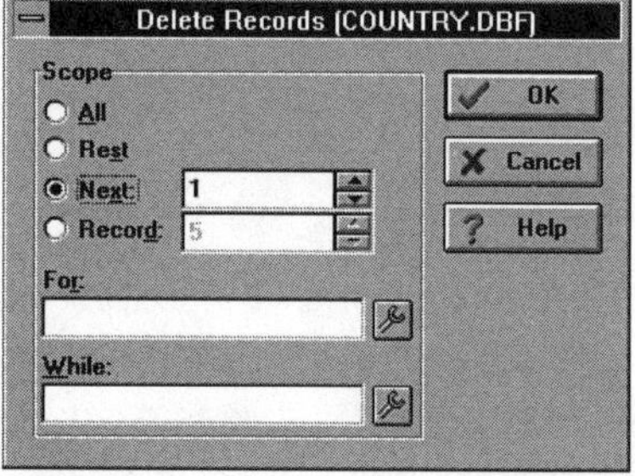

Fig. 14.13
Use the Delete Records dialog box to define which records you want to mark for deletion.

Fig. 14.14
Here's how deleted records appear in the browse layout.

Records marked for deletion

Table Records (CONTACTS.DBF)

Rec	Del	CONTACT_ID	COMPANY_ID	FIRST_NAME	LAST_NAME
1	☐	1	A8331	Martin	Bajhu
2	☒	2	A8331	Chuck	Haddad
3	☐	3	A8331	Martin	Daniels
4	☐	4	A5577	George	Alviston
5	☐	5	A3367	Randy	Flood
6	☒	6	A8101	Ardew	Haldeman
7	☐	7	B4876	Mikey	Rasmussen
8	☐	8	B4876	Martha	Madarasz
9	☐	9	B4876	Dorit	Springer
10	☐	10	B4876	Billy	Barba
11	☐	11	B7930	James	Davis
12	☐	12	C0720	Randal	Fox
13	☒	13	C5973	Reid	Harrell
14	☒	14	C1512	Casimiro	Hedgep
15	☐	15	C1512	Lori	Tartaglio

Note

To delete multiple records from the Command window, use the DELETE command:

```
DELETE [<scope>] [FOR <condition 1>] [WHILE <condition 2>]
```

For example, the following command sequence deletes the last 100 records in the active table:

```
GO BOTTOM
SKIP -100
DELETE NEXT 100
```

Recalling Marked Records

If you make a mistake when marking a record for deletion (and, believe me, you will), you can recover by recalling some or all of the marked records *before* deleting them. You do this by opening the **T**able menu, choosing **T**able Utilities, and then choosing **R**ecall Records. dBASE for Windows displays the Recall Records dialog box shown in figure 14.15. You know the drill by now: Use the Scope controls to define the appropriate scope or to enter Fo**r** and **W**hile conditions, and then choose OK. dBASE for Windows unmarks the selected records.

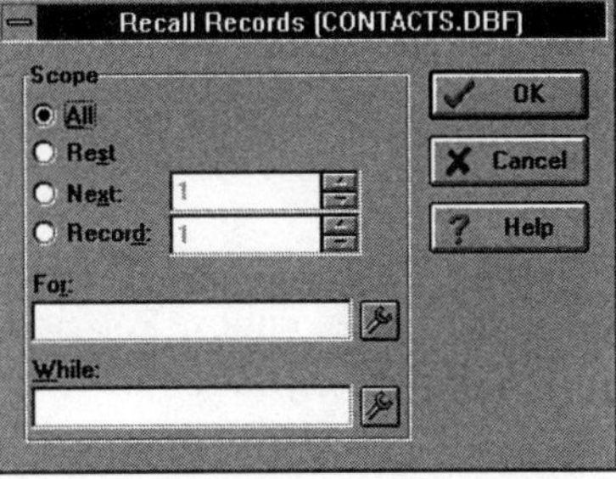

Fig. 14.15
Use the Recall Records dialog box to unmark records that you previously marked for deletion.

Note

In the Command window, you can recall records marked for deletion by using the RECALL command:

```
RECALL [<scope>] [FOR <condition 1>] [WHILE <condition 2>]
```

Deleting Marked Records

If you're sure that the correct records have been marked for deletion, the next step is to physically remove them from the table. This is called *packing* the table.

Caution

After you pack a table, any records that were marked for deletion are gone for good and no amount of huffing and puffing will bring them back. For this reason, before packing a table, make absolutely sure that the marked records are ones you can live without. For large-scale deletions, you might consider making a backup copy of the table before packing it.

To pack the table and permanently remove the marked records, open the **T**able menu, choose **T**able Utilities, and then choose **P**ack Records.

Zapping a Table

If you're sure you want to nuke an entire table, dBASE for Windows includes a Zap Records command that will clean out every record in a table in no time flat. This is handy when you're testing a table layout or if you use a table to temporarily store data. Zap Records skips the marking step and removes the records immediately.

Caution

For obvious reasons, the Zap Records command can be a very dangerous weapon and should be wielded with care. If in doubt, always Browse a table before zapping it to make sure you're not blowing away any crucial information.

Tip
Use the PACK command to pack a table from the Command window.

To remove all records from a table without marking them, open the **T**able menu, choose **T**able Utilities, and then choose **Z**ap Records. The Zap Table dialog box appears to find out whether you're sure that you want to go through with this (see fig. 14.16). Select **Y**es to zap the table or **N**o to cancel.

Fig. 14.16
dBASE for Windows displays this confirmation dialog when you run the Zap Records command.

Troubleshooting

My Browse windows don't have a Del column and dBASE for Windows just seems to delete my records instead of marking them for deletion first. Am I doing something wrong?

No, you just need to change how dBASE for Windows treats deletions. Open the **P**roperties menu, choose **D**esktop, and then select the Table tab in the Desktop Properties dialog box. Deactivate the Dele**t**ed check box and then choose OK. Turning this option off tells dBASE for Windows to add the Del column to the browse layout and show the marked records.

From Here...

To learn more about manipulating data, look at the following chapters:

- Chapter 7, "Indexing and Sorting Data." This chapter takes you through the basic indexing and sorting techniques that can make it much easier to juggle large chunks of data.
- Chapter 8, "Entering, Editing, and Viewing Data." This chapter teaches you the basic techniques for Browsing data as well as for adding and deleting individual records.
- Chapter 13, "Using the Expression Builder." This chapter covers the all-important topic of expressions and shows you how to use the Expression Builder to easily create powerful For and While conditions.
- Chapter 17, "Creating Advanced Queries." This chapter extends the idea of a table subset by showing you how to use query conditions to filter records.

Tip
In the Command window, use the ZAP command to clean out a table.

Chapter 15

Designing Advanced Forms

Chapter 10, "Creating Basic Forms," shows you how to use the Form Expert to set up and run simple data entry forms. This chapter takes you beyond the basics as it delves more deeply into the rich form-design environment provided by dBASE for Windows. The techniques you learn in this chapter will help you create complex forms to handle everything from data entry to dialog boxes.

In this chapter, you learn how to perform these tasks:

- Work with forms and form properties
- Add objects to a form
- Understand the different object types
- Work with object properties

What Is a Form?

If you have used dBASE for DOS, you're probably used to thinking of a form as a data entry screen consisting of one or more fields from a table or view and a few text labels thrown in for good measure. You also can use dBASE for Windows forms as data entry screens, but they go far beyond that. In dBASE for Windows, a *form* can be any kind of window that provides an interface between you and dBASE (or between a user and your dBASE application). A form can be not only a data entry screen, but any of the following items:

- A dialog box that asks the user for information or displays status or error messages
- An MDI (Multiple Document Interface) window. MDI windows enable the user to switch between open windows, and they can be maximized, minimized, moved, or sized. MDI windows are often separate, nondatabase-related utilities, but data entry screens also can fall into this category.
- An application window that users can launch from an icon in Program Manager

◀ "Designing Forms," p. 36

Forms contain one or more *objects* that define what the form does and how you interact with it. A data entry form, for example, may contain text box objects linked to specific fields in a table (see fig. 15.1). A dialog box may contain check box objects, radio button objects, and push button objects (see fig. 15.2). An MDI window may contain push buttons to run the various features of the utility (see fig. 15.3). An application window usually has a menu bar object with pull-down menus to give the user access to the application's features (see fig. 15.4).

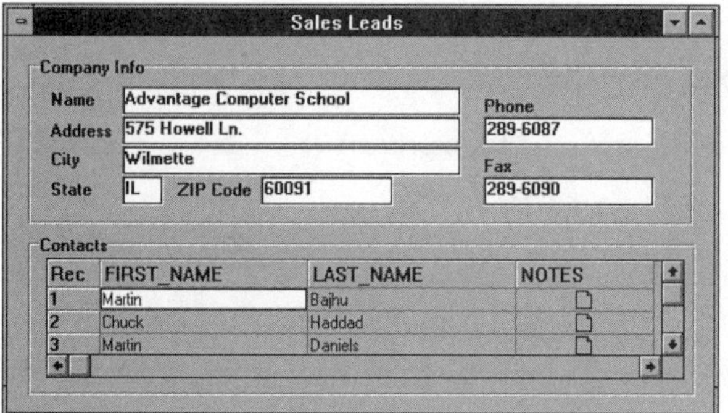

Fig. 15.1
A form designed for data entry.

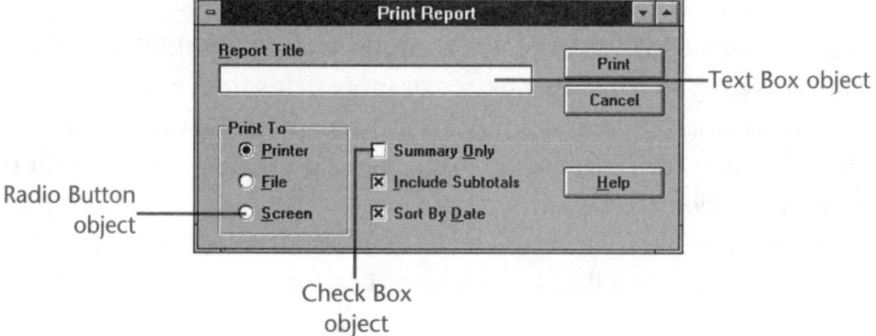

Fig. 15.2
A form used as a dialog box.

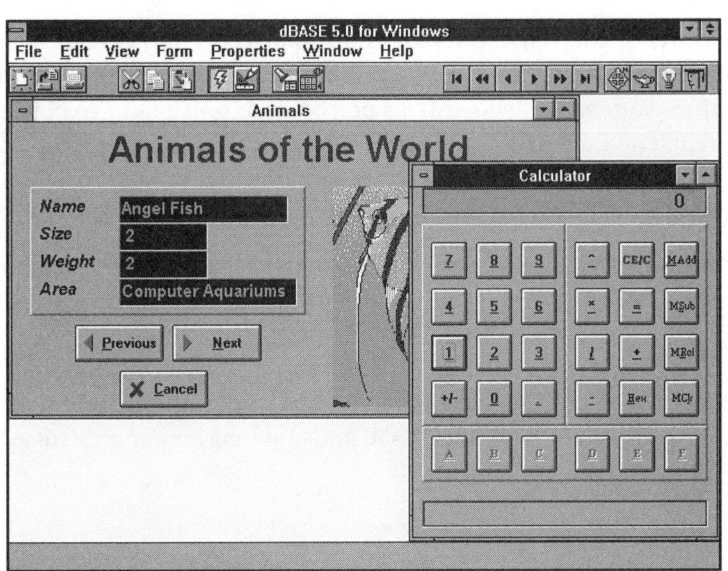

Fig. 15.3
Two forms used as MDI windows.

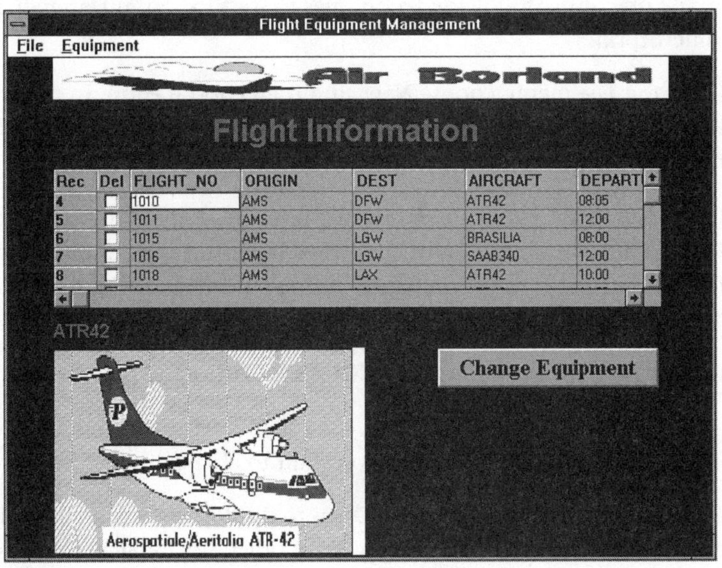

Fig. 15.4
A form used as an application window.

Each of these objects (including the form itself, because a form is also an object) is defined by a collection of *properties*, *events*, and *methods*:

Properties—Characteristics that define the appearance and position of an object. Common properties include the font, width, and color of an object.

▶ "Handling Events," p. 650

Events—Actions that can happen to an object. Typical events include getting and losing the focus and being clicked (left or right). In *event-driven programming,* you assign a procedure or function to an object event, and then that routine runs automatically whenever the event occurs. For example, you can write a routine that validates a field whenever the field loses the focus.

Methods—Actions that an object can perform itself under programmatic control. For example, you can use an object's SetFocus method to give the object the focus.

This chapter looks only at object properties. To work with events and methods, you need to understand the dBASE programming concepts discussed in Part IV of this book.

Starting the Form Designer

You can use one of the following techniques to start the Form Designer and create a new form:

- Open the **F**ile menu, choose **N**ew, and then choose **F**orm. In the Form Expert dialog box that appears, activate the Blank Form option and then choose Create.

- In the Navigator, select the Forms section, and then double-click the Untitled form, or highlight the Untitled form and click the SpeedBar's Design button. In the Form Expert dialog box, activate the **B**lank Form option and then choose Create.
- In the Command window, type **CREATE FORM** and press Enter.

Tip
You also can start a new form by highlighting the Untitled form and pressing Shift+F2.

If you need to modify an existing form, use the following techniques to start the Form Designer and load the form you want to change:

- Open the **F**ile menu and choose **O**pen to display the Open File dialog box. If necessary, use the File **T**ype drop-down list to select the Form (*.WFM) item. In the **F**ile Name list, select the form you want to open and then choose the De**s**ign Form option. Choose OK to open the form in the Form Designer.

- In the Navigator, select the Forms section and highlight the form you want to modify. Then right-click the form and choose Design **F**orm from the SpeedMenu, or click the Design button in the SpeedBar.

- In the Command window, type **MODIFY FORM *<form.wfm>*** (where *<form.wfm>* is the name of the form) and then press Enter.

Tip

You also can load an existing form by highlighting the form and pressing Shift+F2.

Navigating the Form Designer Window

When you open the Form Designer, dBASE for Windows adds the following elements to the screen (see fig. 15.5):

Form Designer menu bar—The new menu bar includes a **L**ayout and P**r**ocedure menu, and new form-related commands appear on the **E**dit, **V**iew, and **P**roperties menus.

Form Designer SpeedBar—The Form Designer has its own SpeedBar that gives you easy access to many of the Form Designer's most commonly used features. Relevant buttons are described in the appropriate sections of this chapter.

Form Designer window—This window is where you add, size, and move objects, as well as work with the object properties. The rulers and grid help you line up your objects.

Control Palette—This window lists the various object types you can add to your forms.

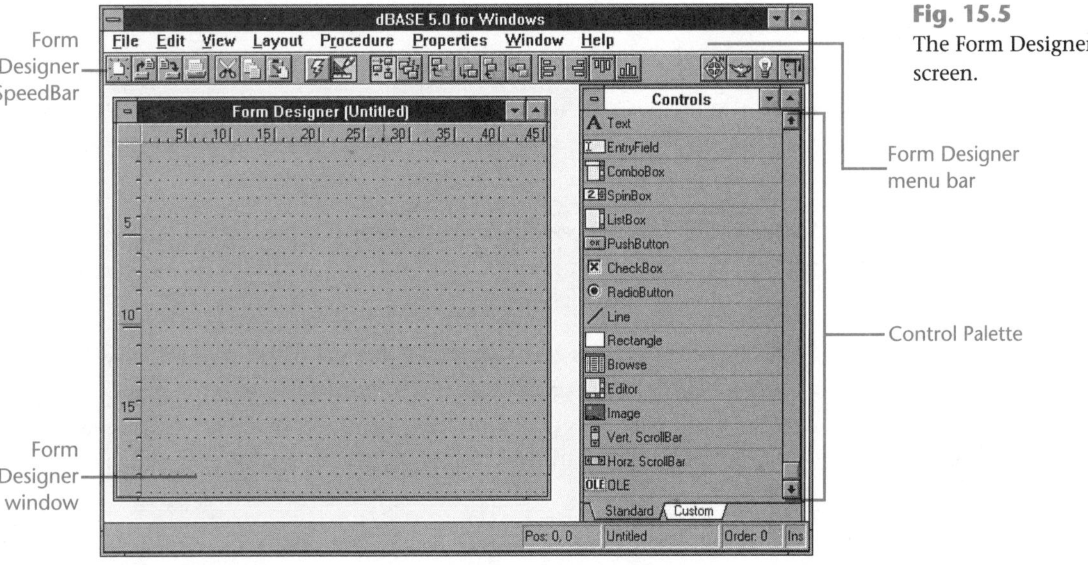

Fig. 15.5
The Form Designer screen.

Setting Form Designer Properties

The Form Designer has several properties you can manipulate to place and align objects on the form more easily. To display these properties, use either of the following techniques:

- Right-click an empty part of the form and choose **F**orm Designer Properties from the SpeedMenu.
- Open the **P**roperties menu and choose **F**orm Designer.

In either case, dBASE for Windows displays the Forms Designer Properties dialog box, shown in figure 15.6.

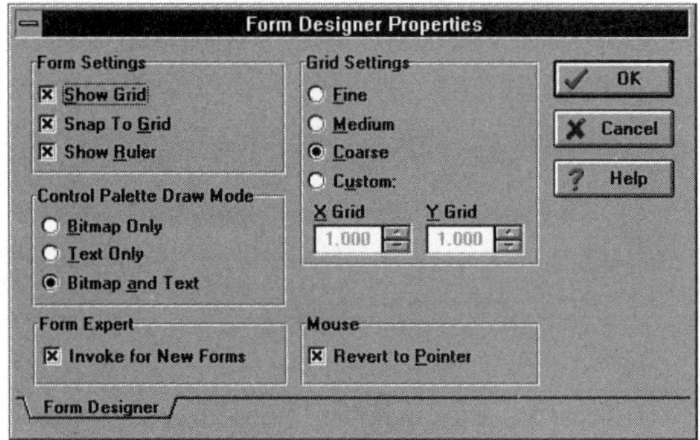

Fig. 15.6
Use the Forms Designer Properties dialog box to change the grid and ruler settings for the Form Designer.

The following list summarizes the available options in this dialog box:

Show Grid—This check box toggles the grid on and off. If the grid is on and the Snap To **G**rid check box is activated, dBASE for Windows aligns your objects with the grid dots as you move or size the object. This feature enables you to easily align your objects neatly.

Snap To Grid—This check box controls how objects align themselves when you change their position. If you activate the check box, moved or sized objects line up automatically with the grid dots.

Show Ruler—This check box toggles the rulers on and off. If the rulers are on, a highlight appears in the top ruler to show you the precise length of an object when you are moving or sizing it. Similarly, a second highlight appears in the left ruler to show you the precise height of the object.

Grid Settings—The controls in this section define the spacing of the grid dots. The spacing is based on the current form font. The default

(**C**oarse) setting means the horizontal distance between two dots is the width of an average character in the form font. (This setting is called the *X Grid* length, and it's given the arbitrary value of 1.000.) Similarly, the vertical distance between two dots is the height of an average character in the form font. (This setting is the *Y Grid* height, and it's also given the value 1.000.) You also can select the **F**ine option (where the X Grid is 0.330 and the Y Grid is 0.330), the **M**edium option (where the X Grid is 0.660 and the Y Grid is 0.660), **C**oarse (where the X Grid is 1.000 and the Y Grid is 1.000), or C**u**stom (where you can enter any value between 0.125 and 9.000 for both the **X** Grid and the **Y** Grid).

Control Palette Draw Mode—These options control the appearance of the objects in the Control Palette. Choose **B**itmap Only to display only the pictures for each object; choose **T**ext Only to display only the name of each object; choose Bitmap **a**nd Text to display both the object's picture and description (this is the default).

Form Expert—Deactivate the Invoke for New Forms check box to prevent dBASE for Windows from starting the Form Expert each time you start a new form.

Mouse—When the Revert to **P**ointer check box is active, dBASE for Windows changes the mouse cursor back to the pointer once you've added an object to the Form Designer. If you deactivate this check box, the current object remains selected after you've added the object to the form.

After you have entered the settings, choose OK to return to the Form Designer. For more information on setting window properties, see the section "Setting the Window Properties" later in this chapter.

Note

Remember that the settings you select in the Forms Designer Properties dialog box affect *all* forms, not just the current one.

Working with a Form as an Object

As mentioned earlier, a form is an object with its own properties, events, and methods. You can use the form's properties to control things like the type of window the form uses, the name that appears in the title bar, and the size and position of the form.

▶ "Handling Events," p. 650

Setting an Object's Properties

All objects have a Properties dialog box (also called an Object Inspector) that lists all the properties, events, and methods associated with the object. To display the Properties dialog box for an object and change its property values, follow these steps:

1. Select the object you want to work with by clicking it or by pressing Tab until the object is selected. (An object is selected when you see grey squares—called *handles*—around the edges of the object.) To select a form, click any empty part of the form or open the **E**dit menu and choose Select **F**orm.

Tip
You also can display the Properties dialog box by right-clicking the object and choosing **O**bject Properties from the SpeedMenu.

2. Open the **V**iew menu and choose **O**bject Properties. dBASE for Windows displays the Properties dialog box for the selected object.

3. Select the Properties page in the Properties dialog box. Figure 15.7 shows the properties for a form. The left side of the dialog box lists the property names and categories, and the right side displays the current settings for each property.

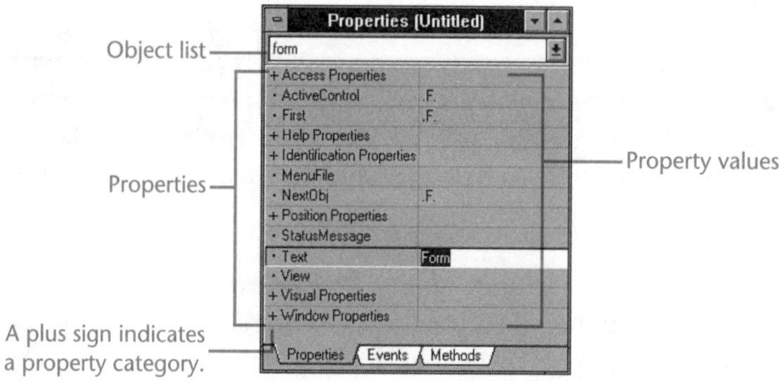

Fig. 15.7
Use the Properties dialog box to set the properties for a form object.

Object list

Properties

A plus sign indicates a property category.

Property values

Properties (Untitled)

form

+ Access Properties	
· ActiveControl	.F.
· First	.F.
+ Help Properties	
+ Identification Properties	
· MenuFile	
· NextObj	.F.
+ Position Properties	
· StatusMessage	
· Text	Form
· View	
+ Visual Properties	
+ Window Properties	

Properties | Events | Methods

4. Click the property you want to change, or use the up and down arrow keys to select the property.

5. If the item has a plus sign (+) beside it, the item is a category that contains a group of related properties. Double-click the category name to display its properties and then select the one you want to manipulate. (You also can display the category's properties by selecting the category name and pressing the plus sign key.)

Note

You can close a category by double-clicking on the category name or by selecting the name and pressing the minus sign key.

6. Enter a new property value using one of the following methods:

   - Type the new value in the edit box.
   - If the property has a drop-down list, use the list to select a value.
   - If the property has a Tool button, choose the Tool button to display a dialog box that enables you to choose the value you want.

7. Repeat steps 4–6 to set other property values.

8. Close the Properties dialog box by pressing Ctrl+F4 or by double-clicking on the Control-menu box.

Tip

To open all the categories, press Ctrl+plus sign (+). To close all the categories, press Ctrl+minus sign (–).

The next few sections show you how to set a few of the form properties.

Note

If you prefer to work in the Properties dialog box without the categories (that is, with an alphabetical list of the property names), open the **P**roperties menu, choose **D**esktop, and then select the Application page in the dialog box that appears. Deactivate the **O**bject Properties Outline check box and then choose OK.

Associating a Table or Query with a Form

Forms often are used to gather or display information from a table or query. Data entry screens, of course, are designed specifically to get and edit table information, but you also may need data in a dialog box form.

For these cases, you need to use the *View* property to associate a table or query with the form. You can type the name of the file (include both the primary name and extension), or you can select a file by following these steps:

1. In the View property, choose the Tool button. dBASE for Windows displays the Choose View dialog box (see fig. 15.8).

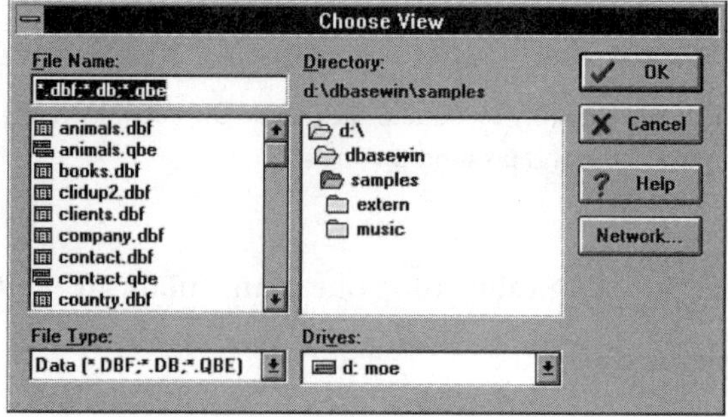

Fig. 15.8
To associate a table or query with a form, use the Choose View dialog box to set the form's View property.

2. In the File **T**ype drop-down list, select the type of file you want to use.
3. If necessary, use the Dri**v**es and **D**irectory lists to select the location of the file.
4. Highlight the file in the **F**ile Name list.
5. Choose OK to return to the Properties dialog box. dBASE for Windows inserts the selected file name in the View property.

Setting the Window Properties

The form Properties dialog box includes several properties that affect how the form window looks and how users can interact with the window. If you double-click the Window Properties category, you see the following properties:

AutoSize—If the form is sizeable (see the Sizeable property), the size of the form depends on the following items:

- The Height and Width properties
- The dimensions the user sets

If you always want the form to open with the same size, set AutoSize to true (.T.). This setting tells dBASE for Windows to adjust the form size automatically to accommodate the objects contained in the form.

EscExit—This property controls whether or not the user can close the form by pressing the Esc key. Set EscExit to true (.T.) to allow the user to exit the form by pressing Esc. Setting this property to false (.F.) disables the Esc key while the form is active.

Maximize—This property determines whether a Maximize button appears in the upper-right corner of the form. Set this property to true (.T.) to display a Maximize button.

MDI—This property determines whether a form is an MDI window. MDI stands for *Multiple Document Interface* and it's a Windows standard that enables programs to open multiple documents within a single application window. You can minimize, maximize, move, or size these open windows, and the window names appear at the bottom of the **W**indow menu. To turn a form into an MDI window, set its MDI property to true (.T.). (This is the default value, so you may not need to change this setting.)

Note

dBASE for Windows, for example, uses one non-MDI window (the main dBASE window) and several MDI windows, including the Navigator, the Command window, and the Form Designer. This format is the basic design of all dBASE applications: you designate one form as the main, non-MDI window (usually with its own menu bar), and the forms the user works with (except dialog boxes) are MDI windows that are subordinate to the application window. Dialog boxes are always non-MDI forms.

Minimize—This property determines whether the form has a Minimize button. Set this property to true (.T.) to display a Minimize button.

Moveable—This property determines whether the form has a title bar (which you can click and drag with a mouse to move the form). Set this property to false (.F.) to hide the title bar and prevent the user from moving the form.

ScaleFontName—This property determines the name of the default form font. This font (along with the ScaleFontSize property) determines the size of the Form Designer grid.

ScaleFontSize—This property determines the size of the default form font. Again, the size of the font determines the size of the Form Designer grid.

Sizeable—This property determines whether the user can size the form with a mouse. Set this property to false (.F.) to change the border to a thin line, which the user cannot drag with the mouse.

SysMenu—This property controls whether a form displays a Control-menu box in its upper-left corner. If you set this property to .T., the Control-menu box appears, and the control menu offers the following commands:

Restore	Restores the form to its original size after being maximized or minimized.
Move	User can move the form using the arrow keys.
Size	User can resize the form using the arrow keys.
Mi**n**imize	Reduces the form to an icon.
Ma**x**imize	Enlarges the form to its largest size.
Close	Closes the form.
Nex**t**	Selects the next open form.
Design **F**orm	Loads the current form into the Form Designer.

Tip
When you set the form's MDI property to .T., dBASE for Windows ignores the SysMenu property and always gives the form a Control- menu box.

The SysMenu property is set to .T. by default, but you normally set it to .F. when you will be using the form as a data entry screen or dialog box.

WindowState—This property determines how the form is displayed. Select *0-Normal* to display the form in its original size; select *1-Minimized* to display the form as an icon; select *2-Maximized* to display the form maximized.

Tip
If MDI is true (.T.), dBASE always treats the Maximize, Minimize, Moveable, and Sizeable properties as true (.T.) and ignores the current values of these properties.

The following table shows some typical window property values for the four kinds of forms:

Property	Data Entry	Dialog Box	MDI Window	Application Window
AutoSize	.T.	.T.	.F.	.F.
EscExit	.T.	.T.	.T.	.F.
Maximize	.T.	.F.	N/A	.T.
MDI	.T.	.F.	.T.	.F.
Minimize	.T.	.F.	N/A	.T.
Moveable	.T.	.F.	N/A	.T.
Sizeable	.T.	.F.	N/A	.T.
SysMenu	.F.	.F.	.T.	.T.

> **Troubleshooting**
>
> *I set my form's Moveable property to true (.T.), but the title bar still appears. What am I doing wrong?*
>
> You probably defined a title for the form. If you give the form a title by entering a value in the Text property (see the next section, "Giving the Form a Title"), the title bar always appears, regardless of the value of the Moveable property. Delete the Text property value and you should be okay.
>
> *Why should dialog boxes be non-MDI windows?*
>
> By definition, MDI windows are nonmodal, meaning they can lose the focus as the user moves to a different window. Dialog boxes, however, are almost always modal; the user must deal with the dialog box first before moving on to anything else. You use MDI windows only when you want to give users the potential to access multiple forms. For example, you may want to let your users enter data in a customer table in one window while browsing a table of orders in another. Because the forms are nonmodal, the user is free to switch back and forth.

Giving the Form a Title

Most forms need a title so the user can identify the form. Also, if the form's MDI property is true (.T.), the form's title appears in the window list at the bottom of the **W**indow menu. The default title for each new form is *Form,* but you can change the title by entering a new value in the Text property (see fig. 15.9).

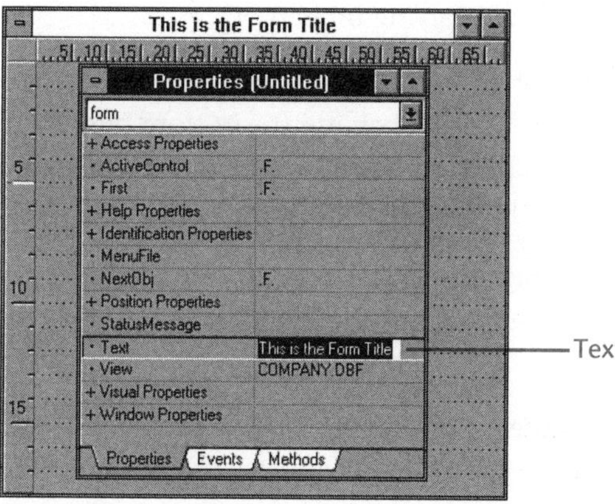

Fig. 15.9
The value in the Text property appears as the form's title.

Setting the Size and Position of the Form

A form's Height and Width properties determine the dimensions of the form, and its Top and Left properties determine the position of the form (or, more specifically, the position of the form's top-left corner). The easiest way to adjust these properties is to size and move the form directly, using your mouse or keyboard.

Note

You can size the form window using either of the following methods:

- With your mouse, position the pointer over one of the window borders (the pointer changes to a two-headed arrow), and then drag the border to the size you want.
- With your keyboard, choose Size from the Control menu, press one of the arrow keys to select a border, and then use the arrow keys to adjust the border. After you finish, press Enter.

You can move a form window using either of the following methods:

- With your mouse, drag the form's title bar.
- With your keyboard, choose **M**ove from the Control menu, use the arrow keys to position the form, and then press Enter.

For more precise adjustments, you can use the Properties dialog box to enter specific values for each property. Double-click the Position Properties category to display the following properties:

Height—Determines the height of the form's usable area (that is, the area between the title bar and the bottom border). The height is measured in character units, where one unit is the height of an average character in the current form font.

Left—Determines the position, in character units, of the left border relative to the left edge of the application window's usable area.

Top—Determines the position, in character units, of the top border relative to the top edge of the application window's usable area. (In dBASE for Windows, the usable area begins just below the SpeedBar.)

Width—Determines the width of the form's usable area in character units.

> **Note**
>
> When you adjust the size and position of the form, make sure the form's borders remain within the confines of the application window. If you need a larger form, you can use the ScrollBar property to add scroll bars to the form. Scroll bars enable the user to scroll to other parts of the form.

Adding a Status Bar Message

In dBASE for Windows, when you highlight a menu item or place the mouse pointer over a SpeedBar button, a message appears in the Status bar that describes the command or button. You can add this convenience to your forms by using the StatusMessage property. In the Properties dialog box, select the StatusMessage property. In the text box provided, type the message you want to appear in the Status bar when the user opens the form.

> **Note**
>
> You also can use the StatusMessage property to define a Status bar message for most other form objects. You can create helpful Status bar prompts that describe objects such as data entry fields and check boxes.

Working with Menus

Most application windows have a menu bar and pull-down menus that give the user access to the application's features. You can add a menu bar to an MDI window, and this menu bar replaces the application menu bar when the MDI window is active (similar to the way the Form Designer menu bar replaces the dBASE for Windows menu bar).

Creating a Menu

To create a menu with the Menu Designer, follow these steps:

1. Open the **L**ayout menu, choose T**o**ols, and then choose Design **M**enu. The Menu Designer window appears, as shown in figure 15.10.

2. Type the name for your menu and then press Enter. To designate a shortcut key for the menu, precede the letter with an ampersand (&). For example, typing **&File** produces a menu where the *F* in File is underlined.

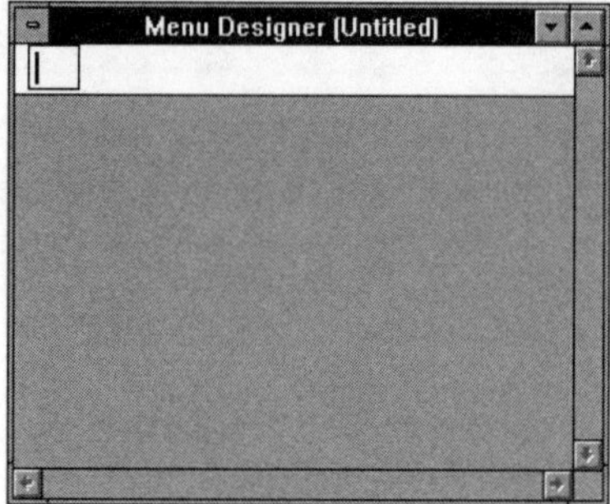

Fig. 15.10
Use the Menu Designer to create a menu for a form.

3. Fill in the menu choices using the following techniques:

   - To enter a command, type the name of the command and press Enter. Again, you can use the ampersand (&) to add a shortcut key to the command name.

   - To enter a separator, open the **M**enu menu and choose Insert Separa**t**or.

   - To create a cascade menu, select the command, open the **M**enu menu, choose Insert **M**enu, and then enter the menu choices for the cascade menu.

Tip
You also can add a separator by pressing Ctrl+T.

Tip
You also can create a cascade menu by pressing Ctrl+M or Tab.

4. To create another menu, select an item in the menu bar, open the **M**enu menu, choose I**n**sert Menu Item (to insert the new menu before the selected menu), or press Tab (to insert the new menu after the selected menu). Then repeat steps 2 and 3 to define the menu.

5. To change the property settings for a menu item, right-click the item to display the SpeedMenu and then choose Object **P**roperties. This list summarizes some common menu properties:

   Enabled (in the Access Properties category)—Set this property to false (.F.) to disable a menu item.

   Checked—Set this property to true (.T.) to place a check mark beside a menu item.

   StatusMessage (in the Help Properties category)—The text you enter for this property appears in the Status bar when the user highlights the menu item.

   Shortcut—This property specifies a shortcut key for the menu item. For example, typing **Ctrl+G** means the user can select the item by pressing Ctrl+G.

Tip
You also can add a menu by clicking on an item in the menu bar and then pressing Ctrl+N.

Note

The Events page in the Properties dialog box has an OnClick item. Use this item to specify the procedure to run when the user selects the menu item.

6. After you finish setting properties, close the Properties dialog box to return to the Menu Designer.
7. To exit the Menu Designer, open the **F**ile menu and choose **C**lose.
8. Choose **Y**es to save your changes.

Adding a Menu to a Form

After you've created a menu file, you can add it to a form by following these steps:

1. Select the MenuFile property in the form's Properties dialog box and click the Tool button. dBASE for Windows displays the Choose Menu dialog box.
2. Click the Tool button to display the Choose Menu dialog box.
3. Highlight the menu file you want to use and then choose OK.

▶ "Creating Procedures," p. 602

▶ "Handling Events," p. 650

Note

The form's MDI property determines where the menu appears. If you want the menu to appear in the form itself (just below the title bar), set MDI to false (.F.). You use this setting if the form is an application window. If you want the menu to appear in place of the application menu bar, set MDI to true (.T.).

Adding Objects to a Form

After you have created your form and its properties are set to your liking, you can start adding objects to the form. These objects are the controls the user will work with and anything else (such as text and graphics) that make the form easier to understand.

Before you start adding objects, however, you need to do some planning to decide what kinds of objects to add to the form. Ask yourself these questions:

What is the purpose of the form? Every form should accomplish a specific task. Whether it's for gathering data or displaying a message, the form's purpose dictates, in a general way, the kinds of objects you will need.

Is this form database-related? If so, you need to associate a table or query with the form (as described earlier in this chapter).

What fields do I need to display? In a database-related form, you need to decide which fields to display for adding and editing information. Also review the data types of the fields you will be using. You can handle character, logical, and memo fields with different objects and in different ways.

Will this be a multiple-table form? If the form will be based on a query of multiple, related tables, you need to decide how to handle the related data. For example, if the relation is one-to-many, do you want to see all the child records that are related to each parent record?

What dialog box controls do I need? If the form is nondatabase-related, you need to decide which dialog box controls (check boxes, list boxes, push buttons, and so on) you need to gather the appropriate information.

◄ "Working with Related Tables," p. 261

What layout should I use? Perhaps the most important design consideration is the layout of the objects. A data entry screen or dialog box with objects scattered willy-nilly is both confusing and frustrating for the user. Follow these guidelines:

- Include only objects that are necessary for accomplishing the goal of the form. Don't clutter the form with unnecessary objects.
- Make sure each object used to gather data has a text label that clearly identifies the object's function. For example, data entry fields should have a label that describes the field.
- If possible, base your form design on a real-world form (such as an invoice or purchase order). Users will feel more comfortable and will be less prone to make mistakes if an electronic form reminds them of its paper counterpart.
- Keep related objects together. For example, if you store an address in several fields (STREET, CITY, STATE, and so on), make sure these fields appear together in the form. To emphasize related objects, surround them with a rectangle.

- Set up your form so the order in which you want the user to fill in the fields is the order in which the fields appear.

Creating an Object

Before examining the specific built-in objects available in dBASE for Windows, first add an object to a form using these steps:

1. In the Control Palette, click the object type you want to use.
2. Move the mouse pointer into the form and position the pointer where you want the top-left corner of the object to appear.
3. Hold down the left mouse button and drag the mouse down and to the right until the object is the size and shape you want. As you drag, an outline of the object appears in the form, and highlights appear in the rulers to show you the object's size (see fig. 15.11).
4. Release the mouse button. dBASE for Windows creates the object (see fig. 15.12).

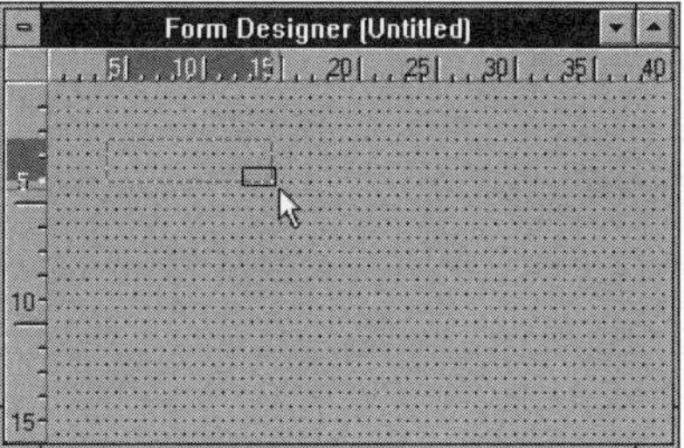

Fig. 15.11
Drag the mouse to create the object.

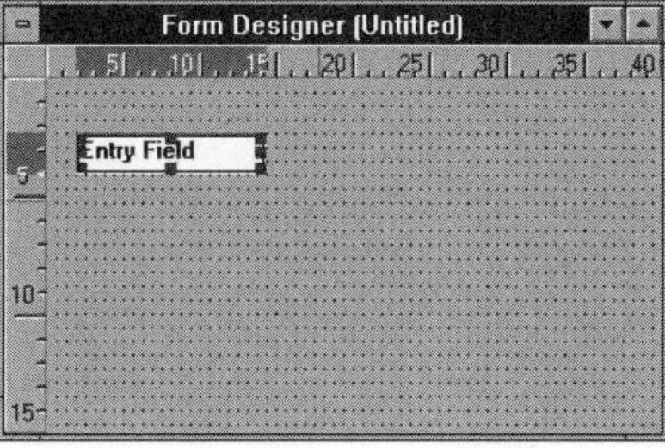

Fig. 15.12
When you release the mouse button, dBASE for Windows creates the object.

Troubleshooting

I don't see the Control Palette on my screen.

To display the Control Palette on your screen, open the **V**iew menu and choose **C**ontrols. Alternatively, you can right-click the form and choose **C**ontrols from the SpeedMenu.

Setting the Initial Value of an Object

When you first run a form, you'll probably want some of the objects to have an initial value. For example, if your form will be used to enter new records in a table, you may want to enter suggested values in some fields. Similarly, you may want to initialize certain dialog box controls (such as a check box, spinner, or scroll bar). Table 15.1 lists the controls that accept initial values.

Table 15.1 Controls That Accept Initial Values

Control	Values Accepted	Comments
EntryField	Anything	Initial value must be of the same data type as the field.
SpinBox	Numeric	Initial value must be between the minimum and maximum values assigned to the spin box.
ScrollBar	Numeric	Initial value must be between the minimum and maximum values assigned to the scroll bar.
CheckBox	.T. or .F.	Use .T. to initially activate the check box; use .F. to initially deactivate the check box.
RadioButton	.T. or .F.	Use .T. to initially activate a radio button; use .F. to initially deactivate a radio button.
List Box	List selection	The Value property is determined by the current list selection. You can't initialize this property directly; instead, you need to set the CurSel property.

Tip
Make sure only one radio button per group is active.

You can set the initial value at runtime within your dBASE code, or you can establish default values at design time. For the latter, follow these steps:

1. Display the Properties dialog box for the object you want to work with.

2. Select the Value property.

3. Type the initial value.

4. Press Enter to accept the value, or press Ctrl+F4 to return to the Form Designer.

Note

The following object types have a Value property: entry fields, spin boxes, scroll bars, check boxes, radio buttons, combo boxes, list boxes, and text editors. If you link any of these objects with a table or query field (as described in the next section), the Value field is automatically set to the field value in the first record.

Linking an Object to a Field or Memory Variable

In your data entry forms, you may use objects such as entry fields and spin boxes to add and edit data from the table or query specified in the form's View property. (See "Associating a Table or Query with a Form," earlier in this chapter, to learn how to set the form's View property.) Similarly, you often may use dialog box objects to modify memory variables. To link an object with a field or variable, follow these steps:

1. Display the Properties dialog box for the object you want to link.

2. Select the DataLink property.

3. Type the name of the memory variable or field you want to link to the object. If you're not sure about a field name, click the Tool button to display the Choose Field dialog box (see fig. 15.13).

4. Use the **T**ables list to select a table, and use the **F**ields list to select the field to link with the object.

5. Choose OK to return to the Properties window. dBASE for Windows enters the field name in the DataLink text box.

Tip

If you want to select a field from a different view, choose the **V**iew button and then select a view from the Choose View dialog box that appears.

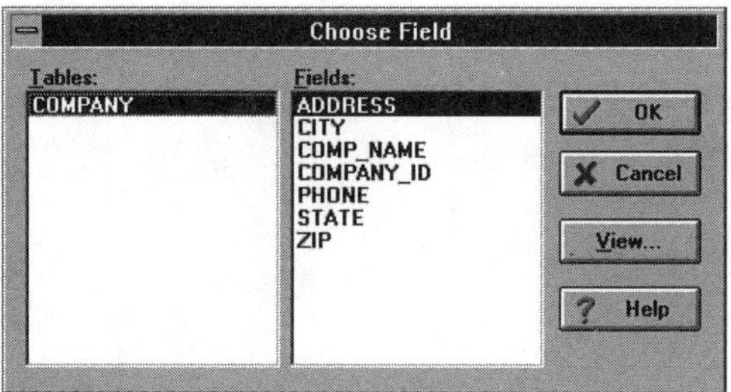

Fig. 15.13
Use the Choose Field dialog box to select the field to use in the DataLink property.

Understanding the Object Types

The Control Palette has over a dozen different object types, each with its own list of properties. Understanding the function of each object and when to use one object instead of another is crucial if you hope to build efficient, attractive forms. The next few sections discuss each object, examine its unique properties, and give you suggestions on when the object is appropriate.

Adding Text with the Text Object

You use the *text object* to add a static text label to a form. In a data entry screen, you almost always use text as a prompt for fields without their own label (such as an entry field or spin box). For example, if you have a field called CUST_NAME on the form, you can create a text object with a prompt such as *Customer Name* and place it beside the field. After you have added a text object to a form, you can change the default label by modifying the object's Text property.

Note

In dBASE for Windows, a text object is equivalent to an @...SAY statement in dBASE for DOS.

You also can use the text object to create shortcut keys for the other form objects. Follow these steps:

1. Add a text object to the form.

2. With the object selected, open the Properties dialog box and select the Text property.

3. Type the prompt you want to use and place an ampersand (&) to the left of the character that will be the shortcut key. For example, if you enter **&Name**, the *N* will be the shortcut key (*N* will appear underlined in the form), as figure 15.14 shows. Close the Properties dialog box when you're done.

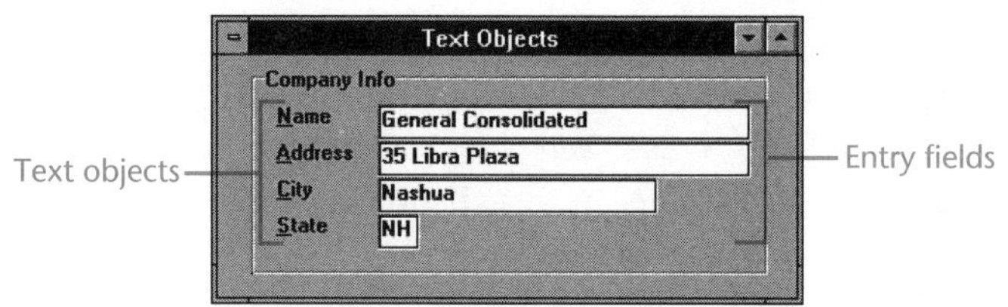

Fig. 15.14
A form displaying several text objects with shortcut keys.

4. Add the object associated with the text object you created earlier. For example, if the *&Name* text is a prompt for a field called CUST_NAME, add the appropriate object for the CUST_NAME field.

By adding the text object and the data entry object consecutively, dBASE for Windows assumes the two are related. When the user presses Alt and the text object's shortcut key, dBASE for Windows automatically selects the data entry object.

Tip
Make sure the text object and the data entry object are located close together so the user knows they're related. You normally position the data entry control to the right or immediately below the text object.

Gathering Data with Entry Fields

Entry field objects are text boxes you can use to enter or edit data in fields and memory variables that accept character, numeric, date, or logical data types. You normally use an entry field when you want to give the user the freedom to enter any appropriate value. Entry fields typically are used to gather data for things like names and street addresses (again see fig. 15.14).

Note

In dBASE for Windows, an entry field object is equivalent to an @...GET statement in dBASE for DOS.

In some situations, an entry field is *not* appropriate, as the following list describes:

- If you want the user to enter a value only from a range of numbers or dates, a spin box or a scroll bar is a better choice. See "Using Spin Boxes and Scroll Bars to Enter a Range of Values" later in this chapter.

- If the field or variable accepts logical values, use a check box to toggle between true (.T.) and false (.F.). The section "Entering Logical Values with Check Boxes" shows you how to add check boxes to a form.
- If you want the user to select from a small number of choices, create a radio button for each choice. The section titled "Using Radio Buttons to Give the User a Choice" helps you create radio buttons.
- If you have a longer list of choices the user can select from, set up a combo box or list box. See "Selecting Data from a List Using Combo Boxes and List Boxes" later in this chapter.

Defining a Data Entry Template

To make data entry easier and more accurate, dBASE for Windows enables you to define an edit *mask* for an entry field. This mask is a template that specifies how you want the entry to look and what kinds of characters are acceptable. With dBASE for Windows, you can use two different kinds of symbols to create the template: picture symbols and function symbols.

The *picture symbols* define how you want each character in the entry field to behave. Table 15.2 lists the available picture symbols.

Table 15.2 Picture Symbols

Symbol	Purpose
Character Data	
!	Converts letters to uppercase.
#	Accepts only numbers, spaces, periods, and signs.
9	Accepts only numbers.
A	Accepts only letters.
X	Accepts any character.
Logical Data	
L	Accepts only T, t, F, f, Y, y, N, or n. Converts t, f, y, and n to uppercase.
Y	Accepts only Y, y, N, or n. Converts y and n to uppercase.

Symbol	Purpose
Numeric Data	
$	Inserts a dollar sign.
*	Inserts asterisks in place of leading blanks.
.	Specifies the position of the decimal point.
,	Separates thousands.
9	Accepts only numbers and plus (+) and minus (–) signs.

Note

Technically, the **$** template character displays whatever currency symbol is defined in the Desktop Properties dialog box. To determine the currency, open the **P**roperties menu, choose **D**esktop, and then select the Country tab. The currency character is displayed in the S**y**mbol text box. The **L**eft and **R**ight option buttons determine which side of the number the **$** character displays the currency symbol.

For example, if you have a numeric field that always uses numbers with two decimal places, you can use the template 99.99. When the user enters **1234**, for example, the number is automatically stored as 12.34.

For even greater flexibility, you can use other characters as literals rather than placeholders. For example, consider the following template: (999)999-9999. If you enter **1234567890**, the template displays the value as (123)456-7890, which is a typical phone number format. dBASE for Windows leaves the literal characters (the parentheses and the dash) as they are and fills in the picture symbols (the 9s).

The *function symbols* are similar to the picture symbols except they operate on the entire field, not just a single character. Table 15.3 lists the function symbols available in dBASE for Windows.

Table 15.3 Function Symbols

Symbol	Purpose
Character Data	
@!	Converts letters to uppercase.
@A	Accepts only letters.
@R	Inserts literal placeholders into the display without including them in the field or variable. For example, if the value in a ZIP_CODE field is 123456789, a template of @R 99999-9999 displays the field as 12345-6789 but stores it as 123456789.
@T	Removes leading and trailing blanks.
Numeric Data	
@$	Inserts a dollar sign. (Again, the currency symbol displayed depends on the value defined in the Desktop Properties dialog box.)
@^	Displays numbers in exponential format.
@Z	Displays a zero value as a blank.
Date Data	
@D	Displays and accepts a date in the current date format defined in the Desktop Properties dialog box.
@E	Displays and accepts a date in European (DD/MM/YY) format.

You can use a function symbol by itself or combine it with the picture symbols.

To define a template for an entry field, follow these steps:

1. Display the Properties dialog box for the entry field object and open the Edit Properties category.

2. To enter function symbols in the Template, select the Function property. To enter picture symbols, select the Picture property.

3. Type the symbols you want for your template. If you're not sure which symbols to use, click the Tool button in either property. dBASE for Windows displays the Choose Template dialog box, as shown in figure 15.15.

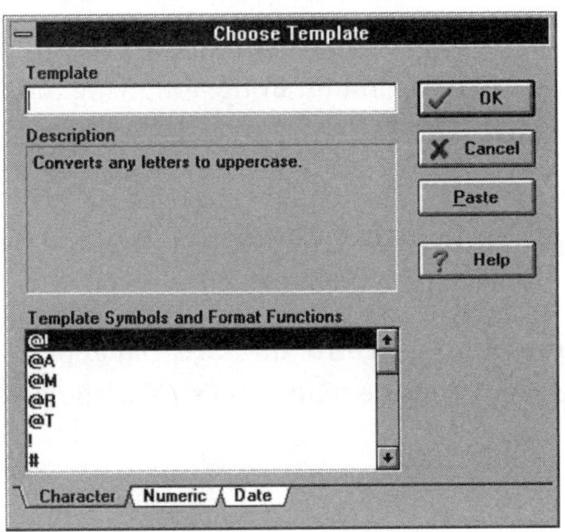

Fig. 15.15
Use the Choose Template dialog box to construct your data entry template.

4. Select the Character, Numeric, or Date page, as appropriate.
5. In the Template Symbols and Format Functions list, highlight the symbol you want to use and then choose **P**aste. dBASE for Windows transfers the symbol into the Template text box.
6. Repeat Step 5 until your template is complete.
7. Choose OK to return to the Properties dialog box.

Tip
You can also use the Template text box to edit the template directly (to add literals and placeholders, for example).

Validating Input

To ensure that data is entered accurately, you can tell dBASE for Windows to validate each entry as the user moves out of the field. If the current field value is invalid, an error message appears and the user is forced back into the field to enter a correct value.

Validation is used constantly in database applications. The test can be simple (such as making sure an order isn't a negative number) to more complicated (such as checking to see if a field value corresponds to a value in a related table).

You set up a field validation by following these steps:

1. Open the Properties dialog box for the data entry object.
2. In the Events page, select the Valid event and then click the Tool button to display the Procedures window.
3. Enter a subroutine that performs the validation.

▶ "Creating Procedures," p. 602

▶ "Handling Events," p. 650

4. Press Ctrl+F4 to return to the Properties dialog box.

5. Select the Properties page and fill in the following properties in the Edit Properties category:

    ValidRequired—This property determines whether dBASE for Windows runs the Valid routine on just new data (.F.), the default, or on both new and edited data (.T.).

    ValidErrorMsg—An error message that appears in the Status bar if the Valid routine returns false (.F.). The default message is `Invalid Input`.

> **Troubleshooting**
>
> *When I move into an entry field and press a key, the entire field value is deleted. Why is this happening and is there any way to prevent it?*
>
> Any time you highlight text and press a key, dBASE for Windows replaces the text with your keystroke. This behavior is normal, and you'll find it happens in most applications. To avoid accidentally deleting the text, press the left or right arrow key to remove the highlight. Alternatively, you can set the entry field's SelectAll property (it's part of the Edit Properties category) to false (.F.). This setting tells dBASE for Windows not to highlight the field when you move into it. This property applies to spin boxes, as well.

Using Spin Boxes and Scroll Bars to Enter a Range of Values

If you need to capture numeric or date data on your form, you can use an entry field, but spin box and scroll bar objects give you the following advantages:

- You can set maximum and minimum values for the field without having to write a Valid procedure.

- The user can adjust the field value with a mouse rather than the keyboard.

Spin Boxes

A *spin box* consists of a text box and up and down arrows (see fig. 15.16). Users can type the numeric or date value in the text box, or they can use the up or down arrows to increase or decrease the current value. The spin box object has the following unique properties:

Rangemax (Edit Properties)—This property sets the maximum value the user can enter in the spin box. The default is 100.

Rangemin (Edit Properties)—This property sets the minimum value the user can enter in the spin box. The default is 1.

RangeRequired (Edit Properties)—This property determines whether dBASE for Windows checks the range values on just new data (.F.), the default, or on both new and edited data (.T.).

SpinOnly—Set this property to true (.T.) to disable the edit box and force the user to enter values using the spin box arrows only. The default is false (.F.).

Step—This property specifies the increments in which the spin box value increases or decreases when the user clicks one of the arrows. The default step value is 1.00.

Tip
Your step values don't have to be whole numbers. You can enter decimal values (such as 1.5 or 6.25), as well.

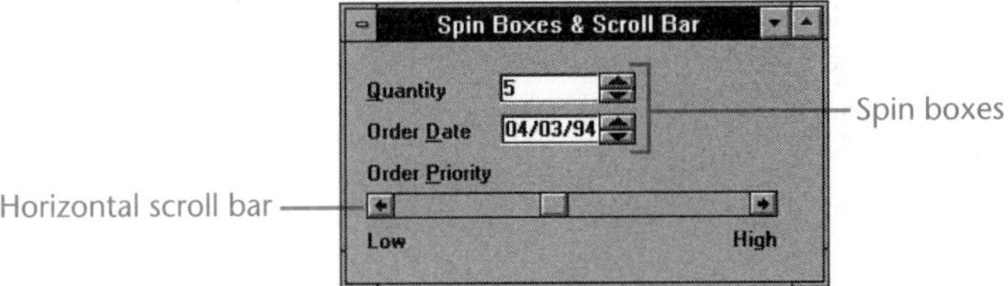

Fig. 15.16
Some example spin box and scroll bar objects.

Note

You can define a data entry template and a Valid routine for a spin box (see "Defining a Data Entry Template" and "Validating Input" earlier in this chapter).

Scroll Bars

Although you normally use *scroll bars* to navigate through a window with a mouse, you can use scroll bars by themselves to enter values between a predefined maximum and minimum. dBASE for Windows offers two kinds of scroll bar objects: a horizontal scroll bar (as shown in figure 15.16) and a vertical scroll bar. In either case, you can increase and decrease the current field value by clicking the arrows or by dragging the scroll box. To set the maximum and minimum values for the object, use the Rangemax and Rangemin properties, respectively.

> **Note**
>
> Unlike spin boxes, scroll bars don't show the current value of the field or variable. For this reason, scroll bars are used more often to enter subjective values. In figure 15.16, for example, the scroll box is used to enter a priority for the order. The values range from 1 to 5, but all the user sees is *Low* at one end and *High* at the other. This kind of scheme has many uses. For example, you can gather questionnaire data where you have Strongly Disagree at one end of the scroll bar and Strongly Agree at the other.

Entering Logical Values with Check Boxes

Logical values toggle a field or variable between true (.T.) and false (.F.), so entering this data with a *check box* makes sense. When the user activates the check box, dBASE for Windows enters true (.T.) in the field; when the user deactivates the check box, the field value becomes false (.F.).

> **Tip**
> To include a shortcut key in the label, precede one of the letters in the Text property with an ampersand (&).

When you add a check box object to a form, the box is checked and the object's label is the same as the object's name (for example, CHECKBOX1). If you want the form to load with the box unchecked, change the object's Value property to false (.F.). To use a different label, modify the object's Text property. Figure 15.17 shows a form with some example check boxes.

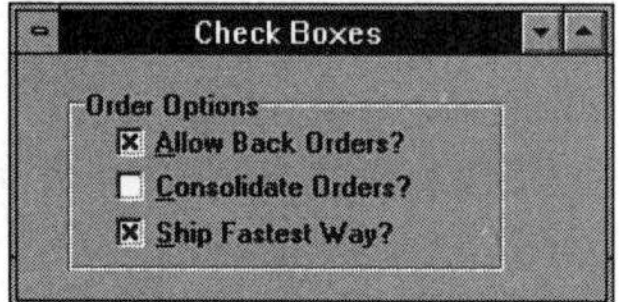

Fig. 15.17
A form with check box objects.

Using Radio Buttons to Give the User a Choice

If a character field can take only a limited number of values, you should, wherever possible, let users select the value they want from a predefined list. This method reduces the data entry errors that may occur if the user had to type the values in an entry field. If the number of possible values is small (for example, from two to five items), a group of *radio buttons* is your best choice.

> **Note**
>
> If you have more than five items, or if form space is limited, present the choices in a combo box or a list box. See "Selecting Data from a List Using Combo Boxes and List Boxes" later in this chapter.

To create a group of radio buttons, follow these steps:

1. Add the first radio button to the form.
2. Open the Properties dialog box for the radio button, display the Access Properties category, and then set the Group property to true (.T.). This setting tells dBASE for Windows that you're starting a group.
3. Set any other properties you need, including the following:

   DataLink—Enter the field or memory variable that stores the text of the active radio button in the group.

   Text—Change the radio button label to reflect the value you want entered in the field or variable if the user activates this radio button. For example, if you change the Text property to *Visa* and the user activates this radio button, dBASE for Windows stores *Visa* in the field or variable.

4. Add the next radio button.
5. Open the Properties dialog box for the new radio button and set its Group property to false (.F.).
6. Repeat steps 3–5 until you have added all the radio buttons in the group.
7. If you want to add another group, repeat steps 1–6.

Tip
To make your radio button groups more organized, surround them with a box. See "Using Graphics Objects" later in this chapter.

Figure 15.18 shows a form with two radio button groups.

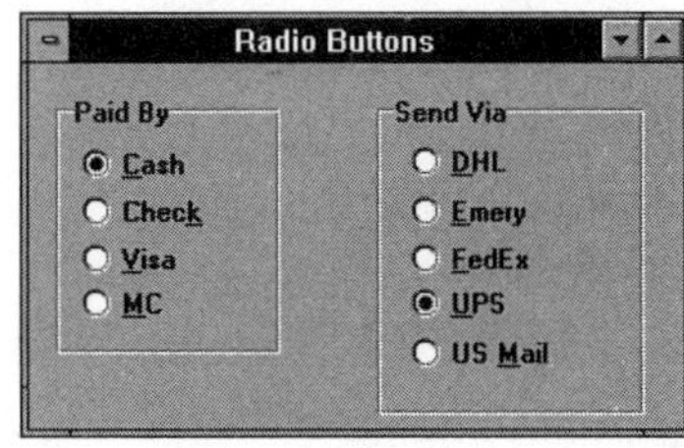

Fig. 15.18
A form with two groups of radio button objects.

Selecting Data from a List Using List Boxes and Combo Boxes

If a field or variable can take any one of a large number of choices (six or more), place the choices in a list box or combo box. A *list box* is a plain list of items that the user selects by clicking an item or by using the keyboard's up and down arrow keys. A *combo box* is a combination of an entry field and a list box. The user can select an item by highlighting it in the list or by typing it in the entry field (see fig. 15.19).

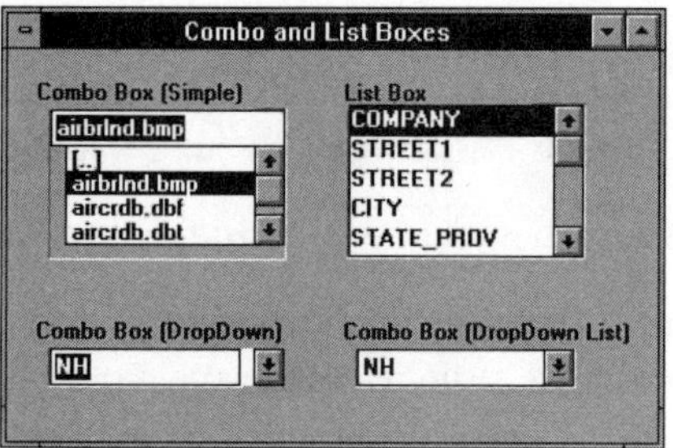

Fig. 15.19
A form with a list box and the three combo box styles.

In both combo boxes and list boxes, you define the items that appear in the list by modifying the object's DataSource property. Follow these steps:

1. Open the Properties dialog box for the combo box or list box object, display the Data Linkage Properties category, and then select the DataSource property.

2. Click the Tool button. dBASE for Windows displays the Choose Data Source dialog box (see fig. 15.20).

Fig. 15.20
Use the Choose Data Source dialog box to select a data source for a combo box or list box.

3. Use the **T**ype drop-down list to select the data source for the list. dBASE for Windows gives you the following choices:

   Array—The list items are the elements of an array.

   Field—The list items are the values contained in a field from the table or query specified in the form's View property.

   File—The list items are files in the current directory.

   Structure—The list items are the field names from the table or query specified in the form's View property.

   Tables—The list items are the tables in the query specified in the form's View property or in the open database file.

4. If necessary, use the **D**ata Source text box to complete the definition of the data source as follows:

   - If you chose Array, type the name of the array.
   - If you chose Field, type the name of the field.
   - If you chose File, type a file mask (for example, *.DBF).

5. Choose OK to return to the Properties dialog box.

You also can customize your combo boxes and list boxes by modifying the following properties:

Tip
You also can select a field by clicking the Tool button and selecting a field from the dialog box that appears. Note that if you haven't yet set the form's View property, dBASE for Windows will ask if you want to open a view.

CurSel—This list box property determines which list item is selected when the user first opens the form. Enter a number between 1 and the number of items in the list.

Multiple (Data Linkage Properties)—Set this list box property to true (.T.) to allow the user to select multiple items in the list.

Sorted (Data Linkage Properties) —Set this property to true (.T.) to display the items sorted alphabetically.

Style (Visual Properties)—This combo box property controls the type of combo box. You have three choices:

- **0-Simple** gives you a normal combo box with an edit box and list.
- **1-DropDown** gives you an edit box with an arrow that drops down the list of items.
- **2-DropDownList** gives you a noneditable box with an arrow that drops down the list of items.

II

Power Skills

Adding a Text Editor to Handle a Memo Field or Text File

Tip
Make sure the editor object is large enough to make it easy for the user to edit the text. See "Moving and Sizing Objects," later in this chapter.

Many forms need to edit a memo field or a text file. For these situations, you need to add an *editor object* to the form and then set the following properties:

DataLink—Use this property to link the editor with either a text file or a memo field from the table or query specified in the form's View property.

Modify (Edit Properties)—Set this property to false (.F.) to prevent the user from making changes to the memo field or text file.

Tip
If you're not sure of the name of the text file or memo field, click the Tool button in the DataLink property to display the Choose Data Link dialog box. Select either File or Field from the **T**ype list, enter a **D**ata Source, and then choose OK.

ScrollBar (Visual Properties)—Use this property to display horizontal and vertical scroll bars for navigating the text. You have the following choices:

0-Off—Does not display the scroll bars.

1-On—Displays the scroll bars.

2-Auto—Displays the scroll bars only when they're needed (that is, when the editor object is not large enough to show the entire memo field or text file).

3-Disabled—Displays the scroll bars, but the user can work with them.

Wrap (Edit Properties)—Set this property to true (.T.) to allow text to wrap inside the editor.

Using the Browse Object in a Multiple-Table Form

► "Using the dBASE Program Editor," p. 561

If your form is based on a multiple-table query, you're free to add any of the fields included in the query to your form. However, if the query is based on a one-to-many relation, you often may want to see all the child records associated with each parent record. For example, if the parent table contains customer information and the child table contains order data, you may want your form to display all the orders for a given customer.

◄ "Working with Related Tables," p. 261

To display the child records associated with each parent record, you need to do two things:

- Add the appropriate parent table fields to the form.
- Add a *Browse object* to the form to display the child records.

Figure 15.21 shows a form with a Browse object. In this case, the parent table contains company information and the child table contains the names of sales contacts within each company.

Note

You also can use the Browse object to display multiple records from a single table (or a single-table query).

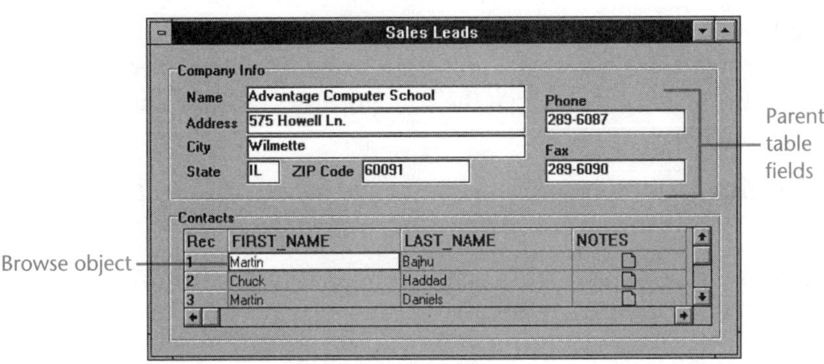

Fig. 15.21
A multiple-table form that uses a Browse object to display the many sides of a one-to-many relation.

Linking the Browse Object to a Table

After you set the form's View property to the appropriate query, you need to link the Browse object to the table you want to use. Open the Properties dialog box, display the Data Linkage Properties, and then enter the table alias in the Alias property.

Tip
If you're not sure which table you want to use, click the Tool button in the Alias property, select a table from the Choose Alias dialog box, and then choose OK.

Setting the Browse Object's Layout Properties

The Browse object has many properties that determine the layout of the Browse window. The following list summarizes these properties:

Fields (Data Linkage Properties)—Type the names of the fields you want in the Browse or click the Tool button to select the fields from the Browse Fields Picker dialog box. In this dialog box, you can also choose the P**r**operties button to enter various properties for each field (such as the Browse heading, a data entry template, the width of the column, and more). If you'd like to add a calculated field, choose the Add **C**alculated Field button and enter a name and expression in the Calculated Field dialog box.

ShowDeleted (Visual Properties)—Set this property to true (.T.) to display the deletion marks (the Del column).

Tip
The order in which the fields appear in the Fields property is the order in which they appear in the Browse window.

ShowHeading (Visual Properties)—Set this property to false (.F.) to hide the field headings.

ShowRecNo (Visual Properties)—Set this property to false (.F.) to hide the record numbers (the Rec column).

Text—Use this property to specify a title for the Browse window.

Setting the Browse Object's Editing Properties

The Browse object also has several properties that control how users edit records in the Browse object. Open the Edit Properties category and adjust the following properties:

Append—Set this property to false (.F.) to prevent the user from adding records in the Browse object.

Delete—Set this property to false (.F.) to prevent the user from marking Browse records for deletion.

Follow—Set this property to false (.F.) to prevent dBASE for Windows from following the current record to its new index location when you modify the key field.

Mode—This property determines the format of the Browse window. *0-Browse* is the normal, multiple-record Browse layout; *1-Form Edit* displays a single record with the fields in columns; *2-Columnar Edit* displays a single record with the fields in a column down the left side of the window.

Modify—Set this property to false (.F.) to prevent the user from making changes to the Browse data.

Toggle—Set this property to false (.F.) to disable the F2 key and prevent the user from toggling between Browse and Edit mode.

Using Graphics Objects

To add some pizzazz to your forms, dBASE for Windows has three objects you can use to create graphics: line, rectangle, and image.

Adding Lines

Use *lines* to separate parts of the form and emphasize important objects. To create a line, select the line control and then click and drag the new line in the Form window. The Properties dialog box for a line enables you to modify the line's style and width with these properties (open the Visual Properties category):

Pen—This property controls the style of the line. The default (*0-Solid*) gives you a solid line, and the other four options create patterned lines consisting of dots and dashes.

Width—This property specifies the width of the line in pixels. The default value is 1. You can type in a value or you can use the spin box.

Adding Rectangles

Rectangles give the user a visual clue as to which objects are related. For example, if you've created a group of radio buttons, surrounding them with a rectangle shows the user that the buttons comprise a group. This list summarizes the properties unique to rectangles:

BorderStyle (Visual Properties)—This property determines the look of the rectangle's border. *0-Normal* produces an etched border; *1-Raised* makes the interior of the rectangle appear to be raised from the form; *2-Lowered* makes the rectangle interior appear to be sunken into the form. Figure 15.22 illustrates each border style.

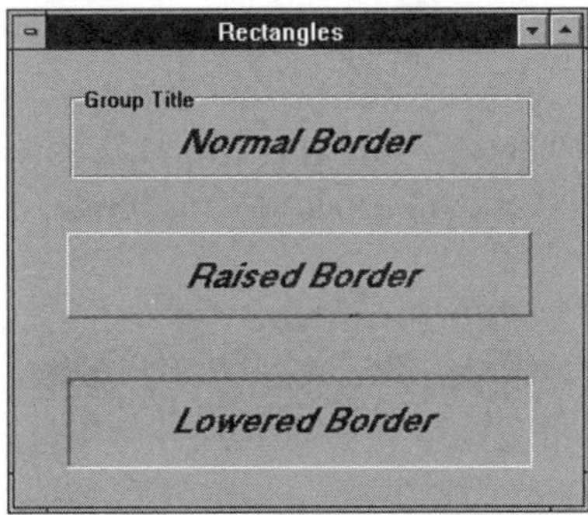

Fig. 15.22 The rectangle border styles.

Text—dBASE for Windows enables you to use the Text property to add a label to the upper-left corner of the rectangle. This property is useful for adding a brief description of the grouped objects.

PatternStyle (Visual Properties)—This property specifies the background pattern for the rectangle. There are seven patterns from which to choose.

Adding Image Objects

If you want to display binary data (such as an OLE object or a bitmap), add an *image object* to the form. To specify the binary data to display in the object, open the Properties dialog box, select the DataSource property, and then click the Tool button. dBASE for Windows displays the Choose Bitmap dialog box (see fig. 15.23). Depending on the image you want to add, use one of the following techniques to specify the data source:

- For a graphic image, select Filename from the Location drop-down list, click the Tool button, and then select a .BMP or .PCX file from the Open File dialog box.
- For an OLE object in a binary field, select Binary from the Location drop-down list, click the Tool button, and then select the binary field from the Choose Field dialog box.

Note

Before you can select a binary field for the image object, you need to set the form's View property to a table or query that contains binary data.

- For a resource object (such as a bitmap image used in dBASE for Windows), select Resource and click the Tool button. In the dBASE for Windows Bitmaps dialog box, select a bitmap from the ID list and then click OK.

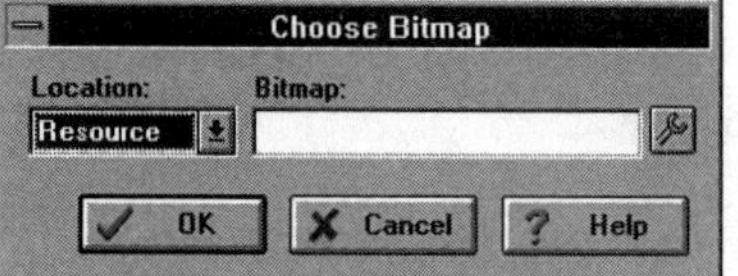

Fig. 15.23
Use the Choose Bitmap dialog box to select the data source for the image object.

Setting Some Common Properties of Objects

Tip
To set properties on multiple objects at one time, see "Selecting Multiple Objects" later in this chapter.

This tour of the dBASE for Windows form objects has examined various properties that are unique to each object. In turn, many properties are common to most, if not all, of the objects. This chapter can't examine every possible property, but a few properties exist that you may work with frequently. The next few sections cover these three property categories: Access Properties, Color Properties, and Font Properties.

Setting the Access Properties

The properties in the *Access* category determine how the user interacts with the form objects. With these properties, you can disable an object, hide it, and place it in a group. This list summarizes the items in the Access Properties category:

Before—This property determines the object that the current object precedes in the form's tab order. The *tab order* is the order in which the objects are selected when the user presses Tab (or Shift+Tab) to navigate the form. This order is normally determined by the order in which you add the objects to the form, but you can use the Before property to change it. For example, suppose that the current object is a radio button and you enter the name of a spin box called SPINBOX1 in the radio button's Before property. Then, whenever the user is on the radio button and presses Tab, SPINBOX1 is selected. To modify the Before property, click the Tool button and use the dialog box that appears to select the object before which you want the current object to appear in the tab order.

Tip
For an easier way to change the tab order, see "Changing the Form's Tab Order" later in this chapter.

Enabled—This property determines whether the user can select and modify an object. If false (.F.), the object is disabled and the user can't select it (and can't change its value). You normally disable an object when you want the user to perform some other action before accessing the object. For example, consider the form shown in figure 15.24. The three disabled radio buttons (**O**vernight, **T**wo-Day, and Three-**D**ay) make sense only when the **C**ourier option is chosen, so they remain disabled while **M**ail is active. If the user chooses **C**ourier, you can write event code that enables the other radio buttons.

▶ "Handling Events," p. 650

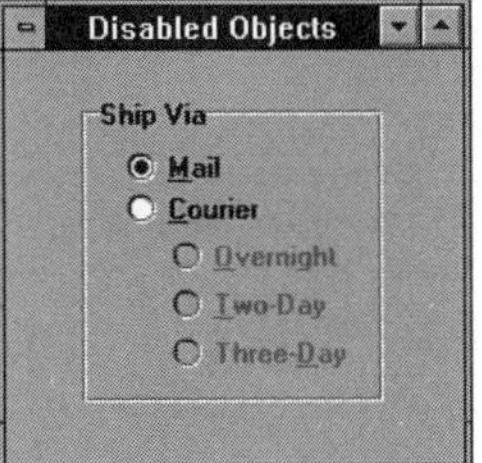

Fig. 15.24
Disabling objects prevents users from selecting them until they perform some other action.

Group—This property was discussed earlier in the radio buttons section (see "Using Radio Buttons to Give the User a Choice").

TabStop—This property determines whether an object appears in the form's tab order. If you set this property to false (.F.), users can't select the object by pressing Tab or Shift+Tab (although they still can click the object with the mouse). You normally use this property to make a form easier to navigate with the keyboard. In a group of radio buttons, for example, you can set the TabStop property to false (.F.) for every button except the first one. This setting enables the user to tab quickly past the entire group. (When they're inside the group, users can use the arrow keys to select a button.)

Visible—This property determines whether an object is visible to the user. Setting Visible to false (.F.) hides the object (and, of course, removes it from the tab order). As with Enabled, you normally hide an object when you want the user to perform some other action before accessing the object.

Setting Colors

The *color properties* control the background and foreground colors of an object. Many objects have a ColorNormal property (in the Visual Properties category) that specifies the color of an object when it doesn't have the focus. Some objects (such as entry fields) also have a ColorHighlight property that determines the object's color when it does have the focus. You can specify a color in two ways: use dBASE for Windows color codes or use the Choose Color dialog box.

Using the Color Codes

dBASE for Windows uses several *color codes* to specify foreground and background colors. These codes are summarized in table 15.4

Table 15.4 dBASE for Windows Color Codes

Code	Color
N	Black
B	Blue
G	Green
GB	Cyan
R	Red
RB	Magenta
RG	Brown
W	Grey
X	Blank

For a high-intensity foreground color, add a plus sign (+) after the code example: W+

For a high-intensity background color, add an asterisk (*) after the code example: N+

Note

These color codes are for color or grey-scale monitors only. They have no effect on monochrome monitors.

You separate foreground and background colors with a forward slash (/). For example, to specify a black foreground over a white background (which is, in most cases, the default setting for ColorNormal), you use the code N/W.

Tip

A form has no foreground, so to change the background color you need only to specify one color code in the form's ColorNormal property.

Using the Choose Color Dialog Box

For a greater variety of colors, you can use the Choose Color dialog box. Follow these steps:

1. In the Properties dialog box, open the Visual Properties category, select the ColorNormal or ColorHighlight property, and then click the Tool button. dBASE for Windows displays the Choose Color dialog box, as shown in figure 15.25.

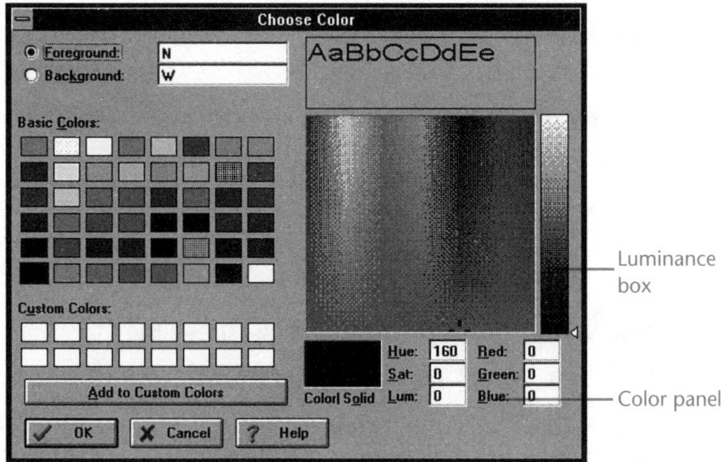

Fig. 15.25
Use the Choose Color dialog box to select a foreground and background color.

2. Select **F**oreground to choose the foreground color, or Bac**k**ground to choose the background color.

3. To select a color, use one of the following methods:

   - Click a color box in the Basic **C**olors section.
   - Click a color in the color panel and click a luminance (brightness) level in the luminance box.
   - Type numbers in the **H**ue, **S**at (saturation), and **L**um (luminance) text boxes (you can type values between 0 and 239). Hue controls the color, saturation controls the amount of grey in the color (the lower the number, the more grey), and luminance controls the brightness of the color (higher numbers produce brighter colors).
   - Type values in the **R**ed, **G**reen, and **B**lue text boxes (you can type values between 0 and 255).

4. Choose OK to return to the Properties dialog box.

Setting the Text Font

Many form objects display text (such as entry fields and list boxes) or have a Text property (such as check boxes and radio buttons). These objects have a Font Properties category that contains several properties you can use to control the font of the text, including the typeface, the type size, and attributes such as bold and italic. In the Properties dialog box, open the Font Properties category to see the following properties:

FontBold—Set this property to true (.T.) to display the object text in bold.

FontItalic—Set this property to true (.T.) to display the object text in italic.

FontName—This property sets the typeface of the object text. You can type a valid font name (such as Arial or Times New Roman) or you can click the Tool button and select a typeface from the Font dialog box.

Tip
You also can use the Font dialog box to modify the other font properties.

FontSize—This property controls the size of the font. You can type a number or use the spin box to adjust the current size.

FontStrikeOut—Set this property to true (.T.) to display a strikeout line through the object text.

FontUnderline—Set this property to true (.T.) to add an underline to the object text.

Working with Objects

When you want to create a functional, attractive form, adding objects and setting their properties is only the beginning. From here, you can add plenty of finishing touches to give your form a polished, professional look. This section looks at a few of these techniques, including how to move and size objects, how to align objects, and how to work with overlapping objects. The first step is to learn how to work with multiple objects simultaneously.

Selecting Multiple Objects

As you learned when working with an object's properties, you need to select the object before you can do anything to it. Selecting a single object is easy; you can click it or press Tab (or Shift+Tab) until the object is selected.

If you want to work with multiple objects at one time, however, you need to select each object. Use one of the following techniques:

- To select every object, open the **E**dit menu and choose Se**l**ect All.
- To select objects randomly, hold down Shift or Ctrl and click each object.
- To select all the objects in a rectangular area of the form, place the mouse pointer at the upper-left corner of the area (make sure it's not over an object), hold down the left mouse button, and then drag the mouse to the bottom-right corner of the area. Every object completely within the rectangular area is selected.

After you select the objects, you can work with them as though they were a single object. In particular, you can use the Properties dialog box to modify any properties the selected objects have in common. Just right-click any one of the selected objects (or open the **V**iew menu) and choose the **O**bject Properties command.

Note

The Properties dialog box for a multiple selection doesn't use the property categories. Instead, all the available properties are listed alphabetically.

Tip

If you need to cancel a selection, click an empty part of the form.

Moving and Sizing Objects

Many of the objects you add to a form may need to be resized and rearranged to get the layout just the way you want it. One way to modify the layout is to use the position properties described earlier in this chapter (see the section

"Setting the Size and Position of the Form" earlier in this chapter). The Top and Left properties control the position of the object's top-left corner, and the Height and Width properties control the dimensions of the object.

Alternatively, you can use your mouse to move and size an object by hand. Follow these steps to move an object:

1. Select the object or objects you want to move. dBASE for Windows displays the selection handles around the object's frame.

2. Position the mouse pointer anywhere inside the object but *not* over one of the selection handles.

3. Drag the object to the position you want. As you drag, the mouse pointer changes to a hand, and dBASE for Windows displays an outline showing the current position.

4. Release the mouse button. dBASE for Windows redraws the object in the new position.

Follow these steps to size an object by hand:

1. Select the object you want to size.

Note

You cannot size a multiple selection by hand. To size multiple objects, select one and then adjust the Height and Width properties for it.

2. Position the mouse pointer over the handle you want to move. The pointer changes to a two-headed arrow. To change the size horizontally or vertically, use the appropriate handle on the middle of a side. To change the size in both directions at one time, use the appropriate corner handle.

3. Drag the handle to the position you want. dBASE for Windows displays an outline showing the new border position.

4. Release the mouse button. dBASE for Windows redraws the object with the new dimensions.

Cutting, Copying, and Pasting Objects

To save time when constructing a form, you can move or copy objects from another form and paste them into the current form. To cut a selected object (or a multiple selection) to the Clipboard, use any of the following techniques:

- Open the **E**dit menu and choose Cu**t**.
- Right-click the selection and choose Cu**t** from the SpeedMenu.
- Click the Cut button in the SpeedBar.

Tip
You also can cut a selection by pressing Ctrl+X.

If you want to copy a selected object (or, again, a multiple selection) to the Clipboard, use any of these techniques:

- Open the **E**dit menu and choose **C**opy.
- Right-click the selection and choose **C**opy from the SpeedMenu.
- Click the Copy button in the SpeedBar.

Tip
Pressing Ctrl+C also copies a selection.

After the objects are on the Clipboard, open the other form and then use any of the following techniques to paste the objects:

- Open the **E**dit menu and choose **P**aste.
- Right-click the selection and choose **P**aste from the SpeedMenu.
- Click the Paste button in the SpeedBar.

Tip
You also can paste the Clipboard contents by pressing Ctrl+V.

Troubleshooting

To save time, I want to make a copy of an object on the same form. When I try this, however, dBASE for Windows reports an error. What's the problem?

dBASE for Windows doesn't allow two objects to share the same name, so it displays an error message if a name collision occurs. To solve the problem, you need to change the name of the original object *before* you paste the copy. Open the Properties dialog box and modify the object's Name property (under the Identification Properties category).

Deleting an Object

If you add an object by mistake, you can delete it from the form to reduce clutter and give yourself more room to work. To delete an object, select it (you can select multiple objects, if necessary), open the **E**dit menu, and then choose **D**elete.

Tip
You also can delete the current selection by pressing Delete.

Aligning Objects

Forms look best when the objects on the left line up neatly on the left, objects on the top line up on top, and so on. You can align objects by moving them or by using the Top and Left properties, but the Form Designer offers several techniques that make this chore much easier. Select the objects you want to align and then use one of the following methods:

- To align the left side of the selected objects with the left side of the leftmost object, click the Align Left SpeedBar button, or open the **L**ayout menu and choose Align **L**eft.

- To align the right side of the selected objects with the right side of the rightmost object, click the Align Right SpeedBar button, or open the **L**ayout menu and choose Align **R**ight.

- To align the top of the selected objects with the top of the topmost object, click the Align Top SpeedBar button, or open the **L**ayout menu and choose Align **T**op.

- To align the bottom of the selected objects with the bottom of the bottommost object, click the Align Bottom SpeedBar button, or open the **L**ayout menu and choose Align **B**ottom.

The Form Designer also has several commands that enable you to center an object on the form. Open the **L**ayout menu, choose **A**lign Special, and then choose one of the following commands:

Absolute **H**orizontal Center—Centers the selection horizontally based on the absolute size of the form (as given by the Width property).

Relative Ho**r**izontal Center—Centers the selection horizontally based on the current size of the form.

Absolute **V**ertical Center—Centers the selection vertically based on the absolute size of the form (as given by the Height property).

Relative Ver**t**ical Center—Centers the selection vertically based on the current size of the form.

Working with Overlapping Objects

You often may have form objects that overlap each other. For example, if you have added a group of radio buttons and you then add a rectangle around the group, the rectangle overlaps and hides the buttons. To fix this problem, you need to send the rectangle behind the radio buttons. This process is called *changing the Z-order* of the objects.

> **Note**
>
> The term *Z-order* comes from the Z-axis concept in 3-D graphs. The Z-axis is traditionally the vertical axis in such graphs, and you can think of the Z-order as the *vertical order* of the form objects. (In this case, "vertical" means perpendicular to the screen; that is, toward the viewer.)

To change the Z-order of an object, use any of the following techniques:

- To bring an object to the front of the Z-order, click the Bring to Front SpeedBar button, or open the **L**ayout menu and choose Bring to **F**ront.

- To send an object to the back of the Z-order, click the Send to Back SpeedBar button, or open the **L**ayout menu and choose Send to Ba**c**k.

- To bring an object closer to the front of the Z-order, click the Bring Closer SpeedBar button, or open the **L**ayout menu and choose Bring Clo**s**er.

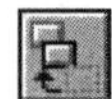

- To send an object farther from the front of the Z-order, click the Send Farther SpeedBar button, or open the **L**ayout menu and choose Send Fart**h**er.

Changing the Form's Tab Order

As mentioned earlier, the form's *tab order* is the order in which users navigate the objects when they press Tab (or Shift+Tab). The tab order is determined by the order in which you add the objects to the form. Users, of course, don't care about the order in which the objects were added to the form. They expect to tab through a form in the order, more or less, in which the objects *appear* in the form. But because you often cannot add objects in the order they appear (you may add new objects or move existing ones), you need some way of adjusting the tab order.

The Form Designer has an Order view that can help you reorder tabs. The Order view shows only the outlines of each object and a number representing the object's current position in the tab order. For example, figure 15.26 shows a form in the normal Layout view and figure 15.27 shows the same form in Order view. Notice that only objects that can receive the focus have a tab order position. Objects that users can't tab to (such as text objects) are left out of the tab order.

> **Note**
>
> You may be wondering why the rectangles in figure 15.27, which cannot receive the focus, have a tab order position. The reason is that the Order view actually shows the entire Z-order of the form (the tab order is a function of the Z-order). In this case, both rectangles had to be sent to the back of the Z-order so you could see the objects they surround. Sending an object to the back of the Z-order automatically gives the object the first position (001). If you send a second object to the back, the old object's position becomes 002, and so on.

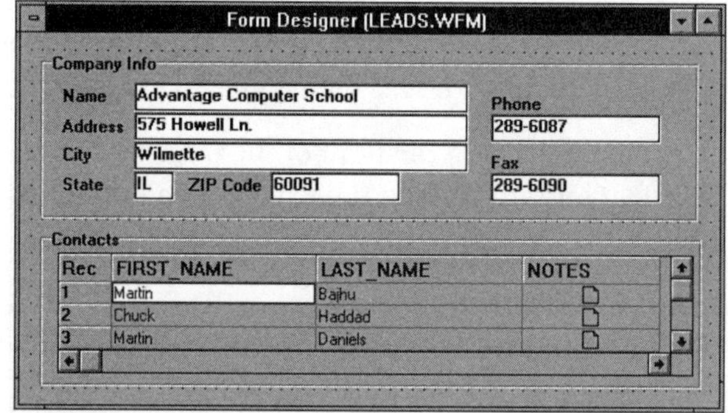

Fig. 15.26 A typical form in Layout view.

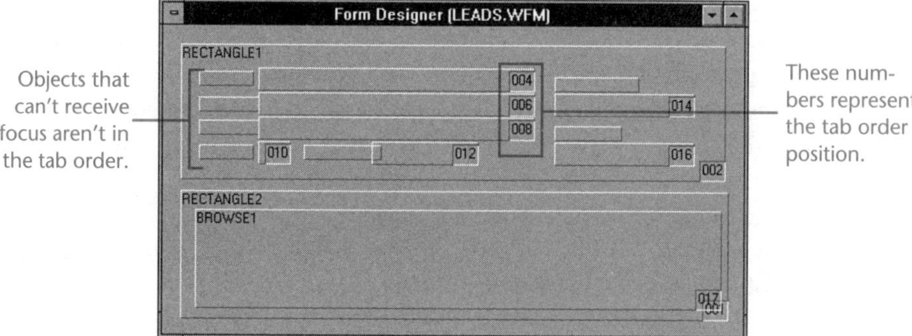

Fig. 15.27 The same form in Order view.

To change to Order view, use either of the following techniques:

- Open the **V**iew menu and choose Or**d**er View.
- Click the Order View button in the SpeedBar.

To change the tab order position of an object, select a number from the Z-order spin box in the SpeedBar and then click the object. Because no two objects can have the same position in the order, the positions of the other objects change accordingly.

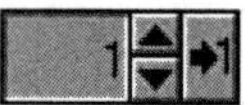

To return to Layout view, use either of the following methods:

- Open the **V**iew menu and choose **L**ayout View.
- Click the Layout View button in the SpeedBar.

From Here...

If you want to build on the material presented in this chapter, here are some reading suggestions:

- Chapter 2, "Moving from dBASE for DOS to dBASE for Windows." This chapter summarizes the differences between the DOS and Windows versions of dBASE. See this chapter for a summary of how forms have changed.
- Chapter 12, "Working with Related Tables." If you want to create multiple-table forms, this chapter shows you how to relate the tables.
- Chapter 24, "Designing a dBASE Application." This chapter gives you the big picture for planning and implementing dBASE for Windows applications. It includes guidelines on visual programming that you can use when designing your forms.
- Chapter 28, "Writing Program Modules." This chapter tells you how to create subroutines in dBASE code. You can then attach these subroutines to events associated with form objects.
- Chapter 31, "Automating Forms." This chapter introduces you to event-driven programming and shows you how to attach dBASE for Windows code to form objects.

Tip

The Form Designer increases the numbers in the Z-order spinner automatically. Therefore, to reset the entire tab order, select 1 in the spinner and then click each object in the tab order you want to use.

Chapter 16

Designing Advanced Reports

Computers are certainly useful beasts and they can even be fun from time to time, but one of their biggest faults is how intangible the work is. You can create huge table structures, design complicated forms, and input data until your fingertips are numb, but at the end of the day you have no palpable proof that you did anything. Computer work can often seem like a lot of smoke and mirrors without some solid evidence that you actually accomplished something.

That's where reports come in. A well-designed report can not only help you make sense of your data, but it's also something concrete that you can get your hands on and show off to other people. This chapter takes you beyond the report fundamentals you learned back in Part I. You'll look at many advanced techniques that will allow you to take full advantage of the power of Crystal Reports.

In this chapter, you learn how to do the following:

- Design a report
- Insert fields and text in a report
- Sort and group report data
- Summarize report data
- Format a report
- Customize Crystal Reports

Designing a Report

◄ "Creating a Report," p. 230

The purpose of a report is to take your raw table or query data and dress it up so that it meets one or more of the following goals:

- The data is presented in a clear, readable format.
- The data is sorted and grouped to make information easy to find.
- The data is summarized so that trends and totals can be easily extracted.

To accomplish these goals, it's not enough merely to add a few fields and labels and then print the report. Before you even start Crystal Reports, you should sit down and plan your report on paper. The next few sections take you through a seven-step program for fool-proof report design.

Step 1: Decide on the Report Audience

Who is going to read your report is every bit as important as *what* they're going to read. Giving a busy manager too much information or a harried data entry operator too little will defeat the purpose of the report. If the report is a request from an individual, make sure that you're clear about what data they want to see and what format they expect. If you're developing the report on your own, put yourself in the reader's shoes. What do you want them to get out of the report? How will the report benefit them? How will it help them with their job?

Many reports are distributed among a number of people in different departments. In these cases, it's usually difficult to tailor the report to meet everyone's exact needs. Instead, you should make sure that you cover all the bases and include enough information to make the report useful to everyone. If you know that some of your readers won't want to dive into the report's detail, Crystal Reports lets you easily add summary data (such as subtotals) to give them the big picture.

Another consideration that will be determined, in part, by the report audience is the overall quality of the report. If you just need a quick and dirty report for a colleague, there's no sense in spending hours formatting the report and perfecting the layout. On the other hand, more formal reports for senior managers or for meetings will require a greater attention to detail.

Step 2: Determine Which Fields Will Appear in the Report

The field data will make up the bulk of the report, but a typical columnar report is only wide enough to hold so many fields. All this means is that you need to give careful thought to which fields you include in the report.

One of the biggest factors in your field selection will be the report audience you identified in Step 1. The data needs of the recipients will often determine the minimum amount of information to include in the report layout. Subsequent fields added to the design should embellish or complement the existing data.

Remember also that you do not want to clutter a report with unnecessary fields. If a table has a primary key, do you really need to insert that field in the report? In a report of, for example, customer orders, will your readers care if the printout includes purchase order numbers or shipping information? As a general rule, include in a report only those fields that support the overall purpose of the report.

Step 3: Determine Which Records Will Appear in the Report

When you know which fields will appear in the report, it's time to think about the records you want to see. Do you need to include every record from the table or query, or just a subset of the records? For example, a monthly inventory report should, of course, include only those records that fall in the appropriate month. Similarly, a sales report for the Western Division Sales Manager should include sales only from the Western division. Crystal Reports has a built-in Expression Builder that lets you set up sophisticated criteria for selecting record subsets.

◄ "Building an Expression," p. 301

Step 4: Decide How You Want the Data Sorted and Grouped

Rare is the report that prints out its records in the natural order determined by the underlying table or query. Most reports display their records using at least an alphabetical or chronological order to make individual items easier to find. Do you need your report records sorted? If so, do you want to sort on a single field or on multiple fields? Should the sort be ascending or descending? When you've answered these questions, Crystal Reports can handle any kind of sorting burden you throw at it.

You also need to think about how you want the records grouped. For example, if you're printing out all the orders for a given time frame, do you want the orders grouped by customer or by sales territory?

Step 5: Determine Whether Your Report Will Need Calculations

Although most of your report data will be culled from existing fields in the underlying table or query, you'll often need to create special calculations for a report. There are two types of calculations you can use:

- A formula field
- A summary calculation

A formula field is a separate field derived by a calculation that involves one or more of the existing fields. For example, if you're creating a purchase order report, you'll likely need to calculate an extended total for each record (quantity sold multiplied by unit price).

A summary calculation is a single formula that you use to compute totals, maximums, minimums, counts, and more. You need to decide if you want these calculations based on the entire report or if you want them subtotalled by page or by group.

Step 6: Decide What Information To Place at the Top and Bottom of Each Page

With the page detail now laid out on paper, you need to decide what information to place at the top (the header) and bottom (the footer) of each page. If you're using a columnar layout, Crystal Reports automatically places the field names in the header. Do you want to use the field names as they are, or change them to something more descriptive? What other information will make the report easier to read? A report title and the date are often useful in headers. Footers are logical places to put summary calculations and page numbers.

Step 7: What Other Finishing Touches Does the Report Need?

Getting the right information and organizing it in a layout that makes sense is only part of the report design battle. To make your creation pleasing to the eye, you need to think about what other finishing touches can be applied. Here are some questions to keep in mind:

- Do you need to add lines or boxes to emphasize and organize certain elements?
- Would a graphic image (such as a logo) or an OLE object break up the monotony of plain text?
- What fonts are you currently using? Would the addition of some bolding or italics, or the use of large type sizes, make the report look more professional?
- Do you need to add some color to the report? This isn't something you need to worry about if you're printing the report on a black and white printer. But if you have access to a color printer, or if you're distributing the report electronically, colors and other formatting options such as borders and drop shadows can do wonders for a drab report.

Understanding Report Concepts and Terms

To make sure that you understand the concepts and terms used throughout the rest of the chapter, this section provides some brief descriptions of some common report terminology:

Database field—A report element that consists of a single field from the underlying table or query. Database fields usually appear in the report's Details section.

Details section—The section of the report that contains the data from the database and formula fields. This section is also sometimes called the *report body*.

Element—A component of a report such as a database field, text field, or formula field.

Formula field—A report field that is derived by an expression involving one or more database fields. For example, if a report includes a QUANTITY field and a UNIT_PRICE field, you could create an EXTENDED formula field defined by QUANTITY*UNIT_PRICE.

Group—A collection of related records. For example, in a report of customer data grouped by city, all the customers located in Boise would form a group.

Group value—The result of a summary calculation based on the records in a single group.

Page Footer section—The section of the report that appears at the bottom of each page.

Page Header section—The section of the report that appears at the top of each page.

Special field—A report element that inserts things like dates, page numbers, and record numbers in the report.

Summary field—A report element that calculates values such as subtotals, maximums, and minimums for pages, groups, and the report as a whole.

Text field—A report element that consists of text only. You normally use text fields to label the report's database fields, but you also can use them for titles and other random text.

Underlying table or query—The table or query upon which the report is based.

Inserting Elements in the Report

In Chapter 11, "Creating Basic Reports," you learned how to insert database fields and text fields into a report. In this section, you look at inserting other report elements such as formula fields, dates, page numbers, and graphics.

Inserting a Formula Field

You use formula fields to display calculated values with each report record. These calculations are based on dBASE for Windows expressions that combine fields from the underlying table or query, functions, and constants with one or more operators. For example, a purchase order report might need a field that multiplies the quantity ordered (QUANTITY) by the unit price (UNIT_PRICE). This new field would use the following formula:

```
QUANTITY*UNIT_PRICE
```

Similarly, a report of customer orders may need to include a field that calculates the due date of each order. If the order date is in the ORDER_DATE field, you'd use the following expression to calculate the due date:

```
ORDER_DATE+30
```

Here are the steps to follow to insert a formula field in a report:

Note

The following steps (and, indeed, the rest of this chapter) assume you have Crystal Reports up and running.

1. Open the **I**nsert menu and choose **F**ormula Field, or click the Insert Formula Field button in the Button Bar. The Insert Formula dialog box appears, as shown in figure 16.1.

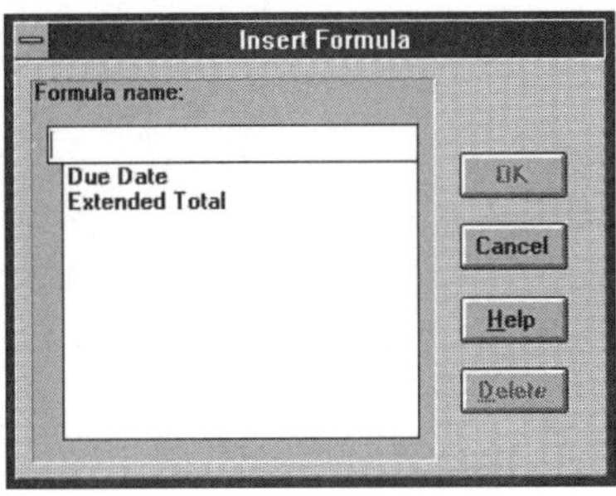

Fig. 16.1
Use the Insert Formula dialog box to enter a name for the formula field you want to create.

2. Type a name for the formula field in the Formula Name text box.
3. Choose OK. The Build Expression dialog box appears (see fig. 16.2).

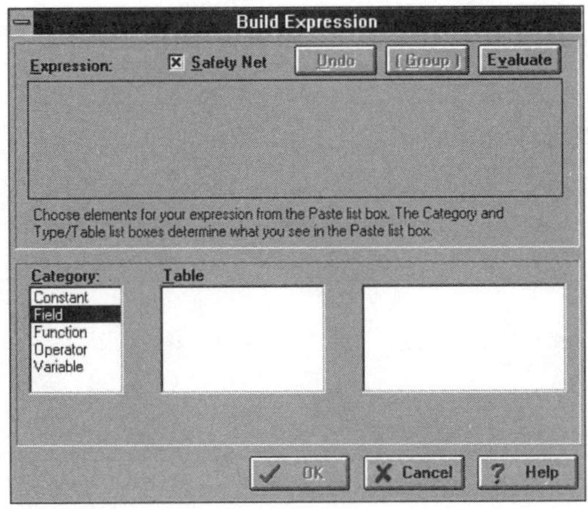

Fig. 16.2
Use the Build Expression dialog box to create the formula expression.

◀ "Building an Expression," p. 301

4. Enter the expression you want to use for the formula.

5. Choose OK to return to the report.
6. Move the mouse to where you want the field to appear and then click. Crystal Reports adds the field to the report.

Editing a Formula

If a formula field isn't working just the way you like, you may need to edit the formula to get the correct values. Here are the steps to follow:

1. Click the formula field to choose it.
2. Open the **E**dit menu and choose **F**ormula. Crystal Reports displays the Expression Builder dialog box and loads the formula into the **E**xpression text box.
3. Make your changes to the formula.
4. Choose OK to return to the formula and put your changes into effect.

Tip
You can also edit a formula by right-clicking the formula field and choosing Edit Formula from the SpeedMenu.

Deleting a Formula

If you no longer need a formula, you can delete it by following these steps:

1. Delete every instance of the formula in the report. (You delete a field by clicking it to choose it and then pressing Delete).
2. Open the **I**nsert menu and choose **F**ormula Field to display the Insert Formula dialog box.
3. Choose the formula name that you want to delete.

> **Caution**
>
> Crystal Reports doesn't ask for confirmation when you delete a formula, so be sure you've chosen the right formula name before continuing.

4. Choose **D**elete. Crystal Reports deletes the formula.

Inserting Special Fields

Crystal Reports has four special fields that you can add to your reports:

***D**ate*—This field displays the current date (or whatever the date is when you print the report). Although you can insert date fields anywhere in the report, they're often placed in the page header so that the reader immediately knows when the report was printed.

Note

If you'd like to add the current time to the report, insert a formula field that uses the TIME( ) function.

***P**age number*—This field displays the current report page number. Although not needed for small reports (one or two pages), page numbers are a must for longer reports to prevent your readers from getting lost.

***R**ecord Number*—This field numbers each report record that appears in the Details section. Note that these record numbers have nothing to do with the table or query record numbers. Instead, they refer only to the record's position in the report. If you change the report's sort order, the record numbers will change as well.

***G**roup Number*—This field numbers each group in the report. See "Sorting and Grouping Report Data" later in this chapter to learn more about groups.

To insert a special field in your report, follow these steps:

1. Open the **I**nsert menu, choose Special Field, and then choose the special field you want from the cascade menu that appears.
2. Move the mouse pointer to where you want the field to appear.
3. Click the mouse to insert the field.

Inserting Lines and Boxes

Lines and boxes are an easy way to separate report sections and to enclose related elements. Figure 16.3 shows an example report design that uses several lines and boxes.

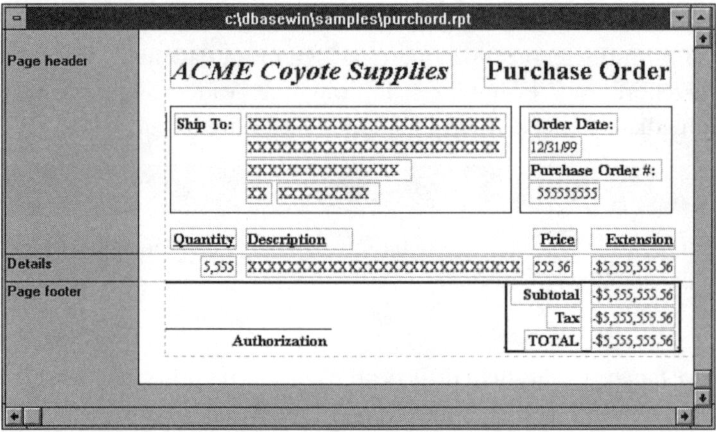

Fig. 16.3
A report with several lines and boxes.

To add a line to your report, follow these steps:

1. Open the **I**nsert menu and choose **L**ine, or click the Insert Line button in the Button Bar.
2. Position the mouse pointer where you want the line to start.
3. Hold down the left mouse button and drag the mouse to the right until the line is the length you want.
4. Release the mouse button.

For information on moving and resizing, see the section "Moving and Sizing Report Elements" later in this chapter.

Adding a box is similar, as the following steps show:

1. Open the **I**nsert menu and choose **B**ox, or click the Button Bar's Insert Box button.
2. Position the mouse pointer where you want the upper-left corner of the box to appear.
3. Hold down the left mouse button and drag the mouse down and to the right until the box is the size and shape you want.
4. Release the mouse button.

Inserting Graphics

To add some pizzazz to your reports, you can insert a graphic image such as a company logo or a design. Here are the steps to follow:

1. Open the **I**nsert menu and choose Grap**h**ic, or click the Insert Graphic button in the Button Bar. The Choose Graphic File dialog box is displayed, as shown in figure 16.4.

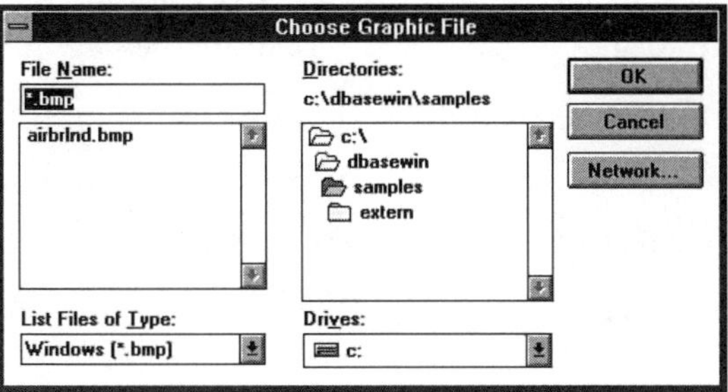

Fig. 16.4
Use the Choose Graphic File dialog box to choose the graphic image to insert in your report.

2. Select the graphic file that you want to insert in the report.
3. Choose OK to return to the report.
4. Position the mouse pointer where you want the graphic to appear.
5. Click the mouse. Crystal Reports displays the graphic image.

Troubleshooting

I added a date field to my report, but I want to post-date a few copies. Is there an easier way to do this other than deleting the date field, adding a formula field, and then reinserting the date field?

You bet there is. Just open the **R**eport menu and choose Set **P**rint Date. In the Print Date dialog box that appears, choose Other, enter the Year, Month, and Day for the date you want to use, and then choose OK. Crystal Reports will use this date in the date field when you print the report. When you need to return to printing the current date, just choose Today's Date in the Print Date dialog box.

Selecting Records to Appear in the Report

Now that you have your report elements in place, you need to think about which records you want to appear in the report. By default, Crystal Reports assumes that you want to include every record from the underlying table or query. You'll often want to print only a subset of the records, however.

For example, if you're creating an accounts receivable aging report for the Eastern division sales manager, you'll want to include invoices only from customers in the Eastern sales territory.

You can use the Expression Builder to create an expression that selects the records you want to appear in the report. Here are the steps to follow:

◀ "Building an Expression," Chapter 13, p. xxx

1. Open the **R**eport menu and choose **R**ecord Selection Formula. The Expression Builder dialog box appears.
2. Enter the expression you want to use for selecting the report records.
3. Choose OK to return to the report.

Sorting and Grouping Report Data

When you have your records selected, your next chore is to decide how you want those records to appear in the report. Crystal Reports gives you two options: sorting and grouping.

Sorting Report Records

Sorting your report records means that you arrange the records alphabetically according to the contents in one or more selected fields. (If the field contains numeric data, the records are sorted numerically.) You can sort either on a single field or on multiple fields. For example, suppose that you choose to sort a report of customer data by three fields: STATE, CITY, and NAME. This will print the records in the following order:

◀ "Sorting Tables," p. 139

- The overall report will be sorted by STATE.
- Records that have the same STATE value will be sorted by CITY.
- Records that have the same CITY value will be sorted by NAME.

Here are the steps to follow to sort your report:

1. Click the Record Sort Order button in the Button Bar, or open the **R**eport menu and choose Record **S**ort Order. The Record Sort Order dialog box appears (see fig. 16.5).

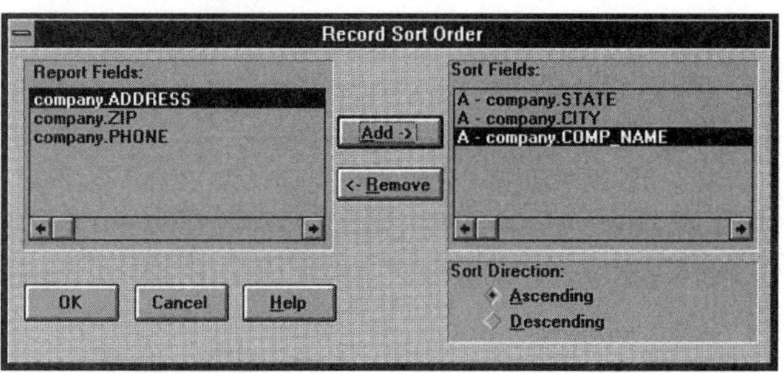

Fig. 16.5
Use the Record Sort Order dialog box to select a sort order for your report.

2. In the Report Fields list, highlight the sort field you want to use.
3. Choose **A**dd. Crystal Reports moves the field into the Sort Fields list.

> **Tip**
> You can also add a field to the sort by double-clicking it.

> **Note**
>
> To remove a field from the sort, highlight it in the Sort Fields list and then choose **R**emove.

4. To create an ascending sort on this field (from 1 to 9 and from A to Z), choose **A**scending; for a descending sort (from 9 to 1 and from Z to A), choose **D**escending.
5. Repeat Steps 2–4 for any other fields you want to include in the sort.
6. When you're done, choose OK to return to the report.

Grouping Report Records

Instead of merely sorting your report records, you can also break them down into distinct groups. For example, you could divide a report of customer information into state groups. Here are some of the advantages you get when you group your data instead of just sorting it:

- Crystal Reports creates two new sections for the group: a header and a footer. You can add text, formulas, graphics, and anything else you can think of into the section header or footer.
- You can start a new page after each group.

- You can reset the report page numbers after each group.
- You can sort the groups and select only certain groups to include in the report.

Crystal Reports differentiates between *simple grouping* and *grouping and summarizing*. Simple grouping divides the report records based on the values in a selected field. For example, if you group by a STATE field, Crystal Reports sorts the records by state and then creates a new group every time the STATE value changes.

Grouping and summarizing divides the records into groups *and* it adds summary calculations for each group (such as a subtotal or a count of the group records). To learn how to group and summarize report data, see the section titled "Summarizing Report Data" later in this chapter.

Here are the steps to follow for simple grouping:

1. Open the **I**nsert menu and choose **G**roup Section. Crystal Reports displays the Insert Group Section dialog box, as shown in figure 16.6.

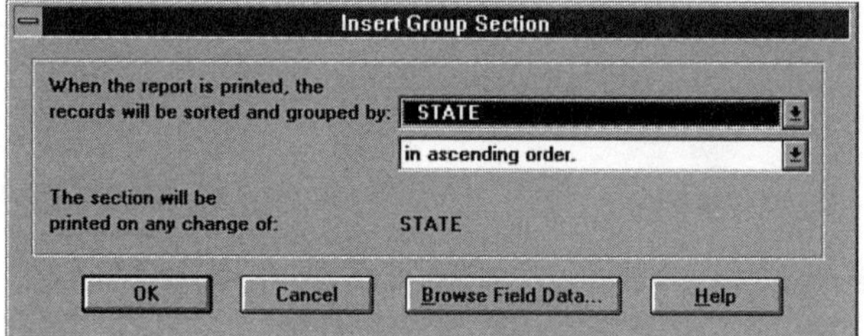

Fig. 16.6
Use the Insert Group Section dialog box to select a field on which to group the report data.

2. Open the first drop-down list and select the field to use for the grouping. The list contains two sections: the Report Fields section contains just the table or query fields you've inserted into the report; the Database Fields contains all the fields from the report's table or query.
3. In the second drop-down list, choose either In Ascending Order or In Descending Order.
4. Choose OK to return to the report. Crystal Reports adds two new group sections (a header and a footer) to the report (see fig. 16.7).

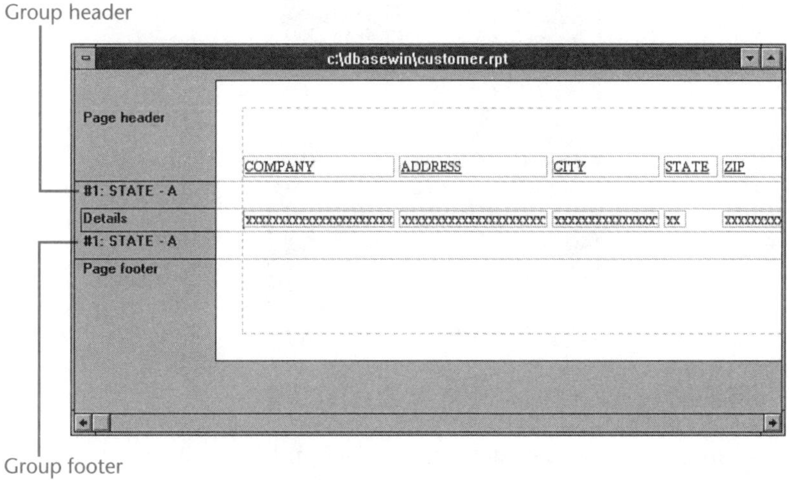

Fig. 16.7
When you group your report records, Crystal Reports inserts two new group sections.

Selecting Report Groups

In the same way that you can select a subset of records to include in the report, you can also select a subset of the groups you've defined. In a report grouped by state, for example, you may want to include only certain states. As you might expect, the techniques you use to select groups are almost identical to those you learned for selecting records (see "Selecting Records to Appear in the Report" earlier in this chapter). In this case, you open the **R**eport menu and choose **G**roup Selection Formula. When the Expression Builder dialog box appears, enter the expression you want to use and then choose OK.

Troubleshooting

How do I delete a group?

Open the **E**dit menu and choose D**e**lete Section. In the Delete Section dialog box, shown in figure 16.8, highlight the group you want to delete and then select OK.

When I created a group, I entered the wrong field by accident. Is there any way to change the field without having to delete the group and start over?

Yes, there is. Open the **E**dit menu and choose **G**roup Section. In the Edit Group Section dialog box that appears, highlight the group and then choose OK. Crystal Reports then displays the Edit Group Section dialog box. Change the group field and then choose OK to return to the report.

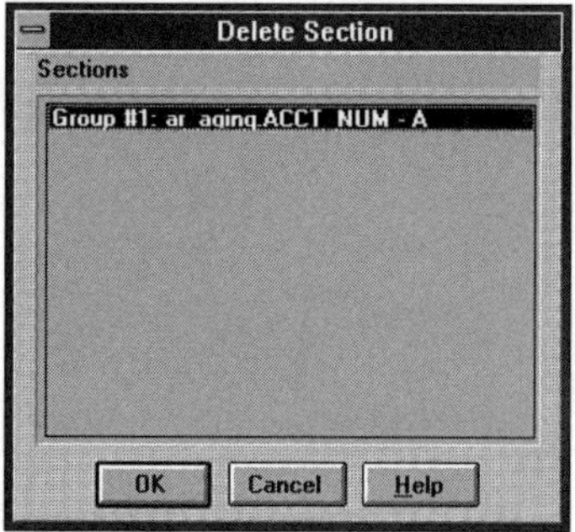

Fig. 16.8
Use the Delete Section dialog box to delete a group you no longer need.

Summarizing Report Data

A good report not only gathers data in one place and makes it easy to digest, but it should also be able to answer questions about the data. What was the largest order last month? How many invoices are more than 90 days past due? What is the sum of the current inventory?

To answer these kinds of questions, Crystal Reports lets you add *summary fields* to your report. These elements operate on a single report field and calculate values such as the field's sum, average, count, maximum, and minimum. You can add these summaries for both grouped data and for the report as a whole.

Inserting a Summary Field

Here are the steps to follow to insert a summary field into your report:

Tip
You can also display the Insert Summary dialog box by right-clicking on the field and choosing Insert Summary from the SpeedMenu.

1. Select the field you want to use for the summary calculation.
2. Click the Insert Summary Field button in the Button Bar, or open the **I**nsert menu, choose Summary Field, and then choose S**u**mmary. Crystal Reports displays the Insert Summary dialog box (see fig. 16.9).
3. In the top drop-down list, select the calculation you want to use for the summary. Table 16.2 lists the available choices for a numeric field (other field types offer a smaller number of choices).

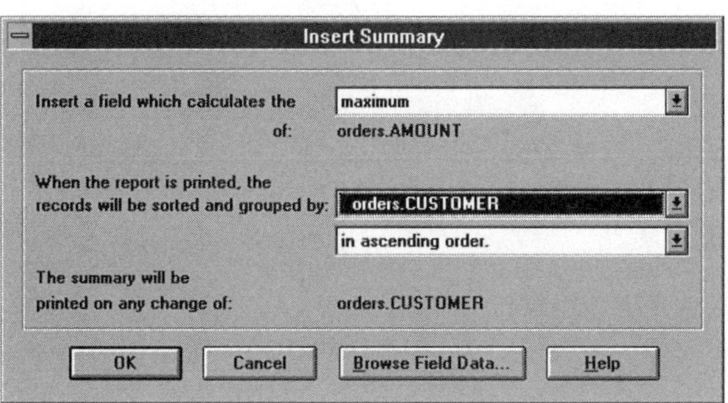

Fig. 16.9
Use the Insert Summary dialog box to select a calculation and the field on which to group the data.

Table 16.2 Summary Field Calculations

Calculation	What It Does
Maximum	Displays the largest value in the selected field for each group.
Minimum	Displays the smallest value in the selected field for each group.
Count	Counts the number of values in the selected field for each group.
Distinct Count	Counts the unique values in the selected field for each group.

4. In the second drop-down list, select the field to use for the groups.
5. Choose OK. Crystal Reports adds the group and inserts the new field in the group's footer.

Inserting a Subtotal

If the summary field you want to insert is a sum calculation, you can save time by creating a subtotal. Here are the steps to follow:

1. Select the field you want to use for the subtotal.
2. Open the **I**nsert menu, choose Summary Field, and then choose **S**ubtotal. Crystal Reports displays the Insert Subtotal dialog box (see fig. 16.10).

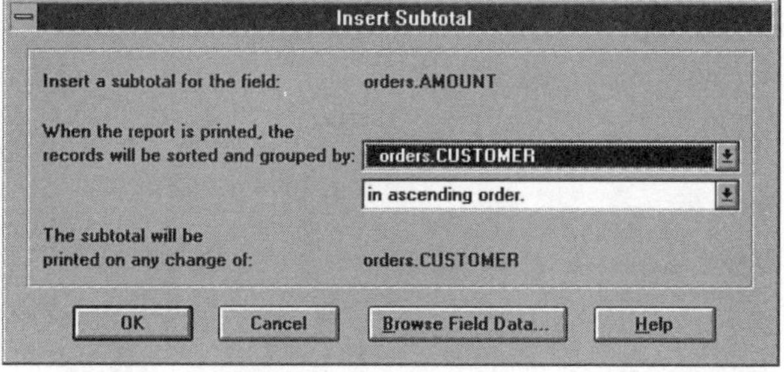

Fig. 16.10 Use the Insert Subtotal dialog box to select a field on which to group the data for the subtotals.

Tip You can also display the Insert Subtotal dialog box by right-clicking the field and choosing Insert Subtotal from the SpeedMenu.

3. In the top drop-down list, select the field to use for the groups.
4. In the second drop-down list, select a sort order.
5. Choose OK.

Inserting a Grand Total

The summary and subtotal fields operate on report groups. If you'd like a calculation for the entire report only, you need to add a grand total. Here are the steps to follow:

1. Select the field you want to use for the grand total.
2. Open the **I**nsert menu, choose Summary Field, and then choose Grand **T**otal. Crystal Reports displays the Insert Grand Total dialog box (see fig. 16.11).

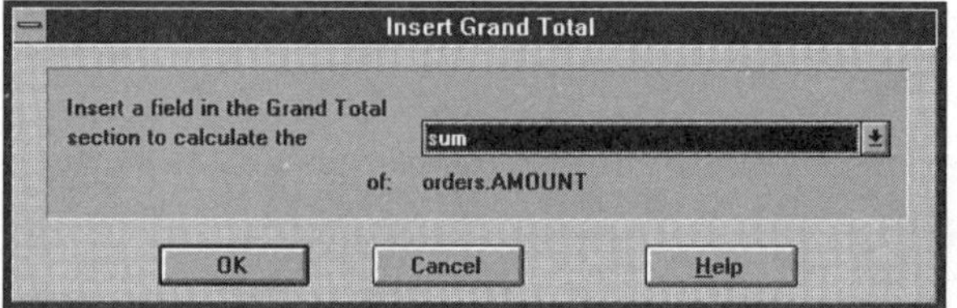

Fig. 16.11 Use the Insert Grand Total dialog box to select a calculation for the grand total.

3. In the drop-down list, select the calculation you want to use for the grand total (see table 16.2 earlier in this chapter for descriptions of the calculations in this list).
4. Choose OK. Crystal Reports creates a Grand Total section and inserts the grand total field.

Troubleshooting

I want to sort my report based on the values in the summary field. Is there any way to do this?

Yes. Just open the **R**eport menu and choose Group Sort **O**rder. The Group Sort Order dialog box that appears looks and operates just like the Record Sort Order dialog you looked at earlier (see "Sorting Report Records").

I inserted a summary field and then realized later that I used the wrong calculation. How can I make changes to a summary field?

Select the summary field, open the **E**dit menu, and then choose S**u**mmary Operation. (Or right-click the field and choose Change Summary Operation from the SpeedMenu.) In the Summary Field dialog box that appears, select the new summary operation and then choose OK.

Tip

You can also display the Insert Grand Total dialog box by right-clicking the field and choosing Insert Grand Total from the SpeedMenu.

Formatting Report Elements

Unlike what the commercials tell us, image may not be everything, but, when it comes to reports, it certainly counts for a lot. Why? Well, because having even the best data in the world won't convince your readers to plow through an unattractive and amateurish-looking report. To help you avoid this fate, Crystal Reports is chock full of tools that can spiff up even the dullest report. The next few sections show you how to wield these tools.

Selecting Report Elements

Before you learn any specific formatting methods, you should know how to select the report elements with which you want to work. Here's a summary of the techniques you can use:

- To select a single element, click it.
- To select multiple elements, hold down Shift or Ctrl and then click each element.

If you want to select multiple fields only (as opposed to other elements such as lines and boxes), follow these steps:

1. Open the **E**dit menu and choose Se**l**ect Fields. The mouse pointer changes to a crosshair.
2. Position the mouse pointer at a point above and to the left of the first field you want to select.
3. Hold down the left mouse button and drag the mouse down and to the right. A rectangle will appear as you drag the mouse.
4. When the rectangle encloses every field you want to select, release the mouse button. Crystal Reports selects every field that lies wholly or partially within the rectangle.

Formatting Fields

Tip
You can also display the formatting dialog box for a field by right-clicking on the field and choosing Change Format from the SpeedMenu.

Fields make up the bulk of your report, so it makes sense to start your formatting tour with them. Crystal Reports' field formatting options control how a field displays its data, how it gets printed, and more. Here are the general steps to follow to format a field:

1. Select the field you want to format.
2. Open the Forma**t** menu and choose F**i**eld. The dialog box that appears depends on the data type of the field. For a character field, for example, Crystal Reports displays the Format String dialog box shown in figure 16.12. (Each dialog box is discussed in detail later in this section.)

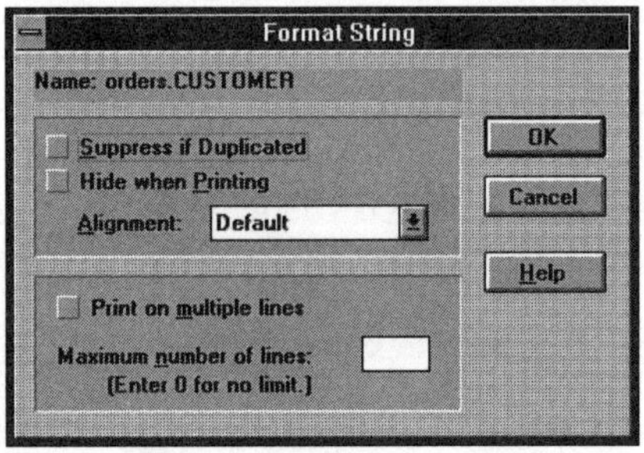

Fig. 16.12
The Format String dialog box appears when you format a character field.

3. Make your dialog box selections.
4. Choose OK to put your changes into effect.

Common Field Formatting Options

Although each type of field has its own unique formatting options, there are a few that are common to all field types:

Suppress If Duplicated—This option controls the printing of duplicate field data. If you activate this option, Crystal Reports prints a blank field value if the value in the current record matches the value in the same field in the previous record. The field value does print whenever the report starts a new page, however.

Hide When Printing—This option controls whether or not a field appears in the printout. If you activate this option, Crystal Reports does not include the field when it prints the report.

Tip
Activate the Hide When Printing option to hide a field that you need only for report calculations.

Alignment—This drop-down list controls how the field values are aligned within the field. The Default option returns the field to its normal alignment (left-aligned for character, logical, and date fields; right-aligned for numeric fields). The other choices are summarized in table 16.3.

Table 16.3 The Field Alignment Options

Alignment	Format Bar Button	Description
Left		Aligns the field values on the left side of the field box
Center		Centers the field values in the field box
Right		Aligns the field values on the right side of the field box

Formatting Character and Memo Fields

When you format a character or memo field, you use the Format String or Format Memo dialog box (fig. 16.12 shows the Format String dialog; Format Memo is identical). These dialog boxes have two unique options:

Print on multiple lines—Activate this option to enable word wrap for the field. This allows the field to print on multiple lines, if necessary.

Maximum number of lines—This option becomes enabled only if you activate the Print on **m**ultiple lines check box. You use this text box to put a limit on the number of lines to print. If you don't want to limit the number of lines, enter 0.

Formatting Numeric Fields

Formatting for a numeric field is handled by the Format Number dialog box shown in figure 16.13. Here's a summary of the options available in this dialog box:

*Use **W**indows Default Format*—Activate this check box to use the numeric formatting options specified in the International settings of the Windows' Control Panel.

*Suppress If **Z**ero*—Activate this check box to display a blank for each field value of zero.

Currency Symbol—Activate this check box to display the currency symbol shown in the text box. If you want to use a different symbol, delete the current symbol and replace it with the one you want to use. You can also display the currency symbol by selecting the field and then clicking on the Currency Symbol button in the Format Bar.

Tip
Press Alt+0162 for a cents sign (¢); Alt+0163 for a British pound sign (£); Alt+0165 for a Japanese yen sign (¥). Use the numeric keypad to enter the numbers.

*One Symbol Per **P**age*—Activate this check box to display the currency symbol only for the first record on each page.

Fixed/Floating—Activate the Fixed radio button to display the currency symbol on the far left of the field. Activate Floating to display the currency symbol to the left of the value.

Position—The options in this list control the position of the currency symbol with respect to the value and the negative symbol.

Decimals—This is a list of the number of decimal places to display in the field. You can also adjust the decimal places using the following Format Bar buttons:

Click this button to increase the number of decimal places.

Click this button to decrease the number of decimal places.

Rounding—The options in this list control the rounding of the field values. For example, 0.01 rounds each value to the nearest hundredth.

Negatives—This is a list of the formats available for negative numbers. You can either place the minus sign (–) at the beginning or end of each value, or you can surround the value with parentheses.

Decimal Separator—This is the symbol used for the decimal place.

Thousands Separator—Activate this check box to separate thousands with the symbol shown in the text box. You can also click the Thousands button in the Format Bar to display the thousands separator.

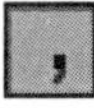

Leading Zero—Activate this check box to display a 0 to the left of the decimal point for values less than one (for example, 0.25).

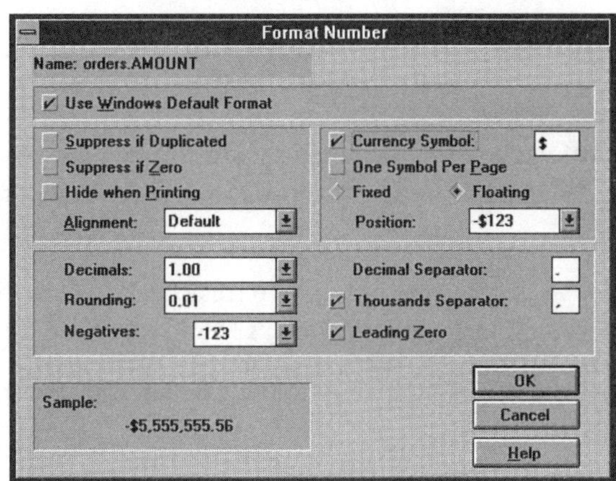

Fig. 16.13
The Format Number dialog box appears when you format a numeric field.

Formatting Logical Fields

The Format Boolean dialog box (see fig. 16.14) appears when you format a logical field. The only unique option in this dialog box is the **B**oolean Text drop-down list. The items in this list control the display of logical values and are summarized in table 16.4.

Table 16.4 The Boolean Text Options

Option	Description
True or False	Displays true values as True; displays false values as False
T or F	Displays true values as T; displays false values as F
Yes or No	Displays true values as Yes; displays false values as No
Y or N	Displays true values as Y; displays false values as N
1 or 0	Displays true values as 1; displays false values as 0

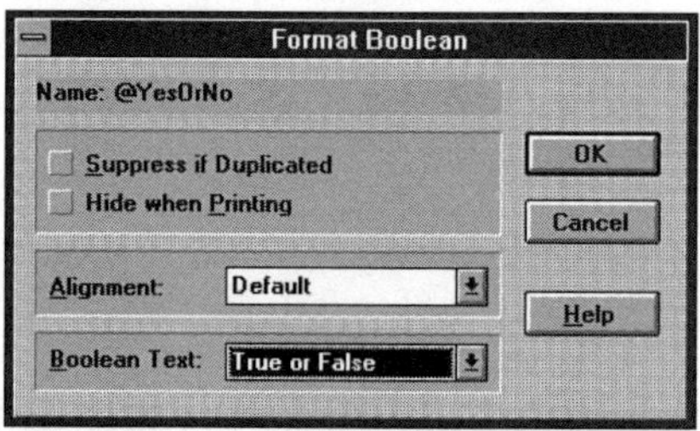

Fig. 16.14
Use the Format Boolean dialog box to format a logical field.

Formatting Date Fields

Date field formatting chores are handled by the Format Date dialog box shown in figure 16.15. Here's a summary of the date-specific options in this dialog box:

*Use **W**indows Default Format*—Activate this check box to use the date format specified in the Control Panel's International settings.

***M**DY*—Activate this radio button to display dates in month/day/year format.

***D**MY*—Activate this radio button to display dates in day/month/year format.

***Y**MD*—Activate this radio button to display dates in year/month/day format.

Month—This list controls how the month component of the date is displayed. Here are the available options:

3	Displays the month as a one- or two-digit number
03	Displays the month as a two-digit number
Mar	Displays the month's three-letter abbreviation
March	Displays the month's full name

Day—This list controls how the day component of the date is displayed. Here are the available options:

1	Displays the day as a one- or two-digit number
01	Displays the day as a two-digit number

Year—This list controls how the year component of the date is displayed. Here are the available options:

99	Displays the year using its last two digits
1999	Displays the year as a four-digit number

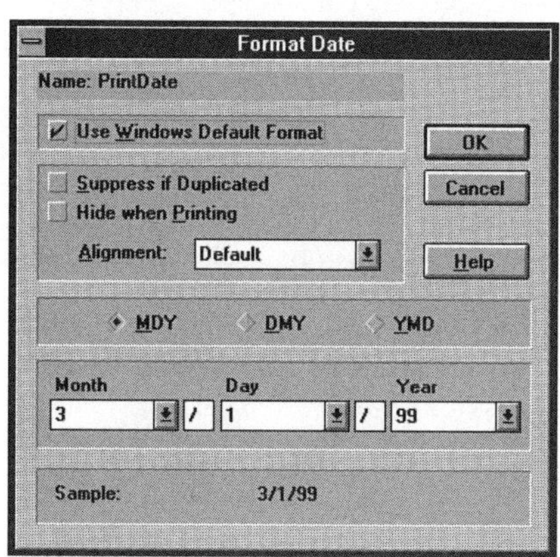

Fig. 16.15
Use the Format Date dialog box to format a date field.

Changing the Font

One of the best ways to spruce up a lackluster report is to change the font used in some of the fields. For example, you can make the field headings bold and Page Header text larger to make it stand out. Follow these steps to change a field's font:

Tip
You can also display the Font dialog box for a field by right-clicking the field and choosing Change Font from the SpeedMenu.

1. Select the field or fields with which you want to work.

2. Open the Forma**t** menu and choose **F**ont. Crystal Reports displays the Font dialog box, as shown in figure 16.16.

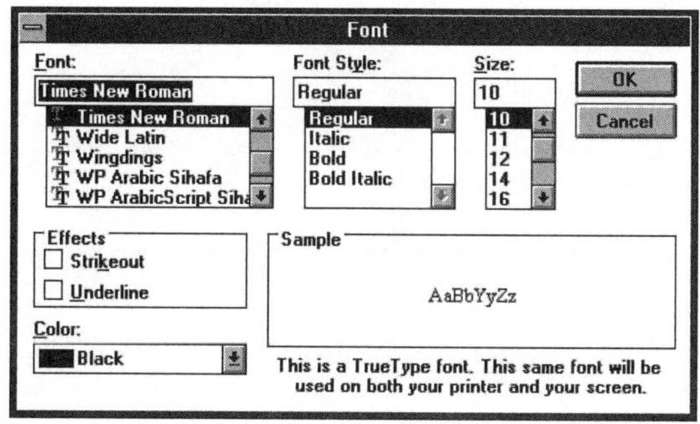

Fig. 16.16
Use the Font dialog box to choose the font options for the selected field.

3. Make your dialog box selections from among the following options:

 Font—This list box displays the available typefaces on your system.

 Font Style—This list box lets you choose a regular, bold, or italic font style.

 Size—This list box displays the available type sizes for the selected typeface.

 Strikeout—Activate this check box to display strikeout characters.

 Underline—Activate this check box to underline the text.

 Color—Use this drop-down list to select a color for the font.

4. Choose OK to put your changes into effect.

Crystal Report's Format Bar also includes several controls for adjusting the font. For the typeface and type size, use the drop-down lists on the left side of the Format Bar (see fig. 16.17). Table 16.5 displays the other Format Bar buttons you can use:

Table 16.5 The Format Bar Font Buttons

Button	Effect on Selected Field
A	Increases the type size by one point
A	Decreases the type size by one point
B	Bolds the text
I	Italicizes the text
U	Underlines the text

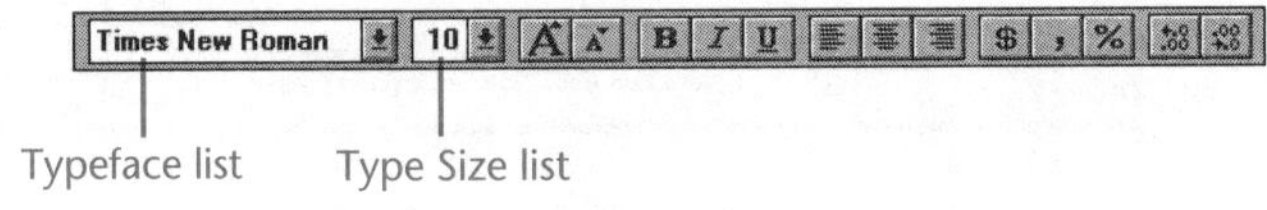

Fig. 16.17
The Typeface and Type Size Format Bar buttons.

Formatting Borders and Colors

When you add a field to your report, Crystal Reports places a light grey box around the field. This box normally doesn't appear when you run or print the report. You can use this box, however, to add borders around your fields and fill them with colors. Here are the steps to follow:

1. Select the field or fields you want to format.
2. Open the Forma**t** menu and choose Bo**r**der and Colors. The Format Border and Colors dialog box appears, as shown in figure 16.18.

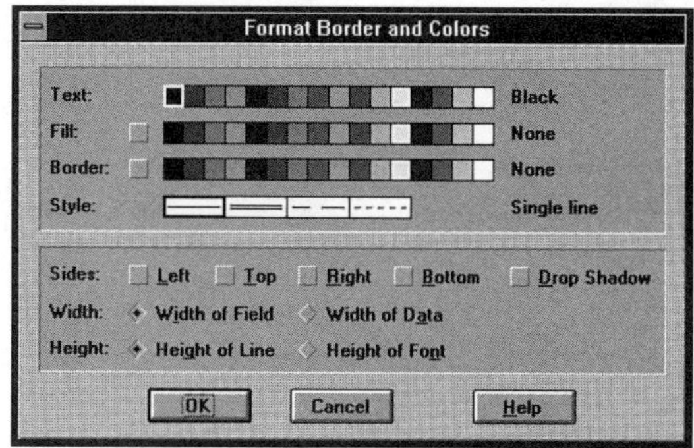

Fig. 16.18
Use the Format Border and Colors dialog box to choose border and color options for the selected field.

Tip
You can also display the Format Border and Colors dialog box for a field by right-clicking the field and choosing Change Border and Colors from the SpeedMenu.

3. Make your dialog box selections from among the following options:

   Text—Click a color square to set the color of the field text.

   Fill—To set the color of the field's background, activate the check box and then click a color square.

   Border—To add a border around the field, activate the check box and then click a color square.

   Style—If you're adding a border around the field, click one of these boxes to set the border style.

   Sides—A border normally surrounds the field. If you want the border to appear only on certain sides, select either **L**eft, **T**op, **R**ight, or **B**ottom.

   ***D**rop Shadow*—Activate this check box to add a drop shadow effect to the field.

Width—These options determine the width of the field box. If you select Width of Field, Crystal Reports makes the field box the same width as is given in the table definition. If you select Width of Data, the box width is determined by the width of the current record.

Height—These options determine the height of the field. If you select Height of Line, Crystal Reports makes the field height the same as the height of the field box. If you select Height of Font, the field height is made large enough to accommodate the field's type size.

4. Choose OK to put your changes into effect.

Formatting Sections

Your formatting work to date has covered only individual fields, but Crystal Reports also lets you format entire sections. You can insert page breaks before and after sections, prevent sections from printing, reset page numbers with each section, and much more.

Follow these steps to format a section:

1. Open the Format menu and choose Section. Crystal Reports displays the Format Section dialog box, as shown in figure 16.19.

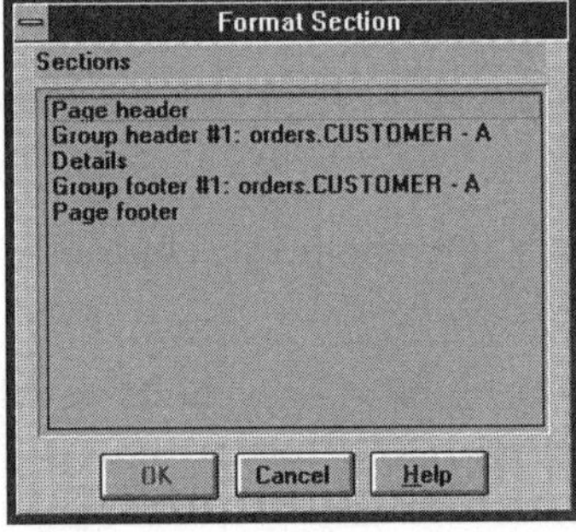

Fig. 16.19
The Format Section dialog box appears so that you can choose the section you want to format.

Tip
An easier way to get to the dialog box shown in figure 16.20 is to right-click the grey area that contains the section name and choose Format Section from the SpeedMenu.

2. Highlight the section you want to format and then choose OK. Another Format Section dialog box appears, as shown in figure 16.20.

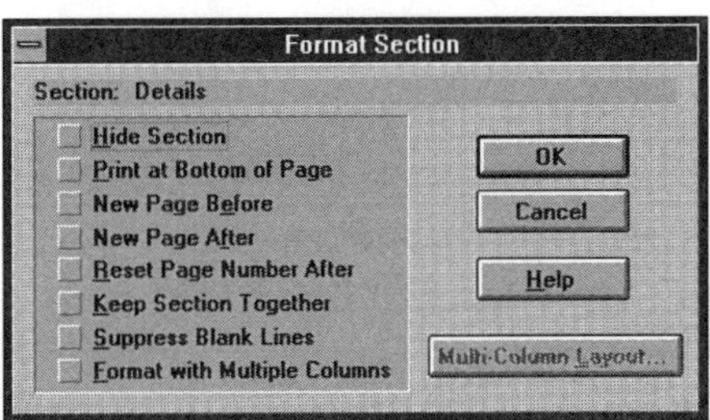

Fig. 16.20
This version of the Format Section dialog box contains the section formatting options.

Note

The number of check boxes that are enabled in the Format Section dialog box depends on which section you're formatting.

3. Make your formatting choices from among the following options:

   ***H**ide Section*—Activate this check box to prevent Crystal Reports from printing the section.

Tip

The fast way to hide a section is to right-click the grey area that contains the section name and choose Hide Section from the SpeedMenu.

Note

If you want to show or hide several sections, you don't need to adjust the **H**ide Section option for each one. Instead, open the **E**dit menu and choose Sho**w**/Hide Sections (or right-click inside the grey area that contains the section names and choose Show/Hide Sections from the SpeedMenu). The Show/Hide Sections dialog box that appears contains a list of your report sections. To the left of each section, you'll see either the letter *S* (meaning Crystal Reports will show the section) or the letter *H* (Crystal Reports will hide the section). To change a section, highlight it and then activate either **S**how Section (to print the section) or **H**ide Section (to prevent the section from printing). Choose OK when you're done.

***P**rint at Bottom of Page*—Activate this check box to print group values only at the bottom of each page.

*New Page **B**efore*—Activate this option to insert a page break before the section. This has no effect on the Page Header and Page Footer sections; they print on every page.

*New Page **A**fter*—Activate this option to insert a page break after the section. Again, this has no effect on the page headers and footers.

Reset Page Number After—Activate this check box to reset the page numbers to 1 after each group prints. This is ideal for invoices and purchase orders where each new group represents a separate report.

Keep Section Together—Activate this check box to avoid splitting a section on a page break. If there is no room left on the current page to print the entire section, Crystal Reports prints the section at the top of the next page.

Suppress Blank Lines—Activate this option to avoid printing records with no data (or records where the field values have been suppressed because of zeros or duplicates).

Format with Multiple Columns—Activate this check box to enable Crystal Reports to print the records in the Details section in two or more columns. Checking this option also enables the Multi-Column **L**ayout button so that you can format the columns (see fig 16.21). Here's a summary of the options in this dialog box:

> *Detail Size*—These options specify the dimension of each record. The **W**idth text box holds the width, in inches, of each detail column. The H**e**ight text box holds the height, in inches, of each detail line.
>
> *Gap Between Details*—These options control the amount of space that appears between each line and each column. The Hori**z**ontal text box holds the gap, in inches, between the columns. The **V**ertical text box holds the gap, in inches, between each detail line.
>
> *Printing Direction*—This is the path used to print the details. Select **A**cross Then Down to print the details across the columns and then down the page. Select **D**own Then Across to print the details down the page and then across the columns.
>
> *Number of Details*—These numbers tell you how many details Crystal Reports can print based on the Detail Size and Gap Between Details settings. Across Page tells you the number of columns, and Down Page tells you the number of details that can print down the page.

4. When you finish, choose OK to put the new formatting into effect.

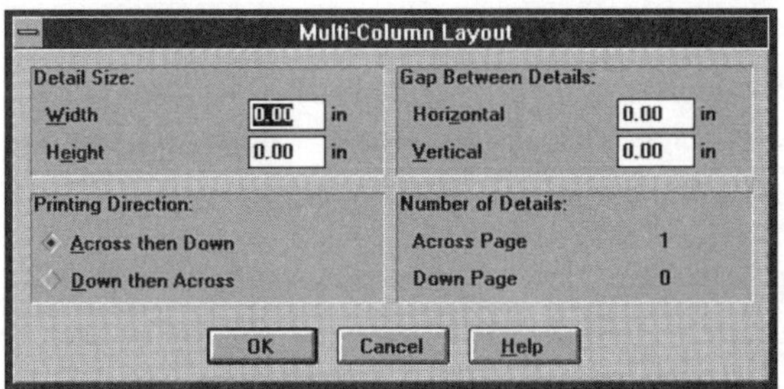

Fig. 16.21
Use the Multi-Column Layout dialog box to set up a report's Details section with multiple columns.

Changing the Report Title

After you save a report, Crystal Reports displays the full pathname of the report file in the Report Designer's title bar. If you'd prefer something more descriptive (if you'll be presenting the report onscreen, for example), you can modify the title bar text. You can also add comments to the report. Comments are an easy way to explain the report more fully and to elaborate on the report's goals and background. Although these comments don't print, they remain attached to the report so that you (or someone you send the file to) can read them at any time.

Follow these steps to change the title bar text and add report comments:

1. Open the Forma**t** menu and choose Report **T**itle. The Edit Report Title dialog box appears, as shown in figure 16.22.

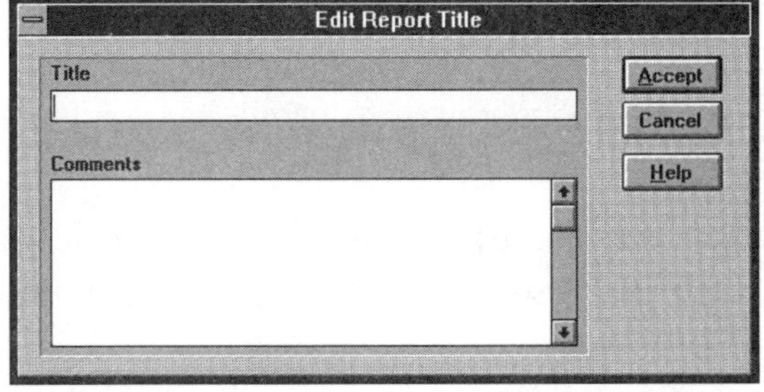

Fig. 16.22
Use the Edit Report Title dialog box to change the title bar text and attach comments to the report.

2. Use the Title text box to enter a title for the report.
3. Use the Comments text box to attach comments to the report.
4. Choose **A**ccept to return to the report.

Moving and Sizing Report Elements

To get your report laid out just right, you'll usually need to move and size some of the report elements. The next few sections give you the scoop on moving fields and on sizing fields and sections.

Moving Fields

To move a field to a different part of the same section or even to an entirely different section, follow these steps:

1. Select the field or fields you want to move.
2. Position the mouse pointer anywhere inside the field (but not over one of the selection handles that appear on either side of the field).
3. Hold down the left mouse button and drag the field to the position you want. As you drag, the field border appears as a grey outline to show you the current position.
4. Release the mouse button. Crystal Reports redraws the field in the new position.

Sizing Fields

Crystal Reports also lets you change the size of a field by making it longer or shorter. Here are the steps to follow to change the size of a field:

1. Select the field or fields you want to size. Crystal Reports displays handles on either side of the field.
2. Position the mouse pointer over the handle you want to move. The pointer changes to a two-headed arrow.
3. Hold down the left mouse button and drag the handle left or right until the field is the size you want. As you drag, a grey outline shows you the new border position.
4. Release the mouse button. Crystal Reports redraws the field with the new dimensions.

> **Caution**
>
> If you're shortening a field, make sure that you don't make the field smaller than the longest field value. If you do, the value will appear truncated in the report.

Sizing Sections

By default, Crystal Reports makes the Page Header and Page Footer sections three lines high and the Details, Group, and Grand Total sections one line high. To change the height of a section, follow these steps:

1. Place the mouse pointer over the grey line at the bottom of the section you want to size. The mouse pointer changes to a two-headed arrow with a horizontal bar through the middle.
2. Drag the mouse up or down until the section is the size you want.
3. Release the mouse button. Crystal Reports redraws the section boundaries.

Troubleshooting

Help! My report is printing each record on a separate page!

Sounds like you've used the Format Section dialog box to activate either the New Page B**e**fore or the New Page A**f**ter check box for the Details section. When you do this, Crystal Reports inserts a page break not for the section as a whole, but for each record in the section. There are times when this can be useful behavior, though. For example, if you have a table with a large number of fields, you may not be able to fit them all across the report page. Instead, arrange the Details section like a form and print each record on a separate page.

I want to start each of my report groups on a new page. In the Format Section dialog box, should I activate New Page Before for the group header or New Page After for the group footer?

It doesn't matter; either one will do the job. The only difference is where Crystal Reports prints the Grand Total section, if you have one. If you activate New Page B**e**fore for the group header, the Grand Total section appears immediately after the last group. If you activate New Page A**f**ter for the group footer, the Grand Total section prints on a separate page at the end of the report.

Customizing Crystal Reports

As you've seen throughout this chapter, Crystal Reports is a powerful tool for creating polished, professional reports. The good news is that the program is chock full of features that make designing these slick reports about as fast and simple as it gets. To make your Crystal Reports life even easier, the program also lets you customize everything from the default file directory to the default formatting used for fields.

To see the customization options, open the **F**ile menu and choose Op**t**ions. The Options dialog box appears, as shown in figure 16.23. Click the buttons on the left side of the dialog box to select the four Options categories: General, Database, Format, and Font. The next few sections discuss each category in detail. When you're done with this dialog box, choose OK to put the options into effect.

Fig. 16.23
Use the Options dialog box to customize Crystal Reports.

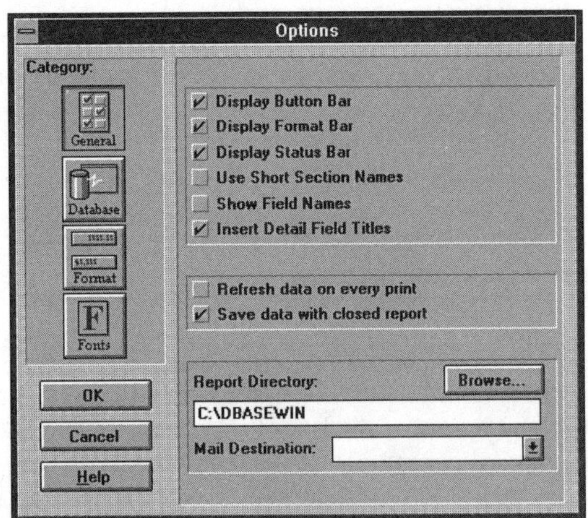

Setting the General Options

The General options control how you work with Crystal Reports. With these options you can show or hide the Button Bar or Format Bar, set the default directory, and select a default data format. Here is a list of these options:

Tip
If you have a large report layout that won't fit on your screen, hiding the Button Bar, Format Bar, and Status Bar will give you a little extra screen real estate to work with.

Display Button Bar—Deactivate this check box to hide the Button Bar.

Display Format Bar—Deactivate this check box to hide the Format Bar.

Display Status Bar—Deactivate this check box to hide the Status Bar.

Use Short Section Names—Activate this check box to display the abbreviated versions of the section names. For example, Page Header is displayed as PH, Details is displayed as D, and Page Footer is displayed as PF. The advantage here is that Crystal Reports also shortens the grey area containing the section names. This gives you more room for your wide reports.

Show Field Names—Activate this check box to display the names of each field instead of their formatting.

Insert Detail Field Titles—When this check box is active, Crystal Reports automatically adds to the report a text field containing the database field name when you insert a database field. Uncheck this option to prevent Crystal Reports from adding the field names.

Refresh Data On Every Print—Activate this check box to retrieve the latest table data every time you print the report.

Save Data With Closed Report—Activate this check box to save the data from the underlying table or query with the report definition. If you deactivate this option, Crystal Reports will have to retrieve the data before you can run the report.

Report Directory—This text box contains the default directory that Crystal Reports uses to store and retrieve your reports. You can either enter the path directly or choose Browse to select the directory using the Set Directory dialog box that appears.

Mail Destination—This drop-down list contains the default destination you want to use when you export a report via E-mail.

Tip
You can also display field names by opening the **E**dit menu and choosing Show Field **N**ames.

Tip
To refresh the table data at any time, open the **R**eport menu and choose Refresh Report **D**ata.

Tip
To save data with the current report only, open the **R**eport menu and activate the Save Data with **C**losed Report command.

Setting the Database Options

If you select the Database category in the Options dialog box, you'll see the controls shown in figure 16.24. These options define how Crystal Reports works with tables and queries. Here's a summary:

Data Directory—This is the default directory that Crystal Reports uses to look for and display table and query files. You can either type the directory into the text box or choose Browse to select the directory from the dialog box that appears.

Database Selector—This text box holds the default file specifications that Crystal Reports uses when displaying database files. If you enter multiple file specs, be sure to separate them with semicolons (;).

Index Selector—This text box holds the default file specifications that Crystal Reports uses when displaying index files.

Use Indexes For Speed—Activate this check box to tell Crystal Reports to use the database indexes when selecting records. If indexes are available, this results in much faster operation.

Translate DOS Strings—Activate this check box to translate ASCII codes in DOS strings to the corresponding ANSI codes for a Windows string.

For example, the ASCII code for the British pound symbol (£) is 156 and its ANSI code is 163.

Translate DOS Memos—This option is identical to Translate DOS Strings except that it operates on memo fields.

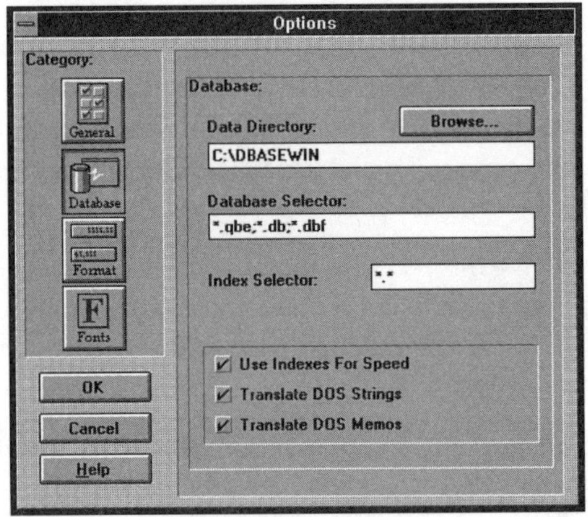

Fig. 16.24
Use the options in the Database category to control how Crystal Reports works with database files.

Setting the Format Options

In the "Formatting Report Elements" section earlier in this chapter, you learned how to format the various field types: character, numeric, date, and logical. The buttons in the Format category of the Options dialog box (see fig. 16.25) allow you to set up default formats for each of these field types. Here are the available buttons:

String—This button displays the Format String dialog box (see fig. 16.12) to set up the default formatting for character fields.

Number—This button displays the Format Number dialog box (see fig. 16.13) to set up the default formatting for numeric fields.

Currency—This button displays the Format Currency dialog box to set up the default formatting for numeric fields containing currency values. This dialog box is identical to the Format Number dialog box.

Date—This button displays the Format Date dialog box (see fig. 16.15) to set up the default formatting for date fields.

Boolean—This button displays the Format Boolean dialog box (see fig. 16.14) to set up the default formatting for logical fields.

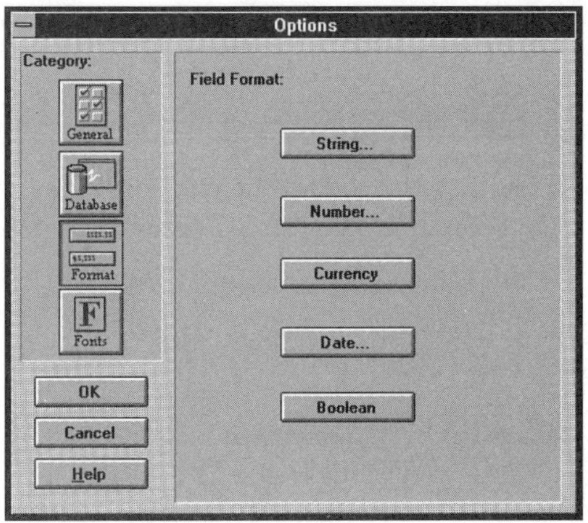

Fig. 16.25
Use the controls in the Format category to set up default formats for the various field types.

Setting the Font Options

Earlier in this chapter (see "Changing the Font"), you learned how to change the font for the text in a field. You can use the controls in the Fonts category to set up default font settings for each section. For example, if you always want your grand totals to appear in 14-point bold Arial, you can set that as the default font for the Grand Total section.

Follow these steps to set your default fonts:

1. Select the Fonts category in the Options dialog box (see fig. 16.26).

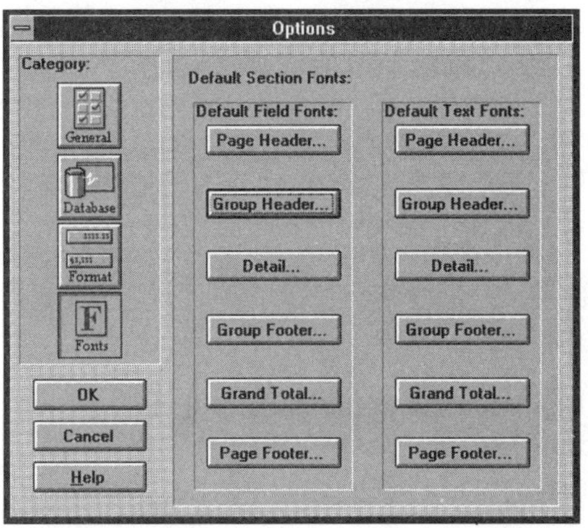

Fig. 16.26
Use the controls in the Fonts category to define default fonts for the different report sections.

2. To set the default font for the fields in a section, click one of the section buttons in the Default Field Fonts box. The Font dialog box appears.

3. Choose your font options and then choose OK to return to the Options dialog box.

4. Repeat Steps 2 and 3 to set the default field font for any other sections.

5. To set the default font for the text in a section, click one of the section buttons in the Default Text Fonts box. Again, the Font dialog box appears.

6. Choose your font options and then choose OK to return to the Options dialog box.

7. Repeat Steps 5 and 6 to set the default text font for any other sections.

Troubleshooting

My reports seem to take forever to print or preview.

This can happen if you don't save the table data with your report definition because Crystal Reports has to retrieve the original data before you can print or preview the report. If you have a large amount of data, this can take a while. If you have enough disk space, you should consider saving the data with the report.

Another thing you should check is that Crystal Reports is using your database indexes when selecting the report records. See "Setting the Database Options," earlier in this chapter, for details.

My report files are huge and I'm running out of disk space.

This is the trade-off for the speed and convenience of saving the table data with the report. The resulting report file contains not only the report definition but also a duplicate copy of the report data. Although Crystal Reports compresses the table data to save space, the report file will still be much larger than normal (how much larger depends on the amount of data with which you're dealing).

From Here...

If you want to learn more about the subjects discussed in this chapter, read the following chapters:

- Chapter 7, "Indexing and Sorting Data." This chapter gives you basic information on indexes and sorting techniques. Using indexes can drastically improve the performance of your reports, and familiarity with sorting can help you sort your report records and groups.

- Chapter 9, "Creating Basic Queries." Many reports are based on query data, so knowing how to create queries is essential. This chapter tells you everything you need to know to get started.

- Chapter 11, "Creating Basic Reports." This chapter gets you started on reports by covering topics such as starting and navigating Crystal Reports, using the Personal Trainer, and designing and printing a basic report.

- Chapter 12, "Working with Related Tables." If you plan to create multiple-table reports, read this chapter to get the lowdown on relating and linking tables.

- Chapter 13, "Using the Expression Builder." This chapter introduces you to dBASE for Windows expressions and shows you how to use the Expression Builder.

- Chapter 19, "Exploring the dBASE Integration Capabilities." If you plan to add OLE objects to your reports, read this chapter to get the full story on OLE.

Chapter 17

Creating Advanced Queries

Chapter 9, "Creating Basic Queries," got you started with queries by showing you how to start and navigate the Query Designer, set up a simple query, and add conditions to filter the query results. In addition, Chapter 12, "Working with Related Tables," showed you how to create multiple-table queries and link tables on a common field. This chapter completes your query education by tackling a few advanced topics, including working with calculated fields, ordering query records with an index, and using the Condition box.

In this chapter, you learn about the following topics:

- Creating calculated fields
- Using calculated fields in multiple-table queries
- Ordering query records using indexes
- Using the Condition box to filter a query
- Equivalent commands for the dBASE for DOS update queries

Creating a Calculated Field

A basic query adds conditions to one or more table fields and then builds the view table by including and excluding certain fields from the query results. In the query examples you've seen so far in this book, the query fields have all come from one of the tables added to the query. But you also can include fields in the query that don't exist in any of the tables. These fields are called *calculated fields* because you use them to derive values based on the contents of one or more of the table fields.

Suppose that you have a table of invoice data that includes a DUE_DATE field (the date the invoice is due to be paid) and you want to see how many days (if any) each invoice is overdue. Ideally, you would like to have a separate field in the table (OVERDUE, for example) that displays the days overdue. This would allow you to filter the table to show, for example, those invoices more than 90 days past due. The hard way to do this is to calculate manually the number of days overdue for each invoice and enter the results in the OVERDUE field. This approach has three problems:

- It is labor-intensive in the extreme because not only must the calculations be performed manually, but each value must be entered into the field. This probably wouldn't be too bad for a dozen or two records, but it becomes just plain silly for the hundreds, or even thousands, of records that most businesses deal with.
- Every record must be changed daily because the number of days overdue changes every day.
- You have to adjust the field value for invoices that are paid and invoices that remain unpaid past their due date.

Calculated fields were designed to solve these types of problems. For this example, you easily could add to a query a calculated field that would derive the number of days overdue using the simple expression

```
DATE()-DUE_DATE
```

Here's how this new field solves the preceding problems:

- The only labor involved is setting up the query and adding the calculated field. dBASE for Windows handles the math, and each record gets updated because a calculated field, by definition, operates on every record in the query.
- The field expression automatically updates the overdue values everyday. All you have to do is run the query to see the new numbers.
- Invoices that remain unpaid are handled automatically by the expression. To deal with invoices that get paid, you can easily add a condition to the query to filter them from the results. You also can add conditions to the calculated field for even greater control over the final results.

The following sections show you how to set up a calculated field.

Adding a Calculated Field to a Query

To create a calculated field, follow these steps:

1. Open a new query or run the Query Designer for an existing query.

◀ "Defining and Using a Basic Query," p. 172

2. If you're creating a new query, the Open Table Required dialog box appears, and you can use it to add the table that contains the fields you want to use in the calculation.

3. In the Query Designer, select Create Calculated **F**ield from the **Q**uery menu. dBASE for Windows adds the calculated field skeleton, as shown in figure 17.1.

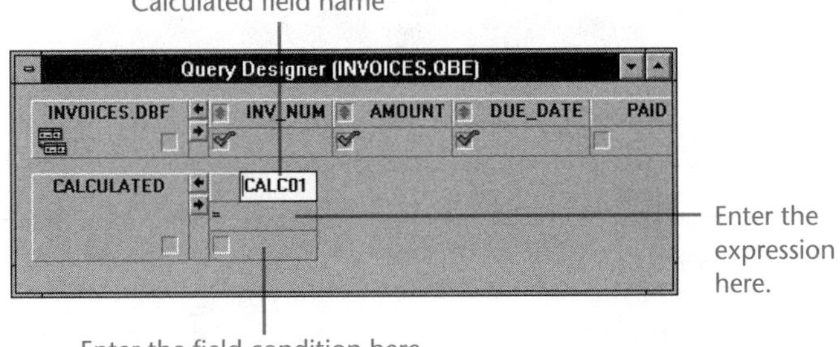

Fig. 17.1 A calculated field added to a query.

Renaming a Calculated Field

When you add your first calculated field to a query, dBASE for Windows gives it a default name of CALC01. Subsequent calculated fields are named CALC02, CALC03, and so on.

You're free to replace these prosaic names with something more descriptive. This usually is a good idea because the field name appears at the top of the Browse column if you include the field in the query results. A descriptive name helps to make the query more readable. In the "days overdue" example, you may want to rename the field as OVERDUE, for example.

To rename the calculated field, click inside the box containing the name, delete the old name, and then type the new one.

Entering the Calculation

The most important part of a calculated field is the calculation. You can use any legitimate dBASE for Windows expression, although most of your calculated fields use field names from one or more tables in the query.

◄ "Using the Expression Builder," p. 283

To enter the calculation, follow these steps:

1. Select the text box beneath the name of the calculated field.

2. Type the expression you want to use for the calculation.

3. Press Enter to accept the expression.

Figure 17.2 shows the previous query with the days overdue calculation entered.

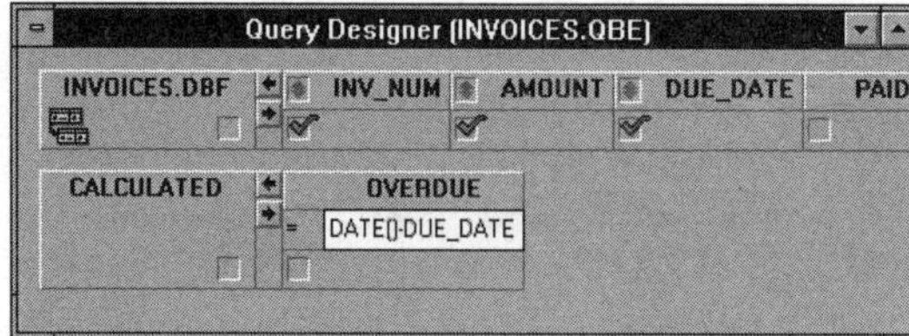

Fig. 17.2
A calculated field with an expression added.

Tip
When you press Enter, watch the Expression text box. If the background turns a different color, it means that dBASE for Windows found an error in the expression. Read the status bar to see what the problem is and then correct it.

Troubleshooting

When I try to run a query with a calculated field, dBASE for Windows displays an error message that says Expecting: Identifier. What could be the problem?

The most likely culprit is an illegal calculated field name. The name you enter for a calculated field must follow the usual dBASE field naming conventions (that is, the name must begin with a letter and cannot be any longer than 10 characters). Unfortunately, the Query Designer doesn't warn you if you enter an illegal name. Everything looks okay, but then you run the query and get an error message. Check the name you're using and then try again.

Adding a Calculation to the Query Results

Tip
You can toggle the selection box for the active calculated field by pressing F5.

In most cases, you'll want the calculated field to appear in the query results. You use the same techniques to include a calculated field in the query as you would any other field:

- To include the calculated field, click the selection box to display the check mark. To exclude the field, click the selection box to hide the check mark.

- If you have multiple calculated fields (see "Using Multiple Calculated Fields," later in this chapter), click the Select All button in the lower-right corner of the CALCULATED box.

For the previous example, figure 17.3 shows the query results with the new OVERDUE calculated field included.

Note

Calculated fields are always displayed as read-only. You can't edit, delete, or make changes of any kind in a calculated field.

Tip
Press F2 to see the query results and Shift+F2 to return to the Query Designer.

Tip
Don't forget to save your query by pressing Ctrl+S.

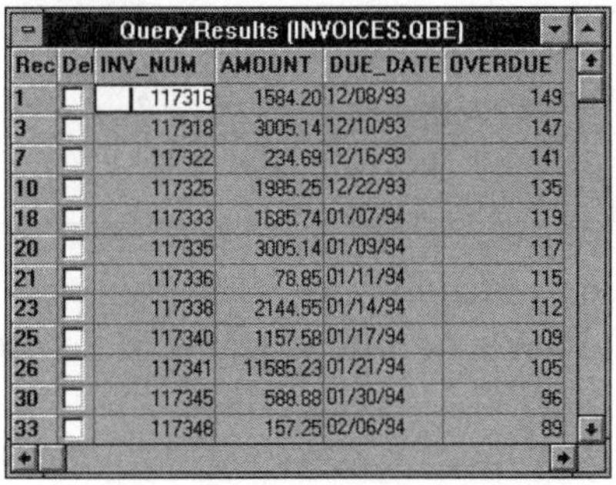

Query Results (INVOICES.QBE)

Rec	Del	INV_NUM	AMOUNT	DUE_DATE	OVERDUE
1		117316	1584.20	12/08/93	149
3		117318	3005.14	12/10/93	147
7		117322	234.69	12/16/93	141
10		117325	1985.25	12/22/93	135
18		117333	1685.74	01/07/94	119
20		117335	3005.14	01/09/94	117
21		117336	78.85	01/11/94	115
23		117338	2144.55	01/14/94	112
25		117340	1157.58	01/17/94	109
26		117341	11585.23	01/21/94	105
30		117345	588.88	01/30/94	96
33		117348	157.25	02/06/94	89

Fig. 17.3
The query results with the calculated field included.

II

Power Skills

Filtering on a Calculated Field

You can add conditions to your calculated fields to filter the query results. You may, for example, want to see only those invoices that are at least 120 days past due. Similarly, you may want to see only invoices where the OVERDUE calculation yields a positive number (a negative number implies that the invoice hasn't yet reached its due date).

Adding conditions in a calculated field is like adding them to regular fields. In a calculated field, select the text box beneath the expression and enter the condition you need. Figure 17.4 shows the INVOICES query with a condition added to the calculated field. In this case, you want to display those invoices where the OVERDUE calculation works out to 120 or more. Figure 17.5 shows the results.

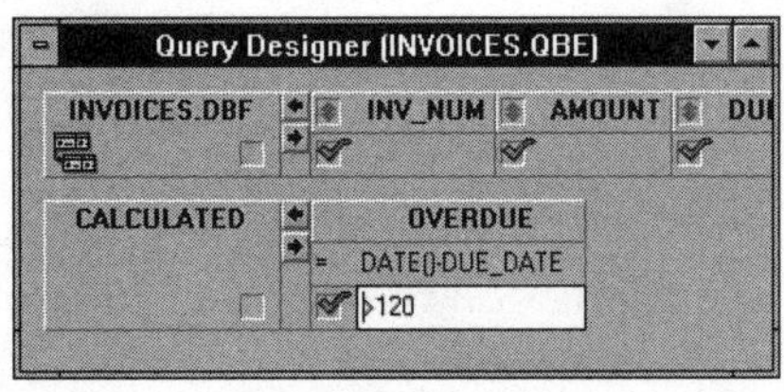

Fig. 17.4
A calculated field with a condition that filters the records.

Query Results (INVOICES.QBE)

Rec	Del	INV_NUM	AMOUNT	DUE_DATE	OVERDUE
1		117316	1584.20	12/08/93	149
3		117318	3005.14	12/10/93	147
7		117322	234.69	12/16/93	141
10		117325	1985.25	12/22/93	135

Fig. 17.5
The filtered query results.

Using Calculated Fields in a Multiple Table Query

◄ "Using a Query to Select Records," p. 181

Many queries are used as the basis for reports. If you want to print out an invoice or purchase order, for example, you'll need the individual line items (the item ordered, its price, and the quantity ordered) for the report detail. These types of queries usually are created from multiple tables. The order data (the item and quantity), for example, may be in one table and the product data (the price) may be in another.

◄ "Designing Advanced Reports," p. 385

Your report also needs the extended price for each line (the unit price of each item multiplied by the quantity ordered). This is a perfect application for a calculated field. Suppose that the unit price is in the UNIT_PRICE field of the PRODUCTS table and the quantity ordered is in the QUANTITY field of the ORDERS table. You then would calculate the extended price with the following expression:

```
ORDERS->QUANTITY*PRODUCTS->UNIT_PRICE
```

◄ "Establishing a Link between Related Tables," p. 272

Notice that when the query contains multiple tables, you have to attach the appropriate table's alias name to each field so that the Query Designer won't get confused. Figure 17.6 shows a multiple-table query with a calculated field (EXT_PRICE) that figures the extended price. Figure 17.7 shows the query results.

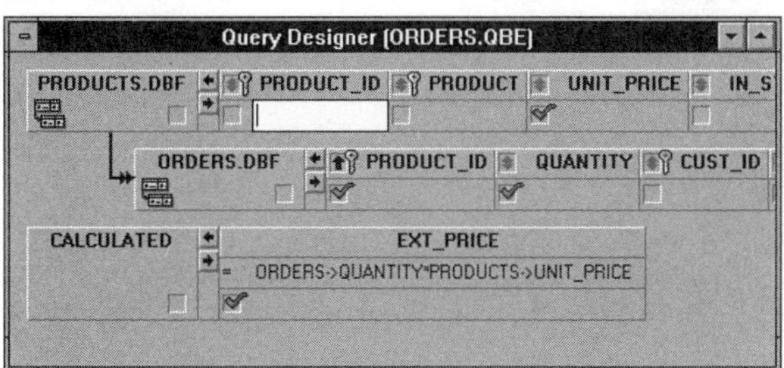

Fig. 17.6
A calculated field in a multiple-table query.

Query Results (ORDERS.QBE)

Rec	Del	PRODUCT_ID	UNIT_PRICE	QUANTITY	EXT_PRICE
1		A123-21	19.95	250	4987.50
2		A456-67	14.95	500	7475.00
3		B567-84	69.95	250	17487.50
4		B345-67	49.95	175	8741.25
10		C012-34	7.95	500	3975.00
15		B987-65	14.95	200	2990.00
25		C678-90	19.95	100	1995.00
29		C111-22	6.95	2500	17375.00
37		D010-10	5.95	1000	5950.00

Fig. 17.7
The query results showing the EXT_PRICE field.

Using Multiple Calculated Fields

dBASE for Windows doesn't restrict you to a single calculated field per query. You're free to add as many fields as you need (subject, as always, to your computer's memory limits). For each field, just repeat the steps outlined earlier in this chapter for adding a single calculated field. After you have multiple fields in the query, you can move them around just like you can with normal fields.

◄ "Changing the Order of Fields and Records," p. 177

As an example, assume that you have a table of invoices and you want to calculate the aging for each record. Ideally, you want to end up with a query result similar to the one shown in figure 17.8. This query uses the following aging scheme:

- Invoices more than 120 days overdue have their amounts displayed in the OVER120 column.
- Invoices between 90 and 120 days overdue have their amounts shown in the OD_90TO120 column.
- Invoices between 30 and 90 days overdue have their amounts shown in the OD_30TO90 column.

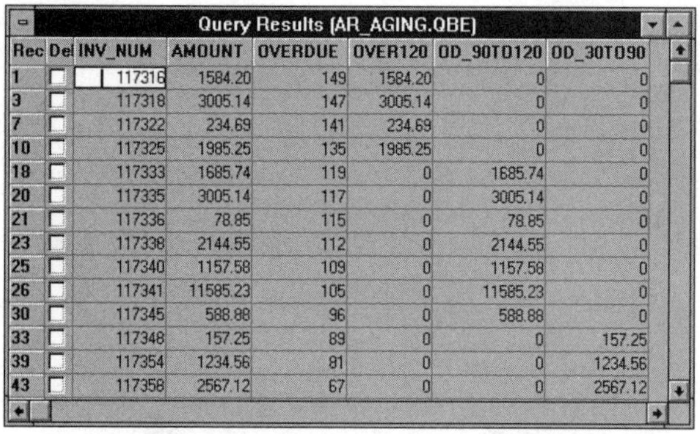

Query Results (AR_AGING.QBE)

Rec	Del	INV_NUM	AMOUNT	OVERDUE	OVER120	OD_90TO120	OD_30TO90
1		117316	1584.20	149	1584.20	0	0
3		117318	3005.14	147	3005.14	0	0
7		117322	234.69	141	234.69	0	0
10		117325	1985.25	135	1985.25	0	0
18		117333	1685.74	119	0	1685.74	0
20		117335	3005.14	117	0	3005.14	0
21		117336	78.85	115	0	78.85	0
23		117338	2144.55	112	0	2144.55	0
25		117340	1157.58	109	0	1157.58	0
26		117341	11585.23	105	0	11585.23	0
30		117345	588.88	96	0	588.88	0
33		117348	157.25	89	0	0	157.25
39		117354	1234.56	81	0	0	1234.56
43		117358	2567.12	67	0	0	2567.12

Fig. 17.8
The results of an accounts receivable aging query.

Figure 17.9 shows the query that produced the results shown in figure 17.8. Although you can see only two calculated fields in figure 17.9, this query actually uses a total of four calculated fields:

- The OVERDUE calculated field determines the number of days overdue with the following expression:

```
DATE()-DUE_DATE
```

- The OVER120 calculated field uses this expression:

```
IIF(DATE()-DUE_DATE>120,AMOUNT,0)
```

If DATE()-DUE_DATE is greater than 120, the OVER120 field displays the value from the AMOUNT field; otherwise, 0 appears.

> **Note**
>
> The IIF( ) function (immediate IF) uses the following syntax:
>
> ```
> IIF(<expL>, <exp1>, <exp2>)
> ```
>
> If the logical expression <expL> is true, the function returns <exp1>. If <expL> is false, the function returns <exp2>.

Tip
You can copy an expression between calculated fields by highlighting some or all of the expression, pressing Ctrl+C, activating the other calculated field, and pressing Ctrl+V.

- The OD_90TO120 calculated field uses the following expression:

```
IIF(DATE()-DUE_DATE>=90 .AND. DATE()-DUE_DATE<=120,AMOUNT,0)
```

If DATE()-DUE_DATE is greater than or equal to 90 and less than or equal to 120, the OD_90TO120 field displays the invoice AMOUNT; otherwise, it displays 0.

- The OD_90TO120 calculated field uses the following expression:

```
IIF(DATE()-DUE_DATE>=30 .AND. DATE()-DUE_DATE<90,AMOUNT,0)
```

If DATE()-DUE_DATE is greater than or equal to 30 and less than 90, the OD_30TO90 field displays the invoice AMOUNT; otherwise, it displays 0.

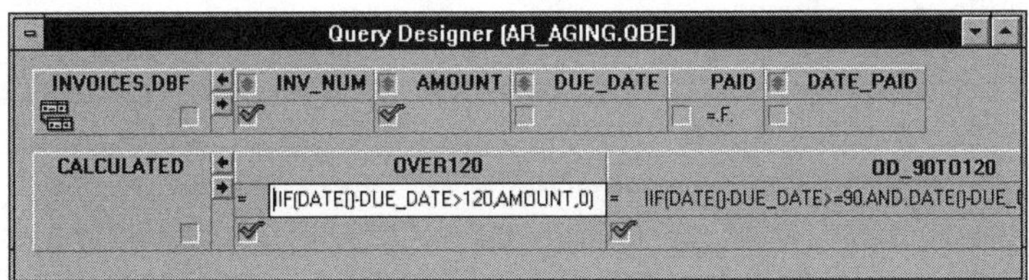

Fig. 17.9
The query that produces the aging calculations.

Deleting a Calculated Field

If you no longer need a calculated field in a query, you can delete it by following these steps:

1. Load the query with which you want to work into the Query Designer.
2. Select the calculated field.

> **Caution**
>
> The Query Designer doesn't ask for confirmation when you delete a calculated field, so be sure you've selected the correct field before continuing.

3. Choose **D**elete Selected Calculated Field from the **Q**uery menu. The Query Designer deletes the field.

If you have multiple calculated fields (see "Using Multiple Calculated Fields," earlier in this chapter) and you want to delete them all, you can use any of the following techniques:

- Select any one of the calculated fields, and then choose **R**emove Selected Table from the **Q**uery menu.
- Click the Remove Table button on the SpeedBar.

Tip
You can also right-click one of the calculated fields and choose **R**emove Selected Table from the SpeedMenu.

Ordering Query Records with an Index

To make it easier to find records in the Query Results window, most queries specify some type of sort order. Ordering the records, however, adds an extra level of complication to a query. In particular, you may have noticed two unusual occurrences in your ordered queries:

- If you're using large tables, some queries seem to take forever to run, while others display their results almost immediately.
- Sometimes your query results are editable and sometimes they're not.

This apparently random behavior actually is the result of the method dBASE for Windows uses to order the query records. If the Query Designer uses the "sort" method, queries run slowly and display their results in a read-only window; if the "index" method is used, the results appear much faster and the records are always editable. To get the optimum performance from your queries, you need to know under which conditions dBASE for Windows orders the query results with a sort and under which conditions it orders the results with an index.

Understanding the Difference between Indexing and Sorting

In Chapter 9, "Creating Basic Queries," you learned how to order a query based on the values in one or more fields. Remember that you order a query by pointing at the Field Order box beside the field name, pressing the left mouse button, and then dragging the mouse to select one of the five orders shown in figure 17.10.

◄ "Changing the Order of Fields and Records," p. 177

> **Note**
>
> The five ordering options shown in figure 17.10 are for character fields only. Numeric and date fields use only the case-sensitive ascending and descending orders, and logical fields cannot be ordered.

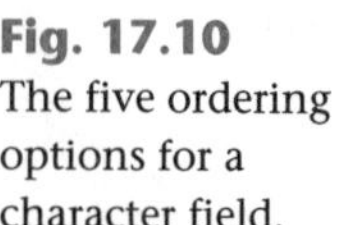

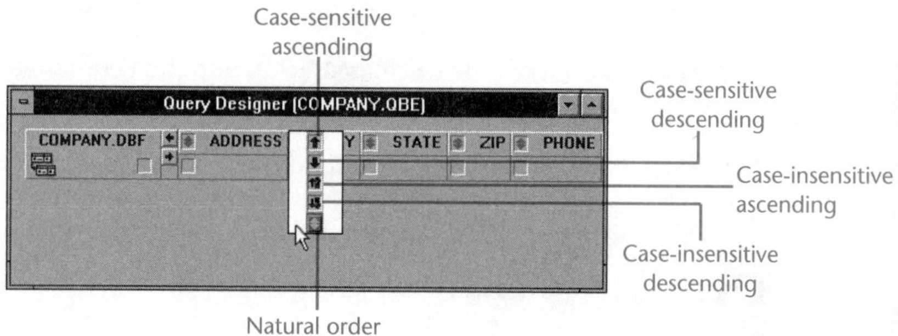

Fig. 17.10
The five ordering options for a character field.

The two case-sensitive orders also are known as *ASCII orders* because they arrange the records according to the ASCII values of the field characters. Table 17.1 summarizes the ASCII values for letters and numbers.

Table 17.1 ASCII Values for Letters and Numbers

Characters	ASCII Values
0 to 9	48 to 57
A to Z	65 to 90
a to z	97 to 122

As you can see, the ASCII order treats uppercase and lowercase letters differently. That is, in an ascending ASCII order, uppercase letters come before lowercase letters.

The case-insensitive orders also are known as *dictionary orders* because they arrange the records as you may see them in a dictionary (that is, uppercase and lowercase letters are treated identically).

When you select an order, dBASE for Windows uses the sort method to arrange the records under the following conditions:

- If you select a dictionary order in a single field
- If you select an order for multiple fields

In either case, dBASE for Windows uses the SORT command to place the records in the selected order. SORT doesn't change the existing table, however. Instead, it creates a temporary table and changes the natural order for this new table. This causes the following two problems:

- It takes time to create the new table and add the records in natural order, so this method is quite slow if you're dealing with a large amount of data.
- Because you no longer are dealing with the original table, you can't make changes to the query results.

To overcome these problems, you need to order the query records using an index. Following are the conditions under which dBASE for Windows uses an index to order the query:

Tip
When you run the query, look in the Status bar. If `Rd Only` appears, it means that you can't make changes to the records.

- If you select an ASCII order in a single field that has a matching index, dBASE for Windows uses the existing index to order the query.
- If you select an ASCII order in a single field that doesn't have an index, dBASE for Windows creates a temporary index that matches the ASCII order and uses the new index to order the query.

The index method is faster because dBASE for Windows doesn't have to create a new table, and the query results are editable because you're working with the original data.

Indexing a Table from the Query Designer

In earlier versions of dBASE, you had to leave the query screen to create a new table index. dBASE for Windows, however, enables you to index the table right from the Query Designer. Here are the steps to follow:

1. Select any field in the table you want to index.
2. Choose Manage **I**ndexes from the **Q**uery menu. The Manage Indexes dialog box appears (see fig. 17.11).

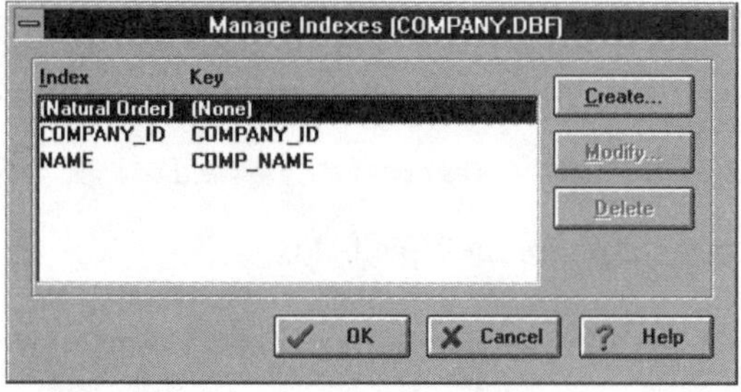

Fig. 17.11
Use the Manage Indexes dialog box to create or modify an index.

3. Select the **C**reate button. dBASE for Windows displays the Create Index dialog box (see fig. 17.12).
4. Enter the options you want for the new index and then choose OK to return to the Manage Indexes dialog box.
5. Choose OK to return to the Query Designer. Your new index appears in the query skeleton as follows:

    - If you created a simple index (such as using a single field with no dBASE for Windows functions), a key icon appears next to the field's order box.

◄ "Creating a Simple Index," p. 128

◄ "Creating a Complex Index," p. 131

- If you created a complex index (such as using multiple fields or dBASE for Windows functions in the key expression), the index appears as a separate field (see fig. 17.13).

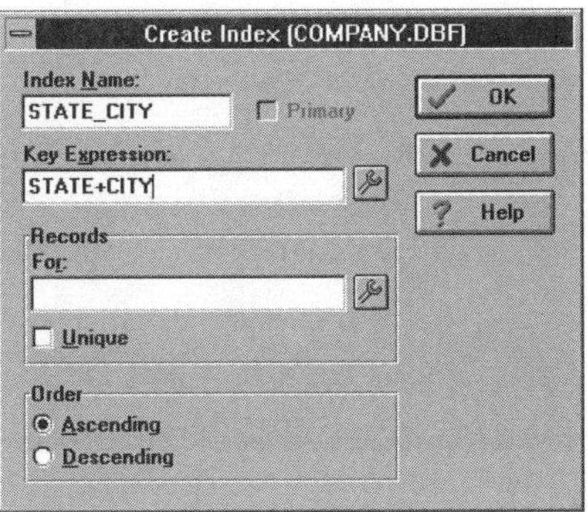

Fig. 17.12
Use the Create Index dialog box to define the new index.

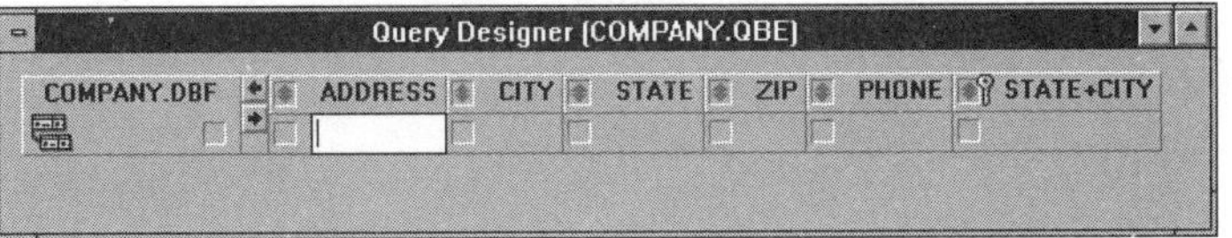

Fig. 17.13
Complex indexes appear in the query skeleton as a separate field.

Troubleshooting

I chose an ASCII order for a field that has an existing index, but dBASE for Windows still used SORT to order the query. Why?

The likely problem is that you didn't choose an ASCII order that matched the index. For example, if the field is indexed in ascending order, you'll only get an indexed query if you choose the ascending ASCII order.

Is there any way to get a dictionary (that is, case-insensitive) order using an index?

There sure is. You need to use the UPPER( ) function in your index key expression to index the field entirely in uppercase. Suppose that you want a dictionary order for a LAST_NAME field (so that the name *deSilva* appears near the name *Desilu,* for example). You would create a new index for the table using the following expression:

```
UPPER(LAST_NAME)
```

This new index appears as an extra field in the table skeleton so that you can use it to set the query order. See the preceding section, "Indexing a Table from the Query

(continues)

(continued)

Designer," to learn how to create a new table index without leaving the Query Designer screen.

I need to order a query based on two fields, but the sort method takes forever thanks to my large tables. Is there a way to use an index order, instead?

Absolutely. You can create a complex index that uses the data from both fields. Suppose that you want the query results ordered by the STATE field and then by the CITY field. You then would create a new index for the table that uses the following key expression:

```
STATE+CITY
```

Again, the Query Designer displays this new index in the table skeleton.

My complex indexes don't appear in the query skeleton.

You need to instruct dBASE for Windows to display them. Choose **Q**uery Designer from the **P**roperties menu. In the dialog box that appears, activate the **D**isplay Complex Indexes check box and then choose OK.

Working with the Condition Box

Tip
You can also display the Query Designer Properties dialog box by right-clicking the Query Designer and selecting **Q**uery Designer Properties from the SpeedMenu.

Chapter 9, "Creating Basic Queries," showed you how to filter the query results by adding conditions to one or more fields in the query skeleton. You also can add conditions by entering an expression in the Condition box (see fig. 17.14). The following is a list of some advantages you have when you use the Condition box:

- You can use the .AND. and .OR. operators to combine multiple conditions in a single expression.
- You can use fields from two or more different tables as part of the condition expression.
- You can use parentheses to indicate precedence.

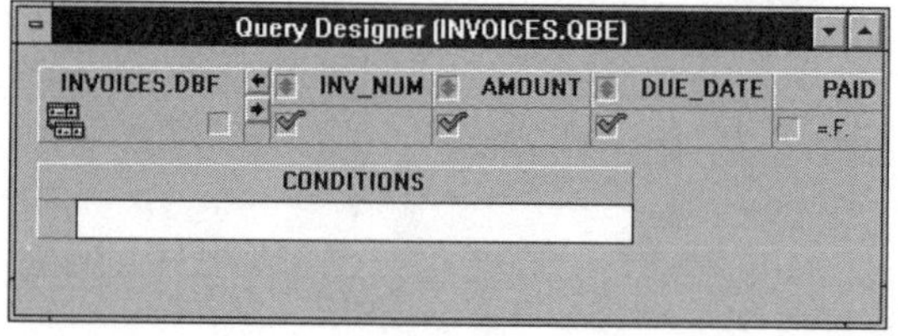

Fig. 17.14
You can use the Condition box to add filter conditions to the query.

To filter the query using the Condition box, follow these steps:

1. Choose Add **C**onditions from the **Q**uery menu. dBASE for Windows displays the Condition box in the Query Designer window.

2. Activate the Condition box by clicking inside it.

3. Enter the filter expression using the following guidelines:

   - Use only standard dBASE for Windows expressions.

   - Be sure to be explicit in entering the appropriate field names and operators. If you enter **"Smith"** as a condition for the LAST_NAME field, for example, it's understood that you want to filter this query to those records where the LAST_NAME field is equal to "Smith". In the Condition box, however, you'd have to spell out the full expression:

```
LAST_NAME="Smith"
```

◄ "Using the Expression Builder," p. 283

   - Be careful how you use the $ operator. In a filter field, $ means "contains," and in the Condition box it means "is contained in." If you enter **$ "Smith"** as a condition for the LAST_NAME field, for example, dBASE for Windows filters those records where the LAST_NAME field *contains* "Smith". In the Condition box, the equivalent expression would be the following:

```
"Smith" $ LAST_NAME
```

     In this case, dBASE for Windows filters those records where "Smith" *is contained in* the LAST_NAME field.

   - If you prefer to use two separate lines rather than the .OR. operator, press the down-arrow key to create a second expression box.

Look at an example of the Condition box in action. Recall that earlier in this chapter you learned how to filter a query based on a calculated field (refer to fig. 17.4). In that example, you created an OVERDUE calculated field and then filtered the query to show only those records that were more than 120 days past due.

You can use the Condition box to achieve a similar result without creating a separate calculated field. The idea is that you use a dBASE for Windows expression to combine both the calculation and the filter. Here's the expression that does the job:

```
DATE()-DUE_DATE>120
```

Figure 17.15 shows the query with this expression entered into the Condition box.

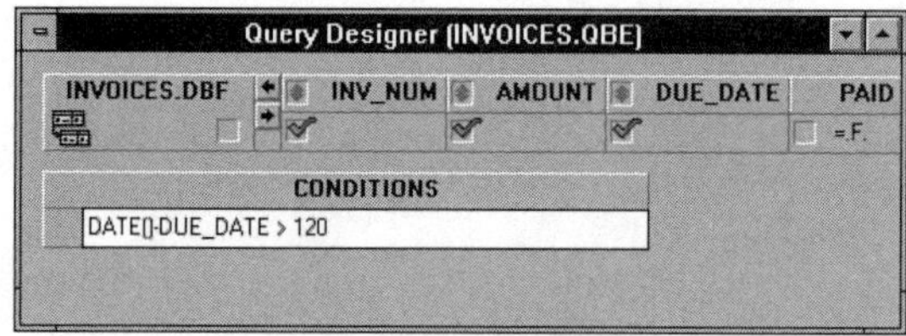

Fig. 17.15 An example expression in the Condition box.

If you need to remove the Condition box from the query, use any of the following techniques:

- Select the Condition box, and then choose Remo**v**e Conditions from the **Q**uery menu.

- Click the Remove Table button on the SpeedBar.

Tip You can also remove the Condition box by right-clicking it and selecting **R**emove Selected Table from the SpeedMenu.

A Note to dBASE for DOS Users about Update Queries

If you've come to dBASE for Windows from dBASE for DOS version IV or earlier, you may be wondering what happened to the powerful Update Query features. Well, they're still there, only dBASE for Windows makes them available for any table, not just a query. Table 17.2 lists the old update commands from dBASE for DOS and the new commands in dBASE for Windows.

Table 17.2 dBASE for Windows Equivalents to dBASE for DOS (Version IV and Earlier) Update Commands

Old Update Command	dBASE for Windows Equivalent
Update, Replace values	**T**able, **R**eplace Records
Update, Append records	**T**able, **T**able Utilities, **A**ppend Records from File
Update, Mark records for deletion	**T**able, **T**able Utilities, **D**elete Records
Update, Unmark records	**T**able, **T**able Utilities, **R**ecall Records

Also, earlier versions of dBASE for DOS enabled you to add summary operators as conditions. If you entered **SUM** as the condition for the AMOUNT field, for example, dBASE would display the sum of the AMOUNT field in the query. In dBASE for Windows, you run the query and then choose one of the following commands:

- To get a count of the records, choose **T**able, **T**able Utilities, **C**ount Records.
- For all other calculations (sum, average, maximum, and so on), choose **T**able, **T**able Utilities, Ca**l**culate Records.

From Here...

You may want to refer to the following chapters for additional information about the concepts discussed in this chapter:

◄ "Manipulating Data," p. 309

- Chapter 7, "Indexing and Sorting Data." If you query a lot, or if you query large tables, indexes can really speed up your work. A basic understanding of how indexes work can help you, and this chapter gives you just that.
- Chapter 9, "Creating Basic Queries." This chapter gets you up and running with queries. You learn how to navigate the Query Designer, how to create a basic query, and how to filter the query with field conditions.
- Chapter 12, "Working with Related Tables." This chapter teaches you about relational database concepts and shows you how to use a multiple-table query to link two tables on a common field.
- Chapter 13, "Using the Expression Builder." Expressions are a crucial part of both calculated fields and the Condition box, and this chapter tells you everything you need to know.
- Chapter 14, "Manipulating Data." This chapter shows you how to work with subsets of data, including update operations such as replacing data, counting records, and performing field calculations.
- Chapter 16, "Designing Advanced Reports." Instead of adding a calculated field to a query, you can add it to a report. This chapter tells you how.

Chapter 18

Using dBASE in a Multiuser Environment

Information has always been remarkably egalitarian. If you can read and write, then you can work with and create information. However, *access* to information has been, historically, notably unegalitarian. If you were lucky, your company's mainframe priesthood *may* have run a report that contained the data you needed, but direct access to the files was at best unthinkable and at worst impossible.

Happily, the increasing popularity of local area networks is changing all that. These networks can make their data and their resources available to anyone else logged on to the system. Provided that you have the appropriate access rights, you get to work with the files directly, so you can browse and edit tables, run your own queries, and create your own reports.

However, database operations that are straightforward in a single-user environment become a little more complex when multiple users get in on the act. This increased complexity occurs because dBASE for Windows has to protect the integrity of the data in a table being accessed simultaneously by two or more people. This chapter examines those dBASE for Windows features that are unique to a multiuser environment. You tackle topics such as sharing data, table and record locking, and setting the program's multiuser options.

In this chapter, you learn about the following topics:

- dBASE for Windows on a network
- Sharing data on a network
- Starting dBASE for Windows from a network server

- Locking database files and records
- The dBASE for Windows multiuser options

dBASE for Windows and Local Area Networks

A *local area network* (LAN, for short) is a collection of computers and peripherals (such as printers and modems) connected by special cables. The LAN enables the computers to communicate with each other, share resources (such as peripherals and programs), and exchange data.

Most networks have at least one computer designated as a *file server* and the other computers are called *workstations.* (In peer-to-peer networks, each machine can act as both a server and a workstation. The individual network nodes can access *shared directories* on the other computers.) The file server usually contains data files, programs, and peripherals, and the workstations log on to the server to access these resources. Suppose that your network administrator has installed dBASE for Windows on the file server. After you log on to the network, you can access the server and then start a copy of dBASE for Windows on your own computer.

The following is a list of the networks that are compatible with dBASE for Windows:

- Novell NetWare, versions 2.2, 3.11, 3.12, and 4.01
- Personal Netware (Novell DOS 7)
- Microsoft Windows for Workgroups 3.11
- Microsoft LAN Manager 2.1
- Artisoft Lantastic 6.0
- Banyan Vines 5.0
- DecNet Pathworks 4.1
- IBM LAN Server 3.0

Note

dBASE for Windows does not support the following dBASE for DOS multiuser commands and functions: ACCESS( ), BEGIN TRANSACTION, COMPLETED( ), DISPLAY USERS, END TRANSACTION, ISMARKED( ), LIST USERS, LOGOUT, PROTECT, RESET, ROLLBACK, SET DBTRAP, SET SQL, and USER( ).

Understanding Data Sharing

Working with dBASE for Windows on a network isn't much different from using the program on a stand-alone machine. You can use, browse, and edit tables, create queries, open forms for data entry, and run reports. In short, anything you can do as a single user, you can do in a multiuser scenario.

The only time you'll notice the network is when there is a sharing conflict. *Sharing* is what LANs are all about. Besides sharing the server's hardware (printers, disk drives, modems, and so on), a network also shares both applications and data files. Sharing conflicts can arise when you're working with a particular file from a shared directory and another user opens and starts working with the same file. If the two of you attempt to modify the same record at the same time, a conflict (or *collision*) will result. As you'll see later in this chapter, dBASE for Windows has some built-in features designed to prevent collisions.

The other sharing issue that networks need to address is giving users access to the most current data. If you open a table of customer data, for example, you want to be sure that the address and phone number you extract is the latest data available. If someone else recently made changes to the record, the changes should be posted to the table in good time.

Troubleshooting

I'm using dBASE for Windows under Windows for Workgroups. As the manual suggests, I've loaded the SHARE program so that I can share data on my local drive. However, dBASE seems to have become unstable and erratic. What's the problem?

The problem is likely a conflict between the SHARE utility and Windows for Workgroups (WFW). WFW uses its own version of SHARE called VSHARE.386 (which is loaded from your SYSTEM.INI file), so you don't have to bother with SHARE. You also are using VSHARE.386 if you installed Microsoft Word for Windows, version 6.0a.

Loading dBASE for Windows from a Network Server

Before starting dBASE for Windows from a network, make sure the file server containing dBASE for Windows is up and running and then log onto it as you normally would by entering the appropriate user name, password, and so on (this procedure depends on the network software you're using).

If your network administrator hasn't already set up a dBASE for Windows icon in your Program Manager group, here are the steps to do so:

1. In Program Manager, open the program group in which you want the icon to appear.

2. Choose **N**ew from the **F**ile menu. The New Program Object dialog box appears (see fig. 18.1).

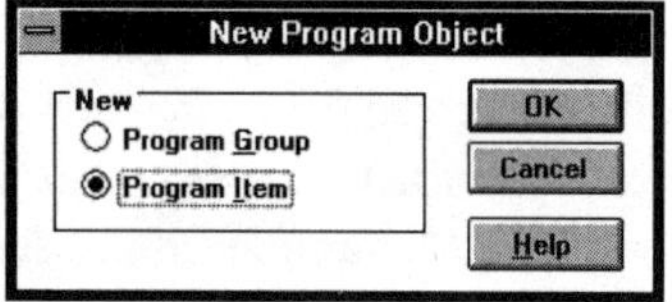

Fig. 18.1
The New Program Object dialog box appears when you choose New from Program Manager's File menu.

3. Make sure the Program **I**tem option is selected and then choose OK. The Program Item Properties dialog box appears (see fig. 18.2).

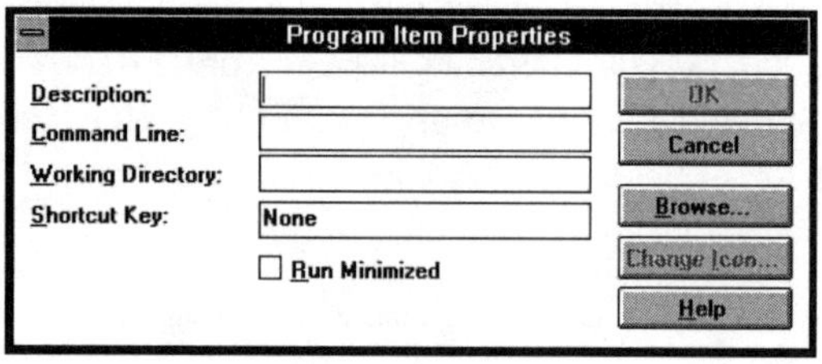

Fig. 18.2
Use the Program Item Properties dialog box to define the program item for dBASE for Windows.

4. In the **D**escription text box, enter a label for the icon.

5. In the **C**ommand Line text box, enter the full path name for the network installation of dBASE for Windows. Be sure to include the following items:

   - The network drive letter.

- The dBASE for Windows executable directory. (This is usually \DBASEWIN\BIN\, but you should either check with the network administrator or choose the **B**rowse button to select the executable from the Browse dialog box.)
- The name of the dBASE for Windows executable file (DBASEWIN.EXE).

If the network drive is drive G, for example, you would type **G:\DBASEWIN\BIN\DBASEWIN.EXE**.

6. In the **W**orking Directory text box, enter the working directory you want to use for dBASE for Windows. (This usually is the directory where you store your database files.)
7. Choose OK. Program Manager adds the icon to the program group.

With the dBASE for Windows icon set up, you can just start the program as you would any other. You don't need to log in to the network version of dBASE for Windows (unlike dBASE for DOS, dBASE for Windows doesn't support the PROTECT command). You can just start it up and use it as though it were a single-user version.

Note

When working in a networked environment, remember that you're dealing with two types of files: those needed by multiple users, and those used only by yourself. Files with multiple users should remain on the server so that other people can access the data. If you'll be creating files for your own use, try, whenever possible, to store them locally. This prevents the server from getting cluttered with dozens of small files from individual users. If you don't have any local hard disk space on which to store your files, ask the network administrator to create a separate subdirectory for you on the server.

Tip

If you're not sure whether dBASE for Windows is running in a networked environment, type **? network()** and press Enter in the Command window. If you see `.T.` in the Results window, a network is present.

Locking Files and Records

As mentioned earlier, using dBASE for Windows in a multiuser environment is, for the most part, identical to using the program on a stand-alone machine. The network comes into play only when two or more users share the same data. In this scenario, you must deal with two concerns:

- Avoiding data sharing conflicts when multiple users attempt to modify the same data
- Giving everyone access to the most current information

Dealing with data-sharing conflicts is the subject of this section. You look at the dBASE for Windows features that *lock* files and records to ensure data integrity. This section approaches *locking* by using the old "5 W's" method that journalists love so much: why, who, what, where, and when.

Why Is Locking Necessary?

In database applications, the idea of *data integrity* is one of the most crucial. After all, merely having information is no big deal. To get the most out of your stored data, you have to put it to work in some way. But let's face it, the data you work with is only as useful as it is accurate. If the information becomes unreliable or corrupted, it is worse than useless—it is potentially dangerous. (Imagine sending your company's sensitive data to the wrong address!)

That's why you do things like back up your data regularly, create fancy forms to make data entry less error-prone, and program validation routines that check the data before committing it to disk.

In a multiuser environment, data integrity is preserved by instituting a system of *locks* that prevent various bad things from happening to a file or record. For example, a busy network can have dozens of users accessing the same data. What happens if two of those users happen to be editing the same record in a table? Whose data gets written to disk? Or, what if one user wants to make changes to an index or a table structure? If you allow other users to access the table's data at the same time, the results could be disastrous.

Locks are designed to handle these sharing conflicts by preventing other users from accessing some or all of a table while another operation that might change the table data is being performed (such as editing a record or reindexing a table).

Who Applies the Lock?

Locks can be applied in one of two ways:

- *Automatic locks* are applied by dBASE for Windows as soon as it detects an operation that could change the data in a table. dBASE for Windows monitors the operation and turns the locks on and off automatically, as needed.

- *Explicit locks* are applied directly by the user. They work just like automatic locks except that you turn the locks on and off yourself. (See "Setting an Explicit Lock," later in this chapter, for instructions.) In most cases, you probably will want to avoid explicit locks and leave automatic locking on all the time because dBASE for Windows is designed to handle this chore smoothly and efficiently. (To learn how to turn automatic locking on and off , see "Working with the Multiuser Options," later in this chapter.)

What Types of Locks Are Available?

Some table tasks have no effect on the overall structure of a table. Operations such as editing a record, marking records for deletion, or sorting the records in the table, leave the table essentially intact. While these types of tasks are under way, dBASE for Windows applies a *read-write lock* to the table. This lock means that the user performing the operation can make changes to the table (that is, they have *write* privileges), but anyone else can only view the data (they have *read-only* privileges).

Other types of operations can have a more drastic effect on the table. Examples include modifying the table structure, changing the table indexes, and packing the table records. For these tasks, dBASE for Windows sets up an *exclusive lock* that allows one, and only one, user access to the table. Other users can't even view the file until the operation is complete and the exclusive lock is removed.

Where Is the Lock Applied?

The easiest way to maintain data integrity in a networked environment would be to always allow only exclusive use of a file. When one user was finished working with a file, he or she would close it and it then would become available to the other users on the network. This certainly is a safe method, but it isn't even remotely practical in today's busy networks where file sharing is a fact of life.

So, if you are forced to deal with the reality of two or more users accessing the same data, you need your locks to be as unobtrusive as possible. dBASE for Windows handles this by applying locks at two levels:

- *Record level locks* apply only to a single record in a table. Other users are free to make changes to any other record, but they're restricted to read-only access for the locked record. dBASE for Windows applies a lock at this level for operations that affect a single record only (such as editing the record).

- *Table level locks* apply to the entire table and they can be either read-write or exclusive. If the table lock is read-write, the other users can open the table, but they can't make any changes to it. If the table lock is exclusive, other users can't open the file.

When Is the Lock Applied?

When the automatic locking feature is activated, dBASE for Windows turns table and record locks on and off based on the current operation being performed on the table.

Table Locks

For table locks, the following operations require exclusive access:

- Opening a table in Design mode
- Creating, modifying, or deleting an index tag
- Reindexing a table
- Packing a table
- Zapping a table
- Importing records into a table

Tip
If you're not sure whether you have exclusive access to the current table, look in the Status bar. dBASE for Windows displays `Excl` in the Status bar for tables opened with exclusive access.

Unless you open the table with exclusive access (see "Working with the Multiuser Options," later in this chapter), when you try to perform an operation that requires an exclusive lock, dBASE for Windows displays a dialog box similar to the one shown in figure 18.3. Choose **O**pen Exclusive to set the exclusive lock, **V**iew Only to create a read-write lock, or **C**ancel to end the operation. (In some cases, dBASE for Windows displays an Exclusive Access Required dialog box in which you choose OK to open the table in exclusive mode.)

Note

The View Only option in the dialog box shown in figure 18.3 is useful when you know someone else is working with the table, and therefore you can't create an exclusive lock. Creating a read-write lock at least enables you to view the current settings of the operation you were trying to perform.

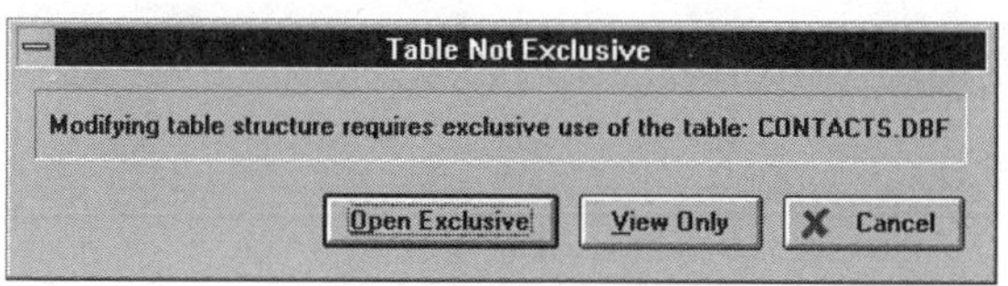

Fig. 18.3
A dialog box similar to this one appears when you attempt to perform an operation that requires an exclusive lock on a table.

If dBASE for Windows can't create the exclusive lock (because someone else is already using the table, for example), then you'll see the error message shown in figure 18.4. You'll have to wait until the other user is finished with the file before you can create the exclusive lock.

Fig. 18.4
This dialog box appears if another user is already working with the table and dBASE for Windows is unable to create an exclusive lock.

dBASE for Windows sets up a read-write lock on the entire table for the following operations:

- Replacing field values
- Marking records for deletion
- Recalling records marked for deletion
- Exporting records
- Sorting records
- Generating records
- Counting records
- Performing field calculations
- Running a report based on the table

Record Locks

dBASE for Windows locks a record as soon as you press any key that will modify data in the record (if you try to insert or delete characters, for example). When the record lock is active, other users can view the data but they can't make changes to it. The record lock is removed when you move to another record.

> **Note**
>
> If you're working with multiple, related tables and you lock a record in the parent table, dBASE for Windows also locks all the related child records in the child table.

◄ "Working with Related Tables," p. 261

If you try to make changes to a record that has been locked by another user, you'll see the error message shown in figure 18.5. dBASE for Windows retries the lock until the record is free. (See "Working with the Multiuser Options," later in this chapter, to see how you can control the time dBASE for Windows spends retrying the record lock.)

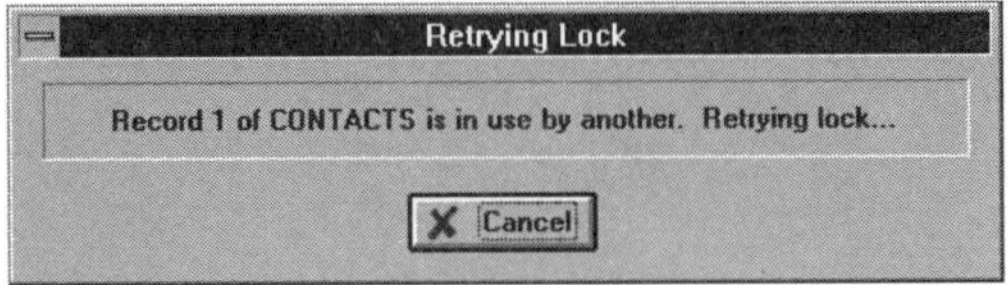

Fig. 18.5
This dialog box appears if the record is already locked by another user.

Setting an Explicit Lock

If you prefer that no one else change some data while you're viewing it, you can explicitly lock one or more records by hand. To do this, follow these steps:

1. Browse the table with which you want to work.
2. Select the record or records you want to lock.
3. Choose **L**ock Selected Record from the **T**able menu. dBASE for Windows locks the records.

Tip
Pressing Ctrl+L also locks the selected records.

> **Note**
>
> You also can use the Command window to establish explicit locks. The RLOCK( ) function, for example, locks records using the following syntax:
>
> ```
> RLOCK([<list expC>][,<alias>])
> ```
>
> Here, <list expC> is a list of record numbers to lock and <alias> is the alias or work area number of the table you want to use. If you run RLOCK( ) without arguments, the function locks the current record in the current table.
>
> To establish a read-write table lock, use the FLOCK( ) function:
>
> ```
> FLOCK([<alias>])
> ```
>
> The optional argument <alias> is, as usual, the alias or work area number of the table you want to lock.

To unlock a table or its records, use the UNLOCK command:

```
UNLOCK [ALL ¦ IN <alias>]
```

Use ALL to unlock tables in all work areas, or IN <alias> to unlock records in a table in a specific work area.

To open a table with an exclusive lock, add the EXCLUSIVE argument to the USE command:

```
USE <filename> EXCLUSIVE
```

Here, <filename> is the name of the table you want to open.

▶ "Working with the Command Window," p. 549

▶ "Automating Other Database Tasks," p. 659

Troubleshooting

I always forget to create an explicit lock. Is there any other way to keep locks on multiple records over a series of operations?

You can try some transaction processing. In dBASE for Windows, a transaction is a series of commands that make changes to a table (such as editing an existing record or adding a new one). When you begin a transaction, dBASE for Windows starts recording each change and adds the appropriate table and record locks as you go along. These locks are kept in place until you end the transaction.

To begin a transaction for the current table, type **begintrans( )** and press Enter in the Command window. To end a transaction, type **commit( )** (to accept the changes you made during the transaction) or **rollback( )** (to undo your changes), and then press Enter. Note that certain operations (such as modifying the table structure, and packing or zapping the table) are not allowed inside a transaction.

To remove the lock on one or more records, select the records and then choose Un**l**ock Selected Record from the **T**able menu (or press Ctrl+L).

Working with the Multiuser Options

By default, dBASE for Windows uses automatic locking and tables are not opened with an exclusive lock. You can modify these settings and more using the Desktop Property Inspector. To do this, follow these steps:

1. Choose **D**esktop from the **P**roperties menu.

2. In the Desktop Properties dialog box that appears, click the Table tab (see fig. 18.6).

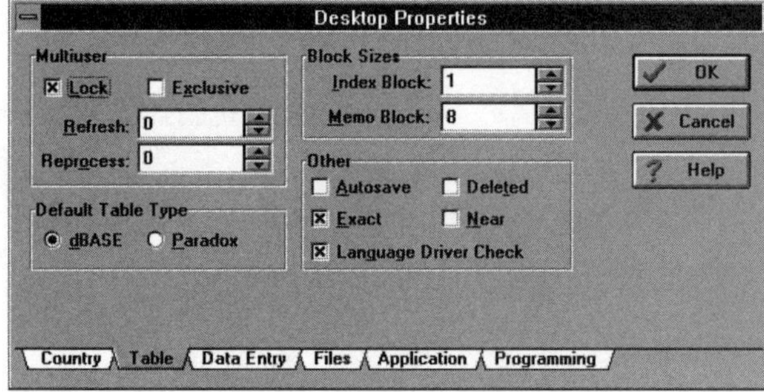

Fig. 18.6
The Table tab contains several options that control dBASE for Windows' multiuser behavior.

3. In the Multiuser box, make your changes to the following options:

***L**ock*—When this check box is activated (the default), automatic locking is turned on. You can disable some (but not all) automatic locks by deactivating this check box. Commands that change data (such as Replace Records) still generate an automatic lock.

*E**x**clusive*—Activate this check box to open all your tables with an exclusive lock.

Tip
If you know you won't be sharing files (or if you're working in a single-user environment), activating the E**x**clusive check box speeds up dBASE for Windows.

***R**efresh*—This option controls the frequency (in seconds) with which dBASE for Windows re-reads the data for the current file. If other people are using the same file, refreshing the data ensures that you're always working with the current information. One caveat, however: faster refresh frequencies lead to slower dBASE for Windows performance.

Note

You can control the data refreshing from the Command window. Just enter the REFRESH command and dBASE for Windows refreshes the data in the current table. (If you want to refresh the data in a different work area, use the REFRESH(<alias>) command, in which <alias> is the alias name or work area number of the other file.)

Reprocess—This option controls the number of times dBASE for Windows retries a table lock before giving up. The minimum value is 0 (in which case the program retries the lock indefinitely) and the maximum value is 32000.

4. Choose OK to put the new settings into effect.

From Here...

You may want to refer to the following chapters for additional information about the concepts discussed in this chapter:

- Chapter 5, "Designing a Database." This chapter shows you how to design databases and, in particular, addresses networking and multiuser concerns.
- Chapter 8, "Entering, Editing, and Viewing Data." This chapter gives you the basics of data entry and editing.
- Chapter 12, "Working with Related Tables." Related tables add an extra level of complication to a networked environment because locks can extend to child tables as well as parent tables. Understanding relational concepts can help simplify things, and this chapter tells you everything you need to know.
- Chapter 22, "Using dBASE for Windows in a Client/Server Environment." This chapter explores client/server issues such as SQL and IDAPI, which have major implications in shared environments.
- Chapter 32, "Automating Other Database Tasks." This chapter discusses, among other things, transaction processing. A transaction locks records and tables until the transaction is either committed or rolled back.

Part III

Integrating dBASE for Windows with Other Applications

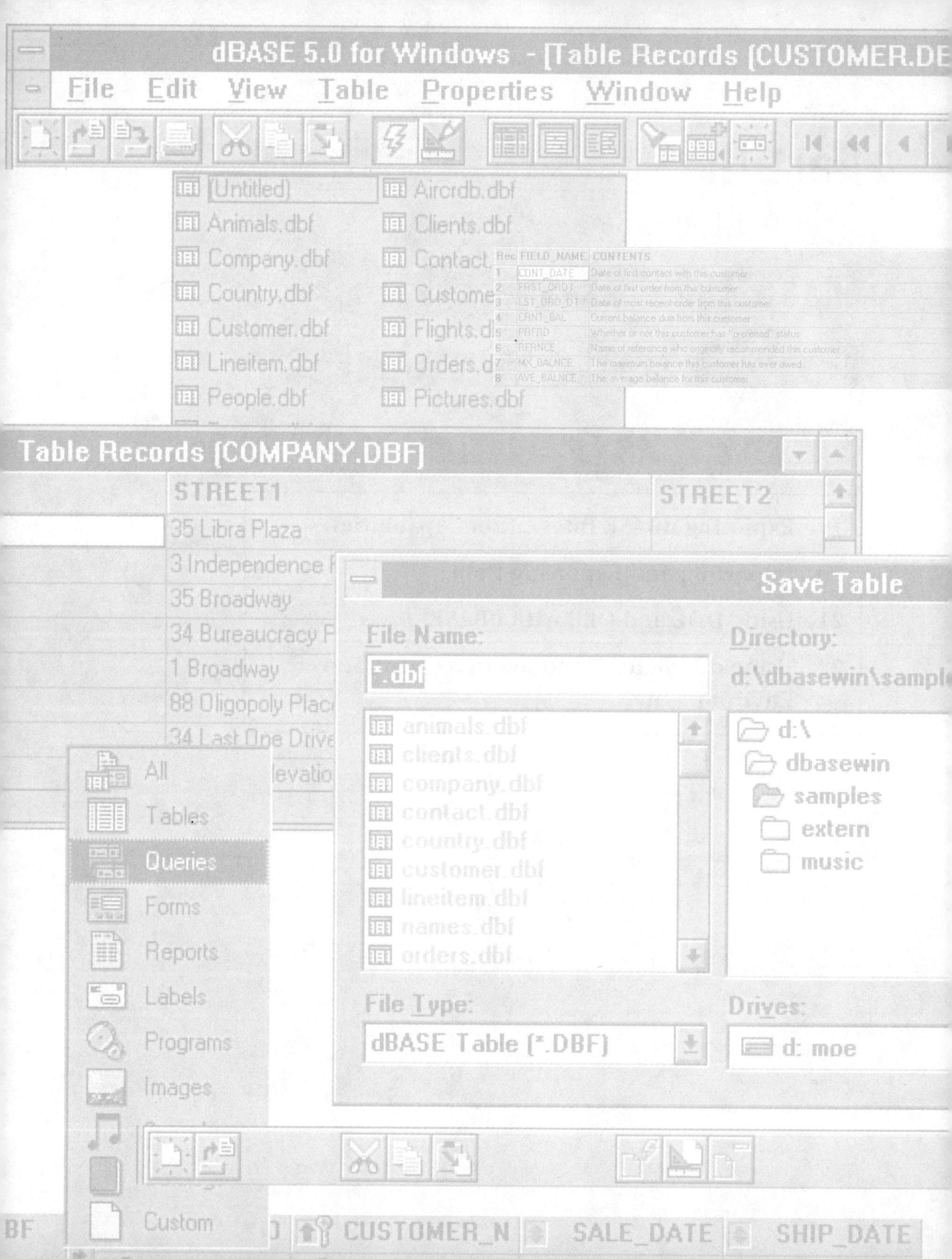
dBASE 5.0 for Windows - [Table Records (CUSTOMER.DE
File Edit View Table Properties Window Help
(Untitled)
Aircrdb.dbf
Animals.dbf
Clients.dbf
Company.dbf
Contact.
Country.dbf
Custome
Customer.dbf
Flights.d
Lineitem.dbf
Orders.d
People.dbf
Pictures.dbf
Rec FIELD_NAME CONTENTS
1 CONT_DATE Date of first contact with this customer
2 FRST_ORDT Date of first order from this customer
3 LST_ORD_DT Date of most recent order from this customer
4 CRNT_BAL Current balance due from this customer
5 PRFRD Whether or not this customer has "preferred" status
6 RFRNCE Name of reference who originally recommended this customer
7 MX_BALNCE The maximum balance this customer has ever owed
8 AVE_BALNCE The average balance for this customer
Table Records (COMPANY.DBF)
STREET1
STREET2
35 Libra Plaza
3 Independence
35 Broadway
34 Bureaucracy
1 Broadway
88 Oligopoly Plac
34 Last One Drive
All
Tables
Queries
Forms
Reports
Labels
Programs
Images
Custom
Save Table
File Name:
*.dbf
Directory:
d:\dbasewin\sampl
animals.dbf
clients.dbf
company.dbf
contact.dbf
country.dbf
customer.dbf
lineitem.dbf
names.dbf
orders.dbf
d:\
dbasewin
samples
extern
music
File Type:
dBASE Table (*.DBF)
Drives:
d: moe
CUSTOMER_N
SALE_DATE
SHIP_DATE

Chapter 19

Exploring dBASE Integration Capabilities

Integration of data is a key factor in computing today. Most businesses and organizations are trying to move into environments that can connect disparate applications across disparate platforms so that information can be shared by everyone who needs it. dBASE for Windows is specifically designed to fit into the integration scheme.

This chapter discusses the following topics in relation to dBASE for Windows integration:

- What is integration?
- dBASE for Windows integration achieved through the client/server relationship
- Connectivity provided by the Borland Database Engine
- The use of Dynamic Data Exchange (DDE)
- The implementation of Object Linking and Embedding (OLE)

What Is Integration?

In simple terms, *integration* is the incorporation of separate parts to form a single entity. The term *integration* as used in the computer industry has had a similar though evolving definition that should be traced through its history for clarity.

The first popular program to use integration was VisiCalc, a spreadsheet program that integrated crude graphing capabilities. When Lotus 1-2-3 became the standard spreadsheet program, graphing was an integral part of the program, but the concept of having a program that performed two separate operations was no longer new and exciting. Graphing simply became a "feature" of the program, and Lotus 1-2-3 was not considered an "integrated" program.

Then Lotus Corporation announced a new, integrated program called Symphony. This DOS-based program integrated several very different programs into one program. It included a spreadsheet/graphing program, a database program, a word processing program, and a telecommunications program. The advantage that an integrated program had over stand-alone programs was the capability to produce data in any one module and use it in a different module without having to reenter the data. Stand-alone programs all used different formats for files, and the files could not be used interchangeably between programs.

Following shortly on the heels of Symphony came similar DOS-based integrated packages, the two most notable being Framework by Ashton-Tate and Enable by Enable Software, Inc. Microsoft Works was the Windows-based entry in the field. Except for Enable, which has endured for more than 11 years, most DOS-based integrated packages did not catch on very well and eventually met their demise. Although people liked the idea of one program that provided all their needs, most of the integrated programs were not robust enough to compete with stand-alone programs. Developers of stand-alone programs took a cue from the integrated programs and began to include import and export filters in their programs so that files could be shared among different programs.

The introduction of local area networks and wide area networks gave the term *integration* an additional meaning. Networking provided integration of data by enabling users to access each other's files as well as programs. Before "real" networks, PC users had to use the "Nike" or "tennis shoe" network to access such files. (In other words, files were hand-carried on disks from one computer to another.)

With the advent of new programming techniques in Windows, integration took on yet another meaning. Through the feature called Dynamic Data Exchange (DDE), separate programs written for Windows (regardless of the vendor) were able to share data. This type of integration is referred to as *client/server*. (The same term is used in a network environment to refer to the relationship between the host computer and the remote computers. In this chapter, however, *client/server* applies to the DDE relationship between programs.)

Note

Computer terms are sometimes used interchangeably in different contexts, creating confusion for users.

Software vendors soon caught on to the fact that they could leverage DDE and the client/server integration into a new product category: software suites. Vendors and developers scurried around to acquire, write, and redesign Windows software that could be "bundled" into a suite. The software in the bundle needed more than DDE going it for it, though. Each program in the suite had to have features and menus that complemented the other programs.

Theoretically, it would seem that making a group of Windows programs compatible with each other would not be too difficult because all Windows programs must conform to a standard look and operation anyway. In fact, the programming demands for creating a suite are tremendous. Two popular software suites are Microsoft Office and Lotus SmartSuite. Microsoft Office includes Word, Excel, PowerPoint, Access, and Mail. Lotus SmartSuite includes 1-2-3, Ami Pro, Approach, Organizer, and Freelance Graphics.

How Does dBASE Fit in?

Although dBASE for Windows is not a suite or part of a suite, it is a program that uses DDE. Therefore, data integration is possible with other Windows programs. With over 15.5 million users worldwide, dBASE is uniquely positioned to become one of the major database applications that provides integration of data. Because dBASE for Windows is designed to leverage existing knowledge, users can move easily to the Windows and client/server platform where integration is an integral part of the program.

Recognizing that integration is such an important part of the future of computing, Borland developers have designed dBASE for Windows so that it meets the integration needs of today *and* tomorrow. The ability to meet future needs is based in dBASE for Windows' "Plug and Play" architecture, which allows it to access the entire Windows Application Programming Interface (API), Dynamic Link Libraries (DLLs), and custom control, including VBX control (created with Visual Basic). This Plug and Play architecture will also accept new features that may be on the horizon in the next version of Windows.

Why Integration Is a Top Priority

The invention and evolution of the PC is really responsible for the emphasis now being placed on integration. Before PCs, all the information of a company or an organization resided on a mainframe or minicomputer. This information was tightly (and sometimes jealously) controlled and parceled out on a need-to-know basis by the IS (Information Systems) or IM (Information Management) department.

When PCs became popular, information fell under the control of individual users. Data became decentralized and segmented. This was a problem because, many times, users in different areas were producing the exact same information. Obviously, the answer to the problem was to connect the PCs. This was accomplished with networks. Once the data became accessible to everyone again, the challenge was to be able to integrate the data produced by so many different programs. Windows answered this challenge with DDE.

Now the role of the Information Management department is to manage the abundance of corporate data, provide security for that data, provide access to users, and support the user with productivity tools for better integration. Access to data and integration of data are key factors that may determine the success or failure of a business. Often, the ability to get the right data to the right people at the right time is the only significant competitive advantage a company has.

Integration of data provides many benefits to a company. One of the primary benefits is the elimination of redundance and duplication—redundance of data in storage, and duplication of effort to record that data—yielding savings in man hours and equipment costs. Another benefit of integration is quick and easy access. The ability to obtain information from other sources and other departments yields quicker turnaround time, faster response to customers, and more intelligent decisions based on a broader spectrum of data.

The Essence of dBASE Integration

The Borland Database Engine (BDE) is the essence of integration for dBASE and all Borland programs. The BDE integrates common database functions across environments and applications. With the BDE established as the basis for common data access for all Borland products and languages, integration of dBASE for Windows is achieved with such products as InterBase, ORACLE, Sybase, Informix, and other DB2 SQL server environments, as well as Quattro Pro and Paradox.

The integration provided by the BDE is *transparent*, meaning that it takes place without the user's knowledge or intervention. If, for example, you want to use dBASE for Windows to access a SQL table, you use the same steps you would use to access a dBASE for Windows table, because the BDE converts the dBASE commands to the proper SQL "dialect" behind the scenes.

The program that interfaces with the BDE is called IDAPI (Integrated Database Applications Programming Interface). This program connects client applications to database servers and allows you to access SQL and Paradox data in the same way you access dBASE data. Borland called an earlier version of this program ODAPI (Open Database Applications Programming Interface).

Note

Look for other programs from other vendors to use the IDAPI in the future. Borland has made the IDAPI specifications available to other developers to enhance the usability of its own products.

The IDAPI Configuration Utility

dBASE provides a utility program that configures the IDAPI and stores the information in a file called IDAPI.CFG. By default, the IDAPI.CFG is configured for dBASE and Paradox. If you need to make changes to the IDAPI.CFG file to change system settings for files such as language drivers, database aliases, and network control files, use the IDAPI Configuration Utility.

The IDAPI Configuration Utility is accessed from Windows, not dBASE. It has its own icon in the dBASE program group window.

▶ "Configuring the IDAPI," p. 504

Taking a Closer Look at the Client/ Server Environment

The client/server environment enables you to integrate applications by moving information between separate applications (programs). As mentioned earlier, this environment is made possible by the protocol referred to as DDE. The DDE protocol is further enhanced by OLE (Object Linking and Embedding). OLE inserts data in the form of "objects." Objects can be text, a spreadsheet, graphics, sounds, animation, or any other type of data created by a server application. As the name Object Linking and Embedding states, the objects can be embedded or linked. Most Windows applications conform to the OLE server requirements. The OLE enhancement to the DDE protocol makes exchanging data much easier for the user than the original DDE protocol, which requires interaction at the programming level.

Two components are necessary in the client/server environment. These are fairly obvious—the client and the server. A *client* is a program that can accept embedded objects. A *server* is a program whose objects can be embedded in other programs. Some Windows programs are both clients and servers; that is, they can accept objects from other programs and give objects to other programs. dBASE functions as an OLE client but not an OLE server. It does, however, function as a server on the DDE level.

Identifying Servers

When an OLE server program is installed under Windows, it is automatically "registered" as a server. Since dBASE for Windows is a DDE server rather than an OLE server, it will not be registered as a server in REGEDIT. You can see which of your installed programs are servers by following these steps:

Tip

You also can see the server applications that are registered on your system when you actually use an OLE field. A dialog box lists all the server applications for you to choose from when you instruct dBASE to insert an object.

1. Start Windows and go to the Program Manager.
2. Open the **F**ile menu and choose **R**un.
3. Type **regedit.exe /v** and choose OK.
4. Open the **S**earch menu and choose **F**ind Key.
5. Type **server** and choose Find **N**ext. The first line that contains the word *server* will be highlighted. The name of the executable file that starts the program is listed with its path. Figure 19.1, for example, shows that Word for Windows (WINWORD) is a server.
6. If you know there are other servers, open the **S**earch menu and choose Find **N**ext again.
7. Repeat step 6 until all server applications have been found.
8. Close the window.

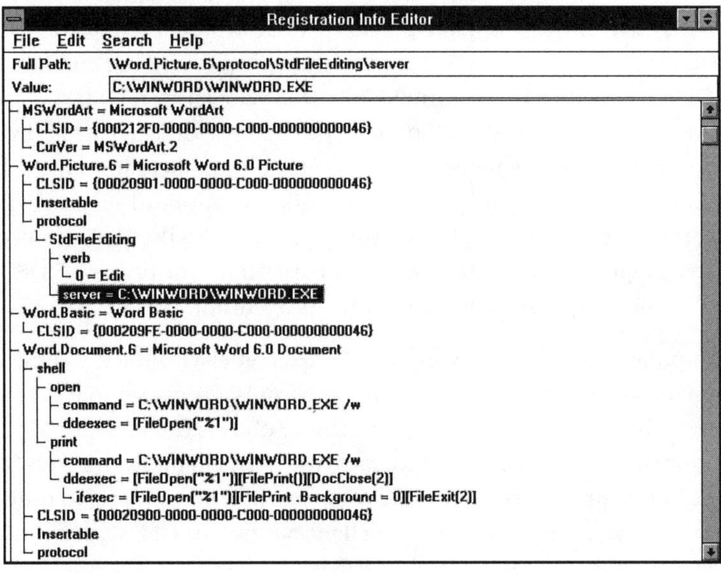

Fig. 19.1
The Registration Info Editor window lists the path and executable file for each server application installed on the system.

Using Data from Other Sources

As a client application, dBASE for Windows can embed or link objects from other programs (that are servers, of course). When an object is embedded, you can choose the object in dBASE, and the source application will open, allowing you to make changes to the object. After you make the changes, you can return to dBASE, and the changes will be updated.

When an object is linked, a reference is created in dBASE to the object in the server application. To change the object, you must edit the object in the server application. When the dBASE file that contains the reference (link) is opened, the link will be updated with the changes if dBASE and the server are both in memory and if link options are set on automatic. Otherwise, you must update the link by making selections from the Links menu.

Implementing OLE in dBASE for Windows

With dBASE for Windows, you can store OLE objects in one or more OLE fields in a table. The objects can be embedded or linked. OLE fields can be placed on forms, but cannot, as yet, be used in Crystal Reports.

When you edit an OLE field, dBASE uses the OLE Viewer window to display the object. When the OLE Viewer is open, the Status bar displays the type of OLE document (embedded or linked) and the application that created it, as shown in figure 19.2.

Tip
Linked objects take up less disk space than embedded objects because linked objects are not duplicated in the table, as embedded objects are.

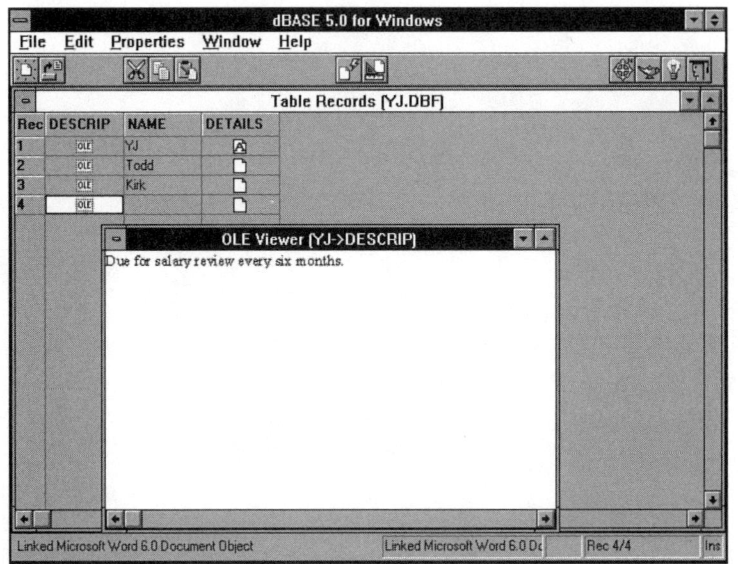

Fig. 19.2
The Status bar showing that the OLE object in the Viewer window is linked from Word 6.0 for Windows.

◀ "Exploring the Field Types," p. 95

Forms can include OLE fields, but they cannot include independent OLE objects. Crystal Reports cannot include OLE fields but can include independent OLE objects. In forms and reports, OLE objects can be positioned and sized as needed.

From Here...

◀ "Creating a Report," p. 230

This chapter covered the concepts of client/server integration and introduced you to embedding and linking objects in dBASE for Windows. If you would like to learn more about the client/server environment, OLE, the actual mechanics of linking and embedding objects, and the traditional methods of integration (importing and exporting files), refer to the following chapters:

- Chapter 20, "Importing and Exporting Data," explores integration achieved through exporting dBASE for Windows files for use with other programs, and importing files from other programs into dBASE for Windows.
- Chapter 21, "Using DDE and OLE with dBASE," covers the mechanics of embedding and linking objects in database fields and reports.
- Chapter 22, "Using dBASE for Windows in a Client/Server Environment," explains the use of SQL tables and explores the IDAPI in more detail.

Chapter 20

Importing and Exporting Data

dBASE for Windows tables are basically compatible with tables created by other Xbase applications such as DOS versions of dBASE, FoxPro (DOS and Windows versions), and Clipper. In addition, dBASE for Windows can export and import data in several formats.

When you export and import data, you can select which records and which fields in those records are to be exported or imported. You can directly or indirectly export data to, and import data from, the following:

- Other database tables
- Spreadsheet files
- Word processing files (saved in text format)
- Text files
- Desktop publishing files

In this chapter, you'll learn how to do the following:

- Export data from a table to another table or a file
- Append data from a file into a table
- Create a new table using data in a spreadsheet

Understanding Xbase Compatibility

Xbase is an informal database standard based on DOS dBASE. Database applications that use this format can usually interchange data in Character, Numeric, Logical, and Date fields, and may be able to interchange information in Float and Memo fields. Some Xbase applications, however, support types of fields that are not supported by others. dBASE for Windows, for example, supports Binary and OLE field types that are not supported by other Xbase applications.

If you try to use data from another Xbase application in dBASE, you may or may not be successful, depending on whether the table from which you are importing uses unique features of the source table. Don't assume that you can use data from other Xbase applications. On the other hand, if you are switching to dBASE for Windows from another Xbase application, you will probably be able to import most of your existing data.

Understanding Database Formats

You can import data from several sources into dBASE tables. You can also export data to other applications. The following is a list of the database file formats that dBASE can import from and export to:

Application	File Type
dBASE (import and export)	DBF
Paradox (import and export)	DB
DBMEMO3 (export only)	DBF, DBT
SDF (import and export)	TXT
Delimited (import and export)	TXT
Quattro Pro for Windows (import only)	WB1
Lotus 1-2-3 (import only)	WK1

▶ "Using DDE and OLE with dBASE," p. 487

Note

In addition to the file formats listed above, dBASE can also exchange information with most Windows applications.

Using dBASE Format

The dBASE format is the native format for DOS versions of dBASE and for dBASE for Windows. dBASE for Windows, though, supports Binary and OLE field types that are not supported by DOS versions of dBASE.

You can export records from a table in dBASE or Paradox format and append them to records in other dBASE tables.

You can open a dBASE for Windows table in the latest DOS version of dBASE, as long as it doesn't contain Binary or OLE fields. You can also open the table in another database application that can read dBASE files, such as Microsoft Access and FoxPro. Note that other applications and dBASE III and III PLUS may have difficulty reading memo fields created in dBASE for Windows.

Note

Microsoft Access can work directly with dBASE tables and can also convert those tables into its own native format.

Using Paradox Format

Using dBASE for Windows, you can create and work with tables in the Paradox format used by DOS and Windows versions of Paradox. You also can do the following:

- Export dBASE-format records in Paradox format
- Export Paradox-format records in dBASE format
- Import dBASE-format records into a Paradox table
- Import Paradox-format records into a dBASE table

The Paradox format supports all the dBASE field types, so exporting from a dBASE table to a Paradox table and importing from a dBASE table into a dBASE table causes no problems. Problems can arise, however, when you change from Paradox to dBASE format.

◄ "Creating a Paradox Table," p. 114

Using DBMEMO3 Format

You can use the DBMEMO3 format to export database and memo fields in a format compatible with dBASE III PLUS. You cannot import data in this format.

Using SDF Format

Records exported in SDF (System Data Format) files are in ASCII text format in which the following are true:

- A carriage-return character followed by a linefeed character terminates each record.
- All records in a table contain the same number of characters, with space characters extending the length of each field to its maximum size.

Note

If a field in the table is full, for example if a character field contains the maximum number of characters, there is no space between that field and the next in the SDF file.

When you import records in this format into a table, the number of characters in each field must match the number of characters in each corresponding table field.

Using Delimited Format

Records exported as delimited files are in ASCII text format in which the following are true:

- A carriage-return character followed by a linefeed character terminates each record.
- A separation character (a comma by default) separates each field from the next.
- A delimiting character (a double quotation mark by default) marks the beginning and end of each character field.

You can accept the default separation and delimiting characters or select others. You should use characters that do not occur within the data you are exporting.

Note

When a comma is used as the separation character, this format is also known as the Comma Separated Value (CSV) format.

You can import data in delimited format into such applications as word processors, text editors, and spreadsheet applications.

Exporting Data

You can export all the fields in all records, or you can selectively export records and fields.

Tip
If you are creating files that will be exported to another format, ensure maximum compatibility by avoiding binary, memo, and OLE fields.

Exporting All Records and Fields

To export all the records and fields from a dBASE or Paradox table, follow these steps:

1. Open the table from which you want to export data.
2. Open the **T**able menu and choose **T**able Utilities to display the submenu shown in figure 20.1.

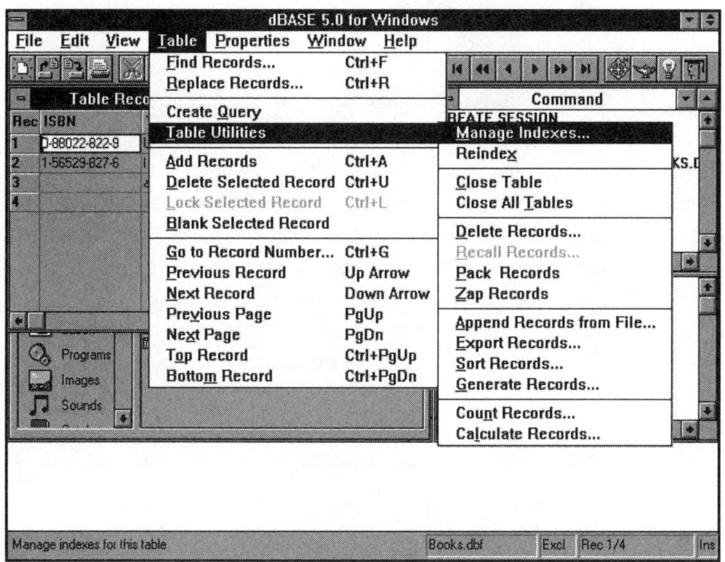

Fig. 20.1
The Table Utilities submenu.

3. In the Table Utilities submenu, choose **E**xport Records to display the Export Records dialog box with the name of the selected dBASE table in the title bar, as shown in figure 20.2.

The Export Records dialog box is where you specify the following:

- A name for the file that will contain the exported records
- The format in which you want the records to be exported

- Which records and which fields in those records you want to export
- Conditions that have to be satisfied for a record to be exported

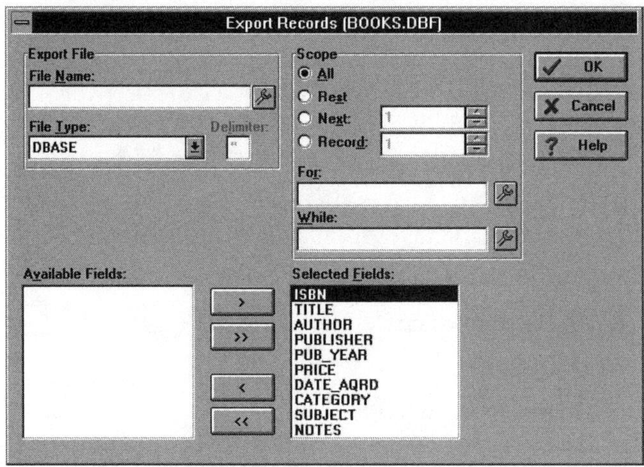

Fig. 20.2
The Export Records dialog box.

Note

When dBASE exports records, it does not verify that the files it creates are compatible with the application in which you intend to use those files. For example, dBASE character fields can contain up to 254 characters, whereas Paradox fields can contain up to 255 characters; Numeric dBASE fields can contain up to 20 digits (including the decimal point and sign), whereas Paradox Number fields can contain up to 15 significant digits. It is your responsibility to make sure that the format you are exporting to is compatible with the type and size of the fields you are exporting.

In the Export Records dialog box, do the following to export all fields in all records:

1. Open the File **T**ype list box, as shown in figure 20.3, and choose the file format for the exported records.
2. If you want to write the exported records into a new file, enter a name for the file into the File **N**ame text box.

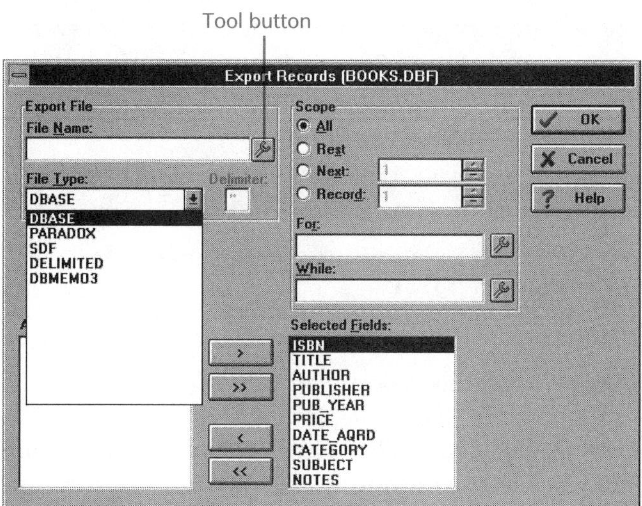

Fig. 20.3
The list of formats in which dBASE can export files.

> **Note**
>
> It is not necessary to type a file name extension. dBASE will automatically add the appropriate extension for the format you choose.

3. If you choose the DELIMITED format and want to change the delimiting character from the default double quotation mark, replace the character in the Delimiter box with a different character.

4. Click the Tool button at the right of the File Name text box to open the Export File dialog box shown in figure 20.4.

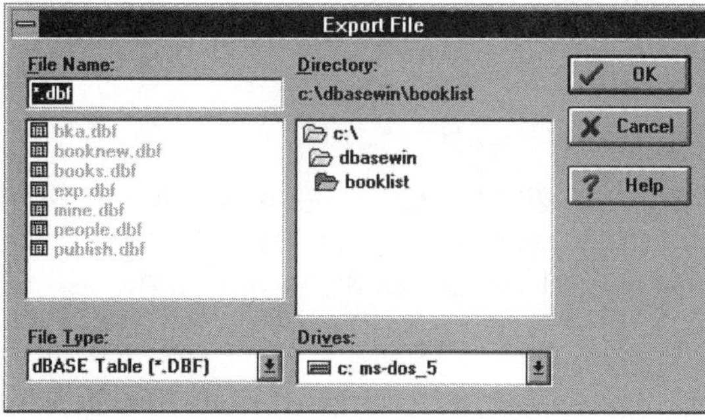

Fig. 20.4
The Export File dialog box.

III

5. Choose the directory in which you want to create the new file and click OK to return to the Export Records dialog box in which the File **N**ame text box now contains the full name of the file into which the exported records will be written.

> **Note**
>
> If you want to write the exported records into an existing file, choose that file in the Export File dialog box.

6. Click OK to export the records.

When you export, dBASE normally creates a destination file and then copies data into it. If you select an existing file, dBASE warns you that data in the existing file will be overwritten and then, if you allow it, copies data over the existing data in that file.

Some of the conditions you may encounter when exporting data are described in the text that follows.

Exporting Indexed Tables

If the table from which you export records is indexed, the exported records are in the indexed order. Otherwise, the exported records are in the natural order of records in the table.

Exporting Tables Containing Memo Fields

If the table being exported contains memo fields and you are exporting in dBASE or Paradox format, a memo file is created with the same name as the destination file but with a .DBT extension in the case of dBASE format, or .MB in the case of Paradox format. If you are exporting in SDF or delimited format, memo fields are not exported.

Exporting Records Selectively

You can select which records to export by clicking one of the option buttons in the top part of the Scope section of the Export Records dialog box. By default, the **A**ll button is selected, so all the records in the selected table are exported.

To export records from a specific record in the table to the last record, follow these steps:

1. Click Cancel to close the Export Records dialog box.
2. Display the table from which you want to export records.

3. Select the first record you want to export.
4. Open the Export Records dialog box using the steps described previously.
5. Select the File **T**ype and File **N**ame for the exported records.
6. Click Re**s**t in the Scope section of the dialog box.
7. Click OK to export the records.

To export a certain number of records, starting at a specific record in the table, use the same steps, with the exception that in step 6, click the Ne**x**t button and enter or choose the number of records in the adjacent text box.

To export a specific record, use the same steps, with the exception that in Step 6, click the Recor**d** button and enter or choose the record number in the adjacent text box.

You also can select records in which a certain field satisfies a specific condition that you specify as an expression. To do this, select the table from which you want to export records and open the Export Records dialog box. Then click the Tool button adjacent to the Fo**r** text box to display the Build Expression dialog box shown in figure 20.5.

◄ "Using the Expression Builder," p. 283

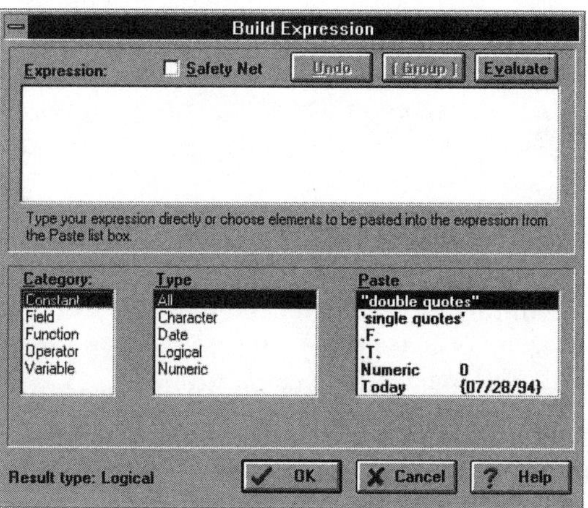

Fig. 20.5
The Build Expression dialog box.

In this dialog box, type the condition that must be satisfied. For example, if you had selected a table that contains a Character field named PUB_YEAR and you want to export only those records in which this field contains 1993, type the condition **PUB_YEAR="1993"**, then click OK to return to the Export Records dialog box that shows the For condition, as shown in figure 20.6.

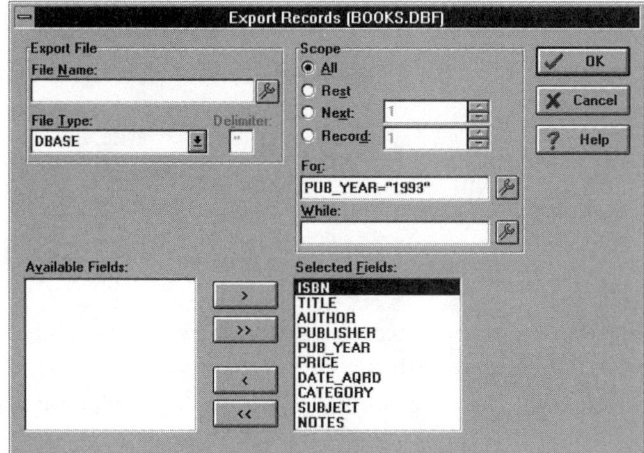

Fig. 20.6 The Export Records dialog box with a For condition.

You also can use a While condition to specify which records are to be exported. Whereas you can use a For expression to export every record in which a certain condition is satisfied, you use a While condition to export a consecutive group of records that satisfy a condition.

Suppose that you open the table that contains a PUB_YEAR field and then enter the While condition in the Export Records dialog box as **PUB_YEAR="1993"**. When you click OK to start exporting, dBASE finds the first record in which the PUB_YEAR field meets the condition and exports that record and all consecutive records in which the condition is true. As soon as dBASE reaches a record in which the condition is not true, it stops exporting records. Only the first consecutive group of records is exported.

Exporting Fields Selectively

When you open the Export Records dialog box, the Selected **F**ields list contains all the fields in the selected table, and these are the fields that will be exported. The A**v**ailable Fields list, which is initially empty, contains fields in the table that are not in the Selected **F**ields list. If the selected table has more than ten fields, only the first ten fields are shown, but you can use the scroll bar to see the remaining fields. If you do not want to export all the fields, you can remove fields from the Selected **F**ields list by using the four buttons in the space between the Selected **F**ields box and the A**v**ailable Fields box. Use these buttons as described in table 20.1.

Table 20.1 Field Control Buttons

Button	Purpose
>	Move the selected field in the A**v**ailable Fields list into the Selected **F**ields list
>>	Move all fields in the A**v**ailable Fields list into the Selected **F**ields list
<	Move the selected field in the Selected **F**ields list into the A**v**ailable Fields list
<<	Move all fields in the Selected **F**ields list into the A**v**ailable Fields list

Note

If you want to export most of the fields from a table, move the fields that you don't want to export from the Selected **F**ields list to the A**v**ailable Fields list by clicking the next-to-bottom field-control button. If you want to export only a few fields, first move all the fields from the Selected **F**ields list to the A**v**ailable Fields list by clicking the bottom button, and then move fields into the Selected **F**ields list by selecting them and clicking the top button.

You can, of course, combine the methods for selecting records with selecting fields to export only certain records and only certain fields in those records.

Exporting Records from Linked Tables

To export records from linked tables, create a query that links those tables and then run the query to display a view of the data in the linked tables. From there, proceed as if the view were a table by opening the Export Records dialog box and choosing which records and fields you want to export and the format in which you want to export them.

◄ "Creating Advanced Queries," p. 425

Note

When you export from a view provided by a query, the Selected **F**ields and A**v**ailable Fields boxes in the Export Records dialog box show table and field names.

Troubleshooting

*Why isn't the **T**able menu showing in my menu bar?*

Table is in the menu bar only when you have an open table or query.

How can I export records from a dBASE table and use them in a word processor document without getting quotation marks around the data from some of the fields?

In the Export Records dialog box, choose no delimiting character. Also, make sure that you use a separation character that does not occur in any of your records (~ or | is often a good choice).

Why does dBASE export records marked for deletion?

Records marked for deletion are normally exported. You can, however, exclude these records by entering **.NOT. DELETED( )** in the For scope box in the Export Records dialog box. Alternatively, you can open the Desktop Properties dialog box and, in the Table tab, uncheck the Dele**t**ed option.

Using Exported Data

If you plan to import data from a dBASE table in other applications, it is usually worth taking the time to do some careful planning before you export the data. The following example illustrates how you can save yourself considerable time and effort.

Importing Data into a Word Processor

If you export data in delimited format, you can easily import it into word processor documents.

When you import data into a word processor, you normally want to arrange the data in columns, with one column for each data field. Rather than just using tabs to set up columns, it is usually better to use the word processor's capability to arrange data in a table so that field data can wrap in the columns.

Some points to consider are as follows:

- Export only those fields you really need in the final document. It is much easier to select fields to be exported than to delete fields after they have been exported.
- Be careful to choose field-separation and field-delimiting characters that are not used within the data.

- If you need many fields, take advantage of leading word processors' capabilities to mix portrait and landscape pages within a document. By printing tables in landscape orientation, you can maximize the number of fields that can be printed without having very deep rows.

Importing Data into a Spreadsheet

You can use your dBASE data in a spreadsheet application. If you plan to do this, you should first examine your spreadsheet application's capabilities to ascertain what type of data it can import. As table 20.2 shows, popular spreadsheet applications can readily import data from dBASE tables.

Table 20.2 Import File Formats for Spreadsheet Applications

Application	Import File Formats
1-2-3 for Windows	Delimited
Quattro Pro	dBASE IV, Paradox, delimited

Importing Data into a Table

You can import data into a dBASE or Paradox table from any of the following:

- Another dBASE or Paradox table
- A text file in delimited format
- A text file in SDF format
- A Quattro Pro spreadsheet file
- A Lotus 1-2-3 spreadsheet file

Note

You can import data from other applications indirectly. For example, to use data from a Microsoft Excel worksheet, save that data in dBASE, delimited, Lotus 1-2-3, or Quattro Pro format and then import the data into dBASE.

Importing Data from a dBASE or Paradox Table

When you import data, the file containing the records to be imported is known as the *source*, and the table into which the records are imported is known as the *target*. You can append data from a dBASE or Paradox table to records already in a dBASE of Paradox table. Records are appended in the order they exist in the source file. All open indexes in the target table are updated as fields are appended.

The name and type of each source field must correspond to the name and type of a field in the target table, although the fields may be in a different order in the two tables. Any records in the source table that do not correspond with those in the target table are ignored.

Note

Date data is an exception to the statement in the preceding paragraph in the case of dBASE tables. Fields of Date type in the source table can be imported into fields of Character type in the target table. Also, Date data in Character fields in the source table can be imported into Date fields in the target table.

When the source table is in dBASE format, fields marked for deletion are appended to the target table unless Deleted is selected in the Tables page of the Desktop Properties dialog box.

To append all records from a source table into a target table, follow these steps:

1. Open the target table.
2. Open the **T**able menu and choose **T**able Utilities to display a submenu.
3. In the submenu, choose **A**ppend Records from File to display the Append Records from File dialog box shown in figure 20.7.
4. Either enter the file name of the source table into the File **N**ame text box, or click the Tool button adjacent to the File **N**ame text box to open the Import File dialog box. Then choose the file name of the source table, and click OK to return to the Append Records from File dialog box.

Fig. 20.7 The Append Records from File dialog box.

5. Open the File **T**ype list box, shown in figure 20.8, and click the type of file from which records are to be appended.

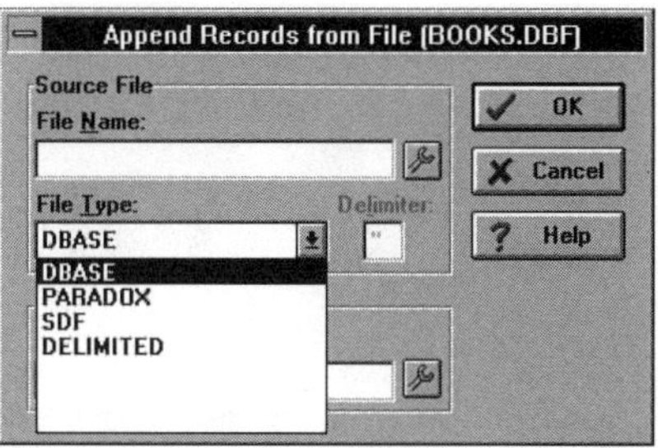

Fig. 20.8
The File Type list box, showing the types of records that can be imported.

6. Click OK to import the records.

> **Note**
>
> If you want to append only some records from the source table, before step 6, click the Tool button adjacent to the Fo**r** text box to open the Build Expression dialog box. In this box, write a condition with which to test records before importing records, then click OK to return to the Append Records from File dialog box.

◀ "Using the Expression Builder," p. 283

Appending Records from SDF and Delimited Files

SDF and delimited files contain ASCII data with no indication of field names and types. The field data for each record in these files, therefore, must be in the order of fields in the target table. Also, the ASCII data in each field in the files must be appropriate for the types of fields in the target table.

With these considerations in mind, proceed in the same manner as you do to append data from a table.

Importing Spreadsheet Data

To create a new dBASE table containing data from a Quattro Pro or Lotus 1-2-3 spreadsheet, follow these steps:

1. Open the **F**ile menu and choose **I**mport to display the Import dialog box shown in figure 20.9.

2. Click the Tool button adjacent to the Spreadsheet text box to open the Choose Spreadsheet dialog box shown in figure 20.10.

3. In the Choose Spreadsheet dialog box, choose the directory that contains the spreadsheet file, open the File **T**ype list box and choose the

type of spreadsheet, click the file name from the list in the **F**ile Name list box, and click OK to return to the Import dialog box.

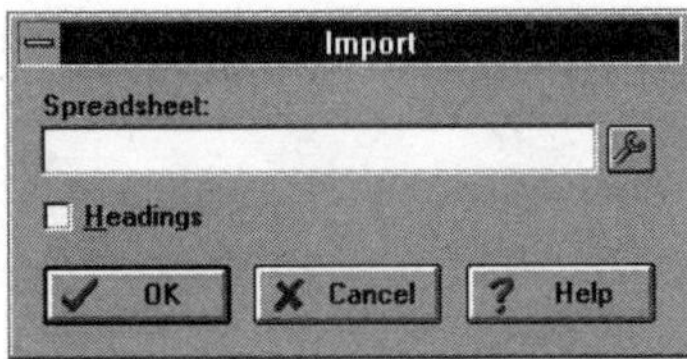

Fig. 20.9
The Import dialog box.

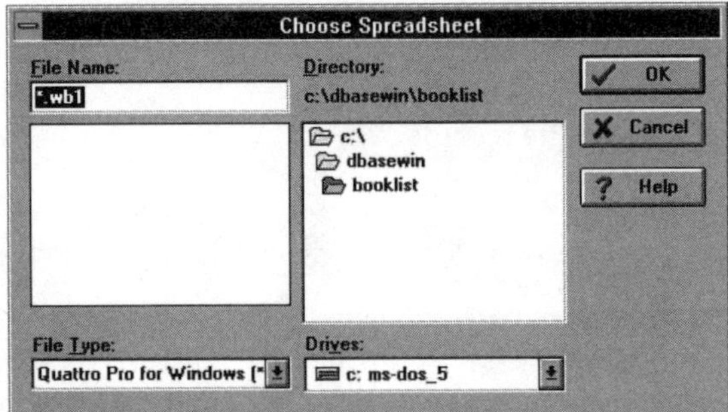

Fig. 20.10
The Choose Spreadsheet dialog box.

4. Click the **H**eadings check box if you want to use the data in the first row of the spreadsheet as field names in the new table.

5. Click OK to create a dBASE table using data from the spreadsheet.

Importing Data from a Word Processor

You can import data from a word processor by saving that text as an unformatted text file and then appending it as a delimited file into a dBASE table. The details depend on the word processor you are using and the type of data with which you are starting.

Suppose, for example, that you have a table in a Word for Windows document and you want to append the data in this table to a dBASE table. This is what you do:

1. Select the table in the Word for Windows document.

2. Copy the table into the Clipboard and then paste it into a new document.

3. With the new document open, open the T**a**ble menu and choose Con**v**ert Table to Text to display the Convert Table to Text dialog box.

4. In the Separate Text With section of the dialog box, click the Co**m**mas option button, then click OK to display the table as text.

5. Open the **F**ile menu and choose Save **A**s.

6. Open the Save File as **T**ype list box and choose Text Only with Line Breaks.

7. Name the file and click OK to save it.

8. In dBASE, open the table to which you want to append data and then display the **A**ppend Records from File dialog box.

9. Enter the name of the file that contains your data into the File **N**ame text box.

10. Open the File **T**ype list box and choose DELIMITED.

11. Click OK to append the data to your table.

You can use similar methods to append data from other word processors.

Working with Binary Data

In addition to text and numbers, you can store binary data representing graphics and sound in dBASE fields. For example, the table that contains a list of books could have a field containing an illustration of book jackets. A table containing information about birds could have a field containing the sound of each bird's cry.

dBASE supports .BMP and .PCX graphics file formats and the .WAV sound format. The actual binary data is stored in the .DBT file associated with the table, the same file that contains the text in memo fields. The actual field in the table has a width of 10 characters and is used to store a pointer to the binary data in the .DBT file.

Adding a Binary Field to a Table

You add a binary field to a table in the same way that you add any other field:

1. With the list of tables displayed in the Navigator window, double-right-click the name of the table to which you want to add a field to display that table's structure.

2. Select the field before which you want to insert the new field.

3. Open the **S**tructure menu and choose **I**nsert Field to display an unnamed field in the structure.

4. Type a name for the new field and press Enter to move to the Type column in the structure.

5. Open the drop-down list of types and choose Binary.

6. Save the new structure.

After you've added the binary field to the structure, click the View Table Data button in the SpeedBar to view the table data. The empty binary fields are shown by eight small ovals, as shown in figure 20.11.

Fig. 20.11
A dBASE table with empty binary fields.

Adding an Image to a Binary Field

To add a graphics image to a binary field, open the table and double-click the binary field in the appropriate record to display the Empty Binary Field dialog box shown in figure 20.12. Alternatively, select the field and press F9.

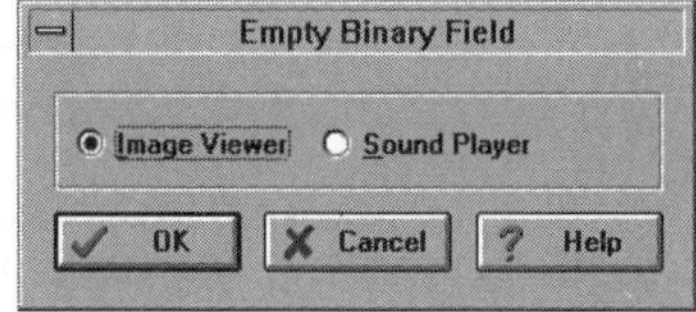

Fig. 20.12
The Empty Binary Field dialog box.

By default, **I**mage Viewer is selected. Click OK to display the empty Image Viewer dialog box shown in figure 20.13.

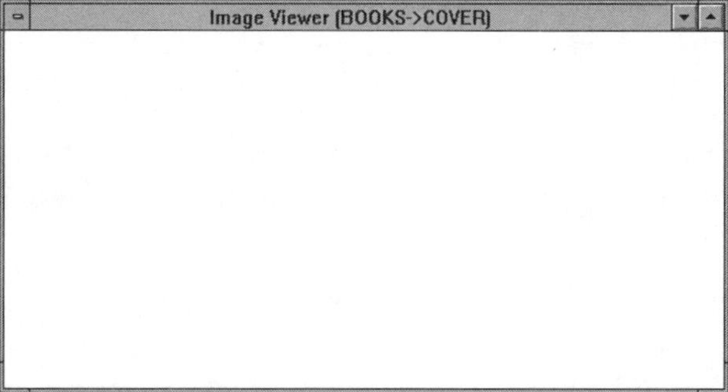

Fig. 20.13
The empty Image Viewer dialog box.

Then follow these steps:

1. Open the **F**ile menu and choose **I**nsert from File to display the Choose Image dialog box.

2. In the drop-down File **T**ype list box, choose either Bitmap TM (*.BMP) or PC Paintbrush TM (*.PCX).

3. In the **D**irectory section of the dialog box, select the directory and subdirectory that contains the graphics file.

4. Click the name of the file and then click OK to display the graphics image in the Image Viewer dialog box.

5. Double-click the menu control box in the Image Viewer dialog box to close that dialog box.

After you have added a graphics image to a field, the presence of the image is indicated in the table by a small colored rectangle, as shown in figure 20.14.

Fig. 20.14
A table with a graphics image stored in a binary field.

When the contents of fields are displayed in a form, an empty binary field is shown by four ovals. When a binary field contains a graphic, this is indicated by a colored rectangle. You can insert a graphic into a field from a form in the same way as when you are working directly with a table.

You can display the image in a graphics field by double-clicking the field in a table or on a form, or by selecting the field and pressing F9.

Adding a Sound to a Binary Field

To add a sound file to an empty binary field, double-click the field or select the field and press F9 to display the Empty Binary Field dialog box. Select **S**ound Player and click OK to display the File Open dialog box. In this dialog box, select the sound (.WAV) file you want to insert; then click OK.

To play the sound in a binary field, you must have a sound board in your computer. When you double-click a field that contains a sound, the Sound Player dialog box appears. Click the Play button to hear the sound.

Troubleshooting

Why is some data missing when I append data from one table into another?

Missing data is most likely because some field names in your source table don't exactly match the field names in your target table. It can also be because field types in the two tables are not the same. Check field names carefully and, if necessary, change them. If mismatched field types are the problem, change the field type in the source or target table.

Why are only parts of some fields from my source table appended into the target table?

This happens in character fields when the target table field is smaller than the source table field. You can solve this problem by opening the target table in design mode and increasing the size of the problem fields.

Why can't I append data from a word processing file into a dBASE table?

Difficulty in appending data from a word processing file occurs probably because you have not created a file in the format that dBASE can correctly read. Make sure that you save the word processing data as an unformatted text file (not in word processor format). To be sure about this, use a text editor such as DOS Edit to look at the file. Also make sure that fields are separated by a character that doesn't occur in the data, and that the same character is set as the separation character in the Append Records from File dialog box.

From Here...

This chapter has covered many aspects of importing data into dBASE tables from files created by other applications, and exporting data from dBASE tables into files that can be read by other applications. For information about how dBASE can directly interact with other applications, see the following chapters:

- Chapter 21, "Using DDE and OLE with dBASE." This chapter shows you how to use DDE and OLE to interact with data in other Windows applications.

- Chapter 22, "Using dBASE for Windows in a Client/Server Environment." Here you will learn how to use dBASE as a front end application to work with SQL databases that exist in other computer platforms.

- Chapter 32, "Automating Other Database Tasks." After you have become skilled in using dBASE interactively, explore this chapter to find out about how you can control integration by programming.

Chapter 21

Using DDE and OLE with dBASE

OLE (Object Linking and Embedding) is an exciting feature that broadens the scope of data that can be stored in databases. With OLE, you can store spreadsheets, word processing documents, drawings, photographs, sounds, scanned images, animations, and any type of file created by an OLE server program. Just think of the possibilities! You could have a database that lists classical compositions and includes a field that plays the first few lines of the piece. You could have a database of all employees with a picture of each employee. A bank could keep a database of its customers that includes scanned images of their signatures.

The concepts of Dynamic Data Exchange (DDE) and OLE were introduced in Chapter 19, "Exploring dBASE Integration Capabilities." In this chapter, you learn the actual mechanics of embedding and linking data. This chapter discusses the following topics:

- Embedding and linking objects in OLE fields
- Editing OLE objects in OLE fields
- Adding OLE fields and independent OLE objects to forms
- Adding independent OLE objects to reports

Using OLE Fields

In Chapter 6, "Creating and Modifying a Table," you learned that an OLE field is used to hold an OLE object, and that you access the field by one of several methods—choosing **V**iew and then Fie**l**d Contents, double-clicking the OLE icon in the field, or pressing F9 when the cursor is on the field. Accessing an OLE field opens the OLE Viewer, as shown in figure 21.1. Notice that the Status bar displays the same information as the Table Records window except that the name of the table is omitted. Instead of displaying the table name, the Status bar displays the type of OLE document (embedded or linked) and the application that created it.

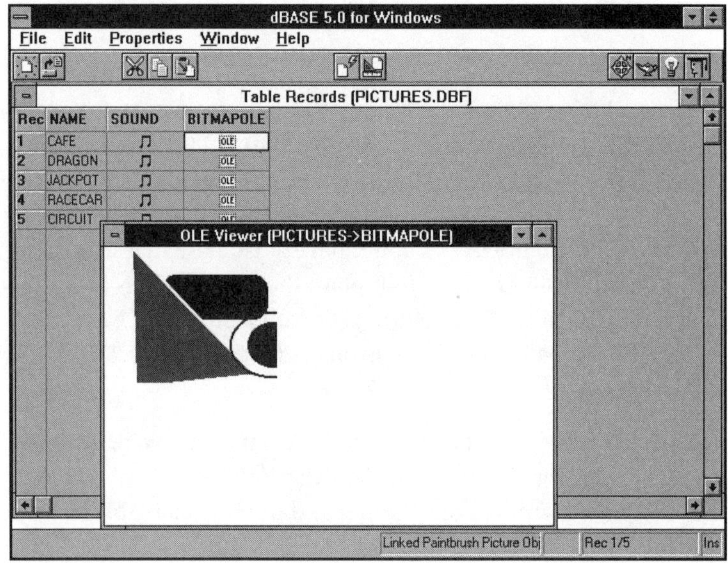

Fig. 21.1
The OLE Viewer, opened by double-clicking the OLE field, is used to embed or link an object.

Tip
If disk storage space is a problem, link files instead of embedding them.

A dBASE table can have one or more OLE fields with unique names. Figure 21.2 shows the OLE field markers in the Browse Layout screen. Notice that one of the markers contains *OLE*, and the rest of the markers are empty. The empty markers denote records that do not have objects in the field.

Note

A file that contains an OLE object is called a *compound document*.

OLE objects can be embedded in a field or linked. Embedded objects are stored in the dBASE file. Linked objects are only referenced in the dBASE file and continue to reside in their original files.

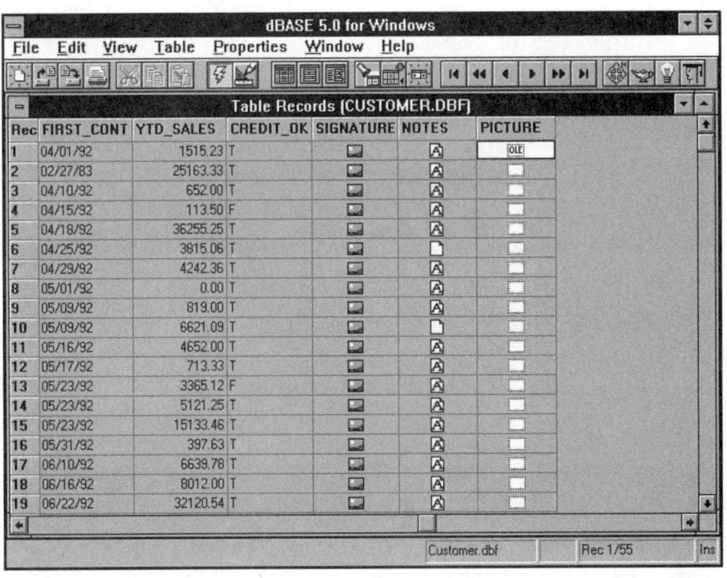

Fig. 21.2
The OLE field marker indicates whether an OLE field contains an object.

Embedding an OLE Document

The steps for embedding an OLE document in a field depend on whether you want to embed an existing document or create a new one. To embed a new OLE document in an OLE field, follow these steps:

1. Open the appropriate table and double-click the OLE field in which you will embed an object.
2. Open the **E**dit menu and choose I**n**sert Object. The Insert New Object dialog box is displayed (see fig. 21.3).
3. Select the application you want to use and choose OK. The application starts.
4. Create the new file in the application.

5. After the file is created in the application, open the **F**ile menu and choose **U**pdate. The contents of the file will be embedded in the dBASE field.

6. Open the **F**ile menu and choose E**x**it. The server application closes, and you return to the dBASE OLE Viewer where the document is displayed.

With this method, no file is saved in the external application.

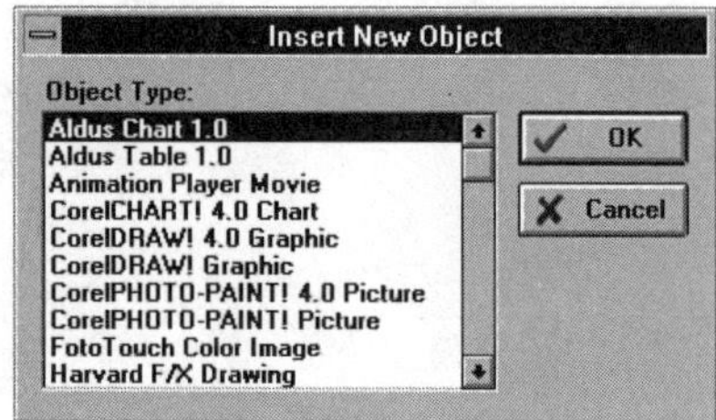

Fig. 21.3
The Insert New Object dialog box displays the applications that can be used as servers to create an object for embedding.

Note

dBASE for Windows can store only Windows sound files (.WAV) and only bitmap image files with the .BMP or .PCX format.

To embed an existing document, follow these steps:

1. Open the appropriate table and double-click the OLE field you want to use.

2. Switch to the Program Manager and open the application you want to use.

Tip
Minimizing dBASE to an icon is an easy way to switch from one application to another. Alternatively, you can switch between applications by pressing Alt+Tab.

3. Open the document that contains the data you want to embed. Figure 21.4 shows a logo created in Paintbrush that can be embedded.

4. Select all or part of the document; then open the **E**dit menu and choose **C**opy.

5. Close the application if you will not be using it again.

6. Switch to dBASE 5.0 for Windows.

7. Open the **E**dit menu and choose **P**aste. The object will be embedded in the field (see fig. 21.5).

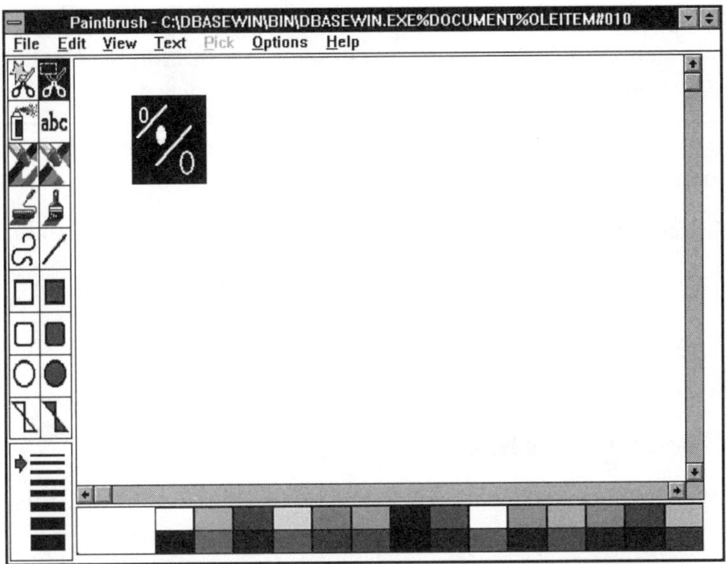

Fig. 21.4
A bitmapped image file opened in Paintbrush that will be embedded in an OLE field.

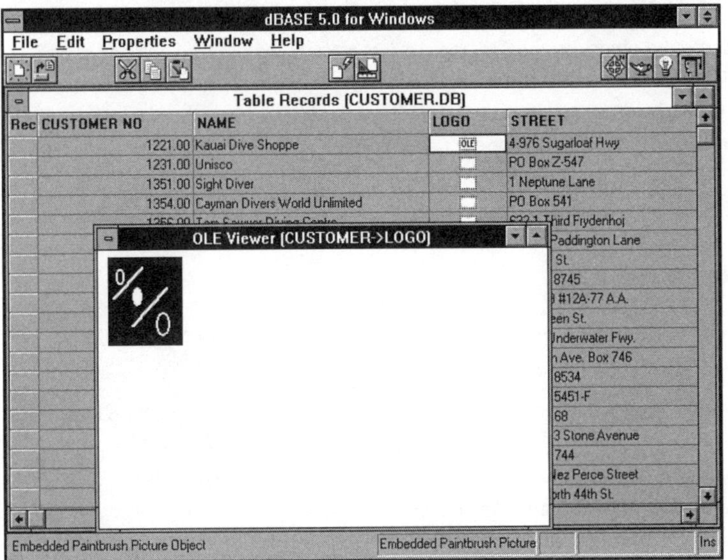

Fig. 21.5
The bitmapped image embedded in the OLE field, as shown in the OLE Viewer window.

Linking an OLE Document

New documents or existing documents in server applications can be linked to dBASE for Windows OLE fields. Follow these steps:

1. Open the appropriate table and double-click the OLE field you want to use.
2. Switch to the Program Manager and start the external application.
3. Create a new document and save it or open an existing document.
4. Select part or all of the document and choose **E**dit, **C**opy.
5. Switch to dBASE 5.0 for Windows.
6. Choose **E**dit, Paste Lin**k**.
7. If the external application will not be used again, return to the window and close it.

Note

Because the object on the Clipboard is not erased when pasted with Paste or Paste Link, the object can be embedded or linked in other fields as long as you do not perform any other operations, such as cut or copy. To paste the object in another field, access the field and choose either **E**dit, **P**aste or **E**dit, Paste Lin**k**.

Troubleshooting

When I select an application from which I want to embed an object, I get the message `File Error. Cannot find LD01.DDL.`

The most likely explanation for this problem is that the application is no longer on your system. It still shows up in the list of servers, though, because it was registered as a server when it was initially installed. When a Windows program is removed from a disk, references to the program, like "fingerprints," still remain in Windows system files. Even though the program you selected from the list has been deleted from the disk, it is still registered as a server and thus shows up in the Insert New Object dialog box.

You might want to invest in a utility program that uninstalls Windows programs and cleans up messy little details like this one. MicroHelp makes a program called UnInstaller 2 that sells for less than $50.

*When I open a file in the server application that I want to embed, there is no **U**pdate command on the **F**ile menu.*

You have used the steps to embed a new OLE object and, after the application is open, opened an existing file. Only the window that was opened first will have the **U**pdate command on the **F**ile menu. Follow the steps to embed an existing document.

*When I try to link a new document to an OLE field, the Paste Lin**k** command is dimmed.*

Return to the external application and save the new file. Then copy the desired portion of the document to the Clipboard again. Do not close the file or the application. When you return to dBASE for Windows, the Paste Lin**k** option should be available. If the option is still not available, you have copied from an application that is not a server application and therefore cannot be linked.

Editing OLE Fields

To edit an embedded or linked object, access the OLE field and double-click the object in the OLE Viewer. The server application that created the object will be opened in a new window, and the object will usually be displayed for editing. Some applications display menu options instead of assuming that you want to edit the object. In this case, choose the option that will edit the file.

Note

Instead of double-clicking the object in the OLE Viewer, you can choose the last option on the **E**dit menu. This option displays the name of the application that will be opened.

If the object is embedded, make the changes and choose **F**ile, **U**pdate. Then choose **F**ile, E**x**it.

If the object is linked, make the changes, save the document, and close the file and the application. The changes will be reflected in the current OLE field in dBASE immediately because both dBASE and the other application were in memory at the same time.

If you revise a linked document in its original program instead of opening the document through the OLE field, the changes that you make may or may not be reflected in the dBASE OLE field that it is linked to. The updating of a link is determined by link settings, which are discussed in the next section.

If you want to delete an embedded or linked object, access the desired OLE field and choose **E**dit, **U**ndo or choose **E**dit, **D**elete. Both commands perform the same function. If you are going to insert a different object in the field, you do not have to delete the current object. Simply insert the new object, and it will replace the old object. (An OLE field can hold only one object at a time.)

Setting Link Options

Link options display information about links and control the way links are updated. In addition, the link options can be used to cancel or change links.

> **Note**
>
> The L**i**nks command, located on the **E**dit menu, is available only if the current OLE field contains a linked object.

To display or change the characteristics of a link, follow these steps:

1. Open the appropriate table and access the OLE field with the linked data.
2. Open the **E**dit menu and choose L**i**nks. The Links dialog box appears (see fig. 21.6).

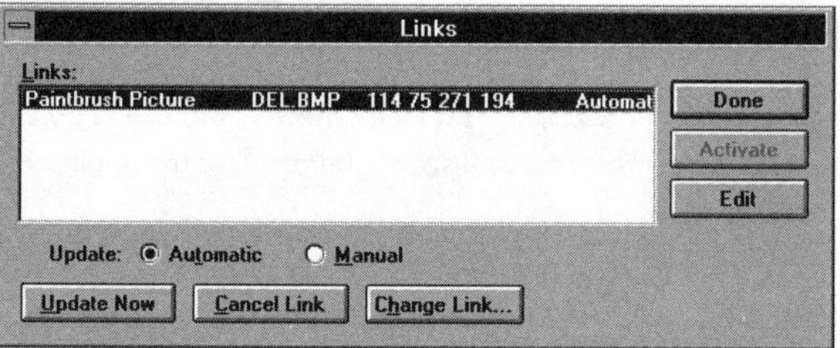

Fig. 21.6
The Links dialog box updates links and changes the characteristics of links.

The Links dialog box shows the link for the current record, including the application name, document type, file name, item identifier (such as a cell range), and update method.

3. Choose the update method you want. The Update methods include Au**t**omatic and **M**anual. If you choose Au**t**omatic, updates are applied to the data automatically only if both dBASE and the external application are in memory. Otherwise, updates must be made with the **U**pdate Now button. The **M**anual option specifies that the **U**pdate Now button must always be used to update changes in the field.

4. If you want to break the link between the OLE field and the object, choose the **C**ancel Link button. The data remains in the field but becomes "static data" that cannot be edited in any way.

5. Choose the C**h**ange Link button to specify a new location for the linked document. You must use this option if you have moved the linked file to a new location. C**h**ange Link also can be used to select a new file for the link, but the new file must be able to support the same item identifier. For example, if the range A1..A10 is used in the original link, the same range will be used in the new file; therefore, the new file cannot be a word processing file because a cell range is not a valid item identifier for a word processing document.

6. If you want to revise the original document, choose the Edit button. Make the changes. Open the **F**ile menu and choose **U**pdate; then open the **F**ile menu and choose E**x**it.

7. When you are finished, click the Done button.

Note

The Activate button in the Links dialog box performs the same operation as double-clicking the object in the OLE Viewer.

Inserting Packaged Objects

A packaged object is an embedded or linked icon that, when double-clicked, opens the application and displays a file or plays a sound or animation file. You embed packaged objects in dBASE fields by dragging the file icon from the dBASE Navigator window or the Windows File Manager window to the OLE Viewer.

To insert a package containing a linked document, you must use the Windows Object Packager. The following steps describe the process:

1. Open the appropriate table and access the OLE field you want to use.

2. Open the **E**dit menu and choose **I**nsert Object. The Insert New Object dialog box is displayed.

3. Choose Package, as shown in figure 21.7, and then choose OK. The Object Packager window is displayed (see fig. 21.8).

4. Switch to the external application and open the document you want to link. Select all or a portion of the document and copy it to the Clipboard.

5. Switch back to the Object Packager window; then open the **E**dit menu and choose Paste **L**ink.

6. Open the **F**ile menu and choose **U**pdate; then open the **F**ile menu and choose E**x**it. The packaged object appears as an icon in the OLE field.

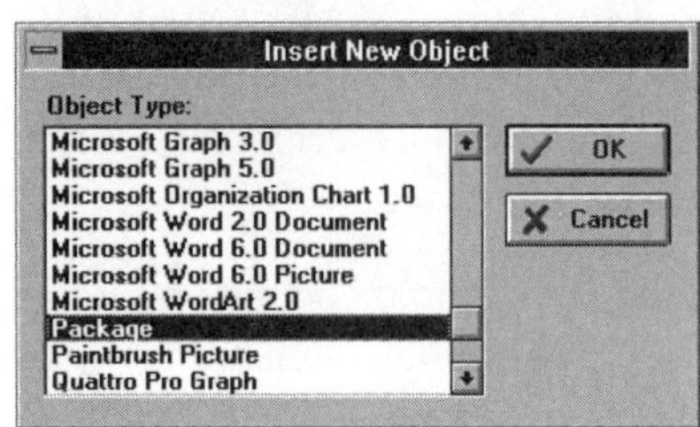

Fig. 21.7
Selecting the Package option in the Insert New Object dialog box opens the Windows Object Packager.

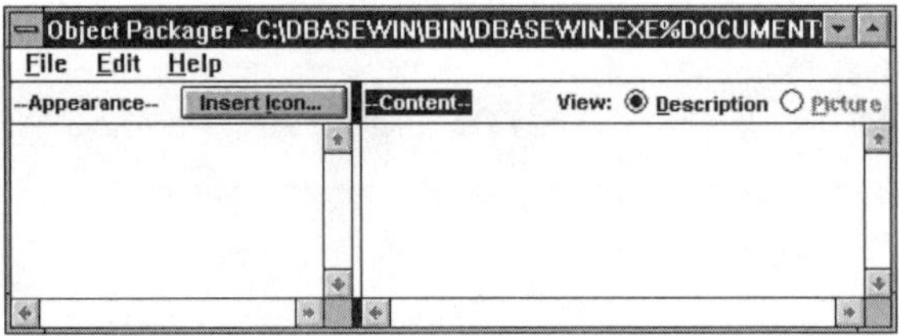

Fig. 21.8
The Object Packager window is divided into two panes: the left pane shows the icon that will be used after an object is packaged, and the right pane shows the description of the file.

Using OLE in Forms

Forms can contain OLE fields, but they cannot contain independent OLE objects—that is, objects stored in a file—like a Quattro Pro spreadsheet. The situation with reports is just the opposite. Reports can contain independent OLE objects, but they cannot contain OLE fields.

Tip
The Object Packager can be used to embed or link objects from non-server applications.

When designing a form that will contain OLE fields, you must place OLE fields in OLE control objects. Do not confuse an "OLE control object" with an "OLE object." An OLE control object is a type of object that can be placed on a form with the Controls palette. Objects include entry fields, combo boxes, spin boxes, and so on. The OLE object is located at the bottom of the palette, so it is usually hidden unless you make the palette window larger (see fig. 21.9).

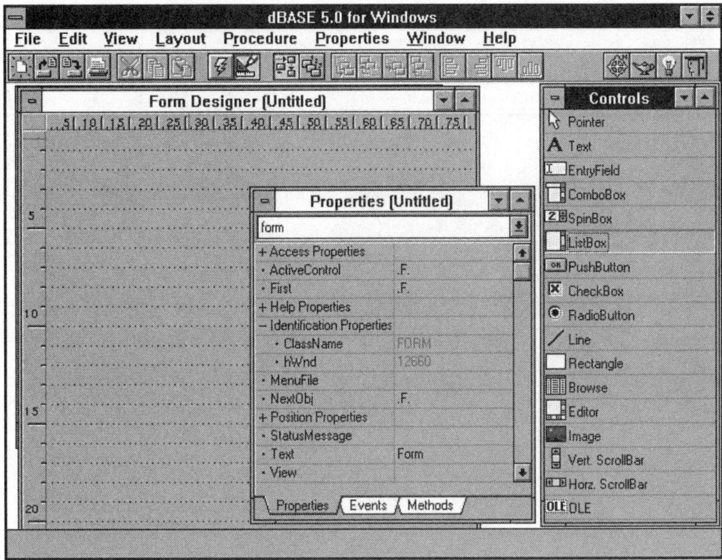

Fig. 21.9
This Controls palette window has been enlarged to show all the control icons.

When you use the Expert to create a form, an OLE field is placed on the form with a field marker. It does not actually show the contents of the OLE field. To place an OLE field on the form that displays the contents of the OLE field and not just the field marker, follow these steps:

1. Click the OLE icon in the Controls palette. Drag to place the field in the desired location.

2. If the object Properties window (as shown in fig. 21.10) is not displayed, right-click the OLE field and choose **O**bject Properties from the SpeedMenu.

3. Click DataLink in the Properties window. Click the Tool button to display a list of fields that are linked to the form. Select the desired OLE field and choose OK.

4. If the field has scroll bars, you know that it is not large enough to display the entire OLE document. If you want to be able to see the entire object in the field, resize the OLE field by dragging a handle on the field border. When resizing the height of the OLE field box, you will notice that the side of the border you are moving jumps to the grid line. It cannot be positioned between the grid lines.

5. If you like, remove the border from the OLE field by changing the Border property (under Visual Properties) to False. (You will probably want to remove the border from OLE fields and other fields if you intend to print the form as a report.)

◀ "Running a Form," p. 209

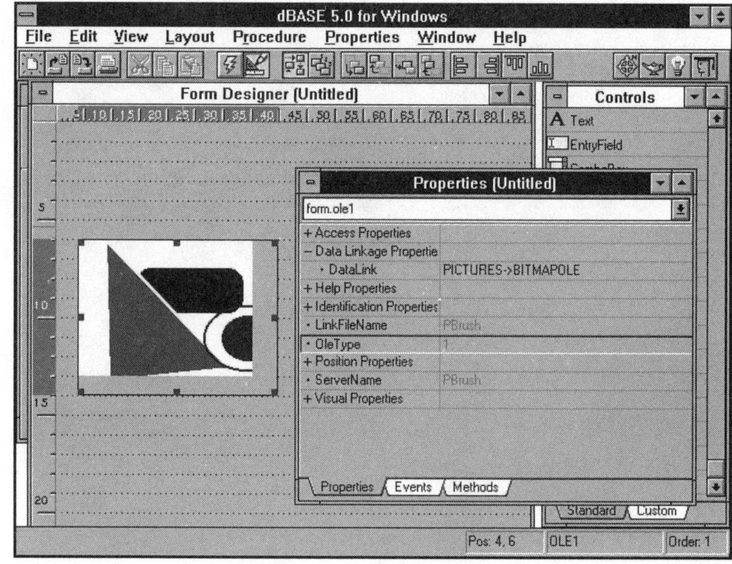

Fig. 21.10
The Properties window assigns characteristics to objects on the form and links the objects to specific fields.

Tip
Format the OLE document in the original application so that it will be the correct size before it is embedded or linked to a dBASE OLE field.

Using OLE in Reports

◄ "Adding Objects to a Form," p. 351

◄ "Understanding the Object Types," p. 356

◄ "Setting Some Common Properties of Objects," p. 372

Crystal Reports do not allow the use of OLE fields in this release of dBASE 5.0 for Windows. No doubt users will lobby for this feature to be added in a later release. In the meantime, you can print OLE fields by printing your forms as reports.

You can insert independent OLE objects in a report by using techniques similar to the embedding and linking techniques discussed earlier in this chapter. To explore these capabilities, consider two examples: you want to include a price sheet on an invoice report, and you want the company logo to be printed in the page footer of the invoice.

The logo will not change, so you simply want to embed it. (Remember that the graphics file must be a .BMP or .PCX file.) Follow these steps:

◄ "Understanding Report Concepts and Terms," p. 389

◄ "Inserting Elements in the Report," p. 390

1. Open the **I**nsert menu and choose Ob**j**ect; or click the OLE icon. The Insert Object dialog box is displayed (see fig. 21.11).

2. Choose Create from **F**ile.

3. Choose **B**rowse to display the file Browse dialog box. Select the logo file and choose OK.

4. Choose OK in the Insert Object dialog box.

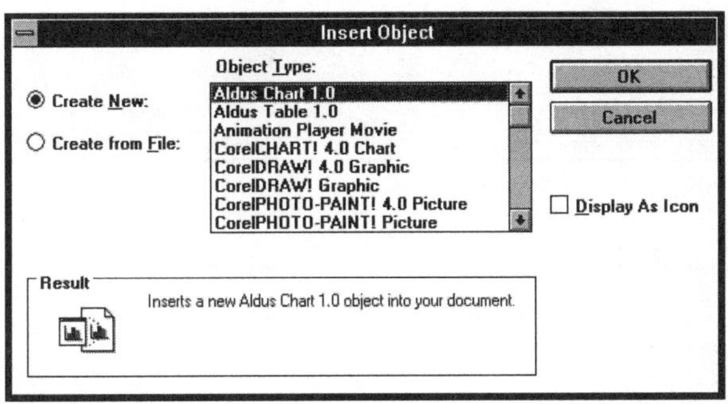

Fig. 21.11
The Insert Object dialog box in Crystal Reports is very similar to the Insert dialog box that you see when using OLE fields in tables.

5. Move the pointer to the desired location in the page footer area and click the primary mouse button. The graphic is embedded.
6. Drag a corner handle to resize the graphic proportionally.

Notice that the name of the application which created the graphic is displayed in the Status bar when the object is selected. Because the object is embedded, double-clicking the object will open the application that created the file and allow you to edit it.

To link the price list to the report, follow the basic steps described earlier and choose **Link** in the Insert Object dialog box. Figure 21.12 shows a price list created in Word for Windows. Figure 21.13 shows that price list linked to a Crystal Report.

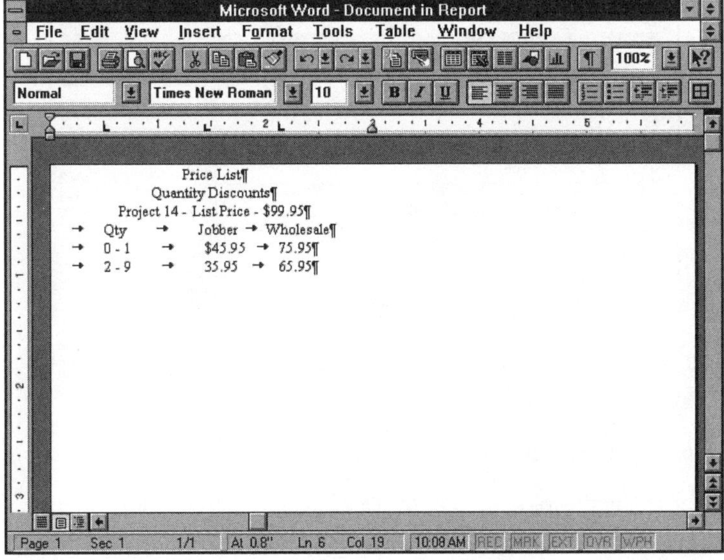

Fig. 21.12
A price list created in Word for Windows that will be linked to a Crystal Report.

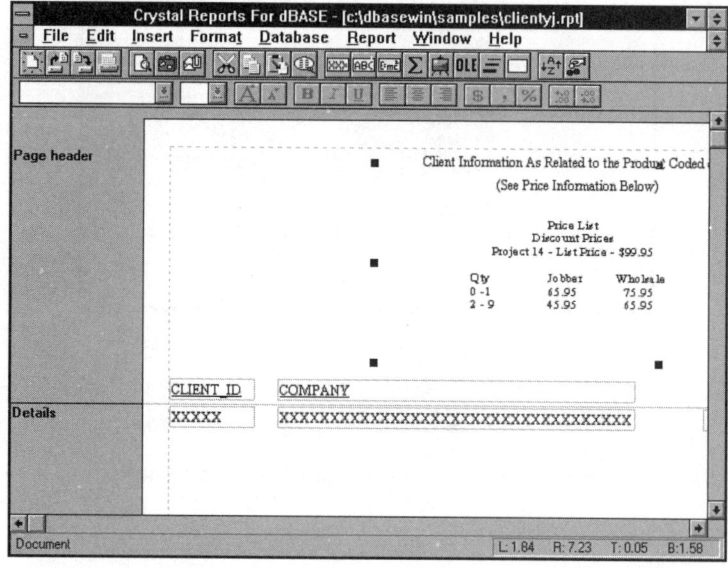

Fig. 21.13
The Word for Windows price list linked to a Crystal Report displays handles when the object is selected.

Remember that link options determine whether a linked object is automatically updated or not. To set link options for an object, select the object and choose **E**dit, L**i**nks. The dialog box displayed in figure 21.14 shows the link options. This dialog box is similar to the one you saw when setting link options for OLE fields.

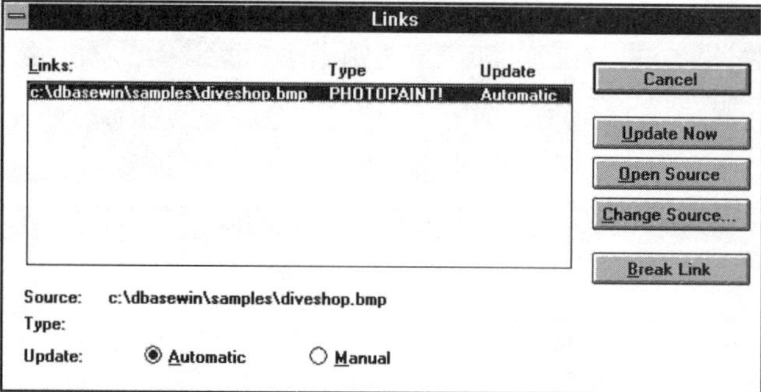

Fig. 21.14
The Links dialog box shows that the default setting for updating links is **A**utomatic.

Both of the previous examples worked with existing files, but you also can embed new files. Follow these steps:

1. Open the **I**nsert menu and choose Ob**j**ect; or click the OLE icon.

2. Choose the desired application to create the new file and then choose OK.

3. Click the pointer on the form where you want the object embedded.

4. Create the new file, open the **F**ile menu, and choose **U**pdate. Then open the **F**ile menu and choose E**x**it.

Using dBASE as a Server

dBASE for Windows functions as a server at the DDE level only. You may recall from Chapter 19, "Exploring dBASE Integration Capabilities," that DDE was the original protocol, but it has since been enhanced with OLE. Most Windows products that are servers are servers at the OLE level. These are the products that are registered by the program REGEDIT.EXE when they are installed. They also are displayed in the Insert New Object dialog box when you embed an object. What this means to you is that for dBASE to function as a server on the DDE level, you must write your own program in order for you to interact with the client application.

◄ "Identifying Servers," p. 464

Note

Remember that the Object Packager can be used to import data from non-OLE server applications, so you could use Object Packager to import a dBASE form, for example, into Word for Windows.

From Here...

Using embedded objects in fields, forms, and reports can enhance the quality of data considerably. Because designing a dBASE form with OLE objects is such a versatile feature, you may want to expand what you know about forms by referring to the following chapter:

- Chapter 31, "Automating Forms," delves into the programming aspect of creating forms. It includes information about creating and manipulating form objects and controls.

Chapter 22

Using dBASE for Windows in a Client/Server Environment

The previous releases of dBASE have supported extensions of the dBASE language for the Structured Query Language (SQL). SQL provides a standard language for accessing databases provided by multiple vendors. In dBASE for Windows, accessing databases on other machines has been made even easier than before. Database applications operate in one of three modes:

- *Single User.* The application and data reside on one machine and are accessed by only one user at a time.
- *Distributed Data.* The data is located on one or more database repositories. Multiple users can access the data by running applications on their machines. All processing is done locally.
- *Client/Server.* The data is located on one or more *servers,* machines that store and process data. Multiple users format queries for records on their machines, the *client,* and send them to the database server. The server processes the query and sends only the requested data back to the client.

Moving to a client/server architecture enables you to use the processing capability of both the local machine and a remote database server. Client/server databases are normally accessed using SQL. dBASE for Windows supports SQL both with explicit calls and through translation of dBASE commands to SQL commands. The SQL Editor routes the SQL commands to the appropriate database server.

All database operations in dBASE for Windows are performed by the Borland Database Engine (BDE). A programmable interface, the Borland Integrated Database Application Programming Interface (IDAPI), is used to translate the commands needed by a specific type of database into commands used by the BDE.

Separate drivers are written to the IDAPI for each server. Only the dBASE and Paradox drivers are shipped with dBASE for Windows. Other drivers must be purchased and installed separately. The SQL Link package provides access to most of the common SQL databases (Interbase, Informix, ORACLE, and Sybase) and is required to access other vendor's SQL databases.

In this chapter, you learn how to do the following:

- Configure the IDAPI
- Access SQL tables
- Issue SQL commands

Choosing an Interface

The BDE and IDAPI provide access to tables from multiple vendors with either dBASE commands or SQL commands. SQL commands are designed to operate in a transaction-oriented environment. As a client, you issue SQL commands to the server. The server maintains a working copy of the data on which any modifications are performed. When all modifications are complete, you have the option of making the changes permanent by *committing* the transaction or discarding all the changes by executing a *rollback*. In addition to using the power of the server to manipulate the data, SQL commands can also perform in a few lines complex operations that may take many lines of dBASE code. For this reason, SQL is used as a standard for accessing many vendors tables in a client/server environment.

Configuring the IDAPI

Before you start using dBASE for Windows to access data files, you need to tell it how to access the files. When you install dBASE for Windows, a default configuration for the IDAPI is installed on your system. The default configuration file is C:\IDAPI\IDAPI.CFG.

The IDAPI enables you to connect to any data source that supports the Open Data Base Connectivity (ODBC) standard. The connection requires the IDAPI driver, the Microsoft ODBC Driver Manager, and the ODBC driver from the database provider. The ODBC drivers must be installed through Windows' Control Panel. You can check which drivers have been installed on your system by selecting the ODBC icon in the Control Panel. The default installation includes the drivers for dBASE and Paradox files. Data tables that are created by dBASE or Paradox are considered *local tables* in dBASE for Windows.

Note

The IDAPI requires version 2 of the ODBC driver.

Once the drivers have been installed for Windows, you may add them to the IDAPI configuration file. The default configuration file used by IDAPI may be changed by modifying WIN.INI. Find the IDAPI section of WIN.INI and change the value of CONFIGFILE01. The configuration file may be any name that is 12 characters or less and has an extension of CFG.

```
IDAPI
     CONFIGFILE01 = C:\IDAPI\IDAPI.CFG
```

Caution

You must exit any applications using IDAPI before modifying the configuration. After you make your modifications, save your changes and restart the application to use your new settings.

Start the IDAPI Configuration Utility by double-clicking the icon in the dBASE for Windows group. The IDAPI Configuration Utility contains two panels: the Driver Name list and the Parameters. Tabs similar to those on file folders provide access to six pages:

IDAPI Configuration Utility

- *Drivers.* Displays the installed drivers for accessing data.
- *Aliases.* Enables you to add a name to use for accessing a data table.
- *System.* Enables you to modify how SQL queries are handled.
- *Date.* Enables you to set the format for the date.
- *Time.* Enables you to set the format for the time (12-or 24-hour, morning and afternoon indicators, and display of seconds or milliseconds).
- *Number.* Determines what separators for thousands and decimals are used in displaying numbers. Also sets the default number of digits to the right of the decimal and whether leading zeros are displayed.

The first three pages determine how dBASE for Windows will handle SQL tables. The last three set the format for display of date, time, and numbers. You may have multiple IDAPI configuration files on your system. Choose **F**ile, **O**pen to open a different file.

◄ "The IDAPI Configuration Utility," p. 463

Setting Up to Use SQL

Tip
All IDAPI configuration files must have an extension of CFG and be less than 12 characters long for the system to find them.

You may need to modify the Drivers page, the Aliases page, and the System page to enable access to your SQL tables. To modify any of the parameters on these pages, select the parameter, enter the new value in the field, and press Enter. When you have made all your changes, you can save the file with the same name or a new name from the **F**ile menu.

Modifying the Drivers Page

The drivers listed on the Drivers page are all the drivers that have been loaded. Two drivers, dBASE and Paradox, are delivered with dBASE for Windows. Other drivers must be provided by the vendor. Figure 22.1 shows the Drivers page for the dBASE driver.

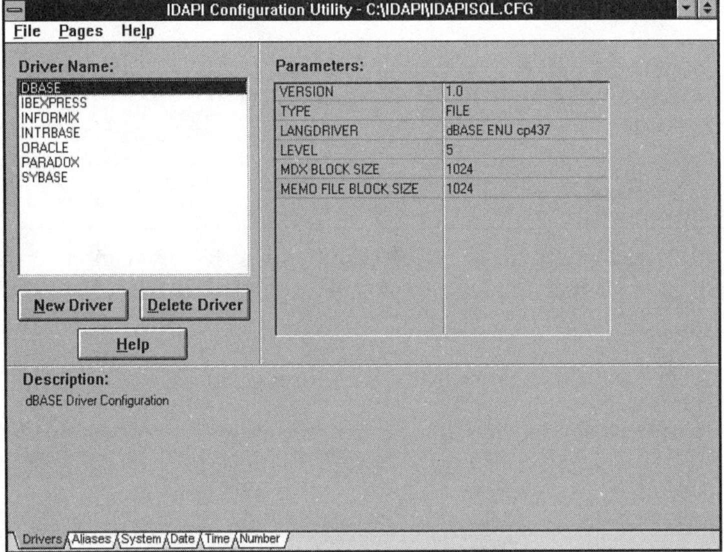

Fig. 22.1
The Drivers page enables you to configure the database drivers to your network.

Tip
If a driver name is not shown for a server you want to access, make sure the SQL Link software for that driver has been loaded on your PC.

Select the driver name from the Driver Name panel. The Parameters panel changes to display the parameters for that driver. Each of the drivers is an object that has specific properties shown in the Parameters panel. Some of the parameters are for internal use only and you should not modify them. The list of all properties is shown in table 22.1. No one driver uses all the properties on this list, but every driver will use some number of them. You will normally only modify a few of these properties. These settings establish the defaults that will be used for each connection made through the driver. Your network and database administrators should have the correct settings for these parameters.

Table 22.1 IDAPI Driver Parameters

Parameter	Driver	Purpose
VERSION	All	Internal label for version of driver. Should not normally be modified.
TYPE	All	Access type, either SERVER or FILE. Should not normally be modified.
DLL	SQL	The name of the Dynamic Link Library used by SQL database drivers. Should not normally be modified.
CONNECT TIMEOUT	SYBASE	The number of seconds to wait for a connection to the server. Defaults to 60.
TIMEOUT	SYBASE	The number of seconds to wait for the server to respond. Defaults to 500.
VENDOR INIT	ORACLE	Initialization sequence for the server. Should not normally be modified.
DRIVER FLAGS	SQL	Internal flags used by the driver for processing. Should not normally be modified.
DATABASE NAME	SQL	Name of the database to open on the server.
SERVER NAME	SQL	Name of the default server to access.
USER NAME	SQL	Default user account to use when logging on to the server.
NET DIR	Paradox	Location of the network control file.
NET PROTOCOL	ORACLE	Protocol being used on the network to the server (SPX/IPX, TCP/IP, Named Pipes).
OPEN MODE	SQL	Access mode for the tables READ ONLY or READ/WRITE.
SCHEMA CACHE SIZE	SQL	Number of tables to cache. The default is 8 and the maximum is 32.
LANGDRIVER	All	The default language used for the data returned. The drivers support multilingual extensions for a number of international languages, in either ASCII or ANSI.

(continues)

Table 22.1 Continued

Parameter	Driver	Purpose
SQLQUERYMODE	SQL	Specifies if queries will be tried locally before being tried on the server.
BLOB EDIT LOGGING	SYBASE	Whether to log all transactions on *BLOBs*, binary large order blocks.
SQLPASSTHRU MODE	SQL	Determines how transactions to a SQL database are handled. Choices are NOT SHARED, SHARED AUTOCOMMIT, SHARED NO AUTOCOMMIT.
LOCK MODE	Informix	Method of locking used.

Several of the properties (NET DIR, NET PROTOCOL, SERVER NAME, DATABASE NAME, USER NAME) determine the method for accessing the network. These are specific for each site and therefore you need to modify them depending on which server driver you are using and how your network is configured. Figure 22.2 shows the ORACLE drivers screen which requires more of the parameters.

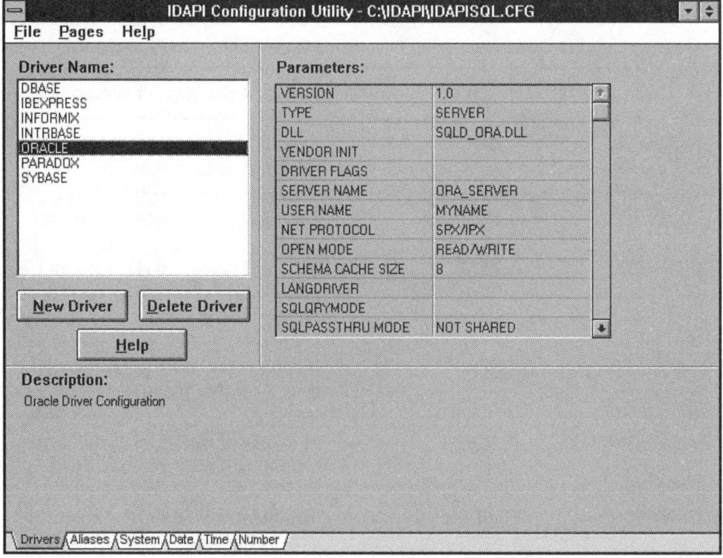

Fig. 22.2
The ORACLE driver enables you to set defaults for connecting to the ORACLE server.

Other properties determine how you access the data in your tables. The Open Mode property determines if you will have the ability to modify data on the server.

If you have SQL data tables on your machine, set the SQLQUERYMODE to LOCAL to have it process the query against your local tables before going to the server. If the requested data is not found in the local tables, the query will be sent to the server for processing. Only then is an error message generated if no data is found. Set the mode to SERVER to have the query processed only by the server. The local tables will not be tried after the server to see if they could satisfy the query.

SQL pass-through commands are those commands issued with the SQLEXEC( ) function. The SQLPASSTHRU MODE determines if the connection through this driver can be used simultaneously by SQL pass-through commands and non-pass-through commands. If you use NOT SHARED, separate connections must be established for each type of command. Using SHARED AUTOCOMMIT enables the commands to use the same connection. Non-pass-through commands issued outside of transaction processing are automatically committed at the end of each statement processing. The final choice, SHARED NO AUTOCOMMIT, allows the non-pass-through commands to be treated the same as the pass-through commands. Both command types share the same connection. No actions are committed until an explicit COMMIT( ) is issued.

Modifying the Aliases Page

After your driver has been established using the Drivers page, you can access the tables on your server. The Aliases page, shown in figure 22.3 for the dBASE driver, enables you to tell the system where to find the tables you will be using and which server to use for accessing them. Aliases may be established for both SQL tables and dBASE/Paradox tables.

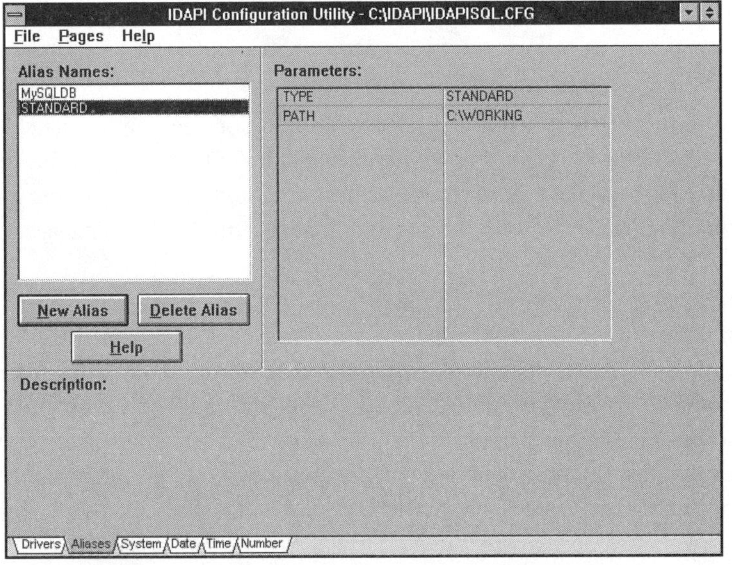

Fig. 22.3
Use the Aliases page to set the path for your tables.

Tip
An alias can be defined for a dBASE or Paradox data table to eliminate the requirement to use a long path to open the file.

To create a new alias, follow these five easy steps:

1. Select the Aliases page and click **N**ew Alias to bring up the Add New Alias dialog box (see fig. 22.4).

2. In the **N**ew Alias Name field, enter the name for the alias.

3. Select the alias type from the scroll list in the Alias **T**ype field. The STANDARD type handles dBASE and Paradox fields. Any other drivers you have loaded will be shown on the list. Choose OK to save the settings.

4. The parameters for the driver type you selected will be shown in the Parameters panel. The TYPE parameter is set from the alias type you selected. As a minimum, you should set the PATH or DATABASE NAME, the SERVER NAME, and the USER NAME to point to your table by typing them into the appropriate fields. The other parameters are similar to the list provided for the driver on the Drivers page and can be adjusted for each connection or left as the defaults.

5. Open the **F**ile menu and choose **S**ave to save the IDAPI configuration file.

Fig. 22.4
You can add an alias from the Add New Alias dialog box.

Once an alias is established in the IDAPI configuration file, the Navigator window in dBASE for Windows has an additional radio button added: Tables From Database. This enables you to choose to have the Navigator show either all the tables in the directory or only those tables that are listed in the database.

Modifying the System Page

The information on the System page, shown in figure 22.5, controls how an application works with the IDAPI when it is first started. To modify any of the parameters, shown in table 22.2, select the parameter and type the new value. The default values are sufficient for most users. Depending on your application and the type of server you are connecting to, you may want to modify the LOCAL SHARE, LANGDRIVER, and SQLQUERYMODE.

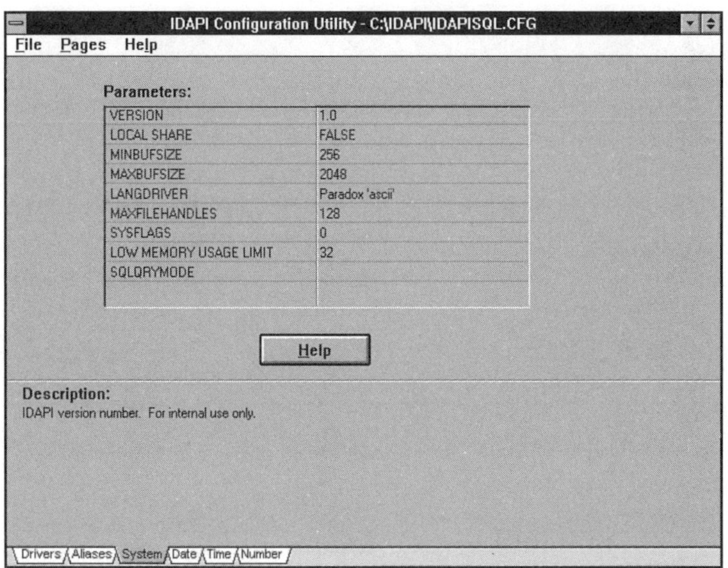

Fig. 22.5
Use the System page to modify the default startup settings.

Table 22.2 IDAPI System Parameters

Parameter	Purpose
VERSION	Internal label for version of driver. Should not normally be modified.
LOCAL SHARE	Determines if a file may be accessed by an IDAPI application and a non-IDAPI application at the same time. Set to TRUE if DOS SHARE is enabled and the applications will both be running at the same time.
MINBUFSIZE	Establishes the minimum buffer size in kilobytes used for caching data for the database. The allowed range is from 32 to 65535 or the maximum RAM available to Windows, whichever is less. The default is 256.
MAXBUFSIZE	Establishes the maximum buffer size in kilobytes used for caching data for the database. The allowed range is from MINBUFSIZE to the maximum RAM available to Windows, in multiples of 128. The default is 2048.
LANGDRIVER	The language used to display data from the database. The default for U.S.A. workstations is ASCII.

(continues)

Table 22.2 Continued

Parameter	Purpose
MAXFILEHANDLES	The maximum number of handles the IDAPI has to access files. The range is from 5 to 256, with a default of 48. Increase the value to improve performance, decrease it to use fewer Windows resources.
SYSFLAGS	Variables used internally by the IDAPI. Do not modify.
LOW MEMORY USAGE LIMIT	Change this value to affect the amount of memory used by IDAPI. The default is 32.
SQLQUERYMODE	The same as the Drivers page. Blank determines that queries should be tried against local tables before server tables. LOCAL specifies that only local tables should be tried. SERVER specifies that only files on the remote server should be accessed.

You must set LOCAL SHARE to TRUE if you are accessing your data tables from both an application that uses the IDAPI interface, like dBASE, and one that does not, like a spreadsheet. In the Windows environment, it is possible to have more than one application active on your machine at the same time. If your applications all access the same data, one application could lock the file, preventing the others from using it, if you do not set LOCAL SHARE to TRUE.

The language driver determines how the special characters are handled in the data. One of the major differences is in the sort order. In the ASCII sequence, *B* immediately follows *A* in an alphabetic sort. In German, however, the *A* is followed by the *Ä*.

Modifying the Date Page

The Date options are used to convert string values to date values (see fig. 22.6). The options determine the separator used, like 9/12/95; the order of the month, day, and year (MODE); whether or not to add 1900 when interpreting a two-digit year; and whether or not to add a leading zero for a one-digit day or month. The defaults are based on the country selected in the Windows Control Panel at the time of installation of the IDAPI. For the U.S., the default separator is /, the default mode is 0 (month, day, year), the default for FourDigitYear is false, YearBiased is TRUE, and both Leading Zeros values are TRUE, which inserts a zero in front of any single-digit month and day entries.

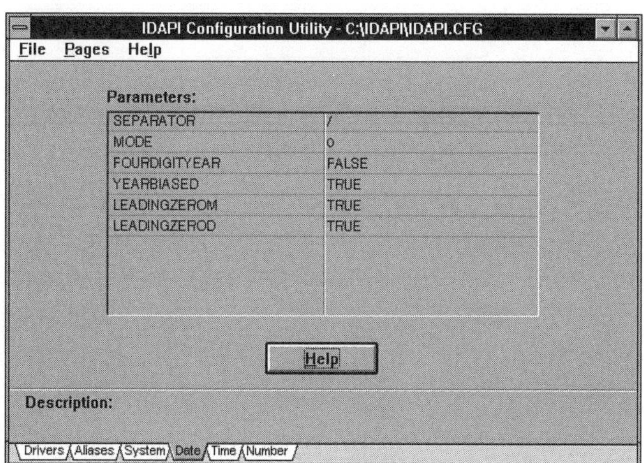

Fig. 22.6
The Date page of the IDAPI Configuration Utility uses the parameters listed to convert string values to date values.

Modifying the Time Page

The Time options are used to convert string values to time values (see fig. 22.7). The options specify whether or not to use a 12-hour clock; what string to use for AM and PM; and whether or not seconds and milliseconds should be included.

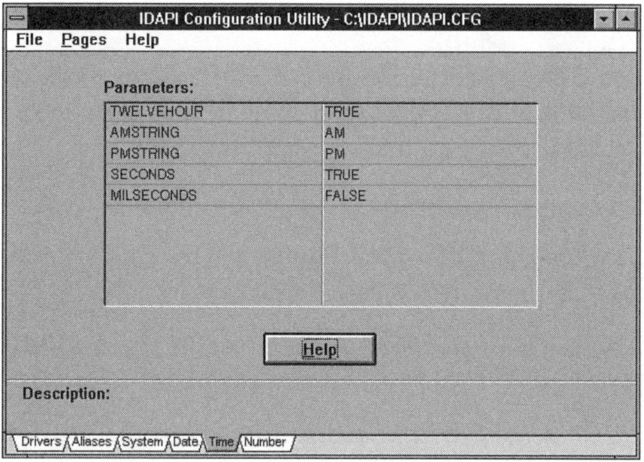

Fig. 22.7
The Time page of the IDAPI Configuration Utility uses the parameters listed to convert string values to time values.

Modifying the Number Page

The options on the Number page, shown in figure 22.8, determine how string values will be converted to number values. Parameters include the decimal separator, the thousand separator, the maximum number of decimal places, and whether or not numbers between 1 and –1 should use leading zeros.

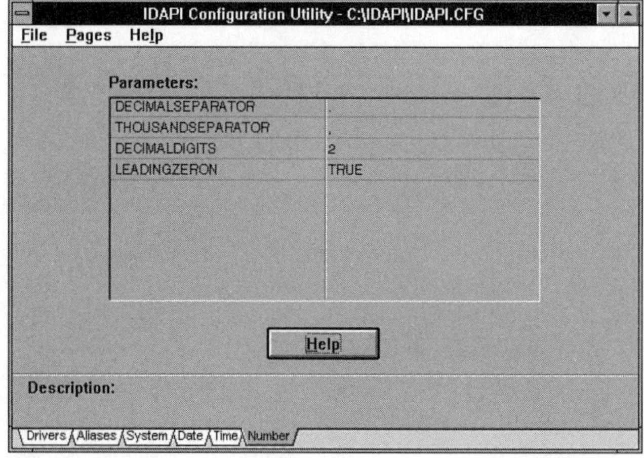

Fig. 22.8
The Number page of the IDAPI Configuration Utility uses the parameters listed to convert string values to number values.

Opening a SQL Table

There are two different methods for accessing a SQL table. Once an alias has been established for a SQL database with the IDAPI Configuration Utility, you may open SQL tables the same as a native dBASE table. You may even combine queries from both dBASE and SQL tables in the same statements.

Using the Navigator

Tip
The Open Database dialog box will be displayed if you click a query or table in the Navigator that requires access to a database that is not open.

When you have defined any aliases in the IDAPI Configuration Utility, an additional radio button, Tables from Database, appears in the Navigator when the All Files or Tables window is displayed.

To access a SQL table using the Navigator, follow these steps:

1. Click the Tables from Database button, and the current database is displayed in the Current **D**atabase field.

2. Click the scroll bar and select an alias from the list of available aliases for databases.

3. Type your username and password in the Open Database dialog box that is displayed and then choose OK.

4. Click any table displayed to open it.

Using the Command Interface

To open a database table using the Command interface, you issue these commands:

```
OPEN DATABASE <database name>
SET DATABASE TO <database name>
```

You then can send SQL commands directly to the table using the SQL command pass-through function SQLEXEC( ). You also can access the table using dBASE commands by opening the table with the dBASE USE command. To specify the name of the database with the table name, place a colon at the beginning and end of the database name. For example:

```
USE :MySQLDB:Customer ORDER CustID
```

> **Caution**
>
> USE causes dBASE to buffer all the records in the SQL table that is opened. For large tables this can be a slow process.

SQL Link requires that each row in a table have a unique identifier in order to allow updates. Normally SQL tables do not have a unique identifier. To allow updating of SQL tables on most database servers (ORACLE and dBASE are exceptions), you use an index providing unique row identification and defined row ordering. Even for those that do not require the index, the performance of the system can be improved through the use of an index.

◄ "Understanding Database Formats," p. 468

> **Troubleshooting**
>
> *Why can't dBASE find my file when I issue the USE command?*
>
> The path in the IDAPI Configuration Utility may be incorrect for your data table. Exit dBASE and check the aliases in the IDAPI Configuration Utility. Ensure all the paths are correctly spelled.

Sending a SQL Statement

SQL statements may be issued from the Command Window or from a procedure. When accessing a SQL table, you can use normal dBASE commands and the IDAPI will automatically convert them to SQL commands to perform the expected function on the table. You may also issue direct SQL statements using the SQLEXEC() function. The SQL commands supported by dBASE for Windows are divided into Data Definition Language (DDL) commands, and Data Management Language (DML) commands.

DDL:

```
CREATE TABLE <table name> ( <column name> <column type>
      [,<column name> <column type> ...]);
CREATE INDEX <index name> ON <table name> (<column name> [ASC/DESC]
      [, <column name> [ASC/DESC]...]);
DROP TABLE <table name>;
DROP INDEX <index name>;
```

DML:

```
SELECT <clause> FROM <clause> [WHERE <clause>][GROUP BY <clause>]
      [HAVING <clause>][ORDER BY <clause>];
UPDATE <table name> SET <column name> = <expression>
      [, <column name> = <expression>...][WHERE <search condition];
INSERT INTO <table name> [(<column name>
      [, <column name>...])] <subselect>/VALUES (value list);
DELETE FROM <table name> [WHERE <condition>];
```

Additional functions provide information on the status of the SQL server.

FUNCTIONS:

```
BEGINTRANS( )
BOOKMARK( )
COMMIT( )
ROLLBACK( )
SQLEXEC(<SQL statement>[, <answer table>])
SQLERROR( )
SQLMESSAGE( )
```

Using the Pass-Through Function SQLEXEC()

You can directly address the SQL server using the pass-through function SQLEXEC(). This is required for performing any SQL commands not directly supported by dBASE for Windows, like GRANT. It also can improve performance in accessing data on a SQL data table, since the server processes the query rather than your local machine. SQLEXEC() commands issued to local data tables must follow the 1989 SQL specification. Commands issued to a remote server must follow the SQL syntax for that server. Refer to the vendor manuals for your server. An example is to grant access privileges on the data tables:

```
?SQLEXEC("GRANT Read, Select ON Customer TO Chris");
```

This command grants read and select privilege to user Chris on a data table, Customer. Note that although the SQLEXEC( ) function can take two arguments, the second one is optional. The second argument provides a storage location for the return message from the SQL server. This would be used in the SELECT command to provide a data table to store the selected rows in:

```
?SQLEXEC("SELECT PartNo, Quantity, Cost FROM Invoices","TEMPINV.DBF");
```

This command requests the PartNo, Quantity, and Cost columns from the Invoices data table and stores the results in the file TEMPINV.DBF in the current directory.

The return value from the SQLEXEC( ) function is the error value, the same values returned by the ERROR( ) function. It is 0 if there was no error. If there was an error, the DBERROR( ) function and the SQLERROR( ) function need to be tested to determine which error occurred.

Checking the Error Return

The error return from SQLEXEC is most often 0 for no error, 239 for an IDAPI error, or 240 for a Server Error. Some additional values are shown in table 22.3.

Table 22.3 SQL Error Messages

Number	Error Message
231	Table already open
232	Database already open
234	Operation not allowed in transaction
236	Operation not allowed on this table
237	Index is not open
239	IDAPI error
240	Server error
241	Database not opened
242	Invalid value for convert size (8-24)
243	Invalid file handle

(continues)

Table 22.3 Continued

Number	Error Message
244	IDAPI not initialized
245	Cannot update a table with itself
246	Invalid catalog
247	Invalid password
248	Access denied
252	Wrong version of IDAPI01.DLL

The DBERROR() and DBMESSAGE() functions will provide additional information on IDAPI errors that occur. The SQLERROR() function and SQLMESSAGE() functions provide information on the errors that occur on the server.

Creating Tables

You may create either local SQL tables or remote SQL tables using the CREATE command:

```
CREATE TABLE <table name> ( <column name> <column type> [,<column
➥name> <column type> ...]);
```

Tip
To change the structure of a SQL table, CREATE a new table with the desired structure, then copy all the records with INSERT...SELECT and DROP the old table.

The structure of SQL tables cannot be modified once created. Table 22.4 lists the valid data types for SQL columns.

Table 22.4 Valid Data Types for SQL Columns

Type	Description
AUTOINC	Autoincrement number
BLOB(*n*,*s*)	Binary large order block, *n* is the number of bytes, *s* is the subtype
BOOLEAN	Logical TRUE or FALSE
BYTES(*n*)	Binary, *n* is the number of bytes
CHARACTER(*n*)	Text, *n* is the number of characters
DATE	Date

Type	Description
DECIMAL(*x*,*y*)	Fixed decimal, *x* is the total length, *y* is the number of digits to the right of the decimal point
FLOAT(*x*,*y*)	Floating point decimal, *x* is the total length, *y* is the number of digits to the right of the decimal point
INT	Integer 32-digit accuracy
MONEY	Currency
NUMERIC(*x*,*y*)	Same as floating point
SMALLINT	Integer, 16-digit accuracy
TIME	Time HH:MM:SS:mmm
TIMESTAMP	Combination of date and time

Retrieving Data

All of the query, form, and report commands for dBASE tables also work with SQL tables. Some SQL tables may have columns with names that are not supported as field names in dBASE tables because of the use of spaces or special characters. To access these columns, you must place colons before and after the column name:

◄ "Importing Data from a dBASE or Paradox Table," p. 479

```
DISPLAY :Part Number:, Qty
```

Since Part Number contains a space, it must be delimited with colons. You can also use the SQL SELECT command to retrieve data from your SQL or local data tables. In the simplest mode, this command can select all the columns (*) and all rows in your SQL table:

```
SELECT * FROM Customer;
```

As your data tables grow, you will probably not want all the records. The main advantage of client/server is to allow the database server to perform the operations to reduce the number of data rows that you look at. By using clauses in your SELECT statement, you can reduce the number of rows that are selected and change the order in the resulting data table.

Tip
BROWSE, LIST, and DISPLAY will not show record numbers for SQL data tables, since the rows are not numbered.

SQL Functions Used in SELECT

Several functions are also supported in dBASE for Windows that can be used in the SELECT command. These commands are shown in table 22.5.

The column name on which the function is to act is placed within the parentheses, as in COUNT(LastName), which counts the LastName column. You can use the column number in the select list, as in SUM(2), which sums the values in the second column in the selection list for the selected rows from the table.

Table 22.5 SQL SELECT Functions

Function	Description
COUNT( )	Counts the number of selected rows.
SUM( )	Sums the values in a numeric column.
MIN( )	Determines the minimum value in the column. The column can be a character, date, or numeric column.
MAX( )	Determines the maximum value in the column. The column can be a character, date, or numeric column.
AVG( )	Determines the average value in a numeric column.

The functions can be very useful in creating complex queries for SQL. For example:

```
SELECT :Invoice Num:,SUM(Quantity*Price)
     FROM Invoices
     WHERE SUM(Quantity*Price)>100
     GROUP BY :Invoice Num:;
```

This query would select the Invoice Number and the total of the items on the invoice where the total is greater than $100.

Adding Data

The SQL INSERT command performs the same function as the dBASE APPEND command. Either can be used with SQL data tables to add records to the table. Here's an example:

```
INSERT INTO <table name> [(<column name> [, <column name>...])]
➥<subselect>/VALUES (value list);
```

Updating Data

The dBASE REPLACE command and the SQL UPDATE command provide the capability to modify the records that are in your SQL data table. To make sure you are changing the correct record with an UPDATE, dBASE for Windows provides the BOOKMARK( ) function. BOOKMARK( ) enables you to set a pointer at a specific record in the data table. Consider this example:

```
USE Customer ORDER CustID
SEEK "A1234"
BookMk1 = BOOKMARK( )
SKIP 10
GO BookMk1
```

The BOOKMARK( ) provides a special data type of bookmark. When used with SQL data tables, the bookmark data type can be used with GO, GOTO, RECORD, LOCK( ), and RLOCK( ). The RECNO( ) function returns a bookmark when used with a SQL data table.

Using the BEGINTRANS( ) function, you can block your operations into transactions, but there are some restrictions. A single transaction can't update multiple table types. The BEGINTRANS( ) function starts the transaction and returns a value of TRUE if there were no errors. The COMMIT( ) function executes all the changes made and stores them in the data table. It returns TRUE if all operations were committed without error. If there were errors in the COMMIT( ), you may want to use the ROLLBACK( ) function to undo all the changes.

Troubleshooting

Why can't I update my file?

SQL records are not numbered, so dBASE must have an index active to allow Write access to a table. You must also have been given Write access to the table by the table owner.

Deleting Data

Unlike dBASE, there is no two-stage operation in a SQL data table for a delete transaction. If you issue the DELETE command on a record, or a DROP on a table or index, there is no way to recover the data without going to the last backup of the data table or to a third-party unerase tool.

From Here...

In this chapter, you got a quick overview of the capabilities of the client/server architecture and SQL. You have seen that once a connection is made to a SQL data table, dBASE for Windows treats it as any other table.

- Chapter 20, "Importing and Exporting Data," discusses transferring data between tables.
- Chapter 23, "Exploring the dBASE Programming Language," discusses how to use the dBASE commands.

Part IV

Building dBASE Applications

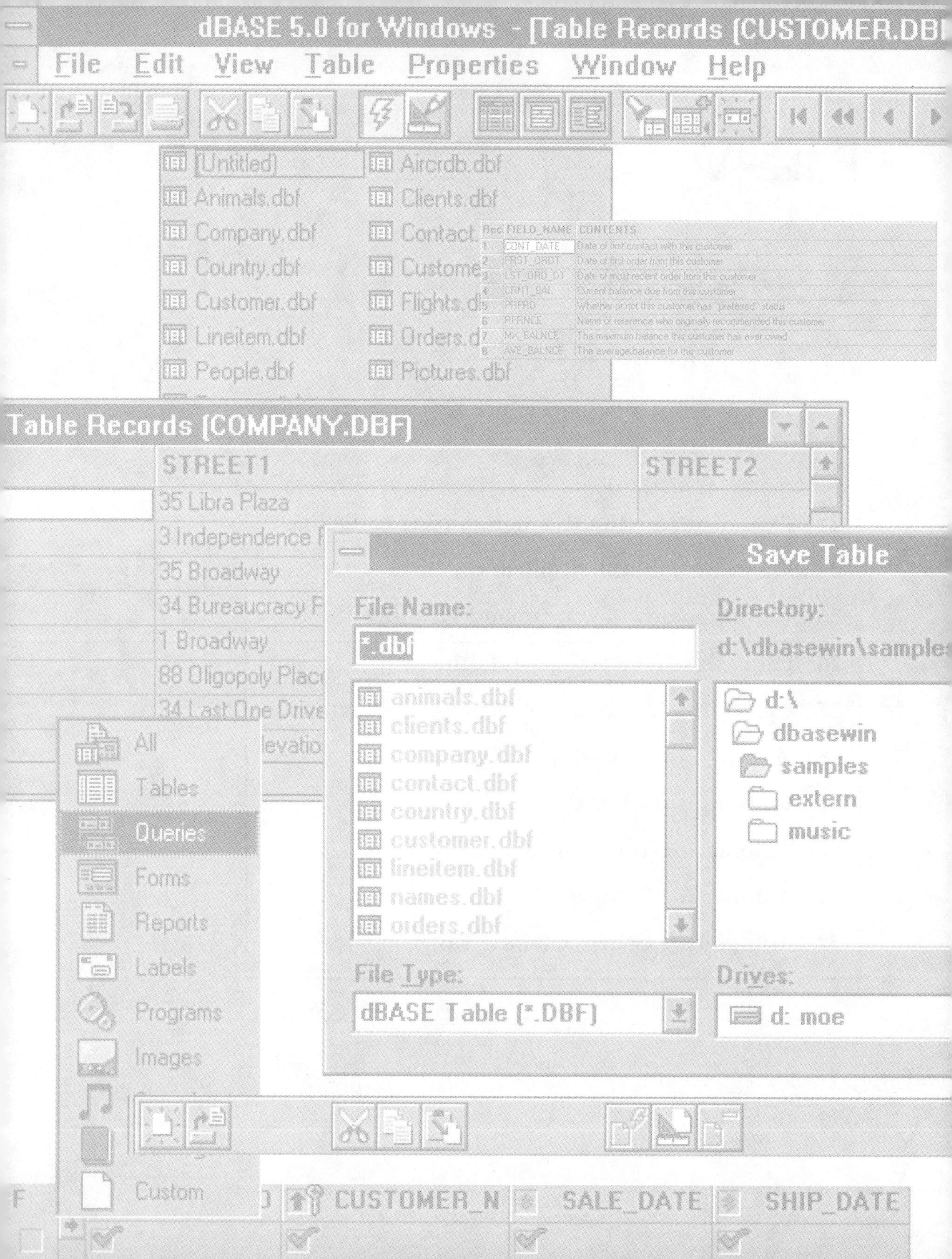

dBASE 5.0 for Windows - [Table Records (CUSTOMER.DBF
File Edit View Table Properties Window Help
(Untitled)
Aircrdb.dbf
Animals.dbf
Clients.dbf
Company.dbf
Country.dbf
Customer.dbf
Lineitem.dbf
People.dbf
Pictures.dbf
Rec FIELD_NAME CONTENTS
1 CONT_DATE Date of first contact with this customer
2 FRST_ORDT Date of first order from this customer
3 LST_ORD_DT Date of most recent order from this customer
4 CRNT_BAL Current balance due from this customer
5 PRFRD Whether or not this customer has "preferred" status
6 RFRNCE Name of reference who originally recommended this customer
7 MX_BALNCE The maximum balance this customer has ever owed
8 AVE_BALNCE The average balance for this customer
Table Records (COMPANY.DBF)
STREET1
STREET2
35 Libra Plaza
35 Broadway
1 Broadway
Save Table
File Name:
*.dbf
Directory:
animals.dbf
clients.dbf
company.dbf
contact.dbf
country.dbf
customer.dbf
lineitem.dbf
names.dbf
orders.dbf
d:\
dbasewin
samples
extern
music
File Type:
dBASE Table (*.DBF)
Drives:
d: moe
All
Tables
Queries
Forms
Reports
Labels
Programs
Images
Custom
CUSTOMER_N
SALE_DATE
SHIP_DATE

Chapter 23

Exploring the dBASE Programming Language

Now that you know how to manage your data with tables, forms, queries, and reports, you are ready to unleash the true power of dBASE: the dBASE programming language. You can use the dBASE programming language to automate repetitive tasks, create custom menus, and develop turn-key database applications. You can even use the dBASE programming language to create stand-alone Windows applications.

dBASE gives you the best of both worlds: the familiarity of structured, linear programming and the power of Windows programming. Existing programs written in dBASE III PLUS and dBASE IV run virtually unchanged in dBASE for Windows. You can continue to write programs, in fact, by using the DOS dBASE programming language and structured event-programming techniques in dBASE for Windows. Your past investment in dBASE is protected.

And when you're ready to venture into the exciting world of Windows programming, you will see that dBASE has a full-featured, event-driven, object-oriented, visual programming language that enables you to exploit the world of Windows. The new object-oriented, event-driven features simplify and speed up application development. The nature of object-based programming requires less programming effort and results in more sophisticated, reusable programs.

This chapter is the first of ten chapters about the dBASE programming anguage. These chapters provide you with an understanding of what the dBASE programming language can do and an introduction to the skills needed to be productive in using dBASE to automate tasks. The dBASE language is discussed from the ground up. That is, a good foundation in the components of the dBASE language is built before you venture into the advanced object-oriented, event-driven programming concepts. Where it's appropriate, cross-references to the new techniques are provided in addition to notes about what is no longer supported.

If you are new to programming, you learn some basic programming concepts while you learn dBASE. If you have programmed in other languages, you learn how to build sophisticated applications with less effort than you experienced in traditional linear programming languages. For experienced dBASE programmers, the following programming chapters provide leverage on your existing knowledge and expand your programming horizons into object-oriented design and event-driven programming.

Note

Before you program in dBASE, you should have a good understanding of using dBASE interactively. The better you understand interactive dBASE for Windows, the better you understand the dBASE programming language and the easier you can create efficient, powerful dBASE applications.

In this chapter, you do the following:

- Identify the programming features of dBASE for Windows
- Explore key components of the dBASE language
- Determine how to run dBASE DOS applications

An Overview of dBASE Programming Features

dBASE has a full-featured programming language, optimized for database management. The dBASE for Windows programming language adds object-oriented and event-driven visual programming capabilities to the power of the dBASE language. You can use dBASE to perform the following tasks:

- Automate a repetitive task
- Mimic the effect of using dBASE interactively
- Manipulate data in ways not possible interactively

- Create custom menus
- Manage data-entry sessions
- Create turn-key database applications

In addition, you can use the dBASE programming language as a stand-alone Windows programming tool. You can write complete Windows applications that run under dBASE without having to learn about the Microsoft Windows Software Development Kit (SDK). In dBASE, you can create all the normal graphical features you have come to expect in a Windows application, such as the ones in this list:

- Dialog boxes
- Buttons
- Windows
- Menu bars
- Pop-up menus
- Drop-down lists
- Animation effects
- Sound effects
- Graphics

Using the tools in this list, you can create an application that enables the user to set a timer as a meeting reminder. You can also write a simple application to manage your time and appointments.

dBASE supports Dynamic Data Exchange (DDE) as a client or as a server, or both simultaneously. This statement means that by programming in dBASE, you can invoke and instruct another application or enable another application to instruct dBASE. dBASE also supports Object Linking and Embedding (OLE) as a client. OLE enables you to link an external document (or other object) to a field in a dBASE table field or embed the document directly into the field. Using the dBASE programming language, you can select the OLE object and invoke the server application, send commands to the client application, or determine whether an OLE field is empty.

Some say that dBASE is difficult to learn. And dBASE diehards wonder how difficult it is to learn the new object-oriented, event-driven development tools. As with any new body of knowledge, it helps to have a guide (this book) and an open mind (a few snacks are OK too) and to use what you learn. Because experience is the best teacher, as you learn new concepts and new commands, try them out in your work environment. The benefit of dBASE and object-oriented design is that you can start slow, on small programs, and add sophisticated features as you have time.

When to Program in dBASE

Before you turn to the dBASE programming language for solutions to your applications needs, look for the solution in the interactive dBASE for Windows product. Many features that require programming in procedural languages and other database products are provided interactively in dBASE for Windows. By using dBASE for Windows interactively, for example, you can provide users with a pop-up list of choices to be entered automatically in a field. No dBASE programming is necessary to provide this feature.

As a general rule, consider programming in dBASE when you encounter these situations:

- You frequently perform the same interactive tasks (such as running a query and then printing a report)
- You want to automate a one-time task that is too time-consuming to do interactively (such as changing an area code for all customers in Edison, New Jersey)
- You want to shield novice users from the power of dBASE (such as creating a menu-driven data-entry form that traps for record deletions)
- You want to develop a custom application (such as creating an inventory tracking system)

Depending on your circumstances and how you want to implement these programs, you can use the familiar procedural, linear programming method or the visual, object-oriented design approach.

What Is Visual Programming?

Traditionally, programs were linear. To automate a task, the programmer wrote lines of code in a programming language that executed line by line. Traditional programs took over the computer, and the programmer therefore had to control everything—the user interface, printing, memory use, and disk access in addition to the data.

In the Windows environment, many of these items (such as printing) are taken care of by Windows. dBASE for Windows extends this assistance to you by managing the user interface and providing *visual* tools to help you automate common database tasks. In a *visual programming* language, you create your application in a graphical interface rather than in a Text Editor.

In a way, when you use any of the design tools in dBASE, you are programming. By placing a ComboBox on a form and interactively setting a few properties, for example, you are programming. The ComboBox is a preprogrammed object that knows how to react when a user arrives on that field and what to do with the data the user enters or selects.

A key benefit to visual programming is that you can instantly see the results of your programming efforts. This capability enables you to build your application piece by piece, one step at a time. While you're working on a new feature, users can benefit from the work you've done to-date.

Where Do You Do dBASE Programming?

Depending on the type of task you want to automate and the programming method you want to use (procedural or object-oriented), you can write dBASE commands in these areas:

- The Command window
- The Program Editor
- The Event Editor

Programming in the Command Window

Tip
Use the Command window to automate tasks on the fly or to test parts of a larger program.

You may have noticed that as you perform actions in dBASE interactively, the Command window displays the corresponding dBASE commands that were sent and the results. Watching the Command window as you work interactively is a great way to learn dBASE commands. When you learn the commands, in fact, you can just type them in the Command window rather than use the menu or SpeedBar. When you choose **F**ile **N**ew **T**able, for example, the CREATE command executes in the Command window and dBASE displays the Table Structure dialog box for an untitled table. Rather than use the dBASE menu, you can enter the command **CREATE** in the Command window. Going one step further, you could follow the command CREATE with a file name for your table.

▶ "Working with the Command Window," p. 549

Note

The dot prompt in dBASE III PLUS and dBASE IV is similar to the input pane of the Command window. The results pane of the Command window is where dBASE DOS programs run (except for programs that open their own windows).

Programming in the Program Editor

When you want to automate a complex task that takes several lines of code, use the dBASE Program Editor or any Text Editor. The advantages of using the dBASE Program Editor is its easy access to the dBASE compiler and debugger.

Tip
You can cut and paste commands from the Command window into the Program Editor to speed your development work.

The programs you write in the Program Editor can be run from the Program Editor, the File Viewer, or the Command window or by choosing the **F**ile **O**pen command and selecting the appropriate File **T**ype. To execute a program from the File Viewer, simply double-click it. To run a program from the Command window, type the dBASE command **DO** followed by the program name (**DO CLIENT_RPT**, for example).

Programming in the Event Editor

Alternatively, you can enter dBASE commands in the Event Editor of a form object; you do event-driven programming in this way. Something happens on the form, and your program runs in response to that event. You can add a button to a form, for example, and attach your program to the OnClick property of that button. Every time the user clicks the button, your program executes.

▶ "Using the dBASE Program Editor," p. 561

Components of the dBASE Programming Language

► "Navigating the Procedure Editor," p. 649

► "Handling Events," p. 650

► "Automating the Sample Form," p. 651

Now that you know the types of programming you can perform with dBASE and where you can do that programming, it helps to have an idea of the scope of the language. As you can imagine, any programming language that provides object-oriented and procedural programming capabilities contains many components. Table 23.1 summarizes the key language components of dBASE.

Table 23.1 dBASE Language Components

dBASE Language Component	Description	Examples
Commands	Reserved words that instruct dBASE to perform a database task. Command words do not have parentheses after the last command word. Some commands take arguments.	IMPORT PRINT CREATE ? SET
Built-in functions	A reserved word (no spaces allowed) followed by parentheses that instruct dBASE to perform an action on something. Functions can return a value and may require arguments.	GETDIRECTORY( ) TIME( ) SUBSTR( ) WINDOW( )
Programming constructs	Reserved words that define an object.	CLASS..ENDCLASS
Control structures CASE	Reserved words that assist you in controlling the flow of your program.	IF...ELSE...ENDIF DO CASE...END FOR...NEXT
Constants	Reserved words which represent a value that does not change (such as the color). dBASE uses constants for property settings.	w/b .t. .f.

(continues)

Table 23.1 Continued

dBASE Language Component	Description	Examples
Operators	Reserved words and symbols that enable you to perform operations.	NEW = > + - * .OR.
System memory variables	Reserved words that temporarily store data about the system.	_PEJECT _PFORM
Object reference variables	Reserved words that enable you to refer to and manipulate an object.	this
Object reference controls	Reserved words that enable you to performan action on an object. Also referred to as event properties.	OnGotFocus

In addition to the built-in programming language elements, dBASE enables you to create your own language components. Using dBASE, you can create the following components:

- User-defined functions (UDFs)
- User-defined procedures
- Statement code blocks
- Expression code blocks
- User-defined objects (new classes)
- User-defined memory variables (local and static)
- User-defined constants
- User-defined methods

► "The Different Types of Program Modules," p. 600

► "Creating Procedures," p. 602

Looking under the Hood

From a technical standpoint (if you've never programmed, it's OK to skip this section and review it later, after you've learned some of the jargon and used these features), dBASE for Windows provides a C-style preprocessor. The preprocessor enables you to instruct the compiler to take certain actions on your code before compiling. You can perform search-and-replace text replacement and conditional compilation or specify compiler options. Using the #DEFINE or #INCLUDE directive, you can define constants and predefine expressions (parameter insertions in identifiers). The preprocessor gives you control over the compilation process, improves overall performance, and increases your productivity.

▶ "Calling Procedures," p. 604

▶ "Creating Codeblocks," p. 610

dBASE also provides a random data generator to help you test your work. The GENERATE command populates any table with random data for testing. GENERATE 10, for example, fills in ten records with random data in all fields (except memos) based on the field type.

The dBASE debugger provides a full set of investigative tools to help you debug your work. You can even launch debugger commands while you view the program execution. Key features include the ones in this list:

- Breakpoints
- Watchpoints
- Data inspector
- Step into and over subroutine execution
- Trace execution

▶ "Setting Breakpoints," p. 592

▶ "Setting Watchpoints," p. 594

▶ "Inspecting Values," p. 595

▶ "Navigating the Debugger," p. 585

▶ "Testing a Program," p. 580

A handy application developer tool, Coverage Analysis, keeps track of which blocks of code execute when you run a program. This tool is essential when you test programs to ensure that all lines of code are tested. Coverage Analysis is a leading-edge programming tool that not many PC development languages provide.

dBASE supports calls to external dynamic link libraries (DLLs) and Windows application program interface (API) calls. The EXTERN command enables you to prototype the external function. After that function is prototyped, you can call it as though it were part of the dBASE language.

◀ "Importing and Exporting Data," p. 467

◀ "Using dBASE for Windows in a Client/Server Environment," p. 503

▶ "Importing and Exporting," p. 670

Last, dBASE provides easy access to other database file types (such as Paradox and SQL tables). Paradox and SQL tables can be opened, created, modified, and queried by using regular dBASE commands. dBASE also enables you to import and export data in a variety of file formats.

Note

To get full access to data stored in SQL databases, you have to purchase and install Borland SQL Link. This product enables you to execute SQL statements directly by using the SQLEXEC( ) function.

Running DOS dBASE Programs

dBASE for Windows provides significant compatibility with dBASE III PLUS and dBASE IV, which preserves your investment in your existing dBASE programs. Of the more than 200 commands in the dBASE IV language, only 36 are unsupported in dBASE for Windows (see table 23.2). Most of the unsupported language elements are no longer needed because of the new Windows interface. For the others (such as the transaction-processing commands), dBASE for Windows provides new language elements to accomplish these tasks better.

Table 23.2 Unsupported DOS dBASE Language

_pecode	RESTORE MACROS
_pscode	ROLLBACK
-pwait	SAVE MACROS
ACCESS( )	SET CLOCK
ASSIST	SET COLOR
BEGIN TRANSACTION..END TRANS	SET DBTRAP
CALL, CALL( )	SET DEBUG
COMPLETED( )	SET ENCRYPTION
DEXPORT	SET HELP
DGEN( )	SET HISTORY
EXPORT	
FIXED	

Table 23.2 Continued

ISMARKED( )	SET HOURS
LIST/DISPLAY HISTORY	SET INSTRUCT
LOAD	SET SCOREBOARD
LOGOUT	SET SQL
PLAY MACRO	
PROTECT	SET TRAP
RELEASE MODULE	
RESET	USER( )
SET PAUSE	
SET STATUS	

In dBASE for Windows, you can run dBASE DOS program source files with a .PRG file extension. You cannot run compiled programs with a .DBO extension or .SCR and .APP files. When you run .PRG files, dBASE compiles the file into a .PRO file.

dBASE DOS programs run by default in the Command Results window by using a fixed-width screen font (as used in DOS). You can use the SET DISPLAY command to change the size of the Command Results window. You can also hide the dBASE application menu and the SpeedBar. Mouse support is automatic. Data format defaults are controlled by the Windows Control Panel. You can use the SET commands in your program, however, to override the Control Panel defaults.

Tip

Use Help to learn more about the unsupported and new language elements. Each Language Reference entry has a "Portability" section that explains the differences between DOS and Windows dBASE versions.

Note

Windows reserves certain keystrokes for common use among all Windows applications you no longer can use in your programs. Pressing Alt+Tab, for example, switches to another Windows application. Your application should not map other behavior to these reserved keypresses. For more information, search for the topic "On Key" in Help.

Any unsupported DOS dBASE commands encountered when a DOS dBASE program runs are ignored. dBASE for Windows just displays a compiler warning message in the Command Results window pane to let you know.

Caution

If your program traps error messages, you may want to update your list of error numbers. Search Help for the topic "Error Messages—Numerical List" for a list of new error numbers.

From Here...

Now that you are familiar with the features of the dBASE for Windows programming language, you are ready to design a dBASE application. To learn how to design a dBASE for Windows application, see the following chapters:

- Chapter 24, "Designing a dBASE Application," builds on what you know about the dBASE programming environment and takes you through the process of designing a custom application.
- Chapter 30, "Automating Table Tasks," shows you how to use dBASE to manage table data in your application.
- Chapter 31, "Automating Forms," describes how to use program forms in your application.
- Chapter 32, "Automating Other Database Tasks," shows you how to use dBASE to manage queries, reports, and data importing and exporting in your application.

Chapter 24

Designing a dBASE Application

Now that you have a basic understanding of what the dBASE programming language can do, you are ready to begin designing your dBASE for Windows application. Time spent up front in planning the components of your dBASE application saves you twice as much time in the long run.

If you haven't developed a database application, you may be a little overwhelmed by the sheer magnitude of the project. On the other hand, if you are an experienced structured programmer, developing an application in the object-oriented environment can seem just as overwhelming.

This chapter reviews the basic steps involved in developing a Windows-based database application. You learn how to incorporate structured programming and object-oriented programming techniques into your application project. Every step, from the design statement to testing the final product, is discussed as it applies to dBASE for Windows.

In this chapter, you learn how to do the following tasks:

- Manage the application-development cycle
- Choose a programming methodology
- Build foundation objects
- Choose a dBASE automation solution for each task to be programmed

Developing a dBASE Application

An *application* is a set of user-interface tools that lead the user through steps necessary to accomplish a task. The *user interface* is the interaction between the user and the application. When you work with dBASE for Windows interactively to create a table, for example, dBASE is the application. However, you can use the dBASE programming language to create your own application that automates the task of creating a table by defining your own user interface. Instead of the user selecting **F**ile **N**ew **T**able and filling out the standard dBASE Table Structure dialog box, you can give the user a button to push and obtain the table structure information by displaying your own custom dialog box.

A dBASE application usually consists of major objects such as tables, queries, forms, and reports which work together as a single, integrated unit to help users effectively and efficiently manage information. These major objects communicate with each other and present themselves to the user as a single unit by virtue of the dBASE programs that you write. With these tools, you can create an environment where users can enter, view, maintain, and report on their data.

Before you start developing your dBASE application, it helps to have a road map to follow. The application-development process generally consists of the following steps:

1. Plan the application.
2. Build the major database objects (tables, forms, queries, and reports).
3. Prototype the task automation.
4. Test the prototype.
5. Debug and make design changes as necessary.
6. Document the task automation.
7. Deliver the application to end users.
8. Gather feedback and redesign as necessary.

◀ "What Is Visual Programming?," p. 529

▶ "Handling Events," p. 650

Remember that the application-development process is dynamic, not static (see fig. 24.1). After you test a prototype, for example, you may have to fix programs that did not perform as expected. After correcting programming errors or implementing design changes, you have to retest the application. In fact, the last step (gather feedback and redesign as necessary) leads you back to step one (plan the application). Luckily, object-oriented programming methods specialize in meeting the needs of dynamic, ever-changing systems.

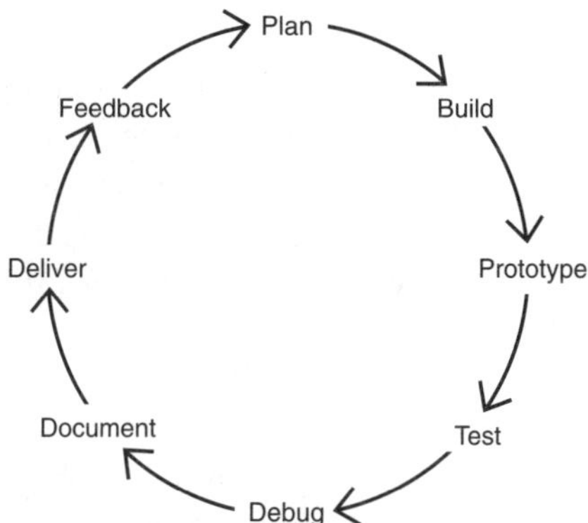

Fig. 24.1
Steps in the dynamic application-development cycle often overlap other steps.

Notice also that the focus of this development process is the task being automated. This is the "divide and conquer" approach to application development. Although your entire project may involve managing information from 25 tables using 10 forms, 30 queries, and countless reports, it is easier if you apply the development steps to the tasks being automated, one task at a time. Again, object-oriented programming helps you accomplish this process.

Planning the Application

The first step in creating a dBASE for Windows application (or any custom application, for that matter) is to turn off your computer. Take out some paper, get a fresh cup of coffee, and block out sufficient time to plan your application. Not enough can be said about how important planning your application is to the success of your project. The time you invest in planning your application saves you time and frustration in the long run.

Tip
Don't skip the planning phase. The more time you spend planning your application, the less time you spend reworking and reprogramming the application.

When you're planning your application, consider the areas in this list:

- Tasks
- People
- Data

Much of the planning stage is spent gathering information. The result of the planning stage is a design statement. The design statement specifies the tasks, people, and data involved. A section usually states the budgeted time and costs along with any necessary approvals. The design statement becomes the road map for the project. Design statements are good in another way too, because they ensure that everyone involved understands the final design specifications, responsibilities, and due dates. It behooves you, therefore, to be as detailed as possible in your design statement.

Tasks

Look to the existing way the task or tasks are being accomplished. Define the tasks you want to automate. Break the task into steps. Look for similarity across tasks and steps. If the Customer data-entry session, for example, needs an automated find customer feature and the Inventory data-entry session needs a find feature too, you may be able to write one program that serves both areas of your application.

People

A major goal of any application-development project is to create user-friendly, easy-to-use automation tools that help users do their work more efficiently. The best way to accomplish this goal is to involve the users in the entire application-development cycle. Begin the planning phase by talking to the people who will use the application. Have the users review the task definition and correct any discrepancies or add any missing items.

Determine the computer literacy and any applicable technical literacy of the users. Novice users may need help screens to assist in their understanding of the application. If the application is technical in nature, identify the user "expert" on whom you can call to guide you in the technical aspects (formulas, technical jargon, task process, and so on).

Work with the users to build the user interface. Menus, dialog boxes, and buttons should be labeled with words that are meaningful to them. If they call the document-retrieval and indexing system the Fileroom program, you should too.

Data

◄ "Exploring Database Concepts," p. 69

◄ "Designing a Database," p. 79

◄ "Understanding Indexes," p. 120

Determine the data your application will manage. Examine the ways in which the data (manual records and computer records) is stored. Gather some samples of the data, forms, and reports being used. Document any calculations being performed. Investigate where the data comes from and how (manually or by way of computer) the data is entered in the existing system. Consider the local and wide-area networking impact on your project.

For the data you will store in dBASE tables, define the table structure. Examine data types and consider adding some of the new data types (binary and OLE). Consider such data-management issues as data integrity, data access, and data security. Define data-validity rules.

Generally, follow the golden rules of database management: Eliminate redundant data storage, divide data into small, manageable tables, and relate tables by using a common field that is indexed (keyed fields).

Building the Database Objects

After you have defined the purpose of the application, you're ready to create the foundation of your database application: the tables, forms, queries, and reports. This process is where your application development begins. Do as much of your work as possible in the interactive side of dBASE. Look for ways to automate tasks with the new graphical user-interface tools. Rather than write a program to extract information, for example, create a query to extract the data and display the results to the user in a pop-up dialog box (modal form).

Caution

Be sure to do your development work in a separate directory from your "live" data. If necessary, copy existing data (tables and queries, for example) into the "safety" directory. Test your interactive work before continuing to program. Back up frequently throughout the development process.

You may find it helpful to explore the sample database objects and programs included with dBASE for Windows. In the SAMPLES subdirectory of dBASE for Windows, BORLAND provides many examples in the \SAMPLES subdirectory). When you look at the sample files, note how graphical elements such as forms are used to interact with the user. Notice also how the database objects interact queries with tables, forms with queries and tables, and tables and queries with reports. Explore the program files and note how programs manipulate the database objects and control their interaction for the user.

In figure 24.2, the Employee form in a typical business application displays table data in an organized format. Graphical tools such as check boxes and drop-down list boxes assist the user in data entry tasks. A custom-designed SpeedBar of buttons automates common tasks such as finding a record.

Figure 24.3 shows that an application's menu bar provides pull-down and cascading menus which guide the user through the application. Custom-defined hot keys and shortcut keys are provided for menu items.

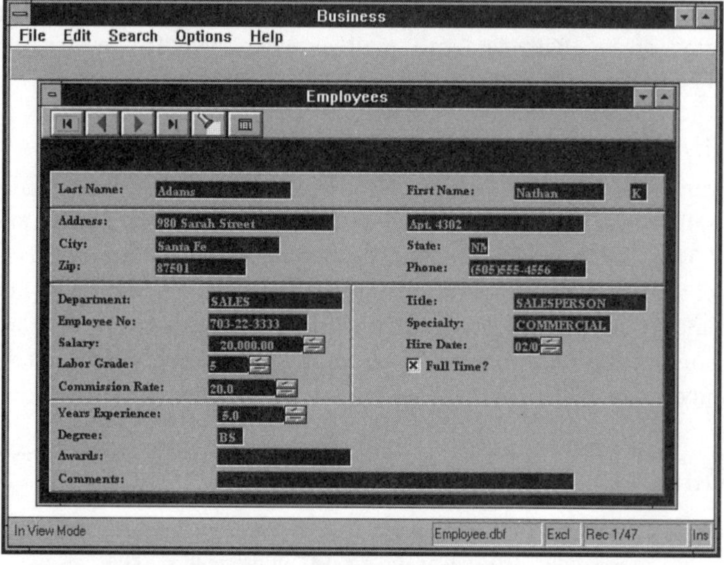

Fig. 24.2
Forms allow you to present table data in a custom format, and automate tasks using graphical user-interface tools.

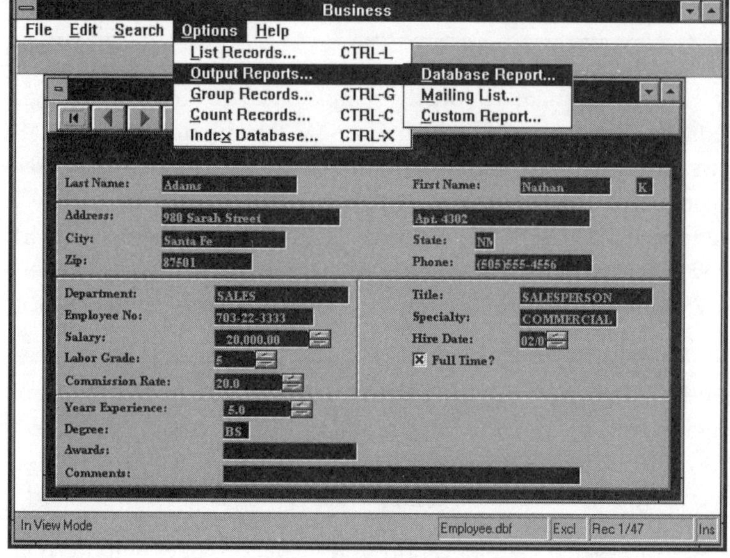

Fig. 24.3
You can create custom menus in dBASE for Windows to guide the user through your custom application.

By pressing the hot key Alt+G, or the shortcut key Ctrl+G, the Business application displays a custom-designed Group Records dialog box (see fig. 24.4).

Fig. 24.4
Your dBASE for Windows application can present custom dialog boxes to gather data from the user at runtime.

Aside from providing working examples, the SAMPLE files included with dBASE provide many pages of ready-to-use code examples that you can cut and paste into your own program. If your application needs a similar feature, you can just cut and paste the code into your program (see fig. 24.5), and then modify the procedure to meet your needs.

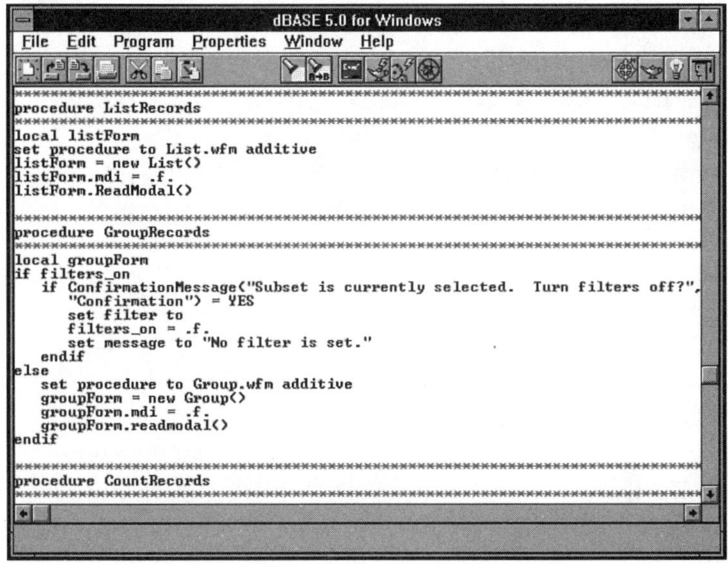

Fig. 24.5
You can cut and paste sample program code into your program.

Another source of sample program code can be found in the forms themselves. Objects have a procedure window (see fig. 24.6) which allows you to write custom routines to respond to events, such as clicking on a button. This illustrates another area of automation which your application plan should consider using.

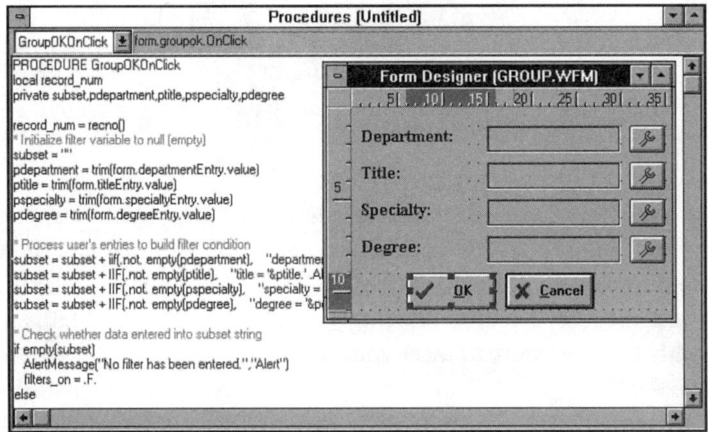

Fig. 24.6 Your dBASE application can respond to events with custom routines that you write.

Prototyping the Task Automation

Tip Leave the English word description at the top of your program as comments to describe what your program does. Add additional comments throughout to further document the "what" and "why."

A *prototype* is a working model of your program. In dBASE for Windows, the time you spend prototyping contributes directly to the final program. Begin by writing down in English what you want the program to do. Then replace the words with the dBASE language elements that accomplish the steps that are listed. Use comments to explain what is going on. Be descriptive in the comments so that anyone can understand what you did and why you chose that methodology.

Testing and Debugging

Testing and debugging is an ongoing process. As you prototype task automation, you should test and debug each program module. As features are added or changed, you should test the modification and retest the prototype.

Try to get users to test the prototypes as you complete your initial testing. In addition to giving you another procedural test, users can provide invaluable feedback about how your prototype works in the real world.

dBASE enables you to prototype, test, and debug one task, a collection of tasks, or the entire application. This modular nature means that you can respond quickly and easily to changes.

Choosing a Programming Methodology

dBASE for Windows enables you to program by following the traditional structured (linear) programming approach or the newer object-oriented approach. Which approach you choose depends on your circumstances and the task being automated.

You generally will find that the object-oriented approach takes less time to program and is easier to maintain. On the other hand, structured programming gives you complete control over users. Often, a combination of the two methodologies is used in developing a custom dBASE application.

The following sections *briefly* summarize the key features and limitations of each methodology. Volumes have been written about each of these programming methods. For a more detailed discussion of structured programming, see *Introduction to Programming* (published by Que Corporation). For more information about object-oriented programming, see Que's *Object-Oriented Programming in C++*.

What Is Structured Programming?

Ever hear the expression *top-down programming*? That term describes in a nutshell the essence of structured programming. Developed in the late 1960s, *structured programming* is a disciplined, consistent style of modular programming. In this "top-down" approach to programming, the application to be developed is broken into components, each of which is broken down even more into components, and so on. A central module controls the other modules, interacts with users, and cleans up when a submodule completes its tasks. A team of programmers usually separately programs the small components (called *subroutines* or *modules*) that are later put together with the main module to assemble the application.

The modular and disciplined approach of structured programming results in well-organized, quality programs. On the other hand, the rigid approach makes mid-project design changes difficult to handle. The division of components often turns out to be incorrect. And because the application cannot be tested in the "real world" until the entire application is assembled, the final application may not meet the needs of the users at that final point. Changes to a top-down system usually mean reworking the system, from the top down—resulting in long turnaround times and costly maintenance.

In dBASE for Windows, you can create your own top-down application complete with custom menus and custom screens. With the implementation of the graphical user interface, however, dBASE for Windows offers many tools, such as forms, that can manage the input and output for you. Rather than write lines and lines of structured program code to create dBASE IV-style windows, you can use forms to display and enable such Windows objects as buttons, check boxes, and drop-down entry fields. In dBASE IV-style windows, you can display only dBASE IV menus and dBASE IV input and output commands such as @..SAY or @...GET. The visual programming approach gives you more options as an application developer, reduces development and revision time, and eliminates maintenance costs.

Tip
Use visual programming tools to speed your development work and then use structured-programming principles to program a custom function or procedure.

Use the new graphical tools whenever possible. In a way, the form has become the new "main module" of visual programming. Then when you want to program a task solution, such as a user-defined function or a user-interface effect that dBASE does not provide interactively, apply the discipline and organization of structured programming to that one task or interface. It's the best of both worlds!

What Is Object-Oriented Programming?

Oddly enough, object-oriented programming (OOP) has its roots in the late 1960s also. A Norwegian computing center created the first object-oriented programming language, called Simula, to simulate real-world situations. In OOP, programs are organized by objects. Objects contain programming instructions and data that define the object's behavior. Each object is self-contained (referred to as *encapsulation*). This term means that one object's data and instructions don't interfere with another object. The Customer form doesn't interfere with the Employee form's data, for example, even though they both contain a field called Last Name.

Tip
Think of OOP as programming objects that communicate with each other.

Another key feature of OOP is *inheritance*. Objects can be contained within other objects, and objects can therefore inherit properties from the objects that contain them. If you color the Employee form red, for example, all contained fields turn red, but the Customer form is not affected (encapsulation). You can, of course, override the inheritance and change the field color to something else with no effect on the container, which is the form.

The last key feature of OOP is *polymorphism*. This concept means that objects which exist in a hierarchy can share program code (instructions) and that the program can execute differently for each object. You can create, for example, a program at the form level (container) that calculates sales tax. Each object on the form can call that program by name. And each object can change the computation performed by the shared program. Polymorphism "hides" the implementation behind a common interface.

Note

The object-oriented features of dBASE are an extension of structured, modular programming. Everything you know about the dBASE language still applies. Object-oriented concepts just give you another way to plan and organize an application.

Everything in dBASE is an object. A form, a table, a window, and a button are all are examples of objects. Objects can be manipulated (moved, copied, and deleted) and have characteristics (properties) that can be changed. A button can be copied from one form to another, for example, by way of the Clipboard. Any programming instructions you added to the button along with all its properties (color and name, for example) move with the button.

The benefits of object-oriented programming (OOP) are numerous. Object-oriented programs are easier to maintain and upgrade, and modules of the code are reusable in the same program or other programs. And because program code, memory variables, and properties are encapsulated within the object being programmed, it is easier to split an application-development project among many programmers without one conflicting with the other.

On the other hand, true OOP is not for every application. You should generally use OOP for these tasks:

- Large, complex application development
- Development projects with more than one programmer
- Application-development projects prone to change

Note

Again, this explanation of the key features of OOP is simplified and brief. For more information about OOP techniques, see *Object-Oriented Programming from Square One* (published by Que Corporation). For a beginner's tour of OOP history and basic concepts, I highly recommend David Taylor's *Object-Oriented Technology: A Manager's Guide* (published by Addison-Wesley).

▶ "Handling Events," p. 650

▶ "Automating the Sample Form," p. 651

▶ "Navigating the Procedure Editor," p. 649

Guidelines for Application Development

As you embark on your application development, remember the following list of general application-development guidelines:

- Document as you work.
- Involve end users.
- Use color to convey meaning to users (red for negative numbers, for example).
- Don't clutter the screen. Spread data input fields over several pages on a form rather than jam it into one screen.
- Label fields, dialog boxes, and windows (to help you write end-user documentation).
- Control the tab order.
- Use buttons and other graphical tools rather than nested menus.
- Spell-check help screens and other text that users (or your boss!) see.

From Here...

Now that you are familiar with how to design your dBASE for Windows application, you are ready to begin programming in the Command window. To learn more about programming, refer to the following chapters:

- Chapter 25, "Working with the Command Window," builds on what you know about the dBASE programming environment and takes you through the process of quick programming in the Command window.
- Chapter 26, "Using the dBASE Text Editor," shows you how to create and save program files.
- Chapter 31, "Automating Forms," shows you how to program in the Event Editor.

Chapter 25

Working with the Command Window

As you work with dBASE for Windows interactively, you may have noticed that words appear in the Command window. The words that appear in the top section of the Command window are the dBASE language elements the dBASE for Windows user interface is sending to the dBASE engine. When you create a form, for example, dBASE sends the command CREATE FORM to the Command window. Watching the Command window as you use dBASE interactively is a great way to begin learning the dBASE language.

Best of all, you can use the Command window. The Command window enables you to enter dBASE language elements in the top section and see the results immediately in the bottom section. You can, for example, test out a formula used in an expression to verify its results.

In this chapter, you learn how to perform the following tasks:

- Display and hide the Command window
- Navigate the Command window
- Set Command window properties
- Enter and execute dBASE commands
- Edit Command window text
- Save Command window text to a program file
- Use popular dBASE commands

Using the Command Window

The Command window gives you direct access to the dBASE engine. You can use the Command window to do the following:

- Learn the dBASE language
- Quickly execute interactive tasks
- Automate tasks not available interactively
- Write and test programming code
- Run DOS dBASE programs without modification

First and foremost, the Command window helps you learn the dBASE programming language. By watching the Command window as you work interactively with dBASE, you pick up a few choice commands and begin using them. That leads to the next use: executing interactive tasks. Rather than choose from menu items or dialog boxes, if you know the proper command, you can just enter it in the Command window. And, using the dBASE language, you can accomplish tasks that would be cumbersome to do interactively or that are not available interactively.

Note

The Command window in dBASE for Windows is similar to the dBASE III PLUS and dBASE IV dot-prompt feature.

For an application developer, the Command window is invaluable. From the Command window, you can write, test, compile, and debug dBASE programs. You can declare memory variables, work with functions, and calculate complex formulas. After the code written in the Command window is perfected, you can cut and paste it into a program file.

Note

If you have existing DOS dBASE programs, you can run them unmodified in the Command window results pane. You may have to resize the window to the proper width, however. You can use the SET DISPLAY command to change the size of the Command Results window. You can also hide the dBASE application menu and SpeedBar. Mouse support is automatic. Data format defaults are controlled by the Windows Control Panel. You can use the SET commands in your program, however, to override the Control Panel defaults.

Navigating the Command Window

Before you venture into using the Command window, take a look at the components: the window, menus, and toolbars.

Tip
Use the Command window to run files by dragging and dropping them from the File Viewer window into the top section of the Command window.

Manipulating the Command Window

By default, the Command window opens when you start up dBASE for Windows. If your Command window is not open, pull down the **W**indow menu and choose Command to open the Command window. To close the Command window when is selected, open the **F**ile menu and choose **C**lose. As with any window in dBASE for Windows, you can minimize, maximize, resize, and move the Command window.

Exploring the Command Window

As shown in figure 25.1, the Command window contains the following components:

◄ "A Quick Tour of dBASE for Windows," p. 45

- *Menu bar*—contains commands to help you work in the Command window.
- *SpeedBar*—contains tools to help you work in the Command window.
- *Input pane*—enables you to enter dBASE commands. When you press Enter, dBASE executes that line of code. The input pane keeps a list of commands that are executed. You can use the scroll bars or cursor keys to move back to a previous command line. Placing the cursor in a previous line and pressing Enter re-executes that line of code (but only that line).
- *Results pane*—displays the output of dBASE commands that do not open their own window or perform disk operations. Some dBASE commands display output in both the results pane and their own window.
- *Divider line*—separates the two panes and enables you to resize each pane relative to the other. Double-click to restore to the center position.
- *Status bar*—displays data about your current session, such as the file name, record locks, record numbers, and insert key status (insert or overwrite).

Tip
Use the Command window for quick calculations. Type **?** and then the mathematical statement. The answer appears in the Results window.

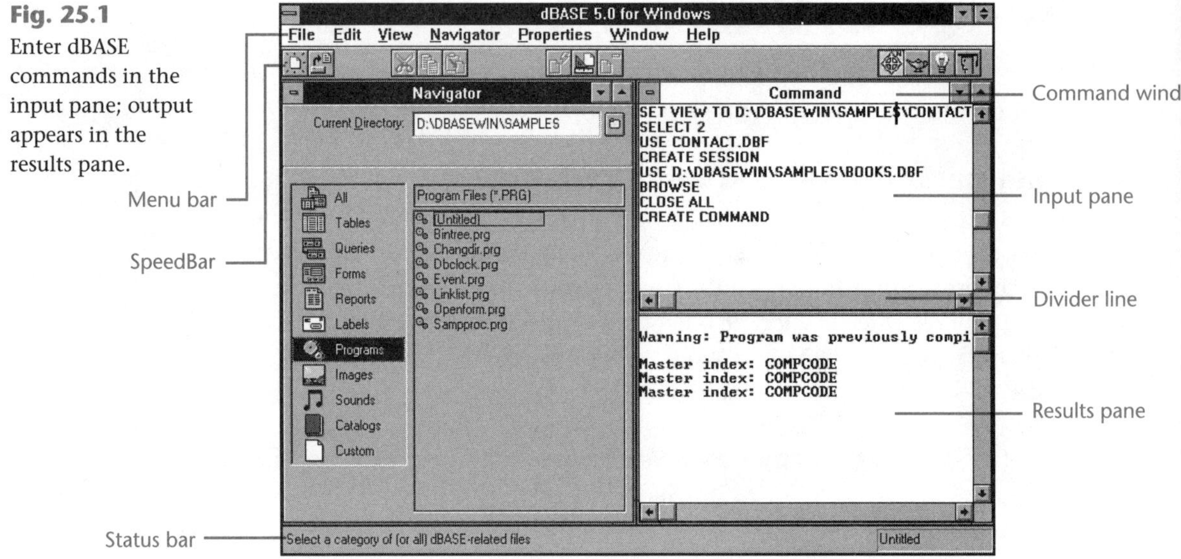

Fig. 25.1 Enter dBASE commands in the input pane; output appears in the results pane.

Instructions entered in the input pane either open a dBASE window or display output in the lower pane of the Control window, the results pane. As you can see in figure 25.2, the BROWSE command issued for the CONTACT.DBF table resulted in dBASE opening a Table Browse window. On the other hand, the ?2+2 statement sent the result, 4, to the results pane.

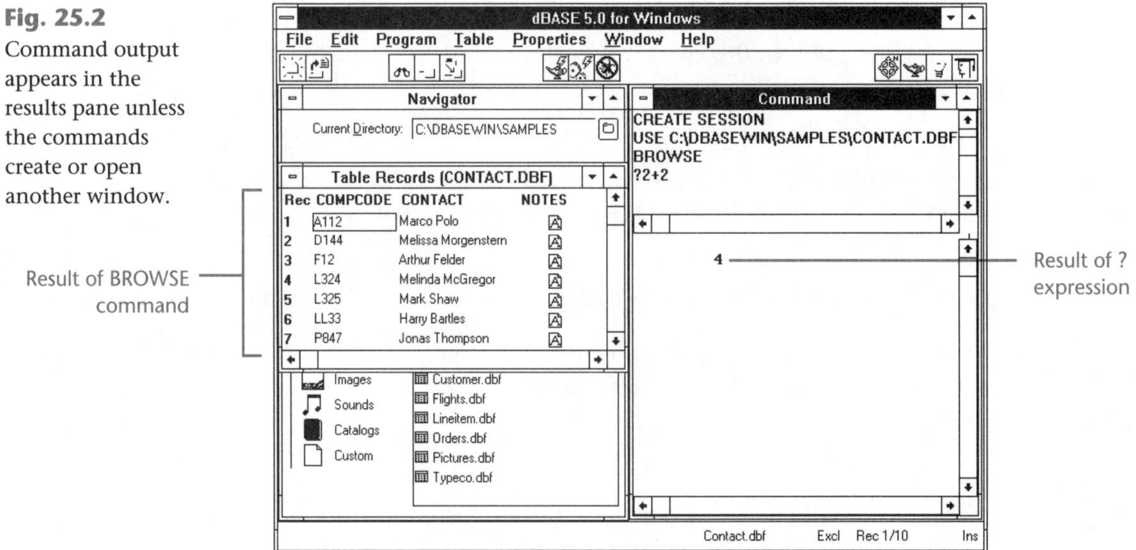

Fig. 25.2 Command output appears in the results pane unless the commands create or open another window.

Working with the Menu Bar

When the cursor resides in the Command window, dBASE changes the menu bar to provide menu options that assist you in your Command window work. Table 25.1 describes each menu.

Table 25.1 Command Window Menu Commands

Menu	Description
File	Enables you to create or open any of the primary dBASE files, close the Command window, or exit from dBASE for Windows.
Edit	Contains commands for undoing, cutting, copying, and pasting text. You can select or clear all text in the input pane. Text can be inserted from a file or copied to a file. A text search-and-replace feature resides on this menu along with access to the Expression Builder and an execute command.
P**r**ogram	A new menu that enables you to run, compile, and debug a program; also displays the results of the Display Coverage feature.
Table	Enables you to perform various operations on table data.
Properties	Enables you to set Desktop and Command window properties.
Window	Rearranges or activates open windows.
Help	Views help information or runs an interactive tutorial.

Working with the SpeedBar

When you're in the Command window, the SpeedBar changes to provide options that assist you in your dBASE command work. Table 25.2 describes what each button does.

Table 25.2 Command Window SpeedBar Buttons

Button	Button Name	Description
	New	Creates any of the primary dBASE files
	Open	Opens any of the primary dBASE file types

(continues)

Table 25.2 Continued

Button	Button Name	Description
	Cut	Moves selected text or control to the Clipboard
	Copy	Copies selected text or control to the Clipboard
	Paste	Copies contents of the Clipboard to the cursor position
	Execute Selection	Executes the current command line
	Do Command	Executes a program
	Debug	Launches the dBASE Debug program
	Navigator	Opens the Navigator window
	Form Expert	Opens the Form Expert
	Tutor	Opens the Interactive Tutors

Tip

To clear the input pane temporarily, make the Command window active and choose **E**dit Select **A**ll, then press Delete. To clear the results pane, type **CLEAR** in the input pane or choose **E**dit **C**lear Results.

Using the SpeedMenu

The Command window provides a SpeedMenu feature. To access the SpeedMenu, click the secondary mouse button (usually the right button, unless you've remapped the buttons) while the input pane of the Command window is displayed. The SpeedMenu conveniently provides a list of the most useful commands. Table 25.3 describes the choices on the SpeedMenu when the Command window is displayed.

Table 25.3 Command Window SpeedMenu Commands

Menu	Description
Command **W**indow Properties	Enables you to set Command window properties
Cu**t**	Moves selected text to the Clipboard

Menu	Description
Copy	Copies selected text to the Clipboard
Paste	Copies Clipboard contents to the current cursor position
Build Expression	Launches the Expression Builder
E**x**ecute Selection	Executes the current command line

Tip
To quickly search for help on a topic, type **HELP** followed by the topic name in the Command window.

Setting Command Window Properties

Just as you can set properties for the dBASE Desktop, you can set properties for the Command window and change the characteristics of the Command window. Choose **P**roperties **C**ommand Window to display the Command Window Properties dialog box (see fig. 25.3). The property settings you choose are stored in the DBASEWIN.INI file.

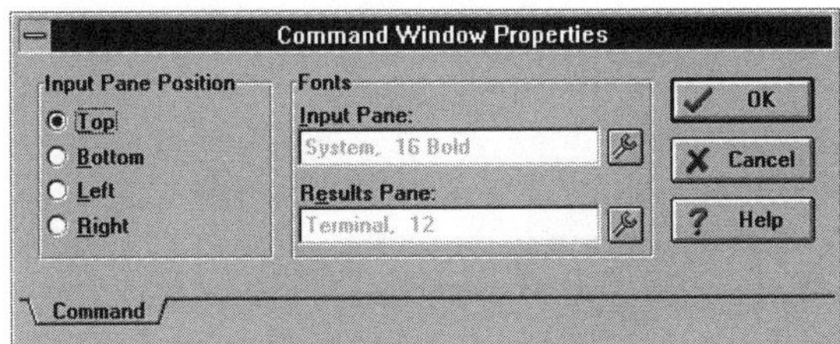

Fig. 25.3
Use the Command Properties Inspector dialog box to rearrange the layout of the Command window or change the fonts.

The following list summarizes the properties you can set:

- *Input Pane position*—enables you to change the layout of the Command window panes. The panes can be split horizontally or vertically and can be swapped.
- *Fonts*—enables you to change the default font, style, size, effects, and color used to display information in the two panes. Click the Tool button to display the Font dialog box and select a font for the **I**nput pane (Command) or R**e**sults pane (Command Results).

Troubleshooting

When I open the Command window, the results pane appears before the input pane.

You can control the order and layout of the two panes by setting the orientation property of the Command window. To change the orientation of the two panes, open the **P**roperties menu and choose **C**ommand Window. Then select the layout you want.

I can't see the entire menu of my DOS dBASE program that runs in the Command window.

Resize the results pane or use the SET command to properly size the window. If necessary, you can adjust the screen display in the Control Panel or change the Results pane font in the Command Window Properties dialog box.

Entering and Executing dBASE Commands

Tip
To stop dBASE from displaying system commands in the Command Results window and messages in the Status bar, issue the command SET TALK OFF.

Entering dBASE commands in the Command window is easy. Just position the cursor in the input pane of the Command window. Pressing Ctrl+End quickly moves you to the last line, which is blank. Now you're ready to type a dBASE command. dBASE is not case-sensitive for language elements; however, quoted text strings are handled exactly as they are typed.

When you press Enter, dBASE executes the current line of code. You can also use the SpeedBar, menu bar, or SpeedMenu to execute the current command line. Because pressing Enter executes the current command line, you cannot type more than one line of code. You can enter as many as 32,767 characters on each line, and you can separate multiple statements on one line with a semicolon (;). The following line of code, for example, clears the results pane and then displays a list of files in the current directory:

```
CLEAR; DIRECTORY
```

To execute a block of command lines, select the command lines and press Enter. Alternatively, you can paste lines of code into the input pane, select the block of commands, and press Enter to execute the command block. You can also execute programs by using the DO command.

IV
Building Applications

Note

The maximum number of lines the input and results panes can contain is limited only by available memory.

▶ "Navigating the Program Editor," p. 563

▶ "Exploring the Program Editor Window," p. 563

Saving Commands to a Program File

If you find that you're frequently typing the same command line or block of command lines, you may want to save the block of commands to a program file. Then, to execute the command (or commands), all you have to do is issue the command DO followed by the program file name.

Tip
To re-execute commands, position the cursor in the appropriate line and press Enter.

To save Command window text to a new program file, follow these steps:

1. Select the command line (or lines).

2. Open the **E**dit menu and choose Copy to **F**ile. dBASE displays the Copy To File dialog box (see fig. 25.4) for the file type Program Source (*.PRG).

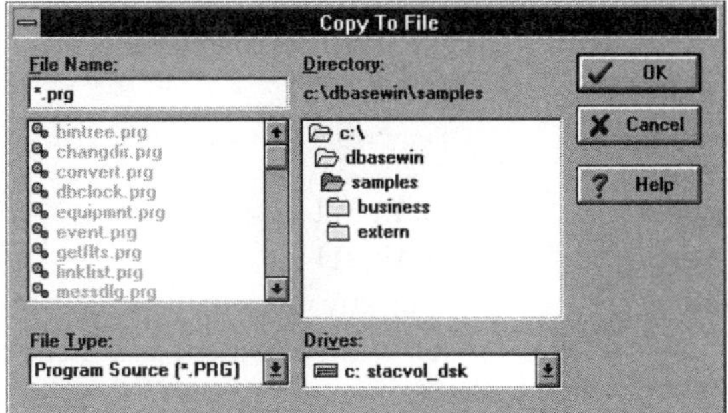

Fig. 25.4
Use the Copy To File dialog box to copy selected commands to a text file.

3. Type a new file name or select an existing file name to be overwritten.

▶ "Navigating the Program Editor," p. 563

▶ "Entering and Executing dBASE Commands," p. 568

To copy Command window text to an existing program file, follow these steps:

1. Select the command line (or lines).

2. Open the **E**dit menu and choose **C**opy. dBASE copies the text to the Clipboard.

3. Open the existing program file and position the cursor at the insertion point you want.

Tip
You can also cut and paste command text from the Help system programming examples.

4. Open the **E**dit menu and choose **P**aste. dBASE inserts the contents of the Clipboard at the current cursor position.

5. Choose **F**ile **S**ave or Save **A**s to save your modified program file.

Using Popular dBASE Commands

Tip
For more information about dBASE commands, type **HELP** followed by the command name in the Command window.

As you begin to use the Command window, keep the following list of popular dBASE commands handy. You can use them to practice programming in the Command window. Or use them to enhance your productivity as you work interactively with dBASE.

Note

dBASE commands are usually written in capital letters to distinguish them from other text in program code. This technique is not a syntax requirement, however. dBASE interprets the command **create** the same as it interprets **CREATE**.

This list shows some popular dBASE commands:

Command: CLEAR
Syntax Example: CLEAR
Description: Clears the results pane

Command: CLEAR ALL
Syntax Example: CLEAR ALL
Description: Clears any open data files, open catalogs, user-defined objects, and memory variables

Command: DO
Syntax Example: DO clients.prg
Description: Executes programs; supply the path if you are not in the current directory

Command: MODIFY COMMAND
Syntax Example: MODIFY COMMAND clients.prg
Description: Opens the specified program in the Program Editor

Command: USE
Syntax Example: USE animals EXCLUSIVE IN SELECT( )
Description: Opens tables and their indexes, but does not display the table; necessary in order to perform BROWSE, EDIT, or MODIFY STRUCTURE

Command: BROWSE
Syntax Example: USE animals BROWSE animals
Description: Displays an open table so that you can view and edit multiple records

Command: EDIT
Syntax Example: USE animals EDIT
Description: Displays an open table so that you can view and edit one record at a time

Command: MODIFY STRUCTURE
Syntax Example: USE animals IN SELECT( ) EXCLUSIVE MODIFY STRUCTURE
Description: Displays the Table Designer for the table in use

Command: DISPLAY STRUCTURE
Syntax Example: USE animals DISPLAY STRUCTURE
Description: Displays the field definitions of a table, number of records, and date of last update

Command: DISPLAY MEMORY
Syntax Example: DISPLAY MEMORY
Description: Displays the values of all memory variables

Command: DISPLAY STATUS
Syntax Example: DISPLAY STATUS
Description: Lists the status of all current dBASE settings

Command: HELP
Syntax Example: HELP EDIT
Description: Launches the Help system

Command: DIRECTORY
Syntax Example: DIRECTORY
Description: Lists the files in the current directory

Command:	SET DIRECTORY TO
Syntax Example:	SET DIRECTORY TO c:\que
Description:	Sets a new search path

Command:	QUIT
Syntax Example:	QUIT
Description:	Closes dBASE

Troubleshooting

The BROWSE command does not display my table.

Before using BROWSE or EDIT, you have to open the table. The USE command followed by the name of the file opens the table.

When I enter a command line into the Command window, an Alert dialog box says that I used an unallowed phrase or keyword.

dBASE is having trouble interpreting your command line. Check your syntax. Make sure that the entire command string fits on one line. Try typing **HELP** followed by the command name to verify syntax and get additional information about using that particular command.

From Here...

Now that you are familiar with how to program by using the Command window, you are ready to begin programming by using the Program Editor. To learn more about writing, executing, and debugging dBASE programs, refer to the following chapters:

- Chapter 26, "Using the dBASE Program Editor," shows you how to create and save program files.
- Chapter 27, "Compiling, Testing, and Debugging Programs," builds on what you know about the dBASE programming and takes you through the process of finding and correcting programming errors (or *bugs*).
- Chapter 28, "Writing Program Modules," shows you how to write modular programs by using the Program Editor and the Event Editor.

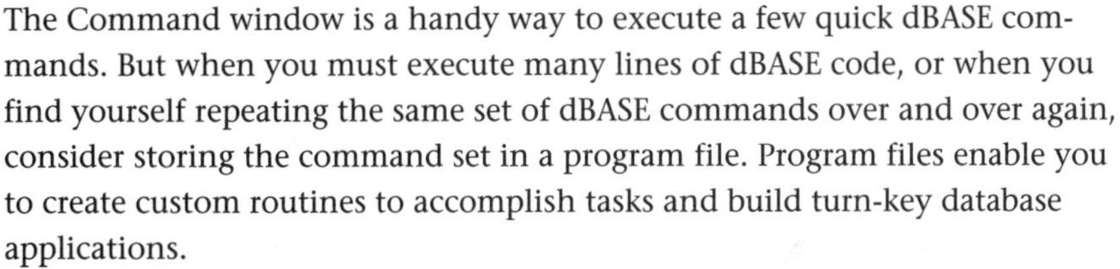

Chapter 26

Using the dBASE Program Editor

The Command window is a handy way to execute a few quick dBASE commands. But when you must execute many lines of dBASE code, or when you find yourself repeating the same set of dBASE commands over and over again, consider storing the command set in a program file. Program files enable you to create custom routines to accomplish tasks and build turn-key database applications.

Program files have a .PRG file extension and store *source code* (dBASE language elements that you can read). When you tell dBASE to execute a program file, dBASE reads the commands one at a time, compiles them into a machine-type language, and processes them. The dBASE language provides language elements such as IF..THEN..ELSE to help you control the flow of your program at runtime.

In this chapter, you learn how to do the following:

- Specify the default Program Editor
- Open the Program Editor
- Navigate the Program Editor window
- Set Program Editor properties
- Enter and execute dBASE commands
- Edit Program Editor text
- Comment and organize dBASE code
- Save program files

Specifying the Default Program Editor

◀ "Using the Text Editor," p. 220

By default, dBASE displays the built-in dBASE Text Editor for creating and editing programs. However, you can use any ASCII Text Editor, such as the Windows Notepad, to create your program files. You can even change the dBASE Program Editor default to another external Text Editor.

To change the default Text Editor for program files, follow these steps:

1. Open the **P**roperties menu and choose **D**esktop.
2. Select the Files tab.
3. In the Editors section (see fig. 26.1), click the Tool button next to the **P**rogram Editor text box. The Choose Program Editor file selection dialog box appears.

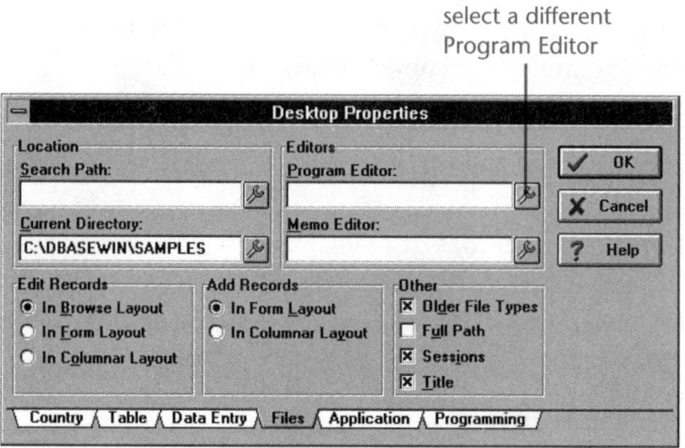

Fig. 26.1
You can use an external Program Editor instead of the built-in dBASE Program Editor.

4. Specify the **F**ile name, **D**irectory, and Dri**v**e of the desired external Text Editor. This setting is stored on the DBASEWIN.INI file.
5. Choose OK to close the Choose Program Editor file selection dialog box.
6. Choose OK again, to close the Desktop Properties dialog box.

Using the built-in dBASE Text Editor provides several significant advantages over an external Text Editor: syntax checking, availability of on-line help (complete with programming examples), access to the dBASE Debugger program, and links to the Coverage Analysis program-testing feature. For these reasons, this chapter focuses on using the dBASE Text Editor to create and edit program files.

Navigating the Program Editor

To open the Program Editor for an existing file, follow these steps:

1. Switch to the Navigator or Catalog window.
2. Specify the directory path.
3. Select Programs.
4. Double-right-click the desired program file. Alternatively, you can select the desired program file and then either click the SpeedBar's Design button, press Shift+F2, or right-click the desired program file and choose Design P**r**ogram from the SpeedMenu.

To open the Program Editor for a new file, follow these steps:

1. Switch to the Navigator window.
2. Specify the directory path.
3. Select Programs.
4. Double-right-click the (Untitled) program item, click the SpeedBar's Design button, press Shift+F2, right-click the desired program and choose Design P**r**ogram from the SpeedMenu, or drag the (Untitled) program item into the Command window.

Before you learn how to use the Program Editor, you need to become familiar with the Program Editor's components: the window, the menus, and the toolbars.

Exploring the Program Editor Window

The Program Editor window opens at the default window size. Like any window in dBASE for Windows, the Program Editor window enables you to minimize, maximize, resize, and move it. To close the Program Editor window, open the **F**ile menu and choose **C**lose.

As figure 26.2 shows, the Program Editor window contains the following components:

◄ "A Quick Tour of dBASE for Windows," p. 45

- The *Program Editor menu bar* contains various commands to help you work in the Program Editor window.

Tip
To modify or create program files quickly, open the Command window and type **MODIFY COMMAND** followed by the name of the program file. You can also type **CREATE COMMAND** to create a new program file.

- The *Program Editor SpeedBar* contains various tools to help you work in the Program Editor window.
- The *Text Editor window* displays the text of your program.
- The *Status bar* displays data about your current session, such as the file name, any record locking active, record numbers, and Insert key status (insert or overwrite).

Note

Editing in the Program Editor works the same as editing in the Memo Field Editor. The only key differences are that the Program Editor menu, SpeedBar, and SpeedMenu contain items that assist you in creating and debugging programs. Also, each program command line can contain up to 32,767 characters, whereas memo field lines impose a 1,024 character limitation. In addition, the Program Editor checks dBASE command syntax when you compile your program.

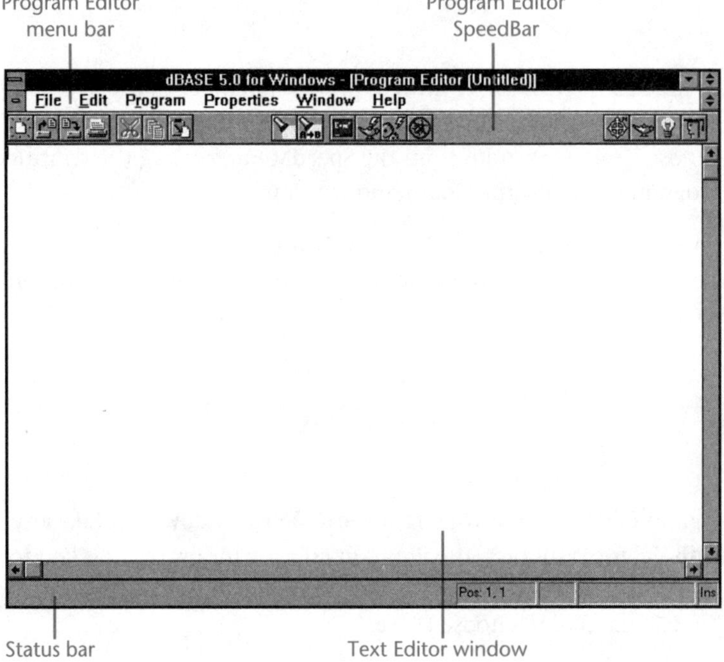

Fig. 26.2
The components of the Program Editor window include a menu bar, the SpeedBar, and a Text Editor window.

Working with the Menu Bar

dBASE changes the menu bar to provide menu options that assist you in your program-editing work. The Program Editor menu bar is similar to the Memo

Field Editor menu bar, with the addition of the program menu choices. Table 26.1 describes each menu.

Table 26.1 Program Editor Window Menu Commands

Menu	Description
File	Enables you to create or open any of the primary dBASE files, close the Program Editor window, save program files, print program files, or exit dBASE for Windows (with or without saving changes).
Edit	Contains commands for undoing, cutting, copying, and pasting text. The menu enables you to insert text from a file or copy text to a file. You can search and replace text, convert case, and join text lines. The menu provides access to the Expression Builder and an execute command.
Program	Enables you to run, compile, and debug a program. This menu also displays the results of the Display Coverage feature.
Properties	Enables you to set Desktop and Program Editor properties.
Window	Rearranges or activates open windows.
Help	Displays help information or runs an interactive tutorial.

Working with the SpeedBar

When you work in the Program Editor window, the SpeedBar changes to provide options that assist you in your dBASE programming work. Table 26.2 describes what each button does.

Tip

To see two views of the same program file, open two Program Editor windows. dBASE automatically updates one window with changes made in the other. Displaying multiple views is handy when you work with large programs.

Table 26.2 Program Editor SpeedBar Buttons

Button	Button Name	Action
	New	Creates any of the primary dBASE files
	Open	Opens any of the primary dBASE file types
	Save	Saves the current file
	Print	Prints the current file

(continues)

Table 26.2 Continued

Button	Button Name	Action
	Cut	Moves the selected text or control to the Clipboard
	Copy	Copies the selected text or control to the Clipboard
	Paste	Copies the Clipboard's contents to the cursor position
	Search>Find text	Finds the specified text and moves the cursor to the first occurrence
	Search>Replace	Searches and replaces the specified text
	Expression Builder	Creates a dBASE expression and inserts it at the cursor position
	Execute Selection	Executes the current command line
	Do Command	Executes the program in the Program Editor window
	Debug	Launches the dBASE Debug program
	Navigator	Opens or switches to the Navigator window
	Command Window	Opens or switches to the Command window
	Form Expert	Opens the Form Expert
	Interactive Tutors	Opens the Interactive Tutors

Tip
When searching for text, press Ctrl+F to display the Search dialog box and Ctrl+L to find the next occurrence.

Using the SpeedMenu

The Program Editor window provides a SpeedMenu feature. To access the SpeedMenu, click the right mouse button while in the Text Editor window. The SpeedMenu conveniently provides a list of the most useful commands. Table 26.3 describes the choices that the SpeedMenu offers while you are using the Program Editor window.

Setting Program Editor Properties

Just as you can set properties for the dBASE Desktop and Command window, you can set properties for the Program Editor and change its characteristics. Open the **P**roperties menu and choose **P**rogram Editor to display the Program Editor Properties dialog box (see fig. 26.3). The property settings that you select are stored in the DBASEWIN.INI file.

Table 26.3 Program Editor SpeedMenu Commands

Menu	Description
Program Editor Properties	Enables you to set Program Editor properties
Cu**t**	Moves selected text to the Clipboard
Copy	Copies selected text to the Clipboard
Paste	Copies the Clipboard's contents to the current cursor position
Find Text	Searches for the specified text
Find **N**ext Text	Searches for the next occurrence of the specified text
Replace Text	Searches for and replaces the specified text
Build Expression	Launches the Expression Builder

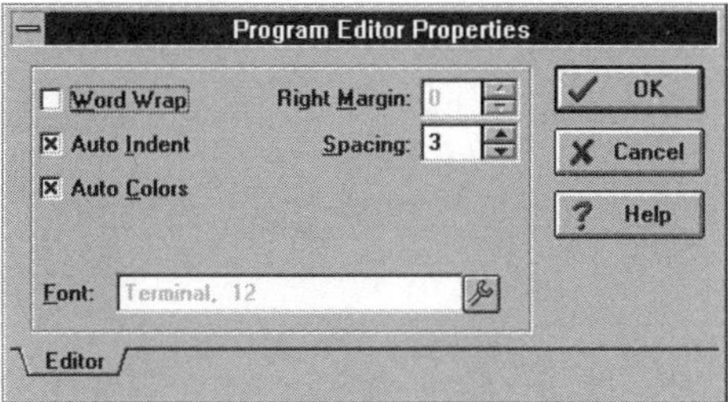

Fig. 26.3
Use the Program Editor Properties dialog box to set defaults for word wrap, text indentation, colors, spacing, and fonts.

Here is a summary of the properties that you can set in the Program Editor Properties dialog box:

- ***W**ord Wrap* controls the insertion of soft carriage returns when the number of characters on a line exceeds the specified right margin. By default, **W**ord Wrap is off (unchecked).

Tip

To convert text quickly to uppercase, lowercase, or initial capital letters, select the text, open the **E**dit menu, choose Con**v**ert Case, and then select the desired case.

- *Right **M**argin* enables you to change the right margin when **W**ord Wrap is on (checked). By default, Right **M**argin is set to 65 characters.
- *Auto **I**ndent* controls whether new lines are automatically indented as far as the previous line. Using indentation to show the flow of logic can make your programs easier to read. The default is on (checked).
- ***S**pacing* controls the number of spaces to insert when the Auto **I**ndent feature is on (checked). The default spacing is four characters.
- *Auto **C**olors* enables you to display programming comments and literal values in different colors. By default, Auto **C**olors is on (checked). Literal values (such as text in quotation marks, braced dates, numbers, and logicals surrounded by periods) appear in blue, syntax errors appear in red, and comments appear in gray.
- ***F**ont* controls the font used in the Text Editor window. The default font is a monospaced font, such as Terminal or Courier. To change the font, click the Tool button, and then choose the desired font, size, style, and effects.

Troubleshooting

As I enter text in quotation marks into the Program Editor window, it appears red.

As you type text in quotation marks, the text appears in red until you type the closing delimiter, the closing quotation mark.

In the Text Editor, I can't open a program text file that has an .ASC file extension.

Open the **E**dit menu and choose **I**nsert from File. This command copies the text into a new program file.

Entering and Executing dBASE Commands

Entering dBASE commands into the Program Editor window is easy. Just position the cursor and start typing. As you type, dBASE reports the cursor position (the column and row) in the status bar.

dBASE is not case-sensitive for language elements. However, text strings within quotation marks are handled exactly as typed.

Each line can be up to 32,767 characters. dBASE requires that command statements reside on a single, unbroken line. For example, you cannot spread the command CREATE over more than one line. If you have to continue a command statement on another line, place a line-continuation character, a semicolon (;), at the end of the line. This character indicates to dBASE that the command continues on the next line.

Commenting Your Program

Take time to document your programming work as you program. Use comments to provide descriptions of the purpose or logic of a series of dBASE commands. Later, when you need to modify the program, you will find that the comments save you time and assist you in implementing the change.

Tip
To execute the program currently in the Program Editor window, press Ctrl+D.

Use comments at the top of a program file to provide a header area. Program headers usually contain such information as the following:

- The name of the program file, and the storage path
- The date that the program was originally written, and the date of its last modification
- The names of the original programmer and the last programmer to modify the file
- Version number information
- A general description of what the program does and which application uses it
- A list of parameters needed
- A list of calls made
- An example, in dBASE code, that demonstrates how to use the program

dBASE provides several ways in which you can add comments in and around your code. The following dBASE language elements, called *command flags*, enable you to enter nonexecuting comment statements:

- An *asterisk (*)*, used as the first character on a line, makes an entire program line a nonexecutable comment.
- *NOTE* is a command word that is identical to the asterisk (*). Placing the word NOTE at the beginning of a line makes the entire program line a nonexecutable comment.

- The *double ampersand (&&)*, which you can use anywhere on a line, tells dBASE to ignore the remaining text on that line. This language element enables you to add comments on program lines that include executable dBASE commands.

Saving the Program File

At any point while you are working in the Program Editor window, you can save your work. dBASE saves your program file as a plain ASCII text file.

To save your program text to a new (unnamed) program file, you can do any of the following:

- Click the SpeedBar's Save File button.
- Open the **F**ile menu and choose Save **A**s.
- Press Ctrl+W to save and close the program file.

dBASE displays the standard Save As dialog box and prompts you for a file name and file type.

To save your program text to an existing (named) program file, do any of the following:

Tip
Use a comment character to deactivate a command line (insert * at the beginning) or part of a line (insert && where needed) temporarily.

- Click the SpeedBar's Save File button.
- Open the **F**ile menu and choose **S**ave.
- Press Ctrl+W to save and close the program file.

dBASE saves the file to its current name.

If you decide that you do not want to keep changes that you made to the program file, open the **F**ile menu and choose A**b**andon and Close, or press Ctrl+O.

Troubleshooting

I have just changed a frequently used memory variable name and need to implement this change in each of my program files.

Use the **E**dit menu's **S**earch feature to search and replace the variable name for you in each file.

I need to disable a section of dBASE code temporarily.

Use the asterisk (*) or the word NOTE at the beginning of each line that you need to disable. Both methods turn the lines into nonexecutable comments. Later, when you need to make those lines executable again, just remove the comment flag (* or NOTE).

Tip
For help regarding command syntax, search for help on that command. Then cut and paste the command syntax to your program file.

From Here...

Now that you are familiar with how to create and edit program files with the Program Editor, you are ready to learn how to test and debug programs with the dBASE Debugger program. To learn more about testing and debugging dBASE programs, refer to the following chapters:

- Chapter 27, "Compiling, Testing, and Debugging Programs." This chapter builds on what you know about dBASE programming and takes you through the process of finding and correcting programming errors (*bugs*).

- Chapter 28, "Writing Program Modules." This chapter shows you how to write and test modular programs using the Program Editor and the Event Editor.

Chapter 27

Compiling, Testing, and Debugging Programs

After you write a program, you need to compile, test, and debug it. *Compiling* is the process of verifying the syntax of program code written in a source file and saving the source code in a format that dBASE for Windows can execute. Source code must be compiled before dBASE can execute the program. *Bugs* are program glitches that produce unexpected results. A *debugger* is a program that helps you find the cause of these unexpected results. (See fig. 27.1)

dBASE for Windows provides a built-in compiler complete with preprocessor features, tools to help you test your program, and a debugger that can help you locate and fix programming errors.

In this chapter, you learn how to do the following:

- Compile programs
- Correct syntax errors
- Test programs
- Start and navigate the Debugger
- Set the Debugger properties
- Inspect and set values
- Control and watch program execution
- Find runtime program errors
- Find program logic errors

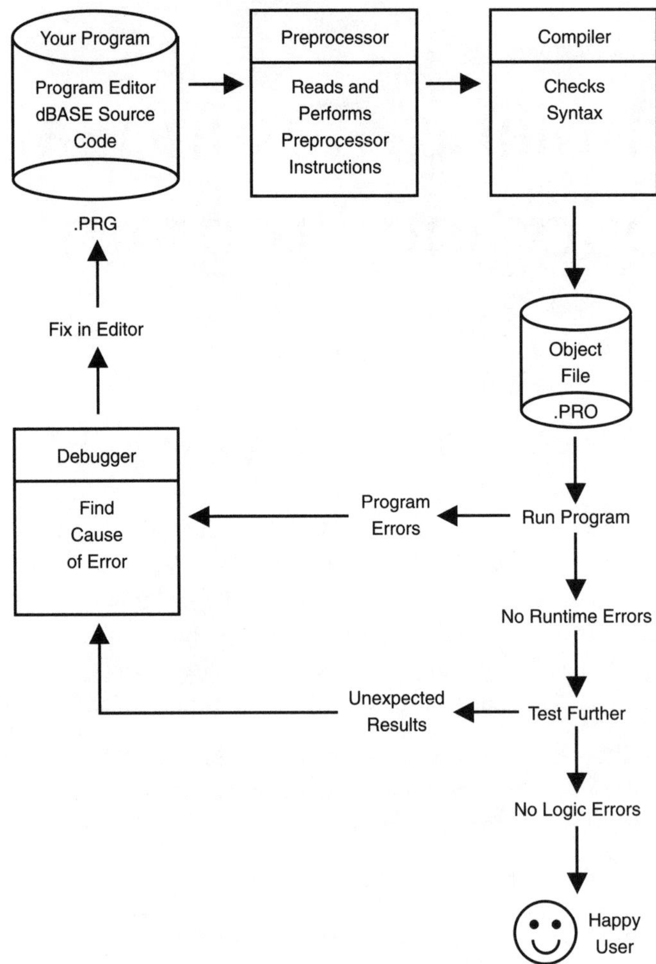

Fig. 27.1 The process of compiling, testing, and debugging is dynamic.

Compiling a Program

dBASE programs that you write, called *source code*, are stored in ASCII text files with a .PRG file extension. For dBASE to execute your program, the source code must be translated into a machine-language (tokenized code) object file. The translated file is saved to the same program name (and in the same directory), but with a .PRO file extension. In fact, forms, queries, and menus generated interactively also have corresponding object files. Table 27.1 lists the source and object file extensions for programs, forms, queries, and menus.

Table 27.1 Source and Object File Extensions

File Type	Source Code File Extension	Object Code File Extension
Program	.PRG	.PRO
Form	.WFM	.WFO
Query	.QBE	.QBO
Menu	.MNU	.MNO

Caution

Because dBASE uses the letter *O* as the last letter of object file extensions, you should not give any program files a name extension that ends with the letter *O*. If you do, dBASE will overwrite the source file while compiling.

Note

Compiled program files cannot be read or edited. Therefore, users cannot change your program unless they have access to the source code. To prevent users of your applications from creating and modifying your program code, issue the command SET DESIGN OFF in your programs. Note that this setting is in effect only while that program (or subroutine) executes. For more information, search for Help on the command topic "SET DESIGN."

Starting the Compiler

dBASE provides many ways to start the compiler:

- Run the program interactively
- Issue a DO command for the program
- Issue a SET PROCEDURE TO command
- Open the P**r**ogram menu and choose **C**ompile
- Issue a COMPILE command for the program

When you run a program interactively, or use the DO or SET PROCEDURE TO command, dBASE checks for a compiled object file. If one is not found, dBASE compiles the program into an object file and then executes the object file. Alternatively, you can compile a program without executing or opening the file, either by using the COMPILE command or by opening the **P**rogram menu and choosing **C**ompile in the Program Editor or Command window. Using the COMPILE command has the advantages of enabling you to use wild cards in file names and to compile more than one program at once.

◄ "Navigating the Program Editor," p. 563

◄ "Entering and Executing dBASE Commands," p. 568

Note

When you compile a dBASE program, the resulting object file with the .PRO extension is not a stand-alone executable; that is, you cannot execute it from DOS. You need dBASE to execute the program.

During compilation, the Compilation Status dialog box (see fig. 27.2) reports the name of the file being compiled, the current line being compiled, and the number of errors found. Table 27.2 describes what each component of the dialog box reports.

Table 27.2 Components of the Compilation Status Dialog Box

Item	Description
Current File Name	The name of the program source file being compiled
Line	The line number of the program currently being compiled
Executable Lines	The number of nonblank lines that contain executable commands
Warnings	The number of warnings given for the program currently being compiled
Routines	The number of subroutines (programs, procedures, or functions) being compiled
Total Lines	The number of lines in the program source files
Total Executable Lines	The number of nonblank lines compiled
Total Files	The number of files compiled, including calls to subroutines in other files
Total Errors	The number of errors found in the files during compilation

Item	Description
Total Warnings	The number of warnings given so far during compilation
Total Routines	The number of subroutines counted and compiled, including the main program
Set Coverage Is	On if a coverage file exists for this programs compilation; otherwise, Off

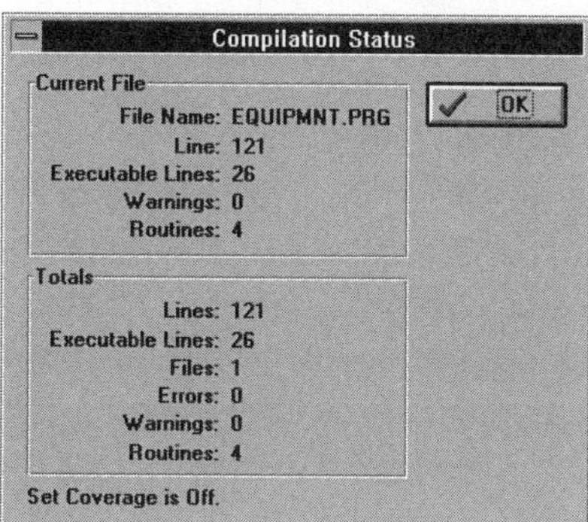

Fig. 27.2
The Compilation Status dialog box keeps you informed on the progress of the dBASE compiler.

Aside from translating your program into a form that dBASE can execute, the compiling process also checks the program's syntax and speeds up processing.

Handling Compiler Errors

When dBASE encounters syntax errors during compilation, a Program Alert dialog box appears (see fig. 27.3). This dialog box describes the error encountered, and lists the file, routine, and line number at which the error occurred. At this point, you have the following options:

- **F**ix switches to or opens the editing window for the source code and places the cursor on the offending line.
- **I**gnore halts compilation of the program that contains syntax errors, but continues to compile any other programs that you specified to be compiled.
- **S**uspend halts execution and returns you to the Editor. This option is not available in compilation errors.
- **D**ebug opens the dBASE Debugger so that you can debug the program line by line. This option is not available in compilation errors.

- Cancel ends compilation (same as pressing Esc).
- Help displays help about compilation errors.

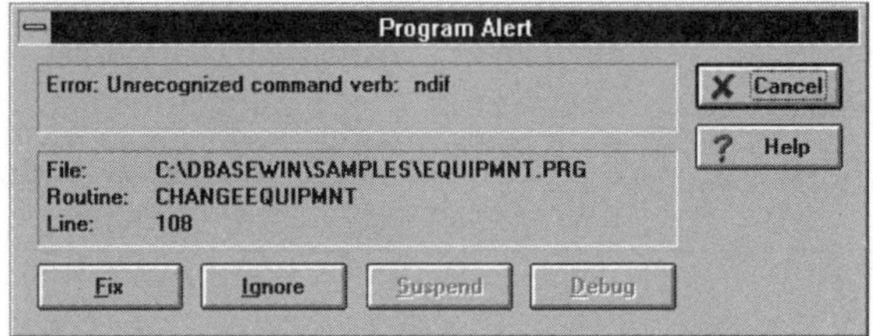

Fig. 27.3
The Program Alert dialog box appears whenever the dBASE compiler encounters a syntax error.

Setting Compilation Properties

Tip
Compile, test, and debug each program module as you complete it instead of waiting until the entire program set or application is completed.

The compiler can compare the modification time and date of the source file to determine whether another compilation is needed. To control this feature, open the **P**roperties menu, choose **D**esktop, and click the Programming tab. You then see the Desktop Properties dialog box as shown in figure 27.4. In the Program Development group, you can set the Ensure **C**ompilation check box. By default, this check box is selected, which tells the dBASE compiler to check the time and date of program, form, or procedure files automatically. If you modify a file but do not compile it, dBASE compiles it when you try to run the file.

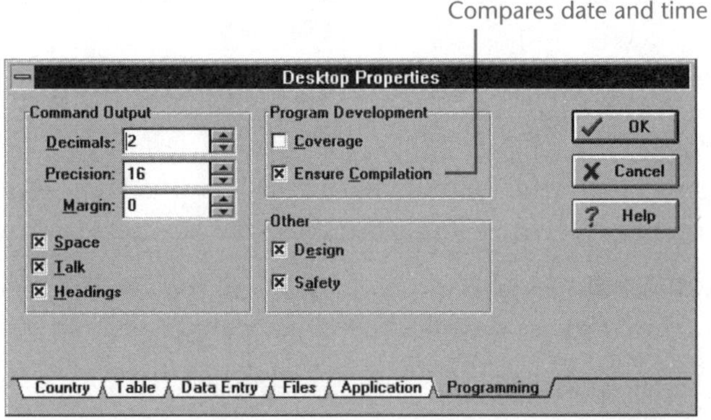

Fig. 27.4
When the Ensure Compilation check box is selected, dBASE compares the date and time of the source and object files.

If you turn off the Ensure **C**ompilation property (by deselecting the check box), dBASE does not check the time and date of the files. Instead, dBASE runs the existing object file or, if no object file exists, compiles one from the source file.

You also can control the Ensure Compilation property with the command SET DEVELOPMENT. To turn on the property, issue the command SET DEVELOPMENT ON in your program; to turn off Ensure Compilation, issue the command SET DEVELOPMENT OFF.

Sending Preprocessor Instructions

Because dBASE uses a preprocessor, you can tell the compiler whether or not to perform certain actions before it compiles your program. For example, you can use the preprocessor to search and replace text, specify compilation conditions, define constants, or set compiler options. To instruct the compiler in this way, you must insert preprocessor statements at the beginning of your program.

Tip
While you are developing your application, turn on the Ensure Compilation property to ensure that you are always working with the latest code. Then, when you deliver your application, issue the statement SET DEVELOPMENT OFF to speed your program's execution.

Preprocessor commands, sometimes called *directives*, begin with a number or pound sign (#). Any line that begins with this character is assumed to be a preprocessor instruction. Table 27.3 lists the preprocessor language commands.

Table 27.3 Preprocessor Language Commands

Command	Description
#define	Defines a name that is used to control program compilation and enables you to search and replace text
#if	Compiles specified code based on the value of the identifier assigned with #define
#ifdef	Compiles specified code if an identifier (defined with #define) exists
#ifndef	Compiles specified code if an identifier (defined with #define) doesn't exist
#include	Inserts the contents of a specified source file (sometimes called a *header file*) into the current program file at the location of the #include statement
#pragma	Sets compiler options, such as coverage analysis
#undef	Undefines an identifier

Tip

Define your constants in a separate header file. Then, during compilation, use the preprocessor command #include to paste the header into your programs. This trick minimizes maintenance; if a constant value changes, you need only change it once in the header file.

Note

If you have a C++ background, you may notice some familiar commands, such as the preprocessor statements just discussed. In this implementation of the dBASE for the Windows environment, you will find many similarities with the C++ language tools that you know and love. When you use the dBASE environment, however, you often are not burdened with the extra work and restrictions that many C++ tools impose. For example, because the dBASE environment is not case-sensitive, you can choose to use lowercase letters when entering commands, but using uppercase letters doesn't cause a compilation error.

Testing a Program

After you successfully compile a program, you must test it. Quality assurance is an ongoing activity during development. As you complete each program module, you must subject it to tests to find problems. Then, as you put the modules together, you test again, looking for problems resulting from the programs interacting with each other or the tables, forms, queries, and reports with which they work. Thorough testing can prevent the implementation of systems that have major structural problems or errors in high-volume, user-critical transactions.

Testing also should push the program to its limits. Such testing is sometimes called *stress testing*. You push high volumes of data through the system to try to locate any stress points and to test performance (memory needs, hard disk access times, and speed).

Depending on the size of the program, testing can be a formidable task. First, you must test in an isolated environment. Do not test your program with live data. Instead, work in a special testing directory separated from your other development work and from any live systems currently being used.

dBASE provides two features to help you test your programs:

- The Generate Records feature, which generates random data
- The Coverage Analysis feature, which monitors the execution of the code

Generating Random Data

You can create test data by copying data in from the live system. Alternatively, you can let dBASE generate random data for you. dBASE's Generate

Records dialog box populates the specified table with randomly generated data of the correct data type. If your table already contains some data, the GENERATE command appends the specified random data to the existing data. This feature is especially helpful when you need to stress test your program with volumes of data.

Note

The GENERATE command cannot generate random data for memo, binary, or Object Linking and Embedding (OLE) fields.

To generate random data, follow these steps:

1. Open the desired table.
2. From the **T**able menu, choose **T**able Utilities and then **G**enerate Records. The Generate Records dialog box appears (see fig. 27.5).

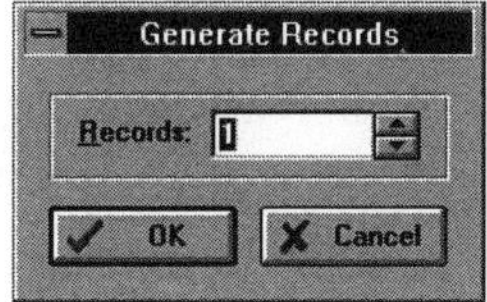

Fig. 27.5
Before stress testing your program for volumes of data, use the Generate Records dialog box to populate your table with random data.

3. Enter the number of records that you want the generator to add.
4. Click OK or press Enter.

Alternatively, you can issue the command GENERATE from a program or the Command window. For example, the following code instructs dBASE to open the ANIMALS table and add 100 new records filled with random data:

```
USE animals
GENERATE 100
```

If you don't first open the table with the USE command, dBASE displays the Select Table dialog box and prompts you to select the table to which to add records. Likewise, if you don't specify the number of records to generate, dBASE displays the Generate Records dialog box and prompts you to enter the number of records to generate.

Monitoring Code Execution

dBASE's Coverage Analysis feature records and reports the execution of codeblocks in your programs. This feature helps you track which lines of code have actually been tested. For example, when you use commands that execute lines of code based on certain conditions (flow-of-control commands), the blocks of code execute only when those conditions are met. In the following example of the IF..ELSE..ENDIF program control language element, the first block of code executes only when the condition tests true (that is, when the value of X is greater than the number 100). Likewise, the second block executes only when the condition tests false.

```
IF X > 100
     Y=X+Z
     ?"Value is over 100."
ELSE
     C=X+B
     ?"Value is under 100."
ENDIF
```

When testing programs, you must test for both the true and false conditions. In large programs, with many conditional tests and numerous calls to other programs, it is very difficult to know whether you have tested each block of code. For such programs, the Coverage Analysis feature comes in handy. If you turn on this feature before you begin testing, dBASE creates a coverage analysis file that records which codeblocks have been executed. The information in the coverage analysis file accumulates each time you run the program.

To start the Coverage Analysis feature, follow these steps:

1. Open the **P**roperties menu and choose **D**esktop.

2. Click the Programming tab.

3. In the Program Development group of the Desktop Properties dialog box (shown earlier in fig. 27.4), select the **C**overage check box to turn on the Coverage Analysis feature.

4. Click OK or press Enter to save the modified desktop property settings.

Alternatively, you can issue the command SET COVERAGE ON in the source program or Command window, or issue the #pragma COVERAGE(ON) preprocessor command in the program. To turn off the Coverage Analysis feature, you can do any of the following:

- Deselect the **C**overage check box

- Issue the SET COVERAGE OFF command

- Issue the #pragma COVERAGE(OFF) preprocessor command

> **Caution**
>
> Issuing the statement SET COVERAGE ON in a program file before compiling turns on coverage only for the other programs (subroutines) that the program may call; the statement doesn't turn on coverage for the program. The only way to turn on coverage from within the same program is to issue the preprocessor command #pragma COVERAGE(ON), issue the command SET COVERAGE ON in the source program or Command window, or select the **C**overage check box in the Desktop Properties dialog box *before* you compile the program.

After you turn on the Coverage Analysis feature, you need to compile the program. As the program is compiled, dBASE creates a new object file that includes special information to assist in the coverage analysis. Then, when you run the program, dBASE creates a binary file with a .COV extension and with the same file name as the program. The coverage analysis file records the line number of the codeblock that executed and the number of times each block of code executed.

To display the coverage analysis file, follow these steps:

1. Open the **P**rogram menu and choose Display Co**v**erage. dBASE displays a standard file selection dialog box.

2. Select a coverage file to view.

3. Click OK or press Enter. dBASE displays the contents of the coverage file in the Command window's results pane (see fig. 27.6).

Alternatively, you can issue the command DISPLAY COVERAGE to display the contents of the coverage file one screen at a time. Also, you can use the command LIST COVERAGE to send the contents to a disk file or the printer. The following statement prints the coverage file:

```
LIST COVERAGE TO PRINTER
```

> **Note**
>
> The only way to stop generating information for the coverage analysis file is to recompile the program with the Coverage Analysis feature turned off.

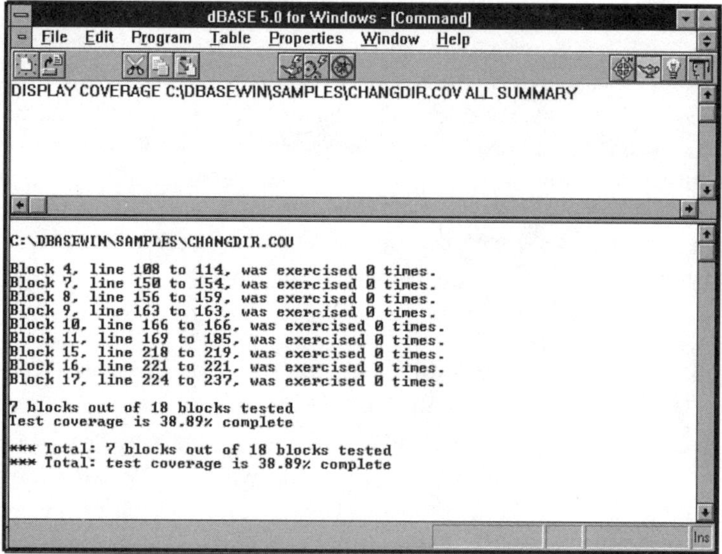

Fig. 27.6
Use the scroll bars to scroll through the coverage analysis file results.

What Is the Debugger?

As hard as you may try to produce perfect, efficient code, programs often produce unexpected results. Programmers refer to these anomalies as *bugs*. Bugs generally come in three species: syntax errors, runtime errors, and logic errors

Syntax errors include missing command words (such as an IF..ELSE structure that is missing the ENDIF keyword), misspelled command words (such as FOR..NXT rather than FOR..NEXT), and missing punctuation (such as a semicolon). The dBASE compiler catches *most* of these types of errors. However, the compiler misses other syntax errors, such as the misspelling of a built-in dBASE property name. dBASE does not find these types of syntax errors until you try to execute the code lines that contain them.

Runtime errors result when dBASE tries to execute a particular line of code. If the compiler cannot make sense of the words on that line (such as a misspelled field name or property name) or cannot find the object to which the code refers (such as a missing table or form), dBASE halts execution and displays a Program Error window.

Often, the program bugs that are most difficult to find are those caused by *logic errors*. Programs with logic errors run without causing dBASE errors, but still do not perform as expected. For example, you may have an Employee application that does not display any dBASE error messages, but prints the incorrect employee data on a W-2 form. Fortunately, the dBASE Debugger program is most helpful when you try to track down these hard-to-find errors.

The dBASE Debugger helps you find the cause of errors in your programs. Using the Debugger, you can do the following:

- Execute programs one line at a time and view program execution
- Inspect the value of variables, fields, objects, and expressions while the program executes
- Change or stop program execution

Note

dBASE for DOS programmers should remember that the SET TRAP, SET DBTRAP, SET PAUSE, and SET DEBUG commands are no longer supported. Instead, use SET ECHO, SET STEP, and DEBUG commands to invoke the Debugger from within a program. All debugging now takes place in the Debugger program.

Navigating the Debugger

The Debugger is the main tool that you use to find errors in programs. To use the Debugger, first you open the Debugger window. Then you run in the Debugger window the program that you suspect contains an error. When you run a program in the Debugger window, you can control program execution. You tell the program when and where to pause execution and when to resume execution. You can execute the program line by line and watch the values of variables, fields, objects, and expressions change. When execution pauses, you can inspect the value of any variables, fields, objects, and expressions as needed. By stepping through the program and investigating value changes, you should be able to determine where and why an error occurs. After you find an error, you must return to the Program Editor to fix the program code; you cannot edit program code in the Debugger.

Before exploring the Debugger features, you need to understand how to open and navigate the Debugger window. To open the Debugger, follow these steps:

1. Switch to the Navigator or Catalog window.

2. Select Programs.

3. Right-click the desired program file and choose De**b**ug from the SpeedMenu. Alternatively, open the desired program file in Design view, open the **P**rogram menu, and choose De**b**ug, or click the SpeedBar's Debug button.

Alternatively, you can start the Debugger by issuing the command DEBUG in the Command window or a program. You can also start the Debugger program from the Windows Program Manager by double-clicking the dBASE Debugger icon. You do not need to select the program that you want to debug before you load the Debugger program; you can do that after the Debugger opens.

Note

The Debugger is actually another application that runs in its own application window. To switch between the Debugger and dBASE, press Alt+Tab.

Before learning how to use the Debugger, you need to get familiar with its components: the window, the menus, and the SpeedBars.

Exploring the Debugger Window

The Debugger window opens at the default window size. As with any window in dBASE for Windows, you can minimize, maximize, resize, and move the Debugger window. To close the Debugger window, you open the **F**ile menu and choose **C**lose.

◄ "Quick Tour of dBASE for Windows," p. 45

As shown in figure 27.7, the Debugger window contains the following components:

- The *Debugger menu bar* provides various commands to help you work in the Debugger application.
- The *Debugger SpeedBar* provides various tools to help you work in the Debugger application.
- The *Module window* displays the source code of the program that you are debugging.
- The *Watch window* displays the watchpoints that you specified.
- The *Break window* displays the breakpoints that you set.

- The *Stack window* lists all program calls to other modules, procedures, and user-defined functions.
- The *Status bar* displays data about your current session, such as the file name, any active record-locking, record numbers, and the Insert key status (whether the key is in insert or overwrite mode).

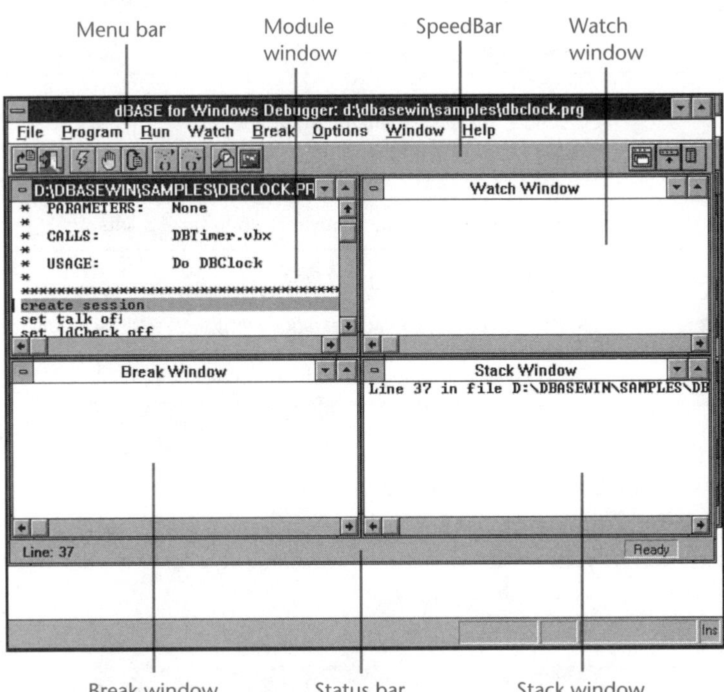

Fig. 27.7 By default, the Debugger application window displays four windows of program information.

> **Note**
>
> You cannot edit your program text in the Debugger. To change the program text, you must return to the applicable Program or Event Editor. You can do this quickly from within the Debugger: simply move to the line of code that you want to edit, open the **P**rogram menu, and choose **F**ix. After the program has been edited, open the **P**rogram menu and choose De**b**ug.

Tip
To see more of your program, maximize or resize the Module window.

Working with the Menu Bar

dBASE changes the menu bar to provide menu options that assist you with your program debugging. Table 27.4 describes each menu.

Table 27.4 Debugger Menus

Menu	Description
File	Enables you to start debugging a program, load new program modules, display text files, change the directory, and exit the Debugger
Program	Enables you to move between lines, find text, return to the origin, go to a procedure, launch the Program Editor, inspect values, and evaluate or modify a value
Run	Enables you to control program execution, trace execution, end execution, and set parameter arguments
Watch	Enables you to add, edit, remove, or change watchpoints
Break	Enables you to add, edit, remove, or go to breakpoints
Options	Sets Debugger properties and defaults
Window	Enables you to tile, cascade, arrange icons, and select windows
Help	Displays help information or runs an interactive tutorial

Working with the SpeedBar

Tip
To quickly locate all occurrences of key words or commands in the program that you are debugging, open the **P**rogram menu and choose **F**ind.

Tip
To view another program or text file, open the **F**ile menu and choose **O**pen Text File.

While you are using the Debugger, the SpeedBar changes to provide options that assist you in your dBASE debugging work. Table 27.5 describes what each button does.

Table 27.5 Debugger SpeedBar Buttons

Button	Button Name	Description
	New	Creates any of the primary dBASE files
	Exit	Exits the Debugger
	Run	Runs or continues execution of the current program
	Stop	Pauses program execution
	Reload	Reloads the current program from disk
	Trace Into	Executes the current program, tracing into procedure calls

Button	Button Name	Description
	Step Over	Executes the current program, stepping over procedure calls
	Inspect	Inspects the value of the item specified
	Evaluate/Modify	Evaluates an expression and modifies the value
	Restore	Restores the Debugger window to a normal size
	Reduce	Reduces the Debugger to just a menu and a SpeedBar
	Palette	Displays the SpeedBar as a vertical palette

Using the SpeedMenu

The Debugger window provides a SpeedMenu feature for each of the four windows. To access the SpeedMenu, click the right mouse button while in one of the four Debugger windows. The SpeedMenu conveniently provides a list of the most useful commands. The Watch window SpeedMenu and the Break window SpeedMenu are identical to their respective menus on the menu bar. The Stack window's SpeedMenu has only one item, **G**o to Source Line, which shows the source code for the highlighted routine.

The Module window's SpeedMenu provides many commands. Table 27.6 describes the choices available from the Module window's SpeedMenu.

Tip

To give yourself easy access to the SpeedBar, you can change it to a free-floating palette of buttons by clicking the Vertical Palette button. Open the **O**ptions menu, choose **D**efault, and check the SpeedBar's **P**opup button.

Table 27.6 The Module Window's SpeedMenu Commands

Menu	Description
Load Module	Enables you to select a new program to debug and loads the program into the Module window
Go to Line	Moves the cursor to a line number that you specify
Previous Line	Moves the cursor to the previous line
Find	Searches for a text string
Find **N**ext	Searches for the next occurrence of the specified text

(continues)

Table 27.6 Continued

Menu	Description
Origin	Moves the cursor to the origin of the call chain
Go to Procedure	Moves the cursor to the specified procedure
Fix	Opens the Program Editor with current program ready for editing
Inspect	Inspects the value of the highlighted item
Evaluate/Modify	Evaluates an expression and modifies the value
Watch	Adds the highlighted expression to the Watch window

Setting Debugger Properties

Tip
To hide the Debugger windows but leave the Debugger visible, click the SpeedBar's Reduce View button. This reduces the Debugger to just a menu and SpeedBar.

Although the Debugger does not have a properties menu item, you can configure the Debugger and save the configuration settings to a file name that you can restore later.

To customize, save, and restore the Debugger's configuration, you use the **O**ptions menu. Table 27.7 describes the options that this menu provides.

Table 27.7 The Options Menu's Commands

Command	Description
Defaults	Enables you to select which Debugger environment option settings to save, and controls the default display of the SpeedBar.
Animation Speed	Enables you to set, by adjusting a button on a slider from slow to fast, the speed at which the **R**un menu's **A**nimation command executes programs.
Display Font	Displays the Font dialog box, which enables you to specify the font, style, and size of the font used in the Debugger windows.
Source File Path	Enables you to change the default drive and directory from which to load files into the Debugger.
Save **O**ptions	Saves the various Debugger configuration settings to a file name that you can restore later. The file extension .CFG is used. The configuration file name DEFAULT.CFG loads automatically when the Debugger starts.
Restore Options	Restores configuration settings from a .CFG Debugger configuration file.

To set Debugger environment options, open the **O**ptions menu and choose **D**efaults. This command displays the Defaults dialog box, as shown in figure 27.8.

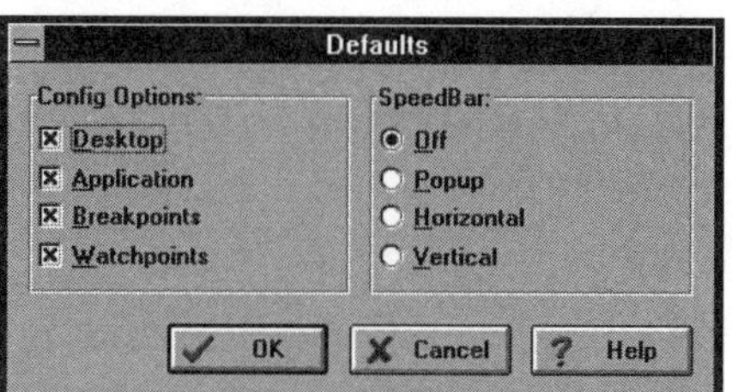

Fig. 27.8
The Defaults dialog box lets you change the default display of the SpeedBar palette.

The Defaults dialog box enables you to set the defaults for both the SpeedBar and the configuration options. The option buttons in the SpeedBar group enable you to change the display and orientation of the SpeedBar palette. With the check boxes under Config Options, you can select the option settings that you want to save to the configuration file:

- **D**esktop saves the current arrangement of the Debugger windows and placement of the SpeedBar.
- **A**pplication saves the current application as the Debugger's default application.
- **B**reakpoints saves the breakpoints currently listed in the Break window.
- **W**atchpoints saves the watchpoints currently listed in the Watch window.

After you select your default option settings, be sure to open the **O**ptions menu and choose Save **O**ptions, to save your settings to the Debugger configuration file.

Locating and Fixing Problems

The Debugger enables you to follow and control program execution. To find and correct program errors, you follow these general steps:

1. Load the program into the Module window.
2. Optionally set breakpoints (to pause execution).
3. Optionally set watchpoints (to display the current values).

4. Execute the program using the SpeedBar buttons Run, Animate, Trace, or Step.
5. Inspect, change, or watch values at breakpoints.
6. Return to the editor to fix discovered problems.
7. Return to Step 1, and repeat the steps until the program runs error free.

Tip
To save the breakpoints and watchpoints that you have set, select the **B**reakpoints and **W**atchpoints check boxes in the Defaults dialog box and save the option settings to a configuration file.

Troubleshooting

Every time that I compile my program, dBASE displays a Program Error dialog box.

The Program Error dialog box appears for each syntax error that the compiler finds. Before you recompile your program, you must correct each error that the compiler found. If you are unsure how to correct the error, search for help on the command. If all else fails, comment out that line or block of code until you find the solution.

I need to debug a different program than I have loaded in the Module window.

Load the other program into the Module window by opening the **F**ile menu and choosing **L**oad Module.

While testing a program, I want to ensure that the Coverage Analysis feature is always turned on, no matter who changes the program.

The best way to be sure that the Coverage Analysis feature is on before compilation is to use the preprocessor command #pragma COVERAGE(ON) at the beginning of the program file.

Setting Breakpoints

Tip
To load another program for debugging, open the **F**ile menu and choose **L**oad Module.

Breakpoints pause execution at locations that you specify and, optionally, under the circumstances that you specify. Pausing execution at predetermined locations enables you to investigate the values of various items at those locations. Setting breakpoints is much easier than trying to click the Stop button at the correct point as the program executes. You can choose to run long programs at full speed or animation speed to bypass error-free code and concentrate your efforts on the problematic code.

Note

Usually you should set breakpoints a few lines before the code line or section that you suspect is causing the error. Then, when execution pauses, use tracing or stepping to observe the program actions that lead to the program error.

In addition to specifying a line at which to pause execution, breakpoints can specify a condition or an action that must be met before execution pauses. For example, you can specify that the breakpoint pause execution only if a field contains a certain value.

To set a breakpoint in the Module window, follow these steps:

1. Move the cursor to the command line at which you want program execution to pause.

2. Open the **B**reak menu and choose **A**dd, or double-click an empty line in the Break window. Either action displays the Add Breakpoint dialog box (see fig. 27.9), in which you can set breakpoint conditions and actions. Alternatively, you can open the **B**reak menu and choose **T**oggle On/Off, or press F2, to set a breakpoint at that line with no conditions or actions.

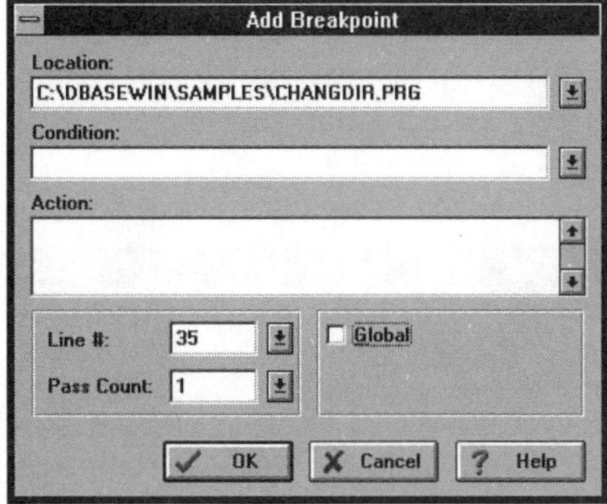

Fig. 27.9
Have dBASE execute a program or change a field value at a breakpoint by specifying a breakpoint action.

In the Module window, the Debugger displays a red highlight bar over each line in which you set a breakpoint. The Break window lists the line number of each breakpoint set. To edit a breakpoint, double-click the breakpoint line in the Break window.

Tip
To set a breakpoint without conditions or actions, move the pointer to the far left of the desired line. After the pointer changes to a hand, click.

The Add Breakpoint dialog box contains the following options:

- The *Location* text box identifies the name of the program that contains the breakpoint. This option does not apply to global breakpoints. (See the ***G**lobal* check box.)

- The *Condition* text box specifies an expression or condition at which to pause execution.

- The *Action* text box instructs the Debugger to perform an action when it reaches the breakpoint.
- The *Line #* drop-down list box specifies the line number of the breakpoint. This option does not apply to global breakpoints. (See the ***G**lobal* check box.)
- The *Pass Count* drop-down list box sets the number of times that the Debugger must reach the breakpoint before pausing execution.
- The ***G**lobal* check box enables you to set a *global breakpoint*, which applies to all lines of the program and any other program that you call.
- The *Expr **T**RUE* option button, which appears only when you have selected the **G**lobal check box (see fig. 27.10), enables you to pause execution whenever the condition that you specified in the Condition box tests true.
- The *Expr **C**hanged* option button, which appears only when you have selected the **G**lobal check box (see fig. 27.10), enables you to pause execution whenever the condition that you specified in the Condition box changes value.

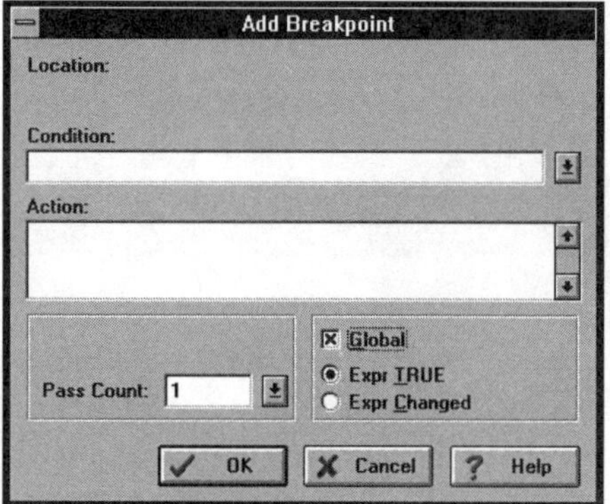

Fig. 27.10
Select the Global check box to pause execution whenever the specified condition occurs anywhere in your program.

Setting Watchpoints

A *watchpoint* enables you to view the changing value of a variable, field, array element, object, or expression as your program executes. To use this feature, you must pause execution. When execution pauses, dBASE updates the watchpoint with the current value.

To set a watchpoint, double-click a blank line in the Watch window or open the **W**atch menu and choose **A**dd. Either action displays the Add Watchpoint dialog box (see fig. 27.11), in which you can set watchpoint conditions and actions. You can also change the value of a watchpoint when execution pauses. Simply open the W**a**tch menu and choose **C**hange, or click the SpeedMenu's **C**hange button, and then enter a new value in the Changing dialog box and click OK or press Enter.

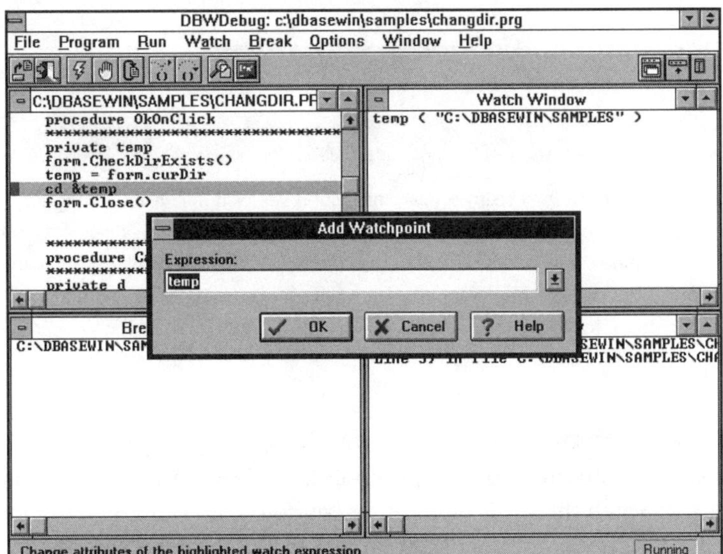

Fig. 27.11
To keep a watch on the values that drive your program, add watchpoints.

Inspecting Values

At any pause in execution, you can inspect values of variables, fields, arrays, objects, or expressions after they have been initialized. To inspect a value at a breakpoint, open the **P**rogram menu and choose **I**nspect, or click the SpeedBar's Inspect button. The Debugger displays the Inspect dialog box (see fig. 27.12). After you type the **N**ame to Inspect, click OK or press Enter. The Debugger displays the current value in the Inspecting dialog box (see fig. 27.13). You can change the value. Press any key to display a Changing dialog box, type the new value, and click OK or press Enter.

Fig. 27.12
Type a value to inspect and then click OK to view the current value.

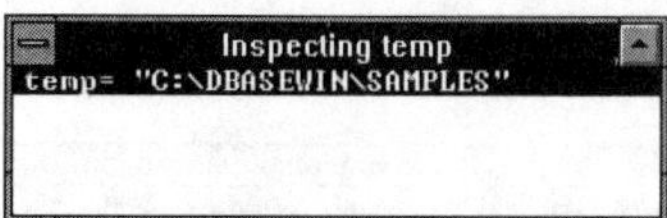

Fig. 27.13
You can change the inspected value and then continue execution.

Note

Although the actions may seem similar, inspecting values differs from setting a watchpoint. Watchpoints do not let you examine the value of arrays or objects, but you can examine these values when you use the Inspect feature. The Inspect feature works only after an item has been initialized, but you can view values at any time when you set watchpoints.

Running a Program in the Debugger

After you load your program, set breakpoints, and set watchpoints, you can sit back and watch the show by running your program from the Debugger. The Debugger provides several ways for you to run the program:

- *Run at full speed*: open the **R**un menu and choose **R**un, click the SpeedBar's Run button, or press F9.
- *Run to the cursor*: open the **R**un menu and choose **G**o to Cursor, or press F4. This runs the program until it reaches the current cursor location.
- *Run until Return*: open the **R**un menu and choose **U**ntil Return. This runs the program until the current routine returns to its caller.
- *Animation*: open the **R**un menu and choose **A**nimate.
- *Trace Into*: open the **R**un menu and choose **T**race Into, click the SpeedBar's Trace button, or press F7.
- *Step Over*: open the **R**un menu and choose St**e**p Over, click the SpeedBar's Step button, or press F8.

Note

Regardless of how you run the program, execution pauses at the breakpoints that you set.

The Animation feature executes the program at the speed that you specify with the **O**ptions menu's **A**nimation Speed command. The Debugger pauses at each command line and updates information in all Debugger windows.

The Trace Into feature executes a program and all lines of any subroutine calls one line at a time. Program execution pauses at the end of each line.

The Step Over feature executes one line at a time. Program execution pauses at the end of each line. Any calls to subroutines are executed as one line; that is, you do not trace the execution line by line into the subroutines.

Tip
To run a program at full speed, or to continue program execution, click the SpeedBar's Run button or press F9.

Troubleshooting

I need to specify parameters at runtime to debug a program properly.

Use the **R**un menu's **P**arameter Arguments command to specify runtime parameters for the program that you are debugging.

I need to test program execution as a variable value changes.

The easiest way to test program execution for various values of a variable is to set a breakpoint and change the value at the breakpoint. Then restart the program from the desired location.

Tip
To stop execution, open the **R**un menu and choose Ter**m**inate. To pause execution temporarily, open the **R**un menu and choose **S**top, or click the SpeedBar's Stop button.

From Here...

Now that you are familiar with how to compile, test, and debug programs, you are ready to learn how to write subroutines. To learn more about writing subroutines, refer to the following chapters:

- Chapter 28, "Writing Program Modules." This chapter builds on what you know about creating dBASE programs and takes you through the process of writing modular programs such as procedures, functions, and codeblocks.

- Chapter 29, "Working with Data." This chapter shows you how to use memory variables and arrays to work with data.

- Chapter 31, "Automating Forms." This chapter takes you through the process of creating and assigning code to object event properties.

Chapter 28

Writing Program Modules

Whether you're using the dBASE for Windows programming language to automate a task in a form, program a button, or create a stand-alone program, you'll probably write code in small, task-specific chunks called modules. The modular approach to programming enables you to share code among programs. For example, suppose that you need a routine that traps and handles record deletions in an employee application. Later you find that you need the same routine in a customer application. By writing generic, independent modules, you can reuse the code and thus speed your development work and reduce program maintenance.

In this chapter, you learn how to do the following:

- Write modular programs
- Create procedures
- Pass information between modules
- Call modules
- Set the scope of a module
- Create statement codeblocks
- Write expression codeblocks

What Is a Program Module?

Modular programming concepts have been around since the late 1960s. Whether your background is spreadsheet macros, C++ programming, or dBASE programming, you have probably been applying modular programming concepts in your work. The main tenet of the modular programming philosophy is that you should break applications down into small, task-oriented components called modules.

A *module* is a block of code that performs a specific task. The small, self-contained nature of modules makes them easy to create, debug, change, and reuse. Applications typically contain many modules that call on each other and share data as needed.

Where Modules Are Created and Stored

Typically, modules are created and stored in program files (.PRG) or in form files (.WFM). In forms, modules usually define how an object reacts to an event. For example, you can write a module to automate the task of finding a record when the user clicks a certain button. Although this and the next few chapters focus on applying basic module and dBASE language skills with program files, remember that the skills are applicable in both program and form files. Chapter 31, "Automating Forms," explains how to apply these skills in the form environment, how to create methods, and how to implement event-driven, object-oriented modules.

Some modules can also be stored in a library. A *library* is simply a program file (.PRG) that contains many modules. Programmers often store generic routines in a library and use them across many applications. A main advantage of storing modules in a library is that you can make many modules available with one call to the library. You also can store all the modules for a particular application in one library, which provides easy access to those modules for ongoing maintenance and design changes.

Tip
Create a toolbox of generic modules by storing them in a program file that you call as a library.

The Different Types of Program Modules

In dBASE for Windows, you can create several different types of programming modules, each of which is described in table 28.1.

Table 28.1 Types of Program Modules

Module Type	Description
Procedure	A module that may or may not return a value.
Function	A module that must return a value.
Statement codeblock	An unnamed module that may or may not return a value.
Expression codeblock	A unnamed module that must return a value.
Method	A module associated with an object through a function pointer. Methods perform actions on an object.

Note

In dBASE for Windows, the term *procedure* refers to procedures and functions. DOS dBASE programmers may find it difficult to get used to this definition. Many of the restrictions and requirements that DOS dBASE places on differentiating these two types of modules do not apply in dBASE for Windows.

If you are used to declaring and using procedures and functions for different purposes, you can continue to do so. dBASE for Windows, however, treats procedures and functions identically. For example, you can call both procedures and functions by using the DO command or the operator parentheses,( ), as in MyModule( ).

This chapter uses the term *procedure* to refer to both procedures and functions.

Tip

If you're not using a library, store application-specific program modules at the bottom of the program file.

▶ "Handling Events," p. 650

▶ "Navigating the Procedure Editor," p. 649

▶ "Programming a Button," p. 652

dBASE for Windows provides several built-in functions (such as the TIME( ) function) that you have probably already used in writing expressions. Custom functions that you create are called *user-defined functions (UDFs).*

Likewise, methods come in two flavors: built-in methods, such as the Move( ) method, perform actions on objects; custom methods are those which you create. This chapter focuses on creating custom functions, procedures, and codeblocks. Chapter 31, "Automating Forms," explains how to create custom methods.

◀ "Using the Expression Builder," p. 283

▶ "Using Custom Controls," p. 652

When you create custom procedures, functions, and methods, you assign names to them. To reuse the code, you can call the named modules from other program modules and objects as needed. Codeblocks do not have names. You usually use codeblocks when you have only a few commands or expressions and do not anticipate that you'll want to reuse the code. For example, you would probably use a codeblock to move a form window to a specific location on the screen.

Creating Procedures

A procedure is a named program module that doesn't have to return a value, although it can.

> **Note**
>
> You cannot call a procedure as an expression in input/output commands such as ? and @..SAY.

To create a procedure, you follow these general steps:

1. Declare the procedure.
2. Name the procedure.
3. Optionally declare parameters.
4. Embed your programming instructions.
5. End the procedure definition and optionally return a value and/or return control to another program module or the Command window.

> **Note**
>
> You cannot declare procedures or functions in the Command window. Using the PROCEDURE or FUNCTION commands in the Command window causes an error. You can create procedures and functions only in program or form files.

Declaring Procedures

Use the dBASE command PROCEDURE to create a procedural program module. The basic syntax is as follows:

```
PROCEDURE yourProcName
     ...your lines of code and comments...
RETURN
```

After the key word PROCEDURE, you provide a procedure name (see the next section, "Naming Procedures," for naming rules). The next code lines consist of your programming instructions and comments. To tell dBASE where this procedure definition ends, you use the key word RETURN. RETURN can return a value to the calling program module, and it can specify a different program file to which to return.

Note

If you prefer to use the DOS dBASE approach of creating user-defined functions (UDFs) rather than procedures that return values, use the FUNCTION command. The syntax is as follows:

```
FUNCTION yourFunctionName
     ...your lines of code and comments...
RETURN
```

Note that functions *must* return a value. All other aspects of procedures described in the following sections (how you name, call, and declare procedures, and how you scope parameters) also apply to functions.

Naming Procedures

Although you can use an unlimited number of characters to name procedures, dBASE for Windows recognizes only the first 32 characters. You can use any combination of letters, numbers, and underscores, but you cannot use spaces or other special characters in procedure names or reserved words. (All dBASE functions and commands are reserved words.)

Caution

Because you can use the command DO to execute both programs and procedures, you should not use the same name for the program file and the procedure.

Note

The naming rules have changed from the DOS versions of dBASE. You are no longer limited to eight- or nine-character names, and the first character doesn't have to be a letter or a number.

Tip

To make names with multiple words easier to read, use underscores in your procedure names or capitalize the first letter of embedded words.

Determining the Maximum Number of Procedures

dBASE gives you access to many more procedures than you will probably ever need to access at one time. Each program file can contain up to 193 procedures, and you can open as many program files (each containing up to 193 procedures) as your system memory allows. In addition, dBASE enables you to open one procedure library, which can contain another 193 procedures.

Using RETURN

The RETURN command serves many purposes. You can use it to signify the end of a procedure, to return a value, and to return control to a specific program module.

The basic syntax of RETURN is as follows:

```
RETURN <expression> <TO MASTER> <TO moduleName> <TO READ>
```

Only the key word RETURN is required. The other elements (called *arguments*)—*expression*, TO MASTER, TO *moduleName*, and TO READ—are optional. Used by itself, RETURN ends the procedure definition and, by default, returns control to the program module that called it. The optional argument *expression* returns an expression that evaluates as a value to the calling module. The argument TO MASTER returns control to the highest-level program module that called this procedure. For example, if procedure A calls procedure B, and procedure B calls procedure C, a RETURN TO MASTER statement returns control to procedure A. (Note, however, that this statement can be hazardous if not used correctly.)

Alternatively, you can use the argument TO followed by the name of a module to which to return control. In the example of procedures A, B, and C, procedure C could return control to another procedure named Z.

The last optional argument to the RETURN command is TO READ, a new feature in dBASE for Windows that is not available in DOS versions of dBASE. The argument TO READ enables you to return control to the last READ command that you issued.

Calling Procedures

To use a procedure, you must first open the file that contains the procedure declaration. If the procedures are stored at the bottom of the current program file, you need only call the procedure using one of the methods described in this section. If the procedures are stored in another program file, use the SET PROCEDURE TO command to open the procedure file.

If the procedures are stored in a library, use the SET LIBRARY TO command to open a library of procedures. Only one library can be open at a time. Libraries offer no clear advantage over procedure files. In fact, when you call procedures, libraries are one of the last places that dBASE looks for them. For this reason, most programmers use procedure files rather than libraries.

By default, dBASE closes all open procedure files before opening another procedure file. To open additional procedure files, without closing currently opened procedure files, use the ADDITIVE key word in your SET PROCEDURE TO statement, as in the following example:

```
SET PROCEDURE TO myProc2 ADDITIVE
```

To close all procedure files, use SET PROCEDURE TO without any options, or use the CLOSE PROCEDURE command to close a specific procedure file:

```
CLOSE PROCEDURE myProc2
```

To close the library, issue the SET LIBRARY TO command without any arguments.

When you call a procedure, dBASE first looks in the program file that calls the procedure. If dBASE doesn't find the procedure, it then looks in the procedure files that were opened with SET PROCEDURE statements. The next place that dBASE looks for the procedure definition is the procedure library that was opened with the SET LIBRARY TO command. Finally, dBASE looks in the current directory for a compiled program (.PRO) or an uncompiled program (.PRG) that has the same name as the procedure that you are calling.

Storing procedures in the program file in which they are used makes maintenance easier, because then all the components of the module are in one place. This storage strategy also shortens the time that it takes dBASE to search for the procedure declaration and thus makes your programs run faster.

Tip

To boost performance, make compiled procedures available to your programs by defining them in the program or in procedure files.

Note

Procedures that you declare in a program are available as long as the program runs.

Using Parameters

You can think of parameters as input to a procedure. Parameters enable procedures to receive data passed by the calling program module. Parameters are optional, and may not always be needed. By declaring parameters in your procedure, however, you can write generic procedures that work with many different values of data. Each time that you run the procedure, you can change the values passed to the procedure to produce different results.

Troubleshooting

The procedure that I created does not work. dBASE simply displays an Alert dialog box that says that the file does not exist.

dBASE cannot find your procedure declaration. For dBASE to have access to a procedure, the procedure must be in the currently running program or form, in a procedure file indicated by the SET PROCEDURE TO command, or in the library indicated by the SET LIBRARY TO command. Check to make sure that any SET commands are at the beginning of your executing program. See the section "Calling Procedures" for more information on where dBASE looks for procedures.

My subroutine does not return a value.

Check for the required RETURN statement and expression argument at the end of your procedure or function. Then use the Debugger to step into the procedure execution. Set a watchpoint for any variables being used. Inspect the value of the expression before, during, and after the subroutine's execution. If applicable, consider whether some other part of the program is interfering with (overwriting) the returned value.

For example, suppose that you are writing a procedure that calculates a discount on a product's list price. Instead of hard coding a list price of $1,000.00, you can set up a parameter. Then, at runtime, you can pass any list price value to the procedure. You could prompt the user for a value, or get the value either from the table currently being browsed or from the form currently being used. In the following example, the procedure discount is passed a parameter value for listPrice. The procedure then calculates the discount and returns the answer to the calling program module.

```
PROCEDURE discount(listPrice)
 salePrice = listPrice - (listPrice*.15)
RETURN
```

The following line calls the discount procedure and returns a salePrice of $850:

```
discount(1000)
```

The process of using parameters is twofold. At the calling program module, you call the procedure providing the appropriate arguments that contain the data being passed down. At the procedure level, the procedure declaration lists parameters that receive the data.

Note

The terms *parameter* and *argument* are often used interchangeably. Either term is adequate for informal usage. Essentially, both parameters and arguments serve the same purpose of providing variable data to do something at runtime. Technically, however, the term *argument* refers to the value provided by the calling program module, and the term *parameter* refers to the values being received by the called program module.

Tip
Declare parameters in your procedures to create generic procedures that work for different values.

Declaring Parameters

Parameters can be any of the following:

- Literal values (numbers, text in quotation marks)
- Fields
- Expressions
- Memory variables

dBASE for Windows provides two approaches for declaring parameters:

▶ "Creating Memory Variables," p. 618

- The call operator: the parentheses, ( )
- The command: PARAMETERS

Depending on the approach that you use, the parameters have a different scope. The term *scope* refers to the availability of the parameter value to other procedures and programs. Parameters declared with the call operator, ( ), have a local scope. Other procedures or programs cannot modify local parameters.

Parameters declared with the command PARAMETERS have a private scope. Private parameters (contrary to the name) can be modified by other procedures and programs. dBASE for Windows supports the PARAMETERS approach for backward compatibility to the DOS versions of dBASE, but the approach is not recommended for future use in dBASE for Windows.

Caution

Wherever possible, avoid using the command PARAMETERS to declare private parameters, because they can result in unintentional overwrites of parameter values. Instead, use the call operator, ( ), to declare local parameters. Other program modules or procedures cannot overwrite local parameters.

Declaring Multiple Parameters

Sometimes you want to pass more than one value to your procedures. You can do so by listing each parameter separated by a comma. Using the call operator, a multiple parameter declaration looks like the following example:

```
PROCEDURE discount(listPrice, disctPercent)
     disctPercent * listPrice
RETURN
```

Using the PARAMETER command, a multiple parameter declaration looks like the following example:

```
PROCEDURE discount
     PARAMETERS listPrice, disctPercent
     disctPercent * listPrice
RETURN
```

Keep in mind that you can list up to 255 parameters. In addition, the number of parameters passed can be fewer or more than the number declared in the procedure. If you send extra parameter values, they are ignored. Missing parameter values are set to the false constant value, .F.

Passing Data to Procedure Parameters

You pass data to procedures at the same time that you call the procedure. For example, in your SALES.PRG program, when you call the discount procedure you would provide the discount percentage and the list price data that the procedure needs to perform its calculation.

dBASE provides two elements that enable you to call the procedure and pass data in the same command statement:

- DO..WITH
- The call operator, ( )

Using DO..WITH

The DO command has an optional key word, WITH, that enables you to pass data to the procedure parameters. With DO..WITH, you can pass to the procedure either the original data or a copy of the original data. When you pass the original data (called *pass by reference*), the procedure can change the original data value. When you pass a copy of the data (called *pass by value*), the procedure cannot change the original data.

To pass the original data value with DO..WITH, you list after the key word WITH the values that you are passing, separating each value with a comma. The following example calls the procedure discount and passes the original values of the memory variables price and percent. The procedure discount can change the value of price or percent.

```
DO discount WITH price, percent
```

To pass a copy of the original data, just place parentheses around the variables that you are passing. The following example calls the procedure discount and passes a copy of the price and percent values. The procedure discount cannot change the value of price or percent.

```
DO discount WITH (price, percent)
```

When you use the call operator (the parentheses) to pass parameter values, the values that you pass to the procedure are *private* to that procedure. When a value is private, changes made to that value in the procedure do not affect the original value. Programmers refer to this method as *pass by value* because you pass the value (not the original data) to the procedure.

Note

When you pass by value, the procedure parameters are actually stored in a different memory address—a physically different place—than the original values. Thus, the procedure parameters and the original values cannot affect each other.

When you pass by reference, the procedure is passed a *reference* to the memory address that contains the original value. Thus, the variable name used in the calling program can differ from the variable name used at the procedure level, but the procedure can still change the original value.

In dBASE, you can pass fields only by value. That is, the procedure cannot change fields that are passed as procedure parameters. When you pass a field as a parameter, dBASE copies the field's value in memory and makes the copy available to the procedure. The actual content of the field is not altered. You can, however, have the procedure return a value and then assign that value to the field in the calling program module.

Using the Call Operator, ( )

To use the call operator, ( ), you change the calling statement as follows:

```
discount(price,percent)
```

If you call a procedure with the call operator, it must return a value.

Creating Codeblocks

Tip
Use codeblocks for one-time, isolated programming needs. Use procedures for more involved, generic routines.

A *codeblock* is an unnamed program module that usually contains only a few command statements or an expression. You use codeblocks primarily when programming form events, although you also can use them in program files. You usually use codeblocks when you have only a few commands or expressions and do not anticipate that you'll need to reuse the code. For example, to move a form window to a specific location on the screen, you would probably use a codeblock.

Codeblock Syntax

Codeblock syntax requires that a codeblock start and end with braces, {}. You prefix each command with a semicolon. The following example programs the Onclick property of an object to open the Customer form:

```
Onclick = {;OPEN FORM Customer}
```

You can also provide more than one command statement, as is shown in the following example, which moves the cursor to the last record:

```
Onclick = {;OPEN FORM Customer ;GO BOTTOM}
```

In addition, you can use program flow control commands such as IF..ENDIF to control execution within a codeblock. The following example uses the IF..ENDIF decision block to determine whether a file exists before using it:

```
Onclick = {;IF FILE(Customer.wfm);OPEN FORM Customer ;GO BOTTOM
          ;ELSE ;missingForm( ) ;ENDIF}
```

Types of Codeblocks

A codeblock that lists commands is called a *statement codeblock*. Statement codeblocks do not have to return a value, although they can.

A codeblock in which you have placed an expression is called an *expression codeblock*. Like an expression, an expression codeblock must return a value. The following example assigns a memory variable, named *discount,* the value of the expression that computes the discount:

```
discount = {listPrice*disctPercent}
```

Tip
Assign codeblocks to memory variables so that you can reuse them in other parts of your program.

Calling Codeblocks

Codeblocks execute when the event to which they are attached executes, or when you call them by using the memory variable to which you assigned them. When you assign a codeblock to a memory variable, you can reuse the codeblock in many locations.

Codeblock Parameters

Codeblocks follow the same parameter and scoping rules as procedures. To declare parameters in a codeblock, use the pipe symbol (¦) to surround the parameter names and place the declaration at the beginning of the codeblock.

The following example assigns values to the variables listPrice and disctPercent. The variable discount is then assigned a codeblock that computes the discount. The fourth line increases the value of listPrice; then, when the codeblock is called in the last line, it recomputes the discount.

```
listPrice = 1000
disctPercent = .10
discount = {¦listPrice, disctPercent¦ listPrice * disctPercent}
listPrice = listPrice + 500
?discount(listPrice,disctPercent) &&Returns 150
```

A Sample Program Module

The CONVERT.PRG sample program module shown in figure 28.1 demonstrates the use of modular programming concepts. This program module is from the dBASE Help topic PARAMETERS. You do not have to retype this sample program. Instead, search for Help on the topic PARAMETERS and click the Example command at the top of the screen. This command opens the example code dialog box, which provides a Copy button. Click the Copy button twice to copy the example to the Clipboard. You can then close the Help screens, if you want. Open the Program Editor for a new program and paste in the sample program. Comment out the top three lines that describe the example, and you're ready to run the sample program.

Some of the modular programming concepts demonstrated in this program module include declaring procedures and parameters and calling a procedure. Note that the procedure call passes a copy of the original data (pass by value) by using the DO..WITH command instead of enclosing the arguments in parentheses. The METRIC procedure uses the PARAMETER command to declare parameters, which makes them local parameters. METRIC uses the command RETURN to denote the end of the procedure, but does not return a value.

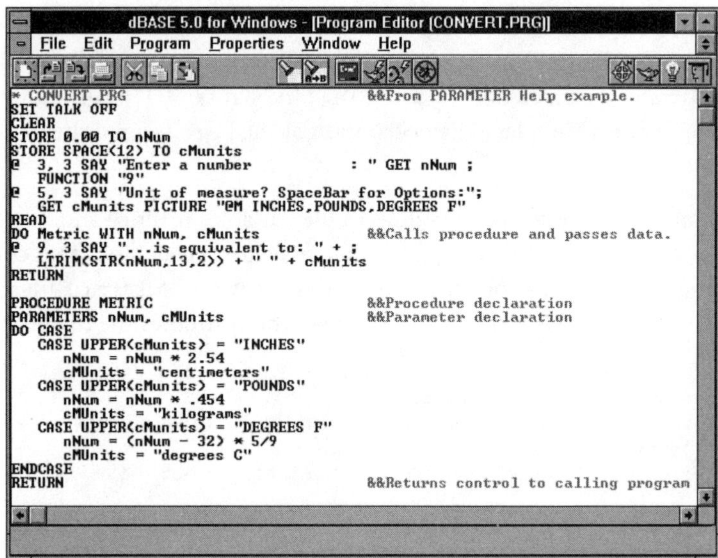
dBASE 5.0 for Windows - [Program Editor (CONVERT.PRG)]
File Edit Program Properties Window Help
* CONVERT.PRG &&From PARAMETER Help example.
SET TALK OFF
CLEAR
STORE 0.00 TO nNum
STORE SPACE(12) TO cMunits
@ 3, 3 SAY "Enter a number : " GET nNum ;
FUNCTION "9"
@ 5, 3 SAY "Unit of measure? SpaceBar for Options:";
GET cMunits PICTURE "@M INCHES,POUNDS,DEGREES F"
READ
DO Metric WITH nNum, cMunits &&Calls procedure and passes data.
@ 9, 3 SAY "...is equivalent to: " + ;
LTRIM(STR(nNum,13,2)) + " " + cMunits
RETURN
PROCEDURE METRIC &&Procedure declaration
PARAMETERS nNum, cMUnits &&Parameter declaration
DO CASE
CASE UPPER(cMunits) = "INCHES"
nNum = nNum * 2.54
cMUnits = "centimeters"
CASE UPPER(cMunits) = "POUNDS"
nNum = nNum * .454
cMUnits = "kilograms"
CASE UPPER(cMunits) = "DEGREES F"
nNum = (nNum - 32) * 5/9
cMUnits = "degrees C"
ENDCASE
RETURN &&Returns control to calling program

Fig. 28.1 Parameters declared for the METRIC procedure enable you to pass various data to METRIC and get different results.

Troubleshooting

The expression codeblock does not update when values change.

For the expression codeblock to re-evaluate the contained expression, it must be called again. Depending on where and how you are using the codeblock, you can have an event (such as the cursor arriving on a field) result in the codeblock being executed again. Otherwise, consider assigning the codeblock to a memory variable and calling the memory variable whenever parameter values change.

A procedure that uses parameters produces unreliable results. Although the data manipulation code is correct, the data returned from the procedure is incorrect.

Either the data input to the procedure is erroneous or some other part of your program is overwriting memory variables used in your procedure. First, check the scope of your parameters. If you used the PARAMETERS key word to declare parameters, they are private and can be overwritten by other modules that have memory variables of the same name. Next, use the Debugger to trace the execution from the source of the parameter values (before they are passed) into the procedure and back to the calling module. Use watchpoints and inspect the values as necessary to locate the source of parameter data corruption.

From Here...

Now that you are familiar with how to create program modules, you are ready to learn how to use them to work with various types of data. To learn more about working with data in program modules, refer to the following chapters:

- Chapter 30, "Working with Data." This chapter builds on what you know about creating dBASE program modules and takes you through the process of using memory variables and arrays to work with data.
- Chapter 31, "Automating Table Tasks." This chapter shows you how to use program modules to manage table data.
- Chapter 32, "Automating Forms." This chapter takes you through the process of working with data in programs using forms. It also explains how to apply certain skills in the form environment, how to create methods, and how to implement event-driven, object-oriented modules.

Chapter 29

Working with Data

When you create a table to store data, you must assign to each category of data (field) a field type such as character, number, or date. In dBASE programming, field types are called *data types*. To work with data stored in tables or data stored temporarily in memory (called *memory variables*), you need to understand and follow the rules governing data types. Data type rules stipulate how you work with data and what a field or memory variable can contain.

dBASE for Windows expands the definition of data beyond the standard field types to include objects and codeblocks. You can create memory variables to manipulate objects (such as a form or a button) and store programming instructions called codeblocks. Data can be information about an event, a record that you print, or a dialog box.

In this chapter, you learn how to do the following:

- Create memory variables
- Declare variable scope
- Create constants
- Create arrays
- Use macro operators
- Save and restore memory variables
- Manipulate various types of data

Working with Memory Variables

A *memory variable* (also called *variable* and *memvar*) is a name that you define to represent a temporary storage area in memory for data. When you create a memory variable, dBASE reserves a spot in memory, labels that spot with the name you provided, and puts whatever data you want in that spot. Variables enable you to make your programs generic. Instead of searching for an exact name *Johnson*, for example, you can ask the user for the name, store it in a variable, and then use that variable to find the data. The contents of a variable can change ("vary") as your application executes. In the name search example, the next time the search routine executes, the user can provide a different name for which to search.

You can create memory variables to store temporarily the following items:

- Data that varies during program execution
- Data that can't change during program execution (called a *constant*)
- A collection of memory variables (called an *array*)
- Programming commands (called a *statement codeblock*)
- An expression (called an *expression codeblock*)

Understanding the Naming Rules

◄ "Creating Codeblocks," p. 610

The following list contains rules for naming variables, arrays, constants, and codeblocks:

- Names can be up to 11 characters long.
- No spaces or tabs are accepted.
- Case does not matter.
- The first character can be a letter or an underline character (but the use of underlines is discouraged; see the accompanying note).
- Subsequent characters can be letters, numbers, ANSI characters, or the following characters:

  $! _

- Names should not be the same as any reserved dBASE words (such as dBASE keywords, commands, objects, events, methods, and properties).

Note

Although you can begin a variable name with an underline character, this use is not recommended because dBASE uses the underline in the names of its built-in memory variables (such as *_app*, a system variable that stores information about the dBASE application).

In addition to following the naming rules, dBASE programmers typically follow certain naming conventions and standards. These guidelines enable dBASE programmers to read each other's code more easily. You should consider the following list of popular naming conventions and establish your own standards across modules and applications:

- Be descriptive. Choose names that describe the variables' contents or purposes (such as *Price* and *inputForm*).
- If the variable works with data in a table, use the same name prefixed with the letter *m* for memory variable (such as *mSSN* for the variable that works with the SSN field).
- Another popular convention for single-letter prefixes is to denote the type of data that the variable can store (such as *wError* to denote this variable as a Window variable).
- Denote the scope of the variable (availability) with a single-letter prefix (such as *lNum* for *local*).

(Remember, these conventions are general guidelines, not rules.)

Note

The dBASE Users Group has issued a report called "Coding Standards and Conventions" that is updated for the new dBASE for Windows. The report adapts the Hungarian notation as outlined by Charles Simonyi of Microsoft Corporation to the dBASE for Windows programming environment. Standard naming and case conventions for all aspects of the dBASE for Windows language, as well as user-defined language elements, are provided. You can obtain this report from the CompuServe dBASE for Windows forum or by contacting your local dBASE users group.

Creating Memory Variables

Tip
Select and consistently follow variable naming conventions throughout your application.

To create a memory variable, you simply assign a value to a variable name. The assignment operator, the equal sign (=), tells dBASE to store the value on the right side in the variable name on the left side of the equal sign. The following statement, for example, stores the number 100 in the variable named X:

```
X = 100
```

This one statement creates the memory variable, reserves a location in memory, labels the location X, and stores the number 100. Note that dBASE automatically determines the data type from the data being stored. Each time you store data in a variable, dBASE analyzes the data type of the data and correctly casts the variable to hold that type of data. You can change the data type of X, for example, by storing character data in X:

```
X="Sun"
```

Note

In dBASE, unlike some programming languages, you don't have to declare variables (except for array variables) before using them.

Variables stay in memory until you close dBASE or until you issue a command to erase memory variables. The RELEASE command releases the variable names that you provide as arguments to the RELEASE command. The CLEAR ALL command releases all variables. The scope of a variable also affects the life of a variable (when it gets released).

Note

You can't store binary, memo, or general (OLE) data in a memory variable. You can store these field types only in a table.

Declaring Memory Variables

In some programming languages, you must declare the variable data type, initial value, and availability (scope) before you use the variable. dBASE doesn't require that you declare memory variables before you use them. But explicitly declaring variable scope and assigning the variable an initial value is considered good programming practice.

Determining Variable Scope

The scope of a memory variable determines

- How long the variable stays in memory (lifespan)
- The availability of the variable to other modules and programs

Table 29.1 describes the different types of variable scopes and the four dBASE commands that you can use to declare variable scope explicitly. By default, undeclared variables created in the Command window are public. Undeclared variables created in a program are private.

Tip

Use local scope (rather than private) to "hide" a variable from other modules.

Table 29.1 Variable Declarations

Declaration Command	Scope	Lifespan
PUBLIC	Global; all modules can access and change the variable.	Lives forever; releases only with RELEASE or CLEAR ALL
PRIVATE	The module that created it, and any modules that module calls, can access and change the variable.	Releases when module that created it ends execution, or when explicitly released/ cleared
LOCAL	Only the module that created it can access and change the variable.	Releases when module that created it ends execution, or when explicitly released or cleared
STATIC	Only the module that created it can access and change the variable.	Lives forever; only releases with RELEASE or CLEAR ALL

In small applications, the default scoping may be sufficient. But in larger applications, scoping improves the modularity and reusability of your work. Declaring a variable scope as local, private, or static offers some protection against having that variable overwritten by another program module in your application.

To declare the variable scope, issue one of the declaration commands listed in table 29.1 followed by the variable name. Here are some examples:

```
PUBLIC nClientID
PRIVATE nSalary
LOCAL dDueDate
STATIC nTaxRate
```

Initializing Variable Values

By default, public and static variables are assigned an initial value of false (.f.) when you declare them. To initialize a variable, assign the variable a value after the declaration statement, as in

```
LOCAL nClientId
nClientId = 100
```

Creating Constants

A *constant* is a memory variable whose value does not change during program execution. Constants provide several advantages over variables. First, constants enable dBASE to generate more efficient code, which makes your application run faster. Second, constants enable you to manage application data in one set place. In a payroll system, for example, you can declare the state withholding tax rate as a constant. Then, if the rate changes next year, you need to change the constant only once rather than in every line of code that uses that piece of data.

◀ "Sending Preprocessor Instructions," p.579

To create a constant, use the preprocessor directive *#define* to declare and initialize the constant. The following example declares nTaxRate as a constant with the value of .15. Then the program uses nTaxRate to compute a withholding tax. When this program is compiled, dBASE replaces all occurrences of the constant nTaxRate with the number .15.

```
#define nTaxRate .15
NetPay = GrossPay - (GrossPay * nTaxRate)
```

Creating Arrays

An *array* is a collection of memory variables. Arrays enable you to work with sets of data. Arrays can be one-dimensional or multidimensional. Arrays are like spreadsheets; the data is organized into rows and columns. One-dimensional arrays have one column and many rows of information. Multi-dimensional arrays have many columns and many rows of information.

Before you can store data in an array, you need to declare the array, using the DECLARE command. When you declare the array, you tell dBASE how many rows and columns you expect to store in the array. Note that you can always expand the array to add more rows and columns later, as needed. The following example declares a one-dimensional array consisting of ten array elements (memory variables), enabling you to store and work with ten items of data:

```
DECLARE [payScale,10]
```

Note the use of brackets around the argument.

To create a multi-dimensional array, you need to provide the number of rows and the number of columns. In the following example, the array named payScale is defined as having 10 rows and 5 columns, storing a total of 50 data elements:

```
DECLARE payScale [10,5]
```

When you declare an array, dBASE assigns a default initial value of false (.f.) to each array element (you can think of an array element as a cell in a spreadsheet).

Tip
Use the ASIZE() command to increase or decrease the array size. For example, ASIZE(payScale,2,1) adds 2 rows and 1 column to the payScale array.

Tip
Use the command AFILL() to assign a value quickly to some or all array elements. For example, AFILL (payScale,100,5,1) assigns the value 100 to the fifth element of the array payScale.

> **Note**
>
> A single array can contain many different types of data: numbers, characters, dates, or any other data type that a memory variable can store.

To refer to an array element, you need to provide its address. An array element's address can be either the cell number (called the *element number*) or the row and column location (called the *subscript*). As you can see in figure 29.1, the first cell has an element number of 1 and a subscript of [1,1].

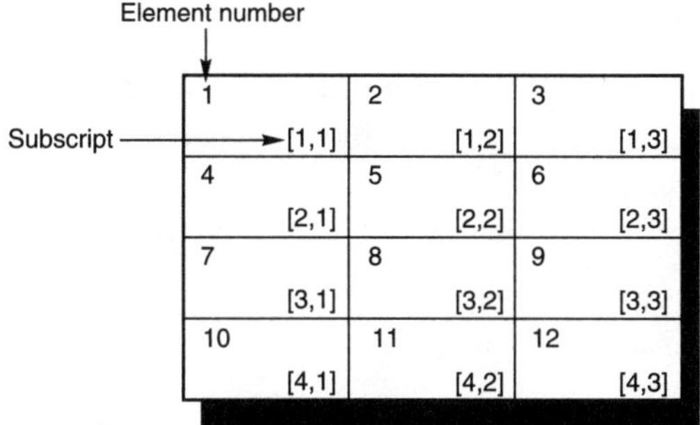

Fig. 29.1
An array is like a spreadsheet, in which data resides in rows and columns.

To assign a value by using the element number, your dBASE statement would look like this example:

```
payScale[1] = 25000
```

To assign a value by using the element subscripts, your dBASE statement would look like this example:

```
payScale[1,1] = 30000VAL
```

dBASE provides many commands and functions to help you manipulate and work with arrays. For a complete list, search for the topic "Memory Variables Language Elements" in the Help system.

> **Caution**
>
> Certain dBASE array functions and commands require that you use the element number, and others require you to provide the element subscripts. Always be sure to check for the syntax requirements in the Help system by searching for help on that command.

Using Macro Operators

Sometimes you need to use a variable as an argument to a dBASE command that is looking for real data. The SET FILTER command, for example, is looking for specific criteria (such as a field name to equal a value), not a variable name. In these cases, you need to use the macro operator & to substitute the data for the variable name upon execution.

In the following example, the macro operator is used to substitute the value of the variable cFilter upon execution of the SET FILTER command:

```
cFilter = 'State_Prov = "CA"'
SET FILTER TO &cFilter
```

When the command statement includes more keywords or arguments after the macro operator variable, use a period (called the macro terminator) to signify the end of the variable name. In the following example, the INDEX command uses two macro expansion variables, and the first one uses the macro terminator:

```
cIndex = "State_Prov"
cTag = "State"
INDEX ON &cIndex. TAG &cTag
```

Generally, you need to use the macro operator only in situations where you want to use a variable as a command argument. The variable you expand can contain command keywords such as IF, FOR, or WHILE.

Caution

You can't use macro operators on local or static variables or on field names. Furthermore, because macro operators expand only at runtime, you can't use macro operators for preprocessor directives.

Saving and Restoring Variables

By nature, variables are temporary. dBASE reserves a temporary space in memory for you to work with data in memory. When your program ends, or when you explicitly request it, variables are removed from memory. But you can decide at any time to save memory variables to a file. This type of file is handy for information such as a user's printer settings or other program configuration items.

Use the SAVE command to save some or all memory variables to a file. In the following example, dBASE creates a memory file called MARYCNF.MEM and stores all memory variables in that file:

```
SAVE TO MARYCNF
```

Caution

You can't store function pointers, system memory variables, or object reference variables to a memory file.

To load the saved memory variables back into memory, issue the RESTORE command. In the following example, dBASE loads the contents of the MARYCNF.MEM file into memory:

```
RESTORE FROM MARYCNF
```

By default, restored memory variables are cast as private in scope. To assign a different scope, add the keyword ADDITIVE to the end of the RESTORE command, and declare the scope before restoring the variables. The following command lines give you an example:

```
PUBLIC marysPrinter
RESTORE FROM MARYCNF ADDITIVE
```

The first line declares the scope, and the second line restores the variables.

Troubleshooting

When I use the macro operator for the following code, I get a variable undefined error message.

```
cName = "David"
LOCATE FOR Name = &cName
```

Not all dBASE commands need the macro operator before a variable name. The LOCATE command enables you to use the variable name without a macro operator. Remove the ampersand (&), and the LOCATE command should return the record number if the name is located. Add ;DISPLAY to the end of your LOCATE statement to see all information stored in the found record.

I created a memory variable to store input from the user. But each time the routine runs, the memory variable seems to retain the value from the last execution.

Your problem seems to indicate that you declared the variable as public or static. You can change the scope to private or local, and the memory variable is automatically cleared each time the module that created the memory variable finishes executing. Otherwise, you need to issue the RELEASE command for that variable name, or use CLEAR ALL if you need to remove all variables from memory.

Exploring Data Types

When you build tables in "interactive" dBASE for Windows, you define the type of data that a field can contain, called the *field type*. In dBASE for Windows programming, you work with data in tables and data stored in memory variables. The field types are expanded into a larger, more diverse set of information types called *data types*. Table 29.2 lists and describes the basic data types.

Note

Number, date, time, and currency formats default to the Windows Control Panel settings. You can override Control Panel settings by altering DBASEWIN.INI or by issuing the appropriate SET command (such as SET CURRENCY).

Table 29.2 dBASE Data Types

Symbol	Data Type	Description
C	Character	Alphanumeric data
M	Memo	Available only in dBASE tables; alphanumeric data
D	Date	Dates
F	Float	Numeric data with or without a decimal point
L	Logical	T, F, Y, or N for True, False, Yes, or No
N	Numeric	Fixed point with or without a decimal point
B	Binary	Available only in dBASE tables; images, sounds, and user-defined data
G	OLE	Available only in dBASE tables; OLE documents
O	Object	Available only for variables; creates object handle
BM	Bookmark	Available only for variables; stores a record pointer
CB	Codeblock	Available only for variables; stores commands or an expression
FP	Function Pointer	Available only for variables; stores the location of a function

Manipulating Character Data

Character data, sometimes called text or string data, is the most common type of data stored in databases. dBASE provides many functions and commands that assist you in working with and manipulating character data. For a complete list of functions and commands that work with character data, search for Help on the topic "String Data Language Elements."

The following sections highlight some of the commonly used string commands and functions.

Changing Case

One of the most common tasks in manipulating text data is the need to change the case from upper- to lowercase or to proper noun format. dBASE provides the following functions for this task:

- UPPER( )
- LOWER( )
- PROPER( )

Combining these functions with the REPLACE command, you can change all the data in a particular field. Suppose, for example, that you downloaded a client list from the mainframe, and the list is all in capital letters. After you import it into your table, you could use the following type of statement to change each field to proper format:

```
REPLACE ALL City WITH PROPER(City)
```

Combining Strings

Another common need is to concatenate (combine) two or more strings into one longer string. You use the + operator to add, or append, strings. You use the – operator to remove extra spaces from the string on the left before appending it to the string on the right. In the following example, both operators are used. Notice that the – operator removes any extra spaces after the first name so that all names listed have just one space between the first and last names.

```
LIST OFF First -" "+Last+" - "+AcctNo
```

Extracting String Subsets

Sometimes you need to extract a certain section of characters embedded within a string. Suppose, for example, that you need only the area code part of a phone number field. dBASE provides the following functions that extract data from strings:

- LEFT( ) extracts from the left.
- RIGHT( ) extracts from the right.
- SUBSTR( ) extracts from any position.

The following section of code gives you an example of each function:

```
mPhone = "201-565-1000"
?LEFT(mPhone,3)              &&Returns 201
?RIGHT(mPhone,4)             &&Returns 1000
?SUBSTR(mPhone,5,3)          &&Returns 565
```

Manipulating Numerical Data

Numeric data can be a fixed-point number (N) or floating-point number (F). The numeric (N) data type is usually used for dollar values that require precision and no rounding errors. The floating (F) data type is usually used for scientific calculations and very small or very large numbers.

dBASE provides many functions and commands that assist you in working with and manipulating numerical data. For a complete list of functions and commands that work with numeric data, search for help on the topic "Numeric Data Language Elements."

The following sections highlight some of the commonly used numeric commands and functions.

Making Financial Calculations

dBASE provides several functions to assist in financial calculations such as calculating loan payments or the present value of an investment:

- FV( ) returns a float that is the future value of an investment.
- PV( ) returns a float that is the present value of an investment.
- PAYMENT( ) returns the periodic amount required to repay a debt.

The following section of code gives you an example of using the PAYMENT( ) function to compute a monthly mortgage payment:

```
Principal = 100000
Interest = .08
NoYears = 30
AmtDue = PAYMENT(Principal, Interest/12, 12*NoYears)
?AmtDue Function "$"          &&Returns $733.76
```

Extracting Integers and Rounding Numbers

Other common tasks when working with numbers include extracting the integer portion of a number (sometimes referred to as *truncating*) and rounding numbers. dBASE provides several functions to assist you in these tasks:

- CEILING( ) returns the nearest integer that is greater than or equal to a specified number.

- FLOOR( ) returns the nearest integer that is less than or equal to a specified number.
- INT( ) returns the integer portion of a specified number.
- ROUND( ) rounds the number to a specified number of decimal places.

The following command lines give examples of what each function returns, given the number 2.49:

```
myNum = 2.49
?CEILING(myNum,1)          &&Returns 2.50
?FLOOR(myNum)              &&Returns 2.00
?INT(myNum)                &&Returns 2.00
?ROUND(myNum)              &&Returns 3.00
```

Making Statistical Calculations

dBASE provides a full range of statistical functions to assist in the calculation of logarithms, square roots, pi, exponents, and absolute values. Some of the most commonly used statistical functions are described in the following list:

- ABS( ) returns the absolute value of a number.
- EXP( ) returns the exponential value.
- LOG( ) returns the natural log.
- LOG10( ) returns the log base 10.
- MAX( ) returns the higher of two numbers.
- MIN( ) returns the lower of two numbers.
- MOD( ) returns the remainder (modulus) of one number divided by another.
- PI( ) returns the approximate value of pi.
- RANDOM( ) generates a random number.
- SIGN( ) returns the sign (+ or –).
- SQRT( ) returns the square root of a number.

The following examples illustrate using financial functions:

```
myNum = -100
?SIGN(myNum)          &&Returns -
?MAX(myNum,2)         &&Returns 2
?ABS(myNum)           &&Returns 100
?SQRT(144)            &&Returns 12
```

> **Note**
>
> dBASE also provides trigonometric functions, formatting functions, and other numeric manipulation functions. For more information on these dBASE functions, search for help on the topic "Numeric Data."

Manipulating Date and Time Data

Dates and times give the rest of the data in a record perspective. Often, users want to see records for a specific period. dBASE stores dates in numeric format. This format enables you to add or subtract a number of days or years to a date. Although dBASE doesn't provide a time data type, you can store time data as a string, using the character data type. For example, you can compute the elapsed number of hours between two times. In the following example, the ELAPSED function computes the number of hours worked based on string data supplied in a specific format. This dBASE statement returns a value of eight hours worked:

```
ELAPSED("09:00","17:00")/-3600
```

For a complete list of functions and commands that work with date and time data, search for Help on the topic "Date and Time Data Language Elements."

The following sections highlight some of the commonly used date and time commands and functions.

Working with Dates

Many of the date functions enable you to determine the number or word that represents the day, month, year, or century with which you need to work:

- DAY( ) returns the day number.
- MONTH( ) returns the month number.
- YEAR( ) returns the century and year number.
- DATE( ) returns the current system date.
- CDOW( ) and DOW( ) return the day of the week as a word or number, respectively.
- DMY( ) and MDY( ) return the date formatted as DD Month YY or Month DD, YY, respectively.

The following commands give some examples of using date functions:

```
myDate={9/1/94}
?DAY(myDate)            &&Returns 1
?MONTH(myDate)          &&Returns 9
?YEAR(myDate)           &&Returns 1994
?CDOW(myDate)           &&Returns Thursday
?DMY(myDate)            &&Returns 1 September 94
```

Working with Times

The dBASE time functions enable you to determine the current system time, track the seconds elapsed, and calculate the time elapsed between two times:

- TIME( ) returns the current system time.
- SECONDS( ) returns the number of seconds elapsed since 12:00 a.m.
- ELAPSED( ) returns the time elapsed between two specified times.

The following example illustrates how to use the ELAPSED function to determine the number of hours worked:

```
cStart = "09:00:00"
cEnd = "17:00:00"
ELAPSED(cEnd,cStart)/3600      &&Returns 8.00
```

Troubleshooting

I need to index a table based on a date and an amount, two variables of different data types.

The INDEX command is looking for character (string) arguments. You need to convert the date and numerical variables to the string data type and use string concatenation to add the two strings together, as in this example:

```
INDEX ON DTOS(myDate)+STR(myAmt,5,2) TO DateAmt
```

For a complete list of data conversion functions, search for Help on the topic "Expression and Type Conversion."

The date variables that I have created appear as numbers, and the dollar amounts appear without currency punctuation.

In dBASE for Windows, the display of numbers and dates is controlled by the Windows Control Panel. You can either make your changes in the Control Panel or override the Windows defaults in dBASE. Open the **P**roperties menu, choose **D**esktop Properties, and change the defaults in the Country tab, which is stored in the DBASEWIN.INI file. Your other option is to use the SET commands to set these attributes from within your program.

From Here...

Now that you are familiar with creating memory variables and working with various types of data, you are ready to learn how to automate table-based tasks. To learn more on working with table data, refer to the following chapters:

- Chapter 30, "Automating Table Tasks." This chapter builds on what you know about working with data and takes you through the process of manipulating tables and their data.
- Chapter 31, "Automating Forms." This chapter takes you through the process of working with table data by using forms.
- Chapter 32, "Automating Other Database Tasks." This chapter shows you how to automate query, printing, and import/export tasks.

Chapter 30

Automating Table Tasks

In database applications, tables are the hub of the wheel, the center of activity. All other functions and actions seem to revolve around the table and its data. Not surprisingly, often the first priority in creating a database application is to automate table tasks.

Common actions such as opening and closing tables, moving between records, and locating records can be automated for the user. This chapter concentrates on the conventional (structured) programming techniques to automate table tasks. In the next chapter, you explore the object-oriented, event-driven approach. Keep in mind, though, that you can use the commands you learn in this chapter in the forms environment as well.

In this chapter, you learn how to do the following:

- Create tables
- Open and close tables
- Navigate records
- Add, delete, and edit records
- Locate records

Manipulating Tables

dBASE enables you to create tables and to open, close, and modify a table's structure from within a program. Tables, as you know from using dBASE interactively, consist of a DBF file and any associated DBT (memo) files. The term *database* refers to the directory where your tables, forms, and so on for an application reside.

Opening and Closing a Table

To work with a table, you must first open the table by issuing the USE command. Opening a table tells dBASE to load the contents of the table into memory. When a table is open, you can access and manipulate the data it contains.

Opening a table doesn't display the table. To display the table, issue the BROWSE command. In the following example, the Customer table is opened by the USE command and displayed to the user in a Table Browse window by the BROWSE command:

```
USE Customer
BROWSE
```

Tip
Use the optional keyword EXCLUSIVE with the USE command when opening tables on a network file server to prevent other users from accessing the table while you work on it.

Because open tables take up precious memory, you should always close tables when you are done working with them. By issuing the USE command without specifying a table name, you close the open table. The CLOSE ALL and CLOSE TABLES commands close all open tables in all work areas. When you exit dBASE, all tables are automatically closed, but explicitly closing tables at the end of your application is considered a good programming practice. (For more information, see the next section, "Using Work Areas.")

Using Work Areas

By default, dBASE is a one-table-at-a-time environment. If you open the Customer table with USE and then issue a BROWSE command, for example, the Customer table appears on-screen. If you then open the Animals table, dBASE closes the Customer table before loading the Animals table into memory. The next BROWSE command displays the Animals table.

dBASE does enable you to open another instance of a table or to open more than one table. But you need to create and manage (select and switch between) work areas. A *work area* is a location in memory that dBASE reserves for an open table and its associated files. Every table that you open needs its own work area. You can have up to 225 work areas open at once.

Tip
To work on more than one table at a time, use work areas.

To create a work area, use the SELECT command. You can name a work area by using a number from 1 to 225, a letter from A to J, or an alias name for the table. The best approach is to use table names or alias names in the SELECT command because then you're not tied to an exact work area number or letter. This method also makes your code easier to read and manage.

You also can use the SELECT( ) function to have dBASE fill in the next available work area number for you, or fill in the work area of the alias provided within the parentheses. Another handy function is the ALIAS( ) function, which returns the alias name associated with a work area.

In the following example, all work areas are cleared. Then, the Customer table is opened into the next available work area (1). The Animals table is opened into the next available work area (2). The BROWSE command displays the table in the first work area. Then the program selects the second work area, which contains the Animals table. The last BROWSE command displays the Animals table.

```
CLOSE ALL
USE Customer IN SELECT( )
USE Animals IN SELECT( )
BROWSE
SELECT Animals
BROWSE
```

Although you could obtain the same functionality by using work area numbers or letters, the approach outlined in the preceding example results in portable code that you can reuse in any work area's environment (just delete or comment out the CLOSE ALL command to insert this code into an existing work area's structure).

Working with a Database

A database in dBASE refers to a location of the database files such as tables and their associated files. A database can be the location of an SQL database or a directory on your hard disk or file server. Interactively, you can change the directory whenever you open a file. And you can create database aliases by using the IDAPI configuration utility. With the exception of the STANDARD DATABASE you specified in IDAPI, you must open a database before you can access its tables.

dBASE provides several commands to help you manage databases: OPEN DATABASE, CLOSE DATABASES, and SET DATABASE. Issue the OPEN DATABASE command to open a database using the name created in IDAPI. Use CLOSE DATABASES to close a specific database, or use the keyword ALL to close all open databases. Use SET DATABASE to select an open database with which to work. If you have multiple databases open, you must use SET DATABASE to tell dBASE which database to look for in the table or other file on which you want to work.

Creating a Table

From a dBASE programming module, you can launch the Table Designer for a table name or create a table by copying the structure of an existing table. To launch the Table Designer, use the CREATE command. In the following example, dBASE opens the Table Design window for a new table called RENTALS.DBF:

```
CREATE RENTALS
```

To create a table by using the structure of another table, add the keyword FROM to the CREATE statement and specify the name of a table definition file. (You can create a table definition file by issuing the COPY TO <filename> STRUCTURE EXTENDED command.) In the following example, the structure of the Customer table is copied to a table called *Struct*. The Struct table is then opened and viewed for editing before it is used to create the new table Employees.

```
USE Customer                          &&Opens the Customer table
COPY TO Struct STRUCTURE EXTENDED     &&Copies the structure to a
                                        new table called Struct
USE Struct                            &&Opens the new Struct table
BROWSE                                &&Displays the table for editing
CREATE Employees FROM Struct          &&Creates the new table Employees,
                                        using the structure in Struct.
```

Alternatively, you could copy the structure and create the table with one command, COPY STRUCTURE. To use this command, you must open the table from which you want to copy the structure before issuing the COPY STRUCTURE command.

```
USE Customer
COPY STRUCTURE TO Employees
```

The COPY STRUCTURE command enables you to specify which fields to include and what type of table you want to create. After the file name, you can list the type of table and fields to include.

Note

By default, dBASE creates new tables by using the table DBASE. You can, as an argument to CREATE, COPY STRUCTURE, or COPY STRUCTURE EXTENDED, specify a different table type such as Paradox.

Modifying Table Structure

After a table is created, you may need to modify the table structure. dBASE provides several commands to assist you in modifying a table's structure.

Use LIST STRUCTURE to display information about a table's structure, the number of records, and the table type. By default, the structure information displays in the Results pane of the Command window. You can, however, output the structure listing to a file or to the printer. In the following example, the structure of the Clients table is saved to a text file named STRUCT.TXT:

```
USE Clients
LIST STRUCTURE TO FILE Struct
```

Use the MODIFY STRUCTURE command to launch the Table Designer and interactively change a table's structure. To modify a table's structure completely under programming control, use the COPY TO STRUCTURE EXTENDED and CREATE FROM commands discussed previously in the "Creating a Table" section.

Renaming, Copying, and Deleting Tables

dBASE provides many commands to rename, copy, and delete tables (see table 30.1). Before using any of these commands, be sure to make a backup copy of the table, and proceed with caution. Nothing can ruin your day more than deleting a critical table when you haven't made a backup.

Table 30.1 Renaming, Copying, and Deleting Tables

Command	Description
RENAME	Assigns a new name to any file
RENAME TABLE	Assigns a new name to a table and any associated files
COPY	Copies an entire table or selected records or fields
COPY TABLE	Copies a table and any associated files
COPY FILE	Copies any type of file
DELETE TABLE	Deletes a table and any associated files
DELETE FILE	Deletes any type of file
ERASE	Erases a file from disk

Troubleshooting

When I erase the PURGE table, I still have DBT memo files on the hard disk.

To delete a table and its associated files, use the DELETE TABLE command rather than ERASE. The ERASE and DELETE FILE commands erase only the named file from the hard disk.

I can't get BROWSE to work.

BROWSE displays the currently open table in the current work area in a Table Browse window. First check to be sure that the table you want to display has been opened with the USE command. Next, verify that you are in the correct work area. Try typing the BROWSE command into the Command window to see whether it works outside the spectrum of your program. Lastly, use the Debugger to trace execution, making sure that the appropriate lines of code are executing as expected.

Navigating a Table

After a table is opened and displayed in a Browse window, you can use dBASE commands to move around in the table. Often you need to determine which record you want to change, or you want to display a certain record based on user input. dBASE provides commands that enable you to move forward and backward in a table, go to a specific record, and determine the number, type, or name of fields in a table.

Determining Where You Are

To determine the record number of the record in which you are currently working, use the RECNO( ) function. RECNO( ) returns the current record number of the active table in the current or specified work area (specify the work area in the parentheses).

To determine whether the record pointer is currently at the beginning of a table, use BOF( ). And to find out whether you're at the end of the table, use EOF( ). Both BOF( ) and EOF( ) enable you to specify a work area in the parentheses.

Moving between Records

dBASE provides two commands to help you move between records: SKIP and GO. SKIP moves the current record pointer forward or backward in the current or alias table. Using SKIP without an argument moves the pointer one record at a time.

In the following example, SKIP moves down 10 records in the alias work area Customer. Then the record pointer backs up five records.

```
SKIP(10) IN Customer
SKIP(-5)
```

Caution

If you issue a SKIP command beyond the end of the table or beyond the beginning of the table, SKIP returns an error. To avoid this problem, use EOF( ) and BOF( ) to test for these conditions.

The GO command (optionally called GOTO) moves the record pointer to a specific location in the table. GO has the following options:

- GO BOTTOM moves the record pointer to the last record.
- GO TOP moves the record pointer to the first record.
- RECORD <#> moves the record pointer to the specified record number, where # is the record number and the keyword RECORD is optional.
- <bookmark> moves the record pointer to the specified marker. (Bookmarks are used instead of record numbers for tables that do not support record numbers.)

In the following example, the record pointer is moved to the top, to the bottom, and finally to the 20th record:

```
USE Clients
GO TOP
GO BOTTOM
GO 20
```

In the next example, the record pointer moves to the fifth record, and then the BOOKMARK command is used to move the record pointer to the specified bookmark:

```
GO 5
X = BOOKMARK( )
GO X
? RECNO( )
```

Automating Data-Entry Tasks

Tip
When you open the table with USE, add the optional keyword NOUPDATE to prevent users from altering, deleting, or recalling any records in the table.

Every day, thousands of records are added, changed, and deleted, and dBASE provides many interactive tools to assist data-entry users in performing these basic tasks. Depending on the environment, the data, and the users, though, you may need to manage these tasks in a program. The next few sections explore the dBASE commands and functions that add, edit, and delete records.

Adding Records

The most popular way to add records to a table is the APPEND command. APPEND adds a new record and displays the new record in a window, ready for data entry. Figure 30.1 shows the new record created by the following commands:

▶ "Automating Forms," p. 645

```
USE Clients
APPEND
```

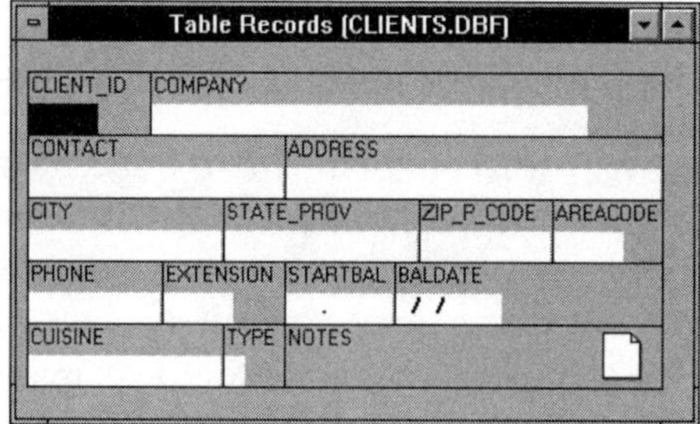

Fig. 30.1
Issuing the APPEND command for an open table adds a new record and displays it, ready for data entry.

APPEND BLANK adds a new record at the end of the table and moves the record pointer to that new record but does not display the new record for data entry. Use APPEND BLANK when you need to enter data behind the scenes, from within the program, by using the REPLACE command. Use APPEND when you want the user to enter the new data.

In the following example, a new client record is added, and the company name, Acme Trucking, is entered into the record by the program. BROWSE displays all table records, with the pointer still on the new record.

```
USE Clients
APPEND BLANK
REPLACE Company WITH "Acme Trucking"
BROWSE
```

Note

You also can add new records by using the INSERT command, which inserts a new record after or before the current record position. But INSERT is rarely used because it requires that you reorganize the table or its index every time you add a new record.

Editing Records

If you want to allow the user to edit records in Browse layout, use the BROWSE command. If you want to allow the user to edit in Form layout, use the EDIT command. To allow the user to edit in Columnar layout, issue the EDIT COLUMNAR command.

Both EDIT and BROWSE provide you with an assortment of optional arguments to customize your table-editing session. The following list describes the most commonly used options:

- SCOPE specifies the number of records to browse or edit.
- FOR restricts BROWSE or EDIT to records that meet the specified condition.
- WHILE browses or edits until the specified condition is met.
- COLOR specifies the color scheme of the Browse or Edit window.
- COMPRESS reduces the number of rows used to display field names, making more room to display an extra record.
- FIELDS specifies the fields to include in the Browse or Edit window.
- FREEZE restricts editing to the specified field.
- NOAPPEND prevents the user from adding new records.
- NODELETE prevents the user from marking records for deletion.
- NOEDIT or NOMODIFY prevents the user from editing in Browse or Edit windows.
- NOFOLLOW keeps the cursor at the record location when the key field changes. Without this option, the cursor follows the record to its new location based on the new key value.
- NOMENU hides the **B**rowse or **E**dit menu.

- NOTOGGLE prevents the user from toggling between Browse and Edit mode.
- TITLE displays the window title as specified.

In the following example, the Company and Phone fields of the Clients table are displayed in an Edit window. Note that the user cannot delete any records or add any records. Figure 30.2 shows the resulting Edit window.

```
USE Clients
EDIT FIELDS Company, Phone NOAPPEND NODELETE
CLOSE Clients
```

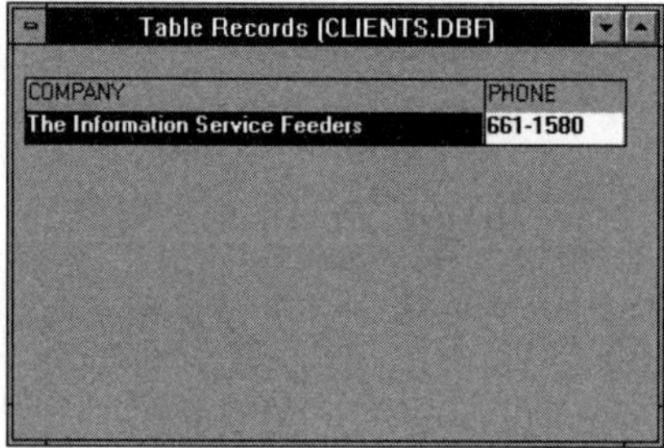

Fig. 30.2 With EDIT and BROWSE command options, you can specify which fields display and which fields can be edited.

Deleting Records

Record deletion in dBASE tables requires two steps:

1. Use the DELETE command to mark a record for deletion.
2. Use the PACK command to remove marked records permanently.

> **Caution**
>
> Be careful with Paradox and SQL tables. The DELETE command immediately and permanently removes records from Paradox and SQL tables. Furthermore, you can't restore deleted records. Your best bet is to use transaction processing (see Chapter 31, "Automating Forms") to verify deletions before committing the deletion to a Paradox or SQL table.

By default, dBASE includes in a table even those records marked for deletion. When you issue a BROWSE command, for example, dBASE lists all records, including those marked for deletion. You can control this situation with the SET DELETED command. The default for SET DELETED is OFF, which means that all records appear in the table. If you issue the command SET DELETED ON, dBASE excludes records marked for deletion.

At any time before issuing the PACK command, you can remove the deletion marker by using the RECALL command. Both DELETE and RECALL enable you to specify records by record number, a range of records, or all records. You also can specify that the DELETE or RECALL applies to all records that meet a FOR condition or to all records until they meet a WHILE condition.

In the following example, all NJ records are deleted:

```
USE Clients                     &&Opens Clients table
DELETE FOR State_Prov = "NJ"    &&Marks all NJ records for deletion
PACK                            &&Deletes all marked records
```

Locating Records

Finding a record quickly in a large database can be a harrowing experience, especially if you are not exactly sure of the name or number for which you are looking. Interactively, dBASE provides the **T**able **F**ind Record command to assist users in locating data. Often, in programming, you need to find records to complete a programming task. dBASE provides several record-search commands:

Tip
If you need to delete all records from a table, quickly use the ZAP command.

- LOCATE enables you to search for specified data in a table, record by record, without using an index.
- SEEK enables you to search for specified data in an indexed table.
- FIND is provided for dBASE III compatibility and enables you to search in indexed tables.

The easiest and, in small tables, the most efficient command is LOCATE. LOCATE is also the most flexible because it accepts expressions of any data type as input and searches any field of a table. The following example illustrates the use of LOCATE to find a customer's phone number:

```
USE Clients
LOCATE FOR Company = "Micro International"
IF FOUND( )
       DISPLAY FIELDS Company, Phone
ELSE
       ?"Company not found."
ENDIF
```

Use SEEK or FIND to speed up searches and to search in large tables. Because both commands use an index to find information quickly (like using the index to a book), you need to issue the INDEX command to create an index for the table before using SEEK or FIND. SEEK provides greater flexibility than

FIND because SEEK accepts dBASE expressions as well as character and numeric input in the specification of the values of the key expression.

You also can use the function SEEK( ) to perform a SEEK operation and return True (.T.) if the record was found or False (.F.) if the record was not found. The following example uses SEEK( ) to find a customer's phone number:

```
USE Clients
INDEX ON Company TAG Co
IF FoundIt = SEEK("Micro International")
       DISPLAY FIELDS Company, Phone
ELSE
       ?"Company not found."
ENDIF
```

Troubleshooting

When I add records to a table that is using an index, the record pointer keeps moving with the new record to its index location.

With APPEND and INSERT, the record pointer follows the added record to its proper position in the index order. To keep the record pointer in the same place, use the NOFOLLOW option when you open the Browse or Edit window.

I need to enter data in a field for the user.

Open the table, move to or locate the appropriate record, then use the REPLACE command to enter data into the field(s). You also could use a SCAN..ENDSCAN block to enter or change data in a field for records meeting a specific condition.

From Here...

Now that you are familiar with working with tables and table data, you are ready to learn how to automate forms. To learn more about forms and automating other database tasks, refer to the following chapters:

- Chapter 31, "Automating Forms." This chapter builds on what you know about working with data and tables and takes you through the process of automating database tasks by using event-driven, object-oriented forms.

- Chapter 32, "Automating Other Database Tasks." This chapter shows you how to automate query, printing, and import/export tasks.

Chapter 31

Automating Forms

The newest and most exciting feature of dBASE for Windows is the introduction of event-driven, object-oriented forms. Instead of writing lines of code to create and display a screen or window, you can interactively design forms complete with push buttons and pull-down menu bars. You can view and modify the code that the Form Designer creates. You can even create a form, and form objects, directly from code.

Forms and the objects that they contain respond to events based on built-in dBASE code. As a dBASE programmer, you can hook into the event engine and attach your own custom event-handling routine. Your event processing can be in addition to, used instead of, or modify the built-in handling of that event by dBASE.

This chapter introduces you to programming with forms. It touches on the fringes of what is possible in object-oriented programming. The goal here is to provide a solid foundation in core concepts and show you how to automate common database tasks, using dBASE for Windows forms. Advanced object-oriented skills such as creating classes are beyond the scope of this introductory level.

In this chapter, you learn how to do the following:

- View and edit form programs
- Navigate the Procedure Editor
- Program a button
- Open a modeless form to display data
- Create a modal form to get user input

- Locate records
- Create a custom menu

Creating the Sample Form

To help you understand how to automate database tasks by using forms, first create a simple form for the Clients table located in the SAMPLES directory. Use the Form Expert to create a basic form that contains all fields. Use the Form Layout, and accept the display properties defaults. Save the form under the name CLIENT.WFM. Figure 31.1 shows what your form should look like with the form window maximized.

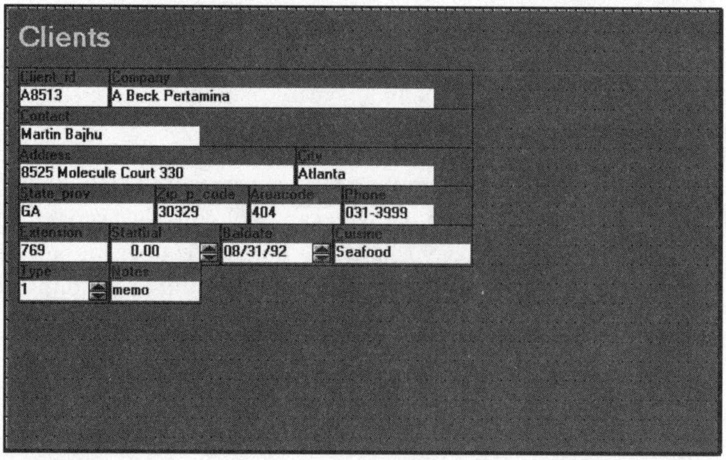

Fig. 31.1
Use the Form Expert to create this form quickly.

Looking under the Hood

When you use the Form Expert or the Form Designer to create a form interactively, dBASE records your design in a program file with a .WFM extension. The Client form you just created, for example, is a dBASE program named CLIENT.WFM.

You can view the generated form code by right-clicking the form in the Navigator window and choosing Edit as Pro**g**ram from the SpeedMenu (see fig. 31.2). The form's Program Editor window appears with the contents of the .WFM file generated by the Form Designer. You can print this file by opening the **F**ile menu and choosing **P**rint. (The file contains about seven pages of code, depending on your printer.)

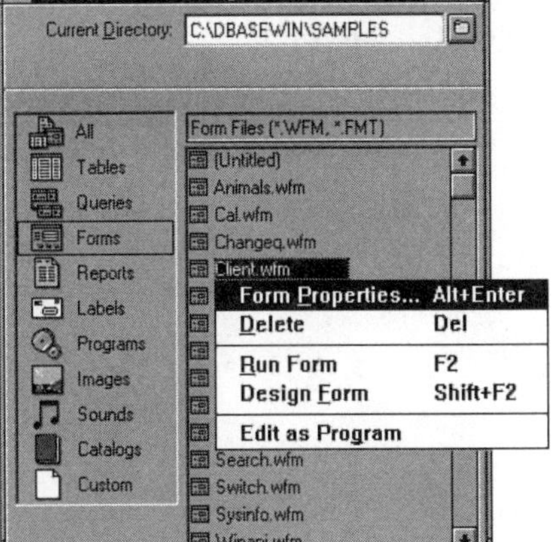

Fig. 31.2
To view generated form code, choose Edit as Program.

Understanding every line of code in the .WFM file is not important at this point, but looking at the .WFM file is a great way to start learning about automating forms, object-oriented programming, and event-driven procedures.

The .WFM file has three main sections:

- *Program header.* The header usually begins with comments describing the form. Then the header lists code that needs to execute before the form is created, such as preprocessor directives, memory variable declarations, and the CREATE SESSION statement. (CREATE SESSION begins a session for the form with a new set of work areas.) The header is also where you declare static and public variables.

- *Class declaration.* The class declaration section, which begins with the keyword CLASS and ends with the keyword ENDCLASS, is the main body of the form program. This area is where the form and the objects it contains (such as fields and buttons) are defined. The Form Designer sets properties and definitions for each control based on defaults or your selections in the designer. Note the following:

  Statements beginning with DEFINE create the control on the form.

  Statements beginning with "this" assign properties.

  Any event-handling procedures that you entered into the Procedure Editor appear after the last control definition and before the ENDCLASS statement.

- *Supporting procedures.* The last section lists any procedure declarations that you've added by using the Procedure Editor in the Form Designer.

Figure 31.3 uses a simple form with only a text and button object to illustrate the main sections of a generated form file.

Fig. 31.3
The class declaration section creates the form.

```
   Program Editor (CODE.WFM)

*This is a sample form to illustrate the three main sections of a
*generated form program (.WFM).
*An event handling procedure has been added to the OK button.
*And a supporting procedure has been added to sound a beep.
** END HEADER — do not remove this line*
* Generated on 05/23/94
*
LOCAL f
f = NEW CODE( )
f.Open( )

CLASS CODE OF FORM
   this.Text = "Form"
   this.Width =          40.00
   this.Height =          15.00
   this.Top =          2.00
   this.Left =          2.00
   this.Minimize = .F.
   this.Maximize = .F.
   this.HelpFile = ""
   this.HelpId = ""
   this.MousePointer =          1

   DEFINE TEXT TEXT1 OF THIS;
       PROPERTY;
         Text "Sample Form Code",;
         Width          24.00,;
         Height          3.00,;
         ColorNormal "N/W",;
         Top          1.00,;
         Left          7.00,;
         MousePointer          0,;
         Border .T.

   DEFINE OKBUTTON OKBUTTON1 OF THIS;
       PROPERTY;
         OnClick CLASS::OKBUTTON1_ONCLICK,;
         Width          8.00,;
         Height          2.00,;
         Top          9.00,;
         Left          18.00
Procedure OKBUTTON1_OnClick
    *This is a sample Event Procedure.
    *This code executes when the user clicks on this button.
    *Before closing the form, the OK button sounds a beep.
    DO SampleProc
    Form.close( )
    RETURN

ENDCLASS
PROCEDURE SampleProc
    *This is a sample supporting procedure.
    *Called by the OKButton's OnClick event procedure.
    ?CHR(7) &&Beep
RETURN
```

Program header

Sets property

Defines control

Class definition

Event procedure

Supporting procedures

Navigating the Procedure Editor

You can use the Form Designer to generate and edit form program code. Or you can use the Program Editor to create a form from scratch and then return to the Form Designer to modify the program interactively.

> **Caution**
>
> If you modify a form program (.WFM) with a text editor, keep the following in mind to ensure your form will still work. First, the Form Designer creates literals for all property settings. Second, the Form Designer automatically generates a class definition for the form, regardless of your modified program code.

While in the Form Designer, you can use the Procedure Editor to edit the program header, declare supporting procedures, or create event-handling procedures. To open the Procedure Editor from within the Form Designer, open the **V**iew menu and choose P**r**ocedures. dBASE opens the Procedures window.

The combo box in the top left corner is called the Method list. When you click the Method list for a new form (see fig. 31.4), two options appear: Header and General. Select Header to enter a program header. Select General to add code after the CLASS..ENDCLASS declaration. Type your comments and code into the Edit pane below the Method list.

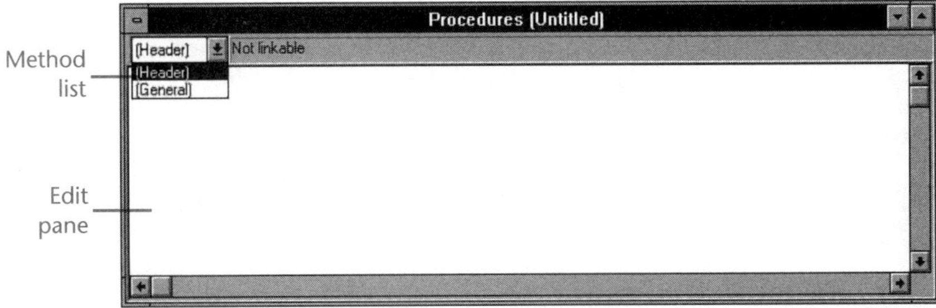

Fig. 31.4 Select Header to enter a program header in the Edit pane.

As you attach code to event procedures and create custom methods, additional items appear in the list. The Procedure Editor Method list for the form code listed in figure 31.3, for example, would list Header, General, and OKBUTTON1_OnClick.

Handling Events

The Object Properties dialog box contains an Events tab that lists the events to which the currently selected object can respond. dBASE tracks these events for you and executes any additional instructions you specify. To enter your own event-processing code, you can type a codeblock directly into the entry field for that event, or click the Tool button to open the Procedure Editor for that event.

An odd concept to grasp is that an event property linked to an event handler (codeblock or procedure) is actually a method. *Methods* are just programming modules that are associated with an object. Objects also have built-in methods that you can use in the event handlers you write.

◀ "What Is Visual Programming," p. 529

This discussion takes you back to the object-oriented programming concepts introduced in Chapter 23, "Exploring the dBASE Programming Language," and Chapter 24, "Planning a dBASE Application." An object consists of data (properties) and instructions (methods) and reacts to events based on those instructions.

Using Codeblocks

◀ "What Is Object-Oriented Programming," p. 546

You can use codeblocks to respond to events when you have only a few commands to issue. You could program a button to go to the next record, for example, by adding this statement codeblock to the button's OnClick event:

```
{SKIP}
```

◀ "Creating Codeblocks," p. 610

Or you could validate data entered into a field by entering an expression codeblock into a field's Valid event property:

```
{DateDue>=DATE( )}
```

To handle an event by using a codeblock in the Form Designer, follow these steps:

◀ "Types of Codeblocks," p. 610

1. Select the object to whose event you want to attach code.
2. Select the Object Properties.
3. Select the Events tab.
4. Click the event. The cursor appears to the right of the event name.
5. Type the codeblock.

Using Event Procedures

For more involved event-handling routines, or event-handling modules that are used by more than one object (such as an error-handling routine), use event procedures. Event procedures follow the same guidelines as procedures created in program files.

When you create an event procedure, dBASE names the resulting method by combining the name of the control with the event. An event procedure created for the Valid property of the DueDate entry field, for example, would be named DueDate_Valid. The combined name helps to document your work and makes the code easier to read.

To handle an event by using an event procedure in the Form Designer, follow these steps:

◀ "Creating Procedures," p. 602

1. Select the object to whose event you want to attach code.
2. Select the Object Properties.
3. Select the Events tab.
4. Click the event. A Tool button appears to the far right of the text box.
5. Click the Tool button. dBASE displays the Procedures window for the newly created event method.
6. Type the programming commands on the line below the PROCEDURE statement.

◀ "Using Parameters," p. 605

Automating the Sample Form

Now you're ready to use the sample form to practice programming a few buttons, validating some data, and searching for some records. In this section, you explore the various ways to automate database tasks by using forms. This text gives you just a sampling of what you can do with dBASE forms. Later in this chapter, you attach a menu to the form.

Programming a Button

The easiest object to program is a button. As with any other object, create the object and then display the list of event properties. In the sample form, you need to create two buttons: one to add new records and one to delete records. In the OnClick property of the Add button, you can enter this codeblock:

```
{APPEND}
```

In the OnClick property of the Delete button, you can enter this codeblock:

```
{DELETE}
```

And to process the final deletions, add the following code to the OnClose property of the form:

```
{PACK}
```

Save and test your work.

Using Custom Controls

The Custom tab of the Controls dialog box provides you with many preprogrammed buttons for use in your application. Add PREVBUTTON and NEXTBUTTON to the sample form to assist the user in navigating among the records.

Validating Data

The Valid property of field objects enables you to verify data entered before it is accepted into the table. In the sample form, you need to validate that the BALDATE is prior to today's date. Add the following code to the Valid property of the BALDATE field:

```
{BalDate<Date( )}
```

Searching for Records

The last database task you need to automate is searching for data based on user input at runtime. To accomplish this task, use the SEARCH.WFM form that comes with dBASE in the SAMPLES directory. Create a Find button, and create an event procedure for the OnClick property. Enter the following lines of code:

```
SET PROCEDURE TO SEARCH.WFM ADDITIVE
local f
f = new search( )
f.mdi = .f.
selected = f.ReadModal( )
seek selected value
```

This code opens the SEARCH.WFM form as a dialog box. The inner workings of dialog boxes, modal windows, and modeless forms are discussed in the next section.

Save and test your work.

Opening Forms

The first thing a non-Windows user notices about a dBASE for Windows form is being able to move around in the form freely. Not only that, but the user is free to click another window or switch over to another Windows application. A form that enables the user to move freely between windows and across applications is called a *modeless* form.

Dialog boxes, on the other hand, are modal. A *modal* window establishes a new "mode" that the user must exit before returning to the modeless environment. Programmers usually use modal windows, such as dialog boxes, to get the user's attention. The user must answer a question or select a setting before proceeding with the task at hand. In modal windows, you should always give the user a way out by displaying a Cancel button or enabling the user to close the window.

To create a modal form, set the MDI property to false (.F.), and open the form with the ReadModal method or READMODAL( ) function. When you open a modal form, program execution pauses until the modal form closes. And the user can't access the dBASE interface.

To create a modeless form, set the MDI property to true (.T.), and open the form with the Open method or OPEN FORM command. Opening a modeless form doesn't interrupt program execution, which means that the program can complete execution and release procedures or memory variables that the still open form needs. Therefore, you should carefully consider scoping the variables and procedures and make sure that any needed by the form are still available. Or, better yet, handle the form's procedure and memory variable needs in the form itself.

Note

MDI windows can't be modal. An MDI form conforms to the Windows Multiple Document Interface (MDI).

Creating a Custom Menu

Tip
If you have old dBASE IV menus, you can use the Component Builder to convert DEFINE MENU, DEFINE POPUP, and other dBASE IV menus to dBASE for Windows menu files with an .MNU extension.

In dBASE for Windows, you can create custom menu bars that work according to the standard Windows conventions. In fact, dBASE provides an interactive Menu Designer to take the drudgery out of creating menus. Using the Menu Designer, you can create a menu bar, pull-down menus, and cascading menus. The menu items can have shortcut keys and can display features such as check marks or greyed-out options. Each menu item has an OnClick property to which you can attach code.

The menu created by the Menu Designer is saved to a program file with an .MNU file extension. To display the menu, you set the form's MenuFile property equal to the menu file's name. Because the menu is a separate file from the form, you can link one menu to many forms.

Starting the Menu Designer

To launch the Menu Designer, follow these steps:

1. Open the form in Form Design mode.
2. Open the **L**ayout menu, choose T**o**ols, and choose Design **M**enu. The Menu Designer window appears for an untitled menu (see fig. 31.5).

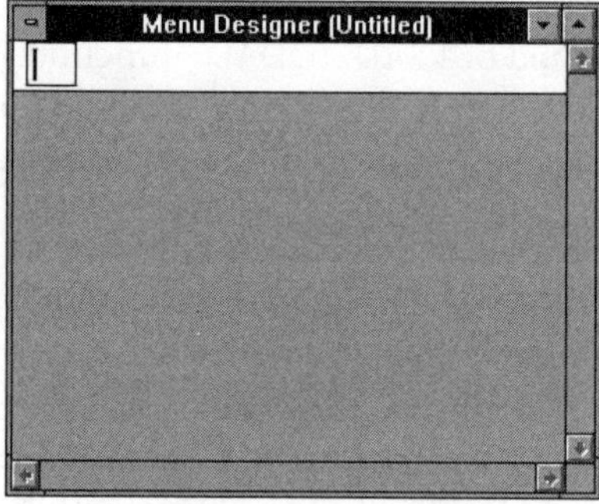

Fig. 31.5
Use the Menu Designer to create complete menu systems for your forms-driven application.

Using the Menu Designer

Tip
To keep menus easy to use, design them with only a few levels.

To build the menu, start by typing the main menu bar. Use the arrow keys or the Tab key to move horizontally across the menu bar. Use the up and down arrows to move vertically through pull-down menus. Use the Tab key from a pull-down menu to create a cascading menu. Figure 31.6 illustrates a menu design in progress.

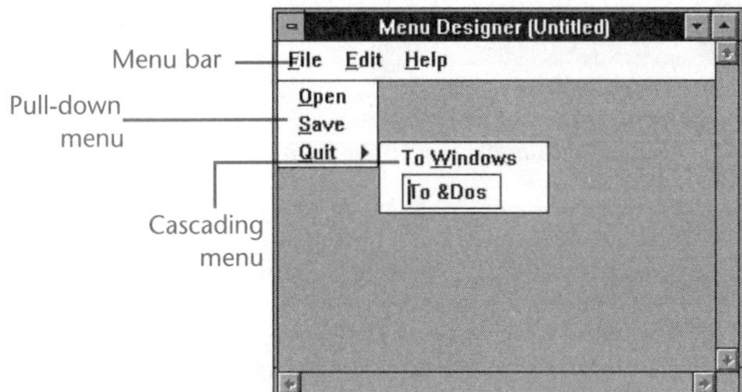

Fig. 31.6
The Menu Builder enables you to work graphically with a menu structure to improve its organization and appearance.

To set properties for each menu item, open the Object Properties, and select a menu item. Figure 31.7 lists properties for the **F**ile **Q**uit To **D**os menu item. Table 31.1 describes the display properties. Keep in mind that you can alter these property settings at runtime. You may, for example, want to disable the **S**ave menu item until a change is made and then enable it.

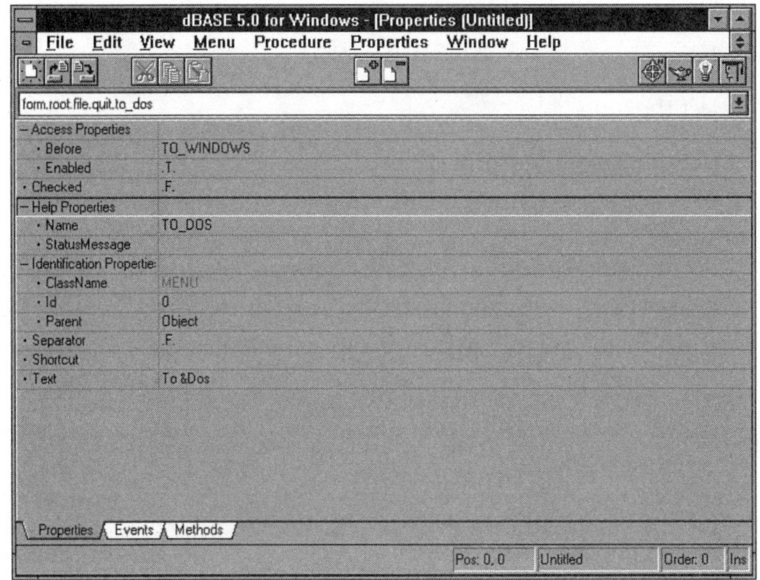

Fig. 31.7
You can set properties for each menu item.

Tip
Use the pull-down list box at the top of the Properties window to move quickly between menu items.

Table 31.1 Menu Display Properties

Property	Description
Checked	Adds a check mark next to the menu item when set to .T.
StatusMessage	Displays the entered text in the status bar when the cursor is on that menu item
Separator	Designates a menu item as a separator bar
Shortcut	Specifies the shortcut key

Tip
To underline the shortcut key, place an ampersand (&) in front of the menu item letter that you want to designate as the shortcut key when you type it in the Menu Designer window.

To program a menu item to perform a task, click the Events tab of the Properties window, and enter the code in the OnClick property. As with forms, you can enter a codeblock or click the Tool button to create an event procedure.

When you have completed your menu design, click the Save button, and save your menu to a valid file name.

To attach a menu to a form's MenuFile property, follow these steps:

1. Select the form object.
2. Select the Object Properties.
3. Select the Properties tab.
4. Click the MenuFile property. A Tool button appears to the far right of the text box.
5. Click the Tool button. dBASE displays the Choose Menu dialog box, which lists all created menus in the current directory.
6. Select the appropriate drive, directory, and menu file.
7. Click OK.
8. Save and run the form.

Figure 31.8 illustrates the completed menu system for the Clients form.

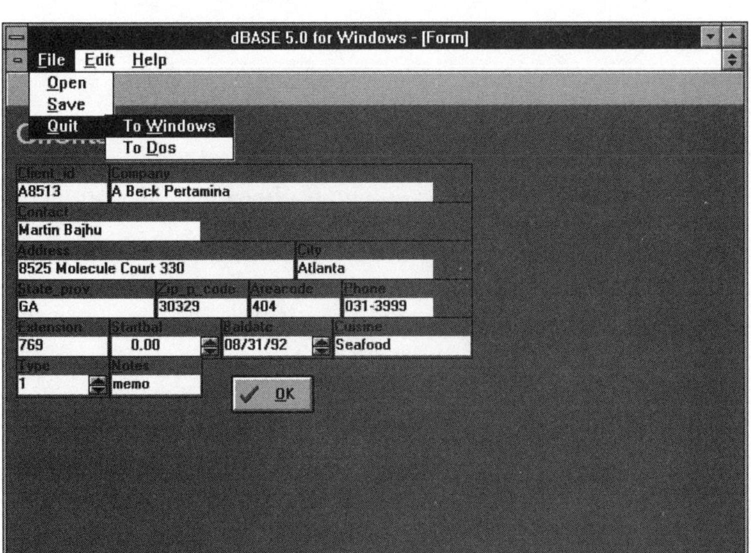

Fig. 31.8
Custom menus completely replace the standard dBASE menus.

Viewing and Editing the Menu Program

As with the generated code for the form, you can view and edit the generated code for a menu. The menu file is a good example of object-oriented concepts. The class definition is borrowed from the built-in menu object. Within that definition, menu choice objects are defined, each with its own properties (data) and instructions (methods). The hierarchy of the menu also illustrates containership—some menu items (objects) contain other menu items (objects).

To edit the menu file as a program, follow these steps:

1. In the Navigator window, click the Custom file type.
2. In the Custom Files text box, type ***.MNU** and press Enter.
3. Right-click the menu file you want to edit. The SpeedMenu appears.
4. Select Edit as Pro**g**ram.

From Here...

Now that you are familiar with working with automating forms, you are ready to learn how to automate other database tasks. To learn more about automating other database tasks, refer to the following chapter:

- Chapter 32, "Automating Other Database Tasks." This chapter shows you how to automate transaction processing, queries, printing, and import/export tasks.

Chapter 32

Automating Other Database Tasks

The power of dBASE programming is just beginning to unfold. In this chapter, you explore many new commands and functions that assist you in automating various database tasks. You can use the skills gained in this chapter in your program modules and in form programs.

In this chapter, you learn how to do the following:

- Process transactions
- Automate queries
- Perform field calculations
- Index and sort data
- Import and export data

Processing Transactions

Sometimes you need to perform data entry tasks and database management tasks as a set. A group of related changes to a database is called a *transaction*. To perform transactions successfully, you must change all records in the set simultaneously; otherwise you should make no changes to any records. The key benefit of transaction processing is that it protects the integrity of your data by preventing partial or failed updates.

Consider a common scenario: multiple users simultaneously using the same database application. Suppose that you want to update a set of records across several tables, but another user on the network is currently using some of the records or tables (that is, those records or tables are currently locked). Because dBASE cannot make your changes to the locked records or tables, only part of your transaction is posted. In these days of mission-critical databases, partial posting of related transactions can lead to erroneous or unreliable data in your database.

dBASE provides several transaction-processing commands that you can use in a structured program or in an object-oriented, event-driven form. In addition to using the transaction-processing commands, you can use several form events to manage transaction events.

Note

dBASE for Windows does not support the DOS dBASE transaction-processing commands BEGINTRANSACTION..ENDTRANSACTION and ROLLBACK. Using these commands does not cause an error, but does produce different results. Instead of using the old transaction-processing commands, use the new event-driven commands and techniques discussed in this chapter.

How dBASE Saves Data

To manage your transaction processing properly, you need to understand how dBASE saves changes or additions to a table. By default, dBASE "commits" changes to a record when you leave that record. The changes are written to the table in a memory buffer. When the buffer is full, dBASE writes the contents to disk.

To have dBASE write changes directly to the disk after you leave each new or edited record, turn on the Autosave property. To do so, you can either issue the dBASE command SET AUTOSAVE ON or select the **A**utosave check box in the Desktop Properties dialog box.

If you turn off the Autosave property, you can use the FLUSH command to write the memory buffer to disk immediately. You can also write changes to the disk by closing a table or its window, ending BROWSE, EDIT, or APPEND, or choosing save or exit options.

When you use transaction processing, you interrupt dBASE's default record change processing by posting changes to a temporary "transaction" area rather than the buffer. When you issue the BEGINTRANS( ) command, dBASE reserves space in memory to store changes. When you issue the COMMIT( ) command, dBASE posts the changes to the normal memory buffer or the hard disk, depending on the status of the Autosave property.

Note

You can define the scope of a transaction to be a field, a group of fields, or an entire record with its related records.

Managing Transactions with Commands

Table 32.1 describes the dBASE commands that control transaction processing. To define a transaction block, you begin by issuing the BEGINTRANS( ) command; the block continues until it reaches a COMMIT( ) or ROLLBACK( ) command. BEGINTRANS( ) initiates record and file locking for the currently open database or table. You can open a table or database before issuing the BEGINTRANS( ) command, or provide the name of the database as an argument to the BEGINTRANS( ) command. If you do not open any table or database, BEGINTRANS( ) applies to the first table or database that you open after invoking BEGINTRANS( ).

Tip
Use SET AUTOSAVE ON or FLUSH to write transaction changes to the disk.

Table 32.1 Transaction Processing Commands

dBASE Command	Description
BEGINTRANS( )	Starts transaction processing
COMMIT( )	Ends transaction processing and posts changes permanently
ROLLBACK( )	Ends transaction processing and discards changes

If the record and file locks succeed, BEGINTRANS( ) returns a true value (.T.). For this reason, you should start your transaction processing with an IF..ENDIF block such as the following:

```
IF BEGINTRANS( )
     ...transaction editing code
ELSE
     ...message to the user indicating that dBASE cannot process
     the transaction because the table or records could not be
     accessed exclusively (someone else may currently be using
     the table); the message also gives the user the choice of
     either retrying or canceling the transaction.
ENDIF
```

COMMIT( ) ends the transaction processing and makes the changes permanently to the tables and indexes involved. dBASE removes all record and table locks. If dBASE can make the change successfully, COMMIT( ) returns a true value (.T.). You also should place the COMMIT( ) command in an IF..ENDIF block, in case the changes cannot be committed. You should then expand your transaction-processing block to the following structure:

```
IF BEGINTRANS( )
     ...transaction editing code
     IF .NOT. COMMIT( )
          ...message telling the user that the changes could not be
          committed to the table(s), and giving the user the choice
          of either retrying or canceling the updates.
     ENDIF
ELSE
     ...message telling the user that dBASE cannot process
     the transaction because the table or records could not
     be accessed exclusively (someone else may currently be
     using the table), and giving the user the option to retry
     or cancel the transaction.
ENDIF
```

Use the ROLLBACK( ) command to discard all transaction changes, restore the tables and indexes to their prior state, and then release table and record locks. If the transaction successfully rolls back, ROLLBACK( ) returns a true value (.T.).

The following example uses transaction processing for the Clients table to increase the starting balances for all clients by $100:

```
ON ERROR DO ErrorTrap      &&If an error occurs, run the ErrorTrap procedure.
USE Clients                &&Open the Clients table.
IF BEGINTRANS( )            &&Start transaction processing
     REPLACE ALL StartBal WITH StartBal+100
     IF .NOT. COMMIT( )     &&Try to commit changes, if can't commit then
          Answer = " "
          DO WHILE .NOT. Answer = "C"
          @20,20 SAY "Unable to save changes at this time."
          @21,20 SAY "Would you like to retry(R) or cancel (C)?";
          GET Answer
          END DO
          ROLLBACK( )       &&When the user decides to Cancel,
                           &&Discard all changes and roll back the table.
     ENDIF
ENDIF
ON ERROR                   &&Clear the error trap.
RETURN                     &&Return to the calling module.
PROCEDURE ErrorTrap
     @20,20 SAY "An error occurred. Unable to save changes."
     ROLLBACK( )
```

Within a transaction block, dBASE tracks only certain updates, such as adding new records (APPEND or INSERT), marking record deletions (DELETE), and changing existing records (EDIT). Furthermore, dBASE prohibits certain commands from executing within a transaction block.

dBASE tracks the following dBASE commands during transaction processing:

@..GET..READ

APPEND

BROWSE

DELETE

EDIT

FLOCK( )

INSERT

RECALL

REPLACE

RLOCK( )

Tip
Before rolling back a transaction, save to a temporary file and give the user the ability to "undo" the rollback.

dBASE prohibits the use of the following dBASE commands within a transaction block:

BEGINTRANS( )

CLEAR ALL

CLOSE ALL

CLOSE DATABASE

CLOSE INDEX

CONVERT

DELETE TAG

INSERT

MODIFY STRUCTURE

PACK

ZAP

Also, remember to issue the PACK command to process any records marked for deletion *after* the transaction processing ends.

> **Note**
>
> You cannot nest transaction blocks within each other.

Managing Transactions with Events

Tip
Create and display a dialog box form that explains transaction errors to the user and gives the user the choice of retrying or canceling transaction changes.

Instead of using the @..SAY..GET.., APPEND, BROWSE, and REPLACE commands to interface with the user when editing records, use forms to provide the user with a more polished graphical user interface. Forms offer a programmer new ways to manage transactions. You can use the transaction commands BEGINTRANS( ), ROLLBACK( ), and COMMIT( ) in form events, or you can attach event-handling code to respond to individual editing events.

The CUSTOMER.WFM form, which comes with dBASE in the SAMPLES directory, provides a good example of using the transaction-processing commands within a form. The ViewEdit procedure executes when the user clicks the View Edit button. This procedure toggles the user between edit and view mode. Transaction processing begins for a single record in the ELSE clause (see fig. 32.1). Note that in figure 32.1 the form is not in edit yet. Changes are processed by the function CheckCommit, which displays a dialog box that enables the user to commit, roll back, or cancel changes.

You can also attach code to event properties to handle specific types of editing events. For example, you could provide transaction processing in the OnChange property of a field, for a record or for a group of related records. You could also display the data in a modal form, and process the "transaction" when the user closes the form or clicks on a button.

Automating Queries

The Query Designer provides an easy, quick method of finding and filtering data. As a dBASE programmer, you might find it beneficial to create and test queries interactively before inserting them into your code. The best part of all is that the Query Designer (like the Form and Menu Designer) makes the design available to you in a program file. To view the generated query code, follow these steps:

1. Open the Navigator or Catalog window.

2. Select Queries as the file type.

3. Right-click on the desired query.

4. Choose the SpeedMenu's Edit as Program selection. dBASE displays the query code in the Program Editor window (see fig. 32.2).

```
PROCEDURE OnAppend
if .not. form.inEditMode
   form.ViewEdit( )        && make form editable and begin transaction
endif

PROCEDURE VIEWEDIT
*** If ending editing, close transaction; otherwise open it.
IF form.inEditMode
   form.CheckCommit( )
   form.inEditMode = .f.
   form.text = "Customer — View Mode"
   form.viewEditButton.text = "&Edit"
   form.viewEditButton.statusmessage = "In View Mode. Click Edit to edit
   ➥data."
ELSE
   BEGINTRANS( )
   form.inEditMode = .t.
   form.text = "Customer — Edit Mode"
   form.viewEditButton.text = "&View"
   form.viewEditButton.statusmessage = "In Edit Mode.  Click
   ➥View to View data."
   form.nameEntry.SetFocus( )     && go to the name entryfield
endif

FUNCTION CheckCommit
if form.inEditMode .and. form.changesMade
   if MessDlg("Confirmation","Commit changes?","Customer ";
         +customer_n,"YesNo") = 6
      commit( )
   else
      rollback( )
   endif
   begintrans( )
else
   rollback( )
endif
form.changesMade = .f.
return .t.
```


Fig. 32.1
You can use transaction-processing commands in forms, too.

After you debug your query code, you can cut and paste it into another program, or an event procedure in a form.

Tip
Edit your query code and use memory variables as criteria to create parameter queries.

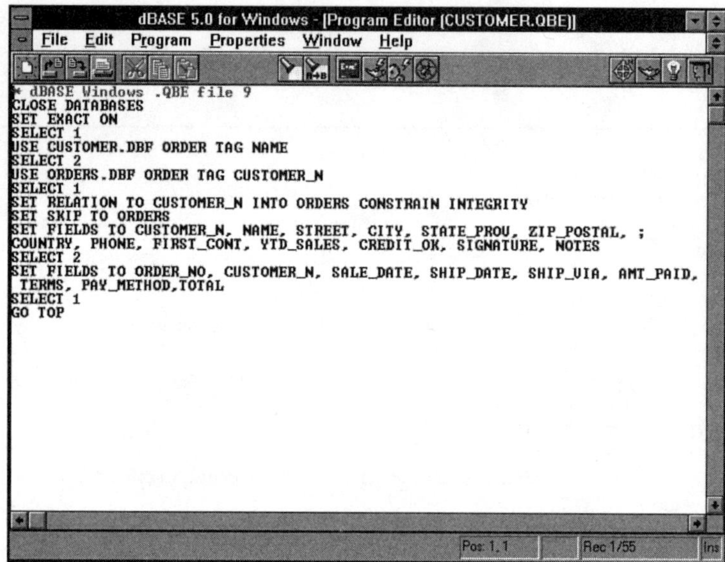
dBASE 5.0 for Windows - [Program Editor (CUSTOMER.QBE)]
File Edit Program Properties Window Help
* dBASE Windows .QBE file 9
CLOSE DATABASES
SET EXACT ON
SELECT 1
USE CUSTOMER.DBF ORDER TAG NAME
SELECT 2
USE ORDERS.DBF ORDER TAG CUSTOMER_N
SELECT 1
SET RELATION TO CUSTOMER_N INTO ORDERS CONSTRAIN INTEGRITY
SET SKIP TO ORDERS
SET FIELDS TO CUSTOMER_N, NAME, STREET, CITY, STATE_PROV, ZIP_POSTAL, ;
COUNTRY, PHONE, FIRST_CONT, YTD_SALES, CREDIT_OK, SIGNATURE, NOTES
SELECT 2
SET FIELDS TO ORDER_NO, CUSTOMER_N, SALE_DATE, SHIP_DATE, SHIP_VIA, AMT_PAID,
TERMS, PAY_METHOD,TOTAL
SELECT 1
GO TOP
Pos: 1, 1
Rec 1/55
Ins

Fig. 32.2
Code generated by the Query Designer.

Performing Field Calculations

Often in applications, you must perform calculations based on data as it exists at that particular moment. dBASE provides several tools to assist you in performing calculations in your programs and forms.

Creating Calculated Fields

Similar to a memory variable, a calculated field shows the results of a mathematical calculation based on other fields in the table. Calculated fields do not exist in the table. In fact, after you close the table, dBASE removes calculated fields from memory (just like memory variables). Unlike memory variables, however, calculated field data cannot be edited.

In dBASE, you can use expressions to create calculated fields interactively in queries and forms. You also can create calculated fields to show dynamically the result of a calculation as dependent field data changes. To create a new calculated field, use the command SET FIELDS TO.

The following example computes the total amount due from the sales price per unit and the quantity ordered. The Total field is the virtual calculated field.

```
USE Orders
SET FIELD TO Orders->Price, Orders->Quantity, Total=Price*Quantity
```

Using the CALCULATE Command

dBASE also provides several commands and functions that perform calculations on fields. In addition to the financial and statistical calculation functions discussed in Chapter 30, "Automating Table Tasks," dBASE provides the CALCULATE command.

The CALCULATE command enables you to perform several different types of computations in one statement. Using CALCULATE, you can compute the total number of, average of, variance of, and standard deviation of the year-to-date sales—all with one statement.

◄ "Manipulating Character Data," p. 625

◄ "Manipulating Numerical Data," p. 627

◄ "Manipulating Date and Time Data," p. 629

The basic syntax of the CALCULATE command enables you to specify a FOR or WHILE condition. You can also specify the record or range of records on which to base the calculations. You can save the result to a list of memory variables or to an array.

You can use one or more of the following functions in your CALCULATE statement:

AVG( )

CNT( )

MAX( )

MIN( )

NPV( )

STD( )

SUM( )

VAR( )

COUNT( )

Note

Although you can use the SUM or AVERAGE commands to find sums and averages, CALCULATE is faster because it runs through the table just once while performing all requested calculations.

The following statement uses the Orders table to calculate the number of orders, average selling price, and total quantity sold for product (stock) number 02390:

```
USE Orders
CALCULATE COUNT( ), AVG(Sell_Price), SUM(Qty);
     FOR Stock_No = 02390;
     TO a,b,c
?a
?b
?c
```

Indexing and Sorting

The order in which you enter records into a table is called the *natural order* or *physical order*. The dBASE record number identifies the physical position of a record in a table. The natural order of a table is not very meaningful.

Indexing and sorting enable you to control the order of records in a table. Using sorts and indexes, you can display and work with records in a more meaningful order. dBASE provides two commands to help you control the order of records from a program module: SORT and INDEX.

Using SORT

A sort creates a completely new table (a copy) in which the physical order of the records is changed to your specifications. Because sorting duplicates data (which usually is considered a waste of disk resources), the sorting feature is rarely used. The following are a few examples of circumstances in which you might consider sorting a table:

- To improve performance of indexes. dBASE can access a table sorted in index order faster than an unsorted table.
- To store an outdated table in a commonly used order.
- To create a new table that is a sorted subset of the original table.

Use the SORT command to sort a table. The command enables you to specify the name of the new table, the table type, the field or fields on which to sort, the sort order (ascending or descending), and conditions under which to sort. You can set the conditions with a FOR or WHILE clause. The following example sorts the Clients table to a new table called CA_Cust, sorted in alphabetical, ascending order by company name:

```
USE Clients
SORT      ON Company;
     TO CA_CUST /A;
     FOR STATE_PROV = CA
USE CA_CUST
```

Note

SORT does not support SEEK, SEEK( ), or FIND. You must use an index for these commands and functions.

Using INDEX

The *indexed* or *logical order* of a table organizes the records numerically or alphabetically in ascending or descending order. The records are ordered by the data in one or more fields, called the *key fields*. Indexes keep track of where records belong in the logical and natural orders. A table can have more than one index, but only one index can be active at any time.

Note

dBASE for Windows enables you to design and maintain multiple index (.MDX) files. The old single index (.NDX) files from dBASE III can be opened in the Command window or in a program, but are available only for compatibility. Old .NDX files should be updated to the new .MDX. To do this, use the COPY INDEXES command.

The syntax of the INDEX command is more involved than most commands, and bears a bit more attention. The following is the basic syntax:

```
INDEX ON <key expression list>
     TAG <tag name>
          OF<.mdx filename>
          FOR <condition>
     DESCENDING
     UNIQUE
```

The *key expression list* is a list of field names on which to index the table. To define the key expression list, you can use up to 100 characters, including operators and functions. The *tag name* is a name by which the index is referenced. The OF clause specifies the file name of the new .MDX index.

The FOR clause is optional and enables you to perform conditional indexing. Note that, unlike the syntax for SORT, the syntax for INDEX does not include a WHILE clause. By default, dBASE creates the index in ascending order. To index in descending order, use the optional keyword DESCENDING. The optional keyword UNIQUE prevents dBASE from including in the index multiple records with the same key value. Without the FOR and UNIQUE clauses, the SORT command includes all records in the index.

The following example indexes the Clients table by company name and only for the State_Prov of CA. A BROWSE command displays the results. Then the example creates an index on the ZIP_P_CODE and saves the index to CUST_ZIP.MDX. Note the use of semicolons to continue the command statement on the next line.

```
USE Clients
INDEX ON Company;
     TAG CA;
     FOR State_Prov = "CA"
BROWSE TITLE "Indexed by Company, CA only"
INDEX ON ZIP_P_CODE TAG ZIP OF CUST_ZIP.MDX
BROWSE TITLE "Indexed by Zip Codes"
```

To open a saved index, use the SET INDEX TO or USE INDEX commands. The following are examples of each command:

```
SET INDEX TO Zip.MDX
USE Clients INDEX Zip.MDX
```

To use an index tag name, use the SET ORDER TO command:

```
SET ORDER TO TAG Zip.MDX
```

To close all open index files except the production .MDX, issue the CLOSE INDEX command.

Importing and Exporting

Little is more tedious than having to enter data into a database from a computer printout. Although in the past users had to overcome many hurdles to share data across applications and hardware platforms, most modern programs enable users to import and export data in standard formats. dBASE enables you to import and export in many formats. You can import and export interactively (by opening the **T**able menu and choosing Table **U**tilities, and then choosing **E**xport or **I**mport) or in programming code (by issuing the IMPORT or EXPORT commands).

Looking at the Standard Formats

dBASE enables you to import and export data in the following formats:

SDF — A *system data format* file is a fixed-length file in which a carriage return and line feed marks the end of the record. This is a type of ASCII file. The default extension is .TXT.

DELIMITED	A text file format in which data is delimited by quotation marks or another character that you specify. This is a type of ASCII file. The default extension is .TXT.
DBASE	A dBASE table with a .DBF extension.
DBMEMO3	A dBASE III PLUS table (.DBF) or memo file (.DBT).
PARADOX	A Paradox table with a .DB extension.
WB1	A Quattro Pro for Windows spreadsheet file. The default extension is .WB1.

Exporting Data

The Export feature copies all or part of a table to a file. If a master index exists, Export organizes the new file based on that index. When exporting to a spreadsheet format, dBASE writes the field names in the first row, as column headers.

Note

Before you export a file, always check the file limitations and requirements of the application that will use the file. For example, you may find that the accounting system with which you want to use the file reads only delimited files in which tabs separate the fields.

You can use the EXPORT command to create a table or file that contains fields from many tables. To do so, you must open the tables in different work areas. Then use SET RELATION to define a relationship between the tables, and use SET FIELDS TO to select the fields that you want to export. Finally, switch to the work area that contains the parent table and issue the EXPORT command.

The following example uses EXPORT to export a text file, called PHONELST.TXT, that is delimited by commas. Only the fields listed in the FIELD clause will be included in the export file.

```
USE Clients
EXPORT TO PhoneLst;
     TYPE DELIMITED WITH , ;
     FIELD Company, Contact, AreaCode, Phone, Extension
```

Importing Data

Use the Import feature to import data from other tables or from non-dBASE for Windows files. The Import feature creates the table into which the data is imported, places the table in the same drive and directory as the original file, and opens the table.

The following example shows how to use IMPORT to create a new dBASE table from a delimited text file.

```
SET DBTYPE TO DBASE
IMPORT FROM PhoneLst.TXT TYPE DELIMITED WITH ,
USE PhoneLst
BROWSE
```

Troubleshooting

I indexed my table on the Names field using the INDEX command. Now I'm missing records.

The good news about indexes is that they are files that are separate from your table. That means that the index cannot alter the natural order (or contents) of your table. Check whether you used the UNIQUE keyword when you created the index. UNIQUE deletes from the index any records that have duplicate key values. For example, if you have two records with the name John, only the first would appear. Also check the FOR clause condition, which may have filtered records out of the index.

The SORT command won't let me re-sort the table to the same table name.

You cannot send the results of a SORT to the same table name, because SORT actually rewrites the natural order of the existing table. To re-sort the table to the same table name, dBASE needs another file name in which to copy the sorted records. If necessary, use a temporary file name and then copy the temporary file to the existing file name. Be very careful, however, because you can filter out records in a SORT command that you may not want to erase permanently. Consider using the INDEX command instead.

From Here...

The best way to learn how to program in dBASE for Windows is simply to do it. Try writing your own program modules and see how they work. If they don't seem to work, use the Debugger to determine where the code goes astray. Use the Help system as you work to help you learn the proper syntax and to give you ideas on how to use dBASE language elements most effectively. Use forms to design the user interface interactively for your application and then review the generated code in the Program Editor.

Appendix A

Using dBASE III and dBASE IV Applications

There are a plethora of database applications that were created using dBASE III, dBASE III Plus, and dBASE IV program packages. Indeed, you may be using some of these even as you read these words. If you are musing over whether to convert these various files into dBASE for Windows format, you probably should. This appendix shows you how.

Most of the tasks inherent in the conversion effort are based upon finding those files on your hard disk and then updating their catalogs. Only a couple of rules need to be observed in this task. First, make sure that you move (or copy) only those files that dBASE for Windows needs—some are redundant, and even though disk space may be less expensive than last year on a dollar-per-byte basis, there's still no point in cluttering your hard disk with superfluous files.

There may be occasions when you will need to update the directory paths of these catalogs so that the computer can access them. When you make the formal conversion, use only the dBASE File Viewer to open these catalog files.

Those files that were formerly used in dBASE III and dBASE IV fall into three main camps when they are applied to dBASE for Windows: those you *need* and can use directly, those you can use *after* conversion, and those you *won't* need.

Files You Can Use Directly

Table A.1 shows the status of these files and their resolution under dBASE for Windows. Unless specifically noted, all these file name extensions are fully interchangeable with the dBASE for Windows software.

Table A.1 Files You Can Use Directly with dBASE for Windows

dBASE File Name Extension	Purpose
.CAT	A catalog file keeps all of the files associated with a particular application together.
.DBF	Database files are now known as tables.
.DBK	Backed-up copies of database tables, similar to .BAK files, can be renamed to .DBF files when needed.
.DBT	Database fields are used for holding memo text.
.FMT	These files house source code for screen formats (.SCR). This code should be updated to accommodate dBASE for Windows by redesigning the screens which, when saved, upgrades the code in the new format.
.FRG	These files house source code for reports. This code should be updated to accommodate dBASE for Windows by redesigning the report through the Report Designer.
.LBG	These files house source code for labels. This code should be updated to accommodate dBASE for Windows by using the Report Designer.
.MBK	These files utilize spare copies of .MDX files that are created when a table was modified in dBASE IV. If the file is renamed with the .MDX extension, they may be used in dBASE for Windows.
.MDX	Multiple index files are available for normal dBASE for Windows use.
.MEM	Both variable and array memory files work in dBASE for Windows. However, these files will not work within dBASE if they contain multidimensional arrays or other specialized memory objects available for the first time within dBASE for Windows.

dBASE File Name Extension	Purpose
.NDX	Index files are fully used in dBASE for Windows.
.PRF	These files house the printer settings as established in the Control Center Print menu of dBASE IV. Such references may be made using the _pform system memory variables. Be aware, however, that the codes used in today's state-of-the-art printers could be quite different from those available during the dBASE III or dBASE IV tenure. In other words, technical obsolescence can force you to start over.
.PRG	These program files contain all of your textual lines of code in ASCII text format. Although these files are usable in dBASE for Windows, you might consider changing the code or using the dBASE design tools to quickly upgrade existing programs.
.QBE	Query-by-Example files were previously made using the Create/Modify Query command. These files contain information for record filtering. They may be executed without any further modification in dBASE for Windows. Any binary information from dBASE IV files is ignored.
.QRY	This extension is applied to files that have been created with dBASE III Create/Modify Query commands. These files may be executed without any modification in dBASE for Windows. Any binary information that exists from dBASE IV files is ignored.
.TBK	Database memo backup files are an additional spare copy of .DBT files. These were created automatically when dBASE IV tables were created or modified. If you rename these files with a .DBT file name extension, they can safely be used within dBASE for Windows. If this method is employed, use care not to overwrite existing files.
.UPD	These Query-by-Example files were generated by dBASE IV. Although they may be used in dBASE for Windows, you will improve your speed and flexibility by using the Query Designer to create new queries prior to running under dBASE for Windows.

(continues)

Table A.1 Continued

dBASE File Name Extension	Purpose
.VUE	View files that were generated using the Create View command in dBASE IV can run unchanged in dBASE for Windows. Although they can be used in dBASE for Windows, you can improve your speed and flexibility by using the Query Designer to create new queries prior to running dBASE for Windows.
.WIN	Not to be confused with any Windows program manager, these are dBASE IV window definition files. Although they work unchanged in dBASE for Windows, any screen forms and windows that *are* created in dBASE for Windows are saved with a .WFM file format.

Files You Won't Need

Table A.2 shows the status of files that you won't need within dBASE for Windows. Before you delete them from your hard disk entirely, however, you might consider copying them or backing them up onto removable media.

Table A.2 Files You Won't Need with dBASE for Windows

dBASE File Name Extension	Purpose
.$$$	Temporary files don't just apply to dBASE for Windows, but can appear scattered throughout your entire hard disk structure. Some have a zero-byte length, but all can be deleted.
.$AB	These are interim file storage files and are not used by dBASE for Windows.
.ACC	These are user count files under dBASE IV.
.APP	Application design object files were created by the Application Generator in dBASE IV.
.ASM	These files used assembly language to create binary files in dBASE IV. They were formerly used to support external subroutines, and are not used in dBASE for Windows.

dBASE File Name Extension	Purpose
.BAR	As the name suggests, these files are used when creating horizontal bar design object files. These files were used internally by the template language compiler, but they have fallen into disuse in dBASE for Windows.
.BCH	These Batch Process design object files were used by the Applications Generator under dBASE IV. They do not apply to dBASE for Windows.
.BIN	Binary files were probably used in external subroutines under dBASE IV. They are not used by dBASE for Windows.
.CAC	Proprietary memory caches are not used in dBASE for Windows.
.COD	Not to be mistaken as a saltwater fish, the template language source code was formerly used to create template files. Such files were used to control the way source code was outputted to the dBASE IV Control Centers code generators. Since dBASE for Windows no longer employs templates to generate code, these files may be deleted.
CONFIG.DB (File)	As the old configuration file under dBASE III and dBASE IV, it was used to control screen colors, automate commands, and help provide program status. Since dBASE for Windows now uses the Windows DBASEWIN.INI initialization file for such configurations, this file is no longer used.
.CPT	Encrypted database memo files were formerly created under the dBASE IV PROTECT command system. These files do not replace the un-encrypted .DBT files. You may want to consider bringing decrypted .DBT files from dBASE IV with you to the dBASE for Windows format.
.CRP	A second set of encrypted database table files were also created under the dBASE IV PROTECT command system. Again, these files replace the un-encrypted .DBF files. You may want to consider bringing decrypted .DBT files from dBASE IV with you to the dBASE for Windows format.
.CVT	Originally, dBASE IV's CONVERT command added a _dBASElock multi-user record-locking field to a table. A duplicate spare of the original file was created. dBASE for Windows can use this file, but the .CVT file—the spare copy—isn't needed.

(continues)

Table A.2 Continued

dBASE File Name Extension	Purpose
.DB2	These files are veterans of the dBASE II program. Although dBASE for Windows doesnt utilize these files directly, a conversion program is available for those purposes within dBASE IV.
DBASE.VMC	A virtual memory configuration file from within dBASE IV Version 2.0 doesn't apply to the Windows environment.
.DBO	These files were used by dBASE IV to create a database object file from a program file. The .DBO files only work within dBASE IV. dBASE for Windows creates its own set of unmodifiable object files from existing .PRG files that you copy into the program.
DBSYSTEM.DB DBSYSTEM.SQL	These two files are encrypted and contain user profiles, including password information (hence the encryption). dBASE for Windows doesn't use a schematic of this nature for security purposes.
.DEF	These files were used internally by dBASE IV's template language compiler.
.DOC	A documentation file that was created by the Applications Generator under dBASE IV to document your application. They are not used by dBASE for Windows.
.ERR	The Error Log file was created by dBASE IV to log and track errors in code compilation. They are not used in the same manner by dBASE for Windows.
.FIL	dBASE IV's Application Generator used this file extension as an organization tool. They do not apply to dBASE for Windows applications.
.FMO	The screen format object files work only within dBASE IV. dBASE for Windows is able to compile source code in screen format files from which the .FMO files are created.
.FNL .LNL .SNL	These files are only employed by DGEN and DEXPORT.
.FRM	dBASE IV alone uses these report design files. dBASE for Windows can use these files in a report format (.FRG) from files generated from .FRM files. You must use Crystal Reports to convert to .RPT format.

dBASE File Name Extension	Purpose
.FRO	dBASE IV used these report form files. dBASE for Windows can use these files in a report format (.FMT) from which the .FRO files are created.
.FW2 .FW3 .RPD	These files represent old Ashton-Tate *Framework* or *RapidFile* files. They are not usable within dBASE for Windows.
.GEN	These were generated files from dBASE IV. Since dBASE for Windows now generates its code without using template files to control code creation, these files become obsolete.
.KEY	These file extensions were a dBASE IV Control Center mechanism. dBASE for Windows employs a Windows Recorder to create the next generation of macro files.
.LBL	These were label files under both dBASE III and dBASE IV schemes. They will only work under dBASE IV's Report Designer. dBASE for Windows can use the code used to generate the old files, but will save your file using a .LBG file extension. If you insist on using the old system, first import the files into dBASE IV and add them to a catalog in the Control Center. Then open them in the Label Designer from the same Control Center. Generate an .LBG file containing the source code for dBASE for Windows. You will be better satisfied, however, if you create a new label file from within the dBASE for Windows range using the Report Designer. You must use Crystal Reports to convert to .RPT format.
.LBO	These files accompanied the label files and work only within dBASE IV. As with the label files, dBASE for Windows can compile source code in label format files from which the .LBO files were created.
.LOG	Transaction log files were used to serve the beginning and ending of transactions under dBASE IV. dBASE for Windows uses transaction processing only under SQL data in a client-server environment.
.NAP	Network Access pack file lists are only used within a multiuser dBASE IV arena.
.PIF	The dBASE IV Program Information File allowed Windows users to use non-Windows applications. dBASE for Windows doesn't use this specification.

(continues)

Table A.2 Continued

dBASE File Name Extension	Purpose
.POP	Pop-up menu design objects were used by the dBASE IV Applications Generator. They don't apply to dBASE for Windows.
.PR2 .PR3	These are Windows printer drivers/devices. None of the dBASE DOS-based printer drivers apply to dBASE for Windows. (See *.TXT* below).
.PRS	Commands for SQL commands and procedures work only with dBASE IV. Although dBASE for Windows is able to access SQL tables, it still needs the correct SQL drivers.
.PRT	dBASE IV used printer output files created by the REPORT FORM command. The resulting output contained little more than a report's contents in text format. They were output to disk as text files, embedded with printer control codes. A new format would create these .PRT files with the REPORT FORM command within dBASE for Windows.
.QBO	The old Query-by-Example format in dBASE IV does not work within dBASE for Windows. Use the Query Designer within dBASE for Windows to create new QBE file queries.
.RTM	Although it doesn't stand for *Read the Manual*, the runtime list files are unsupported in dBASE for Windows.
.SCR	The (old) screen form design under both dBASE III and dBASE IV hold much the same information that dBASE for Windows needs, and thus can be run directly under the new system.
.STR	These structure list design objects were used by dBASE IV's Applications Generator. There is no utility for them within dBASE for Windows.
.T44 .W44	These two files were used as interim holding areas for database table Indexing and Sorting activities. There is no utility for them within dBASE for Windows.

dBASE File Name Extension	Purpose
.TXT	Textual data may be sent to a file name with this extension. Use the REPORT FORM command within dBASE IV or dBASE for Windows. As before, none of the old printer drivers—including the ASCII.PR2 driver that was typically used by this activity—is required, since printer control codes are no longer embedded within text files.
.UPD	dBASE alone uses these Query Update Object files. Use the Query Designer within dBASE for Windows to re-create queries.
.VAL	The dBASE IV Applications Generator used these Values list design object files. They are not used by dBASE for Windows.

Files That Can Be Converted

Some files that were formerly encrypted using the dBASE IV PROTECT command can be used under dBASE for Windows. Typically, the PROTECT command was used to enforce security: a user wanting to employ a PROTECTed file would have to enter a password to gain access to that database/table. This system was also used to protect data from simultaneous, multiple read-writes under networking, and file locking scenarios.

If you want to employ a similar type of system under dBASE for Windows, your file(s) must be decrypted before use.

The following procedure describes what you must do to effectively use file encryption schemes under dBASE for Windows:

1. Make a full backup of all the data you are about to modify. Then make sure that you have EXTEND, DELETE, and UPDATE privileges for the files that you want to access and modify. You must also enjoy FULL field privileges for each field within each file. That's two distinctly different accesses—having one without the other won't work!

2. Find the required files from within your hard disk's subdirectory structure. Enter the dBASE IV database program, and at the dot prompt, type the command **SET ENCRYPTION OFF**.

3. Issue the command **USE *<filename>*** substituting the name of the file that is to be decrypted.

4. Issue the command **COPY TO *<filename>* WITH PRODUCTION**, where *<filename>* is your new file. Always use a different file name to avoid any possible overwriting of your existing data. dBASE IV creates a decrypted copy of your encrypted table, along with an associated memo file (if it existed originally), and the table's production index.

5. Close dBASE IV.

6. Electronically copy the new files into either your dBASE for Windows subdirectory, or the \DATA subdirectory, or wherever you are keeping your application's software. You can also set the file location icon once dBASE for Windows has been launched.

7. Enter dBASE for Windows, and modify your file location under tables to see the new files. They should be fully accessible.

Appendix B

Keystroke Commands Reference

dBASE for Windows, like all well-behaved Windows applications, provides a number of keyboard equivalents for menu operations and certain commands. This appendix presents the most common and frequently used of these keystroke combinations.

The applications you build in dBASE for Windows should conform to the common Window application behaviors described in this appendix. Experienced Windows users learn to expect how certain keystrokes will be interpreted by the applications they use.

In the following table, "Alt+" means to hold down the Alt key while pressing the key following the plus sign. For instance, Alt+Esc means to hold down the Alt key and simultaneously press the Esc key.

Keystrokes Common to All Windows Applications

The following keystrokes are available in essentially all Windows applications. There may be instances, however, where certain keystrokes are disabled by the application that is running at the time.

Action	Keystroke
Open the Windows Control menu	Alt+Spacebar
Open the active window's Control menu	Alt+Hyphen

Action	Keystroke
Close the Control menu, but leave Control menu active	Alt+Esc
Move to another Windows application	Alt+Tab
Open the Windows Task List	Ctrl+Esc
Restore a minimized application (you must highlight the icon first)	Ctrl+Esc
Close an application (Windows will prompt for any object that hasn't been saved yet)	Alt+F4

Keystrokes to Access the Menu Bar

The following keystrokes provide instant access to the dBASE menu bar. These keystrokes apply to all Windows applications.

Action	Keystroke
Move the highlight to the menu bar	Alt
Move the highlight off the menu bar	Alt
Move left and right across the menu bar	Arrow keys
Open the selected menu	Enter
Move off the menu bar	Esc

Dialog Box Keyboard Actions

The following keystrokes apply to virtually all dialog boxes in Windows applications. Dialog boxes are most often used to input values that are needed by the application. For instance, you might use a dialog box to query the user for their user name or ID.

Action	Keystroke
Toggle a check box (check box must be selected)	Spacebar
Toggle a radio button (radio button must be selected)	Spacebar
Activate the selected command button	Enter or Spacebar
Move to the next control on the dialog box	Tab
Move back to the previous control on the dialog box	Shift+Tab
Highlight an item on a selection list	Arrow keys
Select an item on a selection list	Enter
Close dialog box without changing settings	Esc

Menu Hot Keys

The menu bars of most Windows applications include "hot keys" (often called "menu accelerators" or "shortcut keys") that instantly activate certain menu options. You must be careful that the keystroke behavior you build into your applications does not conflict with the following common menu keystrokes.

Action	Keystroke
Copy the highlighted item to the Windows Clipboard	Ctrl+C or Ctrl+Ins
Move the highlighted item to the Windows Clipboard	Ctrl+X or Shift+Del
Delete the highlighted object	Del
Paste the object on the Windows Clipboard	Ctrl+V or Shift+Ins
Create a new object (some applications)	Ctrl+N
Open an object	Ctrl+O
Save	Ctrl+S

(continues)

Action	Keystroke
Undo last action	Ctrl+Z
Print	Ctrl+P
Close a window or application	Alt+F4

Navigator Shortcuts

These keystrokes apply when the Navigator window has the focus.

Action	Keystroke
Delete the highlighted item	Ctrl+U
Add an item to the Navigator window	Ctrl+A
View properties of the selected item	Alt+Enter
Run the item (form, program module, and so on)	F7
View the item in Design mode	Shift+F2
Make highlighted item the first item	Home
Make highlighted item the last item	End
Perform appropriate action depending on the file type	F2

Change Mode Keystrokes

These keystrokes apply to the dBASE environment and involve tables, queries, and forms.

Action	Keystroke
Open object in Design mode	Shift+F2
View object in Run mode	F2
Next Run mode	F2
View properties of selected item	Alt+Enter

dBASE Editing Commands

The dBASE Editor has many hot keys that make it easier for you to find and replace text, move to certain line numbers, and so on.

Action	Keystroke
Move to end of line	End
Move to front of line	Home
Move up a page	Page Up
Move down a page	Page Down
Find text	Ctrl+F
Find next instance of text	Ctrl+K
Replace text	Ctrl+R
Delete word to the right	Ctrl+T
Delete the word to the left	Ctrl+Backspace
Delete the current line	Ctrl+Y
Insert a blank line	Ctrl+N
Execute the current line	Ctrl+J or Ctrl+Enter
Move the cursor one tab width	Ctrl+I
Go to line number	Ctrl+G
Go to top line in module	Ctrl+Page Up or Ctrl+Home
Go to last line of module	Ctrl+Page Down or Ctrl+End
Move to next character	Right arrow
Move to previous character	Left arrow
Move to next word or entry field	Ctrl+Right arrow
Move to previous word or entry field	Ctrl+Left arrow
Select character to the right	Shift+Right arrow
Select character to the left	Shift+Left arrow
Select the same position in previous line	Shift+Up arrow

(continues)

Action	Keystroke
Select to same position in next line	Shift+Down arrow
Select next word	Shift+Ctrl+Right arrow
Select previous word	Shift+Ctrl+Left arrow
Select to beginning of line	Shift+Home
Select to end of line	Shift+End
Select to the point you click	Shift+click
Select up one screen	Shift+Page Up
Select down one screen	Shift+Page Down
Select to beginning of file	Shift+Ctrl+Page Up
Select to end of file	Shift+Ctrl+Page Down
Select all text in file or memo field	Shift+Ctrl+Home or Shift+Ctrl+End

dBASE Table Navigation and Manipulation

The following keystrokes apply to dBASE tables open in Table Records view.

Action	Keystroke
Find records	Ctrl+F
Replace records	Ctrl+R
Add records	Ctrl+A
Delete selected record	Ctrl+U
Lock selected record	Ctrl+L
Go to record number	Ctrl+G
Go to previous record	Up arrow
Go to next record	Down arrow
Go to previous page	Page Down
Go to next page	Page Up

Action	Keystroke
Go to top record in table	Ctrl+Page Up
Go to bottom record in table	Ctrl+Page Down
Go to last field in record	Ctrl+End
Go to first field in record	Ctrl+Home
Move up one set of records	Page Up
Move down one set of records	Page Down
Move left one field	Ctrl+Left arrow
Move right one field	Ctrl+Right arrow
Move to same field in record above	Up arrow
Move to same field in record below	Down arrow
Select character to left of cursor	Shift+Left arrow
Select character to right of cursor	Shift+Right arrow
Save current record	Ctrl+S
Save current record and close window	Ctrl+W
Abandon changes to current record and close window	Ctrl+Q
Close window	Ctrl+F4
Print current record or table	Ctrl+P
Display Table Records window from Table Structure window	F2
Display Table Structure window from Table Records window	Shift+F2
In Table Records window, toggle between layouts	F2
Display contents of memo, OLE, or binary field	F9
Move to next field in record	Tab or Enter
Move to previous field in record	Shift+Tab

dBASE Table Operation Shortcuts

These keystrokes implement common table operations.

Action	Keystroke
Undo change	Ctrl+Z
Find a record	Ctrl+F
Find and replace a record	Ctrl+R
Lock selected record	Ctrl+L
Open memo field	F9
Open binary field	F9

dBASE Table Structure Window Shortcuts

These keystrokes are available in the Table Structure window.

Action	Keystroke
Move to end of current field	End
Move to beginning of current field	Home
Move to next record	Enter
Close Table Structure window	Esc
Move to next cell	Tab or Enter
Move to previous cell	Shift+Tab
Move to same position in previous row	Up arrow
Move to same position in next row	Down arrow
Move to same position in first row	Ctrl+Page Up
Move to same position in last row	Ctrl+Page Down
Save current table structure	Ctrl+S
Save current table structure and close window	Ctrl+W

Action	Keystroke
Abandon changes and close window	Ctrl+Q
Close window	Ctrl+F4
Print current table structure	Ctrl+P
Switch to Table Records window	F2
Add new field at end of table structure	Ctrl+A
Insert new field above insertion point	Ctrl+N
Delete field	Ctrl+U
Go to first cell of specified number	Ctrl+G

dBASE Query Shortcuts

These keystroke commands might be useful as you design and build queries.

Action	Keystroke
Add a table to the query	Ctrl+A
Go to last column of QBE grid	Ctrl+End
Go to first column of QBE grid	Ctrl+Home
Save current query	Ctrl+S
Save current query and close window	Ctrl+W
Abandon changes to current query and close window	Ctrl+Q
Close window	Ctrl+F4
Print current query	Ctrl+P
Run query and display results	F2
Move highlighted item to next field in QBE grid	Tab
Move highlighted item to previous field in QBE grid	Shift+Tab
Move highlighted item to previous table in QBE grid	F3

(continues)

Action	Keystroke
Move highlighted item to next table in QBE grid	F4
Toggle the check mark in the current field of the QBE grid	F5
Toggle the check mark in all fields of the QBE grid	Ctrl+F5
Cycle through the sort order options for the current field	F6

dBASE Form Shortcuts

These keystrokes apply to forms and the fields on forms.

Action	Keystroke
Move to beginning of field	Home
Move to end of field	End
Select everything to the left of the cursor in a field	Shift+Home
Select everything to the right of the cursor in a field	Shift+End
Select the character to the left of the cursor	Shift+Left Arrow
Select the character to the right of the cursor	Shift+Right Arrow
Move up one line in a multi-line field	Up arrow
Move down one line in a multi-line field	Down arrow
Save the current form	Ctrl+S
Save the current form and close the window	Ctrl+W
Abandon changes to current form and close window	Ctrl+Q
Close window	Ctrl+F4
Print the current form	Ctrl+P

Action	Keystroke
Run the form	F2
Display the Form Designer for the current form	Shift+F2

Compatibility Keystrokes

The following keystrokes for compatibility with the dot prompt in dBASE III PLUS and dBASE IV are supported when the Command window is active.

Command	Keystroke
LIST	F3
DIR	F4
DISPLAY STRUCTURE	F5
DISPLAY STATUS	F6
DISPLAY MEMORY	F7
DISPLAY	F8
APPEND	F9

Appendix C

Properties Reference

There are over 170 properties in the standard classes built into dBASE for Windows. Many properties are shared by a number of classes. Properties are commonly used to specify or change characteristics of objects, to specify an object's response to specific events, and to perform certain actions. Consult the dBASE on-line help file to learn how to determine the actions for an OLE object.

Many objects have certain properties (called *methods*) which define actions that may be performed by the object. In the following reference text, methods are indicated by the parentheses which follow the method name. For instance, Add( ) is a method of the *array* class of objects.

ActiveControl

Applies to class: FORM

Data type: Object reference

The *ActiveControl* property refers to the object that currently has the focus.

For example, to display the name of the control that currently has the focus, type

```
? FormName.ActiveControl.Name
```

To set a property of the control that has the focus, type

```
FormName.ActiveControl.Enabled = .T.
```

Add(*value*)

Applies to class: ARRAY

This method adds a single element to a one-dimensional array object. The argument to *Add()* specifies the value to put into the new array element. For instance:

```
ArrayName.Add(20)
```

adds an element to the array named ArrayName and initializes the new element to 20. Please keep in mind that the first element of a dBASE array has an index of 1, not 0 as in many other languages.

Advise(*item*)

Applies to class: DDELINK

Advise( ) creates a hot link to an item in a server topic. The *item* parameter specifies which topic item will be assigned to the DDE link.

Alias

Applies to class: BROWSE

Data type: Character

An *alias* is an alternate name given to a table object and is used to identify the table to display in a Browse object.

Alignment

Applies to class: IMAGE, TEXT

Data type: Numeric

Alignment positions an image or text object when the image or text is smaller than the object containing the image or text.

Append

Applies to class: BROWSE

Data type: Logical

The *Append* property permits or inhibits new records from being added to a table. By default, Append is set to .T.. Set Append to .F. to prohibit new records from being added to a table.

Example:

```
MyTable.Append = .F.
```

AutoSize

Applies to class: FORM

Data type: Logical

The *AutoSize* property determines if the form automatically resizes to accommodate all controls placed on the form.

Before

Applies to class: BROWSE, CHECKBOX, COMBOBOX, EDITOR, ENTRYFIELD, LISTBOX, MENU, OLE, PUSHBUTTON, RADIOBUTTON, SCROLLBAR, SPINBOX, TEXT

Data type: Object reference

Before controls the tabbing order of controls on a form. The current control comes before the control specified in the Before property of the control.

Border

Applies to class: EDITOR, ENTRYFIELD, IMAGE, OLE, RECTANGLE, SPINBOX, TEXT

Data type: Logical

The *Border* property determines if the object displays a border. By default, Border is set to .T.

BorderStyle

Applies to class: RECTANGLE

Data type: Numeric

BorderStyle specifies the appearance of the border displayed around the rectangle. Valid values for BorderStyle are the following:

0 = Normal (the default)

1 = Raised

2 = Lowered

Bottom

Applies to class: LINE

Data type: Numeric

Bottom specifies the row position of the bottom of a line object.

Checked

Applies to class: MENU

Data type: Logical

The *Checked* property causes a check mark to appear next to an entry on a menu. By default, Checked is set to .F. but can be set to .T. to indicate that the menu item has been selected.

ClassName

Applies to class: BROWSE, CHECKBOX, COMBOBOX, DDELINK, EDITOR, ENTRYFIELD, FORM, IMAGE, LINE, LISTBOX, MENU, OLE, PUSHBUTTON, RADIOBUTTON, RECTANGLE, SCROLLBAR, SPINBOX, TEXT

Data type: Character

ClassName returns the name of the class to which the object belongs. ClassName is a read-only property and cannot be changed once the object is created.

Close( )

Applies to class: FORM

The *Close()* method closes an open form. The syntax of the Close( ) method is

```
FormName.Close( )
```

ColorHighlight

Applies to class: ENTRYFIELD, LISTBOX, OLE, SPINBOX

Data type: Character

The *ColorHighlight* property specifies the colors to use for the foreground and background of an object, as well as the color of the object that has focus. The syntax of ColorHighlight is

```
ObjectName.ColorHighlight = "forecolor/backcolor"
```

See the ColorNormal property for a list of acceptable colors.

ColorNormal

Applies to class: BROWSE, CHECKBOX, EDITOR, ENTRYFIELD, FORM, LISTBOX, OLE, SPINBOX, TEXT

Data type: Character

ColorNormal specifies the color of an object that is not selected. The syntax of ColorNormal is

```
ObjectName.ColorNormal = "forecolor/backcolor"
```

Acceptable color values are the following:

Color	Value
Black	N
Blue	B
Green	G
Cyan	GB
Red	R
Magenta	RB
Brown	RG
White	W
Blank	X

Count( )

Applies to class: LISTBOX

The *Count()* method returns the number of items in a list box. The syntax of Count( ) is

```
VariableName = FormName.ListBoxName.Count( )
```

CurSel

Applies to class: LISTBOX

Data type: Numeric

The *CurSel* property determines the number of an item in a list box to highlight. Use CurSel to highlight an item that is not selected by the user. The syntax of CurSel is

```
FormName.ListBoxName.CurSel = 7
```

DataLink

Applies to class: CHECKBOX, COMBOBOX, EDITOR, ENTRYFIELD, OLE, RADIOBUTTON, SPINBOX

Data type: Character

DataLink creates a link between an object on a form and a field in a table. The syntax of DataLink is

```
EntryFieldName = NEW ENTRYFIELD(this)
EntryFieldName.DataLink = "FieldName"
```

DataSource

Applies to class: COMBOBOX, IMAGE, LISTBOX

Data type: Character

DataSource specifies the source of data to display in a combo box, list box, or an image object.

One commonly used syntax of DataSource is

```
ObjectBoxName.DataSource = "STRUCTURE"
```

There are several other common syntaxes for DataSource.

Default

Applies to class: PUSHBUTTON

Data type: Logical

Default specifies whether the pushbutton is the default pushbutton on a form. The default for Default is .F.

The syntax of Default is

```
PushButtonName.Default = .T.
```

Delete

Applies to class: BROWSE

Data type: Logical

Delete specifies if the record in the Browse object can be deleted. The default for Delete is .T. Use Delete to prevent users from accidentally deleting important records.

The syntax is

```
BrowseObjectName.Delete = .T.
```

Delete(*ItemIndex*)

Applies to class: ARRAY

The *Delete()* method deletes an element of a one- or two-dimensional array. The ItemIndex parameter specifies which object to delete.

The syntax of the Delete() method is

```
ArrayName.Delete(12)
```

In the following example, Delete() is used to replace data in the third column of a 2-dimensional array with .F. values:

```
USE EMPLOYEE.DBF
??Create an array of 12 rows by 3 columns
ArrayName = NEW ARRAY(12,3)
COPY TO ARRAY ArrayName FIELDS LastName, FirstName, Reviewed
* Use DELETE( ) to remove the data in the "Reviewed" column
* and replace with false (.F.)
ArrayName .DELETE(3,2)
* Display results of DELETE( ) method on ArrayName array
FOR i=1 TO RECCOUNT( )
? ArrayName [I,1], ArrayName [I,2], ArrayName [i,3]
NEXT i
```

Please keep in mind that the first element of a dBASE array has an index of 1, not 0 as in many other languages.

Dimensions

Applies to class: ARRAY

Data type: Numeric

Dimensions returns the number of dimensions in an array object. Use the Grow() method to add dimensions to an array.

The syntax of Dimensions is

```
VariableName = ArrayName.Dimensions
```

Dir([Wildcards],[FileAttributes])

Applies to class: ARRAY

The *Dir()* method retrieves the DOS file attributes of a file. Dir() fills the array object with the returned values.

The syntax of Dir is

```
ArrayName.Dir("*.*","D")
```

The Wildcards parameter specifies the DOS file name, while FileAttributes specifies which attributes to retrieve. Valid attributes include the following:

Character	FileAttribute
D	Include directories
H	Include hidden files
S	Include system directories
V	Include the disk volume label only

DisabledBitmap

Applies to class: PUSHBUTTON

Data type: Character

DisabledBitmap specifies the image to use on a button that is disabled.

A common syntax is

```
ButtonName.DisabledBitmap = "PICTURE.BMP"
```

DoVerb(*ActionNumber*)

Applies to class: OLE

The *DoVerb()* method determines what action you want from an OLE object. Each OLE object has one or more actions associated with it.

DownBitmap

Applies to class: PUSHBUTTON

Data type: Character

DownBitmap specifies the image to use on a button that is in the "down" position. A common syntax of DownBitmap is

```
ButtonName.DownBitmap = "PICTURE.BMP"
```

There are other syntaxes for DownBitmap as well. Consult the dBASE on-line help for a complete list of syntax for DownBitmap.

Element(ArrayIndex1,ArrayIndex2)

Applies to class: ARRAY

Element() returns the number of an element in an array that is specified by ArrayIndex1,ArrayIndex2. When working with one-dimensional arrays, the value returned by the Element() method is the same as the element's array index. As you work with arrays, please keep in mind that the first element of a dBASE array has an index of 1, not 0 as in many other languages.

Enabled

Applies to class: BROWSE, CHECKBOX, COMBOBOX, EDITOR, ENTRYFIELD, FORM, LISTBOX, MENU, OLE, PUSHBUTTON, RADIOBUTTON, SCROLLBAR, SPINBOX

Data type: Logical

The *Enabled* property specifies if the object can be selected by the user. The default value of Enabled is .T.

EscExit

Applies to class: FORM

Data type: Logical

EscExit determines if a form can be closed by pressing the Esc key. By default, EscExit is set to .T.

Execute(*command*)

Applies to class: DDELINK

The *Execute()* method sends a command to a DDE server. The syntax of the Execute() method is

```
LinkObjectName.Execute('{OPEN C:\FILENAME.DOC}')
```

It is important to note that the syntax of the command parameter varies greatly from application to application.

Fields

Applies to class: BROWSE

Data type: Character

The *Fields* property specifies which fields in a Browse object are displayed. The syntax is

```
BrowseObjectName.Fields = "EMPNAME,EMPNUMBER"
```

Fields( )

Applies to class: ARRAY

The *Fields()* method stores information about a table in an array and returns the number of fields whose characteristics are stored. The syntax of Fields() is

```
USE Tablname.DBF
ArrayName = NEW ARRAY(FLDCOUNT( ), 4)
ArrayName.Fields( )
```

As with all dBASE arrays, the first element of the array in this example has an index of 1.

FieldWidth

Applies to class: BROWSE

Data type: Numeric

FieldWidth specifies the width of a character field in a Browse object.

Fill(value,start,count)

Applies to class: ARRAY

The *Fill()* method fills an array or part of an array with specific values. The *value* parameter specifies the value to insert into the array, while the *start* and *count* parameters specify the starting element and number of array elements, respectively. If start and count are not given, Fill() assigns value to all elements of the array. Please keep in mind that the first element of a dBASE array has an index of 1, not 0 as in many other languages.

First

Applies to class: FORM

Data type: Object reference

The *First* property specifies which object on the form receives the focus as the form opens.

FocusBitmap

Applies to class: PUSHBUTTON

Data type: Character

FocusBitmap specifies the image to use on a button when the button has the focus. A common syntax of FocusBitmap is

```
ButtonName.FocusBitmap = "PICTURE.BMP"
```

There are other syntaxes for FocusBitmap as well. Consult the dBASE on-line help for a complete list of syntax for FocusBitmap.

Follow

Applies to class: BROWSE

Data type: Logical

The *Follow* property specifies whether the display of a Browse object follows a record to its new index order when the Browse object key field value is changed. By default, Follow is .T.

FontBold

Applies to class: BROWSE, CHECKBOX, COMBOBOX, EDITOR, ENTRYFIELD, LISTBOX, PUSHBUTTON, RADIOBUTTON, RECTANGLE, SPINBOX, TEXT

Data type: Logical

The default value for *FontBold* is .F., which means that text is displayed in a normal typeface. Set FontBold to .T. to display text in a bold typeface.

FontItalic

Applies to class: BROWSE, CHECKBOX, COMBOBOX, EDITOR, ENTRYFIELD, LISTBOX, PUSHBUTTON, RADIOBUTTON, RECTANGLE, SPINBOX, TEXT

Data type: Logical

The default value for *FontItalic* is .F., which means that text is displayed in a normal typeface. Set FontBold to .T. to display text in an italic typeface.

FontName

Applies to class: BROWSE, CHECKBOX, COMBOBOX, EDITOR, ENTRYFIELD, LISTBOX, PUSHBUTTON, RADIOBUTTON, RECTANGLE, SPINBOX, TEXT

Data type: Character

The *FontName* parameter specifies the name of the font to use with the object. The FontName syntax is

```
ObjectName.FontName = "Arial"
```

The default FontName is MS Sans Serif for all objects.

FontSize

Applies to class: BROWSE, CHECKBOX, COMBOBOX, EDITOR, ENTRYFIELD, LISTBOX, PUSHBUTTON, RADIOBUTTON, RECTANGLE, SPINBOX, TEXT

Data type: Numeric

FontSize specifies the font size to use with the object.

FontStrikeOut

Applies to class: BROWSE, CHECKBOX, COMBOBOX, EDITOR, ENTRYFIELD, LISTBOX, PUSHBUTTON, RADIOBUTTON, RECTANGLE, SPINBOX, TEXT

Data type: Logical

The default value for *FontStrikeOut* is .F., which means that text is displayed in a normal typeface. Set FontStrikeOut to .T. to display text with a strikethrough on each character.

FontUnderline

Applies to class: BROWSE, CHECKBOX, COMBOBOX, EDITOR, ENTRYFIELD, LISTBOX, PUSHBUTTON, RADIOBUTTON, RECTANGLE, SPINBOX, TEXT

Data type: Logical

The default value for *FontUnderline* is .F., which means that text is displayed in a normal typeface. Set FontUnderline to .T. to display text with each character underlined.

Function

Applies to class: ENTRYFIELD, SPINBOX, TEXT

Data type: Character

The *Function* property formats text displayed in an object. The syntax is

```
EntryFieldName.Function = "@Z"
```

The value of Function is created from the following list:

Symbol	Function
(	Enclose negative number in parentheses
!	Convert all letters to uppercase
^	Display numbers in exponential format
$	Insert a dollar sign or other currency symbol
A	Restrict entry to letters of the alphabet
B	Left-justify an entry

Symbol	Function
C	Display CR (credit) after a positive number
D	Display in current SET DATE format
E	Display date in European format (DD/MM/YY)
I	Center-justify the entry
J	Right-justify the entry
L	Pad numbers with leading zeros
M	Display predefined options each time the user presses the spacebar. Separate the options with commas after "@M"
R	Include literal characters without displaying them
S *n*	Limit the width of the display to *n* characters
T	Remove leading and trailing spaces
V *n*	Wrap entry to width specified by *n*
X	Display DB (debit) after a negative number
Z	Display zeros as blanks

GetTextExtent()

Applies to class: TEXT

The *GetTextExtent()* method returns the width of a text object in units determined by the parent form. GetTextExtent() is useful for calculating the width necessary to display a text object.

Group

Applies to class: CHECKBOX, PUSHBUTTON, RADIOBUTTON

Data type: Logical

The *Group* property starts a logically grouped set of controls on the form. Each object that is linked to the object specified by the DataLink property belongs to the group. The Group syntax is

```
MyYesButton = New RADIOBUTTON(this)
MyYesButton.Text = "Yes"
MyYesButton.DataLink = "Answer"
MyYesButton.Group = .F.
```

```
MyNoButton = New RADIOBUTTON(this)
MyNoButton.Top = 5
MyNoButton.Text = "No"
MyNoButton.DataLink = "Answer"
```

Grow()

Applies to class: ARRAY

The *Grow()* method adds an element, a new row, or a new column to an array object. The syntax of Grow() is

```
ArrayName.Grow(2)
```

If you use 1 as the parameter in Grow(), dBASE will add one new element if ArrayName is a one-dimensional array. If ArrayName is a two-dimensional array, Grow(1) will add a new row to ArrayName.

ArrayName.Grow(2) will add a new column to ArrayName. When 2 is used as the parameter to Grow(), a new column is added to the array and is filled with .F. values.

Height

Applies to class: BROWSE, CHECKBOX, COMBOBOX, EDITOR, ENTRYFIELD, FORM, IMAGE, LISTBOX, OLE, PUSHBUTTON, RADIOBUTTON, RECTANGLE, SCROLLBAR, SPINBOX, TEXT

Data type: Numeric

The *Height* property specifies the height (in characters) of an object on an object. The character size used to determine the height of the object is based on the font selected for the object. By default, these objects use the MS Sans Serif font.

HelpFile

Applies to class: BROWSE, CHECKBOX, COMBOBOX, EDITOR, ENTRYFIELD, FORM, LISTBOX, MENU, OLE, PUSHBUTTON, RADIOBUTTON, SCROLLBAR, SPINBOX

Data type: Character

HelpFile specifies a Windows help file (.HLP) that contains on-line help for the object. The syntax of HelpFile is

```
ObjectName.HelpFile = "MYHELP.HLP"
```

HelpID

Applies to class: BROWSE, CHECKBOX, COMBOBOX, EDITOR, ENTRYFIELD, FORM, LISTBOX, MENU, OLE, PUSHBUTTON, RADIOBUTTON, SCROLLBAR, SPINBOX

Data type: Character

HelpID specifies the help keyword for the object. The syntax for HelpID is

```
ObjectName.HelpID = 23
```

hWnd

Applies to class: BROWSE, CHECKBOX, COMBOBOX, EDITOR, ENTRYFIELD, FORM, IMAGE, LISTBOX, PUSHBUTTON, RADIOBUTTON, RECTANGLE, SCROLLBAR, SPINBOX

Data type: Numeric

hWnd returns the handle applied to the object. The handle is determined by Windows and is a unique number for each object on the screeen. The hWnd of an object is needed by many DLLs and external functions.

ID

Applies to class: BROWSE, CHECKBOX, COMBOBOX, EDITOR, ENTRYFIELD, FORM, IMAGE, LISTBOX, MENU, PUSHBUTTON, RADIOBUTTON, SCROLLBAR, SPINBOX

Data type: Numeric

ID assigns a unique identifier to an object. You must ensure that the ID you assign to an object is unique.

Initiate(DDEServer,Topic)

Applies to class: DDELINK

The *Initiate()* method starts a DDE conversation with a DDE server. The *DDEServer* and *Topic* parameters specify the server application and the topic of the conversation. The syntax of Initiate() is as follows:

```
LinkObj = NEW DDELINK( )
LinkObj.Initiate("WINWORD","MYDOC.DOC");
```

Insert(*Position,2*)

Applies to class: ARRAY

The *Insert()* method inserts an element with a value of .F. into an array at the element specified by Position. If 2 is included in the parameter list, Insert() adds a new row or column to two-dimensional arrays. If the array is one-dimensional, Insert() ignores the second parameter. As always, keep in mind that dBASE arrays start with element 1.

Key

Applies to class: BROWSE, ENTRYFIELD

Data type: Function pointer or Codeblock

The *Key* property executes a subroutine when the user enters a keystroke in a Browse object or EntryField. The Key property syntax is

```
MyObject.Key = MySubroutineName
```

Left

Applies to class: BROWSE, CHECKBOX, COMBOBOX, EDITOR, ENTRYFIELD, FORM, IMAGE, LINE, LISTBOX, OLE, PUSHBUTTON, RADIOBUTTON, RECTANGLE, SCROLLBAR, SPINBOX

Data type: Numeric

The *Left* property specifies the left margin of an object relative to its parent object.

LineNo

Applies to class: EDITOR

Data type: Numeric

The *LineNo* property moves the input cursor to a specific line in the Editor object.

LinkFileName

Applies to class: OLE

Data type: Character

The *LinkFileName* property specifies the name of the file associated with an OLE object.

Maximize

Applies to class: FORM

Data type: Logical

The *Maximize* property determines whether the form contains a maximize button. If the button does not exist, the form cannot be maximized. The default is .T.. Also note that when the MDI property is set to .T., the Maximize setting is ignored; however, you can always maximize the form. To remove the Maximize button, set Maximize to .F..

MaxLength

Applies to class: ENTRYFIELD

Data type: Numeric

The *MaxLength* property specifies the maximum width of an entry into a field.

MDI

Applies to class: FORM

Data type: Logical

The *MDI* property specifies whether the form conforms to the windows multiple document interface (MDI) standard. The default is .T. The MDI property enables you to specify if you want the form to appear as a document form.

MenuFile

Applies to class: FORM

Data type: Character

The *MenuFile* property assigns a predefined menu (stored in a .MNU file) to the form.

Minimize

Applies to class: FORM

Data type: Logical

The *Minimize* property determines whether the form contains a minimize button. If the button does not exist, the form cannot be minimized. The default value is .T. See *Maximize* for further information on setting this property.

Mode

Applies to class: BROWSE

Data type: Numeric

The *Mode* property specifies the appearance of a Browse object. Acceptable values for Mode are these:

Value	Appearance	Shows
0 = Browse	Row and columns	Multiple records (default)
1 = Form edit	Form format	Single record
2 = Column edit	Column format	Single record

Modify

Data type: Logical

The *Modify* property specifies whether the user can modify records in a Browse or Editor object. The default is .T.

MousePointer

Applies to class: BROWSE, CHECKBOX, COMBOBOX, EDITOR, ENTRYFIELD, FORM, IMAGE, LISTBOX, OLE, PUSHBUTTON, RADIOBUTTON, RECT-ANGLE, SCROLLBAR, SPINBOX, TEXT

Data type: Numeric

The *MousePointer* property specifies the appearance of the mouse pointer when working with the object. Acceptable MousePointer values are the following:

Value	Mouse Pointer Appearance
0	Default
1	Arrow
2	Cross
3	I-Beam
4	Icon
5	Size
6	Size (alternate 1)
7	Size (vertical)

Value	Mouse Pointer Appearance
8	Size (alternate 2)
9	Size (horizontal)
10	Up arrow
11	Hourglass

Move(Left,Top,Width,Height)

Applies to class: BROWSE, CHECKBOX, COMBOBOX, EDITOR, ENTRYFIELD, FORM, IMAGE, LISTBOX, OLE, PUSHBUTTON, RADIOBUTTON, RECTANGLE, SCROLLBAR, SPINBOX, TEXT

The *Move()* method repositions and resizes an object within its parent object. The *Left*, *Top*, *Width*, and *Height* parameters specify the new position and size. The units for each of these parameters is the average width and height of the font specified for the object.

Moveable

Applies to class: FORM

Data type: Logical

The *Moveable* property specifies whether a form can be moved by the user. The default is .T. If you don't want the user to reposition a form on the screen, set its Moveable property to .F.

Multiple

Applies to class: LISTBOX

Data type: Logical

The *Multiple* property determines whether a ListBox object is multiple choice. A multiple choice list box enables the user to select more than one item from the list.

Name

Applies to class: BROWSE, CHECKBOX, COMBOBOX, EDITOR, ENTRYFIELD, FORM, IMAGE, LISTBOX, MENU, PUSHBUTTON, RADIOBUTTON, RECTANGLE, SCROLLBAR, SPINBOX, TEXT

Data type: Character

The *Name* property contains the name of the object. The Name property is set when the object is created and is read-only at runtime.

NextCol( )

Applies to class: FORM

The *NextCol()* method returns the next position on a form that an object can be placed without overlapping objects already on the form. Use NextCol( ) in conjunction with *NextRow()* to determine the next available position on a form.

NextObj

Applies to class: FORM

Data type: Object reference

The *NextObj* property references the next object in the tabbing order of a form. `NextObj.Name` will contain the name of that object.

NextRow( )

Applies to class: FORM

The *NextRow()* method returns the next position on a form that an object can be placed without overlapping objects already on the form. Use NextRow( ) in conjunction with *NextCol()* to determine the next available position on a form.

Notify( )

Applies to class: DDETOPIC

The *Notify()* method informs a DDE client that an item in a dBASE server session has changed. An example of Notify( ) is

```
DDEObject.Notify("EMPLOYEE")
```

This example will tell the DDE object specified by DDEObject that the EMPLOYEE item has changed.

OldStyle

Applies to class: CHECKBOX, ENTRYFIELD, LISTBOX, RADIOBUTTON, RECTANGLE, SPINBOX, TEXT

Data type: Logical

The *OldStyle* property determines certain appearance characteristics of the object. When set to .T. (True), the object is displayed in Windows 3.0 style. When set to .F. (the default), the object is displayed in the Windows 3.1 3-D style.

OleType

Applies to class: OLE

Data type: Character

The *OleType* property contains a number that specifies whether the OLE object is an embedded document, contains a link to a document file, or is empty. The default is 0, which means the OLE object is empty. The OleType is established when the OLE object is created and is read only at runtime.

OnAdvise

Applies to class: DDETOPIC

Data type: Function pointer or Codeblock

The *OnAdvise* property executes a subroutine in response to a request from an external application for a hotlink to a dBASE DDE server topic.

OnAppend

Applies to class: BROWSE, FORM

Data type: Function pointer or Codeblock

The *OnAppend* property specifies a subroutine to execute when an item is added to a Browse object or form.

OnChange

Applies to class: BROWSE, CHECKBOX, COMBOBOX, ENTRYFIELD, LISTBOX, OLE, RADIOBUTTON, SCROLLBAR, SPINBOX

Data type: Function pointer or Codeblock

The *OnChange* property specifies a subroutine to execute when an item in the object is changed.

OnClick

Applies to class: MENU, PUSHBUTTON

Data type: Function pointer or Codeblock

The *OnClick* property specifies the subroutine to execute in response to a mouse click on the object.

OnClose

Applies to class: FORM, OLE

Data type: Function pointer or Codeblock

The *OnClose* property specifies the subroutine to execute when the form is closed.

OnExecute

Applies to class: DDETOPIC

Data type: Function pointer or Codeblock

The *OnExecute* property specifies the subroutine to execute when a DDE client sends a command to dBASE.

OnGotFocus

Applies to class: BROWSE, CHECKBOX, COMBOBOX, EDITOR, ENTRYFIELD, FORM, LISTBOX, MENU, PUSHBUTTON, RADIOBUTTON, SCROLLBAR, SPINBOX

Data type: Function pointer or Codeblock

The *OnGotFocus* property specifies the subroutine to execute when the object receives the focus.

OnHelp

Applies to class: BROWSE, CHECKBOX, COMBOBOX, EDITOR, ENTRYFIELD, FORM, LISTBOX, MENU, PUSHBUTTON, RADIOBUTTON, SCROLLBAR, SPINBOX

Data type: Function pointer or Codeblock

The *OnHelp* property specifies the subroutine to execute when the user presses F1 while the object has the focus.

OnLeftDblClick

Applies to class: BROWSE, CHECKBOX, COMBOBOX, EDITOR, ENTRYFIELD, FORM, IMAGE, LISTBOX, MENU, OLE, PUSHBUTTON, RADIOBUTTON, RECTANGLE, SCROLLBAR, SPINBOX, TEXT

Data type: Function pointer or Codeblock

The *OnLeftDblClick* property specifies the subroutine to execute in response to a double-click on the object.

OnLeftMouseDown

Applies to class: BROWSE, CHECKBOX, COMBOBOX, EDITOR, ENTRYFIELD, FORM, IMAGE, LISTBOX, MENU, OLE, PUSHBUTTON, RADIOBUTTON, RECTANGLE, SCROLLBAR, SPINBOX, TEXT

Data type: Function pointer or Codeblock

The *OnLeftMouseDown* property specifies the subroutine to execute when the user left-clicks the mouse button while the pointer is on the object. When used in combination with *OnLeftMouseUp*, this property can be used to implement a drag-and-drop interface feature.

OnLeftMouseUp

Applies to class: BROWSE, CHECKBOX, COMBOBOX, EDITOR, ENTRYFIELD, FORM, IMAGE, LISTBOX, MENU, OLE, PUSHBUTTON, RADIOBUTTON, RECTANGLE, SCROLLBAR, SPINBOX, TEXT

Data type: Function pointer or Codeblock

The *OnLeftMouseUp* property specifies the subroutine to execute when the user releases the left mouse button while the pointer is on the object. When used in combination with *OnLeftMouseDown*, this property can be used to implement a drag-and-drop interface feature.

OnLostFocus

Applies to class: BROWSE, CHECKBOX, COMBOBOX, EDITOR, ENTRYFIELD, FORM, LISTBOX, OLE, PUSHBUTTON, RADIOBUTTON, SCROLLBAR, SPINBOX

Data type: Function pointer or Codeblock

The *OnLostFocus* property specifies the subroutine to execute when the object loses the focus.

OnMiddleDblClick

Applies to class: BROWSE, CHECKBOX, COMBOBOX, EDITOR, ENTRYFIELD, FORM, IMAGE, LISTBOX, MENU, OLE, PUSHBUTTON, RADIOBUTTON, RECTANGLE, SCROLLBAR, SPINBOX, TEXT

Data type: Function pointer or Codeblock

The *OnMiddleDblClick* property specifies the subroutine to execute in response to a middle-double-click of the mouse button on the object.

OnMiddleMouseDown

Applies to class: BROWSE, CHECKBOX, COMBOBOX, EDITOR, ENTRYFIELD, FORM, IMAGE, LISTBOX, MENU, OLE, PUSHBUTTON, RADIOBUTTON, RECTANGLE, SCROLLBAR, SPINBOX, TEXT

Data type: Function pointer or Codeblock

The *OnMiddleMouseDown* property specifies the subroutine to execute when the user middle-clicks the mouse button while the mouse pointer is on the object.

OnMiddleMouseUp

Applies to class: BROWSE, CHECKBOX, COMBOBOX, EDITOR, ENTRYFIELD, FORM, IMAGE, LISTBOX, MENU, OLE, PUSHBUTTON, RADIOBUTTON, RECTANGLE, SCROLLBAR, SPINBOX, TEXT

Data type: Function pointer or Codeblock

The *OnMiddleMouseUp* property specifies the subroutine to execute when the user releases the middle mouse button while the mouse pointer is on the object.

OnMouseMove

Applies to class: FORM

Data type: Function pointer or Codeblock

The *OnMouseMove* property specifies the subroutine to execute whenever the mouse is moved while the mouse pointer is on the form.

OnMove

Applies to class: FORM

Data type: Function pointer or Codeblock

The *OnMove* property specifies the subroutine to execute whenever the user moves the form.

OnNavigate

Applies to class: BROWSE, FORM

Data type: Function pointer or Codeblock

The *OnNavigate* property specifies the subroutine to execute whenever the record pointer in a table is moved.

OnNewValue

Applies to class: DDELINK

Data type: Function pointer or Codeblock

The *OnNewValue* property specifies a subroutine to execute when the item in a hot linked item in a DDE document changes. Hot links, which are created with the Advise( ) method, are designed to notify dBASE when the item changes. Use the OnNewValue property to respond to the change.

OnOpen

Applies to class: BROWSE, CHECKBOX, COMBOBOX, EDITOR, ENTRYFIELD, FORM, IMAGE, LISTBOX, OLE, PUSHBUTTON, RADIOBUTTON, RECTANGLE, SCROLLBAR, SPINBOX, TEXT

Data type: Function pointer or Codeblock

The *OnOpen* property specifies the subroutine to execute whenever the form containing the object is opened.

OnPeek

Applies to class: DDETOPIC

Data type: Function pointer or Codeblock

The *OnPeek* property specifies the subroutine to execute when a DDE client tries to read data from dBASE DDE server item that is involved in a DDE application.

OnPoke

Applies to class: DDETOPIC

Data type: Function pointer or Codeblock

The *OnPoke* property specifies the subroutine to execute when a DDE client tries to insert data into a dBASE DDE server item involved in a DDE application.

OnRightDblClick

Applies to class: BROWSE, CHECKBOX, COMBOBOX, EDITOR, ENTRYFIELD, FORM, IMAGE, LISTBOX, MENU, OLE, PUSHBUTTON, RADIOBUTTON, RECTANGLE, SCROLLBAR, SPINBOX, TEXT

Data type: Function pointer or Codeblock

The *OnRightDblClick* property specifies the subroutine to execute when the user right-double-clicks the mouse button while the mouse pointer is on the object.

OnRightMouseDown

Applies to class: BROWSE, CHECKBOX, COMBOBOX, EDITOR, ENTRYFIELD, FORM, IMAGE, LISTBOX, MENU, OLE, PUSHBUTTON, RADIOBUTTON, RECTANGLE, SCROLLBAR, SPINBOX, TEXT

Data type: Function pointer or Codeblock

The *OnRightMouseDown* property specifies the subroutine to execute when the user right-clicks the mouse button while the mouse pointer is on the object.

OnRightMouseUp

Applies to class: BROWSE, CHECKBOX, COMBOBOX, EDITOR, ENTRYFIELD, FORM, IMAGE, LISTBOX, MENU, OLE, PUSHBUTTON, RADIOBUTTON, RECTANGLE, SCROLLBAR, SPINBOX, TEXT

Data type: Function pointer or Codeblock

The *OnRightMouseUp* property specifies the subroutine to execute when the user releases the right mouse button while the mouse pointer is on the object.

OnSelChange

Applies to class: LISTBOX

Data type: Function pointer or Codeblock

The *OnSelChange* property specifies the subroutine to execute when the highlight is moved from one item to another on a selection list.

OnSelection

Applies to class: FORM

Data type: Function pointer or Codeblock

The *OnSelection* property specifies the subroutine to execute when the user "submits" a form. A form can be "submitted" in three ways: when the Enter key is pressed while the form has the focus, when the spacebar is pressed while a PushButton object has the focus, or when the user clicks a PushButton.

OnSize

Applies to class: FORM

Data type: Function pointer or Codeblock

The *OnSize* property specifies the subroutine to execute when the user resizes the form.

OnUnadvise

Applies to class: DDETOPIC

Data type: Logical

The *OnUnadvise* property specifies the subroutine to execute when the client application in a DDE routine requests that dBASE not notify the user of further changes in the DDE object.

Open( )

Applies to class: FORM

The *Open()* method opens a form and displays the controls and other objects on the form.

The Open( ) method opens a Window as a modeless window. The focus can be switched to another window from a modeless form.

Parent

Applies to class: BROWSE, CHECKBOX, COMBOBOX, EDITOR, ENTRYFIELD, IMAGE, LINE, LISTBOX, MENU, OLE, PUSHBUTTON, RADIOBUTTON, RECTANGLE, SCROLLBAR, SPINBOX, TEXT

Data type: Object Reference

The *Parent* property points to the parent object of the current object. `Parent.Name` will return the name of the parent object.

PatternStyle

Applies to class: RECTANGLE

Data type: Numeric

The *PatternStyle* property specifies the graphic pattern to use for the background of the rectangle object. Valid settings include the following:

Number	Description
0	Solid
1	Backwards diagonal (BDiagonal)
2	Cross
3	Diagonally crossed (Diagcross)
4	Forward diagonal (FDiagonal)
5	Horizontal
6	Vertical

Peek( )

Applies to class: DDELINK

The *Peek()* method gets a piece of information from a DDE server.

Pen

Applies to class: LINE

Data type: Numeric

The *Pen* property specifies the pattern and appearance of a line object. Valid Pen settings are the following:

Setting	Pattern
0	Solid
1	Dash
2	Dot
3	DashDot
4	DashDotDot

Picture

Applies to class: ENTRYFIELD, SPINBOX, TEXT

Data type: Character

The *Picture* property specifies the formatting to apply to the text in the object.

Poke(*item,value*)

Applies to class: DDELINK

The *Poke()* method inserts data into a DDE server application. The *item* parameter specifies the item to be written into the server application (for instance, a worksheet cell), while *value* is the value to be inserted into the item.

Print()

Applies to class: FORM

The *Print()* method prints the current form and all of its objects on the default Windows printer.

RangeMax

Applies to class: SCROLLBAR, SPINBOX

Data type: Date or numeric

The *RangeMax* property specifies the maximum number that can be inserted into the SpinBox or ScrollBar object. Although you cannot insert a number into or display a number with a scrollbar, a Scrollbar object can represent a range of numbers that is indicated by the position of the slider on the scrollbar. Each movement of the scrollbar will increment or decrement the value represented by the scrollbar slider within the limits set by the RangeMin and RangeMax properties of the scrollbar.

RangeMin

Applies to class: SCROLLBAR, SPINBOX

Data type: Date or numeric

The *RangeMin* property specifies the minimum number that can be inserted into the SpinBox or ScrollBar object. Although you cannot insert a number into or display a number with a scrollbar, a Scrollbar object can represent a range of numbers that is indicated by the position of the slider on the scrollbar. Each movement of the scrollbar will increment or decrement the value represented by the scrollbar slider within the limits set by the RangeMin and RangeMax properties of the scrollbar.

RangeRequired

Applies to class: SPINBOX

Data type: Logical

The *RangeRequired* property (default .F.) determines whether the *RangeMax* and *RangeMin* properties of the SpinBox object are enforced.

ReadModal( )

Applies to class: FORM

The *ReadModal( )* method opens a form as a modal window. The focus cannot be moved off the modal window.

Reconnect( )

Applies to class: DDELINK

Use the *Reconnect( )* method to try to restart a DDE conversation that has failed. Reconnect( ) returns .T. if successful. Reconnect( ) can be used to re-establish DDE conversations that were explicitly terminated with the Terminate( ) method.

Release( )

Applies to class: BROWSE, CHECKBOX, COMBOBOX, DDELINK, DDETOPIC, EDITOR, ENTRYFIELD, FORM, IMAGE, LINE, LISTBOX, MENU, OLE, PUSHBUTTON, RADIOBUTTON, RECTANGLE, SCROLLBAR, SPINBOX, TEXT

Use the *Release( )* method to free memory that is occupied by an object.

Resize( )

Applies to class: ARRAY

The *Resize( )* method changes the dimensions of an array object.

Right

Applies to class: LINE

Data type: Numeric

The *Right* property (along with Bottom, Left, and Top) defines the position and dimensions of a line object.

ScaleFontName

Applies to class: FORM

Data type: Character

The *ScaleFontName* property specifies the font that should be used when calculating dimensions based on the form's font. The default ScaleFontName is MS Sans Serif.

ScaleFontSize

Applies to class: FORM

Data type: Numeric

The *ScaleFontSize* property reports the height of each row and the width of each column on a form. The default ScaleFontSize is 8.00.

Scan( )

Applies to class: ARRAY

The *Scan()* method searches an array for a specific value.

ScrollBar

Applies to class: EDITOR, FORM

Data type: Numeric

The *ScrollBar* property specifies whether the object contains a scrollbar. The accepted values for ScrollBar are the following:

Value	Meaning
0	Off. The object does not have a scrollbar.
1	On. The object has a scrollbar.
2	Auto. Display the scrollbar only when needed.
3	Disabled. The scrollbar is not usable even though it is visible.

SelectAll

Applies to class: ENTRYFIELD, SPINBOX

Data type: Logical

The *SelectAll* property specifies whether the entry in an EntryField or SpinBox is initially highlighted. The default is .F..

Selected( )

Applies to class: LISTBOX

The *Selected()* method returns the currently selected option in a ListBox object.

Separator

Applies to class: MENU

Data type: Logical

The *Separator* property determines whether a menu item appears as a separator that divides the menu options into related groups.

Server

Applies to class: DDELINK

Data type: Character

The *Server* property contains the name of the DDELINK object's server application.

ServerName

Applies to class: OLE

Data type: Character

The *ServerName* property contains the name of the application that is started when the OLE object is double-clicked.

SetFocus( )

Applies to class: BROWSE, CHECKBOX, COMBOBOX, EDITOR, ENTRYFIELD, FORM, IMAGE, LISTBOX, OLE, PUSHBUTTON, RADIOBUTTON, SCROLLBAR, SPINBOX

The *SetFocus()* property moves the focus to the object. SetFocus is typically set at runtime.

The *SetFocus()* method moves the focus to the specified object on the form.

ShortCut

Applies to class: MENU

Data type: Character

ShortCut specifies the hot-key combination for a menu option.

ShowDeleted

Applies to class: BROWSE

Data type: Logical

ShowDeleted specifies whether the Browse object should display delete boxes on each column in the Browse object. By default (.T.), delete boxes are shown.

ShowHeading

Applies to class: BROWSE

Data type: Logical

ShowHeading specifies whether the Browse object should display headings on each column in the Browse object. By default (.T.), headings are shown.

ShowRecNo

Applies to class: BROWSE

Data type: Logical

By default (.T.), *ShowRecNo* causes a Browse to display a record number to the left of each record in the Browse object.

Size

Applies to class: ARRAY

Data type: Numeric

Size reports the number of objects contained within the array.

Sizeable

Applies to class: FORM

Data type: Logical

Sizeable specifies whether the user can resize a form at runtime. By default (.T.), dBASE forms are sizeable.

Sort( )

Applies to class: ARRAY

The *Sort( )* method sorts the elements of a two-dimensional array.

Sorted

Applies to class: COMBOBOX, LISTBOX

Data type: Logical

The *Sorted* property determines whether the options in a list box or combo box are displayed in sorted order (.T.) or their natural order (.F., the default).

SpeedBar

Applies to class: PUSHBUTTON

Data type: Logical

SpeedBar specifies whether a pushbutton object should behave as a SpeedBar button (.T.) or as a standard pushbutton (.F., the default).

SpinOnly

Applies to class: SPINBOX

Data type: Logical

SpinOnly specifies if the user can enter an arbitrary value into the SpinBox text area. By default, *SpinOnly* is .F., which permits the user to enter arbitrary values in the text area.

StatusMessage

Applies to class: BROWSE, CHECKBOX, COMBOBOX, EDITOR, ENTRYFIELD, FORM, LISTBOX, MENU, OLE, PUSHBUTTON, RADIOBUTTON, SCROLLBAR, SPINBOX

Data type: Character

StatusMessage specifies the message to display on the status line while the object has the focus. The StatusMessage can be set at runtime to prompt the user appropriately.

Step

Applies to class: SPINBOX

Data type: Numeric

Step specifies how much to increment or decrement the value of a SpinBox each time an arrow is pressed. The default Step is 1.

Style

Applies to class: COMBOBOX

Data type: Numeric

The *Style* property determines certain characteristics of the COMBOBOX object.

0 = Simple (the default). The drop-down list is automatically displayed.

1 = DropDown. The user must click the drop-down arrow to reveal the list.

2 = DropDownList. The user must click the drop-down arrow to reveal the list and input is restricted to entries on the list.

Subscript( )

Applies to class: ARRAY

Subscript() reports the row and/or column index of a specific array object. Unlike some other programming languages, the index of the first element of a dBASE array is 1.

SysMenu

Applies to class: FORM

Data type: Logical

SysMenu specifies whether a form has a Control menu. When set to .F., the form will not have a Control menu and the user will not have access to Maximize, Minimize, Restore, and the other commands on the Control menu.

TabStop

Applies to class: BROWSE, CHECKBOX, COMBOBOX, EDITOR, ENTRYFIELD, LISTBOX, OLE, PUSHBUTTON, RADIOBUTTON, SCROLLBAR, SPINBOX

Data type: Logical

TabStop determines whether the focus can be moved to an object by using the Tab key. When set to .F., the object cannot receive the focus by tabbing to it.

Terminate( )

Applies to class: DDELINK

Terminate() ends a DDE conversation with a DDE server.

Text

Applies to class: BROWSE, CHECKBOX, FORM, MENU, PUSHBUTTON, RADIOBUTTON, RECTANGLE, TEXT

Data type: Character

Text specifies the text string to display on or near the object.

Timeout

Applies to class: DDELINK

Data type: Numeric

Timeout specifies the timeout interval, expressed in seconds, to be used during a DDE conversation.

Toggle

Applies to class: BROWSE

Data type: Logical

Toggle determines whether the user can switch between Browse mode and Edit mode in a Browse object.

Top

Applies to class: BROWSE, CHECKBOX, COMBOBOX, EDITOR, ENTRYFIELD, FORM, IMAGE, LINE, LISTBOX, OLE, PUSHBUTTON, RADIOBUTTON, RECTANGLE, SCROLLBAR, TEXT

Data type: Numeric

In conjunction with the *Left* property, *Top* specifies the upper left corner of an object relative to the object's parent window.

Topic

Applies to class: DDELINK, DDETOPIC

Data type: Character

The *Topic* property is the name of a document to be opened by a DDE server or the topic of a DDETOPIC object.

Unadvise( )

Applies to class: DDELINK

The *Unadvise* method terminates a DDE hot link.

UpBitmap

Applies to class: PUSHBUTTON

Data type: Character

UpBitmap specifies the image to be displayed on a button that is in the "up" position. The UpBitmap value can be a bitmap contained within a DLL, an external .BMP file, or a binary field in a dBASE table.

UpBitmap specifies the image to use on a button that is in the "up" position. A common syntax of UpBitmap is

```
ButtonName.UpBitmap = "PICTURE.BMP"
```

There are other syntaxes for UpBitmap as well. Consult the dBASE on-line help for a complete list of syntax for UpBitmap.

Valid

Applies to class: ENTRYFIELD, SPINBOX

Data type: Function pointer or Codeblock

Valid specifies a condition that must be met before the user can move the focus off a control. Valid is typically used for checking the validity of new data being entered into the database.

ValidErrorMsg

Applies to class: ENTRYFIELD, SPINBOX

Data type: Character

The *ValidErrorMsg* is displayed in the Status bar when the Valid event property returns .F.. The Valid event property is used for input checking.

ValidRequired

Applies to class: ENTRYFIELD, SPINBOX

Data type: Logical

The *ValidRequired* property specifies whether the Valid event property applies to all data or just new data. The Valid event property specifies the condition that data must meet.

Value

Applies to class: CHECKBOX, COMBOBOX, EDITOR, ENTRYFIELD, LISTBOX, RADIOBUTTON, SPINBOX, SCROLLBAR

Data type: Numeric, Float, Character, or Date

Value is the property holding the value of an object. The data type for *value* is determined by the type of object.

Vertical

Applies to class: SCROLLBAR

Data type: Logical

Vertical specifies whether the scrollbar object appears as a vertical (.T., the default) or horizontal (.F.) scrollbar.

View

Applies to class: FORM

Data type: Character

The *View* property specifies the name of the table or query on which a form is based. All tables and queries specified in the View property are opened each time the form is opened.

Visible

Applies to class: BROWSE, CHECKBOX, COMBOBOX, EDITOR, ENTRYFIELD, FORM, IMAGE, LINE, LISTBOX, OLE, PUSHBUTTON, RADIOBUTTON, RECTANGLE, SCROLLBAR, SPINBOX, TEXT

Data type: Logical

The *Visible* property determines whether the object is visible (.T., the default) or invisible (.F.).

When

Applies to class: BROWSE, CHECKBOX, COMBOBOX, EDITOR, ENTRYFIELD, LISTBOX, PUSHBUTTON, RADIOBUTTON, SCROLLBAR, SPINBOX

Data type: Function pointer or Codeblock

When specifies a condition that must evaluate to .T. before the user is given access to an object.

Width

Applies to class: BROWSE, CHECKBOX, COMBOBOX, EDITOR, ENTRYFIELD, FORM, IMAGE, LINE, LISTBOX, OLE, PUSHBUTTON, RADIOBUTTON, RECTANGLE, SCROLLBAR, SPINBOX, TEXT

Data type: Numeric

The *Width* and *Height* properties determine the sizes of objects on the screen.

WindowState

Applies to class: FORM

Data type: Numeric

The *WindowState* property specifies the appearance of forms.

0 = Normal (default) Works the same as Restore in the Windows Control menu.

1 = Minimized

2 = Maximized

Wrap

Applies to class: EDITOR

Data type: Logical

By default, *Wrap* is set to .F., enabling the user to determine where carriage returns appear in text in the Editor. When set to .T., the Editor will automatically insert carriage returns to consistently wrap text at the same place in each line.

Index of Common Problems

Expression Builder

Forms

(continues)

Forms (continued)	
If you have this problem...	**You'll find help here...**
Form Expert won't display in the Available Files list in the table you want to use.	209
Moveable property in your form is set to true (.T.), but the title bar still appears.	347
Save commands aren't listed in the **F**ile menu.	227

Integration	
If you have this problem...	**You'll find help here...**
Can't append data from a word processing file into a dBASE table.	486
Can't update your file.	521
Data is missing when you append data from one table into another.	486
dBASE can't find your file when you issue the USE command.	515
Error message `File Error. Cannot find LD01.DDL` appears when you try to embed an object.	492
Need to export records to a word processor document without getting quotation marks around the data.	478
Only parts of some fields from your source table are appended into the target table.	486
Paste Link command is dimmed when you try to link a new document to an OLE field.	493
Records you marked for deletion are exported.	478
Table menu doesn't show in your menu bar.	478
Update command on the **F**ile menu disappears when you open a file in the server application that you want to embed.	493

Manipulating Data

If you have this problem...	You'll find help here...
Average calculation keeps reporting inaccurate results.	321
Count doesn't appear in status bar when you choose OK in the Count Records dialog box.	318
Need to calculate how much disk space a subset of records takes up.	318
Records seem to be deleted rather than first marked for deletion.	333
Searches are quick on some fields and slow on others when you have a large table.	327

Multi-User Environment

If you have this problem...	You'll find help here...
dBASE is unstable and erratic when you use it under Windows for Workgroups.	445
Need to keep locks on multiple records over a series of operations.	453
Need to share data on local drive.	445

Programming

If you have this problem...	You'll find help here...
Alert box says that file doesn't exist in procedure you created.	606
Alert box says you used an unallowed phrase or keyword when you enter a command line into the Command window.	560
BROWSE command doesn't display your table.	560
Can't get BROWSE to work.	638
Can't open a program text file that has an .ASC file extension in the Text Editor.	568

(continues)

If you have this problem...	You'll find help here...
Record pointer keeps moving with the new record to its index location when you add records to a table.	644
Records are missing after you index your table on the Names field using the INDEX command.	672
Results pane appears before the input pane when you open the Command window.	556
SORT command won't let you re-sort the table to the same table name.	672
Subroutine doesn't return a value.	606
Text appears red when you enter it in quotation marks into the Program Editor window.	568

Queries

If you have this problem...	You'll find help here...
Complex indexes don't appear in the query skeleton.	438
Error message `Expecting: Identifier` appears when you try to run a query with a calculated field.	428
Need to get a dictionary (that is, case-insensitive) order using an index.	437
Need to order a query based on two fields, but sort method takes forever because of large tables.	438
SORT is used to order your query even though you chose an ASCII order for a field that has an existing index.	437
View displays more dates than it should after you run a query that has a date condition.	190
View doesn't contain the records you expect after you run a query.	190
View is empty when you run a query.	190

Related Tables

If you have this problem...	You'll find help here...
Child table field that you need for your link doesn't appear in the I**n**dex list.	277
Error message tells you that dBASE can't define a "cyclic relation" when you try to create a relation.	277
Need to establish a link between two tables that share a common field, but field name is different.	277
Need to link fields where parent table includes date information in character format, and child table uses normal date data type.	277

Reports

If you have this problem...	You'll find help here...
Added a date field to your report, but you need to post-date a few copies.	395
Entered the wrong field by accident when you created a group.	399
Need to delete a group.	399
Need to sort your report based on values in the summary field.	403
Need to start each report group on a new page.	417
Nothing happens when you change the alignment of a field by clicking a SpeedBar button.	254
Printed reports are missing first two or three characters from every line.	254
Report Designer window doesn't open.	244
Report Designer window doesn't show all three of the Page header, Details, and Page footer sections.	244
Report Designer window looks different from the one shown in this book.	244
Report files are huge, and you're running out of disk space.	422

Tables

Index

Symbols

A

B

D

E

F

G

H

I-J

K

L

M

N

O

P

Q

R

S

T

U

V

X–Y

Z